Lecture Notes in Computer Science 3790

Commenced Publication in 1973
Founding and Former Series Editors:
Gerhard Goos, Juris Hartmanis, and Jan van Leeuwen

Gustavo Alonso (Ed.)

Middleware 2005

ACM/IFIP/USENIX
6th International Middleware Conference
Grenoble, France, November 28 - December 2, 2005
Proceedings

 Springer

Volume Editor

Gustavo Alonso
Swiss Federal Institute of Technology (ETHZ)
Department of Computer Science, ETH Zentrum
8092 Zürich, Switzerland
E-mail: alonso@inf.ethz.ch

Library of Congress Control Number: 2005935949

CR Subject Classification (1998): C.2.4, D.4, C.2, D.1.3, D.3.2, D.2, H.4

ISSN   0302-9743
ISBN-10   3-540-30323-5 Springer Berlin Heidelberg New York
ISBN-13   978-3-540-30323-7 Springer Berlin Heidelberg New York

Springer is a part of Springer Science+Business Media

springeronline.com

© IFIP International Federation for Information Processing 2005
Printed in Germany

Typesetting: Camera-ready by author, data conversion by Scientific Publishing Services, Chennai, India
Printed on acid-free paper   SPIN: 11587552   06/3142   5 4 3 2 1 0

Preface

Today, middleware is a key part of almost any application. Gone are the days when middleware was only used in the IT industry for high-end applications. Rather than middleware being part of the IT world, today IT applications represent only one aspect of middleware. With the increase in distribution, network capacity, and widespread deployment of computing devices (in homes, automobiles, mobile phones, etc.), middleware has surpassed the importance of operating systems as the platform where application development and deployment take place. This makes middleware very exciting as a research area but also a very challenging one since it encompasses many different concepts and techniques from a wide variety of fields: networking, distributed systems, software engineering, performance analysis, computer architecture, and data management.

Middleware 2005 in Grenoble, France, was the 6th edition of an increasingly successful conference. The scope of the conference has been slowly widening with every edition to accommodate new fields and applications. This year we made a considerable effort to reach out to other communities who are also active in the general area of middleware — sensor networks, networks in general, databases, software engineering— a fact that is reflected in the variety of submissions.

The program this year was selected from over 112 submissions. From these, the Program Committee selected 18 full papers and 6 short papers. Each paper had at least four reviews and the selection was made based on technical merit, relevance, originality of the contribution, and degree of innovation. Preference was given to papers with new ideas or covering novel application areas. Among the accepted papers, there was a fair number of PC papers. For the record, PC papers had to be clearly above other papers to be considered for acceptance. In this Call for Papers, we did not include work–in–progress papers. Instead, we introduced short papers — selected from the regular submissions as papers that had interesting ideas but were not ready for publication as full papers — and a demo session with a separate Call for Papers — which should give a venue to present systems-oriented research.

As in the past, the review process was highly selective and the source of many interesting discussions on the nature of middleware and its general applicability. The exciting program that was prepared reflects these discussions and created the perfect background for similar discussions during the conference. Together with the workshops that accompanied the conference, Middleware 2005 covered a wide range of issues and topics related to all aspects of middleware, from software engineering to low-level implementation details.

Finally, I would like to thank Richard van de Stadt, in charge of the conference review system, who was at all moments most helpful and made sure the review process ran flawlessly. I would also like thank all the Program Committee members and external reviewers for their time and effort during the review process. Writing good, informative, and fair reviews is not easy and takes a considerable amount of time. I am proud to say that this year's PC has done an excellent job with the reviews, thereby continuing the tradition of excellence in the Middleware conferences. The result of their efforts is an excellent and very interesting program that no doubt made the 2005 edition of the conference a success.

April 2005   Gustavo Alonso
                                          Middleware 2005 Program Chair

Organization

Middleware 2005 was organized under the auspices of IFIP TC6WG6.1 (International Federation for Information Processing, Technical Committee 6 [Communication Systems], Working Group 6.1 [Architecture and Protocols for Computer Networks]).

Steering Committee

Joe Sventek (Chair)	University of Glasgow, UK
Gordon Blair	Lancaster University, UK
Markus Endler	PUC-Rio, Brazil
Rachid Guerraoui	EPFL, Switzerland
Peter Honeyman	CITI, University of Michigan, USA
Guy LeDuc	University of Liege, Belgium
Jan de Meer	IHP-Microelectronics, Germany
Doug Schmidt	Vanderbilt University, USA

Sponsoring Institutes

IFIP (International Federation for Information Processing)
www.ifip.or.at

Advanced Computing Systems Association
www.usenix.org

INRIA Rhône-Alpes
www.inrialpes.fr

Organizing Committee

General Chair	Jean-Bernard Stefani (INRIA, France)
Program Chair	Gustavo Alonso (ETH Zürich, Switzerland)
Local Arrangements Chairs	Sébastien Jean (UPMF, France)
	Noel De Palma (INPG, France)
Workshops Chair	Geoff Coulson (University of Lancaster, UK)
Doctoral Symposium Chairs	Jacques Mossière (INPG, France)
	Edward Curry (NUI Galway, Ireland)
Publicity Chair	Gilles Muller (École des Mines de Nantes, France)

Program Committee

Christiana Amza	University of Toronto, Canada
Roger Barga	Microsoft Labs, USA
Alberto Bartoli	Trieste University, Italy
Gordon Blair	Lancaster University, UK
Christof Bornhoevd	SAP Labs, USA
Roy Campbell	Urbana-Champaign, USA
Fabio Casati	HP Labs, USA
Geoff Coulson	Lancaster University, UK
Peter Druschel	Rice University, USA
Johann Eder	University of Klagenfurt, Austria
Markus Endler	PUC-Rio, Brazil
Dana Florescu	BEA, USA
Rachid Guerraoui	EPFL, Switzerland
Thomas Gschwind	IBM, Switzerland
Monika Henzinger	EPFL, Switzerland
Peter Honeyman	CITI, University of Michigan, USA
Wei Hong	Intel Berkeley, USA
Valérie Issarny	INRIA, France
Arno Jacobsen	University of Toronto, Canada
Bettina Kemme	McGill University, Canada
Anne-Marie Kermarrec	INRIA- Rennes, France
Fabio Kon	IME/USP, Brazil
Donald Kossmann	ETH, Zurich
Frank Leymann	Stuttgart University, Germany
Cecilia Mascolo	UCL, UK
Ken Moody	University of Cambridge, UK
Elie Najm	ENST, France
Marta Patino	UPM, Spain
Evvagelia Pitoura	University of Ioannina, Greece
Calton Pu	Georgia Tech, USA
Krithi Ramamritahn	IIT Bombay, India
Peter Steenkiste	CMU, USA
Doug Schmidt	Vanderbilt University, USA
Rick Schlichting	ATT Research, USA
Stefan Tai	IBM Watson, USA
Doug Terry	Microsoft Research
Peter Trantafillou	Patras University, Greece
Yu-Chee Tseng	National Chiao Tung University, Taiwan
Steve Vinoski	IONA, USA
Werner Vogels	Amazon, USA

Referees

Ioannis Aekaterinidis
Jalal Al-Muhtadi
Trevor Armstrong
Khaled Barbaria
Irina Carabus
Renato Cerqueira
Agnes de La Chapelle
Jin Chen
Alex Cheung
Arlindo Flávio da Conceição
Isabelle Demeure
Michael Derntl
Catalin Drula
Cristian Duda
Vladimir Dyo
Joao Eduardo Ferreira
Kathrin Figl
Renato Fileto
Peter Fischer
Ayalvadi Ganesh
Alfredo Goldman
Paul Grace
Irfan Hamid
Guoli Li
Matt Medland
Shouang Hou
Ryan Huebsch
Danny Hughes
Jérôme Hugues
Jürgen Mangler
Irum Godil
Enping Tu
Taimur Javed
Ricardo Jiménez-Peris
Gueyoung Jung
José de Ribamar B. P. Junior
Mejdi Kaddour
Marek Lehmann
Apu Kapadia
Xin Li
Alexander Keller

Chih-Yu Lin
Jinshan Liu
Boon Thau Loo
Kaloian Manassiev
Eli Fidler
Vinod Mathusamy
Matt Medland
Giuliano Mega
Thomas A. Mikalsen
Mirco Musolesi
Nikos Ntarmos
Barry Porter
Anand Ranganathan
Sylvia Ratnasamy
Pierre-Guillaume Raverdy
Francisco Reverbel
Etienne Riviere
Ricardo C.A. da Rocha
Hana Rubinsztejn
Daniele Sacchetti
Vagner Sacramento
Marcos Vaz Salles
Geetanjali Sampemane
Erich Schikuta
Lenin Singaravelu
James Skene
Gokul Soundararajan
Mudhakar Srivatsa
Heinz Stockinger
Galen S. Swint
Ferda Tartanoglu
Helmut Wanek
Jinpeng Wei
Thomas Weishäupl
Eric Wohlstadter
Qinyi Wu
Stefanos Zachariadis
Jiaying Zhang
Apóstolos Zarras
Ying Zhu
Jianjun Zhang

Table of Contents

Securing Publish/Subscribe for
Multi-domain Systems

Jean Bacon, David Eyers, Ken Moody, and Lauri Pesonen

University of Cambridge Computer Laboratory,
JJ Thomson Avenue, Cambridge, CB3 0FD, UK
firstname.lastname@cl.cam.ac.uk

Abstract. Two convincing paradigms have emerged for achieving scalability in widely distributed systems: *role-based*, policy-driven control of access to the system by applications and for system management purposes; and *publish/subscribe communication* between loosely coupled components. Publish/subscribe provides efficient support for mutually anonymous, many-to-many communication between loosely coupled entities. In this paper we focus on securing such a communication service (1) by specifying and enforcing access control policy at the service API, and (2) by enforcing the security and privacy aspects of these policies within the service itself. We envisage independent but related administration domains that share a pub/sub communications infrastructure, typical of public-sector systems. Roles are named within each domain and role-related privileges for using the pub/sub service are specified. Intra- and inter-domain, controlled interaction is supported by negotiated policies. In a large-scale publish/subscribe service, domains are not expected to trust all message brokers fully. Attribute encryption allows a single publication to carry both confidential and public information safely, even via untrusted message brokers across a vulnerable communications substrate. Our approach provides the application designer with fine-grained expressiveness while, at the same time, improving system fault tolerance by allowing a single shared messaging network to route both public and confidential information. Early simulations show that our approach reduces the overall traffic compared with a secure publish/subscribe scheme that encrypts whole messages.

Keywords: publish/subscribe, loosely coupled applications, content-based routing, role-based access control, attribute encryption, message confidentiality, trust.

1   Introduction

We are concerned with how communication within and between large-scale, independent, widely distributed application domains should be supported and managed. Two recently emerging paradigms for achieving scalability are asynchronous, publish/subscribe-based communication and role-based access control (RBAC). In the EDSAC21 project we aim to extend and integrate these

G. Alonso (Ed.): Middleware 2005, LNCS 3790, pp. 1–20, 2005.

paradigms to achieve a scalable, secure middleware capable of supporting fine-grained control of communication within and between domains. In this paper we present our multi-domain architecture and an interim evaluation based on simulation.

We define a domain to be an independently administered unit in which a domain manager has, or may delegate, responsibility for naming and policy specification. The following motivating scenarios have in common a communication infrastructure shared by independently administered domains, some of which are strongly related and have similarly named roles. The bulk of the communication is likely to be within a domain but there is also a clear need for inter-domain communication. (1) A global company has branches (e.g. sales) in California, London and Tokyo. Some (sales) data and events should be shared between branches. (2) A number of county-level police domains need support for intra- and inter-domain messages. (3) A national health service's communication infrastructure is shared by many independent hospitals, clinics, primary-care practices etc. (4) An "active city" has independent public services such as police, fire, ambulance, hospital, and utilities. As well as communicating with similar services nationally (e.g. police with police) the different services need to cooperate, especially in emergencies. Examples are common in the public sector, where systems have been particularly susceptible to expensive failure or curtailment.

The concept of role is well established for providing scalable security administration. Role-based access control (RBAC) separates the administration of people, and their association with roles, from the control of privileges for the use of services (including service-managed data). Service developers need only be concerned with specifying access policy in terms of roles, and not with individual users. Here we focus on securing the communication service. Domain managers, or their delegates, specify communication policy in terms of message types and roles; that is, which roles may create, advertise, send and receive which types of message. Inter-domain communication is achieved through negotiated agreements, expressed as access control policy, on which role(s) of one domain may receive (which attributes of) which types of message of another.

Publish/subscribe [1] is emerging as an appropriate communication paradigm for large-scale systems. It allows loose coupling between mutually anonymous components and supports many-to-many communication. In this paper we focus on securing publish/subscribe within and between domains. For consistency with other publish/subscribe systems we use *event* as synonymous with the more general term *message*. The notion of role is ideally suited to a multicast communication style. For example, the Cambridge police domain may define a role *sergeant-on-duty* and message topics such as *traffic-accident (attribute-list)*. Authorisation policy will indicate which roles can advertise, subscribe to and publish each topic. Inter-domain communication is supported, after human negotiation, by indicating in policy that a specified role of some domain may subscribe to certain (attributes of) topics published by some other domain.

Authentication into roles must be securely enforced to control the use of all protected services. We have addressed this in earlier papers. For the communication service, RBAC policy indicates the visibility (to roles, intra- and inter-domain) of specified attributes of message types. The fact that advertisement is required before messages can be published, and both are RBAC-controlled, prevents the spam that pervades email communication between humans. Without such control denial-of-service through publication or subscription flooding could degrade large-scale inter-software communication in the same way that it consumes resources in email management. In our system a spammer could only be an authorised, authenticated member of a role and therefore could be held accountable.

If the network and message brokers could be guaranteed 100% secure and trustworthy, then RBAC would achieve precisely the visibility specified by policy. In practice, we have to protect confidential data on the wire and in the brokers by means of encryption. We offer fine-grained security, in that message attributes are encrypted selectively, with key management transparent to the client level. We assume that some form of message encryption is always needed, since nodes of a communication service are not likely to be trusted universally with all data and the network is vulnerable to listeners. Encryption overhead per se does not need to be justified, and our evaluation indicates that our approach incurs less overhead than using whole-message encryption.

The contribution of this paper is to show how role-based access control, together with fine-grained data encryption and the associated key management, can be integrated with publish/subscribe based communication to create a secure middleware suitable for a wide range of large-scale, widely distributed application domains. First, we set the scene by discussing related research on secured publish/subscribe in Section 2. Section 3 gives background in publish/subscribe systems and role-based access control, emphasising, without loss of generality, the systems we have used for our implementation and evaluation, Hermes and OASIS. We then outline how RBAC and publish/subscribe are integrated. Section 4 presents our multi-domain architecture in more detail. Section 5 uses a multi-domain, networked city as a case study and describes the scenarios evaluated in Section 6. Section 7 presents our conclusions in the context of our ongoing and future research.

2   Related Work

To our knowledge, the architecture we outlined in [2] was the first to consider access control for a publish/subscribe service. There, we took a typical private-sector application, a newsfeed service, comprising a single naming and protection domain. We did not consider public-sector, multi-domain examples, where it becomes natural for a message-broker substrate to be shared, and where different levels of trust in brokers must be accommodated. This work did not address data encryption and key management.

Some authors explicitly exclude security as being orthogonal to the design issues of publish/subscribe [3]. Others have limited their work to the communications level [4]. Others have discussed how publish/subscribe systems might be secured but without explicit design details and evaluation. Wang et al. present a number of considerations for publish/subscribe access control in [5] but without proposing an architecture to solve the problems they raise. Similarly, in [6], Miklós provides semantics defining a security ordering based on event attribute values, but does not describe a practical test prototype. The approach of Miklós is likely to be too restrictive in practice; it will not scale well due to the detailed specifications required to define event security classes and how they interact.

Opyrchal and Prakash concentrate on the separate problem of providing confidentiality for events during the last hop from the local broker to the event subscriber in an efficient manner, with as few encryptions as possible [7]. Limiting the number of last hop encryptions is valuable if the local brokers have poor resources. We assume that the local brokers are powerful enough to deliver events to their subscribers over TLS connections [8]. While more resource-intensive, TLS provides us with strong client and server-side authentication and key management in addition to data encryption.

In sentient and ubiquitous computing environments privacy should be a major concern, for example, when individuals can be recognised automatically and tracked. This issue is not often considered. An exception is the Gaia project where the approach is to guarantee anonymity [9]. [10] is also concerned with anonymity in location systems. Publish/subscribe is based on mutual anonymity at the client level. Parametrised RBAC gives the option of anonymity or identification. However, principals are not anonymous to the system when authenticated into roles and the privileges of misbehaving principals can be withdrawn promptly. Attribute-level policy expression controls the selective propagation of identity attributes at a fine grain.

3   Background and Integration

Although our approach is generally applicable, our design and implementation are based on *Hermes* publish/subscribe and OASIS RBAC. This section provides a brief overview of publish/subscribe systems and role-based access control, describing the features specific to Hermes and OASIS. We then show how a publish/subscribe system can be secured by RBAC.

3.1   Publish/Subscribe Systems

Large-scale, publish/subscribe messaging technology typically comprises a network of brokers, which provide a communication service, and lightweight clients, which use the service to advertise, subscribe to and publish messages [11,12]. Such systems are subject to failures of nodes and links, and their components may join and leave dynamically. A communication service must be robust under these conditions, fault-tolerant and dynamically reconfigurable. For this reason the message brokers are often built above a peer-to-peer overlay network [13], since peer-to-peer naming and protocols provide the necessary robustness.

Publish/subscribe systems are classified as type/topic- or content/attribute-based. Hermes [13,14] is a distributed, content-based publish/subscribe architecture with an integrated programming model and strong message typing. It is built on a peer-to-peer routing substrate to provide scalable event dissemination and fault tolerance.

A Hermes system consists of two kinds of component: *event brokers* and *event clients*, the latter being *publishers* and *subscribers*. Event brokers form the application-level overlay network that performs event propagation by means of a content-based routing algorithm. Event clients publish, or subscribe to, events in the system. An event client has to maintain a connection to a *local event broker*, which then becomes *publisher-hosting*, *subscriber-hosting*, or both. An event broker without connected clients is called an *intermediate broker*.

Hermes supports *event typing*: every published event (or *publication*) in Hermes is an instance of an *event type*. An event type has an *event type owner*, an *event type name* and a list of typed *event attributes* so that, at runtime, publications and subscriptions can be type-checked by the system. Hermes event types are organised into inheritance hierarchies, but our work does not depend on this. We show later how inheritance can be used within domains when it is available.

Each event type defined within a domain is registered by its owner via a local event broker. This causes encryption status and keys to be set up within the domain and a rendezvous node to be selected for peer-to-peer routing. Before a publisher can publish an event instance, it must submit an *advertisement* to its local event broker, indicating the event type that it wishes to publish. Subscribers express their interest in the form of *subscriptions* that specify the desired event type and a conjunction of (content-based) filter expressions over the attributes of this event type.

The rendezvous node for an event type is selected by hashing the type name to a broker identifier – an operation that is supported by the peer-to-peer routing substrate [15]. Advertisements and subscriptions are routed towards the rendezvous node, and brokers along the path set up filtering state for them.

Most publish/subscribe systems, including Hermes, optimise content-based routing of events with a *subscription coverage relation*, that states which subscriptions are subsumed by others [11]. This allows brokers to reduce the number of events sent through the system by enabling them to filter non-matching events as close as possible to the publisher; these filters become increasingly specific as events approach subscribers.

For reliability reasons, rendezvous nodes are replicated for each event type (for example, broker instances can be selected by concatenating a *salt value* to the type name before hashing [16]). In Hermes, a rendezvous node keeps an authoritative copy of the event type definition, which is cached at other brokers throughout the system for type-checking advertisements, subscriptions, and publications. In our current work, authoritative, domain-specific type information is stored within the originating domain and rendezvous nodes hold a copy.

3.2 Role-Based Access Control

Role-Based Access Control (RBAC) [17] is an established technique for simplifying scalable security administration by introducing *roles* as an indirection between *principals* (i.e. users and their agents) and *privileges*. Privileges, such as the right to use a service or to access an object managed by a service, are assigned to roles. Separately, principals are associated with roles. The motivation is that users join, leave and change role in an organisation frequently, and the policy of services is independent of such changes.

The *Open Architecture for Secure Interworking Services* (OASIS) [18,19], provides a comprehensive rule-based means to check that users can only acquire the privileges that authorise them to use services by activating appropriate roles. A role activation policy comprises a set of rules, where a role activation rule for a role r takes the form

$$r_1, .., r_n, a_1, .., a_m, e_1, .., e_l \vdash r$$

where r_i are prerequisite roles, a_i are appointment certificates (most often persistent credentials) and e_i are environmental constraints. The latter allow restrictions to be imposed on when and where roles can be activated (and privileges exercised), for example at restricted times or from restricted computers. Any predicate that must remain true for the principal to remain active in the role is tagged as a *role membership condition*. Such predicates are monitored, and their violation triggers revocation of the role and related privileges from the principal. An authorisation rule for some privilege p takes the form

$$r, e_1, .., e_l \vdash p$$

An authorisation policy comprises a set of such rules. OASIS has no negative rules, and satisfying any one rule indicates success.

OASIS roles and rules are parametrised. This allows fine-grained policy requirements to be expressed and enforced, such as exclusion of individuals and relationships between them, for example *treating-doctor(doctor-ID, patient-ID)*. Without parametrisation it becomes necessary to define an unmanageably large number of roles for an organisation of any size.

3.3   Integration

In OASIS RBAC, the authorisation policy for any service specifies how it can be used in terms of roles and environmental constraints. Here, we use OASIS to protect the publish/subscribe service in this way at a local broker. The service's methods include *define(message-type), advertise(message-type), publish(message-type, attribute-values)* and *subscribe(message-type, filter-expression-on-attribute-values)*. OASIS policy indicates, for each method, the role credentials, each with associated environmental constraints, that authorise invocation. *define* is used to register a message type with the service and specify its security requirements at the granularity of attributes. On *advertise, publish* and *subscribe* these requirements are enforced. We can therefore support secure publish/subscribe within a domain in which roles are named, activated and administered.

A domain-structured OASIS system is engineered with a per-domain, secure OASIS server, as described in [18], and a per-domain policy store containing all the role activation and service-specific authorisation policies. This avoids the need for small services to perform authentication and secure role activation. The domain's OASIS server carries out all per-domain role activation and monitors the role membership rule conditions while the roles are active. This optimisation concentrates role dependency maintenance within a single server and provides a single, per-domain, secure service for managing inter-domain authorisation policy specification and enforcement.

4   A Multi-domain Architecture

In this section we present an architecture for an RBAC-secured, multi-domain publish/subscribe system based on a shared event-broker network. We assume that domains are given unique names within the system as a whole and that roles are named and managed within a domain. We assume that each domain provides a management interface through which role activation policies and services' authorisation policies can be specified and maintained.

A group of domains may have a parent domain from which an initial set of role names and policies is obtained. For example, county police domains may agree to use a nationally defined set of police roles; health service domains may start from an initial national role-set. The domain management interface allows local additions and updates, for example, when government changes national policy. Parametrised roles allow domain-specific parameters, for example *sergeant(Cambridgeshire)*. This avoids the role explosion when non-parametrised RBAC is used on a large scale.

4.1   The Event-Broker Infrastructure

RBAC enforces authorisation policy at the level of clients of the publish/subscribe service. At the service level we have to protect confidential data on the wire and in the broker network. Publisher-hosting brokers must encrypt messages to secure confidential information, first checking against policy that the publisher is authorised to send the attribute values. Subscriber-hosting brokers must decrypt messages and deliver to the subscriber the attributes that it is allowed by policy to read. These policies are specified when the message type is defined.

We distinguish between trusted and untrusted brokers. For example, a national police service may comprise some tens of county-level domains, deploying a (sub)network of brokers, trusted by all police domains. Statically, these brokers are trusted by police to encrypt and decrypt police data. Dynamically, under monitoring, some broker may come under suspicion and have trust withdrawn from it. The police domains may choose to route data through the untrusted brokers of other services, for example in rural regions. In general, police domains may interoperate with other emergency service domains and with the media or public via parts of the broker network that are untrusted.

A shared broker infrastructure may be built up when public sector domains agree to interoperate. Alternatively, a broker infrastructure may be provided commercially or as a public service, and independent, distributed applications may use it to communicate intra- or inter-application. In both scenarios the domains/applications will have different levels of trust in the various brokers.

A shared event-broker infrastructure offers both direct and indirect benefits: management overheads are reduced by operating only a single broker network instead of a separate one for each domain, with federation via gateways (as in [20]). Untrusted brokers can augment trusted brokers' routing abilities, ensuring better resilience to failures. These direct benefits are particularly significant when the network has many domains, and/or the domains are small. The indirect benefits of using a shared network are equally important: networks of trust can be established and reconfigured more easily, since the privileges of brokers and clients are controlled dynamically within a homogeneous access control scheme. Also, encrypting attributes separately allows a single event to contain both public and private information.

Key Management for Trust Groups. A broker network comprising multiple trust groups must have a key manager for each group. Some domains' OASIS servers will maintain key-groups of trusted brokers and distribute keys to them, transparently to the clients of the publish/subscribe service. A broker must be provided with credentials that allow it to join a trust group. Intermediate trusted brokers decrypt messages to achieve efficient content-based routing. Untrusted brokers participate in routing at the message, rather than attribute, level; details are given below. When a broker becomes untrusted, new keys must be distributed to the remaining group members. We do not address malicious brokers with byzantine behaviour that may corrupt routing state.

In Fig. 1 the brokers are annotated with the encryption keys to which they have access; **P** for the *police* key, **F** for the *fire* key. The broker to which the reporter is attached can deliver only unrestricted public data.

Suppose inter-domain communication is negotiated and an authorised subscription is made from an external domain that has brokers in a different trust group. The police and fire services of Fig. 1 are an example. Such a negotiated agreement, that events of one domain may be subscribed to from another, implies that the local brokers of publishers and subscribers are trusted to encrypt and decrypt the authorised attributes, and have the appropriate keys.

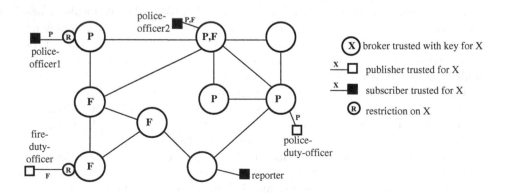

Fig. 1. Illustration of Secure Publish/Subscribe

4.2 Policy

Policy and enforcement mechanisms must be in place to support:

(i) Secure connection by a new broker in order to become part of a group of trusted brokers.
(ii) Secure connection by a client to any trusted local broker.
(iii) Secure propagation of messages through the broker network with confidentiality of attributes enforced as specified by policy.
(iv) RBAC-controlled use of the publish/subscribe service by clients.

For (i) and (ii), publishers, subscribers and brokers hold public key pairs, bound to identity certificates (e.g. X.509 [21]), to connect to their local OASIS service. Successful authentication will allow brokers to become part of a trusted group for key management purposes, and will allow clients to proceed to request activation of the roles that authorise advertisements, subscriptions and publications.

The authentication key pairs are also used in creating client and server-side authenticated TLS connections between nodes. This prevents simple network sniffing attacks by outsiders, thus helping to achieve data confidentiality and integrity, contributing to (iii). For (iii) the key management service controls the propagation of attribute decryption keys to trusted brokers.

(iv) was introduced in Section 3. The authorisation policy for the *define(type)* operation specifies the credentials and constraints required for registering new message types with the publish/subscribe service in a domain, and subsequently for managing the registered types. It controls the ability to modify and remove existing types and, in Hermes, to create sub-types. When a parent domain exists it is likely that an initial set of message types will be used by all child domains, similar to the use of nationally agreed role-names within related domains. A type-specific *read-write policy*, if present, augments and refines the advertisement and subscription policies. It defines, at the attribute level, the roles that can read and/or write the various attributes of a type and can also restrict access by attribute value, see below.

An *advertisement policy* defines which roles are allowed to advertise, and then to publish, events of each given type. Environmental constraints may also be included, see Section 3. Their actions may be subject to further *restriction*, see below, as indicated by the type-specific *read-write policy*. A *subscription policy* defines the authorised receiver roles and conditions in a similar fashion. If required, individual clients can be identified using role parameters.

Restriction. A publisher or subscriber role may be authorised by the *publication* or *subscription* policies, but restricted by the type-specific *read-write policy* to a subset of the attributes of some event type that it requests, and/or for a subset of the values of certain attributes. Rather than reject the request outright, the local broker may allow the request after applying a restriction.

In the case of a publisher, any attribute value whose *read-write policy* does not include write access is ignored. A simple approach is to omit the attribute from the marshalled data, and supply a null value to subscribers. With a type hierarchy it may be possible to restrict publications to a super-type of the requested type, if *advertisement policy* allows that. In the case of a subscriber, the natural restriction is to suppress the attribute value whenever the subscriber does not have read access to an attribute under *read-write policy*.

Authorisation to advertise, publish or subscribe may also depend on conditions such as event type or content, date, time or frequency of publication. Thus a publisher may be restricted to publish certain events between 9am and 5pm. OASIS environmental constraints can specify and enforce some of these conditions, and publish/subscribe filtering may implement some forms of restriction by attribute value. In general, specific predicates must be computed by the local broker of the client to which the restrictions apply, see Section 5.

4.3   Attribute Encryption

Real-world occurrences often include confidential data that should be accessible only to authorised subjects, e.g. the press should know about a car accident on a highway, but the names of the victims should stay confidential to the police and health services. This is achieved by RBAC policy and mechanism at application level, and by encrypting attributes (in publications) and filter expressions (in subscriptions) with symmetric keys at the message service level, as outlined above. Although our approach introduces run-time overhead due to the cryptographic operations on attributes of publications and subscriptions, it allows the same publication to be disseminated to subscribers with different privileges, thus using the event dissemination tree efficiently. Section 6 shows that attribute encryption can decrease the overall cryptographic overheads.

Event Types with Attribute Encryption in Hermes.   To indicate attribute encryption within the Hermes type system, we annotate the event type hierarchy with the keys that are used to encrypt specific attributes, reflecting defined policy. Local brokers of publishers and subscribers implement this security policy; clients are not concerned with encryption. Each attribute of an event type is either *public*, indicated by the empty key (0), or it must be encrypted using one or more keys. Fig. 2 shows annotated type hierarchies for Police and Fire Service domains. The `location` attribute in a `PoliceEvent` may be encrypted using both *police* and *fire* keys. This would result in two instances of the same attribute in a single event, each instance encrypted with a different key.

The standard inheritance sub-typing relation between event types must still hold: a subtype has to be more specific than its parent type. As a result, encryption keys can only be removed from inherited attributes but not added. This is illustrated in Fig. 2 with the `location` attribute, whose access becomes more restrictive as new event types are derived.

Coverage Relations with Encrypted Filters.   In order to take advantage of subscription coverage (described in Section 3), we extend this relation to handle subscriptions that refer to encrypted attributes.

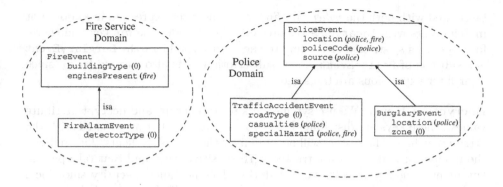

Fig. 2. Per-Domain Event Type Hierarchies with Attribute Encryption

A filter expression encrypted under a particular key is covered by a previous filter expression if this previous filter is the same or more general, and is encrypted under the same key (including the case where neither expression is encrypted). A subscription is then covered by another subscription if all its filter expressions are covered. More formally, if s_1 and s_2 are two subscriptions with a conjunction of filter expressions f^i and g^j encrypted under the keys k_i and l_j, respectively,

$$s_1 = f_{k_1}^1 \wedge f_{k_2}^2 \wedge \ldots \wedge f_{k_n}^n \tag{1}$$
$$s_2 = g_{l_1}^1 \wedge g_{l_2}^2 \wedge \ldots \wedge g_{l_m}^m, \tag{2}$$

then s_1 covers ($\sqsupseteq$) s_2 is defined as follows:

$$s_1 \sqsupseteq s_2 \iff \forall i \exists j. \, f_{k_i}^i \sqsupseteq g_{l_j}^j \wedge k_i = l_j \tag{3}$$

We assume above that each subscription includes empty filters encrypted with all available keys by default.

The coverage relations between the example subscriptions s_1 to s_4 are shown in Fig. 3. Subscription s_1 is the most general because it does not specify any filter expressions. It covers the second subscription s_2, which specifies a filter f_1 over the location attribute encrypted under the *police* key or the *fire* key. Subscribers can only provide meaningful filters for encrypted attributes if they have read access, and in addition the broker handling the s_2 subscription must

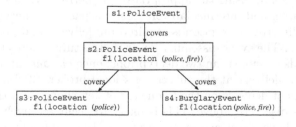

Fig. 3. Subscription Coverage with Attribute Encryption

be trusted with both the *police* and *fire* keys. The filter expression in s_3 does not match events with `location` attributes encrypted under the *fire* key and therefore s_2 covers s_3 strictly. According to the event type hierarchy `BurglaryEvent` is a subtype of `PoliceEvent`, hence subscription s_4 is also covered by s_2, since their filter expressions are the same.

Encryption Keys. We use symmetric keys to encrypt and decrypt attribute values. These keys are distributed only to the brokers that are trusted with the attribute values. The system will never deliver these keys to clients. This reduces the number of nodes that are trusted with sensitive keys, and that take part in key management protocols. Note that this does not affect security since local brokers encrypt and decrypt attribute values on behalf of connected clients, and deliver events to clients over secure links.

To support cryptographic properties such as key freshness, and forward and backward secrecy [22], the system requires key management service(s). The most suitable key management strategy depends on the broker-network architecture. For EDSAC21 we assume a stable configuration with static, multi-hop, inter-broker connections and are investigating a tree-based approach [22]. However, the dynamic nature of a peer-to-peer routing layer presents special problems, and we are also evaluating an alternative, ad-hoc network based approach [23].

Efficient group key management [24] is not the focus of this paper. Overall, the efficiency of key distribution will have little impact on performance, since symmetric keys are distributed only to brokers, as opposed to publishers and subscribers. Relatively few entities are involved in key dissemination, and changes will be infrequent. However, correct key management is essential for the security of the system.

4.4   Security Overheads

When compared with basic publish/subscribe, our secured publish/subscribe introduces three types of processing overhead: *one-time only*, *per event*, and *key management related*. (1) One-time only overheads include node authentication and authorisation when new nodes connect to the network, and subscription-filter encryptions. (2) Per event overheads include those caused by encrypting and decrypting attributes, and applying restriction predicates at local brokers. One encryption is required for each instance of a secure attribute in a published event (see Section 4.3), using the appropriate symmetric key; this happens only once at the source, and intermediate brokers can pass the encrypted event to the next node directly. Decryption is required on delivery, and possibly at each routing step, too. The event dissemination tree structure ensures that each new subscription adds no more than two decryptions: once *en route* at a filtering broker, and once on delivery at the subscriber's local broker. (3) Finally, the cost of key management depends on the frequency of key change and the dissemination method, as discussed above. This is likely to occur relatively infrequently, as clients never have direct access to encryption keys, and key management is handled at broker-level only.

In addition to processing overheads, attribute encryption increases the size of events in two ways: (1) a single attribute value encrypted with multiple keys results in multiple instances of that value, each encrypted with a different key; (2) encryption algorithm mechanisms dictate that the encrypted data must be at least of some minimum length, depending on the encryption algorithm. Common minimum lengths would be 64 bits and 128 bits. Thus, a single 8 bit attribute value encrypted with three keys grows in size to 192 bits because of padding and multiple attribute instances. This might be avoided by using a stream cipher, which operates on a stream of data one bit at a time, rather than a block cipher.

5   Case Study: Public Services Within a City

We now illustrate our architecture for a city in which the publish/subscribe systems of different emergency services interoperate securely and efficiently. We use a break-in to a university building as an example. Fig. 4 shows the principals, brokers and messages discussed below. We assume that equipment failure has left the police network partititioned, and that broker **b1** is connected only through the fire network.

1) We focus on two police officers on night shift; part of their duty is to respond to notifications of burglaries. We assume that the event-type BurglaryEvent is already advertised when the officers come on duty. This means that a rendezvous node **b5** is assigned for the type and subscriptions can be made. We shall see that further advertisements, and subsequent publications, can be made as burglaries are detected in different areas.

We assume that both officers authenticate with their local OASIS service on coming on duty and, assuming that their credentials are valid, acquire the role with associated privilege to send subscription messages: $s1$ and $s2$ respectively.

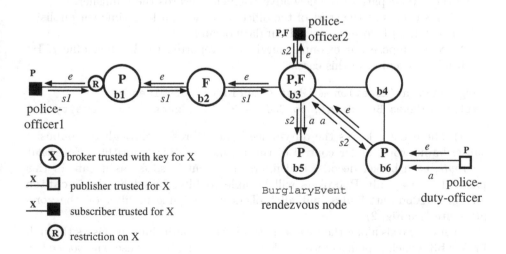

Fig. 4. Notifying two police officers of a BurglaryEvent

Officer 1 is a probationary officer, who moves between different parts of the city. Officer 2 is located in West Cambridge. Suppose that at the start of her shift officer 2 subscribes to `BurglaryEvent(location = 'West Cambridge')`. Since this subscription requires filtering on the `location` attribute, and this attribute is encrypted with the *police* key (recall the event type hierarchy shown in Fig. 2), the officer knows that her local broker must be trusted with the *police* key, i.e. a **P** broker.

Officer 1 tries to subscribe to all burglary events with a police code less than 4, `BurglaryEvent(polCode < 4)`, but the request is only partially granted. Instead, the subscription is restricted, as described in Section 4, to deliver only those events that occur in the officer's current location. This restriction, which is based on a dynamically checked environmental constraint, is shown in Fig. 4, attached to his broker connection.

2) Any broker through which $s1$ and/or $s2$ travel (towards their rendezvous node and then along the reverse path of advertisements) will update its internal routing state appropriately. Note that our security architecture augments standard Hermes subscription setup behaviour when we reach broker **b2**. Whilst $s1$ travels through this broker, the broker is not part of the police network, and thus will not have access to the *police* key. Therefore this broker will be forced to degrade routing efficiency by ignoring police officer 1's filter on the `polCode` attribute, which it cannot decrypt, and routing all events forward.

3) We show a duty-officer at a police station who must notify police officers of reported burglaries. Like officers 1 and 2, the duty-officer authenticates himself with his local OASIS service, and acquires privileges to advertise `BurglaryEvents`. Again, his local broker needs access to the *police* key. The consequent advertisement message is shown as a in Fig. 4. This step could occur in parallel with a subscription, see Step 1. If a broker notices that an existing subscription matches a new advertisement, it will resend the subscription message along the reverse path of the new advertisement towards the publisher.

All this occurs at the start of the officers' sessions, a long time (in publish/subscribe terms) before the actual burglary occurs.

4) Now suppose our example burglary is reported to the duty-officer. He publishes an event e, in this case:

```
BurglaryEvent(location = 'West Cambridge', premises =
'William Gates Building', polCode = 3, ..., zone = 'university').
```

5) The event e leaves the duty-officer's local broker, through the publish/subscribe network, under control of the Hermes routing algorithm. Note that *en route*, each broker decodes and filters the event in so far as it can. In this particular case, only **P** brokers will be able to filter based on the `location` and/or `polCode` attributes, but all brokers will be able to filter on the `zone` attribute (see Fig. 2).

6) As e travels along the reverse path of the subscriptions, it passes through broker **b3**, which is police officer 2's local broker. The broker uses the *police* key to decrypt the `location` and `polCode` attributes before delivering the event to officer 2 over the secure 'final hop' set up as described in Step 1 above.

7) In order to reach police officer 1, e needs to be routed through **b2**. While this is not the most desirable mode of operation, since the event passes through a broker that does not have access to the *police* key, it is crucially better than the situation in which the police network remains partitioned.

As mentioned in Step 2, since broker **b2** cannot decrypt *police* encrypted attributes, it cannot apply filtering on fields such as `location`. Thus for routing e, the event appears as `BurglaryEvent(location = ?, polCode = ?, ...,` `zone = 'university')`, and it is passed on to **b1** regardless of its `location` value.

8) Finally, the local broker **b1** of police officer 1, which is trusted with the *police* key, will receive e from **b2**, and decrypt the `location` attribute. It will then apply the restriction, checking whether officer 1 is currently in West Cambridge. If so, **b1** will decrypt the entire event and pass it over the secure 'final hop' to officer 1. We have assumed for simplicity that although officer 1 is mobile he remains connected to the same local broker. The alternative is that he creates a new OASIS session whenever he needs to connect to a different broker.

6 Evaluation

The EDSAC21 project is substantial and still at an early stage. We have carried out the following simulation studies to validate the approach. Fig. 5 and Fig. 6 compare the performance of our attribute encryption implementation with the more common approach (such as [4]) that encrypts multiple instances of entire events with each of the relevant keys. Each figure shows the average result of three simulations for each data point.

These experiments all used the Hermes publish/subscribe system for message routing, running over a simulated network topology of 1000 IP routers (organised

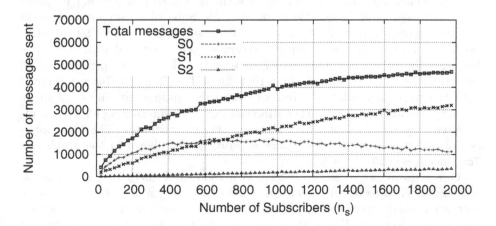

Fig. 5. Total number of messages with attribute encryption

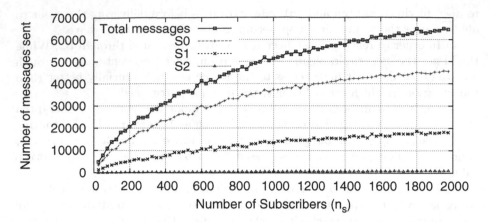

Fig. 6. Total number of messages without attribute encryption

into ten autonomous subnetworks), with fifty randomly chosen event brokers. In this overlay network we randomly introduced ten event publishers, who, in each iteration of the test, published a total number of 1000 events.

We used the case study scenario of Section 5 as a basis for the simulation, generating events of type PoliceEvent. There were three groups of subscribers: (1) public information services (S0) that filtered only on a single unencrypted attribute (severity); (2) police officers (S1) who filtered on a single *police* encrypted attribute (location); (3) police trainers (S2) who held both *police* and *policeTraining* keys and filtered on isDrill and location. For the attribute encrypted case, publishers encrypted the individual message attributes as shown in Fig. 2. The implementation that encrypts whole events had to send up to three instances of each event, one for each of the independent security domains covered by a message.

The events were delivered to the subscribers, whose number (n_s) we gradually increased from 25 to 2000 in steps of 25. Subscribers set random filters on event attribute values. Five per cent of all subscriptions were S2 subscriptions that filtered on two encrypted attributes, one encrypted with the *police* key, and the other with the *policeTraining* key. Thirty five per cent of all subscriptions were S1 subscriptions that filtered on one attribute encrypted with the *police* key, while the rest were S0 subscriptions filtering on a single unencrypted attribute. Note that subscriptions with filtering on encrypted attributes may also include filters on unencrypted attributes. The total number of events sent within the broker network is also shown in the graphs, as Total messages = S0 + S1 + S2.

Our performance results show that with 1000 subscribers, only about 39300 messages needed to be sent when using attribute encryption, while 51400 were sent when events were encrypted atomically with one key at a time – a 24% saving in bandwidth. For 2000 subscribers, the savings had increased further to 27%.

As the number of subscribers increases, the network with attribute encryption eventually becomes saturated by complex filtering; this is because it becomes increasingly likely that there is a local S1 or S2 subscriber at each broker for any given event. Thus the number of events that need to be decrypted (S1 and S2) grows in Fig. 5, initially because of new event dissemination routes, but later also because events previously counted under S0 now need at least one attribute decrypted; they contribute instead to S1 or S2, which explains the eventual fall-off of the S0 tally as the number of subscribers increases. However, even with 2000 subscribers there were over 11000 event hops for which no attribute decryptions were needed.

Attribute encryption slightly increases the number of times that events need to be decrypted for filtering. However, this is largely compensated by the fact that we then need fewer point-to-point encryptions and decryptions within a TLS connection (total decryptions $= 2 \times S2 + S1$). For 2000 subscribers, whole event encryption needed about 87400 decryptions, while attribute encryption required a grand total of approximately 88500, – an increase of 1.2%. However, for a less saturated network with 1000 subscriptions, overall encryptions decreased by 2.7%.

Note that generally the overall load on event brokers is decreased still further in our approach, since less data needs to be decrypted at each filtering decryption step (a few attributes, as opposed to the whole event).

7   Conclusions and Future Work

Security is a crucial concern for the development of scalable messaging systems, particularly those for the public sector where data is often highly confidential and privacy must be guaranteed. Publish/Subscribe communication is recognised as appropriate for large-scale systems, yet most research on it excludes security. This paper presents our architecture for a secure publish/subscribe middleware. Our system builds on the performance and fault-tolerance of publish/subscribe messaging, and augments it with scalable security administration based on decentralised Role-Based Access Control. We assume a multi-domain architecture for administration of roles, message types and policies.

Although our implementation uses Hermes and OASIS, our design is applicable to publish/subscribe systems in general. To secure a topic-based publish/subscribe system, whole event encryption would be used, with given events being sent multiple times, encrypted under different keys. Our simulation takes this approach as a basis for comparison. To secure a content-based publish/subscribe system, whole event encryption could be used, but we have shown that it is practicable to encrypt the different attributes of an event separately.

Using an "Active City" example, we show how various public-sector, emergency service notifications can be captured in an event type hierarchy, and how access control and attribute encryption can facilitate secure and efficient communication. If a type hierarchy is not available, our design equally well supports separate services using a shared publish/subscribe system with a flat message type-space.

We have simulated attribute encryption and whole-event encryption for a scenario based on the case study in Section 5. We show that our approach reduces the number of events sent in the system, as well as the processing required for decryptions performed by brokers. Efficiency was not the main focus of our design; rather, we were concerned to demonstrate that the expressiveness of fine-grained access control need not incur undue implementation overhead.

Current and Future Work. This research is part of a project, EDSAC21, to provide secure middleware for large-scale, widely distributed applications. The system mechanisms themselves are used to maintain role membership rules and push changes of policy, thus facilitating immediate response to changes in security predicates.

In [25] we present current work on ensuring the system-wide uniqueness and integrity of message type names and versions, and [26] discusses how a broker network is assembled securely and maintained. We are currently integrating active databases and publish/subscribe. Database message types are defined as described in Section 4.2. Database instances can then advertise the events they are prepared to publish, and subscribers use the standard subscription mechanism [27].

We are also working on how to support communication patterns other than the anonymous multicast of publish/subscribe, while retaining the efficiency and resilience of a broker network. Natural requirements are for an individual member of a role to be selected on publication, and for any recipient to be able to reply to a publication, either anonymously (as in voting) or identified.

We shall continue to assume stationary rather than mobile brokers. Since OASIS is session-based we have so far assumed that mobile clients will remain connected to a single broker during their period of subscription. We envisage natural extensions that allow detached operation while a subscription persists, where a local broker (or a separate service) will buffer messages on behalf of detached clients. Future work is to investigate how best to support client mobility during a period of subscription.

In this paper we have demonstrated the synergy between roles and publish/subscribe communication within and between domains, and have shown the feasibility of expressing and enforcing fine-grained security policy.

Acknowledgements

We acknowledge the contributions of Peter Pietzuch, Brian Shand and András Belokosztolszki. The EDSAC21 project builds on their research as graduate students and they were involved in the design of the architecture presented here. EPSRC GR/T28164 supports Lauri Pesonen and EPSRC GR/S94919 supports David Eyers.

References

1. Eugster, P.T., Felber, P.A., Guerraoui, R., Kermarrec, A.M.: The many faces of publish/subscribe. ACM Computing Surveys **35** (2003) 114–131
2. Belokosztolszki, A., Eyers, D.M., Pietzuch, P.R., Bacon, J.M., Moody, K.: Role-based access control for publish/subscribe middleware architectures. In: 2nd International Workshop on Distributed Event-Based Systems (DEBS'03). ICDCS, ACM SIGMOD (2003)
3. Baldoni, R., Contenti, M., Virgillito, A.: The evolution of publish/subscribe communication systems. In: Future Directions of Distributed Computing. Volume 2584 of LNCS., Springer (2003) 137–141
4. Yan, Y., Huang, Y., Fox, G., Pallickara, S., Pierce, M., Kaplan, A., Topcu, A.: Implementing a prototype of the security framework for distributed brokering systems. In: Proceedings of the International Conference on Security and Management (SAM'03). (2003) 212–218
5. Wang, C., Carzaniga, A., Evans, D., Wolf, A.: Security issues and requirements in internet-scale publish-subscribe systems. In: Proceedings of the 35th Annual Hawaii International Conference on System Sciences (HICSS'02), IEEE (2002) 303
6. Miklós, Z.: Towards an access control mechanism for wide-area publish/subscribe systems. In: 1st International Workshop on Distributed Event-Based Systems (DEBS'02). ICDCS, IEEE (2002) 516–524
7. Opyrchal, L., Prakash, A.: Secure distribution of events in content-based publish subscribe systems. In: 10th USENIX Security Symposium. (2001)
8. Dierks, T., Allen, C.: The TLS protocol, version 1.0, RFC-2246. Internet Engineering Task Force (1999)
9. Campbell, R., Al-Muhtadi, J., Naldurg, P., Sampemane, G., Mickunas, M.D.: Towards security and privacy for pervasive computing. In: Software Security – Theories and Systems, Mext-NSF-JSPS International Symposium, ISSS 2002. Volume 2609 of LNCS., Springer (2002) 1–15
10. Beresford, A., Stajano, F.: Location privacy in pervasive computing. IEEE Pervasive Computing **2** (2003) 46–55
11. Carzaniga, A., Rosenblum, D.S., Wolf, A.L.: Design and evaluation of a wide-area event notification service. ACM Transactions on Computer Systems **19** (2001) 332–383
12. Banavar, G., Kaplan, M., Shaw, K., Strom, R.E., Sturman, D.C., Tao, W.: Information flow based event distribution middleware. In: Middleware Workshop at the International Conference on Distributed Computing Systems 1999. (1999)
13. Pietzuch, P.R., Bacon, J.M.: Peer-to-peer overlay broker networks in an event-based middleware. In: 2nd International Workshop on Distributed Event-Based Systems (DEBS'03). ICDCS, ACM SIGMOD (2003)
14. Pietzuch, P.R., Bacon, J.M.: Hermes: A distributed event-based middleware architecture. In: 1st International Workshop on Distributed Event-Based Systems (DEBS'02). ICDCS, IEEE Press (2002) 611–618
15. Rowstron, A., Druschel, P.: Pastry: Scalable, decentralized object location and routing for large-scale peer-to-peer systems. In: Middleware '01, IFIP/ACM International Conference on Distributed Systems Platforms. (2001) 329–350
16. Zhao, B.Y., Kubiatowicz, J.D., Joseph, A.D.: Tapestry: An infrastructure for fault-tolerant wide-area location and routing. Technical Report UCB/CSD-01-1141, UC Berkeley (2001)

17. Sandhu, R., Coyne, E., Feinstein, H.L., Youman, C.E.: Role-based access control models. IEEE Computer **29** (1996) 38–47
18. Bacon, J., Moody, K., Yao, W.: Access control and trust in the use of widely distributed services. In: Middleware '01, IFIP/ACM International Conference on Distributed Systems Platforms. Volume 2218 of LNCS., Springer (2001) 295–310
19. Bacon, J., Moody, K., Yao, W.: A model of OASIS role-based access control and its support for active security. ACM Transactions on Information and System Security (TISSEC) **5** (2002) 492–540
20. Hombrecher, A.B.: Reconciling Event Taxonomies Across Administrative Domains. PhD thesis, University of Cambridge Computer Laboratory, Cambridge, UK (2002)
21. ITU-T (Telecommunication Standardization Sector, International Telecommunication Union): ITU-T Recommendation X.509: The Directory – Authentication Framework. (2000)
22. Kim, Y., Perrig, A., Tsudik, G.: Tree-based group key agreement. ACM Transactions on Information and System Security **7** (2004) 60–96
23. Hietalahti, M.: Efficient key agreement for ad-hoc networks. Master's thesis, Helsinki University of Technology, Department of Computer Science and Engineering, Espoo, Finland (2001)
24. Rafaeli, S., Hutchison, D.: A survey of key management for secure group communication. ACM Computing Surveys **35** (2003) 309–329
25. Pesonen, L., Bacon, J.: Secure event types in content-based, multi-domain publish/subscribe systems. In: Fifth International Workshop on Software Engineering and Middleware (SEM05). (2005) To appear.
26. Pesonen, L., Eyers, D., Bacon, J.: A capability-based access control architecture for multi-domain publish/subscribe systems. (2006) Submitted for publication.
27. Vargas, L., Bacon, J., Moody, K.: Integrating databases with publish/subscribe. In: 4th International Workshop on Distributed Event-Based Systems (DEBS'05). ICDCS, IEEE Press (2005) 392–397

ABACUS: A Distributed Middleware for Privacy Preserving Data Sharing Across Private Data Warehouses*

Fatih Emekci, Divyakant Agrawal, and Amr El Abbadi

Department of Computer Science,
University of California at Santa Barbara
{fatih, agrawal, amr}@cs.ucsb.edu

Abstract. Recent trends in the global economy force competitive enterprises to collaborate with each other to analyze markets in a better way and make decisions based on that. Therefore, they might want to share their data with each other to run data mining algorithms over the union of their data to get more accurate and representative results. During this process they do not want to reveal their data to each other due to the legal issues and competition. However, current systems do not consider privacy preservation in data sharing across private data sources. To satisfy this requirement, we propose a distributed middleware, ABACUS, to perform intersection, join, and aggregation queries over multiple private data warehouses in a privacy preserving manner. Our analytical evaluations show that ABACUS is efficient and scalable.

1 Introduction

Recent trends in the global economy force competitive enterprises to collaborate with each other for the purpose of market analysis. One of the most important examples of such collaboration is data sharing to mine and understand the market trends to be used in decision making. However, although enterprises are willing to share information with each other, they do not want to reveal their data. Due to the legal issues and competition in the market, datasources want to preserve the privacy of their data while sharing them. For example, consider a scenario consisting of two hotels, H_1 and H_2, and two airlines, A_1 and A_2. Assume hotel H_1 wants to offer a new deal to each of its customers including hotel and flight expenses based on his/her flight history. Therefore, hotel H_1 needs to learn flight history of its customers from airlines A_1 and A_2. One method to learn flight history of customers is that airlines send all of their data to hotel H_1 so that hotel H_1 can extract desired information. However, these airlines also work with hotel H_2, which is a competitor of hotel H_1, and thus they may not want to send all of their data to hotel H_1. That is because hotel H_1 can discover the customers of hotel H_2 and try to attract them. Therefore, if airlines want to work with both hotels, they cannot send their data to any of these hotels. Similarly, hotel H_1 cannot send its data to airlines so that airlines can extract the information that hotel H_1 needs since airlines will discover

---

* This research was funded in parts by NSF grants IS-02-23022 and CNF-04-23336.

G. Alonso (Ed.): Middleware 2005, LNCS 3790, pp. 21–41, 2005.

each other's customers. In order to be able to collaborate, hotel H_1 should take its customers' information from airlines in a way that airlines A_1 and A_2 share their data with hotel H_1 by only revealing common customers (i.e., revealing $H_1 \cap A_1$ to H_1 and A_1 and $H_1 \cap A_2$ to H_1 and A_2). By using such a method hotel H_1 cannot discover new customers which may be customers of hotel H_2 and also airlines cannot discover new customers which may be customers of the other airline. In addition to this, hotel H_1 may want to know the total amount of its customers' travel expenses or total expenditure of a customer for its future business decisions and offers. Other enterprises may be willing to collaborate with hotel H_1, if they can preserve their privacy. The essential operations to perform these collaborations are privacy preserving intersection, join and aggregation queries. Unfortunately, we cannot use traditional query processing techniques since they do not consider privacy issues. Therefore, there is a need for privacy preserving query processing and data sharing across multiple private data warehouses.

Data integration and sharing has emerged as an important practical problem from a data management point of view [3,4,7,8,9]. Techniques used for this purpose commonly assume that the data sources are willing to allow access to all their data without privacy concerns during query processing. This assumption, however, is unrealistic in real life since most of the time data sources are competing enterprises. There have been several techniques in the areas of database and cryptography for privacy preserving data sharing. One of them is to use trusted third parties such that data sources hand over their data and a third party performs the computation on their behalf [1,10]. The level of trust may not be acceptable in these methods. Another approach is using secure multi-party computation where given m parties and their respective inputs $x_1, x_2, .., x_m$, a function $f(x_1, x_2, ..., x_m)$ is computed such that all parties can only learn $f(x_1, x_2, ..., x_m)$ but nothing else [6,7,11]. The computation and the communication costs make this method impractical for database operations working over a large number of elements.

In this paper, we address the problem of privacy preserving data sharing over multiple private data warehouses. We propose a distributed middleware, ABACUS, to perform intersection, join, and aggregation queries over multiple private data warehouses in a privacy preserving manner. Privacy preservation means that parties involved in the query would only be able to learn the query result but nothing else. In addition, we introduce new types of aggregation queries needed in this context and propose efficient techniques to process them. ABACUS operates as a proxy among private data warehouses and allows users to pose queries over multiple private data warehouses. Our analytical evaluations demonstrate that ABACUS provides an efficient and scalable scheme to perform intersection, join, and aggregation queries.

The rest of the paper is organized as follows. Section 2 formulates the problem and presents the architecture overview. Section 3 describes intersection and join query processing. Aggregation query processing is discussed in Section 4 and the analysis is presented in Section 5. The last section concludes the paper.

2 Problem Definition and Architecture Overview

Enterprises gather data from their multiple operational databases into a data warehouse, which is one the most popular ways of storing data to support decision-making in or-

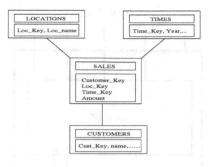

Fig. 1. An Example of Star Schema

ganizations. Data warehouse systems or OLAP (Online Analytical Processing) systems are different than OLTP (On-Line Transaction Processing) systems which are designed for fast updates. Thus, large enterprises have both OLAP and OLTP systems to support both an on-line community who expect fast response time for executing transactions and off-line users who expect to analyze the data in a reasonable amount of time. Most enterprises create a large data warehouse, and periodically extract data from OLTP systems into data warehouse to be able to analyze data without interfering with online users. Data Warehouses usually use star schema for fast execution of queries over aggregated data. Star schema has dimension tables and a fact table containing a foreign key for each of the dimension tables. Furthermore, it is usually not normalized for efficient query response time since fewer joins, a bottleneck in query processing, are performed. Figure 1 shows an instance of a star schema with the fact table, *Sales*, and the dimension tables, *Customers*, *Times*, and *Locations*. Current commercial data warehouses support efficient methods to examine data. However, they do not support privacy preserving data sharing across multiple private data warehouses, which is useful for analyzing the market instead of a single company's data.

The problem of query processing across multiple private data warehouses is defined as follows:

> Let D_1, D_2, ..., D_m be the data warehouses (defined with a star schema) of a set of m data sources $P = \{P_1, ..., P_m\}$ and q be a query spanning D_1 through D_m. The problem is to compute the answer of q without revealing any additional information to any of the data sources.

Agrawal et al. [2] solved the problem of privacy preserving query processing across private databases by restricting it to two data sources with some relaxation in an honest-but-curious environment [6] for intersection and equijoin operations. The honest-but-curious environment means that parties follow the protocols correctly but keep all messages sent and received during the course of the query processing. The relaxation reveals the sizes of the tables or lists in the database to the other party. However, the proposed technique has two shortcomings: 1) Encryption is a computation intensive operation which is not suitable for database operations where large numbers of items need to be processed. 2) It does not support aggregation queries, which are among the most important queries.

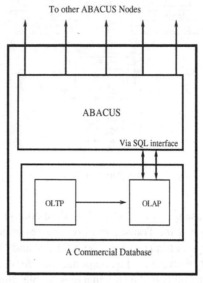

To other ABACUS Nodes

ABACUS

Via SQL interface

OLTP → OLAP

A Commercial Database

An ABACUS Node

Fig. 2. The architecture of a ABACUS node

In this paper, we propose ABACUS for privacy preserving data sharing across multiple private data warehouses. ABACUS eliminates the need for third parties by taking advantage of the star schema and executes intersection, join and aggregation queries in a privacy preserving manner. In addition, we introduce new types of aggregation operators which are useful in the context of data warehouse and solve them efficiently. ABACUS also operates in an honest-but-curios environment and it reveals the size of tables and lists similar to [2].

ABACUS is a distributed middleware operating on top of any commercial database as shown in Figure 2. It provides a user interface where users can pose queries over multiple private data warehouses. ABACUS executes queries by running ABACUS nodes operating on different data warehouses. Each ABACUS node interacts with its data warehouse via SQL interface supplied by the underlying commercial database. Then, it contacts other ABACUS nodes and shares its data with them to process queries in a privacy preserving manner using the protocols proposed in this paper.

ABACUS does not aim to solve the problem of revealing additional information to a datasource which poses multiple queries and combines their results in order to obtain additional information about the data. In addition, it does not solve the problem of data discovery and schema mediation. Solutions to these problems are discussed briefly in [2] and they could be used in ABACUS.

3   Intersection and Join Query Processing

Intersection and join queries are the two important types of queries supported by current commercial databases without privacy concerns. However, in the context of data sharing across multiple private data warehouses we need privacy preserving intersection and join queries. Therefore, we will define the problems of privacy preserving intersection, and join queries and also show how to solve them efficiently in Section 3.1 and Section 3.2 respectively.

3.1 Aggregated Intersection

Intersection queries constitute the first step for collaboration over common data items. For example, a company may need to know other companies' opinions about its customers. For this kind of collaboration, two companies need to find the common customers as a first step, i.e., intersection. The intersection of two customer lists can be found easily unless they do not hesitate to reveal their customers to each other. However, most of the time companies may not want to reveal their customer lists but only common customers to each other due to legal issues or competition. To support such a type of collaboration, a method for privacy preserving intersection where parties can only learn items in the intersection but nothing else is needed. Therefore, we first define the problem of finding the intersection of lists in the context of data warehouse while preserving the privacy called *aggregated intersection query processing* as follows:

> Let L_1, L_2,..., L_m be the lists containing secret data stored by a set of datasources $P = \{P_1, P_2, ..., P_m\}$ respectively. For each data source P_i, the problem is to find all other data sources, P_j, with $e \in L_j$ for each item $e \in L_i$ in a privacy preserving manner, i.e., if P_j does not have e in L_j, then P_j will not know $e \in L_i$.

Example 1. We illustrate the aggregated intersection problem with an example. Consider three datasources P_1, P_2 and P_3 involved in executing aggregated intersection query with customer tables T_1, T_2 and T_3 respectively as shown in Figure 3. At the end of aggregated query processing, datasources will only learn the common customers they share with other data sources but nothing else. In this example, all data sources will know 6565 exists in tables T_1, T_2, and T_3. P_1 and P_2 will also know that 8080 is common in their tables. Similarly, P_1 and P_3 will know that 7070 is common in tables T_1 and T_3. However, P_2 should not be able to know that P_1 and P_3 have 7070 in their tables. Similarly, P_3 must not know that P_1 and P_2 have 8080 in their tables.

Our solution to the above problem is based on using one-way secure cryptographic hash functions. These hash functions are widely used in many real life applications such as password protection, message authentication, and digital signatures. The examples of such hash functions include *SHA-1, MD4,* and *MD5* [12]. A simple solution to the aggregated intersection problem could use one-way hash functions and compare hashed values of items to determine whether they are the same or not. Basically, data source P_i computes the hashed list of list L_i by computing the hash value of each item in L_i. Then, it sends the hashed list to data source P_j so that it can compare the incoming hashed list with its own hashed list to find the common items in L_i and L_j. According to this scheme, in Example 1, data source P_1 uses a hash function H and sends the list of hashed values, $\{H(6565), H(7070), H(8080)\}$, to P_2 and P_3. Then, P_2 compares the hashed list with its own hashed list, $\{H(6565), H(8080)\}$, and determines that 6565 and 8080 are common. Since the hash function is a one-way hash function, P_2 will not

Costumers

SSN	Name	Surname	Address	Phone
6565	Jack	Brial	6616 K Rd. Xyz 93090 ZT	890–908–4545
7070	...	...	...	...
8080	...	...	...	...

T_1

SSN	Name	Surname	Address	Phone
6565	Jack	Brial	6616 K Rd. Xyz 93090 ZT	890–908–4545
8080				

T_2

SSN	Name	Surname	Address	Phone	E–mail
6565	Jack	Brial	6616 K Rd. Xyz 93090 ZT	890–908–4545	bj@utz.edu
7070					

T_3

Fig. 3. Illustration of Aggregated Intersection

be able to know 7070 is in L_1. This basic solution, however, suffers from the following two problems: 1) If the domain size is small, then item x whose hash value is $H(x)$ could be computed by exhaustively searching the whole domain. 2) Hash collisions might produce inaccurate results.

In the context of data warehouses, data sources usually have more information about the secret items. For example, all data sources in Example 1 keep *name, last name, phone* and *address* information as well as *SSN* (Social Security Number) of a customer in their customers tables. If all of these information is used in hashing, then the domain will become large. For instance, instead of hashing SSN, a concatenation of SSN, name, last name, phone and address could be used in hashing, i.e., $H(6565|Jack|Brial|6616KRD$ $XyzZT93090|8909084545)$ could be used instead of $H(6565)$ for a customer with an SSN 6565. This method allows us to enlarge the domain size and makes exhaustive search impossible. The aggregated intersection problem is to find the common secret items in the dimensions tables in the context of data warehouse. ABACUS uses the common attributes in all of the tables to hash secret items i.e., the values of common attributes are used instead of a value of a primary key. For example, the attributes *SSN, Name, Surname, Phone,* and *Address* are common in T_1, T_2 and T_3 in Example 1. If 5 attributes each of which is 10 characters long are used in hashing, the domain size would be $28^{50} \approx 2^{250}$ which makes exhaustive search impossible.

As mentioned before, hash collisions might result in sharing a secret item which is not in the intersection. H maps values to $| DomH |$ which is assumed to be arbitrarily large compare to the intersection size. Let $N = | DomH |$; in the random oracle model, the probability that n hash values have at least one collision equals [2]: $Pr[collision] = 1 - exp(\frac{-n(n-1)}{2N})$. For 1024 bit hash values and $n = 1$ million, this probability is 10^{-295}

[2]. Thus, the solution to expand the domain size minimizes the probability of data vulnerability by exhaustive search and also helps in reducing the probability of hash collisions, and therefore, errors in the queries are significantly reduced.

3.2 Aggregated Join Queries

One of the most important query operators supported by current commercial database systems is the join operator. Privacy preserving join operations have not been previously considered in database research or in current database management systems. However, they might be needed in data sharing across private data sources. For example, a company (e.g. a hotel) might want to know the transaction details of its customers in other companies (e.g. airlines) in the market to classify them according to their transactions. For instance, a hotel can identify the customers that travel frequently and offer special promotions to them. To be able to do this, it needs to join its customers table with other companies' sales tables. Since other companies may benefit from this process, they might be willing to share transaction details. However, during this process companies are not willing to reveal any information about a customer who is not a customer of the other company as well as his/her existence. Traditional join query processing techniques cannot be used to process these queries since they do not consider privacy issues. In order to satisfy these requirements, we propose a new join operator, the *aggregated join query operator*, to be used for privacy preserving data sharing across private data warehouses. We first formally define the *aggregated join query processing* problem and then propose a solution.

The aggregated join query processing problem is formally defined as follows:

Assume data source P_1 has a dimension table $P_1.T_d$ and data sources $P_2, P_3, ..,$ P_m have fact tables $P_2.T_f, P_3.T_f, ..., P_m.T_f$ respectively with common attribute A. Then, the goal is to compute $P_1.T_d \bowtie P_2.T_f \cup P_1.T_d \bowtie P_3.T_f \cup .... \cup P_1.T_d \bowtie P_m.T_f$ such that none of the data sources learn any extra information other than the query result. Query poser P_1 will learn only the tuples t such that $t \in P_i.T_f$ for which $t.A \in P_1.T_d.A$. In other words, P_i shares a list, L_v, of tuples in $P_i.T_f$ for each value $v \in P_i.T_f.A$ with P_1 if $\exists t \in P_1.T_d$ such that $t.A = v$, and nothing else where $i = 2, 3..., m$.

We illustrate the problem with an example. Assume the three data warehouses in Example 1 want to execute an aggregated join query. And assume P_1 poses the aggregated join query to find the aggregated join of its dimension table, *Customers Table*, with the fact tables, *Sales Table*, of the other data sources as shown in Figure 4. The problem is to provide an answer to this query without revealing any additional information. For this example, P_2 will return the tuples with SSN 6565 and 8080 in its Sales table without knowing P_1 has 7070 in its customers table. Similarly, P_3 will return all tuples with SSN 6565 and 7070 without knowing P_1 has a customer with an SSN 8080. In addition, P_1 will not be revealed the transaction details of other customers which are not in its Customers table, e.g. a customer with an SSN 9090.

ABACUS executes the aggregated join query, $\bigcup_{i=2}^{m} P_1.T_d \bowtie P_i.T_f$, in two phases: *Intersection Phase* and *Join Computation Phase*. In the intersection phase, P_1 and P_j compute the intersection of their dimension tables, $P_1.T_d \cap P_j.T_d$ with the method discussed in Section 3.1 (i.e., P_1 sends a hashed list of its customers so that P_j can know

SSN	Date	Amount
6565	7/21/2004	10
6565	9/27/2004	48
8080	1/1/2004	23

Sales Table at P_2

SSN	Date	Amount
6565	7/9/2004	23
6565	9/7/2004	84
7070	2/2/2004	79
9090	2/2/2004	92

Sales Table at P_3

SSN	Name	Surname	Address	Phone
6565	Jack	Brial	6616 K Rd. Xyz 93090 ZT	890–908–4545
7070				
8080				

Customers Table at P_1

Fig. 4. Illustration of Aggregated Join

common customers). Then, P_j sends all tuples $t \in P_j.T_f$ where $t.A \in \Pi_A(P_1.T_d \cap P_j.T_d)$ to P_1.

During the query processing, no extra useful information gets revealed. In the intersection phase, all data sources compute the intersection of the dimension tables and in the join computation phase, all data sources other than the query poser send the related tuples from their fact tables. As a result, no site gains extra useful information other than the intersection and the join results.

4 Aggregate Query Processing

The traditional aggregation operation is generally used to compute the aggregate of a list of values such as SUM, AVERAGE or MIN/MAX. One kind of privacy preserving aggregation can be thought of as computing the aggregation of values in the union of lists coming from different data sources such that each data source will only know the final aggregate but nothing else. To execute these queries, each data source can compute its local aggregate and the final aggregate can be computed in such a way that none of the data sources will know the local aggregate of other data sources (*Secure multiparty computation* or the technique described in this section can be used to compute the final aggregate value for SUM and AVERAGE). However, data sources may not be willing to execute aggregation operations over their whole data or may want to know more than the sum of the values in several lists. Therefore, there is a need for new types of aggregation queries. In this section, we will introduce *Row-Based Aggregation* and *Column-Based Aggregation* queries. We formally define *Row-Based Aggregation* queries and show how to process them in Section 4.1. Then, we will present *Column-Based Aggregation* queries and techniques to execute them efficiently in Section 4.2.

4.1 Row-Based Aggregation

Enterprises may want to know the total expenditure of a customer in the market. For example, hotels and airlines may want to classify their customers based on their travel expenses. Without privacy concerns it is easy to perform this classification task. One of the enterprises may collect data from all enterprises and perform the computation. However, they may not be willing to reveal their value during this operation. For example, an airline company may not be willing to reveal an expenditure of a customer to other airlines since other airlines may try to attract this customer. For instance, if a customer's expenditure in company C_1 is 80, and another company C_2 knows that his/her expenditure in C_1 is 80, then C_2 can offer a new deal to this customer and try to attract him/her using this information. Although enterprises may not be willing to reveal their earnings from a customer, they may want to know the total expenditure of the customer without revealing their values. For example, these hotels and airlines may be willing to know the total expenditure of a customer in these hotels and airlines (i.e., total expenditure in the market) without revealing their earnings from this customer so that competing hotels and airlines protect their private information from each other. Since the traditional aggregation operation is not strong enough to support these needs, ABACUS proposes a new type of aggregation queries, *Row-Based Aggregation* queries, and a new technique to execute them in a privacy preserving manner in the context of data warehouses.

For the sake of this discussion, we will first define the row-based aggregation on a table with two attributes namely *Key* and *Value*. Then, we will discuss how this can be generalized to support queries in data warehouses. The *Row-Based Aggregation* query processing problem is defined as follows:

Let $T_1, T_2, ..., T_m$ be the tables stored by a set of source peers $P = \{P_1, P_2, ..., P_m\}$ ($m \geq 3$) respectively containing a *Key* and a *Value* attributes. Each data source, P_i, would like to learn the aggregate for each $Key \in T_i$, $\sum_{j=1}^{m} Value$ $\exists [Key, Value] \in T_j$. Then, the problem is to obtain the answer of the query without revealing any additional information.

The above problem formulation is for SUM queries. We solve the above problem with some relaxation. The relaxation is that a data source with *Key* in its database can learn who else has the same *Key* (Note that this information is the same as the result of aggregated intersection). However, it is impossible to learn the *Value* associated with that *Key* at the other data warehouses. Extending our solution to support AVERAGE queries is straightforward and discussed briefly at the end of this section.

Example 2. Let us illustrate the problem with an example. Consider four companies, P_1, P_2, P_3 and P_4, that want to classify their customers according to their total expenditures from these companies. They have tables T_1, T_2, T_3 and T_4 each of which with two attributes *customer SSN* and the *amount of expenditure* as $[Key, Value]$ pairs. The contents of the tables are as follows:

$T_1 = \{[6565, 10], [7070, 20], [8080, 30]\}$
$T_2 = \{[6565, 50], [8080, 30]\}$
$T_3 = \{[6565, 10], [7070, 20], [8080, 30]\}$
$T_4 = \{[6565, 10], [7070, 20]\}$

To classify customers, one should know their total expenditures in the market. In other words, a row-based aggregation is needed for this process so that at the end of query processing P_1, P_2, P_3 and P_4 will get the following lists respectively as an answer without knowing any additional information: $\{[6565, 80], [7070, 60], [8080, 90]\}$, $\{[6565, 80], [8080, 90]\}$, $\{[6565, 80], [7070, 60], [8080, 90]\}$, $\{[6565, 80], [7070, 60]\}$. The first item in the above first list, $[6565, 80]$ means that the customer with SSN 6565 has a total expenditure of 80 in companies P_1, P_2, P_3 and P_4. ABACUS can process row-based aggregation queries in a privacy preserving manner while revealing some information which is typically acceptable in an honest-but-curious environment. For example, each company will learn who else has a customer with the same SSN as in its list. For instance, P_1 will know that 6565 exists in all data sources, while 7070 also exists in P_3 and P_4, and 8080 exists in P_2 and P_3. During this query processing, none of the data sources will be able to learn the value of a specific key of the other data sources. For example, P_1 will not learn that 6565 has an expenditure of 50 in P_2, but will learn that 80 is the total expenditure of 6565 in all of the companies. Note that, if only two data sources have the same key, they may not share their values with each other by rejecting aggregation on that key (because they can learn each other's value for that key). ABACUS allows users to configure their privacy policies for this kind of policy related issues and handle them efficiently. We will discuss these issues later in this section.

A simple technique to compute the sum of values (i.e., $V_1 + V_2 + V_3 + V_4$) for a specific key Key in four key-value pairs $[Key, V_1]$, $[Key, V_2]$, $[Key, V_3]$, and $[Key, V_4]$ residing at four different parties P_1, P_2, P_3 and P_4 respectively without revealing V_1, V_2, V_3 and V_4 could be circulating a token with a label $H(Key)$. Using secure one-way hash function can prevent others from learning Key if they do not have Key. The process consists of two circulations. During the first circulation, every party, P_i, would add its value, V_i, and a random number, r_i, and pass the token to the next party. Therefore, P_1 creates a token with a label $H(Key)$ and adds $V_1 + r_1$, then passes it to P_2. The other parties follow the same protocol and pass the token to the next one. At the end of first circulation, P_1 will get $V_1 + r_1 + V_2 + r_2 + V_3 + r_3 + V_4 + r_4$ for a token with a label $H(Key)$. There is no way to determine the value of a specific party during the course of the first circulation because of the random numbers added. In the second circulation, all parties subtract the random numbers they added during the first circulation. Therefore, at the end of second circulation, P_1 would have a token with a label $H(Key)$ and the sum of the values for that Key, $V_1 + V_2 + V_3 + V_4$. Although it seems secure, this basic technique has two problems. Since this process is needed for every item in the list, using the same random number for every item in the list may result in information leakage such as the difference between two values. To prevent this information leakage, parties should use a different random number for each item in their lists. Therefore, every data source should maintain a list of random numbers it used during this process which is not scalable for large lists. Another problem is that any two of the data sources could collude and learn the value of another data source. For example, P_2 and P_4 could learn the value of P_3, V_3. In the first circulation, P_4 would pass the token with a label $H(Key)$ and $V_1 + r_1 + V_2 + r_2 + V_3 + r_3 + V_4 + r_4$ to P_1 and in the second circulation, P_1 would pass $V_1 + V_2 + r_2 + V_3 + r_3 + V_4 + r_4$ to P_2. Since P_2 and P_4 know $V_1 + r_1 + V_2 + r_2 + V_3 + r_3 + V_4 + r_4$ and $V_1 + V_2 + r_2 + V_3 + r_3 + V_4 + r_4$ they could figure out r_1, and thus V_1(Note that P_1 passed $V_1 + r_1$ to P_2 in the first circulation). Therefore, P_2 and P_4

could collude and reveal the value of P_1 without revealing their values to each other or to the other parties.

In order to compute aggregation securely, ABACUS uses Shamir's secret sharing technique, which allows one to compute any linear combination of secret values. ABACUS uses this property to perform SUM and AVERAGE queries thus computing aggregation without revealing individual values.

Shamir's Secret Sharing

Shamir's secret sharing method [13] allows a dealer D to distribute a secret value v_s among n peers $\{P_1, P_2, ..., P_n\}$, such that knowledge of any k ($k \leq n$) peers is required to reconstruct the secret. Since, even complete knowledge of $k - 1$ peers cannot reveal any information about the secret, Shamir's method is information theoretically secure. Dealer D chooses a random polynomial $q(x)$ of degree $k - 1$ where the constant term is the secret value, v_s, and a publicly known set of n random points. The dealer computes the share of each peer as $q(x_i)$ and sends it to peer P_i. The method is summarized in Algorithm 1.

Algorithmus 1. Shamir's Secret Sharing Algorithm

1: *Input:*
2: v_s: Secret value;
3: D: Dealer of secret v_s;
4: P: set of peers $P_1, ..., P_n$ to distribute secret;
5: *Output:*
6: $share_1, ..., share_n$: Shares of secret, v_s, for each peer P_i;
7: *Procedure:*
8: D creates a random polynomial $q(x) = a_{k-1}x^{k-1} + ... + a_1 x^1 + a_0$ with degree $k - 1$ and a constant term $a_0 = v_s$.
9: D chooses publicly known n random points, $x_1, ... x_n$, such that $x_i \neq 0$.
10: D computes share, $share_i$, of each peer, P_i, where $share_i = q(x_i)$ and sends it to P_i.

In order to construct the secret value v_s, any set of k peers will need to share the information they have received. After finding the polynomial $q(x)$, the secret value $v_s = q(0)$ can be reconstructed. $q(x)$ can be found using Lagrange interpolation such that $p(x_i) = share_i$ where $i = 1, ..., k$. The key observation is that at least k points and the respective shares are required to determine a unique polynomial $q(x)$ of degree $k - 1$.

Row-Based Aggregation in ABACUS

ABACUS executes row-based aggregation queries in three phases: *Distribution phase*, *Intermediate-Computation phase*, and *Final-Computation phase*.

Distribution Phase

After the query is posed, m data sources decide on the degree of the polynomial that is going to be used in Shamir's secret sharing (the degree of the polynomial should be greater than or equal to $m - 1$). They also choose $n \geq m$ random values $X = \{x_1, ..., x_n\}$. Without loss of generality, we will use a polynomial of degree of $m - 1$ and $n = m$ in our setting. Each data source P_i has a list of *Key-Value* pairs, $L_i = \{[K_1, V_1], ..., [K_{|L_i|}, V_{|L_i|}]\}$; P_i creates m shares from L_i, $share(L_i, P_1), ... , share(L_i, P_m)$, one for each of the data sources P_1 through P_m respectively (including itself).

P_i creates the shares by applying a one-way hash function and Shamir's secret sharing algorithm to each of the elements in L_i. For every element $[Key, Value]$ in L_i, P_i computes the share of data source P_j, $sh([Key, Value], P_j) = [H(Key), q(x_j)]$, using a hash function H and Algorithm 1 with $q(x)$ and X (the constant term in $q(x)$ will be replaced by the secret value, $Value$, to compute $q(x)$ in Shamir's secret sharing). Therefore, the list of shares of data source P_j from L_i is $share(L_i, P_j) = \{sh([K_1, V_1], P_j), ...,$ $sh([K_{|L_i|}, V_{|L_i|}], P_j)\}$. Then, P_i sends $share(L_i, P_j)$ to the data source P_j. Note that P_i keeps its share, $share(L_i, P_i)$, for itself and since using the same $q(x)$ would results in information leakage, a random polynomial is used for each of the item in the list. Therefore, random polynomials q_1 through $q_{|L_i|}$ are used for the items 1 through $| L_i |$ in L_i.

In Example 2, assume P_1 with a list, $L_1 = \{[6565, 10], [7070, 20], [8080, 30]\}$ and four data sources decided on four random points $X = \{27, 65, 90, 123\}$. Since there are four data sources, a polynomial $q(x)$ of a degree three would be used with a hash function H while calculating the share of each data source. As a first step, P_1 chooses three random polynomials for each item in its list: $q_1(x) = 2x^3 - 2x^2 + 10$, $q_2(x) = x^3 - 5x^2 + 20$, $q_3(x) = x^3 - 13x^2 + 30$. Observe that the constant term of polynomial q_i is value of the ith item in L_1 and q_i is used for the ith item in L_1. Then, the shares of key-value pairs in L_1 for data source P_2 are calculated as follows:

$sh([6565, 10], P_2) = [H(6565), q_1(x_2)] = [H(6565), q_1(65)]$

$sh([7070, 20], P_2) = [H(7070), q_2(x_2)] = [H(7070), q_2(65)]$

$sh([8080, 30], P_2) = [H(8080), q_3(x_2)] = [H(6565), q_3(65)]$.

Therefore, the share list for P_2, $share(L_1, P_2)$, is: $share(L_1, P_2) = \{[H(6565), q_1(65)],$ $[H(7070), q_2(65)], [H(8080), q_3(65)]$. Similarly, other data sources' share lists are computed and are sent to them. P_1 would keep $share(L_1, P_1)$ for itself and sends $share(L_1, P_2)$, $share(L_1, P_3)$, and $share(L_1, P_4)$ to P_2, P_3, and P_4 respectively.

Distribution phase at data source P_i is summarized in Algorithm 2.

Algorithmus 2. Distribution Phase

1: *Input:*
2: X: Random Values $X = \{x_1, .., x_m\}$;
3: H: Secure one-way hash function
4: L_i: Secret list of *Key-Value* pairs at data source P_i;
5: *Output:*
6: $share(L_i, P_1), ..., share(L_i, P_m)$: Shares of secret list, L_i, for each data source P_j;
7: *Procedure:*
8: **for** Each secret *Key-Value* pair $[Key, V_s] \in L_i$ **do**
9:    Find share $sh([Key, V_s], P_j)$ of each data source P_j for $[Key, V_s]$ with Algorithm 1 using a random polynomial $q(x)$ where $q(x) = a_{k-1}x^{k-1} + ... + V_s$ and the hash function H such that $sh([Key, V_s], P_j) = [H(Key), q(x_j)]$.
10:    Add $sh([Key, V_s], P_j)$ into $share(L_i, P_j)$.
11: **end for**
12:
13: **for** For each data source P_j **do**
14:    Send $share(L_i, P_j)$ to data source P_j
15: **end for**

Intermediate-Computation Phase

After receiving their shares from the data sources, $P_1, ..., P_m$, each data source, P_i, calculates intermediate result lists, $IR(L_1, P_i), ..., IR(L_m, P_i)$, corresponding to the lists

$share(L_1, P_i)$,....,$share(L_m, P_i)$ respectively. The kth element of $share(L_j, P_i)$ is a key-value pair i.e., $share(L_j, P_i)[k] = [H(Key), Value^*]$ which is the share of P_i from the $[Key, Value]$ pair in L_j ($share(L_j, P_i)[k][1] = H(Key)$ and $share(L_j, P_i)[k][2] = Value^*$). P_i computes the intermediate result lists as follows:

$IR(L_j, P_i)[k][1] = share(L_j, P_i)[k][1]$

$IR(L_j, P_i)[k][2] = \sum_{h=1}^{m}(share(L_h, P_i)[g][2]$ s.t. $\exists\ g$ where $share(L_h, P_i)[g][1] = IR(L_j, P_i)[k][1])$,

i.e., $INTER - RES_i$.

In Example 2, P_1 would have lists $share(L_1, P_1)$, $share(L_2, P_1)$, $share(L_3, P_1)$ and $share(L_4, P_1)$ where

$share(L_1, P_1) = \{[H(6565), 120], [H(7070), 320], [H(8080), 400]\}$

$share(L_2, P_1) = \{[H(6565), 100], [H(8080), 600]\}$

$share(L_3, P_1) = \{[H(6565), 3500], [H(7070), 900], [H(8080), 90]\}$

$share(L_4, P_1) = \{[H(6565), 110], [H(7070), 80]\}$

Then, in the intermediate computation phase, P_1 will compute $IR(L_1, P_1)$ $IR(L_2, P_1)$, $IR(L_3, P_1)$ and $IR(L_4, P_1)$ and send them to data sources P_1, P_2, P_3 and P_4 respectively. For example, $IR(L_3, P_1)$ is computed as follows: Since $H(6565)$ exists in all lists, the values associated with it, 120, 100, 3500 and 110 in $share(L_1, P_1)$ through $share(L_4, P_1)$ respectively, are added. Therefore, $IR(L_3, P_1)[1] = H(6565)$ and $IR(L_3, P_1)[2] = 120+100+3500+110 = 3830$. The same calculation is performed for all items in the list resulting in $IR(L_3, P_1) = \{[H(6565), 3830], [H(7070), 4900], [H(8080), 1090]\}$.

The intermediate computation process at data source P_i is summarized in Algorithm 3.

Algorithmus 3. Intermediate Computation Phase

1: *Input:*
2: $Share_L$: Set of share lists, $Share_L = \{share(L_1, P_i), .., share(L_m, P_i)\}$;
3: *Output:*
4: Set of intermediate result lists $\{IR(L_1, P_i), .., IR(L_m, P_i)\}$ to send back to the data sources $P = \{P_1, ..., P_m\}$ respectively;
5: *Procedure:*
6: **for** each list $share(L_k, P_i) \in Share_L$ **do**
7:   **for** $j = 1; j \leq |share(L_k, P_i)|$ **do**
8:     $IR(L_k, P_i)[j][1] = share(L_k, P_i)[j][1]$
9:     **if** $share(L_k, P_i)[j][1] = share(L_l, P_i)[o][1]$ such that $\exists\ l$ and o where $l \leq m$ and $1 \leq o \leq |share(L_l, P_i)|$ **then**
10:        $IR(L_k, P_i)[j][2] = IR(L_k, P_i)[j][2] + share(L_l, P_i)[o][2]$
11:     **end if**
12:   **end for**
13: **end for**
14: Send $IR(L_1, P_i), ..., IR(L_m, P_i)$ to $P_1, ..., P_m$ respectively

---

Final-Computation Phase

In the final computation phase, data source P_i retrieves its intermediate result lists, $IR(L_i, P_1)$,....,$IR(L_i, P_m)$ from all m data sources. Since all data sources compute the sum of their shares for a specific *Key*, the kth entry of an intermediate list contains $H(Key)$ and the sum of shares for *Key*. Therefore, for a *Key-Value* pair in L_i, the corresponding entry k in the intermediate result lists are: $IR(L_i, P_1)[k] = [H(Key), INTER - RES_1]$, $IR(L_i, P_2)[k] = [H(Key), INTER - RES_2], ..., IR(L_i, P_m)[k] = [H(Key), INTER - RES_m]$.

In the final computation phase, data sources calculate the sum for each *Key* from the m intermediate results. Since all data sources use a random polynomial degree of $m-1$ and compute the shares of all data sources using m points, $X = \{x_1, x_2, .., x_m\}$, these result in a polynomial $P(x) = a_{m-1}x^{m-1} + ... + a_1x^1 + a_0$ where constant term, a_0, is the sum of the values for *Key* and $P(x_i) = INTER - RES_i$. The coefficients of $P(x)$ and thus the sum of the values could be computed because the values of $P(x)$ are known at m different points ($P(x_i) = INTER - RES_i$).

Proof of Correctness

A data source P_j constructs a random polynomial $a_jx_i^{m-1} + b_jx_i^{m-2} + ... + Value$ to hide the secret values for each $[Key, Value]$ pair. After generating this random polynomial, it computes the share of P_i as $(H(Key), [a_{P_j}x_i^{m-1} + b_{P_j}x_i^{m-2} + ... + v_{P_j}])$ for each secret key-value pair, where $v_{P_j} = Value$ and sends the shares of the other data sources. After P_i receives the shares from all m data sources, it sends the sum of values which have the same key. Without loss of generality, assume l of the m data sources have the same *Key* with the secret values v_1 through v_l respectively. Then the sum for that *Key* is in the following form:

$$a_1x_i^{m-1} + b_1x_i^{m-2}... + v_1 +$$
$$a_2x_i^{m-1} + b_2x_i^{m-2}... + v_2 +$$
$$\vdots$$
$$a_lx_i^{m-1} + b_lx_i^{m-2}... + v_l$$

Therefore, P_i sends its results $INTER - RES_i = (a_1 + a_2 + ... + a_l)x_i^{m-1} + ... + SUM$ to the parties having *Key* in their lists, where SUM is the sum of the secret values ($SUM = v_1 + v_2 + ... + v_l$) for the values that have the same key, *Key*.

Each data source receives m results from each of the data sources (including itself) for each key in its *[Key-Value]* list:

$$INTER - RES_1 = (a_1 + a_2 + ... + a_l)x_1^{m-1} + ... + SUM$$
$$INTER - RES_2 = (a_1 + a_2 + ... + a_l)x_2^{m-1} + ... + SUM$$
$$\vdots$$
$$INTER - RES_m = (a_1 + a_2 + ... + a_l)x_m^{m-1} + ... + SUM$$

Since $X = \{x_1, x_2, .., x_m\}$ is known by all data sources, there are a total of m unknown coefficients including SUM and m equations in the above system of equations. Therefore, SUM can be derived by using the above equations. The data source, P_j, cannot know the value of the other data sources, since the coefficients of the polynomials used by other data sources are not known by P_j.

For the average query, P_i sends $INTER - RES_i = [(a_1 + a_2 + ... + a_l)x_i^{m-1} + ... + SUM]/l$ where $INTER - RES_i = \frac{(a_1 + a_2 + ... + a_l)}{l}x_i^{m-1} + ... + AVG)$ and $AVG = \frac{v_1 + v_2 + ... + v_l}{l}$. Therefore, each data source receives m results:

$$INTER - RES_1 = \frac{(a_1 + a_2 + ... + a_l)}{l}x_1^{m-1} + ... + AVG$$
$$INTER - RES_2 = \frac{(a_1 + a_2 + ... + a_l)}{l}x_2^{m-1} + ... + AVG$$
$$\vdots$$
$$INTER - RES_m = \frac{(a_1 + a_2 + ... + a_l)}{l}x_m^{m-1} + ... + AVG$$

Again, since $X = \{x_1, x_2, .., x_n\}$ is known by the data sources, there are m unknown coefficients including AVG and m equations and thus, AVG can be derived from the above equations.

Row-Based Aggregation in Data Warehouses

After the query is posed, data sources create lists of *[Key, Value]* pairs using their fact and dimension tables so that row-based aggregation can be performed over them with the above technique. All information in the dimension table about a tuple in the fact table is used to form a *Key* for that tuple. The tuple from a fact table is added into the list as *[Key, Value]* pairs where *Value* is the value associated with that tuple. For example, data source P_2 in Figure 4 creates *[Key-Value]* pairs as follows: for a tuple with SSN 6565, it retrieves other information about 6565 from the customers table such as name, surname and address. Then, it combines those information to create the *Key* for this tuple and the amount is used as the *Value*.

Properties of the Algorithm

Data sources use a one-way hash function to hide *Key*, and thus all of the data sources will learn $H(Key)$. Only those data sources which have *Key* would be able to know *Key* and its existence at data source P_i. In addition, P_i uses Shamir's secret sharing to hide the value associated with *Key* from other data sources. It uses a polynomial degree of $m - 1$ and m random points to compute shares of the m data sources. Then, it keeps one of these shares for itself and sends the remaining $m - 1$ shares to the other parties. Since all of the m shares are needed to reveal the secret value in Shamir's secret sharing method, the other data sources would not be able to compute the value, even if they combine their shares coming from P_i.

In general, for any *Key* at any data source P_j, any data source P_i can prevent execution of aggregation for that *Key*. Since one of the m shares is sent to P_i, P_i can prevent aggregation on *Key* by not sending the intermediate result to the other data sources. Therefore, other data sources would not be able to learn SUM for *Key*. Using this property, ABACUS allows data sources to control sharing the value of *Key* with other data sources. This might be needed since if only two data sources have *Key*, performing row-based aggregation will result in revealing the values to these two data sources (the result is the sum of the two values, and since these data source know their values, they can figure out the other value from the result). Note that, if *Key* exists in only one data source, then the owner can protect it from other data sources This can easily be done by preventing aggregation on *Key*. In addition to these, data sources cannot figure out something from their shares using the distribution of values since they are random values (i.e., a random polynomial is used for each item in the list to compute the shares).

4.2 Column-Based Aggregation

Enterprises might want to know the size of the market and some statistical information about the market where they compete. In addition, they might be interested in expenditures of their customers such as the ratio of their expenditures in their companies to their total expenditures in the market. In other words, a company might want to know how much it satisfies the needs of customers. Therefore, companies might be willing to collaborate to perform these kinds of operations however, they might not want to reveal extra information, for example a company might not want to reveal how much it satisfies the needs of its customers. One way to compute the market size in a privacy preserving manner is to aggregate the expenditures of all customers in that market. Formally, data sources $P_1, P_2, .., P_m$ might want to know sum of their local sums $LS_1, LS_2, ..., LS_m$ respectively, and the global sum $GS = LS_1 + ... + LS_m$, without revealing their local sums. This problem could be solved with the technique discussed in Section 4.1. However, in a competitive environment it is unrealistic to expect enterprises to share their local sums. For example, a big company with 1000 customers might not be willing to share its local sum which is the sum of its 1000 customers with a small company with 10 customers. Instead, it might want to collaborate for the common customers to compute their total expenditures, so that both companies could learn how much they satisfy the needs of their customers. However, during this process they do not want to reveal any additional information. In order to satisfy these needs, we introduce *column-based aggregation*.

Formally, the column-based aggregation query processing problem is defined as follows:

> Let $T_1, T_2, ..., T_m$ be the tables stored by a set of data warehouses $P = \{P_1, P_2, ..., P_m\}$ ($m \geq 3$) respectively containing a key and a value field. The data source P_i would like to learn the aggregation of values for all *Keys* in T_i, i.e., $\sum_{\forall Key \in T_i} \sum_{k=1}^{m} (Value\ s.t.\ \exists[Key, Value] \in T_k \land \exists Key \in T_i)$. Then the problem is to obtain the answer by only providing the aggregation result to P_i while revealing only the common *Keys* to other data sources.

The goal of the query processing is to compute *column-based aggregation* such that the data source posing the query, P_i, would only know the result of the query, $\sum_{\forall Key \in T_i} \sum_{k=1}^{m} (Value\ s.t.\ \exists[Key, Value] \in T_k \land \exists Key \in T_i)$, while other data sources would only know the *Keys* in T_i if they have those *Keys*. The query processing consists of three steps:

- *Intersection Phase:* Data source P_i sends the list of hash values of *Keys* in T_i. On P_j receiving this list, P_j computes the common keys in tables T_i and T_j (by hashing its keys in T_j and comparing them with the list coming from P_i).
- *Local Aggregation for Intersection Phase:* Data source P_j, computes the local sum of values, *local sum*, for the common keys between P_i and P_j. Formally, the local sum, LS_j, at data source P_j is: $LS_j = \sum_{\forall Key \in T_i} (Value\ s.t.\ \exists[Key, Value] \in T_j \land \exists Key \in T_i)$.
- *Global Aggregation Phase:* Data sources compute the *global sum*, GS, which is the sum of *local sum* of m data sources. They compute $GS = \sum_{i=1}^{m} LS_i$ without revealing the local sums with the technique discussed in Section 4.1 (One could think of the data sources, $P_1, ..., P_m$, have the following *[Key, Value]* pairs $[P_i, LS_1], ..., [P_i, LS_m]$ respectively and they want to compute the *row-based aggregation* for the key P_i, which is the global sum).

The proposed query processing method computes column-based aggregation queries correctly. The answer to the column-based aggregation query for data source P_i is $\sum_{\forall Key \in T_i} \sum_{k=1}^{m} (Value \ s.t. \ \exists [Key, Value] \in T_k \wedge \exists Key \in T_i)$. The proposed technique computes the local sum at each data source in *local aggregation for intersection phase* where $LS_j = \sum_{\forall Key \in T_i} (Value \ s.t. \ \exists [Key, Value] \in T_j \wedge \exists Key \in T_i)$. Then, in *global aggregation phase* the sum of all the local aggregations are computed as answer which is $\sum_{k=1}^{m} LS_k$, i.e., $\sum_{\forall Key \in T_i} \sum_{k=1}^{m} (Value \ s.t. \ \exists [Key, Value] \in T_k \wedge \exists Key \in T_i)$.

At the end of the query processing other data sources will only know their common *Keys* with the query poser P_i and P_i will only know the result of the column based aggregation query result but nothing else. After *intersection phase*, the other data sources will know the common elements between P_i and them but nothing else, since one-way hash function is used to hide *Keys*. During *local aggregation for intersection phase*, the data sources would compute their local aggregates. Then, in the *global aggregation phase*, they compute the sum of the local aggregations without revealing their local aggregations to anybody with the *row-based aggregation*. Therefore, P_i would only know the global aggregation result, which is column based aggregation result but not the local aggregations. And the other data sources would not know any other local aggregation and the global aggregation results unless P_i wants them to know (Note that if P_i does not send its intermediate result to other data sources, they cannot compute the global sum in the row-based aggregation in Section 4.1).

5   Analytical Evaluation

In this section, we compute the query response times for the proposed query processing techniques. The query responses time for intersection and join queries are studied in Section 5.1. Then, the query execution costs of row-based aggregation and column-based aggregation queries are calculated in Section 5.2. Finally, we show the query response times of the queries over a sample scenario to demonstrate the scalability of our technique in Section 5.3.

5.1   Cost of Intersection and Join Query Processing

Data source P_i hashes its list and sends to m data sources. Then, it compares its list with other datasources to find the intersection. Therefore, the computation cost is the cost of hashing the list and the cost of comparisons. Let C_h be the cost of hashing a single item and every hashed word is b bits long. The computation time for hashing is: $C_h \times |L_i|$. The number of comparisons to compare the hashed list, L_i, with the other lists coming from other data sources is (assuming lists are sorted) less than $(m - 1) \times |L_i|$ without loss of generality assume L_i is the longest list. The time needed for this comparison is: $\frac{(m-1) \times |L_i|}{CPU \ Speed}$ seconds. Therefore, total computation time is: $C_h \times |L_i| + \frac{(m-1) \times |L_1|}{CPU \ Speed}$ The communication time is the sum of the time needed to send its own hashed list and the time to receive the $m - 1$ hashed lists from other data sources. Therefore, total communication time is: $\frac{b \times (|L_1| + ... + |L_m|)}{Bandwidth}$. The query response time, the sum of the computation and communication cost, is:

$$C_h \times |L_i| + \frac{(m - 1) \times |L_i|}{CPU \ Speed} + \frac{b \times (|L_1| + ... + |L_m|)}{Bandwidth}$$

In the aggregated join, the first step is aggregated intersection. After this first step, data source P_j sends the related tuples to P_i. The query response time is sum of the cost of aggregated intersection and the cost of sending related tuples. Therefore, the query response time for aggregated join is:

$$\text{The cost of intersection} + \frac{m \times |L| \times v}{Bandwidth}$$

where v is the size of a tuple $t \in T_R$.

5.2   Cost of Aggregation Query Processing

The Cost of Row-Based Aggregation Query Processing

In the distribution phase, data sources compute the hash value of keys and the shares of m data sources. Therefore, the computation cost is $\frac{m \times |L|}{CPU speed} + C_h \times |L|$. The communication cost is sending these shares to other data sources and receiving shares from other data sources, which is $\frac{2 \times m \times |L| \times b}{Bandwidth}$, where b is the size of a *Key-Value* pair.

In the local aggregation phase, the computation cost is scanning all lists and adding the values for a specific key (computation of intermediate result lists). The amount of addition is less than $m \times |L|$. Thus the cost of computation in the local aggregation phase is $\frac{m \times |L|}{CPU speed}$ (assuming that lists are sorted and are of the same size). After this computation, P_i sends intermediate results lists to m data sources and receive its intermediate result lists from m data sources. The communication cost for this operation is $\frac{2 \times m \times |L| \times b}{Bandwidth}$ (note that the size of intermediate lists is equal to the size of lists).

In the final aggregation phase, P_i solves an equation system for each element in the list. Thus, the computation time is $|L_i| \times C_{eq}$, where C_{eq} is the cost of solving an equation with m unknowns.

The query response time for row-based aggregation query is (without loss of generality, assume all lists are size of $|L|$):

$$\approx |L| \times C_h + \frac{4 \times m \times b \times |L|}{Bandwidth} + \frac{2 \times m \times |L|}{CPU speed} + |L| \times C_{eq}.$$

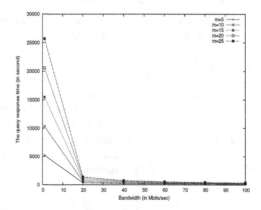

Fig. 5. The Query Response Time for Intersection Queries

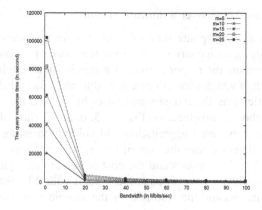

Fig. 6. The Query Response Time for Row-based Aggregation Queries

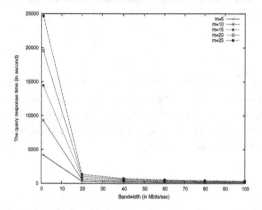

Fig. 7. The Query Response Time for Column-based Aggregation Queries

The Cost of Column-Based Aggregation Query Processing

The column-based aggregation query processing consists of three phases: 1) intersection phase 2) local aggregation for intersection 3) global aggregation. In the intersection phase, data source P_i sends its hashed lists to m data sources. The communication and computation cost for this phase is:

$$C_h \times |L_i| + \frac{m \times b \times |L_i|}{Bandwidth}$$

The cost of computation in local aggregation for intersection phase is $\frac{|L_i|}{CPU speed}$ (data sources calculates the sum of values in the intersection). Remember that there is no communication in this phase. The cost of global aggregation phase is negligible since the cost of the summation of m values using m parties is negligible in this context. Therefore, the cost of *column-based aggregation* query processing is:

$$\approx C_h \times |L_i| + \frac{m \times b \times |L_i|}{Bandwidth} + \frac{|L_i|}{CPU speed}.$$

5.3 Query Response Times over a Sample Scenario

We demonstrate the query response time of ABACUS for intersection and row-based and column based aggregation queries over a sample scenario to show that it is scalable and efficient. We compute the response times for queries in an environment where m data warehouses each of which with a dimension table and a fact table size of 1 million. We execute the queries over these data warehouses by varying the bandwidth and the number of data warehouses involved, m. Figures 5, 6, and 7 show the query response time for intersection, row-based aggregation and column-based aggregation queries. During these calculations we take the size of key-value pair, b, as 1024 bits, the cost of hashing, C_h, as 10^{-4} [5] seconds and the cost of solving an equation, C_{eq}, as 10^{-5} seconds (the time needed to solve an equation system with 20 unknowns in Matlab). The analytical evaluations and the results over the sample scenario demonstrate that ABACUS is scalable in terms of the number of parties participating in queries and the cost is increasing linearly with the number of parties involved. In addition as results show that the query processing is communication intensive operation since ABACUS uses light-weight computations.

6 Conclusion

In this paper, we propose a distributed middleware, ABACUS, to perform intersection, join and aggregation queries over multiple private data warehouses in a privacy preserving manner. In addition to this, we present new types of aggregation queries which are needed for privacy preserving data sharing. Analytical evaluations demonstrate that the proposed scheme is efficient and scalable.

References

1. G. Aggarwal, M. Bawa, P. Ganesan, H. Garcia-Molina, K. Kenthapadi, N. Mishra, R. Motwani, U. Srivastava, D. Thomas, J. Widom, and Y. Xu. Enabling privacy for the paranoids. In *Proc. of the 30th Int'l Conference on Very Large Databases VLDB*, pages 708–719, Aug 2004.
2. R. Agrawal, A. Evfimievski, and R. Srikant. Information sharing across private databases. In *Proc. of the 2003 ACM SIGMOD international conference on on Management of data*, pages 86–97, 2003.
3. S. Bergamaschi, S. Castano, M. Vincini, and D. Beneventano. Semantic integration of heterogeneous information sources. *Data Knowl. Eng.*, 36(3):215–249, 2001.
4. U. Dayal and H. Hwang. View definition and generalization for database integration in a multidatabase system. In *IEEE Transactions on Software Engineering*, volume 10, pages 628–644, 1984.
5. P. Ganesan, R. Venugopalan, P. Peddabachagari, A. Dean, F. Mueller, and M. Sichitiu. Analyzing and modeling encryption overhead for sensor network nodes. In *Proc. of the 2nd ACM international conference on Wireless sensor networks and applications*, pages 151–159. ACM Press, 2003.
6. O. Goldreich. Secure multi-party computation. *Working Draft*, jun 2001.
7. L. M. Haas, R. J. Miller, B. Niswonger, M. T. Roth, P. M. Schwarz, and E. L. Wimmers. Transforming heterogeneous data with database middleware: Beyond integration. *IEEE Data Engineering Bulletin*, 22(1):31–36, 1999.

8. A. Y. Halevy, Z. G. Ives, D. Suciu, and I. Tatarinov. Schema mediation in peer data management systems. In *Proc. of the 19th ICDE*, pages 505–516, 2003.

9. A. Kementsietsidis, M. Arenas, and R. J. Miller. Mapping data in peer-to-peer systems: Semantics and algorithmic issues. In *Proc. of the 2003 ACM SIGMOD*, pages 325–336, 2003.

10. M. W. N. Jefferies, C. Mitchell. A proposed architecture for trusted third party services. *Cryptography Policy and Algorithms Conference*, July 1995.

11. M. Naor and K. Nissim. Communication preserving protocols for secure function evaluation. In *ACM Symposium on Theory of Computing*, pages 590–599, 2001.

12. Secure Hash Standart. http://www.itl.nist.gov/fipspubs/fip180-1.htm.

13. A. Shamir. How to share a secret. *Commun. ACM*, 22(11):612–613, 1979.

Causeway: Support for Controlling and Analyzing the Execution of Multi-tier Applications

Anupam Chanda[1], Khaled Elmeleegy[1],
Alan L. Cox[1], and Willy Zwaenepoel[2]

[1] Rice University, 6100 Main Street, Houston, Texas 77005, USA
{anupamc, kdiaa, alc}@cs.rice.edu
[2] Ecole Polytechnique Fédérale de Lausanne, 1015 Lausanne, Switzerland
willy.zwaenepoel@epfl.ch

Abstract. Causeway provides runtime support for the development of distributed *meta-applications*. These meta-applications control or analyze the behavior of multi-tier distributed applications such as multi-tier web sites or web services. Examples of meta-applications include multi-tier debugging, fault diagnosis, resource tracking, prioritization, and security enforcement.

Efficient online implementation of these meta-applications requires meta-data to be passed between the different program components. Examples of metadata corresponding to the above meta-applications are request identifiers, priorities or security principal identifiers. Causeway provides the infrastructure for injecting, destroying, reading, and writing such metadata.

The key functionality in Causeway is forwarding the metadata associated with a request at so-called transfer points, where the execution of that request gets passed from one component to another. This is done automatically for system-visible channels, such as pipes or sockets. An API is provided to implement the forwarding of metadata at system-opaque channels such as shared memory.

We describe the design and implementation of Causeway, and we evaluate its usability and performance. Causeway's low overhead allows it to be present permanently in production systems. We demonstrate its usability by showing how to implement, in 150 lines of code and without modification to the application, global priority enforcement in a multi-tier dynamic web server.

1 Introduction

Many applications, e.g., web sites generating dynamic content and web service applications, have multi-tiered implementations. A multi-tier application is composed of multiple program components communicating among themselves to execute incoming requests. In such applications, a request is executed by multiple threads of control on different application components, the threads of control

G. Alonso (Ed.): Middleware 2005, LNCS 3790, pp. 42–59, 2005.

exchanging data among themselves along communication channels. For example, an application may be composed of a web server, an application server, and a database server: requests are executed by all three programs communicating with each other to exchange request data.

Often, systems to control or analyze the execution of multi-tier applications are written to perform tasks like multi-tier debugging, fault diagnosis, resource tracking, prioritization, and security enforcement. Examples include Pinpoint [5], Magpie [4,9], and Domain and Type Enforcement (DTE) [3] for Unix systems. We term these and similar systems that control or analyze the execution of multi-tier applications as *meta-applications*.

Traditionally, there have been two approaches to writing such meta-applications: a log-based approach, and a metadata-passing approach. The log-based approach operates in two phases — first, execution events of the application are recorded in logs, and next, the log records are analyzed. Magpie [4,9] and TraceBack [2] are examples of systems employing this approach. The log-based approach cannot affect the execution of requests in an online manner because processing of a log record lags the corresponding execution event by a positive time delay. Additionally, the execution events on the different tiers belonging to the same request need to be identified and connected while processing the log records.

The metadata-passing approach propagates *metadata* — arbitrary, out-of-band data — in addition to request data along execution paths. The meta-application accesses and utilizes this metadata to achieve its goal. Often, the metadata also serves in connecting a request's execution events spread across the tiers of the system, e.g., if it contains a request identifier. Several examples of meta-applications using this approach exist in the literature, e.g., Pinpoint [5] and DTE [3]. Pinpoint and DTE use request identifiers and security principal identifiers as metadata respectively. These meta-applications use hand-crafted code to handle and propagate metadata.

Unlike the log-based approach, the metadata-passing approach can affect the execution of requests in an online manner, e.g., Real-Time CORBA [10] which propagates priorities among application components to affect scheduling. Hence, we adopt the metadata-passing approach to building meta-applications. Our objective is to provide a framework that makes development of meta-applications using this approach easier.

In this paper we introduce Causeway, a framework to facilitate the association and propagation of metadata along request execution paths in a multi-tier application. Causeway provides an interface to associate metadata with threads of control and facilitates the propagation of metadata across communication channels. Causeway aids the development of meta-applications by performing all necessary management to handle and propagate metadata. This obviates the need for hand-crafted code for the common requirements of different meta-applications employing the metadata-passing approach.

The alternative to Causeway, propagating metadata at application level, involves augmenting all application-level inter-process communication protocols — a tedious solution. By making propagation of metadata a system-level function, it becomes independent of the application-level communication protocol used. Further, in a multi-tier application, it is possible that some individual components are unaware of the presence of metadata or choose to ignore it. Consider a three-tier system, where the middle tier component is unaware of metadata. The front and the back-end tiers may still, however, need to access metadata. In this scenario, system support for metadata propagation is required in the middle tier.

Causeway performs automatic propagation of metadata across *system-visible* communication channels. Such channels are those implemented in the operating system kernel and system libraries, e.g., pipes and sockets. Augmented kernel and system libraries provide Causeway's support for system-visible channels. Causeway provides an API to be called from application code to perform metadata propagation across *system-opaque* channels, e.g., shared memory. Support for system-opaque channels is the essential difference between Causeway and Stateful Distributed Interposition (SDI) [11].

We have implemented a prototype of Causeway, measured its overhead, and built a useful meta-application using Causeway. We summarize our experience with Causeway as follows:

- Adding support to propagate metadata across system-visible channels required modest effort.
- The measured overhead of Causeway to propagate metadata was small in absolute cost (order of microseconds) and it scaled well with increasing metadata size. The overhead of Causeway, while not propagating any metadata, was insignificant — less than 3% for a microbenchmark involving the pipe channel. Thus Causeway may reasonably remain a part of a production environment whether implementing a meta-application or not.
- Using Causeway we could rapidly implement a distributed priority enforcement system where the priority of a request is injected and propagated as metadata, and accessed to implement global priority scheduling. This required writing only about 150 lines of code on top of Causeway to change the priority of threads executing requests. We evaluated this system on an implementation of the TPC-W [12] benchmark.

The rest of the paper is organized as follows. We describe the design of Causeway in Section 2. In Section 3 we measure Causeway's overhead with two microbenchmarks. In Section 4 we evaluate Causeway's complexity to support system-visible channels, and measure the overhead of Causeway on an implementation of the TPC-W benchmark. We describe the distributed priority enforcement system using Causeway in Section 5. Related work is covered in Section 6. We conclude in Section 7.

2   Causeway Design

At an abstract level, Causeway works as follows. A request to an application is executed by one or more threads of control, possibly in one or more tiers. Threads exchange request data along communication channels, e.g., sockets, pipes and shared memory. Causeway's interface supports injection, inspection, modification and removal of metadata. Metadata is assigned to a thread when it performs injection. When a thread sends request data to another thread along a channel, Causeway transfers metadata from the former thread to the latter. Support for metadata propagation is required at *transfer points* where an application thread sends to or receives data from a channel. In this way, metadata, once injected, is propagated along the request execution paths.

Causeway has two parts: (1) a set of interfaces that are used by applications to manage and utilize metadata, and (2) mechanisms that implement propagation of metadata. First, we describe the structure and composition of metadata.

2.1 Metadata

Metadata in Causeway consists of a two-tuple containing the metadata type and the metadata value. Examples of metadata types include request priority, request identifier, and security principal identifier. Meta-applications can define new metadata types, if required.

2.2 Interfaces

Meta-applications can interact with Causeway in two ways — through an interface to inject and access metadata and through a callback interface in which Causeway calls handlers registered by the meta-application.

Metadata Interface. Causeway provides interfaces for injection, inspection, modification, and removal of metadata. These interfaces may be called from user-level or kernel-level.

Causeway manages metadata in a dictionary keyed by the address of the associated *entity*. An entity is either a thread of control or data that is read from or written to a channel. A thread's metadata is propagated to the data written on a write operation, subsequently this metadata is propagated from the data to a thread performing a read operation. Further, a thread can remove metadata associated with itself or a data entity. Table 1 shows the function signatures of the Causeway API. The Causeway API performs metadata operations in the following manner:

Table 1. The Causeway API

int cw_type_query(void *addr, int types[], int ntypes)
int cw_data_lookup(void *addr, int mtype, struct cw_metadata *md_p)
int cw_data_insert(void *addr, int mtype, struct cw_metadata md)
int cw_data_remove(void *addr, int mtype)

- cw_type_query retrieves the collection of *all* metadata types associated with addr in the types array of size ntypes. On successful completion, cw_type_query returns the number of metadata types retrieved and -1 on error. The types array must be large enough to hold all the metadata types associated with addr otherwise an error is flagged.
- cw_data_lookup retrieves the metadata of type mtype associated with addr. It returns 0 on successful completion and -1 on error.
- cw_data_insert inserts the given metadata md of type mtype and associates it with addr, overwriting any prior metadata of that type. It returns 0 on successful completion and -1 on error.
- cw_data_remove removes any existing metadata of type mtype associated with addr. It returns 0 on successful completion and -1 on error.

Callback Interface. Using Causeway's callback interface the meta-application can register a *transfer-point* callback method. A transfer point is a point where data is read from or written to a channel by a thread. At a transfer point Causeway determines if the type of the metadata being passed has a callback method registered. If a callback method exists, it is invoked with the metadata as an argument. The callback method reads and possibly modifies the metadata. The callback method can call arbitrary operating system code, e.g., to change the priorities of threads.

The signatures of a callback method and the callback interface are shown in Table 2. A callback method is of type callback_t. The callback interface, reg_callback_method, registers a given callback method for a given metadata type at a transfer point.

Table 2. The Callback Interface

```
typedef void (*callback_t)(struct cw_metadata **md, int mtype);
callback_t    callback_method;
void          reg_callback_method(int mtype, callback_t callback_method);
```

2.3   Support for Propagation of Metadata

When a thread performs a write on a channel, the thread's metadata is associated with the data written into the channel. On a subsequent read on the channel by a thread, metadata is propagated from the data and assigned to the thread.

There are two ways metadata can be assigned to a thread — injection and propagation across a channel. Newly assigned metadata replaces the thread's existing metadata of the same type.

Transfer Points. Places where a thread writes to or reads from a channel are transfer points. Channels are of two types: system-visible channels that occur in the operating system kernel and system libraries, e.g., sockets and pipes, and system-opaque channels that occur in the application, e.g., shared memory.

Causeway exports a Systems Programming Interface (SPI) consisting of a single function cw_metadata_xfer for the purpose of implementing transfer points. cw_metadata_xfer takes a source entity and a destination entity as arguments. It obtains the source entity's metadata and assigns the obtained metadata to the destination entity. At a transfer point for either a system-visible or system-opaque channel, a single call to cw_metadata_xfer is performed.

2.4 System-Visible Channels

For system-visible channels, the metadata transfer SPI is automatically called from an augmented kernel and system libraries to implement Causeway's support for metadata propagation. Sockets and pipes are system-visible channels supported by Causeway. Further, for a multi-threaded program, metadata needs to be propagated between the user-level thread and the kernel-level thread on entry to and exit from the kernel because multiple user-level threads may be multiplexed on top of a kernel-level thread. Metadata propagation between a user-level thread and a kernel-level thread constitutes additional system-visible channels in Causeway. We enumerate below the transfer points for system-visible channels:

1. *User-level thread to kernel-level thread:* On entry to the kernel, Causeway transfers metadata from the user-level thread to the kernel-level thread running it.
2. *Kernel-level thread to user-level thread:* On exit from the kernel, Causeway transfers the kernel-level thread's metadata to the user-level thread.
3. *Kernel-level thread to message:* When a kernel-level thread writes a message on a socket or a pipe, its metadata is transferred to the message.
4. *Message to kernel-level thread:* When a kernel-level thread receives a message from a socket or a pipe, metadata is transferred from the received message to the kernel-level thread.

These transfer points occur in the operating system kernel and the threading library.

Causeway handles sockets and pipes similarly. When a thread writes to a socket (or a pipe), Causeway associates metadata from the thread to the data written via the metadata transfer SPI described above. Similarly, on a subsequent read from the socket by another (or the same) thread, metadata is propagated from the data to the thread.

The above applies for LOCAL sockets only. For INTERNET sockets, data is encapsulated in IP packets for send and receive across sockets. Causeway encapsulates metadata, in addition to data, in the IP packets. For IPv4, Causeway encapsulates metadata in the IP header as IP options. In particular, Causeway defines a new IP option type, populates the IP header with the option type, length, and payload. At the receiver side, metadata, if any, is extracted from the received IP options. Since IP options can be a maximum of 40 bytes only, with 1 byte each for the type and length fields, via this mechanism Causeway can transfer at most 38 bytes of metadata in IP packets. This limit on metadata size is deemed enough for most practical purposes. This limitation is an artifact of Causeway's implementation and not its design. A general purpose tunneling protocol could be used to overcome this limitation, if required. For IPv6, Causeway uses the destination options in the IP header which does not have any size limitation. Further details about that are outside the scope of this paper.

2.5　Shared Memory — System-Opaque Channel

For system-opaque channels, the application must be modified to call the metadata transfer SPI to perform propagation of metadata. Causeway supports metadata propagation across shared memory — a system-opaque channel implemented in user-space. A transfer point needs to be inserted in the application where a user-level thread reads from or writes to shared memory. Producer-consumer is a popular model of shared memory usage. At an abstract level, the model works as follows. Producers and consumers share a buffer or queue of objects. A producer creates an object, acquires a lock to enter the critical section, adds the object to the shared buffer or queue, and releases the lock. A consumer acquires a lock to enter the critical section, retrieves and removes an object from the shared buffer or queue, releases the lock, and then accesses the retrieved object. The use of system-supported synchronization primitives, like `pthread_mutex` or `pthread_rwlock`, simplifies the task of identifying the producer-consumer communication channels through shared memory.

Two transfer points, one in the producer code and the other in the consumer code are inserted. Both transfer points use the metadata transfer SPI. The producer transfer point associates the producer thread's metadata with the produced object. The consumer transfer point retrieves the metadata associated with the consumed object and propagates it to the consumer thread. Causeway provides a user-level library that exports the metadata transfer SPI and manages the metadata associated with shared memory objects.

2.6　Heterogeneity of Operating System Kernel and Hardware

It is quite common for a multi-tier application to be spread across machines running heterogeneous operating system kernels on diverse hardware platforms. The design of Causeway mandates that all inter-machine metadata propagation be typed and be transmitted in network byte order. This ensures correct interpretation of metadata at the receiver. Further, our implementation of Causeway in FreeBSD lays out a blueprint for its implementation in other operating system kernels. In Section 4.1 we list the transfer points in the FreeBSD kernel required for the system-visible channels. An equivalent set of transfer points is required in another operating system kernel, such as Linux.

2.7　Operating System Specific Meta-applications

Sometimes, parts of a meta-application may require modifications to the operating system kernel. Under such circumstances, the meta-application becomes operating system specific. For example, we implemented a distributed priority enforcement system on top of Causeway which may alter priorities of threads and processes in a system — an operating system specific task. Thus, this meta-application is operating system specific. On the other hand, if all we wanted in a meta-application is to tag identifiers with requests, it would require no operating system modification other than Causeway itself.

3 Microbenchmarks

In this section we quantify the overhead imposed by our implementation of Causeway at the transfer points for two system-visible channels. We chose light-weight applications to provide maximum exposure to Causeway's overhead. We wrote two microbenchmarks: the first measuring the overhead associated with the transfer points for metadata propagation between a user-thread and a kernel thread, and the second measuring the overhead for the transfer points for the pipe channel.

In the first microbenchmark, a process creates a `pthread` which invokes a `getpid` call. This test brings out the cost of metadata propagation across the user-kernel boundary, because on each entry to and exit from the kernel, metadata is transferred from user space to kernel and vice versa. We repeat the `getpid` call multiple times and measure its average cost. We perform this experiment under the following scenarios: (1) without inserting the transfer point, which is the base case, (2) inserting the transfer point but transferring 0 bytes of metadata, (3) transferring 1 byte of metadata, and (4) transferring 32 bytes of metadata.

Table 3 shows the results of the above experiment. The cost of `getpid` increased by about 840 machine cycles when a transfer point was introduced. We used a 2.4 GHz Pentium 4 Xeon, so this overhead translates to about 0.35 microseconds. This result shows the cost of having the Causeway framework but not using it to propagate any metadata. The overhead increased by about 1500 machine cycles or about 0.6 microseconds when transferring 1 byte of metadata. To transfer 32 bytes of metadata, the further increase in overhead was small: about 40 machine cycles or 0.02 microseconds. In relative terms, the overhead with respect to the base case ranged from about 12% to less than 35% to transfer metadata in the above test.

The results of the above experiment show that the overhead of using Causeway is small. The overhead of inserting a transfer point is less than half of a microsecond. The overhead of transferring 32 bytes of metadata is about 1 microsecond, and the overhead scales well with increasing metadata size.

Table 3. Causeway Overhead (`getpid` test)

Description	Cost (machine cycles)	Cost (microseconds)	Overhead (%)
Base case	7001	2.92	-
0 byte metadata	7841	3.27	12.0
1 byte metadata	9369	3.90	33.8
32 bytes metadata	9409	3.92	34.4

Table 4. Causeway Overhead (pipe test)

Description	Cost (machine cycles)	Cost (microseconds)	Overhead (%)
Base case	35782	14.9	-
0 byte metadata	36807	15.3	2.9
1 byte metadata	49858	20.8	39.3
32 bytes metadata	54383	22.66	52.0

The second microbenchmark measures the cost of transferring 1 byte of data between two processes across a pipe. As before, we perform this experiment under the four scenarios used in the previous microbenchmark. Table 4 shows the result for the pipe test. The overhead of inserting a transfer point but passing no metadata is similar to that of the `getpid` test. The overhead of passing metadata is higher because the metadata is propagated across address spaces. Nevertheless, the overhead of propagating up to 32 bytes of metadata is less than 8 microseconds, a small amount. Finally, the overhead scales well with increasing metadata size. In this test Causeway's overhead ranged from less than 3% to about 52% over the base case.

Note that for the above measurements we could not use a microbenchmark consisting of a network server and client as the cost of sending messages over the network is several orders of magnitude higher than the overhead of Causeway in terms of absolute cost and we would not have been able to detect the overhead of Causeway with such a microbenchmark.

4 Evaluating Causeway

In this section we quantify the complexity involved in Causeway to insert transfer points for system-visible channels, and transfer points in an implementation of the TPC-W [12] benchmark. We also measure Causeway's overhead on TPC-W.

4.1 Transfer Points for System-Visible Channels

Sockets, pipes, and user-level thread/kernel-level thread boundary are the system-visible channels supported by Causeway. Six transfer points in the FreeBSD 5.2 kernel support metadata propagation across these channels as shown in Table 5. The user thread to kernel thread and kernel thread to user thread transfer points are required if the application is multithreaded. The socket and pipe transfer points are required if the application performs interprocess communication. Transfer points within system-visible channels do not require reimplementation for each new application.

4.2 Transfer Points for Apache and MySQL

We used Causeway to propagate metadata in an implementation of the TPC-W [12] benchmark. Our implementation of the TPC-W benchmark used the

Table 5. Transfer Points for System-visible Channels in the FreeBSD Kernel

Location	Description	File name	Function name
Kernel	User thread to kernel thread	`kern/kern_kse.c`	`thread_user_enter`
Kernel	Kernel thread to user thread	`kern/kern_kse.c`	`thread_userret`
Kernel	Kernel thread to socket message	`kern/uipc_socket.c`	`sosend`
Kernel	Socket message to kernel thread	`kern/uipc_socket.c`	`soreceive`
Kernel	Kernel thread to pipe message	`kern/sys_pipe.c`	`pipe_write`
Kernel	Pipe message to kernel thread	`kern/sys_pipe.c`	`pipe_read`

Apache web server (version 1.3.31) built with the PHP module (version 4.3.6) and the MySQL database server (version 4.0.16). The TPC-W interactions are implemented as PHP scripts.

Apache is a multi-process web server and does not use shared memory communication among the different processes. Thus, no transfer points are required in Apache.

MySQL is a multi-threaded program and it uses the libpthread library on FreeBSD. Inspection of the MySQL source code revealed that though individual MySQL pthreads access some shared data structure in a synchronized manner, there is no communication between threads to exchange data corresponding to a single request. In other words, a request in MySQL is executed in its entirety by a single pthread. An incoming database connection is accepted by a listener thread and handed over to a worker thread. The worker thread reads the request, executes it and sends back the response. Hence, no transfer points are required in MySQL as well.

In TPC-W, Apache and MySQL exchange messages across sockets. MySQL uses user-level thread on top of kernel-level threads. Thus Causeway's support for metadata propagation across system-visible channels, viz., sockets, and user-level thread and kernel-level thread boundary, suffices for our implementation of TPC-W using Apache and MySQL. This support is provided in an augmented FreeBSD kernel.

4.3   Overhead of Causeway on TPC-W

We conducted an experiment to evaluate the overhead imposed by Causeway on our implementation of TPC-W under a realistic workload. We subjected TPC-W to a workload consisting of emulated clients exercising the *shopping mix* [12] workload. Apache, MySQL and the load generator ran on separate machines. All the machines were 2.4 GHz Pentium Xeon with 2 Gigabytes of memory, and were connected by switched Gigabit ethernet. We varied the number of concurrent emulated clients and measured the throughput (interactions per minute) obtained from TPC-W. We compare the throughput obtained with the Causeway framework with that obtained without the Causeway framework (base case). Under Causeway we transferred 4 bytes of metadata across each transfer point for TPC-W. Table 6 shows the results of this experiment; Causeway's overhead on TPC-W's throughput remains less than 5%, further it does not increase with

Table 6. TPC-W Throughput (interactions/minute) for Shopping Mix

No. of concurrent emulated clients	Throughput (base case)	Throughput using Causeway	Causeway Overhead(%)
10	89.4	89	4.91
50	424.8	411	3.25
100	844.2	826.4	2.11

increasing load on the system and remains fairly constant. This result shows that Causeway may be used in a production environment without any substantial performance degradation.

5   Example Use of Causeway: Multi-tier Priority Propagation

Meta-applications to control and analyze the execution of applications can be built easily using Causeway. We illustrate one such meta-application here.

Using Causeway we could rapidly implement a priority propagation system, enabling a multi-tier application to prioritize the execution of requests. Under this system, upon receiving a request the application injects a priority as metadata, Causeway propagates this priority metadata with the execution of the request to each of the tiers, and the meta-application uses the priority metadata to enforce priority scheduling on each tier. The meta-application is automatically invoked on each tier by Causeway's transfer point callback mechanism.

The implementation of the multi-tier priority propagation system on top of Causeway required writing about 150 lines of code. We tested the multi-tier priority propagation system with an implementation of the TPC-W benchmark [12]. No modifications were required in the TPC-W application code, other than the injection of priority metadata.

5.1   Metadata Access

The priorities are injected into the system when a request arrives, using the metadata access API of Causeway. We register transfer point callback methods at the transfer points from a kernel thread to a user thread, and from a socket to a kernel thread. These callback methods change the priorities of the user thread and the kernel thread respectively. The first callback method affects the scheduling of MySQL `pthreads` while the second one achieves the same for Apache processes.

5.2   Application

We use the TPC-W [12] benchmark as our application. TPC-W simulates an online bookstore. Its implementation consists of a front-end web server, providing an HTTP front-end and serving static content, a middle-tier application that implements the business logic, and a back-end database server that stores the dynamic content of the site. The benchmark defines 14 interactions with the web site, 13 of which access the database. 6 interactions write to the database, while the others are read-only. Our hardware and software platforms are the same as described earlier in Section 4.

5.3 Experiment

The goal of the experiment is to demonstrate that multi-tier priority propagation using Causeway, without application modification, has considerable benefits. Our performance metric is the response time of the high-priority requests. We show that the response time of high priority requests is relatively independent of the load imposed on the system. We also demonstrate that enforcing priority at both tiers (web server and database server) is superior to only enforcing it at the first tier.

We define a foreground load as a sequence of 100 instances of each TPC-W interaction, spaced out in time by one second. We define a background load that directs a steady stream of read-only requests at the site. The background load simulates visitors browsing the web site, while the foreground load simulates customers performing the actions that may lead to purchases at the site, thereby deserving higher priority. We use two different levels of background load: one which overloads the system and one which imposes a moderate load without, however, saturating the system.

We have two levels of priority in the system: a default priority and a high priority. Requests originating from the background load are always tagged with metadata indicating the default priority. To demonstrate the effect of priorities, we perform two experiments, with requests from the foreground load tagged with metadata either indicating the high priority or the default priority. In addition, to demonstrate the difference between single-tier and multi-tier priority enforcement, we run an experiment in which on the web server the priorities are enforced by the transfer point callback methods as described above, but on the database server they are ignored.

5.4 Results

Table 7 shows the average response times (along with the 95% confidence intervals) in milliseconds for each of the interactions under the following conditions:

1. No background load: This case shows the baseline response time for each interaction.
2. No priority: The background load is present, but neither of the tiers enforce priority scheduling based on the metadata.
3. Priority in first tier: The background load is present, and the first tier (the web server) enforces priority scheduling based on the metadata.
4. Priority in both tiers: The background load is present, and both tiers enforce priority scheduling based on the metadata.

Table 7. Average Response Time and 95% Confidence Interval (in milliseconds) for the TPC-W Interactions under High Background Load

Inter-action	No background load	No priority	Priority in 1st. tier	Priority in all tiers
admin-confirm	60 (±0.2)	1936 (±3.8)	1993 (±38)	342 (±71)
admin-request	59 (±0.01)	1617 (±120)	868 (±85)	68 (±13)
best-sellers	918 (±49)	3173 (±986)	3016 (±234)	940 (±33)
buy-confirm	85 (±1.3)	1951 (±36)	1992 (±67)	1457 (±131)
buy-request	60 (±1)	1930 (±4.5)	1915 (±59)	81 (±36)
customer-reg	55 (±1.2)	931 (±88)	61 (±1.5)	60 (±1.6)
home	61 (±1.7)	1737 (±93)	1095 (±102)	63 (±2.2)
new-product	81 (±1.7)	1933 (±3)	1969 (±28)	85 (±4)
order-display	60 (±0.8)	1930 (±3)	1970 (±4)	64 (±4)
order-inquiry	40 (±0.01)	42 (±2.2)	40 (±1)	40 (±0.3)
product-detail	60 (±0.6)	1516 (±127)	966 (±100)	68 (±14)
search-request	60 (±0.03)	1533 (±127)	987 (±102)	61 (±0.7)
search-result	670 (±0.6)	2628 (±314)	2528 (±5.3)	671 (±1.5)
shopping-cart	70 (±0.9)	1931 (±4)	1984 (±6)	217 (±40.5)

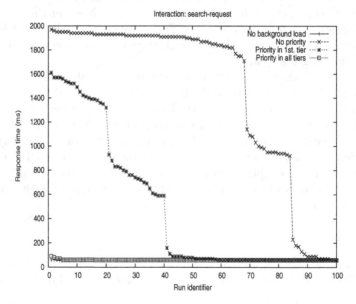

Fig. 1. Response Time Distribution (Sorted in Descending Order) for Search-Request Interaction (High Background Load)

As further illustration of the results, we show in Figure 1 the response times, sorted in descending order, for the execution of the 100 requests of the search-request interaction under the four cases as described above.

Table 8. Average Response Time and 95% Confidence Interval (in milliseconds) for the TPC-W Interactions under Moderate Background Load

Inter-action	No back-ground load	No priority	Priority in 1st. tier	Priority in all tiers
admin-confirm	60 (±0.2)	95 (±6)	90 (±6)	65 (±1.3)
admin-request	60 (±0.2)	92 (±6)	65 (±2.7)	60 (±0.15)
best-sellers	918 (±49)	1092 (±165)	1137 (±158)	912 (±0.9)
buy-confirm	85 (±1.3)	136 (±6)	123 (±6)	94 (±1.8)
buy-request	60 (±1)	103 (±7)	99 (±6)	63 (±1.7)
customer-reg	55 (±1.3)	78 (±4.4)	62 (±2.6)	59 (±1.1)
home	61 (±1.9)	98 (±6.2)	82 (±5.5)	62 (±2)
new-product	81 (±1.7)	125 (±9.6)	101 (±7)	84 (±3.4)
order-display	60 (±0.8)	102 (±6.9)	101 (±6.5)	62 (±1.5)
order-inquiry	40 (±0.01)	40 (±0.15)	40 (±0.01)	40 (±0.01)
product-detail	60 (±0.6)	94 (±6)	64 (±2.4)	60 (±0.2)
search-request	60 (±0.04)	97 (±6.3)	65 (±2.8)	60 (±0.14)
search-result	670 (±0.62)	715 (±19.7)	728 (±11.8)	667 (±3.2)
shopping-cart	70 (±0.86)	110 (±6.2)	83 (±4.1)	73 (±1.1)

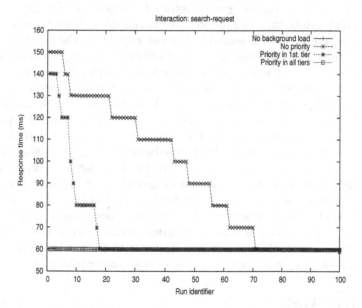

Fig. 2. Response Time Distribution (Sorted in Descending Order) for Search Request (Moderate Background Load)

Table 7 and Figure 1 reflect the behavior under a background load that pushes the system into overload. The same results for a moderate background load are shown in Table 8 and Figure 2.

5.5 Discussion

The results overall confirm the benefits of multi-tier priority enforcement. With priorities enforced at both tiers the response times approximate those under no load, and they are substantially better than those in the absence of priorities or in the presence of priorities only at the first tier. The results for single-tier priority enforcement are better than with no priorities, but inferior to using priorities at both tiers. The differences are more outspoken in the case of overload, but remain present even under more moderate loads. Given that Causeway allows multi-tier priority propagation without modification of the application and without noticeable overhead, we argue that this serves as a convincing demonstration of its merits.

More detailed inspection of the results on a per-interaction basis leads to some additional observations. First, in looking at Table 7 we see that for a large number of the interactions the response time under load with multi-tier priorities is almost identical to the response time under no load. For a few interactions, however, the response under load is higher, even with the priorities. This observation is explained by the fact that the background load acquires read locks on a certain table in the database, and the fact that the interactions that show a slowdown under load acquire an exclusive lock on that table. As a result, independent of priorities, the foreground interactions need to wait for all current readers to finish before they can proceed at the database. Under overload, there can be a large number of such reads in progress, explaining the marked increases in response time for the admin-confirm, buy-confirm, buy-request and shopping-cart interactions. For the moderate load where only a very few such readers are present, the differences almost vanish (see Table 8). For foreground interactions that have no conflicts with the background load, there is almost no difference between the the no-load case and the case of load and with multi-tier priorities.

Second, in a few cases, namely the customer-registration and the order-inquire interactions, there is no difference between single-tier and multi-tier priorities. This is the result of the fact that for these interactions there is no access to the database or the cost is mainly governed by application execution and not by database access. Conversely, for the interactions whose cost is primarily governed by database access or for the interactions that acquire exclusive locks on the database, there is a more pronounced difference between single-tier and multi-tier priorities. In these cases, the benefit of enforcing priority at the first tier is also limited relative to the case of not having priorities at all.

6 Related Work

Several meta-applications to control or analyze multi-tier applications exist in the literature. The use of request tagging has been utilized to determine faults in Internet services [5]. The resulting Pinpoint system uses instrumentation of the J2EE platform to pass on request identifiers among the different components of the system. Each component registers information in a log about the request identifier, the component identifier and whether a particular operation results in success or failure. Failure is defined as throwing a Java exception, a runtime exception, an infinite loop, etc. The log is statistically analyzed using data clustering techniques to find faulty components. Pinpoint does not support applications spanning multiple machines, but the authors state that the Java RMI libraries can be extended to pass request identifiers across machines. Unlike Causeway, Pinpoint does not track execution events in the kernel as its instrumentation does not extend beyond the J2EE platform.

Aguilera et al. [1] infer causal paths from message traces to locate nodes causing performance bottlenecks; their implementation is based on the Pinpoint system [5]. They collect traces of messages between nodes, process them offline to find causal relationships among them, and study the delay patterns of the messages to infer which node is causing the bottleneck. Their system is intended to operate in a "black-box" environment, and therefore tries to be minimally invasive. Causeway is more invasive, requiring kernel and library changes, but in turn provides more functionality. In particular, it's deterministic rather than being heuristic, and much more fine-grained.

Magpie [4,9] logs events, and extracts events belonging to a particular request execution by performing temporal joins over the log of events. These joins are based on application-specific schemas, which may require considerable expertise and knowledge about the application. Magpie and request identification using Causeway present an interesting set of tradeoffs. Magpie does not require kernel or library modifications, and leverages event logging facilities already present in Windows. In contrast, Causeway accepts the premise of such modifications, and as a result avoids the need for detailed knowledge about the application.

TraceBack [2] provides a debugging facility in production systems. It can identify what first went wrong in the event of a program crash, hang or exception. It instruments the program to record control flow information at runtime, which is later analyzed to locate the occurrence of the first fault.

DTE [3] propagates domain and type information among communicating processes providing security and access control for interprocess communication. While DTE provides security mechanisms, Causeway may be used to implement arbitrary meta-applications.

Perhaps the work closest to Causeway is Stateful Distributed Interposition (SDI) [11] which propagates contextual information along request execution paths in a multi-tier application. Resource constraints and security classification are examples of contextual information. Contextual information in SDI and metadata in Causeway are analogous. SDI assumes all communication channels in a multi-tier program to be system-visible, and thus it does not propagate contextual information across system-opaque channels. Causeway supports metadata propagation across shared memory, a system-opaque channel.

7   Conclusions

We have designed Causeway, operating system support for facilitating development of meta-applications to control and analyze multi-tier applications. Causeway provides interfaces for metadata injection and access which can be used for propagation of metadata in multi-tier applications. Propagated metadata can be accessed and used to implement the desired meta-application. We have implemented Causeway in the FreeBSD operating system kernel. The complexity of adding transfer points in the FreeBSD kernel for system-visible channels was modest. Causeway's support for system-visible channels suffices for metadata propagation in an implementation of the TPC-W [12] benchmark using Apache and MySQL — no modification to Apache or MySQL was required. We measured the overhead of Causeway and found it small enough so that it can be used in a production environment. Further, the overhead scales well with increasing metadata size and load on the application. We have demonstrated the use of Causeway by implementing a multi-tier priority enforcing system and using it to achieve global priority enforcement on our implementation of the TPC-W benchmark. This required adding only about 150 lines of code on top of Causeway.

As ongoing and future work we are implementing call path profiling of distributed programs on top of Causeway. Call path profiling [7,8] associates resource consumption of program execution with call paths. At any point in the program execution, a call path is defined as the sequence of call sites used to activate each of the procedure frames on the call stack when the given point of execution is reached. Call path profilers are superior to call-graph profilers like gprof [6] because they can distinguish resource consumption of a procedure based on the call paths leading to it.

In a distributed program whose components perform Remote Procedure Calls (RPCs) among themselves, we can use Causeway to propagate the context information (call path) from the caller to the callee, and use this propagated context information to annotate the callee's profiles. Profiles of the caller and the callee may then be stitched together in a single call path tree using these annotations. The end result is an end-to-end call path profile of a distributed program — such a profiler does not exist in the literature. This profiling system illustrates another useful meta-application on top of Causeway.

References

1. M. K. Aguilera, J. C. Mogul, J. L. Wiener, P. Reynolds, and A. Muthitacharoen. Performance Debugging for Distributed Systems of Black Boxes. In *Proceedings of the 19th ACM Symposium on Operating Systems Principles (SOSP '03)*, pages 74–89, Oct. 2003.
2. A. Ayers, R. Schooler, C. Metcalf, A. Agarwal, J. Rhee, and E. Witchel. TraceBack: First Fault Diagnosis by Reconstruction of Distributed Control Flow. In *Conference on Programming Language Design and Implementation (PLDI) 2005*, pages 201–212, June 2005.
3. L. Badger, D. F. Sterne, D. L. Sherman, K. M. Walker, and S. A. Haghighat. A Domain and Type Enforcement UNIX Prototype. In *Fifth USENIX UNIX Security Symposium*, June 1995.
4. P. Barham, A. Donnelly, R. Isaacs, and R. Mortier. Using Magpie for Request Extraction and Workload Modelling. In *OSDI*, pages 259–272, Dec. 2004.

5. M. Y. Chen, E. Kiciman, E. Fratkin, A. Fox, and E. Brewer. Pinpoint: Problem Determination in Large, Dynamic Internet Services. In *Proceedings of the International Conference on Dependable Systems and Networks (IPDS Track)*, pages 595–604, June 2002.
6. S. L. Graham, P. B. Kessler, and M. K. McKusick. gprof: a call graph execution profiler. In *SIGPLAN Symposium on Compiler Construction*, pages 120–126, 1982.
7. R. J. Hall. Call path profiling. In *Proceedings of the 14th International Conference on Software Engineering*, pages 296–306, 1992.
8. R. J. Hall and A. J. Goldberg. Call path profiling of monotonic program resources in UNIX. In *Proceedings of the USENIX Summer Technical Conference*, 1993.
9. R. Isaacs, P. Barham, J. Bulpin, R. Mortier, and D. Narayanan. Request extraction in Magpie: events, schemas and temporal joins. In *SIGOPS EW'04: ACM SIGOPS European Workshop*, Sept. 2004.
10. Jon Currey. Real-Time CORBA Theory and Practice : A Standards-based Approach to the Development of Distributed Real-Time Systems. At http://www.uninova.pt/~jmf/aptr/Documentos/CorbaRT.pdf.
11. J. Reumann and K. G. Shin. Stateful Distributed Interposition. *ACM Transactions on Computer Systems*, 22(1):1–48, Feb. 2004.
12. T. P. P. C. (TPC). TPC BENCHMARK W (web commerce). At http://www.tpc.org/tpcw/, Feb. 2002.

MINERVA∞: A Scalable Efficient Peer-to-Peer Search Engine

Sebastian Michel[1], Peter Triantafillou[2], and Gerhard Weikum[1]

[1] Max-Planck-Institut für Informatik, 66123 Saarbrücken, Germany
{smichel, weikum}@mpi-inf.mpg.de
[2] R.A. Computer Technology Institute and University of Patras, 26500 Greece
peter@ceid.upatras.gr

Abstract. The promises inherent in users coming together to form data sharing network communities, bring to the foreground new problems formulated over such dynamic, ever growing, computing, storage, and networking infrastructures. A key open challenge is to harness these highly distributed resources toward the development of an ultra scalable, efficient search engine. From a technical viewpoint, any acceptable solution must fully exploit all available resources dictating the removal of any centralized points of control, which can also readily lead to performance bottlenecks and reliability/availability problems. Equally importantly, however, a highly distributed solution can also facilitate pluralism in informing users about internet content, which is crucial in order to preclude the formation of information-resource monopolies and the biased visibility of content from economically-powerful sources. To meet these challenges, the work described here puts forward MINERVA∞, a novel search engine architecture, designed for scalability and efficiency. MINERVA∞ encompasses a suite of novel algorithms, including algorithms for creating data networks of interest, placing data on network nodes, load balancing, top-k algorithms for retrieving data at query time, and replication algorithms for expediting top-k query processing. We have implemented the proposed architecture and we report on our extensive experiments with real-world, web-crawled, and synthetic data and queries, showcasing the scalability and efficiency traits of MINERVA∞.

1 Introduction

The peer-to-peer (P2P) approach facilitates the sharing of huge amounts of data in a distributed and self-organizing way. These characteristics offer enormous potential benefit for the development of internet-scale search engines, powerful in terms of scalability, efficiency, and resilience to failures and dynamics. Additionally, such a search engine can potentially benefit from the intellectual input (e.g., bookmarks, query logs, click streams, etc.) of a large user community participating in the sharing network. Finally, but perhaps even more importantly, a P2P web search engine can also facilitate pluralism in informing users about internet content, which is crucial in order to preclude the formation of information-resource monopolies and the biased visibility of content from economically powerful sources.

G. Alonso (Ed.): Middleware 2005, LNCS 3790, pp. 60–81, 2005.

Our challenge therefore was to exploit P2P technology's powerful tools for efficient, reliable, large-scale content sharing and delivery to build a P2P web search engine. We wish to leverage DHT technology and build highly distributed algorithms and data infrastructures that can render P2P web searching feasible.

The crucial challenge in developing successful P2P Web search engines is based on reconciling the following high-level, conflicting goals: on the one hand, to respond to user search queries with high quality results with respect to precision/recall, by employing an efficient distributed top-k query algorithm, and, on the other hand, to provide an infrastructure ensuring scalability and efficiency in the presence of a very large peer population and the very large amounts of data that must be communicated in order to meet the first goal.

Achieving ultra scalability is based on precluding the formation of central points of control during the processing of search queries. This dictates a solution that is highly distributed in both the data and computational dimensions. Such a solution leads to facilitating a large number of nodes pulling together their computational (storage, processing, and communication) resources, in essence increasing the total resources available for processing queries. At the same time, great care must be exercised in order to ensure efficiency of operation; that is, ensure that engaging greater numbers of peers does not lead to unnecessary high costs in terms of query response times, bandwidth requirements, and local peer work.

With this work, we put forward MINERVA∞, a P2P web search engine architecture, detailing its key design features, algorithms, and implementation. MINERVA∞ features offer an infrastructure capable of attaining our scalability and efficiency goals. We report on a detailed experimental performance study of our implemented engine using real-world, web-crawled data collections and queries, which showcases our engine's efficiency and scalability. To the authors' knowledge, this is the first work that offers a highly distributed (in both the data dimension and the computational dimension), scalable and efficient solution toward the development of internet-scale search engines.

2   Related Work

Recent research on structured P2P systems, such as Chord [17], CAN [13], Skip-Nets [9] or Pastry [15] is typically based on various forms of distributed hash tables (DHTs) and supports mappings from keys to locations in a decentralized manner such that routing scales well with the number of peers in the system. The original architectures of DHT-based P2P networks are typically limited to exact-match queries on keys. More recently, the data management community has focused on extending such architectures to support more complex queries [10,8,7]. All this related work, however, is insufficient for text queries that consist of a variable number of keywords, and it is absolutely inappropriate for full-fledged Web search where keyword queries should return a ranked result list of the most relevant approximate matches [3].

Within the field of P2P Web search, the following work is highly related to our efforts. Galanx [21] is a P2P search engine implemented using the Apache HTTP server and BerkeleyDB. The Web site servers are the peers of this architecture; pages are stored only where they originate from. In contrast, our approach leaves it to the peers to what extent they want to crawl interesting fractions of the Web and build their own local indexes, and defines appropriate networks, structures, and algorithms for scalably and efficiently sharing this information.

PlanetP [4] is a pub/sub service for P2P communities, supporting content ranking search. PlanetP distinguishes local indexes and a global index to describe all peers and their shared information. The global index is replicated using a gossiping algorithm. This system, however, appears to be limited to a relatively small number of peers (e.g., a few thousand).

Odissea [18] assumes a two-layered search engine architecture with a global index structure distributed over the nodes in the system. A single node holds the complete, Web-scale, index for a given text term (i.e., keyword or word stem). Query execution uses a distributed version of Fagin's threshold algorithm [5]. The system appears to create scalability and performance bottlenecks at the single-node where index lists are stored. Further, the presented query execution method seems limited to queries with at most two keywords. The paper actually advocates using a limited number of nodes, in the spirit of a server farm.

The system outlined in [14] uses a fully distributed inverted text index, in which every participant is responsible for a specific subset of terms and manages the respective index structures. Particular emphasis is put on minimizing the bandwidth used during multi-keyword searches. [11] considers content-based retrieval in hybrid P2P networks where a peer can either be a simple node or a directory node. Directory nodes serve as super-peers, which may possibly limit the scalability and self-organization of the overall system. The peer selection for forwarding queries is based on the Kullback-Leibler divergence between peer-specific statistical models of term distributions.

Complementary, recent research has also focused into distributed top-k query algorithms [2,12] (and others mentioned in these papers which are straightforward distributed versions/extensions of traditional centralized top-k algorithms, such as NRA [6]). Distributed top-k query algorithms are an important component of our P2P web search engine. All these algorithms are concerned with the efficiency of top-k query processing in environments where the index lists for terms are distributed over a number of nodes, with index lists for each term being stored in a single node, and are based on a per-query coordinator which collects progressively data from the index lists. The existence of a single node storing a complete index list for a term undoubtedly creates scalability and efficiency bottlenecks, as our experiments have showed. The relevant algorithms of MINERVA∞ ensure high degrees of distribution for index lists' data and distributed processing, avoiding central bottlenecks and boosting scalability.

3   The Model

In general, we envision a widely distributed system, comprised of great numbers of peers, forming a collection with great aggregate computing, communication, and storage capabilities. Our challenge is to fully exploit these resources in order to develop an ultra scalable, efficient, internet-content search engine.

We expect that nodes will be conducting independent web crawls, discovering *documents* and computing *scores* of documents, with each score reflecting a document's importance with respect to *terms* of interest. The result of such activities is the formation of *index lists*, one for each term, containing relevant documents and their score for a term. More formally, our network consists of a set of nodes N, collectively storing a set D of documents, with each document having a unique identifier *docID*, drawn from a sufficiently large name space (e.g., 160 bits long). Set T refers to the set of terms. The notation $|S|$ denotes the cardinality of set S. The basic data items in our model are triplets of the form *(term, docID, score)*. In general, nodes employ some function $score(d,t) : D \to (0,1]$, which for some term t, produces the score for document d. Typically, such a scoring function utilizes tdf*idf style statistical metadata.

The model is based on two fundamental operations. The $Post(t,d,s)$ operation, with $t \in T$, $d \in D$, and $s \in (0,1]$, is responsible for identifying a network node and store there the (t,d,s) triplet. The operation $Query(T_i,k) :$ $return(L_k)$, with $T_i \subseteq T$, k an integer, and $L_k = \{(d, TotalScore(d)) : d \in D, TotalScore(d) \geq RankKscore\}$, is a top-k query operation. $TotalScore(d)$ denotes the aggregate score for d with respect to terms in T_i. Although there are several possibilities for the monotonic aggregate function to be used, we employ summation, for simplicity. Hence, $TotalScore(d) = \sum_{t \in T_i} score(d,t)$. For a given term, $RankKscore$ refers to the k-th highest TotalScore, s_{min} (s_{max}) refers to the minimum (maximum) score value, and, given a score s, $next(s)$ ($prev(s)$) refers to the score value immediately following (preceding) s.

All nodes are connected on a *global* network G. G is an *overlay network*, modeled as a graph $G = (N,E)$, where E denotes the communication links connecting the nodes. E is explicitly defined by the choice of the overlay network; for instance, for Chord, E consists of the successor, predecessor, and finger table (i.e., routing table) links of each node.

In addition to the global network G, encompassing all nodes, our model employs term-specific overlays, coined *Term Index Networks (TINs)*. $I(t)$ denotes the TIN for term t and is used to store and maintain all (t,d,s) items. TIN $I(t)$ is defined as $I(t) = (N(t), E(t))$, $N(t) \subseteq N$. Note that nodes in $N(t)$ have in addition to the links for participating in G, links needed to connect them to the $I(t)$ network. The model itself is independent of any particular overlay architecture.

$I(t).n(s_i)$ defines the node responsible for storing all triplets (t,d,s) for which $score(d,t) = s = s_i$. When the context is well understood, the same node is simply denoted as $n(s)$.

4 Design Overview and Rationale

The fundamental distinguishing feature of MINERVA∞ is its high distribution both in the data and computational dimensions. MINERVA∞ goes far beyond the state of the art in distributed top-k query processing algorithms, which are based on having nodes storing complete index lists for terms and running coordinator-based top-k algorithms [2,12]. From a data point of view, the principle is that the data items needed by top-k queries are the triplets $(term, docID, score)$ for each queried term (and not the index lists containing them). A proper distributed design for such systems then should appropriately distribute these items controllably so to meet the goals of scalability and efficiency. Thus, data distribution in MINERVA∞ is at the level of this, much finer data grain. From a system's point of view, the design principle we follow is to organize the key computations to engage several different nodes, with each node having to perform small (sub)tasks, as opposed to assigning single large task to a single node. These design choices, we believe, will greatly boost scalability (especially under skewed accesses).

Our approach to materializing this design relies on the employment of the novel notion of Term Index Networks (TINs). TINs may be formed for every term in our system, and they serve two roles: First, as an abstraction, encapsulating the information specific to a term of interest, and second, as a physical manifestation of a distributed repository of the term-specific data items, facilitating their efficient and scalable retrieval. A TIN can be conceptualized as a *virtual* node storing a *virtually global* index list for a term, which is constructed by the sorted merging of the separate complete index lists for the term computed at different nodes. Thus, TINs are comprised of nodes which collectively store different horizontal partitions of this global index list. In practice, we expect TINs to be employed only for the most popular terms (a few hundred to a few thousand) whose accesses are expected to form scalability and performance bottlenecks.

We will exploit the underlying network $G's$ architecture and related algorithms (e.g., for routing/lookup) to efficiently and scalably create and maintain TINs and for retrieving TIN data items, from any node of G. In general, TINs may form separate overlay networks, coexisting with the global overlay G^1.

The MINERVA∞ algorithms are heavily influenced by the way the well-known, efficient top-k query processing algorithms (e.g., [6]) operate, looking for docIDs within certain ranges of score values. Thus, the networks' $lookup(s)$ function, will be used using scores s as input, to locate the nodes storing docIDs with scores s.

A key point to stress here, however, is that top-k queries $Q(\{t_1, ..., t_r\}, k)$ can originate from any peer node p of G, which in general is not a member of any $I(t_i)$, $i = 1, ..., r$ and thus p does not have, nor can it easily acquire, the necessary routing state needed to forward the query to the TINs for the query terms. Our infrastructure, solves this by utilizing for each TIN a fairly small number (relative to the total number of data items for a term) of nodes of G

---

[1] In practice, it may not always be necessary or advisable to form full-fledged separate overlays for TINs; instead, TINs will be formed as straightforward extensions of G: in this case, when a node n of G joins a TIN, only two additional links are added to the state of n linking it to its successor and predecessor nodes in the TIN. In this case, a TIN is simply a (circular) doubly-linked list.

which will be readily identifiable and accessible from any node of G and can act as *gateways* between G and this TIN, being members of both networks.

Finally, in order for any highly distributed solution to be efficient, it is crucial to keep as low as possible the time and bandwidth overheads involved in the required communication between the various nodes. This is particularly challenging for solutions built over very large scale infrastructures. To achieve this, the algorithms of MINERVA∞ follow the principles put forward by top-performing, resource-efficient top-k query processing algorithms in traditional environments. Specifically, the principles behind favoring sequential index-list accesses to random accesses (in order to avoid high-cost random disk IOs) have been adapted in our distributed algorithms to ensure that: (i) sequential accesses of the items in the *global, virtual* index list dominate, (ii) they require either no communication, or at most an one-hop communication between nodes, and (iii) random accesses require at most $O(log|N|)$ messages.

To ensure the at-most-one-hop communication requirement for successive sequential accesses of TIN data, the MINERVA∞ algorithms utilize an *order preserving hash function*, first proposed for supporting range queries in DHT-based data networks in [20]. An order preserving hash function $h_{op}()$ has the property that for any two values v_1, v_2, if $v_1 > v_2$ then $h_{op}(v_1) > h_{op}(v_2)$. This guarantees that data items corresponding to successive score values of a term t are placed either at the same or at neighboring nodes of $I(t)$. Alternatively, similar functionality can be provided by employing for each $I(t)$ an overlay based on skip graphs or skip nets [1,9]. Since both order preserving hashing and skip graphs incur the danger for load imbalances when assigning data items to TIN nodes, given the expected data skew of scores, load balancing solutions are needed.

The design outlined so far, leverages DHT technology to facilitate efficiency and scalability in key aspects of the system's operation. Specifically, posting (and deleting) data items for a term from any node can be done in $O(log|N|)$ time, in terms of the number of messages. Similarly, during top-k query processing, the TINs of the terms in the query can be also reached in $O(log|N|)$ messages. Furthermore, no single node is over-burdened with tasks which can either require more resources than available, or exhaust its resources, or even stress its resources for longer periods of time. In addition, as the top-k algorithm is processing different data items for each queried term, this involves gradually different nodes from each TIN, producing a highly distributed, scalable solution.

5   Term Index Networks

In this section we describe and analyze the algorithms for creating TINs and populating them with data and nodes.

5.1   Beacons for Bootstrapping TINs

The creation of a TIN has these basic elements: posting data items, inserting nodes, and maintaining the connectivity of nodes to ensure the efficiency/scalability properties promised by the TIN overlay.

As mentioned, a key issue to note is that any node p in G may need to post (t, d, s) items for a term t. Since, in general, p is not a member of $I(t)$ and does not necessarily know members of $I(t)$, efficiently and scalably posting items to $I(t)$ from any p becomes non-trivial. To overcome this, a bootstrapping process for $I(t)$ is employed which initializes an TIN $I(t)$ for term t. The basic novelty lies in the special role to be played by nodes coined *beacons*, which in essence become gateways, allowing the flow of data and requests between the G and $I(t)$ networks.

In the bootstrap algorithm, a predefined number of "dummy" items of the form $(t, \star, s_i)$ is generated in sequence for a set of predefined score values s_i, $i = 1, ..., u$. Each such item will be associated with a node n in G, where it will be stored. Finally, this node n of G will also be made a member of $I(t)$ by randomly choosing a previously inserted beacon node (i.e., for the one associated with an already inserted score value s_j, $1 \leq j \leq i - 1$) as a gateway.

The following algorithm details the pseudocode for bootstrapping $I(t)$. It utilizes an order-preserving hash function $h_{op}() : T \times (0, 1] \rightarrow [m]$, where m is the size of the identifiers in bits and $[m]$ denotes the name space used for the overlay (e.g., all 2^{160} ids, for 160-bit identifiers). In addition, a standard hash function $h() : (0, 1] \rightarrow [m]$, (e.g. SHA-1) is used. The particulars of the order preserving hash function to be employed will be detailed after the presentation of the query processing algorithms which they affect. The bootstrap algorithm selects u "dummy" score values, i/u, $i = 1, ..., u$, finds for each such score value the node n in G where it should be placed (using $h_{op}()$), stores this score there and inserts n into the $I(t)$ network as well. At first, the $I(t)$ network contains only the node with the dummy item with score zero. At each iteration, another node of n is added to $I(t)$ using as gateway the node of G which was added in the previous iteration to $I(t)$. For simplicity of presentation, the latter node

---

Algorithm 1. Bootstrap $I(t)$

```
 1: input: u: the number of "dummy" items (t, ⋆, s_i), i = 1, ..., u
 2: input: t: the term for which the TIN is created
 3: p = 1/u
 4: for i = 1 to u do
 5:     s = i × p
 6:     lookup(n.s) = h_op(t, s) { n.s in G will become the next beacon node of I(t) }
 7:     if s = p then
 8:         N(t) = {n.s}
 9:         E(t) = ∅ {Initialized I(t) with n.s with the first dummy item}
10:     end if
11:     if s ≠ p then
12:         n_1 = h_op(t, s − p) {insert n(s) into I(t) using node n(s − p) as gateway}
13:         call join(I(t), n_1, s)
14:     end if
15:     store (t, ⋆, s) at I(t).n(s)
16: end for
```
---

can be found by simply hashing for the previous dummy value. A better choice for distributing the load among the beacons is to select at random one of the previously-inserted beacons and use it as a gateway.

Obviously, a single beacon per TIN suffices. The number u of beacon scores is intended to introduce a number of gateways between G and $I(t)$ so to avoid potential bottlenecks during TIN creation. u will typically be a fairly small number so the total beacon-related overhead involved in the TIN creation will be kept small. Further, we emphasize that beacons are utilized by the algorithm posting items to TINs. Post operations will in general be very rare compared to query operations and query processing does not involve the use of beacons.

Finally, note that the algorithm uses a *join*() routine that adds a node $n(s)$ storing score s into $I(t)$ using a node n_1 known to be in $I(t)$ and thus, has the required state. The new node $n(s)$ must occupy a position in $I(t)$ specified by the value of $h_{op}(t, s)$. Note that this is ensured by using $h(nodeID)$, as is typically done in DHTs, since these node IDs were selected from the order-preserving hash function. Besides the side-effect of ensuring the order-preserving position for the nodes added to a TIN, the join routine is otherwise straightforward: if the TIN is a full-fledged DHT overlay, join() is updating the predecessor/successor pointers, the $O(log|N|)$ routing state of the new node, and the routing state of each $I(t)$ node pointing to it, as dictated by the relevant DHT algorithm. If the TIN is simply a doubly-linked list, then only predecessor/successor pointers are the new node and its neighbors are adjusted.

5.2   Posting Data to TINs

The posting of data items is now made possible using the bootstrapped TINs. Any node n_1 of G wishing to post an item (t, d, s) first locates an appropriate node of G, n_2 that will store this item. Subsequently, it inserts node n_2 into $I(t)$. To do this, it randomly selects a beacon score and associated beacon node, from all available beacons. This is straightforward given the predefined beacon score values and the hashing functions used. The chosen beacon node has been made a member of $I(t)$ during bootstrapping. Thus, it can "escort" n_2 into $I(t)$.

The following provides the pseudocode for the posting algorithm. By design, the post algorithm results in a data placement which introduces two characteristics, that will be crucial in ensuring efficient query processing. First, (as the bootstrap algorithm does) the post algorithm utilizes the order-preserving hash function. As a result, any two data items with consecutive score values for the same term will be placed by definition in nodes of G which will become one-hop neighbors in the TIN for the term, using the join() function explained earlier. Note, that within each TIN, there are no 'holes'. A node n becomes a member of a TIN network if and only if a data item was posted, with the score value for this item hashing to n. It is instructing here to emphasize that if TINs were not formed and instead only the global network was present, in general, any two successive score values could be falling in nodes which in G could be many hops apart. With TINs, following successor (or predecessor) links always leads to

---

Algorithm 2. Posting Data to $I(t)$

1: **input:** t, d, s: the item to be inserted by a node n_1
2: $n(s) = h_{op}(t, s)$
3: n_1 sends (t, d, s) to $n(s)$
4: **if** $n(s) \notin N(t)$ **then**
5:     $n(s)$ selects randomly a beacon score s_b
6:     $lookup(n_b) = h_{op}(t, s_b)$ { n_b is the beacon node storing beacon score s_b }
7:     $n(s)$ calls $join(I(t), n_b, s)$
8: **end if**
9: store $((t, d, s)$

---

nodes where the next (or previous) segment of scores have been placed. This feature in essence ensures the at-most-one-hop communication requirement when accessing items with successive scores in the global virtual index list for a term.

Second, the nodes of any $I(t)$ become responsible for storing specific segments (horizontal partitions) of the global virtual index list for t. In particular, an $I(t)$ node stores all items for t for a specific (range of) score value, posted by any node of the underlying network G.

5.3   Complexity Analysis

The bootstrapping $I(t)$ algorithm is responsible for inserting u beacon items. For each beacon item score, the node $n.s$ is located by applying the $h_{op}()$ function and routing the request to that node (step 5). This will be done using G's lookup algorithm in $O(log|N|)$ messages. The next key step is to locate the previously inserted beacon node (step 11) (or any beacon node at random) and sending it the request to join the TIN. Step 11 again involves $O(log|N|)$ messages. The actual join() routine will cost $O(log^2|N(t)|)$ messages, which is the standard join() message complexity for any DHT of size $N(t)$. Therefore, the total cost is $O(u \times (log|N| + log^2|N(t)|)$ messages.

The analysis for the posting algorithm is very similar. For each $post(t, d, s)$ operation, the node n where this data item should be stored is located and the request is routed to it, costing $O(log|N|)$ messages (step 3). Then a random beacon node is located, costing $O(log|N|)$ messages, and then the join() routine is called from this node, costing $O(log^2|N(t)|)$ messages. Thus, each post operation has a complexity of $O(log|N|) + O(log^2|N(t)|)$ messages.

Note that both of the above analysis assumed that each $I(t)$ is a full-blown DHT overlay. This permits a node to randomly select any beacon node to use to join the TIN. Alternatively, if each $I(t)$ is simply a (circular) doubly-linked list, then a node can join a TIN using the beacon storing the beacon value that is immediately preceding the posted score value. This requires $O(log|N|)$ hops to locate this beacon node. However, since in this case the routing state for each node of a TIN consists of only the two (predecessor and successor) links, the cost to join is in the worst case $O(|N(t)|)$, since after locating the beacon node with the previous beacon value, $O(|N(t)|)$ successor pointers may need to be followed in order to place the node in its proper order-preserving position. Thus, when

TINs are simple doubly-linked lists, the complexity of both the bootstrap and post algorithms are $O(log|N| + |N(t)|)$ messages.

6 Load Balancing

6.1 Order-Preserving Hashing

The order preserving hash function to be employed is important for several reasons. First, for simplicity, the function can be based on a simple linear transform. Consider hashing a value $f(s) : (0, 1] \rightarrow I$, where $f(s)$ transforms a score s into an integer; for instance, $f(s) = 10^6 \times s$. Function $h_{op}()$ can be defined then as

$$h_{op}(s) = (\frac{f(s) - f(s_{min})}{f(s_{max}) - f(s_{min})} \times 2^m) \ mod \ 2^m \qquad (1)$$

Although such a function is clearly order-preserving, it has the drawback that it produces the same output for items of equal scores of different terms. This leads to the same node storing for all terms all items having the same score. This is undesirable since it cannot utilize all available resources (i.e., utilize different sets of nodes to store items for different terms). To avoid this, $h_{op}()$ is refined to take as input the term name, which provides the necessary functionality, as follows.

$$h_{op}(t, s) = (h(t) + \frac{f(s) - f(s_{min})}{f(s_{max}) - f(s_{min})} \times 2^m) \ mod \ 2^m \qquad (2)$$

The term $h(t)$ adds a different random offset for different terms, initiating the search for positions of term score values at different, random, offsets within the namespace. Thus, by using the $h(t)$ term in $h_{op}(t, s)$ the result is that any data items having equal scores but for different terms are expected to be stored at different nodes of G.

Another benefit stems from ameliorating the storage load imbalances that result from the non-uniform distribution of score values. Assuming a uniform placement of nodes in G, the expected non-uniform distribution of scores will result in a non-uniform assignment of scores to nodes. Thus, when viewed from the perspective of a single term t, the nodes of $I(t)$ will exhibit possibly severe storage load imbalances. However, assuming the existence of large numbers of terms (e.g., a few thousand), and thus data items being posted for all these terms over the same set of nodes in G, given the randomly selected starting offsets for the placement of items, it is expected that the severe load imbalances will disappear. Intuitively, overburdened nodes for the items of one term are expected to be less burdened for the items of other terms and vice versa.

But even with the above hash function, very skewed score distributions will lead to storage load imbalances. Expecting that exponential-like distributions of score values will appear frequently, we developed a hash function that is order-preserving and handles load imbalances by assigning score segments of exponentially decreasing sizes to an exponentially increasing number of nodes. For instance, the sparse top $1/2$ of the scores distribution is to be assigned to a single node, the next $1/4$ of scores is to be assigned to 2 nodes, the next $1/8$ of scores to 4 nodes, etc. The details of this are omitted for space reasons.

6.2 TIN Data Migration

Exploiting the key characteristics of our data, MINERVA∞ can ensure further load balancing with small overheads. Specifically, index lists data entries are small in size and are very rarely posted and/or updated. In this subsection we outline our approach for improved load balancing.

We require that each peer posting index list entries, first computes a (equi-width) histogram of its data with respect to its score distribution. Assuming a targeted $|N(t)|$ number of nodes for the TIN of term t, it can create $|N(t)|$ equal-size partitions, with $lowscore_i, highscore_i$ denoting the score ranges associated with partition i, $i = 1, ..., |N(t)|$. Then it can simply utilize the posting algorithm shown earlier, posting using the $lowscore_i$ scores for each partition. The only exception to the previously shown post algorithm is that the posting peer now posts at each iteration a complete partition of its index list, instead of just a single entry.

The above obviously can guarantee perfect load balancing. However, subsequent postings (typically by other peers) may create imbalances, since different index lists may have different score distributions. Additionally, when ensuring overall load balancing over multiple index lists being posting by several peers, the order-preserving property of the placement must be guaranteed. Our approach for solving these problems is as follows. First, again the posting peer is required to compute a histogram of its index list. Second, the histogram of the TIN data (that is, the entries already posted) is stored at easily identifiable nodes. Third, the posting peer is required to retrieve this histogram and 'merge' it with his own. Fourth, the same peer identifies how the total data must now be split into $|N(t)|$, equal-size partitions of consecutive scores. Finally, it identifies all data movements (from TIN peer to TIN peer) necessary to redistribute the total TIN data so that load balancing and order preservation is ensured.

Detailed presentation of the possible algorithms for this last step and their respective comparison is beyond the scope of this paper. We simply mention that total TIN data sizes is expected to be very small (in actual number of bytes stored and moved). For example, even with several dozens of peers posting different, even large, multi-million-entry, index lists, in total the complete TIN data size will be a few hundred MBs, creating a total data transfer movement equivalent to that of downloading a few dozen MP3 files. Further, index lists' data posting to TINs is expected to be a very infrequent operation (compared to search queries). As a result, ensuring load balancing across TIN nodes proves to be relative inexpensive.

6.3 Discussion

The approaches to index lists' data posting outlined in the previous two sections can be used competitively or even be combined. When posting index lists with exponential score distributions, by design the posting of data using the order-preserving hash function of Section 5.1, will be adequately load balanced and nothing else is required. Conversely, when histogram information is available and can be computed by posting peers, the TIN data migration approach will yield load balanced data placement.

A more subtle issue is that posting with the order-preserving hash function also facilitates random accesses of the TIN data, based on random score values. That is, by hashing for any score, we can find the TIN node holding the entries with this score. This becomes essential if the web search engine is to employ top-k query algorithms which are based on random accesses of scores. In this work, our top-k algorithms avoid random accesses, by design. However, the above point should be kept in mind since there are recently-proposed distributed top-k algorithms, relying on random accesses and more efficient algorithms may be proposed in the future.

7 Top-k Query Processing

The algorithms in this section focus on how to exploit the infrastructure presented previously in order to efficiently process top-k queries. The main efficiency metrics are query response times and network bandwidth requirements.

7.1 The Basic Algorithm

Consider a top-k query of the form $Q(\{t_1, ..., t_r\}, k)$ involving r terms that is generated at some node n_{init} of G. Query processing is based on the following ideas. It proceeds in phases, with each phase involving 'vertical' and 'horizontal' communication between the nodes within TINs and across TINs, respectively. The vertical communications between the nodes of a TIN are occuring in parallel across all r TINs named in the query, gathering a threshold number of data items from each term. There is a moving coordinator node, that will be gathering the data items from all r TINs that enable it to compute estimates of the top-k result. Intermediate estimates of the top-k list will be passed around, as the coordinator role moves from node to node in the next phase where the gathering of more data items and the computation of the next top-k result estimate will be computed.

The presentation shows separately the behavior of the query initiator, the (moving) query coordinator, and the TIN nodes.

Query Initiator

The initiator calculates the set of *start nodes*, one for each term, where the query processing will start within each TIN. Also, it randomly selects one of the nodes (for one of the TINs) to be the initial coordinator. Finally, it passes on the query and the coordinator ID to each of the start nodes, to initiate the parallel vertical processing within TINs.

The following pseudocode details the behavior of the initiator.

Processing Within Each TIN

Processing within a TIN is always initiated by the start node. There is one start node per communication phase of the query processing. In the first phase, the

---

Algorithm 3. Top-k QP: Query Initiation at node $G.n_{init}$

1: **input:** Given query $Q = \{t_1, .., t_r\}, k$:
2: **for** $i = 1$ to r **do**
3:     $startNode_i = I(t_i).n(s_{max}) = h_{op}(t_i, s_{max})$
4: **end for**
5: Randomly select c from $[1, ..., r]$
6: $coordID = I(t_c).n(s_{max})$
7: **for** $i = 1$ to r **do**
8:     send to $startNode_i$ the data $(Q, coordID)$
9: **end for**

---

start node is the top node in the TIN which receives the query processing request from the initiator. The start node then starts the gathering of data items for the term by contacting enough nodes, following successor links, until a threshold number γ (that is, a batch size) of items has been accumulated and sent to the coordinator, along with an indication of the maximum score for this term which has not been collected yet, which is actually either a locally stored score or the maximum score of the next successor node. The latter information is critical for the coordinator in order to intelligently decide when the top-k result list has been computed and terminate the search. In addition, each start node sends to the coordinator the ID of the node of this TIN to be the next start node, which is simply the next successor node of the last accessed node of the TIN. Processing within this TIN will be continued at the new start node when it receives the next message from the coordinator starting the next data-gathering phase.

Algorithm 4 presents the pseudocode for TIN processing.

Algorithm 4. Top-k QP: Processing by a start node within a TIN

1: **input:** A message either from the initiator or the coordinator
2: $tCollection_i = \emptyset$
3: $n = startNode_i$
4: **while** $|tCollection_i| < \gamma$ **do**
5:     **while** $|tCollection_i| < \gamma$ AND more items exist locally **do**
6:         define the set of local items $L = \{(t_i, d, s) \text{ in } n\}$
7:         send to $coordID : L$
8:         $|tCollection_i| = |tCollection_i| + |L|$
9:     **end while**
10:     n = succ(n)
11: **end while**
12: $bound_i$ = max score stored at node n
13: send to $coordID : n$ and $bound_i$

Recall, that because of the manner with which items and nodes have been placed in a TIN, following succ() links, items are collected starting from the item with the highest score posted for this term and proceeding in sorted descending order based on scores.

Moving Query Coordinator

Initially, the coordinator is randomly chosen by the initiator to be one of the original start nodes. First, the coordinator uses the received collections and runs a version of the *NRA* top-k processing algorithm, locally producing an estimate of the top-k result. As is also the case with classical top-k algorithms, the exact result is not available at this stage since only a portion of the required information is available. Specifically, some documents with high enough TotalScore to qualify for the top-k result are still missing. Additionally, some documents may also be seen in only a subset of the collections received from the TINs so far, and thus some of their scores are missing, yielding only a partially known TotalScore.

A key to the efficiency of the overall query processing process is the ability to prune the search and terminate the algorithm even in the presence of missing documents and missing scores. To do this, the coordinator first computes an estimate of the top-k result, which includes only documents whose TotalScores are completely known, defining the RankKscore value (i.e. the smallest score in the top-k list estimate). Then, it utilizes the *bound*$_i$ values received from each start node. When a score for a document d is missing for term i, it can be replaced with *bound*$_i$ to estimate the $TotalScore(d)$. This is done for all such d with missing scores. If $RankKscore > TotalScore(d)$ for all d with missing scores then there is no need to continue the process for finding the missing scores, since the associated documents could never belong to the top-k result. Similarly, if $RankKscore > \sum_{i=1,...,r} bound_i$, then similarly there is no need to try to find any other documents, since they could never belong to the top-k result. When both of these conditions hold, the coordinator terminates the query processing and returns the top-k result to the initiator.

If the processing must continue, the coordinator starts the next phase, sending a message to the new start node for each term, whose ID was received in the message containing the previous data collections. In this message the coordinator also indicates the ID of the node which becomes the coordinator in this next phase. The next coordinator is defined to be the node in the same TIN as the previous coordinator whose data is to be collected next in the vertical processing in this TIN (i.e., the next start node at the coordinator's TIN). Alternatively, any other start node can be randomly chosen as the coordinator.

Algorithm 5 details the behavior of the coordinator.

7.2 Complexity Analysis

The overall complexity has three main components: the cost incurred for (i) the communication between the query initiator and the start nodes of the TINs, (ii) the vertical communication within a TIN, and (iii) the horizontal communication between the current coordinator and the current set of start nodes.

The query initiator needs to lookup the identity of the initial start nodes for each one of the r query terms and route to them the query and the chosen coordinator ID. Using the G network, this incurs a communication complexity of $O(r \times log|N|)$ messages. Denoting with *depth* the average (or maximum) number

---

Algorithm 5. Top-k QP: Coordination
___
1: **input:** For each i: $tCollection_i$ and $newstartNode_i$ and $bound_i$
2: $tCollection = \bigcup_i tCollection_i$
3: compute a (new) top-k list estimate using $tCollection$, and RankKscore
4: $candidates = \{d | d \notin \text{top-}k \text{ list}\}$
5: **for** all $d \in candidates$ **do**
6:     $worstScore(d)$ is the partial TotalScore of d
7:     $bestScore(d) := worstScore(d) + \sum_{j \in MT} bound_j$ {Where MT is the set of term ids with missing scores }
8:     **if** $bestScore(d) < RankKscore$ **then**
9:        remove d from $candidates$
10:     **end if**
11: **end for**
12: **if** $candidates$ is empty **then**
13:     exit()
14: **end if**
15: **if** $candidates$ is not empty **then**
16:     $coordID_{new} = pred(n)$
17:     calculate new size threshold γ
18:     **for** $i = 1$ to r **do**
19:        send to $startNode_i$ the data $(coordID_{new}, \gamma)$
20:     **end for**
21: **end if**
___

of nodes accessed during the vertical processing of TINs, overall $O(r \times depth)$ messages are incurred due to TIN processing, since subsequent accesses within a TIN require, by design, one-hop communication. Each horizontal communication in each phase of query processing between the coordinator and the r start nodes requires $O(r \times log|N|)$ messages. Since such horizontal communication takes place at every phase, this yields a total of $O(phases \times r \times log|N|)$ messages. Hence, the total communication cost complexity is

$$cost = O(phases \times r \times log|N| + r \times log|N| + r \times depth) \qquad (3)$$

This total cost is the worst case cost; we expect that the cost incurred in most cases will be much smaller, since horizontal communication across TINs can be much more efficient than $O(log|N|)$, as follows. The query initiator can first resolve the ID of the coordinator (by hashing and routing over G) and then determine its actual physical address (i.e., its IP address), which is then forwarded to each start node. In turn, each start node can forward this from successor to successor in its TIN. In this way, at any phase of query processing, the last node of a TIN visited during the vertical processing, can send the data collection to the coordinator using the coordinator's physical address. The current coordinator also knows the physical address of the next coordinator (since this was the last node visited in its own TIN from which it received a message with the data collection for its term) and of the next start node for all terms (since these are the last nodes visited during vertical processing of the TINs, from which it received a message). Thus, when sending the message to the next start nodes to continue vertical processing, the physical addresses can be used. The end result of this is that all horizontal communication requires one message, instead of $O(log|N|)$ messages. Hence, the total communication cost complexity now becomes

$$cost = O(phases \times r + r \times log|N| + r \times depth) \tag{4}$$

As nodes are expected to be joining and leaving the underlying overlay network G, occasionally, the physical addresses used to derive the cost of (4) will not be valid. In this case, the reported errors will lead to nodes using the high-level IDs instead of the physical addresses, in which case the cost is that given by (3).

8   Expediting Top-k Query Processing

In this section we develop optimizations that can further speedup the performance of top-k query processing. These optimizations are centered on: (i) the 'vertical' replication of term-specific data among the nodes of a TIN, and (ii) the 'horizontal' replication of data across TINs.

8.1   TIN Data Replication

There are two key characteristics of the data items in our model, which permit their large-scale replication. First, data items are rarely posted and even more rarely updated. Second, data items are very small in size (e.g. < 50 bytes each). Hence, replication protocols will not cost significantly either in terms of replica state maintenance, or in terms of storing the replicas.

Vertical Data Replication. The issue to be addressed here is how to appropriately replicate term data within TIN peers so to gain in efficiency. The basic structure of the query processing algorithm presented earlier facilitates the easy incorporation of a replication protocol into it. Recall, that in each TIN $I(t)$, query processing proceeds in phases, and in each phase a TIN node (the current start node) is responsible for visiting a number of other TIN nodes, a successor at a time, so that enough, (i.e., a batch size of) data items for t are collected. The last visited node in each phase which collects all data items, can initiate a 'reverse' vertical communication, in parallel to sending the collection to the coordinator. With this reverse vertical communication thread, each node in the reverse path sends to its predecessor only the data items its has not seen. In the end, all nodes in the path from the start node to the last node visited will eventually receive a copy of all items collected during this phase, storing locally the pair $(lowestscore, highestscore)$, marking its lowest and highest locally stored scores. Since this is straightforward, the pseudocode is omitted for space reasons.

Since a new posting involves all (or most) of the nodes in these paths, each node knows when to initiate a new replication to account for the new items.

Exploiting Replicas. The start node selected by the query initiator no longer needs to perform a successor-at-a-time traversal of TIN in the first phase, since the needed data (replicas) are stored locally. However, vertical communication was also useful for producing the ID of the next start node for this TIN. A subtle point to note here is that the coordinator can itself determine the new start node for the next phase, even without receiving explicitly this ID at the end of vertical communication. This can simply be done using the minimum score value ($bound_i$) it has received for term t_i; the ID of the next start node is found hashing for score $prev(bound_i)$.

Additionally, the query initiator can select as start nodes the nodes responsible for storing a random (expected to be high score) and not always the maximum score, as it does up to now. Similarly, the coordinator when selecting the ID of the next start node for the next batch retrieval for a term, it can choose to hash for a score value that is lower than the score $prev(bound_i)$. Thus, random start nodes within a TIN are selected at different phases and these gather the next batch of data from the proper TIN nodes, using the TIN DHT infrastructure for efficiency. The details of how this is done, are omitted for space reasons.

Horizontal Data Replication. TIN data may also be replicated horizontally. The simplest strategy is to create replicated TINs for popular terms. This involves the posting of data into all TIN replicas. The same algorithms can be used as before for posting, except now when hashing, instead of using the term t as input to the hash function, each replica of t must be specified (e.g., $t.v$, where v stands for a version/replica number). Again, the same algorithms can be used for processing queries, with the exception that each query can now select one of the replicas of $I(t)$, at random.

Overall, TIN data replication leads to savings in the number of messages and response time speedups. Furthermore, several nodes are off-loaded since they no longer have to partake in the query processing process. With replication, therefore, the same number of nodes overall will be involved in processing a number of user queries, except that each query will be employing a smaller set of peers, yielding response time and bandwidth benefits. In essence, TIN data replication increases the efficiency of the engine, without adversely affecting its scalability. Finally, it should be stressed that such replication will also improve the availability of data items and thus replication is imperative. Indirectly, for the same reason the quality of the results with replication will be higher, since lost items inevitably lead to errors in the top-k result.

9   Experimentation

9.1   Experimental Testbed

Our implementation was written in Java. Experiments were performed on 3GHz Pentium PCs. Since deploying full-blown, large networks is not an option, we opted for simulating large numbers of nodes as separate processes on the same PC, executing the real MINERVA∞ code. A 10,000 node network was simulated.

A real-world data collection was used in our experiments: GOV. The GOV collection consists of the data of the TREC-12 Web Track and contains roughly 1.25 million (mostly HTML and PDF) documents obtained from a crawl of the .gov Internet domain (with total index list size of 8 GB). The original 50 queries from the Web Track's distillation task were used. These are term queries, with each query containing up to 4 terms. The index lists contained the original document scores computed as tf * log idf. tf and idf were normalized by the maximum tf value of each document and the maximum idf value in the corpus, respectively. In addition, we employed an extended GOV (XGOV) setup, with a larger number of query terms and associated index lists. The original 50 queries were expanded by adding new terms from synonyms and glosses taken from the WordNet thesaurus (http://www.cogsci.princeton.edu/~wn). The expansion yielded queries with, on average, twice as many terms, up to 18 terms.

9.2   Performance Tests and Metrics

Efficiency Experiments. The data (index list entries) for the terms to be queried were first posted. Then, the GOV/XGOV benchmark queries were executed in sequence. For simplicity, the query initiator node assumed the role of a fixed coordinator. The experiments used the following metrics:

Bandwidth. This shows the number of bytes transferred between all the nodes involved in processing the benchmarks' queries. The benchmarks' queries were grouped based on the number of terms they involved. In essence, this grouping created a number of smaller sub-benchmarks.

Query Response Time. This represents the elapsed, "wall-clock" time for running the benchmark queries. We report on the wall-clock times per sub-benchmark and for the whole GOV and XGOV benchmarks.

Hops. This reports the number of messages sent over our network infrastructures to process all queries. For communication over the global DHT G, the number of hops was set to be $log|N|$ (i.e., when the query initiator contacts the first set of start nodes for each TIN). Communication between peers within a TIN requires, by design, one hop at a time.

To avoid the overestimation of response times due to the competition between all processes for the PC's disk and network resources, and in order to produce reproducible and comparable results for tests ran at different times, we opted for simulating disk IO latency and network latency. Specifically, each random disk IO was modeled to incur a disk seek and rotational latency of 9 ms, plus a transfer delay dictated by a transfer rate of 8MB/s. For network latency we utilized typical round trip times (RTTs) of packets and transfer rates achieved for larger data transfers between widely distributed entities [16]. We assumed a RTT of 100 ms. When peers simply forward the query to a next peer, this is assumed to take roughly 1/3 of the RTT (since no ACKs are expected). When peers sent more data, the additional latency was dictated by a "large" data transfer rate of 800Kb/s, which includes the sender's uplink bandwidth, the receivers downlink bandwidth, and the average internet bandwidth typically witnessed.[2]

Scalability Experiments. The tested scenarios varied the query load to the system, measuring the overall time required to complete the processing of all queries in a queue of requests. Our experiments used a queue of identical queries involving four terms, with varying index lists characteristics. Two of these terms had small index lists (with over 22,000 and over 42,000 entries) and the other two lists had sizes of over 420,000 entries. For each query the (different) query initiating peer played the role of the coordinator.

The key here is to measure contention for resources and its limits on the possible parallelization of query processing. Each TIN peer uses his disk, his uplink bandwidth to forward the query to his TIN successor, and to send data to the coordinator. Uplink/downlink bandwidths were set to 256Kbps/1Mbps. Similarly, the query initiator utilizes its downlink bandwidth to receive the batches of data in each phase and its uplink bandwidth to send off the query to the next TIN start nodes. These delays define the possible parallelization of query execution. By involving the two terms with the largest index lists in the queries, we ensured the worst possible parallelization (for our input data), since they induced the largest batch size, requiring the most expensive disk reads and communication.

9.3   Performance Results

Overall, each benchmark experiment required between 2 to 5 hours for its real-time execution, a big portion of which was used up by the posting procedure.

Figures 1 and 2 show the bandwidth, response times, and hops results for the GOV and XGOV group-query benchmarks. Note, that different query groups have in general mutually-incomparable results, since they involve different index lists with different characteristics (such as size, score distributions etc).

In XGOV the biggest overhead was introduced by the 8 7-term and 6 11-term queries. Table 1 shows the total benchmark execution times, network bandwidth consumption, as well as the number of hops for the GOV and XGOV benchmarks.

Generally, for each query, the number of terms and the size of the corresponding index list data are the key factors. The central insight here is that the choice of the NRA algorithm was the most important contributor to the overhead. The adaptation of more efficient distributed top-k algorithms within MINERVA∞ (such as our own [12], which also disallow random accesses) can reduce this overhead by one to two orders of magnitude. This is due to the fact that the top-k result can be produced without needing to delve deeply into the index lists' data, resulting in drastically fewer messages, bandwidth, and time requirements.

---

[2] This figure is the average throughput value measured (using one stream – one cpu machines) in experiments conducted for measuring wide area network throughput (sending 20MB files between SLAC nodes (Stanford's Linear Accelerator Centre) and nodes in Lyon France [16] using NLANR's iPerf tool [19].

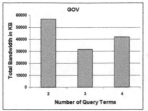
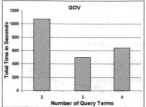
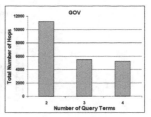

Fig. 1. GOV Results: Bandwidth, Execution Time, and Hops

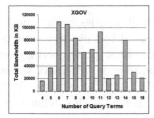
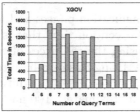
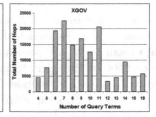

Fig. 2. XGOV Results: Bandwidth, Execution Time, and Hops

Table 1. Total GOV and XGOV Results

Benchmark	Hops	Bandwidth(KB)	Time(s)
GOV	22050	130189	2212
XGOV	146168	744700	10372

The 2-term queries introduced the biggest overheads. There are 29 2-term, 7 3-term, and 4 4-term queries in GOV.

Figure 3 shows the scalability experiment results. Query loads tested represent queue sizes of 10, 100, 1000, and 10000 identical queries simultaneously arriving into the system. This figure also shows what the corresponding time would be if the parallelization contributed by the MINERVA∞ architecture was not possible; this would be the case, for example, in all related-work P2P search architectures and also distributed top-k algorithms, where the complete index lists at least for one query term are stored completely at one peer. The scalability results show the high scalability achievable with MINERVA∞. It is due to the "pipelining" that is introduced within each TIN during query processing, where a query consumes small amounts of resources from each peer, pulling together the resources of all (or most) peers in the TIN for its processing. For comparison we also show the total execution time in an environment in which each complete index list was stored in a peer. This is the case for most related work on P2P search engines and on distributed top-k query algorithms. In this case, the resources of the single peer storing a complete index list are required

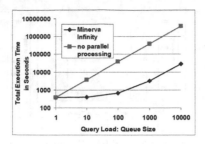

Fig. 3. Scalability Results

for the processing of all communication phases and for all queries in the queue. In essence, this yields a total execution time that is equal to that of a sequential execution of all queries using the resources of the single peers storing the index lists for the query terms. Using this as a base comparison, MINERVA∞ is shown to enjoy approximately two orders of magnitude higher scalability. Since in our experiments there are approximately 100 nodes per TIN, this defines the maximum scalability gain.

10   Concluding Remarks

We have presented MINERVA∞, a novel architecture for a peer-to-peer web search engine. The key distinguishing feature of MINERVA∞ is its high-levels of distribution for both data and processing. The architecture consists of a suite of novel algorithms, which can be classified into algorithms for creating Term Index Networks, TINs, placing index list data on TINs and of top-k algorithms. TIN creation is achieved using a bootstrapping algorithm and also depends on how nodes are selected when index lists data is posted. The data posting algorithm employs an order-preserving hash function and, for higher levels of load balancing, MINERVA∞ engages data migration algorithms. Query processing consists of a framework for highly distributed versions of top-k algorithms, ranging from simple distributed top-k algorithms, to those utilizing vertical and/or horizontal data replication. Collectively, these algorithms ensure efficiency and scalability. Efficiency is ensured through the fast sequential accesses to index lists' data, which requires at most one hop communication and by algorithms exploiting data replicas. Scalability is ensured by engaging a larger number of TIN peers in every query, with each peer being assigned much smaller subtasks, avoiding centralized points of control. We have implemented MINERVA∞ and conducted detailed performance studies showcasing its scalability and efficiency.

Ongoing work includes the adaptation of recent distributed top-k algorithms (e.g., [12]) into the MINERVA∞ architecture, which have proved one to two orders of magnitude more efficient than the NRA top-k algorithm currently employed, in terms of query response times, network bandwidth, and peer loads.

References

1. J. Aspnes and G. Shah. Skip graphs. In *Fourteenth Annual ACM-SIAM Symposium on Discrete Algorithms*, pages 384–393, Jan. 2003.
2. P. Cao and Z. Wang. Efficient top-k query calculation in distributed networks, PODC 2004.
3. S. Chakrabarti. *Mining the Web: Discovering Knowledge from Hypertext Data*. Morgan Kaufmann, San Francisco, 2002.
4. F. M. Cuenca-Acuna, C. Peery, R. P. Martin, and T. D. Nguyen. PlanetP: Using Gossiping to Build Content Addressable Peer-to-Peer Information Sharing Communities. Technical Report DCS-TR-487, Rutgers University, Sept. 2002.
5. R. Fagin. Combining fuzzy information from multiple systems. *J. Comput. Syst. Sci.*, 58(1):83–99, 1999.
6. R. Fagin, A. Lotem, and M. Naor. Optimal aggregation algorithms for middleware. *J. Comput. Syst. Sci.*, 66(4), 2003.
7. P. Ganesan, M. Bawa, and H. Garcia-Molina. Online balancing of range-partitioned data with applications to peer-to-peer systems. In *VLDB*, pages 444–455, 2004.
8. A. Gupta, O. D. Sahin, D. Agrawal, and A. E. Abbadi. Meghdoot: content-based publish/subscribe over p2p networks. In *Proceedings of the 5th ACM/IFIP/USENIX international conference on Middleware*, pages 254–273, New York, NY, USA, 2004. Springer-Verlag New York, Inc.
9. N. Harvey, M. Jones, S. Saroiu, M. Theimer, and A. Wolman. Skipnet: A scalable overlay network with practical locality properties. In *USITS*, 2003.
10. R. Huebsch, J. M. Hellerstein, N. Lanham, B. T. Loo, S. Shenker, and I. Stoica. Querying the internet with pier. In *VLDB*, pages 321–332, 2003.
11. J. Lu and J. Callan. Content-based retrieval in hybrid peer-to-peer networks. In *Proceedings of CIKM03*, pages 199–206. ACM Press, 2003.
12. S. Michel, P. Triantafillou, and G. Weikum. Klee: A framework for distributed top-k query algorithms. In *VLDB Conference*, 2005.
13. S. Ratnasamy, P. Francis, M. Handley, R. Karp, and S. Schenker. A scalable content-addressable network. In *Proceedings of ACM SIGCOMM 2001*, pages 161–172. ACM Press, 2001.
14. P. Reynolds and A. Vahdat. Efficient peer-to-peer keyword searching. In *Proceedings of International Middleware Conference*, pages 21–40, June 2003.
15. A. Rowstron and P. Druschel. Pastry: Scalable, decentralized object location, and routing for large-scale peer-to-peer systems. In *IFIP/ACM International Conference on Distributed Systems Platforms (Middleware)*, pages 329–350, 2001.
16. D. Salomoni and S. Luitz. High performance throughput tuning/measurement. http://www.slac.stanford.edu/grp/scs/net/talk/High_perf_ppdg_jul2000.ppt. 2000.
17. I. Stoica, R. Morris, D. Karger, M. F. Kaashoek, and H. Balakrishnan. Chord: A scalable peer-to-peer lookup service for internet applications. In *Proceedings of the ACM SIGCOMM 2001*, pages 149–160. ACM Press, 2001.
18. T. Suel, C. Mathur, J. Wu, J. Zhang, A. Delis, M. Kharrazi, X. Long, and K. Shanmugasunderam. Odissea: A peer-to-peer architecture for scalable web search and information retrieval. Technical report, Polytechnic Univ., 2003.
19. A. Tirumala et al. iperf: Testing the limits of your network. http://dast.nlanr.net/projects/iperf/. 2003.
20. P. Triantafillou and T. Pitoura. Towards a unifying framework for complex query processing over structured peer-to-peer data networks. In *DBISP2P*, 2003.
21. Y. Wang, L. Galanis, and D. J. de Witt. Galanx: An efficient peer-to-peer search engine system. *Available at http://www.cs.wisc.edu/ yuanwang*.

An Optimal Overlay Topology for Routing Peer-to-Peer Searches

Brian F. Cooper

Center for Experimental Research in Computer Systems,
College of Computing, Georgia Institute of Technology
cooperb@cc.gatech.edu

Abstract. Unstructured peer-to-peer networks are frequently used as the overlay in various middleware toolkits for emerging applications, from content discovery to query result caching to distributed collaboration. Often it is assumed that unstructured networks will form a power-law topology; however, a power-law structure is not the best topology for an unstructured network. In this paper, we introduce the *square-root topology*, and show that this topology significantly improves routing performance compared to power-law networks. In the square-root topology, the degree of a peer is proportional to the square root of the popularity of the content at the peer. Our analysis shows that this topology is optimal for random walk searches. We also present simulation results to demonstrate that the square-root topology is better, by up to a factor of two, than a power-law topology for other types of search techniques besides random walks. We then describe a decentralized algorithm for forming a square-root topology, and evaluate its effectiveness in constructing efficient networks using both simulations and experiments with our implemented prototype. Our results show that the square-root topology can provide a significant performance improvement over power-law topologies and other topology types.

Keywords: peer-to-peer search, overlay topology, random walks.

1 Introduction

Peer-to-peer search networks have gone from serving as application-specific overlays to become generally useful components in systems for finding and distributing content. In particular, "unstructured" peer-to-peer networks, such as those in Gnutella and Kazaa, continue to remain popular and widely deployed. Even with the advent of more "structured" networks for content-based routing (such as [1,2,3]), unstructured networks continue to be important, both because of their usefulness for content discovery [4] and because they can be used together with structured networks in so-called hybrid systems [5,6]. Several types of systems have an unstructured topology as a sub-network: superpeer networks [7] use an unstructured topology to connect the superpeers, caching networks [8] use an unstructured topology to connect caches, scientific collaboration networks [9] use an unstructured topology to locate data sets, and so on. Since a variety of middleware tools implement an unstructured peer-to-peer network, it is important to investigate techniques for optimizing unstructured topologies.

G. Alonso (Ed.): Middleware 2005, LNCS 3790, pp. 82–101, 2005.

Unstructured networks tend toward power-law topologies, and several techniques for searching in power-law topologies have been developed. One especially effective technique is to conduct a "random walk," where each peer forwards a search message to a random neighbor until results have been found [10,11,12]. This technique requires far fewer messages than Gnutella's original flooding-based algorithm, and results have shown that random walk searches are a scalable and effective way to find content in a peer-to-peer network.

Although these techniques have been developed to work with power-law topologies, a power-law network is not the best network for a random walk. Implementing a protocol that causes the network to converge to a more efficient topology can significantly improve search performance. In this paper, we introduce the *square-root topology*, where the degree of each peer is proportional to the square root of the popularity of the content at the peer (measured in terms of the number of submitted searches that match the peer's content). We present analysis based on random walks in Markov chains to show that the square-root topology is not only better than power-law networks, it is in fact optimal in the number of hops needed to find content. Intuitively, the probability that a random walk quickly reaches a peer is proportional to the degree of the peer, and if peers with popular content have correspondingly high degrees, then most searches will quickly reach the right peers and find matching content. Simulation results confirm our analysis, showing that a random walk requires up to 45 percent fewer hops in a square-root topology than in a power-law topology.

We also present simulation results to show that several other walk-based techniques perform better in a square-root topology than in a power-law topology. One technique is suggested by Adamic et al [10], who propose biasing random walks toward high degree peers. If peers track their neighbors' content, then high degree peers will have knowledge of the content of many peers, and searches will quickly be evaluated over a large amount of content. Another technique is suggested by Lv et al [11], who argue for starting multiple parallel random walks for the same search. This technique reduces the time before searches complete, though it requires roughly the same total number of messages. A third technique is to bias random walks based on previous results from peers, as suggested by Yang and Garcia-Molina [13]. In each case, the square-root topology performs better than a power-law topology, decreasing the number of messages per search by as much as 50 percent.

Next, we introduce a decentralized algorithm, *square-root-construct*, for building and maintaining the square-root topology as peers join and leave the system. Each peer uses purely local information to estimate the popularity of its content, avoiding the need for tracking the global distribution of popularities among peers. Then, each peer adds or drops connections to other peers to achieve its optimal degree. Simulation results as well as experiments using our implemented peer-to-peer system prototype demonstrate the performance advantages of the square-root topology. For example, in a network of 1,000 peers running on a cluster in our lab, a random topology required more than twice the bandwidth of a topology maintained using *square-root-construct*.

A related result to the square-root topology was obtained by Cohen and Shenker [14], who suggested that content be replicated proactively to improve search efficiency. Their result showed that the optimal replication was the *square-root replication*, where the number of copies of a content object is proportional to the square root of the object's popularity. Our results are complementary, as we deal with the number of neighbors each peer has rather than the number of copies of each document. In particular, our square-root topology can be used in cases where a square-root replication is not feasible, such as applications where there are high storage and bandwidth costs for replicating content. Moreover, in cases where square-root replication is used, a square-root topology still provides better efficiency than a power-law topology, with an improvement of more than 50 percent.

We are implementing a flexible peer-to-peer content location middleware toolkit, called *Overlay-Dynamic Information Networks (ODIN)*. ODIN can be layered on top of existing data repositories (such as document repositories, local filesystems or scientific databases) to connect these repositories into a large scale searching network for use by different applications. The square-root topology forms the basis of the overlay networks constructed in ODIN. In this paper, we focus on the square-root topology, and show its usefulness for a wide range of different searching techniques that might be employed by peer-to-peer middleware like ODIN. In particular, our contributions include:

- We define the *square-root topology*, and give analysis based on random walks in Markov chains to show that a square-root topology is optimal for random walk searches. (Section 2)
- We present simulation results to show that a square-root topology is better than a power-law topology for a variety of search techniques, and when square-root replication is used. (Section 3)
- We develop a distributed algorithm, *square-root-construct*, for dynamically building the square-root topology based on purely local information available to a peer. (Section 4)
- We present results from simulations and from our prototype that demonstrate the effectiveness of *square-root-construct* for constructing efficient topologies. (Section 5)

We examine related work in Section 6, and present our conclusions in Section 7.

2 Network Topologies

Random walk searches were initially introduced as a way to optimize searches in power-law networks [10], and recent research often takes the power-law topology as a given (see for example [11,7]). While random walk searches are better than Gnutella-style search broadcasts in power-law networks, power-law networks are not the best structure for random-walk searches. In this section, we provide analysis showing that square-root networks provide optimal performance for random walk searches, and thus are better than power-law networks. Our analysis is backed up with simulation results for different scenarios in Section 3.

2.1 Background

A peer-to-peer search network is a partially connected overlay of peers, sitting on top of a fully connected underlying network (such as the Internet.) The main reason to keep the overlay network partially connected is to reduce the state that each peer must maintain. Since each peer only has to stay connected to a few neighbors, no peer has to know about all of the peers in the system or understand the whole topology. Furthermore, a peer only needs to react to changes concerning its immediate neighbors; changes to remote parts of the topology do not directly affect peers. This limited state and localized impact of changes improves scalability, even when there is a high amount of peer *churn*, with many peers joining and leaving the system.

The topology of the overlay network is built up over time in a decentralized way. Peers that join the system connect to peers that are already in the system, and the choice of neighbors is essentially random in many existing systems. Topologies in these systems tend toward a power-law distribution, where some long-lived peers have many connections while most peers have a few connections. Formally, in a power-law network, the number of neighbors of the ith most connected peer is proportional to $1/i^\alpha$, where α is a constant that determines the skew of the distribution. Larger α results in more skew.

A simple random walk search starts at one peer in the network, and is processed over that peer's content. That peer then forwards the search to one or a subset of its neighbors, who each process and forward the query. In this way, the search "walks" around the network, until it terminates according to some stopping criterion. There are several alternatives for terminating the walk [11]: a walk can be given a *time-to-live* which limits the number of hops the walk makes, or the walk can terminate after G results have been found, where G is a user-defined parameter (the "goal"). Several researchers have adapted random walk searches in various ways to make them less random and more efficient. We examine these adaptations in more detail in Section 3.

2.2 The Square-Root Topology

Consider a peer-to-peer network with N peers. Each peer k in the network has degree d_k (that is, d_k is the number of neighbors that k has). The total degree in the network is D, where $D = \sum_{k=1}^{N} d_k$. Equivalently, the total number of connections in the network is $D/2$.

We define the square-root topology as a topology where the degree of each peer is proportional to the square root of the popularity of the peer's content. Formally, if we define g_k as the proportion of searches submitted to the system that are satisfied by content at peer k, then a square-root topology has $d_k \propto \sqrt{g_k}$ for all k.

We now show that a square-root topology is optimal for random walk searches. Imagine a user submits a search s that is satisfied by content at a particular peer k. Of course, until the search is processed by the network, we do not know which peer k is. How many hops will the search message take before it arrives at k, satisfying the search? The expected length of the random walk (called the *hitting time* or *mean first passage time*) depends on the degree of k:

Lemma 1. *If the network is connected (that is, there is a path between every pair of peers) and non-bipartite, then the expected number of hops for search s to reach peer k is D/d_k.*

This result is shown in [15], and is derived using the properties of Markov chains. We now briefly summarize the reasoning behind the lemma. A Markov chain consists of a set of states, where the probability of transitioning from state i to state j depends only on i and j, and not on any other history about the process. For our purposes, the states of the Markov chain are the peers in the system, and $1 \leq i, j \leq N$. Associated with a Markov chain is a transition matrix T that describes the probability that a transition occurs from a state i to another state j. In our context, this transition probability is the probability that a search message that is at peer i is next forwarded to peer j. With simple random walks, the transition probability from peer i to peer j is $1/d_i$ if i and j are neighbors, and zero otherwise. The result in [15] depends only on the node degrees, and not on the structure; that is, the expected length of a walk does not depend on which peers are connected to which other peers. This property follows from the fact that the Markov chain converges to the same stationary distribution regardless of which vertices are connected.

This model assumes peers forward search messages to a randomly chosen neighbor, even if that search message has just come from that neighbor or has already visited this neighbor. This assumption simplifies the Markov chain analysis. Previous proposals for random walks [11] have noted that avoiding previously visited peers can improve the efficiency of walks, and we examine this possibility in simulation results in the next section.

Using the transition matrix, we can calculate the probability that a search message is at a given peer at a given point in time. First, we define an N element vector V_0, called the *initial distribution vector*; the kth entry in V represents the probability that a random walk search starts at peer k. The entries of V sum to 1. Given T and V_0, we can calculate V_1, where the kth entry represents the probability of the search being at peer k after one hop, as $V_1 = TV_0$. In general, the vector V_m, representing the probabilities that a search is at a given peer after m hops, is recursively defined as $V_m = TV_{m-1}$.

Under the conditions of the lemma (the network is connected and non-bipartite), V_m converges to a *stationary distribution vector* V_s, representing the probability that a random walk search visits a given peer at a particular point in time. Most importantly for our purposes, it can be shown [15] that the kth entry of V_s is d_k/D. In other words, in the steady state, the probability that a search message is at a given peer k is d_k/D.

What is the expected number of hops before a search reaches its goal? We can treat the search routing as a series of experiments, each choosing a random peer k from the population of N peers with probability d_k/D. A "successful" experiment occurs when a search chooses a peer with matching content. The expected number of experiments before the search message successfully reaches a particular peer k is a geometric random variable with expected value $\frac{1}{d_k/D} = \frac{D}{d_k}$. This is the result given by Lemma 1.

If a given search requires D/d_k hops to reach peer k, how many hops can we expect an arbitrary search to take before it finds results? For simplicity, we assume that a search will be satisfied by a single unique peer. We define g_k to be the probability that peer k is the goal peer; $g_k \geq 0$ and $\sum_{k=1}^{N} g_k = 1$. The g_k will vary from peer to peer. The proportion of searches seeking peer k is g_k, and the expected number of hops that will be taken by peers seeking peer k is D/d_k (from Lemma 1), so the expected number of hops taken by searches (called H) is:

$$H = \sum_{k=1}^{N} g_k \cdot \frac{D}{d_k} \tag{1}$$

How can we minimize the expected number of hops taken by a search message? It turns out that H is minimized when the degree of a peer is proportional to the square root of the popularity of the documents at that peer. This is the square-root topology.

Theorem 1. *H is minimized when*

$$d_k = \frac{D\sqrt{g_k}}{\sum_{i=1}^{N}\sqrt{g_i}} \tag{2}$$

Proof. We use the method of Lagrange multipliers to minimize equation (1). Recall the constraint that all degrees d_k sum to D; that is, the constraint for our optimization problem is $f = (\sum_{k=1}^{N} d_k) - D = 0$. We must find a Lagrange multiplier λ that satisfies $\nabla H = \lambda \nabla f$ (where ∇ is the gradient operator). First, treating the g_k values as constants,

$$\nabla H = \sum_{k=1}^{N} -D \cdot g_k \cdot d_k^{-2} \cdot \hat{\mathbf{u}}_\mathbf{k} \tag{3}$$

where $\hat{\mathbf{u}}_\mathbf{k}$ is a unit vector. Next,

$$\lambda \nabla f = \lambda \sum_{k=1}^{N} \hat{\mathbf{u}}_\mathbf{k} = \sum_{k=1}^{N} \lambda \hat{\mathbf{u}}_\mathbf{k} \tag{4}$$

Because $\nabla H = \lambda \nabla f$, we can set each term in the summation of equation (3) equal to the corresponding term of the summation of equation (4), so that $-D \cdot g_k \cdot d_k^{-2} \cdot \hat{\mathbf{u}}_\mathbf{k} = \lambda \hat{\mathbf{u}}_\mathbf{k}$. Solving for d_k gives

$$d_k = \frac{\sqrt{D \cdot g_k}}{\sqrt{-\lambda}} \tag{5}$$

Now we will eliminate λ, the Lagrange multiplier. Substituting equation (5) into f gives

$$\sum_{k=1}^{N} \left(\frac{\sqrt{D \cdot g_k}}{\sqrt{-\lambda}} \right) = D \tag{6}$$

and solving gives

$$\frac{1}{\sqrt{-\lambda}} = \frac{D}{\sqrt{D} \sum_{k=1}^{N} \sqrt{g_k}} \tag{7}$$

If we change the dummy variable of the summation in equation (7) from k to i, and substitute back into equation (5), we get equation (2). $\qquad\square$

Theorem 1 shows that the square-root topology is the optimal topology over a large number of random walk searches. Our analysis shows that D, the total degree in the network, does not impact performance: substituting equation (2) into equation (1) eliminates D. Thus, any value of D that ensures the network is connected is sufficient. Note also that our result holds regardless of which peers are connected to which other peers, because of the properties of the stationary distribution of Markov chains.

Finally, peer degrees must be integer values; it is impossible to have a third of a connection for example. Therefore, the optimal peer degrees must be calculated by rounding the value calculated in equation (2).

3 Experimental Results for the Square-Root Topology

Our analysis of the square-root topology is based on an idealized model of searches and content. Real peer-to-peer systems are less idealized; for example, searches may match content at multiple peers. In this section we present simulation results to illustrate the performance of a square-root topology for realistic scenarios. We use simulation because we wish to examine the performance of large networks (i.e., tens of thousands of peers) and it is difficult to deploy that many live peers for research purposes on the Internet.

Our primary metric is to count the total number of messages sent under each search method. Searches terminate when "enough" results were found, where "enough" is defined as a user specified goal number of results G. In summary, our results show:

- Random walks perform best on the square-root topology, requiring up to 45 percent fewer messages than in a power-law topology. The square-root topology also results in up to 50 percent less search latency than power-law networks, even when multiple random walks are started in parallel.
- The square-root topology is the best topology when proactive replication is used, and the combination of square-root topology and square-root replication provides higher efficiency than either technique alone.
- Other search techniques based on random walks, such as biased high-degree [10], biased towards most results or fewest result hop neighbors [13], and random walks with statekeeping [11] performed best on the square-root topology, decreasing the number of messages sent by as much as 52 percent compared to a power-law topology.
- The square-root topology performed better than other topology structures as well, including a constant degree network, and a topology with peer degrees directly proportional to peer popularity. In super-peer networks [7] the square-root was the best topology for connecting the supernodes.

In this section, we first describe our experimental setup, and then present our results.

3.1 Experimental Setup

Our experimental results were obtained using a discrete-event peer-to-peer simulator that we have developed. Our simulator models individual peers, documents and queries, as well as the topology of the peer-to-peer overlay. Searches are submitted to individual peers, and then walk around the network according to the specified routing algorithm. Our simulations used networks with 20,000 peers. Simulation parameters are listed in Table 1.

Because the square-root topology is based on the popularity of documents stored at different peers, it is important to accurately model the number of queries that match each document, and the peers at which each document is stored. It is difficult to gather accurate and complete query, document and location data for tens of thousands of real peers. Therefore, we use the content model described in [16], which is based on a trace of real queries and documents, and more accurately describes real systems than simple uniform or Zipfian distributions. In particular, we downloaded text web pages from

Table 1. Experimental parameters

Parameter	Value
Number of peers	20,000
Documents	631,320
Queries submitted	100,000
Goal number of results	10
Average links per peer	4
Minimum links per peer	1

1,000 real web sites, and evaluated keyword queries against the web pages. We then generated 20,000 synthetic queries matching 631,320 synthetic documents, stored at 20,000 peers, such that the statistical properties of our synthetic content model matched those of the real trace. The resulting content model allowed us to simulate a network of 20,000 peers. In our simulation, we repeatedly submitted random queries chosen from the set of 20,000 to produce a total of 100,000 query submissions. In [16] we describe the details of this method of generating synthetic documents and queries, and provide experimental evidence that the content model, though synthetic, results in highly accurate simulation results. Most importantly, the synthetic model retains an accurate distribution of the popularity of peer content, which is critical for the construction of the square-root topology.

3.2 Random Walks

First, we conducted an experiment to examine the performance of random walk searches in different topologies. In this experiment, queries matched documents stored at different peers, and had a goal $G = 10$ results. We compared three different topologies:

- A *square-root topology*, generated by assigning a degree to each peer based on equation (2), and then creating links between randomly chosen pairs of peers based on the assigned degrees.
- A *low-skew power-law topology*, generated using the PLOD algorithm [17]. In this network, $\alpha = 0.58$.
- A *high-skew power-law topology*, generated using the PLOD algorithm, with $\alpha = 0.74$.

The results of our experiment are shown in Figure 1. As the figure shows, random walks in the square-root topology require 8,940 messages per search, 26 percent less than random walks in the low-skew power-law topology (12,100 messages per search) and 45 percent less than random walks in the high-skew power-law topology (16,340 messages per search). In the power-law topologies, searches tend toward high degree peers, even if the walk is truly random and not explicitly directed to high degree peers (as in [10]). Unless these high degree peers also have the most popular content, the result is that searches have a low probability of walking to the peer with matching content, and the number of hops and thus messages increases. If the power-law distribution is more skewed, then the probability that searches will congregate at the wrong peers is higher and the total number of messages necessary to get to the right peers increases.

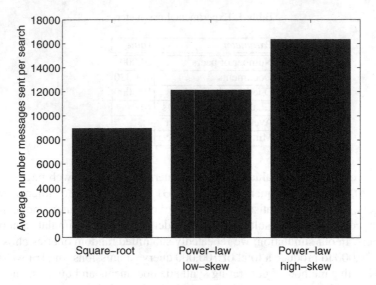

Fig. 1. Random walk searches on different topologies

Table 2. Parallel random walks: search latency (ticks)

Walks	Square-root	Power-law low-skew	Power-law high-skew
1	8930	12090	16350
2	4500	6210	8970
5	1800	2490	3740
10	904	1250	1880
20	454	630	947
100	96	130	194

Even though random walks perform best in the square-root topology, a large number of messages need to be sent (8,940 messages in a network of 20,000 peers in the above results). However, this result is a significant improvement over traditional Gnutella-style search: flooding in a high-skew power-law network, with a TTL of five in order to find at least ten results on average, requires 17,700 messages per search. Moreover, the above results are for simple, unoptimized random walks. Adding optimizations such as proactive replication or neighbor indexing significantly reduces the cost of a random walk search, and results for these techniques (presented in the next sections) show that the square-root topology is still best.

Another issue with random walks is that the search latency is high, as queries may have to walk many hops before finding content. To deal with this, Lv et al [11] propose creating multiple, parallel random walks for each search. Since the network processes these walks in parallel, the result is significantly reduced search latency (even though the total number of messages is not reduced). We ran experiments where we created 2, 5, 10, 20, and 100 parallel random walks for each search, and measured search latency as the number of simulation time ticks required to find the goal content (one tick represents the time to process a search and forward it one hop.) These results are shown in Table 2.

As the table shows, the square-root topology provided the lowest search latency, regardless of the number of parallel walks that were generated. The improvement for the square-root topology was consistently 27 percent compared to the low-skew power-law topology, and 50 percent compared to the high-skew power-law topology. Even when searches are walking in parallel, the square root topology helps those search walks quickly arrive at the peers with the right content.

3.3 Proactive Replication

The square-root topology is complementary to the square-root replication described in [14]. In situations where it is feasible to proactively replicate content, the square-root replication specifies that the number of copies made of content should be proportional to the square root of the popularity of the content. The square-root topology can be used whether or not proactive replication is used, but the combination of the two techniques can provide significant performance benefits.

We conducted an experiment where we proactively replicated content according to the square-root replication. Each peer was assigned capacity equal to twice the content they were already storing, and this extra capacity was used to store proactively replicated copies. We then connected peers in the square-root, high-skew power-law, and low-skew power-law topologies, and measured the performance of random walk searches. Again, $G = 10$.

The results are shown in Figure 2. As expected, proactive replication provided better performance than no replication (e.g., Figure 1). Proactive replication performs best with the square-root topology, requiring only 2,830 messages per search, 42 percent

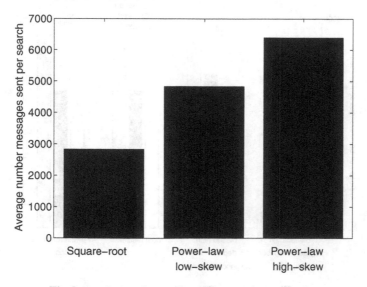

Fig. 2. Random walk searches with proactive replication

less than in the low-skew power-law network (4,830 messages) and 56 percent less than in the high-skew power-law network (6,390 messages). Proactive replication makes more copies of the documents that a search will match, while the square-root topology makes it easier for the search to get to the peers where the documents are stored. The combination of the two techniques provides more efficiency than either technique alone. For example, in our experiment, the square root topology with proactive replication required 68 percent fewer messages than the square root topology without replication.

3.4 Other Search Walk Techniques

Next, we examined the performance of other walk-based techniques on different topologies. We compared three other techniques based on random walks:

- *Biased high degree*: messages are preferentially forwarded to neighbors that have the highest degree [10].
- *Most results*: messages are forwarded preferentially to neighbors that have returned the most results for the past 10 queries [13].
- *Fewest result hops*: messages are forwarded preferentially to neighbors that returned results for the past 10 queries who have travelled the fewest average hops [13].

In each case, ties are broken randomly. For the biased high degree technique, we examined both neighbor-indexing (peers track their neighbors' content) and no neighbor-indexing. Although [13] describes several ways to route searches in addition to most results and fewest result hops, these two techniques represent the "best" that the authors studied: fewest result hops requires the least bandwidth, while most results has the best chance of finding the requested number of matching documents.

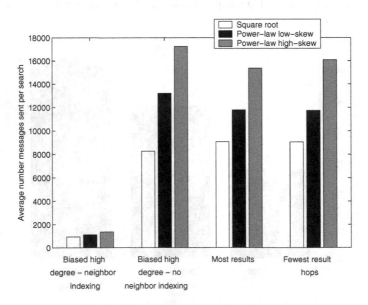

Fig. 3. Other walk-based search techniques

The results are shown in Figure 3. As the figure shows, in each case the square-root topology is best. The most improvement is seen with the biased high degree technique, where the improvement on going from the high-skew power-law topology (17,250 messages on average) to the square-root topology (8,280 messages on average) is 52 percent. Large improvements are achieved with the fewest result hops technique (44 percent improvement versus the high-skew power-law topology) and most results (41 percent improvement versus the high-skew power-law topology). The smallest improvement observed was for the biased high degree technique with neighbor indexing; the square-root topology offers a 16 percent decrease in messages compared to the low-skew power-law topology. Overall, the square-root topology provides the best performance, even with the extremely efficient biased high degree/neighbor indexing combination. Moreover, the square-root topology can be used even when neighbor indexing is not feasible.

The combination of square-root topology, square-root replication and biased high degree walking with neighbor indexing provides even better performance. Our results (not shown) indicate that this approach is extremely efficient, requiring only 248 messages per search on average. Again, the square-root topology is better than the power-law topology when square-root replication and neighbor indexing are used. Using all three techniques together results in a searching mechanism that contacts less than 2 percent of the system's peers on average while still finding sufficient results.

Finally, the results so far assume *state-keeping* [11], where peers keep state about where the search has been. Then, peers can avoid forwarding searches to neighbors that the search has already visited. We also ran experiments for no statekeeping. The results (not shown) demonstrate that the square-root topology is better than power-law topologies, whether or not statekeeping is used.

3.5 Other Topologies

We also tested the square-root topology in comparison to several other network structures. First, we compared against two simple structures:

- *Constant-degree topology*: every peer has the same number of neighbors. In our simulations, each peer had five neighbors.
- *Proportional topology*: every peer had a degree proportional to their popularity g_k (rather than proportional to $\sqrt{g_k}$ as in the square-root topology).

Our results show that the square-root topology is best, requiring 10 percent fewer messages than the constant degree network, and 7 percent fewer messages than the proportional topology. Although the improvement is smaller than when comparing the square-root topology to power-law topologies, these results again demonstrate that the square-root topology is best. Moreover, the cost of maintaining the square-root topology is low, as we discuss in Section 4, requiring easily obtainable local information. Thus, it clearly makes sense to use the square-root topology instead of constant degree or proportional topologies.

A widely used topology in many systems is the super-peer topology [7,18]. In this topology, a fraction of the peers serve as super-peers, aggregating content information from several "leaf" pears. Then, searches only need to be sent to super-peers. The super-peers are connected using a normal unstructured topology (which, like other topologies, tends to form into a power-law structure). We ran simulations using a standard super-peer topology, in which searches are flooded to super-peers. We compared this standard topology to a super-peer topology that used the square-root topology and random walks between super-peers. The results indicate a significant improvement using our techniques: the square-root super-peer network required 54 percent fewer messages than a standard super-peer network.

4   Constructing Square-Root Networks

In order for the square-root topology to be useful in peer-to-peer systems, there must be a lightweight, distributed algorithm for constructing the topology. We cannot expect a centralized planner to organize peers into the square root topology, nor can we expect individual peers to keep a large amount of state about the rest of the network. In particular, it is too costly in a large network to expect each peer to track all of the queries in the network or the popularity of content at all the other peers in order to compute equation (2). In this section, we describe an algorithm, called *square-root-construct*, that allows peers to construct the square-root topology in a distributed manner, using only local information.

In our algorithm, when peers join the network, they make random connections to some number of other peers. The number of initial connections that peer k makes is denoted d_k^0. The actual value of d_k^0 is not as important as the fact that peers make enough connections to keep the network connected. Then, as peer k is processing queries, it gathers information about the popularity of its content. From this information, peer k calculates its first estimate of its ideal degree, d_k^1. If the ideal degree d_k^1 is more than d_k^0, peer k adds $d_k^1 - d_k^0$ connections, and if the ideal degree is less than d_k^0, peer k drops $d_k^0 - d_k^1$ connections. Over time, peer k continues to track the popularity of its content, and recomputes its ideal degree ($d_k^2, d_k^3...$). Whenever its ideal degree estimate is different from its actual degree, peer k adds or drops connections. As in other peer-to-peer systems, peers can find new neighbors using a hostcatcher at a well known address, or by caching peer addresses from network messages.

Peers use purely local information to estimate the popularity of their content. In particular, each peer k maintains two counters: Q_{total}^k, the total number of queries seen by k, and Q_{match}^k, the number of queries that match k's content. Then, peers can estimate g_k in equation (2) as $Q_{match}^k / Q_{total}^k$. As peer k sees more and more queries, it can continue to recompute its estimate of g_k in order to calculate successive estimates of its ideal degree.

It is much more difficult to estimate the denominator of equation (2), which is the sum of the square roots of the popularity of all of the peers. Luckily, we can avoid this problem, since we have another degree of freedom: D, the sum of the d_k values for all peers. Recall from our analysis in Section 2.2 that D does not impact the overall performance of the system, as long as the system remains connected. Therefore, we can choose $D \propto \sum_{i=1}^{N} \sqrt{g_i}$, and substituting such a D into equation (2) eliminates $\sum_{i=1}^{N} \sqrt{g_i}$. More formally, we choose a maximum degree d_{max}, representing the degree we want for a peer whose popularity $g_k = 1$. Of course, it is unlikely that any peer will have content matching all queries, so the actual largest degree will almost certainly be less than d_{max}. Then, we define D as:

$$D = d_{max} \cdot \sum_{i=1}^{N} \sqrt{g_i} \tag{8}$$

Substituting equation (8) into equation (2) gives the ideal degree of a peer as:

$$d_k = d_{max} \cdot \sqrt{g_k} \approx d_{max} \cdot \sqrt{Q_{match}^k / Q_{total}^k} \tag{9}$$

If the popularity of a peer's content is very low, then d_k will be very small. If peer degrees are too small, the network can become partitioned, which will prevent content at some peers from being found at all. In the worst case, because d_k must be an integer, we must round equation (9), so the ideal degree might be zero. Therefore, we define a value d_{min}, which is the minimum degree a peer will have. The degree a peer will aim for is:

$$d_k = \begin{cases} \text{round}(d_{max} \cdot \sqrt{Q_{match}^k / Q_{total}^k}) & \text{if greater than } d_{min} \\ d_{min} & \text{otherwise} \end{cases} \tag{10}$$

Our algorithm *square-root-construct* can be summarized as follows:

- We choose a maximum degree d_{max} and minimum degree d_{min}, and fix them as part of the peer-to-peer protocol.
- Peer k joins, and makes some number d_k^0 of initial connections; $d_{min} \leq d_k^0 \leq d_{max}$.
- Peer k tracks Q_{match}^k and Q_{total}^k, and continually computes d_k according to equation (10).
- When the computed d_k differs from peer k's actual degree, k adds or drops connections.

Eventually, this method will cause the network to converge to the square root topology; as peers see more queries their estimates of their popularity will become increasingly accurate. Simulation results in the next section show that the network converges fairly quickly to an efficient structure.

Our algorithm also deals with situations where peer popularities change. Then peers will see more or fewer matching queries for their content, and will adjust their g_k estimates and degrees accordingly. In this situation, we may decide to use a decay factor μ to decrease the importance of older information in the estimate of g_k ($0 \leq \mu \leq 1$). Periodically, peer k would multiply both Q_{match}^k and Q_{total}^k by μ. Then, newer samples would have greater weight, and the network would converge more quickly according to the new distribution of popularities.

5 Experimental Results for the *Square-Root-Construct* Algorithm

We conducted two experiments to evaluate the effectiveness of square-root-construct. First, we ran simulations with 20,000 peers. Then, we validated our simulation results by running an experiment with our implemented peer-to-peer prototype in a network with 1,000 peers. Both experiments show that the *square-root-construct* algorithm effectively produces an efficient square-root topology.

5.1   Simulation Results

We ran simulations to measure the performance of searches over time as the topology adapted under the *square-root-construct* algorithm, and compared the performance to searches in square-root and power-law topologies constructed *a priori* using complete knowledge about peers and queries. We used the same experimental setup as described in Section 3. The parameters for the *square-root-construct* algorithm are shown in Table 3. We experimented with several parameter settings, and found that these settings worked well in practice. In particular, they produced connected networks with approximately the same total degree as the networks from experiments in Section 3.

Figure 4 shows the number of messages per search, calculated as a running average every 1,000 queries. As the figure shows, initially the performance of the network being adaptively constructed with the *square-root-construct* algorithm is not quite as good as the *a priori* square-root topology. However, the performance quickly improves, and after about 8,000 queries the performance of the adaptive square-root topology is consistently as good as the topology constructed *a priori*. (Other experiments show that the time for convergence to the performance of the *a priori* structure varies linearly with the number of peers in the network.) The *square-root-construct* network already performs

Table 3. Parameters for *square-root-construct*

Parameter	Value
d_{max}	160
d_{min}	3
d_k^0	4

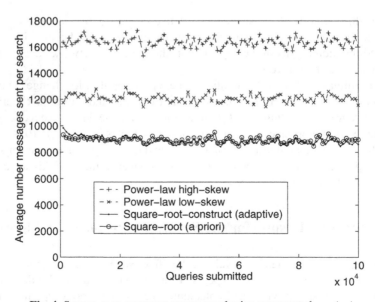

Fig. 4. Square-root-construct versus topologies constructed *a priori*

better than the power-law networks after 1,000 queries (the first data point). Although 1,000 queries are only enough to provide rough estimates of peer popularity, even rough estimates are able to produce a more efficient topology than a power law network.

5.2 Prototype Measurements

We have implemented a prototype peer-to-peer middleware toolkit, called *Overlay-Dynamic Information Networks (ODIN)*, and we used it to test the square-root topology and *square-root-construct* algorithm with queries over real data. ODIN is implemented in C++, and communicates using XML messages over HTTP connections. Each peer connects to randomly chosen peers, whose addresses are gathered from a "host-catcher" at a well known address or from the headers of messages observed in the network. Our peers used the *square-root-construct* algorithm (with parameters from Table 3) to adapt the network topology as they processed searches. We compared this network to one constructed using a traditional (i.e. Gnutella) unstructured topology policy. In this policy, peers connected to random remote peers, always trying to keep at least five connections alive but without aiming for a particular topology.

For our experiment, we downloaded 169,902 HTML pages (4.04 GB total) from 1,000 web sites. We then started 1,000 peers on cluster machines in our lab, and each peer stored the content from one web site. Peers processed queries over the full text of web pages using standard techniques (the cosine distance and TF/IDF weights [19]). We generated 20,000 keyword queries from the downloaded data with query terms matching the distribution observed in several real user query sets [20]. Each query was submitted to a randomly chosen peer.

Figure 5 shows a running average (every 1,000 queries) of the total network bandwidth required per search. As the figure shows, the network using the square-root

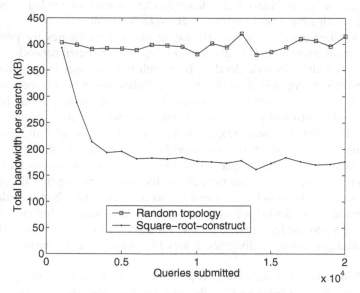

Fig. 5. Bandwidth required for search messages

construct algorithm initially performs poorly but then improves significantly, eventually requiring half the bandwidth on average of the network constructed randomly. Once each peer builds an accurate estimate of the popularity of its content, and adjusts its degree accordingly, the total bandwidth used drops below 180 KB per search, compared to 415 KB per search for the random topology.

In return for this higher efficiency, the *square-root-construct* network must send more control traffic (connect and disconnect messages) between peers. In fact, the square-root network requires 5.4 times as much bandwidth for control messages than in the random network. However, this cost is far outweighed by the savings in search bandwidth; an extra 4.6 KB per search on average for control messages results in a savings of 238 KB in search bandwidth per search on average. We can conclude that the extra control traffic is insignificant compared to the benefits of the square-root-topology.

6   Related Work

Random walk searches in peer-to-peer networks were proposed by Adamic et al [10] in order to cope with the unique characteristics of power-law networks. Follow-on work by others showed how to enhance performance by using replication [11,14], parallel random walks [11] and biased random walks of various types [13]. Most of this work assumes an existing topology, either power-law, random, or some other organization. In our results sections we examined each of these techniques. Other techniques have been proposed, such as "intelligent search" [21], routing indices [22], result caching [23] and so on. We have not yet tested the square-root topology against an exhaustive list of techniques, although we are continuing to gather data about its effectiveness for various techniques. Gkantsidis, Mihail and Saberi [24] discuss how to use random walks and flooding together to achieve high efficiency. Our square-root topology can be used together with their techniques to achieve even higher performance.

Some investigators have looked at building efficient topologies for peer-to-peer searches. Pandurangan et al [25] discuss building low diameter networks, although their focus is on Gnutella-style flooding for which low diameter is important. Lv et al [12] presented a dynamic algorithm for load balancing in peer-to-peer networks. Their goal is to shift load onto high capacity nodes. To achieve this load balancing, overloaded nodes must find nearby nodes to take over some of their connections. Our approach, while similarly using adaptivity, has a different goal of shifting load onto the most popular nodes. Moreover, our algorithm allows a peer to simply drop a connection without having to find a peer to take it over. While our approach can reduce overall load in the system, it does not achieve the load balancing that Lv et al's approach does. It may be possible to extend our techniques to take both popularity and capacity into account. Gia [4] is a system that combines several techniques, including topology adaptation and biasing random walks toward high-capacity nodes. Their goal is load balancing to improve efficiency. It may be possible to combine our techniques with theirs.

Several investigators have examined peer-to-peer systems analytically; examples include models for peer behavior [26], download traffic [27], data semantics [28], and so on. Gkantsidis, Mihail and Saberi [29] demonstrate analytically that random walks are useful to locate popular content in two cases: a) when the topology forms a super-peer network, and b) when the same search is issued repeatedly. We expand on their work in several ways. First, our analysis holds for both popular and rare items; in fact, the square root topology is specifically optimized to provide efficient searching over a wide range of item popularities. Second, while their analysis and simulation is limited to pure random walks, we demonstrate that the square-root topology is efficient for a wide range of search techniques, such as biased random walks, random walks with proactive replication, and so on. Third, we show that the square-root topology is useful both in the case of super-peer networks and in flat networks.

Several investigators have proposed more structured peer-to-peer networks, some-times known as distributed hash tables (DHTs). Examples include CHORD [1], CAN [2], Pastry [3], and others. In these systems, the topology is structured accord-ing to protocol rules in order to ensure high efficiency. Despite the advent of DHTs, research in and deployment of unstructured systems continues. One reason is the con-tinuing popularity of unstructured systems such as Gnutella and Kazaa, and another rea-son is the difficulty experienced, at least until recently [5,30], with using DHTs for key-word search. Chawathe et al [4] discuss several reasons why both unstructured networks and DHTs are worthy of study. Loo et al [5,6] discuss a hybrid structured/unstructured architecture for information discovery, and our work could impact the design of the unstructured part of such a hybrid system.

In a previous workshop paper [31], we have examined a narrow application of the square root topology in situations where it is not feasible to replicate data or in-dexes. Here, we examine the usefulness of the square root topology for a wide range of searching techniques (including proactive replication, supernode networks, and other approaches to using replication).

7   Conclusions

We have presented the square-root topology, and shown that implementing a protocol that causes the network to converge to the square root topology, rather than a power-law topology, can provide significant performance improvements for peer-to-peer searches. In the square-root topology, the degree of each peer is proportional to the square root of the popularity of the content at the peer. Our analysis shows that the square-root topology is optimal in the number of hops required for simple random walk searches. We also present simulation results which demonstrate that the square-root topology is better than power-law topologies for other peer-to-peer search techniques. Next, we presented an algorithm for constructing the square-root topology using purely local information. Each peer estimates its ideal degree by tracking how many queries match its content, and then adds or drops connections to achieve its estimated ideal degree. Results from simulations and our prototype show that this locally adaptive algorithm quickly converges to a globally efficient square-root topology. Our results show that the combination of an optimized topology and efficient search mechanisms provides high performance in unstructured peer-to-peer networks.

References

1. Stoica, I., Morris, R., Karger, D., Kaashoek, M.F., Balakrishnan, H.: Chord: A scalable peer-to-peer lookup service for internet applications. In: Proc. SIGCOMM. (2001)
2. Ratnasamy, S., Francis, P., Handley, M., Karp, R., Shenker, S.: A scalable content-addressable network. In: Proc. SIGCOMM. (2001)
3. Rowstron, A., Druschel, P.: Pastry: Scalable, decentralized object location and routing for large-scale peer-to-peer systems. In: Proc. IFIP/ACM International Conference on Distributed Systems Platforms. (2001)
4. Chawathe, Y., Ratnasamy, S., Breslau, L., Lanham, N., Shenker, S.: Making Gnutella-like P2P systems scalable. In: Proc. SIGCOMM. (2003)
5. Loo, B., Hellerstein, J., Huebsch, R., Shenker, S., Stoica, I.: Enhancing P2P file-sharing with an Internet-scale query processor. In: Proc. Conference on Very Large Data Bases. (2004)
6. Loo, B., Huebsch, R., Stoica, I., Hellerstein, J.: Enhancing P2P file-sharing with an Internet-scale query processor. In: Proc. International Workshop on Peer-to-Peer Systems. (2004)
7. Yang, B., Garcia-Molina, H.: Designing a super-peer network. In: Proc. ICDE. (2003)
8. Kalnis, P., Ng, W., Ooi, B., Papadias, D., Tan, K.: An adaptive peer-to-peer network for distributed caching of OLAP results. In: Proc. SIGMOD. (2002)
9. Agarwal, D., Berket, K.: Supporting dynamic ad hoc collaboration capabilities. In: Proceedings of the 2003 Conference for Computing in High-Energy and Nuclear Physics (CHEP 03). (2003)
10. Adamic, L., Lukose, R., Puniyani, A., Huberman, B.: Search in power-law networks. Phys. Rev. E **64** (2001) 46135–46143
11. Lv, Q., Cao, P., Cohen, E., Li, K., Shenker, S.: Search and replication in unstructured peer-to-peer networks. In: Proc. of ACM Int'l Conf. on Supercomputing (ICS'02). (2002)
12. Lv, Q., Ratnasamy, S., Shenker, S.: Can heterogeneity make Gnutella scalable? In: Proc. of the 1st Int'l Workshop on Peer to Peer Systems (IPTPS). (2002)
13. Yang, B., Garcia-Molina, H.: Improving search in peer-to-peer networks. In: Proc. ICDCS. (2002)
14. Cohen, E., Shenker, S.: Replication strategies in unstructured peer-to-peer networks. In: Proc. SIGCOMM. (2002)
15. Motwani, R., Raghavan, P.: Randomized Algorithms. Cambridge University Press, New York, NY (1995)
16. Cooper, B.F.: A content model for evaluating peer-to-peer searching techniques. In: Proc. ACM/IFIP/USENIX Middleware Conference. (2004)
17. Palmer, C., Steffan, J.: Generating network topologies that obey power laws. In: Proc. GLOBECOM. (2000)
18. Nejdl, W., Wolpers, M., Siberski, W., Schmitz, C., Schlosser, M., Brunkhorst, I., Loser, A.: Super-peer-based routing and clustering strategies for RDF-based peer-to-peer networks. In: Proc. WWW. (2003)
19. Baeza-Yates, R., Ribeiro-Neto, B.: Modern Information Retrieval. ACM Press, New York, N.Y. (1999)
20. Cahoon, B., McKinley, K.S., Lu, Z.: Evaluating the performance of distributed architectures for information retrieval using a variety of workloads. ACM Transactions on Information Systems **18** (2000) 1–43
21. Kalogeraki, V., Gunopulos, D., Zeinalipour-Yazti, D.: A local search mechanism for peer-to-peer networks. In: Proc. CIKM. (2002)
22. Crespo, A., Garcia-Molina, H.: Routing indices for peer-to-peer systems. In: Proc. ICDCS. (2002)

23. Bhattacharjee, B.: Efficient peer-to-peer searches using result-caching. In: Proc. IPTPS. (2003)
24. Gkantsidis, C., Mihail, M., Saberi, A.: Hybrid search schemes for unstructured peer-to-peer networks. In: Proc. INFOCOM. (2005)
25. Pandurangan, G., Raghavan, P., Upfal, E.: Building low-diameter P2P networks. In: Proc. IEEE Symp. on Foundations of Computer Science. (2001)
26. Ge, Z., Figueiredo, D., Jaiswal, S., Kurose, J., Towsley, D.: Modeling peer-peer file sharing systems. In: Proc. INFOCOM. (2003)
27. Gummadi, K., Dunn, R., Saroiu, S., Gribble, S., Levy, H., Zahorjan, J.: Measurement, modeling and analysis of a peer-to-peer file-sharing workload. In: Proc. SOSP. (2003)
28. Bernstein, P., et al: Data management for peer-to-peer computing: A vision. In: Proc. WebDB. (2002)
29. Gkantsidis, C., Mihail, M., Saberi, A.: Random walks in peer-to-peer networks. In: Proc. INFOCOM. (2004)
30. Reynolds, P., Vahdat, A.: Efficient peer-to-peer keyword searching. In: Proc. ACM/IFIP/ USENIX International Middleware Conference. (2003)
31. Cooper, B.F.: Quickly routing searches without having to move content. In: Proc. IPTPS. (2005)

Combining Flexibility and Scalability in a Peer-to-Peer Publish/Subscribe System

Chi Zhang[1], Arvind Krishnamurthy[2], Randolph Y. Wang[1],
and Jaswinder Pal Singh[1]

[1] Princeton University
[2] Yale University

Abstract. The content-based publish/subscribe model has been adopted by many services to deliver data between distributed users based on application-specific semantics. Two key issues in such systems, the semantic expressiveness of content matching and the scalability of the matching mechanism, are often found to be in conflict due to the complexity associated with content matching. In this paper, we present a novel content-based publish/subscribe architecture based on peer-to-peer matching trees. The system achieves scalability by partitioning the responsibility of event matching to self-organized peers while allowing customizable matching functionalities. Experimental results using a variety of real world datasets demonstrate the scalability and flexibility of the system.

Keywords: publish/subscribe, matching, peer-to-peer.

1 Introduction

The deployment and application of event-based publish/subscribe services has increased considerably over the past years. A number of emerging applications, ranging from simple personal tools to large-scale and critical systems, benefit from this paradigm. Examples include stock quote notification, Internet news feeds, real-time traffic control, and various monitoring/management systems. Publish/subscribe systems deliver events from publishers to subscribers based on their interests. Publishers and subscribers can be completely unaware of one another and communicate via the message brokers that match events to interested data users. This decoupling provides an attractive communication mechanism for building large scale distributed systems.

The expressiveness of subscriber interests is a key factor in such middlewares. Early publish/subscribe systems like TIBCO [20] and CORBA event channels [13] are subject-based. Subscribers join a set of subject groups that they are interested in and receive all messages associated with the subjects.

Content-based publish/subscribe systems allow more flexibility in specifying subscriber interests. Subscriptions specify filters on event contents. Only those events with attributes matching the filters are delivered to the subscriber. A typical application is stock quote notification. The events carry attributes of prices and trade volumes of individual stocks. Subscribers may specify triggering ranges of price or volume for the stocks that they are interested in. They get notification once events matching their subscriptions occur. Another scenario is literature reference tracking. Researchers may subscribe to new publications matching certain keywords in their titles, abstracts or bodies.

G. Alonso (Ed.): Middleware 2005, LNCS 3790, pp. 102–123, 2005.

They may also choose to track new papers from certain authors or citing certain previous works. In both examples, content-based filtering provides fine-grained control on the relevance of messages.

However, the power of expressiveness introduces an additional cost of matching events to the complex filters specified by subscribers. As the system scales with the number of subscriptions and the volume of event messages, a centralized matching solution cannot meet the computation and communication requirements. Therefore, we seek a solution to the scalability issue by distributing the matching responsibility to many machines. In particular, we leverage peer-to-peer overlay techniques to build a highly scalable publish/subscribe system. In our system, broker nodes self-organize and maintain a decentralized data structure that stores the subscriptions, match the events to the subscriptions, and deliver the events to relevant subscribers. Broker nodes may be added to or removed from the system without global coordination. A key problem facing such a scalable system is how to partition the workload among participating peers in a load-balanced fashion.

The flexibility provided by content expressiveness creates challenges to system scalability. While a subject-based publish/subscribe system can easily partition the workload of event delivery to a large set of servers by hashing the subjects among the servers, content-based systems have more complex subscription structures that impede the workload partition. Three factors contribute to this difficulty:

1. **High dimensionality of the content space:** a general publish/subscribe system might have to operate in a setting that involves a large number of attributes. To make things even worse, subscribers and publishers do not always speak the same schema. Subscribers seldom know in advance the schemas used by (potentially many) publishers. Even if they do, they might be interested in only a subset of it.
2. **Type flexibility:** attributes may have various types that require different filtering tests.
3. **Skewed data distribution:** is common in real world subscriptions and events. It can create a load imbalance in the system that throttles the scalability.

Previous work on workload partitioning usually impose restrictions on the flexibility of subscriptions and events. In [22] and [19], the set of attributes and their values are hashed to decide the servers managing the subscriptions. This requires events and subscriptions to follow certain pre-defined schemas, and only works well with equality tests. It is difficult to efficiently support range subscriptions in such systems. Meghdoot [9] leverages CAN [15] to partition the multi-attribute space. Though it can support range subscriptions, it is still confined to numerical attributes and also can not handle skewed distributions efficiently.

Our Solution

In this paper, we propose a peer-to-peer architecture that achieves high scalability and generality. We address the expressiveness problem with a modular matching tree structure. This tree organizes the subscriptions into hierarchical groups based on their similarity. It supports flexible schemas and multiple attribute types in subscriptions and events, and allows customization of new attributes and filtering types. We distribute this matching tree in a peer-to-peer system where each peer processor manages a small fragment of the tree. They maintain the distributed tree by peer-wise communications without global coordination.

Events can enter the system from any processor. A decentralized tree navigation algorithm is used to forward the events to those tree fragments that may contain matching subscriptions. In experiments using several real world data sets, the proposed system demonstrates excellent scalability: the distributed event matching only visits a small number of processors, processors maintain a small amount of state about peers, and the workload is well-balanced across the processor set.

The next section gives a survey of related work. Section 3 details the structure of the matching tree. Section 4 discusses how the tree is distributed and how to navigate the tree in a decentralized manner. Section 5 focuses on how the distributed tree is maintained in the face of churn and changing load conditions. Section 6 presents experimental results.

2 Related Work

Several centralized algorithms for content-based publish-subscribe [8,7,2,10] have been proposed to address the efficiency of the matching operation. Our matching tree bears some similarity to previous work, such as [2,10], which also use search tree structures. The key differences are: 1) Our matching tree is more flexible, partitioning the subscriptions by both schema content and attribute value, while [2,10] only partition by the attribute value specified in subscriptions. 2) We distribute the matching tree amongst peer processors to address the scalability problem.

Distributed content-based publish/subscribe systems deploy a network of broker servers to efficiently match and deliver events. Examples include Elvin [17], Siena [4], and Gryphon [2]. Elvin uses a central server to store subscriptions and match events. Therefore, it still imposes a bottleneck at the matching engine. Siena and Gryphon distribute the responsibility of matching events to a set of distributed servers. Events follow a multicast tree to reach all matching subscribers. However, they require the subscriptions to be replicated on all servers. This causes a burden on server management and is a stumbling block to scalability.

To address this scalability problem, several systems consider the partitioning of content-space and the subscription set. Riabov et al. have proposed clustering algorithms that partition similar subscriptions into multicast groups. EDN [22] partitions the content space subject to the restriction that the schema is fixed. For equality test, the attribute IDs and values are hashed to generate a key to locate the server managing it. For inequality tests, EDN uses an R-tree to decide offline how to assign subscriptions to processors, and requires each processor to maintain a complete map of this assignment. This approach is limited to small-scale systems with a fixed set of subscriptions, and it is also unclear as to whether it works efficiently for high dimensional content space.

Peer-to-peer overlays have emerged as a promising approach to realizing highly scalable distributed systems. Several systems provide application-level multicast [12,3] that divides the data dissemination responsibilities amongst peers. They do not, however, address the selective delivery of events. Recently, Distributed Hash Tables (DHTs) have been employed to build scalable publish/subscribe systems. Scribe [5] uses

Pastry [16] to build a subject-based publish/subscribe service. It hashes each topic to a peer, which then acts as the rendezvous point. The routing paths from subscribers to the rendezvous point form a multicast tree for this subject. This approach, however, can not be adapted to efficiently support the content-based publish/subscribe model.

A few previous projects have addressed content-based publish/subscribe in peer-to-peer systems. [19] partitions the content-space by hashing a set of selected attributes and their values into peer processors. The domain of attribute values are partitioned into intervals for the hashing. A range subscription may need to be decomposed to multiple intervals, resulting in storage and matching inefficiency. Furthermore, the subscriptions and events are limited by the pre-selected attribute sets. Meghdoot [9] relaxes the restrictions on subscriptions. It uses CAN [15] to manage the multi-attribute content-space. A subscription defines a rectangular region in the D-attribute content space bounded by the minimal and maximal value specified. Unspecified attributes take the whole value range. The hyper-rectangle is projected to a point in a $2D$-dimension CAN constructed from the minimal and maximal values of the D-dimension rectangle. An event is then mapped to a rectangle in the $2D$ space, and the mapping is performed in a manner such that the rectangle covers all subscription points relevant to the event. This novel approach reduces the subscription matching problem into a range query operation in CAN. The drawback with this approach is that subscriptions are limited to numerical comparisons. Other tests like keyword subset can not be supported. Furthermore, the subscriptions are only mapped to the upper-left side of the diagonal hyper-plane of the CAN space, which may create load imbalance.

3   Content-Based Event Matching

In this section, we start by describing the specification of events and subscriptions in our system. We then present the main data structure, the matching tree, used in the system.

We also note that we focus primarily on the logical organization and navigation of the matching tree in this section. The distributed operation and maintenance of the tree will be presented in following sections.

3.1   Content-Based Publish/Subscribe Model

We adopt a general event-space model with multiple attributes, based on the models used in previous systems [7,4,2]. The contents of an event message is represented by a set of attribute-value pairs. Each attribute has a unique name or ID. We support several types of attributes: *numerical* (integer, floating point, and date/time), *string*, and *set*. The event message can be represented as $e = \{A_1 = v_1, A_2 = v_2, \ldots, A_k = v_k\}$. Events from different publishers may use different schemas, but we assume a consistent assignment of unique attribute IDs and their types across the publishers to avoid naming confusion. One could also employ hierarchical namespaces to achieve this coordination.

As an example, consider an event from a research reference database. Its contents may be formulated as $[title = $ TTT$, date = $ YY/MM$, authors = \{A, B, C\}$, $references = \{D_1, D_2, \ldots D_n\}]$, where *title* has *string* type, *date* is *numerical*, and *authors* and *references* fields are both of type *set*, meaning they include an unordered list of keys.

Table 1. Predicates supported in the system

type	tests
Numerical	$=, <, \leq, >, \geq$
String	$=, <, \leq, >, \geq$, prefix match
Set	$\ni, \supseteq$

A subscription is a conjunction of predicates over the attributes. Each predicate specifies a boolean test over an attribute. The test specified by a predicate depends on the type of the attribute. Table 1 lists the type of tests supported in our system. Disjunction of predicates can be expressed by the "OR" of multiple conjunctions, so we treat a disjunctive subscription as a set of independent conjunctive subscriptions.

We do not require events and subscriptions to use the same schemas. There may be a large number of possible attributes, while any event and subscription may specify only a subset of attributes. An event matches a subscription if every predicate specified is satisfied by the attribute-value content of the event message. Not all attributes in the event need to appear in the matching subscription. The additional attributes do not affect the matching results, since the subscription does not care about the values of these attributes. However, the event does not match a subscription if an attribute specified in the subscription's predicates is missing from the event. This semi-structured matching capability is important for environments with heterogeneous publishers. Some systems, like EDN [22], require all events to use the same schema. Such restrictions limit the generality of the system and thus is not desirable.

3.2 Content-Space Partition with a Matching Tree

We propose a matching tree algorithm to partition a general event space. A hierarchical tree structure is used to partition the set of subscriptions based on their predicates. Each internal node partitions the subscriptions by a similarity test, so similar subscriptions can be grouped to the same tree branch. In order to adapt to flexible attribute sets and schemas, we build the similarity tests dynamically.

Two types of similarities are used in the tests. The first is the similarity of the attribute set. The test takes an attribute from the subscriptions and hashes its name. The subscriptions are assigned to one of two branches based on the hash value. After recursive partitioning with several levels of internal nodes, each branch will have subscriptions sharing the same attribute. The second type groups subscriptions having similar value constraints for a common attribute. Depending on the type of this attribute, the test assigns the subscriptions to two branches. For convenience, we label the child branches of an internal node L and R. In addition, there is a wildcard branch, labeled as *, for subscriptions that do not contain the attribute specified by the internal node.

Figure 1 gives an example of the matching tree used for subscriptions to research publications. The root node partitions the subscriptions based on attributes specified in their predicates. It takes the first attribute in the subscription (A_1), hashes the name ($A_1.name$), and assigns the subscription to one of two branches based on the demarcating value of 5 for the result of the hash. The left child node of the root further partitions the subscriptions based on the value of the *date* attribute. If a subscription has a predicate that tests the *date* attribute, then it is stored in one or both of the L and R branches.

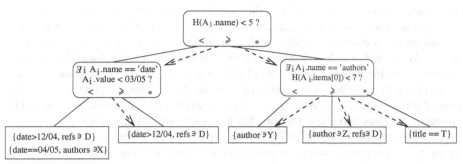

Fig. 1. Matching Tree

For instance, if the range of the predicate on the 'date' attribute intersects with the range $(0, 03/05)$, the subscription would be inserted in the left branch; if it intersects with the range $[03/05, \infty)$, it would be inserted in the right branch; and a subscription that covers a broad range, like $\{date > 12/04, authors \ni X\}$, would be inserted in both branches. If a subscription's first attribute hashes to a value less than 5 and if that subscription does not have any predicates referring to the $date$ attribute, then it is stored in the wild-card * branch. The right child of the root node partitions the subscriptions based on how they test the $authors$ attribute. Since $authors$ is a set attribute, we pick any of the keys specified in the predicate testing the $authors$ attribute, and hash it to decide the branch the subscription belongs to. The subscription $\{title == T\}$ falls into the default branch *, since it does not contain any predicates testing the $authors$ attribute.

Event messages also navigate the same matching tree to find matching subscriptions. Figure 1 gives an example of how an event is handled. The event starts from the root node. It is passed on to both branches, because the attributes in the event, $date$ and $authors$, hash to the L and R branches respectively. The event is further propagated through the R branch at the left child node based on its $date$ value. At the right child node, both L and R branches are followed, because the elements in the $authors$ field hash to either side of the pivot value 7. At the leaf nodes, a centralized matching algorithm like the counting algorithm [7] is used to match the event to the set of matching subscriptions.

Next, we give further details regarding the two partitioning methods.

3.3   Partitioning the Attribute Set

The first type of partitioning tries to group together subscriptions that test similar attributes. We first order the predicates of a subscription based on their selectivity. For simplicity, we order equality tests before subset tests, and consider inequalities as the least selective. More sophisticated techniques that take into account data distribution to order predicates regarding their selectivity are also possible. We then take the most selective predicate in the subscriptions, and hash the attribute name into a bin $H(A_1.name)$.

Each child branch manage a sequence of hash bins and the subscriptions falling into the sequence. A pivot value separates the hash bins of the left and right branches.

While a subscription only descends into either the left or the right branch of this internal node, an event may follow both branches. Given an event $\{A_1 = v_1, A_2 = v_2, \ldots, A_k = v_k\}$, the left branch is taken if any of the hash values $H(A_i.name)$ corresponds to the bins on the left side of the pivot. Similarly, the right branch is taken if any of the hash values corresponds to right-hand side bins. In general, when this form of partitioning is performed iteratively at multiple internal nodes, an event with k attributes navigates into at most k branches under attribute set partitioning.

Given a set of subscriptions in a leaf node, we choose the pivot value that evenly partitions the subscriptions. When the subscriptions' most selective attribute is the same, either because of user subscription pattern or due to prior partitioning of the attribute set, we partition based on the second and third most selective attributes. Therefore, the state information maintained in an attributed set partitioning node includes the order of the attribute being hashed, the range of hash bins owned by this node, and the pivot value used for partitioning.

3.4 Partitioning Attribute Content

After partitioning the attribute set, each branch of the matching tree contains subscriptions with similar attributes. We can therefore partition further using the value ranges of their common attributes. We apply different strategies based on the attribute's data type.

- **Value range partition** applies to numerical attributes. It splits the value range of the attribute by a pivot value. The value range specified by predicates in the subscriptions are compared to the pivot. If the whole range falls to the left/right of the pivot, the subscription is assigned to the left/right branch. Otherwise, the subscription is replicated into both branches. This strategy is therefore suitable for subscriptions specifying narrow value ranges, for example, equality tests. The attribute set partitioning policy that gives priority to highly selective predicates also improves efficiency of value range partition. While subscriptions may be replicated in both branches, an event only descends into one of them. So this approach reduces matching cost by using additional storage.
- **Min/max partition** divides the set of subscriptions instead of the value space. The minimal/maximal value in the constraints is used to decide the branch it belongs to. Therefore, a subscription is only assigned to one of the left/right branches. Consequently, an event may need to navigate into both branches to locate matching subscriptions. Figure 2 illustrates differences between the three strategies used to partition range constraints on a numerical attribute.
- **String value partition** is similar to value range partitioning. A subscription with a prefix predicate may be assigned to both branches if the prefix includes the pivot string.
- **Set partition** hashes the keys specified in the subscriptions and divides the hashed key space into two halves across a pivot key. A subscription specifying several keys for the set attribute may choose to follow the branch decided by any of the keys. An event message would have to navigate into all branches that its set members

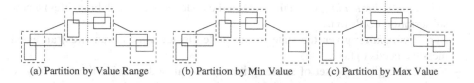

(a) Partition by Value Range   (b) Partition by Min Value   (c) Partition by Max Value

Fig. 2. Partitioning options based on a numerical attribute

hash to. This is necessary to ensure that all related subscriptions can be reached. Therefore, an event message specifying k keys for the set attribute may navigate into up to k branches under multiple levels of set partitioning.

In all of the above mentioned types of attribute content based partitioning, the default $*$ branch may be taken if a subscription does not specify the attribute. An event always traverses into the $*$ branch if it exists, unless the attribute being partitioned is the only one specified in the event.

3.5 Choosing Partition Method

The matching tree grows by splitting leaf nodes. We aim at distributing the subscriptions in the leaf node evenly to the branches of the newly formed internal node. The two partitioning methods described above have different levels of effectiveness under different situations. When the subscriptions carry sets of attributes that differ significantly, partitioning the value space of any single attribute may only work on a small part of subscriptions while leaving the majority in the wildcard branch. Attribute set partitioning is more effective in this case. After subscriptions with the same attributes are grouped together, partitioning the content of this attribute will yield more balanced results.

When a leaf node needs to be partitioned, we scan the subscriptions in the node, and count the number of subscriptions associated with each attribute. We try to partition the attributes that appear in at least half of the subscriptions, and choose the partition method that yields best load balance, defined as the largest number of subscriptions in the branches after split. If such attributes do not exist, we partition the attribute set.

Besides the partitioning approaches discussed above, we also use a special "partition" method that replicates the set of subscriptions to both children branches. An event may choose to follow any of the mirrored branches. As the branches are assigned to different processors, this replication spreads out the load of event matching. We use this method when the processor managing the leaf node is saturated by the event traffic targeting the leaf node. Such event hot spots may be found in some subscriptions that match a broad range of events, for example, $\{Volume \geq P_1\}$ in stock quote notification service (Section 6.1).

3.6 Extensibility

The above discussion illustrates that several different partitioning methods are used in our system. Generally, for each data type, the system needs at least one partitioning method to decide how the subscriptions and the events navigate the matching tree. Each partitioning method is implemented as a module that provides three interface functions:

- *Subscription branching*: given the state in the node, decide which branch(es) a new subscription needs to take.
- *Event branching*: given the state in the node, decide which branch(es) an event message needs to take.
- *Node split*: given the set of subscriptions in a leaf node, decide the best way to partition the subscriptions once the leaf node gets overloaded.

This modular design allows new data and predicate types to be introduced into our system, therefore ensuring generality.

4   Peer-to-Peer Matching Tree with Brushwood

In this section, we present the design of our peer-to-peer architecture. We distribute the matching tree using peer-to-peer overlay techniques in order to achieve the following:

- **Balanced distribution:** We partition the matching tree into a set of subtrees, so that the workload of managing subscriptions and matching events can be divided among peer processors in a balanced manner.
- **Locality and ability to support complex event filtering:** Since the distribution is at the granularity of subtrees, related subscriptions are stored on the same processor. Furthermore, the generality of the matching tree ensures that our system can handle subscriptions with range predicates and efficiently match events to such subscriptions.
- **Symmetric distribution that avoids hotspots:** We ensure that no processor in the system is subject to inordinately high load. We avoid distribution schemes that assign the root of the matching tree to a single processor, which is then subject to handling every new event or subscription. Instead, we make all subtrees self-contained and independent. Each processor maintains the path from the root of the matching tree to the root of the subtree in addition to maintaining the full set of internal nodes and leaf nodes of the subtree. An event or subscription could be routed to any one of the processors, which can either handle it locally or forward it to the appropriate processor(s).
- **Scalability:** We require that processors maintain small amounts of state regarding the current state of the system. In particular, each processor in our system keeps track of a logarithmic number of peers in the system. Peers periodically exchange information regarding their portion of the matching tree, so that they can maintain a weakly consistent partial view of the global matching tree. This partial view allows the processors to forward subscriptions and event messages to relevant matching tree nodes.

4.1   Brushwood

We extend the Brushwood framework described in our position paper [24] to build the peer-to-peer matching tree. Brushwood is a peer-to-peer search tree designed for scalable indexing of high dimensional data. Here we adapt its distributed organization for the publish-subscribe needs.

Tree Distribution: Brushwood partitions a search tree into self-contained fragments cooperatively managing the distributed tree. Figure 3 (a) illustrates our approach in distributing a matching tree. The edges are labeled as 'L', 'R' and '*' for left, right and default branches. We linearize the tree nodes by pre-order traversal and then partition them into eight fragments separated by the dotted vertical bars. This partitioning method preserves locality of similar subscriptions since the low level subtrees are not split. The tree fragments are assigned to eight processors A - H, shown as the rectangles below the tree. We identify the fragments, and the processors managing them, with its *left boundary*. The left boundary is defined as the the left-most tree node in the partition under pre-order traversal. This boundary can be uniquely identified by the sequence of edge labels along the path from the root of the matching tree to the boundary node. We use this sequence as the *Tree ID* of the tree fragment. The Tree ID of each of the fragments are shown in the processor rectangles.

Data Structure Maintained by Each Processor: In a dynamic peer-to-peer system, processor joins and departures are frequent events. Each join/departure changes the location of some subtree. Therefore, we can not afford to replicate across all processors the global map of which processor owns which portion of the tree. Instead, a processor only maintains a *partial tree view*, which is a sub-graph of the global matching tree. This partial tree of a processor consists of the following: 1) all the leaf nodes managed by the processor, 2) the left boundary nodes of some selected peer processors, and 3) all internal tree nodes along the paths from the root of the matching tree to the nodes specified above in (1) and (2). Information about the peer boundary nodes are collected by contacting peer processors. The construction of the partial view is, therefore, a localized operation with cost proportional to the number of peers. The selection of peer processors is discussed later in this section. Figure 4 shows the partial view of A and D.

Event Handling: When a new event is received by a processor, the event is processed using the partial tree view. The event is propagated through the partial tree view, starting from the root of the partial tree, to determine which portions of the tree are related to the event. During this process, one or more of the following types of actions are performed:

- The event is relevant to one or more of the *local* leaf nodes managed by this processor. The matching can be then performed locally.
- The event needs to be routed to a *remote* leaf node managed by a peer.
- The event is relevant to some *obscure* nodes corresponding to unknown portions of the matching tree that is not managed by any peer. The event is then routed to some peer that is more likely to be aware of the obscure node.

Example: Now we show how to perform event matching in a distributed tree with an example event message $\{A_1 = 20, A_2 = 90\}$. Assume the event enters the system from processor A. A navigates its partial tree to find all subtrees that may contain subscriptions matching this event. In this case, subtrees RR, $R*$ and $*$ are involved. A forwards the query to the processors managing these regions. RR is managed by peer D. Obscure nodes $R*$ and $*$ have to be reached by overlay routing. We route the messages to the peer that is farthest in the same direction as the obscure node (given the pre-order

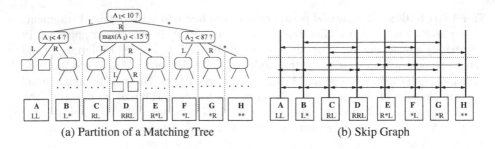

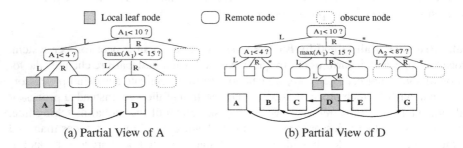

Fig. 3. Peer-to-peer Matching Tree

Fig. 4. Partial Tree Views from Processor A and D

linearization of tree nodes) without passing over the target. In this example, all three subtrees are forwarded to peer D for further matching. D further navigates its partial tree to identify related regions to be searched. It performs local matching in subtree RR, and forwards the message to E and G for further matching. Event matching is therefore performed starting from any processor by "jumping" among the processors instead of traversing a distributed tree path from the root to the target. Each forwarding step refines the subtrees that need to be searched. The number of hops is logarithmic in the number of processors, regardless of tree depth. Subscription insertion follows a similar procedure.

4.2   Routing Substrate

We now consider the question of establishing peers. To ensure system scalability, we limit the amount of state information managed by individual processors. Each processor only maintains $\log N$ peers and their partition boundaries in an N-processor system. Therefore, each node join and departure can be handled efficiently by contacting only $\log N$ processors. A tree navigation can be done within $\log N$ steps regardless of the shape of the tree. We extend Skip Graphs/Nets [1,11] to achieve such an efficient lookup.

Conceptually, a processor in a Skip Graph maintains $\log N$ levels of peer pointers, pointing to exponentially farther peers in the linear ordering of N processors. Figure 3 (b) depicts the overlay structure of the Skip Graph among the eight processors. Each

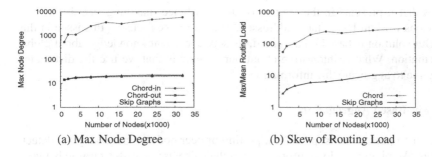

(a) Max Node Degree   (b) Skew of Routing Load

Fig. 5. Routing Imbalance under Skewed Key Distribution

processor uses a random membership vector to decide its peers. At level i, the peers are the nearest processors on the left and right sides with membership vectors that match the processor's membership vectors for the first i bits.

Brushwood routing depends on a linear ordering of partitions. In this sense, any linear space DHT routing facility can be used. We choose Skip Graphs for two reasons. First of all, Skip Graphs do not impose constraints on the nature and structure of keys. It can work with complex keys, like the variable-length Tree IDs, as long as there is a total ordering. Second, even if one can encode tree nodes into key values, such unhashed and often skewed keys can cause routing imbalances in some DHTs, as they use key values to decide the peering relation. Skip Graphs do not suffer from this problem because its peering is decided by purely random membership vectors, even though the keys are unhashed.

We simulated Chord [18] and Skip Graphs with a skewed key distribution to show the imbalance in routing. Figure 5 (a) depicts the maximal processor degrees of Chord and Skip Graphs with 1K~32K processors. The processor keys are derived from a normal distribution with standard deviation 0.125 in the range $[0, 1]$. With such unhashed keys, Chord processors falling into the sparsely populated regions will manage larger portions of the keyspace, and are therefore likely to have a large number of in-bound peers. Furthermore, the imbalance in peer distribution also leads to imbalance in routing costs. We route 1000 messages between random pairs of nodes. Figure 5 (b) shows the imbalance as the ratio of maximal routing load to mean load. We observed similar routing imbalances in Meghdoot, which employs CAN for routing in (skewed) subscription content space. We present this result in Section 6.

5   Maintaining the Partition Tree

In this section, we discuss the maintenance of the dynamic matching tree in a peer-to-peer setting. The major challenges are: 1) the frequent processor joins and departures, typically referred to as churn, and 2) balancing the workload among the dynamic processor set. Our design leverages Skip Graphs to achieve efficient routing while maintaining only a logarithmic number of peers. Therefore, the processor joins and departures only result in small maintenance overheads. Balancing the workload associated with publish/subscribe events is important for the scalability of the system. The challenges that it presents in the context of the distributed matching tree differ from what previous work in DHTs have addressed. Therefore, we focus on this issue in this section. Our solution is based on a limited, loosely consistent knowledge about global load distribution. What is interesting about our scheme is that we use the distributed matching tree to aggregate this information.

5.1 Gossip-Based Aggregation

In most peer-to-peer systems, periodical polling of peer nodes is necessary for detecting failures. We piggyback load information in the pair-wise heart-beat traffic between peers. Peer processors aggregate the global load information from these gossip messages. This approach is inspired by previous work [21].

Each processor maintains load summaries for the nodes in its partial tree view. This summary corresponds to the workload of the matching subtree rooted at the node and the resources available on the processors that maintain the subtree. In particular, it includes the following information: 1) the total number of subscriptions in the subtree; 2) the total rate of events visiting the subtree; 3) the total capacity of processors managing the subtree. The first two items show the load associated with subscription storage and event matching. The third summarizes the resource devoted for managing the load. We define capacity as the network bandwidth of the processor instead of storage, since this is the limiting factor for matching and delivering events. This information reflects the heterogeneity of participating processors. The load-to-capacity ratio in the summary indicates whether the subtree is overloaded or underloaded.

Periodically, a processor sends to peers its load summaries about nodes along its Tree ID path (Section 4.1). Recall that this path stretches from the root to the first node (under pre-order) belonging to the processor. Figure 6 illustrates the Tree ID paths of peer B and D, and the gossip messages they send to A.

A maintains the storage and event processing load for the subtree it manages locally. After receiving load summaries from its peers, A can aggregate the load for the internal nodes in its partial tree. The summary about the root node gives the global load information. This information is loosely consistent. It is easy to see that the aggregation converges within $O(\log N)$ steps in a N-processor system, because information about one processor reaches all other processors within $O(\log N)$ forwarding steps, the

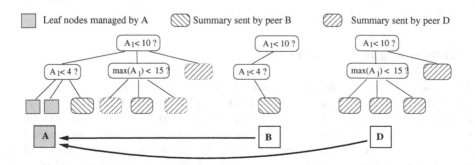

Fig. 6. Gossiping and aggregation of load information

diameter of a Skip Graph. With a typical heart-beat interval of 30 seconds, the aggregation converges within several minutes, during which time the overall load is unlikely to change by a substantial amount.

5.2   Processor Join

When a new processor joins the system, it contacts a known processor P that is currently in the system. P uses the load summary in its partial tree view to direct the join request. It navigates the tree, locally, to find a subtree with a high load level, as determined by the ratio of total load to capacity associated with the subtree. If this subtree is remote or obscure (defined in Section 4.1), the join request is forwarded towards that subtree, and eventually reaches a peer Q with high load level. This forwarding process is similar to the distributed tree navigation for inserting subscriptions and matching events.

After receiving the join request, Q divides the set of leaf nodes it manages and hands over one half to the joining processor. If there is only one leaf node, or if one leaf node has significantly higher load than others, this leaf is partitioned using algorithms described in Section 3.5. The joining processor receives from Q the leaf nodes, which also determines the new Tree ID of the joining processor. The processor then joins the Skip Graph and establishes its partial tree view by contacting the peers.

Section 3.5 describes two strategies of leaf node partitioning: split or replicate. If the high load is caused by larger than average number of subscriptions, we choose one of the various options to partition the set of subscriptions among the new branches. If the load is caused by high event rate to the subscriptions, we may replicate the subscriptions in the new branches to spread out the event processing load.

5.3   Processor Departure and Failures

Processors in the system may leave gracefully or fail/quit silently without warning. In the former case, it notifies its peers of the intention to leave and hands over the set of leaf nodes and subscriptions to its left-hand side peer, and the Skip Graph will route corresponding messages to this peer after the processor's departure.

Failures and non-cooperative departures are detected by periodic heart-beat messages. If a processor P does not hear from a peer for several consecutive heart-beat intervals, this peer is marked as failed and is excluded from the partial tree view. If the peer is the immediate right-hand side peer, P takes over the responsibility of managing the leaf nodes of the failed peer. In order to avoid data loss, we can replicate subscriptions to left hand side peers during normal operation. This replication strategy is used in many peer-to-peer systems [16,18,15].

5.4   Reactive Load Balancing

Besides the load-balanced join process, reactive load balancing of heavily loaded processors is also desirable. Such imbalance may be caused by insertion of new subscription, transfer of data after peer departure, or change of event traffic pattern. Processors in the system detect load imbalance from the global load information. If a processor sustains significantly higher load than global average, it can start a load balancing process by navigating the distributed tree to find an underloaded processor. This processor is forced to quit its current position, offload its work to its neighboring processor, and rejoin the system as the overloaded processors' neighbor in order to take over half of the load from the overloaded processor.

6   Experimental Results

In this section, we present our experimental results. We use two very different real world datasets for publish/subscribe workload. We also evaluate system scalability with larger synthetic workloads. We start by describing the example applications and the datasets before presenting the experimental results.

6.1   Example Applications

Stock quote alert is a popular publish/subscribe service. Users subscribe to events about stock price changes and transaction volume fluctuations. Such services are usually implemented with DBMS triggers in a centralized server. Similar subscriptions that specify numerical data ranges may be found in other systems like monitoring and sensor networks. Therefore, we use stock quote alert as one of our representative applications.

We use the stock quote dataset collected by Gupta *et al.* to evaluate Meghdoot [9]. It was obtained from Yahoo! Finance [23] by downloading the daily quotes of 100 stocks from 2/Jan/1998 to 31/Dec/2002. This event set contains 115,353 events. The schema and value range of the events are summarized in Table 2. The data distribution is highly skewed. Most stock prices/volumes are within a relatively narrow range, except for a few high price/volume stocks quotes.

We follow the method used in [9] to generate stock subscriptions. Subscriptions randomly select one of five templates designed to model common user interests in stock events. Table 3 lists the subscription templates and their probabilities. The parameters are generated using random draws from uniform distributions over the data ranges of the corresponding fields, while maintaining the constraints. The fifth template is a "rare" case of a broad subscription that matches any stock with trading volume above a given parameter. In the real world, users are usually interested in events specific to a narrow group of stocks. Therefore, this template is assigned a relatively low probability.

While stock quote events exhibit a well-formed schema with numerical attributes, a number of applications use semi-structured data representations. We use the CiteSeer scientific literature digital library [6] as a representative data source for such applications. CiteSeer uses the Open Archives Initiative [14] protocol to publish the metadata of its literature collection. This metadata is encoded in XML, which accomodates semi-structured data and allows for efficient data manipulation. We parse the XML records

Table 2. Schema of Stock Quote Events

Attribute	Date	Symbol	Open	High	Low	Close	Volume
Type	String	String	Float	Float	Float	Float	Integer
Minimal	2/Jan/98	aaa	0	0	0	0	0
Maximal	31/Dec/02	zzzzz	500	500	500	500	310000000

Table 3. Templates of Stock Quote Subscriptions

Subscription	Prob.	Description
$\{Symbol = P_1 \wedge P_2 \leq Open \leq P_3\}$	20%	Notify when stock P_1 opens with price between P_2 and P_3.
$\{Symbol = P_1 \wedge Low \leq P_2\}$	35%	Notify when the price of stock P_1 is at most P_2.
$\{Symbol = P_1 \wedge High \geq P_2\}$	35%	Notify when the price of stock P_1 is at least P_2.
$\{Symbol = P_1 \wedge Volume \geq P_2\}$	5%	Notify when stock P_1 is traded at least P_2.
$\{Volume \geq P_1\}$	5%	Notify when any stock is traded more than P_1.

published by CiteSeer to generate events one per publication, with the following extracted attributes: *Date, Title, Authors, Subject*, and *References*. We further extract *Keywords* from the subject line by removing stop words and obtaining the stems of the remaining words. The *Authors, Keywords*, and *References* fields are represented with the *Set* type defined in Section 3.1. Note that some fields, like *References*, might be missing in some cases due to incomplete records. A total of 574,128 events are extracted.

We generate three types of subscriptions for our experiments:

– $\{Authors \ni P\}$: notify when the author list of a newly published paper includes P. We select parameter P from the list of authors appearing in the data set, with probability proportional to the occurrence frequency.
– $\{Keywords \supseteq P\}$: notify when a newly published paper includes the keyword list P. P is a set of one to three keywords selected randomly from the set of keywords in the data set, with probability proportional to keyword occurrence frequencies.
– $\{References \ni P\}$: notify when a newly published paper cites another document P. Again, P is randomly chosen according to data distribution.

Besides the above two publish/subscribe data sets, we also use a synthetic workload to test system scalability, similar to that used in [4]. This workload uses events and subscriptions that specify one of more of 1000 numerical attributes. This synthetic workload models a general purpose publish/subscribe system that does not limit the users to a small set of pre-defined schemas. Each subscription specifies 1 to 10 predicates. Each predicate randomly selects an attribute, a comparison operator of $=, >, <, \leq$ or $\geq$, and a value between 0 to 999. We use either an uniform or a zipf distribution ($\alpha = 0.8$) to select the attributes. The operator and value fields are chosen uniformly randomly. Published events randomly specify between 1 to 20 attributes and their values, under the same distribution as for subscriptions.

We compare Brushwood matching tree against Meghdoot for the stock quote alert experiments. Meghdoot uses CAN to partition the multi-dimensional content-space to peer nodes. Meghdoot does not support the CiteSeer data set (due to the presence of set predicates) or the synthetic workload (due to the large number of attributes and the flexible event schema). So for these datasets, the experiments only evaluate our system under different parameters.

6.2 System Scalability

We first use the synthetic workload to evaluate system scalability. We simulate from 1024 to 16384 peer processors. The number of subscriptions is fixed at 1 million. The

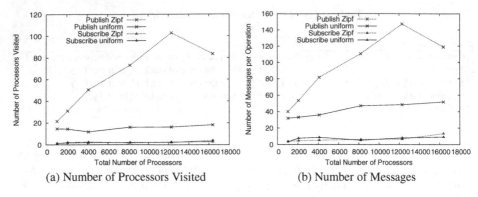

(a) Number of Processors Visited   (b) Number of Messages

Fig. 7. Synthetic workload: cost vs. system scale

number of event messages is 110000. We start with a single processor and add the remaining at random intervals, in order to simulate a peer join process. In the mean time, we insert the subscriptions into the system. We count the number of messages forwarded for inserting subscriptions and publishing events as a measure of the communication cost. Some of the messages require further processing at the recipients: to insert a subscription or to match an event to local subscriptions. We measure this cost as the number of processors processing the request. We refer to this number as the *textitspan* of the operation, and the processors as *visited* by the operation. For subscriptions, it is the number of sites the subscription is replicated to. For events, it is the number of nodes that need to perform predicate evaluation or matching.

Figure 7 depicts the average number of processors visited and the average number of messages forwarded for a subscription/event. Even with 16384 nodes, a typical publishing event spans less than 1% of the processors, showing good scalability. The maximal span we observed is about 250.

When attributes are selected using the Zipf distribution, the span of publishing events increases much faster than under uniform distribution. The reason is that a skewed distribution generates many similar subscriptions and events. In order to balance the load, these closely related subscriptions are partitioned across different processors. Events matching such subscriptions have to visit more partitions.

An interesting trend in Figure 7 is that the event span decreases when the number of processors increase from 12288 to 16384 (for Zipf distributed attributes). Meanwhile, the degree of subscription replication (indicated by the number of processors visited for subscription insertion) increases from 2 to 4. This is because that as more processors join, while the total number of subscriptions remains the same, our tree partitioning algorithm devotes the newly joined processors to store replicated subscriptions, thereby decreasing the number of processors that an event has to visit.

6.3 Stock Quote Alert

Next we evaluate the performance of our system and Meghdoot using the stock quote dataset. We scale the system from 128 processors to 8192 (the N parameters in the graphs). We also scale the number of subscriptions proportionally to the number of processors (100N).

Figure 8 shows the number of messages forwarded by subscription insertion and event matching as we increase the number of peer processors. Compared to Meghdoot, our scheme shows a substantially lower cost for processing events. This is first because we partition the subscription set based on data distribution. Meghdoot uses CAN's partitioning method that splits a zone into halves of equal sizes (The reason for this regular split is to avoid interleaving of the zone spaces that can significantly increase the number of peering zones.) Therefore it suffers load imbalance under the highly skewed dataset. In order to alleviate this imbalance, Meghdoot replicates the overloaded nodes, resulting in a higher number of subscription messages. Another reason is the flexible value partitioning method used in the matching tree (Section 3.4). Meghdoot partitions the subscriptions by Min/Max range specified for the attributes. This approach splits the subscriptions into non-overlapping sets, but an event may need to visit both zones after the split. We use value range partitioning method that allows events to visit only one branch after the partition. Our approach also replicate some subscriptions, but only limited to broad ones. So the subscription cost is still lower than that of Meghdoot.

Figure 9 shows the histogram of event spans (the number of processors visited by the event). Under all three settings of system scale, our scheme demonstrates relatively small and stable span, due to reasons discussed above.

Next, we compare the load balance of the two systems. We consider several aspects of load balance: subscription storage, event matching, and routing state. Routing state is represented by the number of peers that processors maintain.

Figure 10 (a) presents the cumulative distribution (CDF) of the number of subscriptions managed by the processors. Our system exhibits evenly balanced storage loads, while most of the subscriptions in Meghdoot are managed by a small number of nodes. The imbalance in Meghdoot is due to the fact that only some of the zones (the portion of the CAN space above the diagonal plane) are used to store subscriptions. Moreover, the constraint of equal-space partitioning also limits its ability to achieve balanced load under skewed data distribution.

Figure 10 (b) depicts the CDF of the percentage of events prcessed by the processors. Note that each event may be examined by multiple processors, so the total is higher than the number of events submitted to the system. Our system shows better load bal-

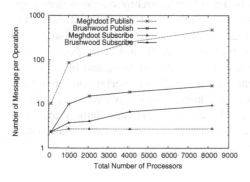

Fig. 8. Stock: Number of Messages vs. System Scale

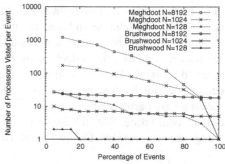

Fig. 9. Stock: Distribution of Number of Processors Visited for Publishing an Event

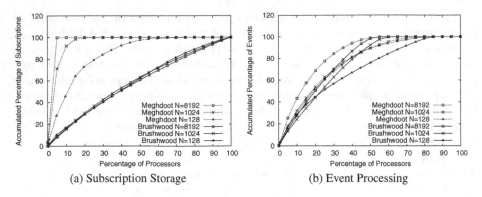

(a) Subscription Storage   (b) Event Processing

Fig. 10. Stock: load distribution

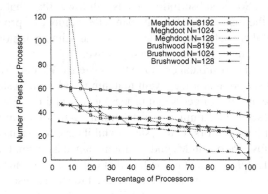

Fig. 11. Stock: Distribution of Number of Peers per Node

ance in event processing, because the subscriptions are more evenly partitioned among the peers. Some of the subscriptions match very broad range of events (like those only specifying *Volume* in Table 3), Both Brushwood and Meghdoot replicate some subscriptions to share the event matching load. Therefore, there is not a significant difference between the two schemes in balancing the loads associated with event processing.

We discussed the routing state balance problem in Section 4.2. In Skip Graphs, the peering relationship is decided by random membership vectors, and hence is not affected by skewed key distributions. Meghdoot uses CAN for overlay routing, which decides peering by zone neighborhood. Therefore, larger zones may have more peers if the zones are partitioned into different sizes under a skewed data distribution. In a high dimensional space, this imbalance is more significant since zones can make contact along more dimensions. Figure 11 confirms this intuition.

6.4 Literature Reference Notification

Now we present the results of the CiteSeer experiments. We use simulation settings similar to the above tests, except that the subscriptions choose parameter values based on a real distribution derived from the data set, instead of using uniform random distributions. Figure 12 shows the CDF of the subscription storage and event matching load on the processors. Although the contents of subscriptions and events have skewed distributions, the load balancing mechanisms in Brushwood ensure good load balance.

Figure 13 (a) (b) shows the cost of inserting subscriptions and the cost of processing events. Both the number of messages and the number of nodes visited are small. Since the attributes *Authors*, *Keywords*, and *References* are of *Set* type, the span of subscription and event messages is mainly decided by the number of items specified. In this real-world data set, the number of authors, keywords and references are usually small. Therefore the Brushwood approach performs well. However, we do observe a sharp increase in publishing cost as the number of processors is increased from 4096 to 8192. This is due to the dynamic load balancing mechanism discussed in Section 5.4. As the peer population increases, popular subscriptions can receive a significant number of subscribers. Therefore, peers maintaining them get overloaded and split their load to more processors. As a result, events involving such subscriptions have to flood more

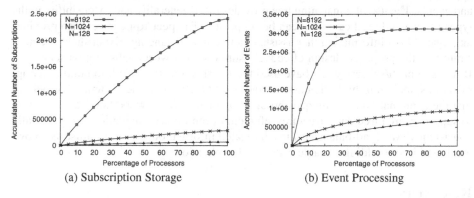

(a) Subscription Storage   (b) Event Processing

Fig. 12. CiteSeer: cumulative load distribution

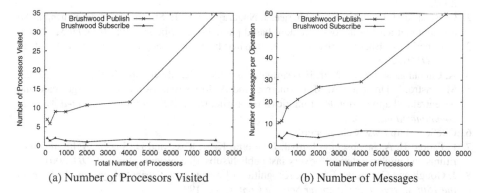

(a) Number of Processors Visited   (b) Number of Messages

Fig. 13. CiteSeer: cost of operations vs. system scale

peers, while each peer still maintains a reasonable share of load (Figure 13). We did not observe such a trend in previous experiments because their subscription values are drawn from a uniform distribution. Though there is an increase in publishing cost, we do note that the reactive load balancing mechanism manages to balance load even in the face of skewed subscription patterns.

7 Conclusions

In this paper, we propose a content-based publish/subscribe middleware built by distributing a matching tree over a peer-to-peer system. The main contribution is in the decentralized navigation and management algorithms for the distributed matching tree in peer-to-peer settings. Our system achieves efficient event matching while requiring only small amounts of state to be maintained by the peers. Processors in the system build partial views of the global tree based on information about only a logarithmic number of peers. Therefore, the system provides high scalability. Compared to other peer-to-peer approaches, it imposes no restrictions over the schemas associated with subscriptions and events. The use of a matching tree provides more generality and extensibility in the types of data and predicates that can be supported. The peer-to-peer tree also provides aggregated load information that assists reactive load balancing. Experiments demonstrate that the proposed design effectively supports real world subscription scenarios. Besides publish/subscribe, we have used the Brushwood framework to build other applications, including high dimensional index and distributed file systems. We believe that the combination of techniques brought together in Brushwood (such as the ability to support search tree data structures, efficient decentralized navigation using partially consistent views, load-balance using aggregated information) shows promise as a powerful toolkit for building scalable distributed applications.

References

1. J. Aspnes and G. Shah. Skip Graphs. In *Proceedings of Symposium on Discrete Algorithms*, 2003.
2. G. Banavar, T. Chandra, B. Mukherjee, J. Nagarajarao, R. E. Strom, and D. C. Sturman. An efficient multicast protocol for content-based publish-subscribe systems. In *ICDCS*, 1999.
3. S. Banerjee, B. Bhattacharjee, and C. Kommareddy. Scalable application layer multicast. In *SIGCOMM*, 2002.
4. A. Carzaniga and A. L. Wolf. Forwarding in a content-based network. In *SIGCOMM*, 2003.
5. M. Castro, P. Druschel, A.-M. Kermarrec, and A. Rowstron. SCRIBE : A large-scale and decentralized application-level multicast infrastructure. *IEEE Journal on Selected Areas in communications*, 2002.
6. CiteSeer. http://www.citeseer.org/.
7. F. Fabret, H. A. Jacobsen, F. Llirbat, J. Pereira, K. A. Ross, and D. Shasha. Filtering algorithms and implementation for very fast publish/subscribe systems. In *SIGMOD*, 2001.
8. J. Gough and G. Smith. Efficient recognition of events in a distributed system. In *Proc. of the 18th Australasian Computer Science Conference*, 1995.
9. A. Gupta, O. D. Sahin, D. Agrawal, and A. E. Abbadi. Meghdoot: content-based publish/subscribe over p2p networks. In *Proc. of the 5th ACM/IFIP/USENIX International Conference on Middleware*, 2004.

10. E. N. Hanson, M. Chaabouni, C.-H. Kim, and Y.-W. Wang. A predicate matching algorithm for database rule systems. In *SIGMOD*, 1990.
11. N. J. A. Harvey, M. B. Jones, S. Saroiu, M. Theimer, and A. Wolman. SkipNet: A Scalable Overlay Network with Practical Locality Properties. In *USITS*, 2003.
12. Y. hua Chu, S. G. Rao, and H. Zhang. A case for end system multicast. In *SIGMETRICS*, 2000.
13. Object Management Group. Corba event service specification (version 1.1), March 2001.
14. Open Archives Initiative. http://www.openarchives.org/.
15. S. Ratnasamy, P. Francis, M. Handley, R. Karp, and S. Shenker. A scalable content addressable network. In *Proceedings of ACM SIGCOMM*, 2001.
16. A. Rowstron and P. Druschel. Pastry: Scalable, decentralized object location and routing for large-scale peer-to-peer systems. In *Middleware*, 2001.
17. B. Segall and D. Arnold. Elvin has left the building: A publish/subscribe notification service with quenching. In *Proceeding of AUUG97*, 1997.
18. I. Stoica, R. Morris, D. Karger, F. Kaashoek, and H. Balakrishnan. Chord: A scalable peer-to-peer lookup service for internet applications. In *SIGCOMM*, 2001.
19. D. Tam, R. Azimi, and H.-A. jacobsen. Building content-based publish/subscribe systems with distributed hash tables. In *Internation Workshop on Databases, Information Systems and Peer-to-Peer Computing*, 2003.
20. TIBCO. http://www.tibco.com/.
21. R. van Renesse and K. P. Birman. Scalable management and data mining using astrolabe. In *IPTPS*, 2002.
22. Y.-M. Wang, L. Qiu, D. Achlioptas, G. Das, P. Larson, and H. J. Wang. Subscription partitioning and routing in content-based publish/subscribe networks. In *16th International Symposium on Distributed Computing*, 2002.
23. Yahoo! Finance. http://finance.yahoo.com/.
24. C. Zhang, A. Krishnamurthy, and R. Y. Wang. Brushwood: Distributed trees in peer-to-peer systems. In *IPTPS*, 2005.

WReX: A Scalable Middleware Architecture to Enable XML Caching for Web-Services

Junichi Tatemura[1], Oliver Po[1], Arsany Sawires[2,*],
Divyakant Agrawal[1], and K. Selçuk Candan[1]

[1] NEC Laboratories America,
10080 North Wolfe Road,
Suite SW3-350, Cupertino, CA 95014
{tatemura, oliver, agrawal, candan}@sv.nec-labs.com
[2] Department of Computer Science,
University of California Santa Barbara,
Santa Barbara, CA 93106
arsany@cs.ucsb.edu

Abstract. Web service caching, i.e., caching the responses of XML web service requests, is needed for designing scalable web service architectures. Such caching of dynamic content requires maintaining the caches appropriately to reflect dynamic updates to the back-end data source. In the database, especially relational, context, extensive research has addressed the problem of incremental view maintenance. However, only a few attempts have been made to address the cache maintenance problem for XML web service messages. We propose a middleware solution that bridges the gap between the cached web service responses and the back-end dynamic data source. We assume, for generality, that the back-end source has a general XML logical data model. Since the RDBMS technology is widely used for storing and querying XML data, we show how our solution can be implemented when the XML data source is implemented on top of an RDBMS. Such implementation exploits the well-known maturity of the RDBMS technology. The middleware solution described in this paper has the following features that distinguish it from the existing technology in this area: (1) It provides declarative description of Web Services based on rich and standards-based view specification language (XQuery/XPath); (2) No knowledge of the source XML schema is assumed, instead the source can be any general well-formed XML data; (3) The solution can be easily deployed on RDBMS, and (4) The size of the auxiliary data needed for the cache maintenance does not depend on the source data size, therefore, the solution is highly scalable. Experimental evaluation is conducted to assess the performance benefits of the proposed approach.

Keywords: web services, caching, XML views, path expressions, XML-relational mapping.

---

* This work has been done during the author's summer internship at NEC.

G. Alonso (Ed.): Middleware 2005, LNCS 3790, pp. 124–143, 2005.
© IFIP International Federation for Information Processing 2005

1 Introduction

Performance degradation of a Web Service can significantly impact the response times of front-end applications that use it. Especially for Web Services that provide dynamic content to many users (such as product information services), latency observed by the users is caused not only by the network transmission, but mainly by server overload at the back-end application. Offloading processing from the back-end applications is thus essential in providing Web Services scalability. Therefore, caching is a key enabling technology for scalable Web Service delivery.

A Web Service cache must handle request and response messages (typically formatted using XML); thus the cache must process (e.g., parse XML content of) a request message to identify the response message to be returned. Therefore, a standard HTTP cache cannot be directly employed when caching Web Services. Furthermore, in order to achieve loose coupling of remote services, Web Services usually handle messages with coarser granularities than traditional distributed object messaging such as CORBA. This fact makes it more difficult to map data source updates to the cached messages. Caching messages for data-driven Web Services thus requires middleware support for appropriate propagation of updates from the source to the cache.

It is commonly understood that an XML data/query model can be implemented on a relational model to leverage from the proven and highly-optimized storage and query capabilities already provided by existing relational database systems [15]. Thus, one approach to caching Web Service could be to apply existing technologies that manage data dependency between web content and data in relational databases, such as Data Update Propagation (DUP)[3], view invalidation [2], invalidation based on query templates [4], and many other works on view maintenance. However, these relational approaches will be very inefficient because an XML query can involve too many join operations when translated into SQL.

In this paper, we propose a middleware architecture, WReX, that bridges the semantic gaps among Web Service messages, a relational data model, and an XML data model, for caching Web Services. To make the proposed middleware solution applicable to various data sources, the WReX represents the source data in the caches as XML views and provides a declarative way to define Web Services to access the data. The WReX architecture (Sections 3 and 4) aims at resolving the impedance mismatch between the cached data content and the underlying database technology by applying recent XML-specific view maintenance techniques transparently in a relational setting.

Consequently, the WReX introduced in this paper consists of two complementary components: (1) Web Service Content Description (WSCD) mechanism fills the gap between Web Service messages and XML views of the source data and (2) XML view maintenance mapped to relational storage fills the gap between XML views and updates to the source data. This novel middleware architecture has the following features that distinguish it from the previous works: (1) It provides declarative description of Web Services based on rich and standards-based view specification language (XQuery/XPath); (2) No knowledge of the source XML schema is assumed, instead the source can be any general well-formed XML data; (3) The solution can be easily deployed on RDBMS, and (4) The size of the auxiliary data needed for the cache maintenance does not depend on the source data size, therefore, the solution is highly scalable. Experimental evaluation is conducted to assess the performance benefits of the proposed approach. Experimental evaluations presented in Section 5 establish the performance benefits of the WReX middleware approach.

2   Cache-Enabled Service Middleware Architecture

Figure 1 illustrates WReX, a Web Service middleware architecture enhanced with *web service caching*. WReX consists of a Web Service Application Server, an XML Data Source, and an Update Manager, which are implemented on top of a common Web computing platform (e.g., a J2EE application server and a relational database server). WReX lets users describe and deploy Web Services that deliver content generated from their own data sources. Given the description of a Web Service, the middleware manages request/response message caches.

A Web Service application is deployed on top of the WS Application Server and the XML Data Source as can be seen Figure 1. The application has three major parts: (1) data (data source to be published), (2) content logic (description of message content to be generated from the data source) , and (3) management logic (user authentication, logging, and metering). The *cache-enabled* Web Service application server consists of the following components: (1) Various management components, (2) a message content cache component, (3) a content processor, and (4) an XPath cache. Management components manipulate messages (e.g., insert data in the header) genereted by the content processor.

Management components handle management tasks such as user accounting and monitoring with approprite transformation of message content. Web service

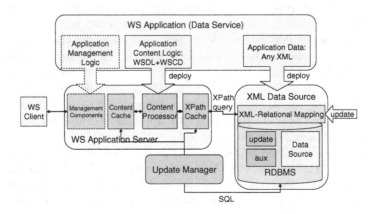

Fig. 1. WReX: Web Service Caching Architecture

messages that contain management information are much less reusable even if actual content delivered to the user (e.g., product information) is reusable. By separating management functions as these components, WReX lets the other components focus on managing relationships between message content and the source data and makes cache more applicable.

The content logic specifies how to generate content of a message in response to a request message from a Web Service client. A shortcoming of the existing technologies is that, the Web Service definition language (WSDL) only defines interfaces (such as data types) of request/response messages, but does not provide content relationship between request and response messages [18]. To bridge this gap, we introduce a description platform, Web Service Content Description (WSCD), which provides a template of a response message that can contain references to data in a request message and queries to the source data. When the application server receives a request message, it generates a response message by integrating a message template and content fragments retrieved from the data source. Caching is applied to both generated response messages (Content Cache) and retrieved content from the source (XPath Cache).

This approach is similar to JSP (Java Server Pages) or ESI (Edge Side Includes). JSP provides a template of dynamic web pages and lets the application server construct a page from the template and content fragments generated by applications. Several application servers provide caching functionality for such content fragments in order to reduce application overload. ESI is a markup language used to define web content components for dynamic assembly and delivery of web pages at edge servers. The edge server dynamically integrates fragments into a web page and needs to retrieve only non-cacheable or expired fragments from the original servers. Datta et al. [5] has extended this approach to enable more flexible content composition on the edge server resulting in enhanced cacheability and reusability of content. In this sense, our approach can be seen as an extension of the JSP/ESI concept from HTML to XML context with XML cache update management. Another related example is the Weave management system [19] that enables the user to create Web content using declarative specification and caches various intermediary data such as views of relational data, XML page fragments, and HTML pages. Although it supports XML content generation from relational databases, update maintenance between cached XML content and data source is based on time stamps and specified with event-condition-action rules.

To enable caching of XPath queries to the data source as well as the message responses from the Web Service itself, the Update Manager needs to monitor updates in the data source and identify changes in the cached results. Here, note that an XML-aware data source is commonly implemented on an XML-aware RDBMS, which can leverage from the maturity of RDBMS implementations, extensive tuning, proven scalability, sophisticated query processing and query optimizers. However, even though the underlying DBMS is relational, traditional view/cache management solutions for relational data can not be directly applied to an XML data/query model. For example, CachePortal [2] automates cache update management based on a view invalidation technique in a relational model. However, when a query involves many join operations, which is the case of XML queries in a relational model, it is very inefficient due to costs from an extra database snapshot and over invalidation. Therefore, we introduce an update management middleware component which benefits from the relational nature of the back-end database, while deploying XML-specific view management techniques (i.e., the Update Manager that accesses the data source through SQL queries (Figure 1)).

2.1   Web Service Content Description (WSCD)

Given a service request, the Web Service generates response messages based on the service logic. The interface between the request and response is usually defined using WSDL (Web Service Definition Language). WSDL, on the other hand, does not describe content relationships between request and response messages, which are needed for managing updates. We propose Web Service Content Description (WSCD) language that describes how a response message is generated for a given operation specified in WSDL. Formally, the WSCD for a service operation o consists of three parts: (V, T, S), where V is the variable assignment definition, T is the template definition, and S is the source references.

- The variable assignment definition V defines how to extract data from a request message. Mapping from a request message to variables is given by pairs of name and XPaths: $V = \{(name_i, xpath_i)\}$. Given a request message, which can be seen as an XML document, V generates a specific variable assignment $v = \{name_i = value_i\}$. In addition to the generation of a response message, v is used as the identity of the message cache: the identity consists of an operation name and a variable assignment (o, v).
- The template T defines the content of a response message with references to the variables V. The template can contain XQuery expressions to dynamically insert data derived from the data source.
- The source reference S maps URIs of data source service endpoints to document URIs referred to by XQuery expressions in T.

Figure 2 shows an example of a WSCD description. Elements `<cd:Variables>`, `<cd:Template>`, `<cd:ServiceEPR>` correspond to (V, T, S), respectively.

A variable is defined with a part of the request message (i.e. input) of a WSDL operation and an XPath expression that indicates data within the part. Combined with WSDL binding information, it is translated to a full XPath expression applied to a request message, for example:

```
"/Envelope/Body/GetBookRequest/Category/text()"
```

in case of the SOAP literal binding. A template specifies an XML content of a part of the response message (i.e., output) of a WSDL operation. It can contain an XQuery specified in `<cd:Query>`. The query may refer to variables defined in the variables part.

```
<cd:WSCD xmlns:cd=... operation="GetBook">
 <cd:Variables>
  <cd:Let name="category" part="body"
     path="/GetBookRequest/Category/text()"/>
  <cd:Let name="maxprice" part="body"
     path="/GetBookRequest/Max/text()"/>
  <cd:Let name="minprice" part="body"
     path="/GetBookRequest/Min/text()"/>
 </cd:Variables>
 <cd:Template part="body">
  <GetBookResponse>
    <cd:Query>FOR ... LET... WHERE... RETURN...</cd:Query>
  </GetBookResponse>
 </cd:Template>
 <cd:ServiceEPR .../>
</cd:WSCD>
```

Fig. 2. Example of Web Service Content Description

Note that WSCD is meant to provide a simple specification of message content in a request-response Web Service operation. If the user wants a full set of programming functionality to create Web Service (such as event handling), a special programming language for Web Services, such as XL [8], could be used instead of WSCD. In fact, since XL uses XQuery expressions to access data, a possible extension of WReX is to support the XL language, in addition to WSCD, for services with complicated interactions.

Our WSCD approach is also related to "declarative web services" [1], used for composing dynamic XML documents by importing fragments. For optimized data management, a declarative web service that provides fragments is defined as an XQuery on data sources. Although they focus on data replication issues in a distributed environment, they also state possibility of querying cost reduction through an update propagation mechanism, on which we focus in this paper.

2.2 Cache Management Using WSCD

The WSCD description of Web Service messages provides a framework to manage Web Service caching. First, the system needs to identify the matching incoming requests and cached response messages. This task is done by extracting values from an incoming message with XPath expressions in the variable definition V since the cache identity is given as a variable assignment (o, v). Efficient filtering [7] can be applied to process multiple XPath matching results in a scalable manner. Then we focus on the second task: to manage update dependencies between cached messages and the data at the source.

As described above, the WSCD template contains a set of XQuery expressions $XQ = \{xq_i\}$ to insert dynamic data from the source into response messages. Since an XQuery expression xq contains references to the variables V and the source S, what the system needs to manage is an XQuery instance (xq, v, S):

when the result of an XQuery instance is updated, the message cache items that contain this result must be updated or invalidated.

An XQuery statement accesses documents (i.e., the source data) through XPath expressions. Thus, a set of XPath expressions $XP = \{xp_i\}$ is extracted from XQueries XQ and is given to the XPath cache component, which caches an XPath instance: (xp, v, S). The XPath Cache receives an XPath query from XQuery Processor and returns the query result from the cache. If it is not cached, the XPath Cache issues an XPath query to the data source. The data source returns the query result and makes available *auxiliary data* required to maintain XPath cache (Section 3).

When the Update Manager observes updates in the data source, it determines the impact of the source update to cached XPath results. During this process, the Update Manager uses the auxiliary data and update data to identify the cache updates. It may also access the source data if needed. Then it maintains cached results in the XPath Cache affected by the update. Consequently, message cache items that refer to the affected XPath instances are also either invalidated or maintained. In order to effectively manage update dependency between message cache and the data source, the WReX uses our XML-specific view maintenance techniques described next.

3   XPath Cache Maintenance

In this section we describe the data model and the incremental XPath maintenance technique WReX relies on. Further details of both are presented in [13].

3.1   Data Model

As described earlier, the underlying logical model of the data source is XML. Each XML data source is represented as an ordered tree in which every node n is a pair $\langle n.id, n.label \rangle$ where $n.id$ is a node identifier that uniquely identifies the node and $n.label$ is a string that describes the node type and/or value. We use upper-case letters to represent the node labels. For example, A, B, and C are node labels. We use numeric subscripts to distinguish different nodes that have the same label. Thus, A_i and A_j refer to two distinct nodes with the same label A. Figure 3 shows an example document tree and path expression that will be used as a running example to illustrate the incremental maintenance technique.

3.2   Update Model

A source update is a transformation of the source XML document. Any source transformation can be expressed in terms of the two primitive operations of addition and deletion of leaf nodes. Thus, for simplicity, in this section, we focus on the maintenance operations needed to handle these two types of source updates. Formally, we model a source update $\mathcal{U}$ as a pair $\langle \mathcal{U}.type, \mathcal{U}.path \rangle$ where $\mathcal{U}.type$ is the type of the update: *Add* (add a leaf node) or *Delete* (delete a leaf node). $\mathcal{U}.path$ is the path of all the ancestors of the added or deleted node

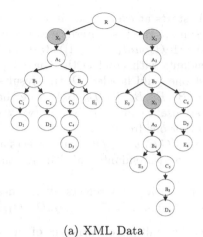

(a) XML Data

/A//B[Count(//E) ≥ 1 ∨ Count(/D) ≥ 1]//C[Count(//E) = 0]//D

(b) XPath Query

Fig. 3. (a) An Example XML Tree and (b) a path-expression $\mathcal{E}$

starting with the document root and ending with the added or deleted node itself. The added or deleted node itself is referred to as $\mathcal{U}.node$. For example, $\mathcal{U} = \langle Add, (R, X_1, A_1, B_1, Z)\rangle$ represents the addition of node Z as a child node of node B_1 in the XML document shown in Figure 3(a).

3.3 Query Model

Path expressions are the basic building blocks of XML queries and therefore are fundamental to implementing Web Services in our framework. The cache content is the result of applying path expression-based queries to the source document. A path expression $\mathcal{E}$ of size N is a sequence of N steps: $(s_1, s_2, \cdots s_N)$. A step s_i is a triple $\langle s_i.axis, s_i.label, s_i.pred\rangle$ where (i) $s_i.axis$ is an axis test (child '/' or descendent '//'); (ii) $s_i.label$ is a label test; and (iii) $s_i.pred$ is an optional predicate test which can be any complex condition examining the labels and the structure of the nodes in the subtree of the node being tested. $Pred_i(n)$ is said to be *true* if and only if (1) Node n belongs to the source tree, and (2) $s_i.pred$ evaluates to *true* at node n or step s_i does not have a predicate test. For example, $Pred_3(C_1)$ in the example is *true* because C_1 satisfies the condition $s_3.pred$ since C_1 has no descendants labeled E.

Given an expression $\mathcal{E}$, a document tree $\mathcal{D}$, and a sequence of context nodes $\mathcal{C}$ (the set of staring nodes from $\mathcal{D}$), a query, $\mathcal{Q} = q(\mathcal{E}, \mathcal{C}, \mathcal{D})$ returns a sequence of nodes $\mathcal{R}$ as a result. For example, consider the query $\mathcal{Q} = q(\mathcal{E}, \mathcal{C}, \mathcal{D})$ where: $\mathcal{D}$ is the document tree shown in Figure 3(a), $\mathcal{C} = (X_1, X_2, X_3)$ are the shaded nodes the same figure, and $\mathcal{E}$ is the path expression specified in Figure 3(b). Given this query,

1. the first step s_1 ($/A$) starts at every node in $\mathcal{C}$ and selects all the children
   with label A; this results in the first intermediate result $\mathcal{R}_1 = (A_1, A_2, A_3)$.
2. s_2 ($//B[Count(//E) \geq 1 \vee Count(/D) \geq 1]$) starts at every node in $\mathcal{R}_1$ and
   selects all the descendants with label B that have at least one descendant
   labeled E or at least one child labeled D; this results in the second intermediate result $\mathcal{R}_2 = (B_2, B_3, B_4, B_4, B_5, B_5)$. Note that B_4 - and also B_5 -
   occurs twice in $\mathcal{R}_2$ because it can be derived in two ways from nodes of $\mathcal{R}_1$,
   one from A_2 and another one from A_3.
3. starting at $\mathcal{R}_2$, step s_3 ($/C[Count(//E) = 0]$) selects all the descendants labeled C that have no descendants labeled E; this results in $\mathcal{R}_3 = (C_3, C_4, C_5, C_5, C_5)$.
4. finally, s_4 ($//D$) starts at $\mathcal{R}_3$ and selects all the descendants labeled D.
   Hence, the final result of $\mathcal{Q}$ is $\mathcal{R} = \mathcal{R}_4 = (D_3, D_3, D_4, D_4, D_4)$.

We differentiate between the multiple occurrences of the same node in a result
by using a numeric superscript. For example, we denote the result $\mathcal{R}$ as $\mathcal{R} = (D_3^1, D_3^2, D_4^1, D_4^2, D_4^3)$.

For a node $n \in \mathcal{R}$, the sub-sequence of the ancestors of a node n that matched
the steps of $\mathcal{E}$, and thus caused n to appear in $\mathcal{R}$ is referred to as the *result
path* of n and denoted as $ResultPath(n)$. $ResultPath_i(n)$, where $i \geq 0$, is the
i^{th} element in $ResultPath(n)$. In the example query above, $ResultPath(D_3^1) = (X_1, A_1, B_2, C_3, D_3)$ and $ResultPath(D_3^1)_2 = (X_1, A_1, B_2, C_3, D_3)$ is B_2.

3.4   Incremental Maintenance of Path Expression Results

A source update $\mathcal{U}$ can affect the cached result $\mathcal{R}$ by adding or deleting nodes to any
of the intermediate results $\mathcal{R}_i$. The primary reason of such additions and deletions is
changing the truth values of the expression predicates at the steps of the expression:

> If an update changes a predicate $Pred_i(n)$ from $false(true)$ to $true(false)$,
> we say that the update directly adds (deletes) node n at step i.

A direct addition (deletion) at step i can induce other indirect additions (deletions)
in steps $j > i$. The final result $\mathcal{R}$ is affected if and only if the effect propagates all
the way to step N. For example, if $\mathcal{U} = (Add, (R, X_1, A_1, B_1, E_5))$, then $Pred_2(B_1)$
changes from *false* to *true*. The direct effect of this is to add B_1 to $\mathcal{R}_2$. The resulting
indirect effects are the addition of C_1 and C_2 to $\mathcal{R}_3$ and then the addition of D_1 and
D_2 to $\mathcal{R}_4$. For each step, the incremental maintenance process first discovers all the
direct effects and then uses these effects to discover the indirect ones.

Discovering the Direct Effects of the Updates. We identify the direct effects
of the updates in two phases: **Axis&Label test** and the **predicate test**.

Phase I - Axis&label test: Let us define δ_i^+ and δ_i^- as the sequences of all nodes
that $\mathcal{U}$ directly adds/deletes at $\mathcal{R}_i$ respectively. Let also $\delta_i = \delta_i^+ \sqcup \delta_i^-$. The job
of this phase is to identify a sequence Δ_i such that we can guarantee, without
any source queries, that $\delta_i \sqsubseteq \Delta_i$.

In [13], we showed that every node n in δ_i must also belong to $\mathcal{U}.path$. Moreover, for a node n to be directly added to be in δ_i, it must have an ancestor

in every $\mathcal{R}_j$, $j < i$. Since n itself belongs to $\mathcal{U}.path$, then all its ancestors also belong to $\mathcal{U}.path$. This suggests that $\mathcal{U}.path$ has much of the information needed to identify the nodes of δ_i. In fact, applying the axes and labels tests to $\mathcal{U}.path$, ignoring the predicate tests, provides a sequence Δ_i which is guaranteed to be a supersequence of δ_i. This is because this process uses a relaxed selection condition (it ignores the predicate tests, which evaluation requires querying the source) over the branch $\mathcal{U}.path$ which is guaranteed to include all the nodes of all the δ_i's. Computing the Δ_i's from $\mathcal{U}.path$ proceeds very similar to computing the $\mathcal{R}_i$'s from the source tree $\mathcal{D}$. For example, consider an update $\mathcal{U}$ of adding a node D_6 as a child of D_4. In this case, $\mathcal{U}.path$ is the tree branch that starts with the root R and ends with D_6. Computing the different Δ_i's as described above results in: $\Delta_0 = (X_2, X_3)$, $\Delta_1 = (A_2, A_3)$, $\Delta_2 = (B_3, B_4, , B_4, B_5, B_5)$, $\Delta_3 = (C_5, C_5, C_5)$, $\Delta_4 = (D_4, D_4, D_4, D_6, D_6, D_6)$. Note that the only nodes that will be directly added are the three occurrences of D_6 that appear in Δ_4; all the other nodes n in all the computed Δ_i's will not be added or deleted because $\mathcal{U}$ did not affect $Pred_i(n)$. Note that, because D_6 did not exist before $\mathcal{U}$ occurred, the value $Pred_i(D_6)$, $\forall i$ is $false$ before $\mathcal{U}$. Similarly, if an update deletes a node n from the source tree, the value $Pred_i(n)$, $\forall i$ is $false$ after $\mathcal{U}$.

Phase II - Predicate test: This phase identifies the exact sequence δ_i by determining which nodes in Δ_i had their predicate values changed due to the update.

To detect such changes we need to compare, for every node in δ_i, the values of $Pred_i(n)$ before and after $\mathcal{U}$ occurred. Let us denote the value of the predicate before the update occurred as $Pred_i^{before}(n)$ and the value after the update as $Pred_i^{after}(n)$. The value of $Pred_i^{after}(n)$ can be easily calculated by querying the source. The value of $Pred_i^{before}(n)$, on the other hand, cannot be computed by a source query because the update $\mathcal{U}$ has already been incorporated at the source. Once again, in [13], we showed that we can deduce the value of $Pred_i^{before}(n)$ using the information of the result paths. Specifically, we showed that if we define $RP_i(n)$ to be $true$ if and only if n is the ith element of the result path of some node in $\mathcal{R}$, then we can take $Pred_i^{before}(n) = RP_i(n)$. Therefore, we keep the result paths' information as auxiliary data with the cached result $\mathcal{R}$. With that, we compute $Pred_i^{before}(n)$ without issuing any source queries. To compute the size of this auxiliary data, recall that each result path is of length $N + 1$; if M is the size of the cached result $\mathcal{R}$, then the size of the auxiliary data is clearly $O(M * N)$. Thus the auxiliary data size is bounded by the expression size and the result size and it does not depend on the source data size.

Discovering the Indirect Effects of the Updates To discover the indirect effects from the direct ones, we need to handle two cases:

1. *Indirect additions due to direct additions:* when a node n is directly added to $\mathcal{R}_i$ then, in order to retrieve the indirect additions at $\mathcal{R}$, the maintenance algorithm issues a source query with context as n and with the steps sequence $(s_{i+1}, s_{i+2}, \cdots, s_N)$. This query is denoted as $q((s_{i+1}, s_{i+2}, \cdots, s_N), (n), \mathcal{D})$.

Incremental_Maintenance (Expression $\mathcal{E}$, Update $\mathcal{U}$)

1- $\Delta_0 = \mathcal{C} \cap \mathcal{U}.path$
      $\mathcal{R}^+ = \mathcal{R}^- = ()$ //Empty sequences
      $i = 1$ // loop variable
2-   WHILE $(i \leq N$ AND Δ_{i-1} is not empty)
   2-1 $j = i$
      WHILE $(s_j$ has no predicate test AND $j < N)$ j++
   2-2 $\Delta_j = q((s_i, s_{i+1}, \cdots, s_j).axis\&label, \Delta_{i-1}, \mathcal{U}.path)$
   2-3 Let $\mathcal{T}_j = (n | n \in \Delta_j \wedge Pred_j^{after}(n) = true)$
   2-4 $\delta_j^+ = (n | n \in \mathcal{T}_j \wedge RP_j(n) = false)$
   2-5 $\mathcal{R}^+ = \mathcal{R}^+ \sqcup q((s_{j+1}, s_{j+2}, \cdots, j_N), \delta_j^+, \mathcal{D})$
   2-6 $\mathcal{R}^- = \mathcal{R}^- \sqcup (n | n \in \mathcal{R} \wedge ResultPath_j(n) \in (\Delta_j - \mathcal{T}_j))$
   2-7 $\Delta_j = \mathcal{T}_j - \delta_j^+$
   2-8 $i = j + 1$
3- $\mathcal{R} = \mathcal{R} \sqcup \mathcal{R}^+$
      $\mathcal{R} = \mathcal{R} - \mathcal{R}^-$

Fig. 4. Incremental View Maintenance Algorithm for XML Path Expressions

2. *Indirect deletions due to direct deletions:* when a node n is directly deleted from $\mathcal{R}_i$, then all the nodes $r \in \mathcal{R}$ that came to $\mathcal{R}$ due to n belonging to $\mathcal{R}_i$ must also be deleted from $\mathcal{R}$. These are the nodes $r \in \mathcal{R}$ which have $ResultPath_i(r) = n$. Thus, using the auxiliary data described above, we can discover the indirect deletions without issuing any source queries.

The Full Algorithm. Figure 4, shows an algorithm based on the ideas presented above. Step 1 initializes some algorithm variables. $\mathcal{R}^+$ and $\mathcal{R}^-$ are the sequences of nodes to be added and deleted, respectively, in $\mathcal{R}$. The loop in step 2 computes the different Δ's. Step 2-1 assigns the value of j such that the range $i : j$ spans all the expression steps starting at i that do not have predicate tests. For this range, no predicate tests are needed because all the predicates are known to be *true*, by definition, before and after $\mathcal{U}$. Thus, there are no direct effects in this range. Therefore, the algorithm combines all the axis&label tests of this range in one step, namely, step 2-2. Step 2-3 identifies $\mathcal{T}_j$ as the sequence of the nodes of Δ_j that have $Pred_j^{after}(n) = true$. Step 2-4 then discovers the direct additions at $\mathcal{R}_j$. These direct additions are then used by step 2-5 to discover the indirect effects on $\mathcal{R}$. Step 2-6 discovers all the ultimate deletions at $\mathcal{R}$, it implicitly discovers the direct deletions and uses them to discover the indirect ones. Step 2-7 excludes from Δ_j the nodes that will not have effects on later iterations, this is formally proved in [13]. Step 2-8 increments the loop variable to start after j in the next step. Finally, step 3 updates $\mathcal{R}$ using $\mathcal{R}^+$ and $\mathcal{R}^-$.

Note that the algorithm does not differentiate between source addition and deletion updates, the only case that needs to make such distinction is when $\mathcal{U}.node$ itself belong to Δ_N, this case is implicitly taken care of in the computation of $Pred_i(n)$ before and after $\mathcal{U}$.

In addition to the result $\mathcal{R}$, the auxiliary data also need to be maintained. This is not shown here for simplicity.

In the following section, we show how this algorithm is implemented when the source XML document is stored in an RDBMS and hence, queried by SQL queries.

4   Implementation over RDBMS

Although there have been several efforts to build native XML database systems [10,11], a common consensus is to use RDBMS technology to leverage from the proven and highly-optimized storage and query capabilities already provided by existing relational database systems [15].

Therefore, in this section, we show how the incremental XPath maintenance algorithm described in Section 3 can be implemented when RDBMS technology is used for the storage of the XML source data, the auxiliary data, and the cached results. This requires an update management middleware which bridges the gap between the XML logical data model at one side, and the relational database implementation at the other side.

First, we will describe the XML-to-RDBMS and XPath-to-SQL mapping schemes the middleware uses (Section 4.1). Then we will describe how to employ this relational framework for incremental view maintenance of XPath queries to support efficient Web Service caching (Section 4.2).

4.1   Storing and Querying XML over RDBMS

XML Data to Relational Data Mapping. Given the mismatch between the XML data model (which has a nested structure) and the relational data model (which is flat), several techniques have been proposed for storing and querying XML documents using relational database systems [6,9,16,15]. These approaches typically work as follows. The first step is *relational schema generation*, where relational tables are created for the purpose of storing XML documents. The next step is XML document *shredding*, where XML documents are stored by shredding them into rows of the tables that were created in the first step. The final step is XML query processing (XPath queries in our case), where XPath queries over the stored XML documents are converted into SQL queries over the created tables.

One simple approach of shredding is to store each node in the XML tree as a tuple in a relational table, which maintains all the necessary information, such as the node label, and node type. *Node identifiers* are used to capture and represent the structure of the XML source in the relational database. In order to efficiently maintain path-expression views over XML documents, two essential properties must be provided by node identifiers: First, element(s) updated in the source XML document should be easily identified. Secondly, structural (parent, child, descendent, sibling) relationships among the elements of the XML document should be easily determined using the node identifiers. These are critical for efficient query processing and also in facilitating effective view maintenance in the presence of updates.

Several approaches are proposed to assign node identifiers to the nodes in XML document. We apply one such approach called, the ORDPATH [12] scheme (also used in the upcoming version of Microsoft SQL Server). ORDPATH identifiers can be assigned to the nodes of an XML tree without requiring a schema. ORDPATHs are conceptually similar to the Dewey Order introduced in [17]. The resulting identifiers have the property that ancestor relationships between

id	label	type	value	parent
1	Manuscripts	element	NULL	0
1.1	Category	attribute	Fiction	1
1.3	Book	element	NULL	1
1.3.1	ISBN	attribute	1-555860-438-3	1.3
1.3.3	Title	element	NULL	1.3
1.3.3.1	NULL	value	A Story	1.3.3
1.3.5	Author	element	NULL	1.3
1.3.5.1	Country	attribute	USA	1.3.5
1.3.5.3	NULL	value	John Doe	1.3.5
1.5	Monograph	element	NULL	1
1.5.1	ISBN	attribute	1-888570-843-5	1.5
1.5.3	Title	element	NULL	1.5
1.5.3.1	NULL	value	Another Story	1.5.3
1.5.5	Author	element	NULL	1.5
1.5.5.1	Country	attribute	Canada	1.5.5
1.5.5.3	NULL	value	Tom Alter	1.5.5

Fig. 5. SrcTBL: The XML Document Table

the nodes is captured by the prefix relationship between the corresponding node identifiers: $ancestor(n_i, n_j) \leftrightarrow prefix(n_i.nid, n_j.nid)$.

Consider the following sample XML document:

```
<Manuscripts Category="Fiction">
    <Book ISBN="1-555860-438-3">
        <Title>A Story</Title>
        <Author Country="USA">John Doe</Author>
    </Book>
    <Monograph ISBN="1-888570-843-5">
        <Title>Another Story</Title>
        <Author Country="Canada">Tom Alter</Author>
    </Monograph>
</Manuscripts>
```

Figure 5 shows the table SrcTBL in which an XML document is stored in an RDBMS

- **id:** The ORDPATH identifier originally proposed is implemented as a bit string, and an RDBMS is supposed to implement primitive functions for structural relationships and query plans optimized for ORDPATHs. In our prototype, we have implemented an ORDPATH id as a character string, as shown in Figure 5, for experimental purpose without implementing primitive functions in RDBMSs. The primitive $ancestor(n_i.id, n_j.id)$ is implemented as a string prefix matching: "$n_i.id$ LIKE $n_j.id$ || '%'". Note that the node id column captures the order of the XML document, thus this XML order semantics are not lost when the document is stored in an unordered relational system.
- **parent:** To identify a parent-child relationship effectively in our experimental prototype, we additionally store the parent node id in the table. The primitive $parent(n_i.id, n_j.id)$ is in fact implemented as "n_i.id = n_j.parent".
- **label, type, value:** A node type is specified in **type**, which is either an **element**, **attribute**, or **value**. An **element** node has its tag name in **label**. An **attribute** node has its name and value in **label** and **value** respectively. A **value** node has its value in **value**. Although our view maintenance algorithm is presented on a simplified document model (i.e., $\langle n.id, n.label \rangle$), it can be easily mapped in this node model.

With this table schema in place, XPath queries can be processed by translating them into SQL queries against a table of this schema, as illustrated next.

4.2 XML Document Update Management

For each cached XPath expression, the system stores the following data required for incremental maintenance (Section 3): (1) `CntxtTBL`: a table of the nodes that comprise the query context, (2) *Query Statement:* an SQL representation of the original XPath expression, (3) *Individual query step:* an SQL representation of each step in the incremental maintenance algorithm, and (4) `AuxTBL`: the auxiliary data (i.e. the result paths), whose schema is `AuxTBL(id0, id1, id2, ⋯, idN)` (where N is the number of steps in the cached expression, each row in this table stores a result path of the result, and the nodes in the last column idN comprise $\mathcal{R}$).

In the maintenance process, the whole auxiliary data (i.e., `AuxTBL`) needs to be maintained, not only the final result $\mathcal{R}$ which is stored in the last column of that table. We have implemented that simply by projecting more columns in the SELECT clauses of the following SQL statements. With that, the rows resulting from these SQL statements represent partial path expressions. Therefore, we use join operations to concatenate these partial result paths to form full result paths to maintain `AuxTBL`. For simplicity, we do not show the concatenation queries here.

In addition to these tables, we maintain an update table (`UpdtTBL`) that stores the source update being processed. As mentioned before, each update $\mathcal{U}$ is represented by $\mathcal{U}.path$ which is a branch of the source tree. Thus, we use the same schema as for the `SrcTBL`.

The View Maintenance Process. We illustrate the view maintenance process with the following expression as an example:

$$/site/person[LIKE(@id, "person\%")]/name$$

To construct the SQL query representing this expression, the hierarchical relationships between the nodes can be represented by either nested SQL queries or as self-join operations on the source table, `SrcTBL`, shown in Figure 5. We adopted the second option in our solution because it allows the query optimizer to generate more efficient query plans. Thus, the expression is transformed into the following SQL query by the middleware:

```
SELECT A.id, B.id, C.id, E.id
FROM CntxTBL A, SrcTBL B, SrcTBL C, SrcTBL D, SrcTBL E
WHERE parent(B.id)=A.id AND parent(C.id)=B.id AND parent(D.id)=C.id
AND parent(E.id)=C.id
AND B.type = 'element' AND A.label = 'site'
AND C.type = 'element' AND B.label = 'person'
AND D.type = 'attribute' AND D.label = 'id' AND LIKE(D.value,'person%')
AND E.type = 'element' AND E.label = 'name'
```

In this query, the final result is the set of nodes in the last projection E.id, the other projections A.id, B.id and C.id represent the result path information which is used as auxiliary data for the maintenance process.

The algorithm in Figure 4 starts by initializing Δ_0 in step 1 by an intersection operation:

```
CREATE TABLE Δ₀(id0) AS
(SELECT id FROM CntxtTBL INTERSECTION SELECT id FROM UpdtTBL)
```

Then, in the first iteration of the loop, step 2-1 assigns to j the value 2 because s_1 has no predicate test. Then, step 2-2 computes Δ_2 by the following SQL statement:

```
CREATE TABLE Δ₂(id0, id1, id2) AS
SELECT A.id, B.id C.id FROM Δ₀ A, UpdtTBL B, UpdtTBL C
WHERE parent(B.id)=A.id AND parent(C.id)=B.id
AND B.type = 'element' AND B.label = 'site'
AND C.type = 'element' AND C.label = 'person'
```

The projection of A.id and B.id here are to get partial result paths. In step 2-3, T_2 is computed by:

```
CREATE TABLE T₂ AS SELECT A.id FROM Δ₂ A, SrcTBL B
WHERE parent(B.id)=A.id
AND B.type = 'attribute' AND C.label = 'id'
AND LIKE(B.value,'person%')
```

Then step 2-4 computes the direct additions at $\mathcal{R}_2$ as follows:

```
CREATE TABLE δ₂⁺ AS
SELECT T.id FROM T₂ T
WHERE NOT EXISTS (SELECT * FROM AuxTBL WHERE id2 = T.id)
```

Step 2-5 then uses δ_2^+ to discover the ultimate additions at $\mathcal{R}$, the SQL query used to discover these additions is:

```
SELECT A.id, B.id FROM δ₂⁺ A, SrcTBL B
WHERE parent(B.id)=A.id
AND B.type = 'element' AND B.label = 'name'
```

(A.id, B.id) in this query result is a partial result path starting at $\mathcal{R}_2$ until $\mathcal{R}_3$. Then step 2-6 computes the ultimate deletions at $\mathcal{R}$ as follows:

```
SELECT DISTINCT A.id3 FROM AuxTBL A
WHERE A.id2 IN
SELECT id2 FROM Δ₂ DIFFERENCE SELECT id FROM T₂
```

step 2-7 simply reduces Δ_2 by a DIFFERENCE operator.

In the second (also, last) iteration of the loop, we have $i = j = 3$. In step 2-2, Δ_3 is computed from the reduced Δ_2. Since this iteration is processing the last expression step, then if $\mathcal{U}.node$ belongs to Δ_3 then the computation of $Pred_3(\mathcal{U}.node)$ takes into account $\mathcal{U}.type$. This is computed as follows: If

$\mathcal{U}.type = Add$, then $Pred_3^{before}(\mathcal{U}.node) = false$ because $\mathcal{U}.node$ did not exist in the source before $\mathcal{U}.node$. If $\mathcal{U}.type = Del$, then $Pred_3^{after}(\mathcal{U}.node) = false$ because $\mathcal{U}.node$ does not exist in the source after $\mathcal{U}.node$. These two cases are implicitly taken care of in the algorithm without testing $\mathcal{U}.type$ in the computation of $Pred_3(\mathcal{U}.node)$ before and after $\mathcal{U}$. Finally, all the ultimate additions and deletions in AuxTBL are determined by joining the partial result paths discovered by the SQL queries shown above.

5 Experimental Evaluation

In this section, we experimentally show that the proposed scheme provides a large performance impact, while incurring a small storage and processing overhead. For this purpose, we used the XMARK benchmark [14] to generate a data set of 325,236 nodes. Experiments are done using an Oracle 9i database on a PC with Linux 8.0, Pentium 4 1800 MHz CPU with 1 GB memory. We evaluated the caching performance by using the following XPath queries:

- *XP1*: /site/people/person[like(@id,"person%")]/name/text()
- *XP2*: /site/closed_auctions/closed_auction[price>40]/price/text()
- *XP3*: /site//item[contains(description,"gold")/name/text()
- *XP4*: /site/closed_auctions/closed_auction/annotation/description/ parlist/listitem/parlist/listitem/text/emph/ketword/text()

Overhead of Auxiliary Data. Table 1 shows the overhead of auxiliary data (i.e., AuxTBL) in terms of storage requirements and execution time. In addition to cached XPath results (denoted as columns R-VAL and R-ID), the system needs to store result paths as auxiliary data(AUX). As can be seen in the AUX column, the storage overhead does not depend on the data size, but depends on the number of steps in the XPath query and the cached data size. Then, to observe the query processing in WReX, we compared the original full query execution time with the execution time of the modified query that also retrieves result paths to be used as auxiliary data. As shown in the Table 1, the overhead is less than 10% in each case.

Table 1. Overhead in Auxiliary Data Maintenance: R-VAL: Result Set Value Storage, R-ID: Result Set Node ID Storage, AUX: Auxililary Data Storage, SOV: Storage Overhead (=AUX/(R-VAL+R-ID)), FQ: Full Source Query Execution Time, FQA: Full Source Query with Aux. Data Execution Time, EOV: Execution Time Overhead (=FQA/FQ).

	R-VAL (byte)	R-ID (byte)	AUX (byte)	SOV	FQ (msec)	FQA (msec)	EOV
XP1	36538	30103	85199	1.28	532	551	1.04
XP2	2366	8312	24267	2.27	802	876	1.09
XP3	3080	2327	6096	1.13	3933	4019	1.02
XP4	964	752	5525	3.22	3520	3556	1.01

Performance Impact of Cache-enabled Middleware. To observe the benefit of WReX in reducing the execution time observed by the users, we have compared the execution time requirements for incremental cache update and full recomputation on the following cached queries:

– *XP5*: /site/people/person[like(@id,"person2%")]/name/text()
– *XP6*: /site/people[person[like(@id,"person1%")]]/
  person[like(@id,"person2%")]/name/text()

For each query, 100 source updates were randomly generated. The results of the time comparison for all the updates are shown in Figures 6(a) and 6(b). In short, full queries take 10 to 20 times longer to execute on average. The figures clearly establish the advantage of the proposed incremental view maintenance middleware.

Finally, consider Figure 7, which shows the caching impact analysis for query XP4, which has 13 steps, but no predicate. Since there are no predicates in XP4,

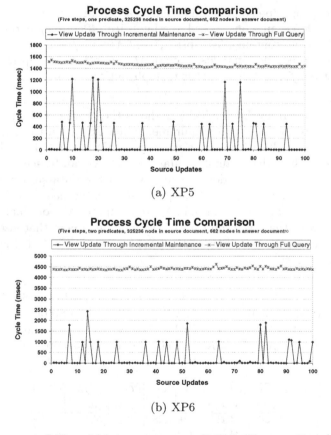

(a) XP5

(b) XP6

Fig. 6. Incremental View Maintenance versus Full Re-Computation (Queries XP5, XP6)

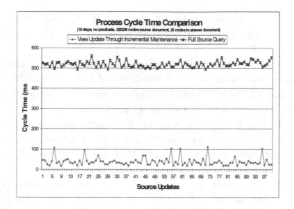

Fig. 7. Incremental View Maintenance versus Full Re-Computation (Query XP4)

no queries to the source need to be issued for predicate checking. Therefore, the time needed for incremental maintenance is rather constant, whereas the need for accessing sources for predicate tests had introduced a higher variability to the incremental maintenance time for queries XP5 and XP6 in Figures 6(a) and 6(b). Nevertheless, since predicate evaluation is only a part of the overall processing needed for reevaluation of queries XP5 and XP6, incremental maintenance was consistently cheaper even when sources are accessed for predicate checking.

6   Conclusion

In this paper, we have proposed WReX, a Web Service middleware architecture that enables cache management by bridging the gap between Web Service message caching and updates in the source data. Our solution consists of two components: (1) Web Service Content Description (WSCD) that fills the gap between Web Service messages and XML views of the source data; and (2) XML-specific view maintenance that fills the gap between XML views and updates in the source data. Cache-enabled Web Services are easily described and deployed on a common platform with proven RDBMS technology. Through experimental evaluation, we have demonstrated the performance benefits of our incremental view maintenance. Future work includes more effective maintenance of multiple XPath views and multiple updates, extension of our approach to other XML-to-RDBMS mapping schemes (such as schema-aware mappings), and more detailed studies on the entire middleware performance.

References

1. S. Abiteboul, A. Bonifati, G. Cobena, I. Manolescu, and T. Milo. Dynamic XML documents with distribution and replication. In *SIGMOD Conference*, pages 527–538, 2003.

2. K. S. Candan, D. Agrawal, W. Li, O. Po, and W. Hsiung. View invalidation for dynamic content caching in multitiered architectures. In *The 28th Very Large Data Bases Conference*, 2002.

3. J. Challenger, P. Dantzig, and A. Iyengar. A scalable system for consistently caching dynamic web data. In *In Proceedings of IEEE INFOCOM'99*, 1999.

4. C. Y. Choi and Q. Luo. Template-based runtime invalidation for database-generated web contents. In *APWeb 2004*, 2004.

5. A. Datta, K. Dutta, H. M. Thomas, D. E. Vandermeer, and K. Ramamritham. Proxy-based acceleration of dynamically generated content on the world wide web: An approach and implementation. *ACM Trans. Database Syst*, 29(2):403–443, 2004.

6. A. Deutsch, M. Fernandez, and D. Suciu. Storing Semi-structured Data with STORED. In *Proceedings of the 1999 ACM International Conference on Management of Data (SIGMOD'1999)*, 1999.

7. Y. Diao, M. Altinel, M. J. Franklin, H. Zhang, and P. Fischer. Path sharing and predicate evaluation for high-performance XML filtering. *ACM Trans. Database Syst*, 28(4):467–516, 2003.

8. D. Florescu, A. Grunhagen, and D. Kossmann. XL: An XML programming language for web service specification and composition. In *WWW2002, International World Wide Web Conference*, 2002.

9. D. florescu and D. Kossman. Storing and Querying XML Data using an RDBMS. *IEEE Data Engineering Bulletin*, 22(3):27–34, 1999.

10. Roy Goldman, Jason McHugh, and Jennifer Widom. From Semistructured Data to XML: Migrating the Lore Data Model and Query Language. In *Proceedings of the ACM International Workshop on the Web and Databases (WebDB'99)*, 1999.

11. J. Naughton, D. DeWitt, D. Maier, A. Aboulnaga, J. Chen, L. Galanis, J. Kang, R. Krishnamurthy, Q. Luo, N. Prakash, R. Ramamurthy andJ. Shanmugasundaram, F. Tian, K. Tufte, S. Viglas, C. Zhang, B. Jacksonand A. Gupta, and R. Chen. The Niagara Internet Query System. *IEEE Data Engineering Bulletin*, 24(2), 2001.

12. Patrick E. O'Neil, Elizabeth J. O'Neil, Shankar Pal, Istvan Cseri, Gideon Schaller, and Nigel Westbury. Ordpaths: Insert-friendly xml node labels. In *SIGMOD Conference*, pages 903–908, 2004.

13. Arsany Sawires, Junichi Tatemura, Oliver Po, Divyakant Agrawal, and K. Selçuk Candan. Incremental Maintenance of Path-Expression Views. In *SIGMOD Conference*, 2005.

14. Albrecht Schmidt, Florian Waas, Martin L. Kersten, MichaelJ. Carey, Ioana Manolescu, and Ralph Busse. Xmark: A benchmark for xml data management. In *VLDB*, pages 974–985, 2002.

15. Jayavel Shanmugasundaram, Rajashekhar Krishnamurthy, Igor Tatarinov, Eugene Shekita, Efstratios Viglas, Jerry Kinman, and Jefferey Naughton. A General Technique for Querying XML Documents using a Relational Database System. In *Proceedings of the 2001 ACM International Conference on Management of Data (SIGMOD'2001)*, 2001.

16. Jayavel Shanmugasundaram, Eugene J. Shekita, Rimon Barr, Michael J. Carey, Bruce G. Lindsay, Hamid Pirahesh, and Berthold Reinwald. Efficiently publishing relational data as xml documents. In *Proceedings of 26th International Conference on Very Large Data Bases (VLDB'2000), September 10-14, 2000, Cairo, Egypt*, pages 65–76, 2000.

17. Igor Tatarinov, Stratis Viglas, Kevin S. Beyer, Jayavel Shanmugasundaram, Eugene J. Shekita, and Chun Zhang. Storing and querying ordered XML using a relational database system. In *Proceedings of the 20002 ACM International Conference on Management of Data (SIGMOD'2002)*, pages 204–215, 2002.
18. D. B. Terry and V. Ramasubramanian. Caching xml web services for mobility. *ACM Queue*, 1(3):70–78, 2003.
19. K. Yagoub, D. Florescu, V. Issarny, and Patrick Valduriez. Caching strategies for data-intensive web sites. In *The VLDB Journal*, pages 188–199, 2000.

Inflatable XML Processing

Rohit Fernandes[1] and Mukund Raghavachari[2]

[1] Department of Computer Science, Cornell University
rohitf@cs.cornell.edu
[2] IBM T.J. Watson Research Center
raghavac@us.ibm.com

Abstract. The past few years have seen the widespread adoption of
XML as a data representation format in various middleware: databases,
Web Services, messaging systems, etc. One drawback of XML has been
the high cost of XML processing. We present in this paper InflateX, a system that supports efficient XML processing. InflateX advances the state
of the art in two ways. First, it uses a novel representation of XML,
called *inflatable trees*, that supports lazy construction of an XML document in-memory in response to client requests, as well as, more efficient
serialization of results. Second, it incorporates a novel algorithm, based
on the idea of *projection* [8], for efficiently constructing an inflatable tree
given a set of XPath expressions. The projection algorithm presented in
this paper, unlike previous work, can handle all axes in XPath, including complex axes such as `ancestor`. While we describe the algorithm in
terms of our inflatable tree representation, it is portable to other representations of XML. We provide experiments that validate the utility of
our inflatable tree representation and our projection algorithm.

Keywords: XML, XPath, Performance, Projection.

1 Introduction

The past few years have seen the widespread adoption of XML as a data in-
terchange format in various middleware: databases, Web Services, messaging
systems, etc. The popularity of XML has been accompanied by its main drawback — the high cost of XML processing. One of the factors affecting XML
processing is the memory footprint of XML documents — when documents are
large or many documents are processed simultaneously, XML processors may
operate inefficiently or not execute at all.

Consider the following (common) situation — a web service receives an XML
document over the network. In processing the document, the web service accesses
certain portions of the document (possibly by executing queries in a language
such as XQuery [14] or XPath [12] on the document). Based on the result of
processing, the web service constructs a new XML document and publishes it
over the network. In such a situation, the cost of loading an instance of the
XML document into main memory and serializing the constructed output can
dwarf the cost of query evaluation during the execution of the web service.

G. Alonso (Ed.): Middleware 2005, LNCS 3790, pp. 144–163, 2005.

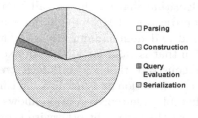

Fig. 1. Breakdown of query processing time in terms of parsing time, construction time, query evaluation time, and result serialization time

Figure 1 presents a breakdown of the cost of executing a query on a DOM [13] representation of an XML document.[1]

In this paper, we describe a system, InflateX, that addresses the high cost of XML processing. At the heart of the InflateX system is a novel representation of XML, called *inflatable tree*, that builds portions of an XML document lazily in memory in response to traversals of the document initiated by clients. The remaining portion of the XML document is stored in binary form, which can be up to five times more concise than the DOM representation of XML [8]. To a client, InflateX provides a DOM view of the XML document — the client may manipulate this view as one would any DOM representation. We will show that the inflatable tree representation is more efficient (in general) than full DOM materialization of a document in all aspects of XML processing : construction of an instance of a document in memory, query evaluation, and serialization of output.

To optimize the lazy construction of inflatable trees, InflateX allows clients to specify a set of XPath expressions with respect to which the document should be *projected* [8]. In one pass over the document, the InflateX system materializes those portions of the document that are relevant to the provided set of XPath expressions and retains the remaining portions in binary form. Traversals of the inflatable tree that are contained in the set of XPath expressions can be processed efficiently (since those nodes are already materialized in memory). Traversals that access portions that are not materialized will cause the InflateX system to materialize those portions on-demand. We will provide a novel projection algorithm that can handle all XPath axes — previous work could handle only XPath expressions with `child` and `descendant` axes.

1.1 Contributions

The contributions of the paper are the following:

- A novel representation of XML, called *inflatable tree*, that supports lazy construction of an XML document in memory. The representation allows for more efficient construction, query evaluation and serialization of XML data.

---

[1] The figure reports the execution of the Java equivalent of the XQuery `for $i in /site/regions/namerica/item return $i` on a 10MB XMark [11] document.

- A novel projection algorithm that can handle all XPath axes. We will show that the definition of projection of Marian and Siméon is not sufficient when axes other than `child` and `descendant` are used, and provide a general definition of projection that is valid for all XPath axes.
- Experiments that demonstrate that the *inflatable tree* representation substantially reduces the construction and serialization time in XML processing. Furthermore, the inflatable tree representation allows an XML processor to handle larger documents than it might otherwise (approximately, 2-5 times the corresponding DOM representation).

1.2 Related Work

Bohannon *et al.* [4] describe a virtual DOM interface that delivers navigable XML views of relational data. Like inflatable trees, their interface supports lazy materialization of an XML document. Their system, however, relies on the existence of an underlying database that acts as a persistent store for the XML data. The system also relies on the database for query execution. In many situations, for example, for some web services, such a store may not be available. Our inflatable tree representation provides a mechanism for efficient XML processing in memory, without any requirements of an underlying database.

Marian and Siméon have introduced the idea of *projection* which constructs a DOM representation of a document based on a set of XPath expressions [8]. One drawback to projection as defined by Marian and Siméon is that it assumes that all queries that will be executed on the document are known in advance. The inflatable tree representation is robust in that it can be used even when the full set of XPath expressions that will be evaluated on the document is not known in advance. Second, their projection algorithm cannot handle XPath expressions involving axes such as `parent` and `ancestor`. Finally, their approach does not reduce the cost of serialization of results which, as observed in Figure 1, can be high.

Compressed XML [5] is a concise representation of an XML document. The tree skeleton of an XML document — the portion of an XML document obtained by ignoring all string information — is compressed. String information is not stored directly, but if the queries are known in advance, compressed XML encodes information about the strings that may be required to evaluate the queries on the document. Unlike compressed XML, our representation retains all information relevant to an XML document.

Streaming algorithms [3,6,7] reduce the memory overhead of XML processing by not constructing the document in memory, but processing it as it is parsed. They can be applied in constrained circumstances where all queries evaluated in the document are known in advance and are independent of each other. As with projection, streaming algorithms support only limited subsets of query languages; for complex queries involving joins or nested queries, it is necessary to manifest portions of the document in memory [8].

1.3 Structure of Paper

The paper is structured as follows. In Section 2, we describe our system architecture and the *inflatable* tree representation. In Section 3, we present a new definition of projection that is valid when all XPath axes are allowed. In Section 4 we present our algorithm for document projection. In Section 5, we give an overview of our implementation. In Section 6, we provide experimental results. Finally, in Section 7, we conclude and describe future work.

2 System Architecture

The architecture of our system is depicted in Figure 2. A client passes a reference to a data stream, and optionally, a set of XPath expressions called the *projection set* to the InflateX system. The projection set is an approximation of the traversals that will be executed over the XML document; it is used as a hint to optimize the construction of the inflatable tree representation of the document. The projection set need not be complete — the client may execute XPath expressions over the document that are not covered by the projection set. The InflateX system uses the projection set and the XML data stream to construct an initial inflatable tree representation of the XML document. The client may determine the initial projection set using various mechanisms, for example, static analysis of the client application, profiling information of the most common XPath expressions or traversals used, etc. In this paper, we will focus on mechanisms for building the inflatable tree efficiently given a projection set.

We now describe our inflatable tree representation and how a client interacts with it in greater detail. For simplicity, we will focus on elements, though our implementation can handle the other XML nodes, such as attribute nodes.

2.1 Inflatable Trees

Our representation of XML documents, *inflatable tree*, is based on the observation that the binary representation of an XML document (as a sequence of bytes)

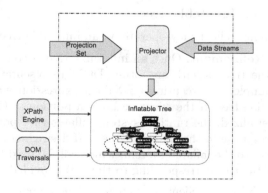

Fig. 2. System architecture

can be 4-5 times more concise than constructing a DOM model instance of the
document. Given a reference to an XML document, we store the sequence of
bytes corresponding to the XML document in an array of bytes in memory. Our
representation of the XML document in memory consists of two sorts of nodes:
materialized nodes and *inflatable* nodes. A *materialized* node corresponds to an
element in the document and contains all information relevant to the element,
such as its tag. An *inflatable* node represents an unexpanded portion of the XML
document; it contains a pair of offsets into the byte array representation of the
document corresponding to the start and end of the unexpanded portion. For
example, Figure 3a depicts the inflatable tree representation of an XML document tree. The materialized nodes are shown with a label, and the nodes that
have a dashed border are inflatable nodes. They contain offsets into the binary
array of bytes.

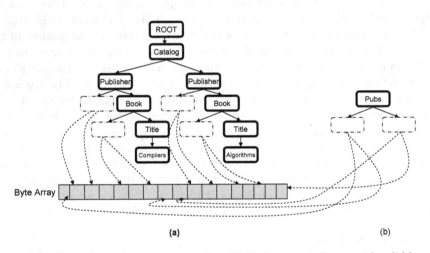

Fig. 3. (a) Inflatable tree epresentation of an XML document. Boxes with solid borders
represent materialized nodes. Boxes with dashed borders represent inflatable nodes. (b)
Representation of a constructed XML document.

2.2   Operations on Inflatable Trees

We now describe how a client may operate on an inflatable tree.

Inflatable Tree Refinement. Once an inflatable tree is constructed, a client
may operate on the tree as with any other DOM representation of an XML
document, for example, by executing an XPath expression with respect to a
node of the inflatable tree. If the client accesses a portion of the tree that has
not yet been materialized, the runtime system inflates that portion of the tree
automatically in response to the client's request. If desired, the client may pass
a new projection set to the InflateX system, which will be used by the system to
inflate portions of the tree corresponding to the new provided set of XPaths.

Construction of XML. A client may construct new nodes and trees, which
are always constructed in materialized form. When construction refers to sub-

trees from existing documents, InflateX constructs an inflatable node with the appropriate offsets. For example, Figure 3b shows the result of constructing a tree based on the input XML document of Figure 3a. The children on the Pubs element in Figure 3b are the two Publisher subtrees in Figure 3a.

Serialization of Results. Since the byte array representation of the input XML documents is retained in memory, portions of the results that are derived from the input document can be serialized directly from the byte array. As we will show in Section 6, this direct serialization can be substantially more efficient than explicit traversal of a tree to perform serialization. For example, in Figure 3b, the inflatable nodes corresponding to the Publisher elements can be serialized directly from the input document byte array.

3 Preliminaries

We define the abstractions of XML documents and XPath expressions that will be used in this paper. We will then provide a definition of projection that is valid when all XPath axes are supported.

3.1 Tree Model of XML Documents

An XML document can be represented as a tree whose nodes represent the structural components of the document — elements, text, attributes, etc. Parent-child edges in the tree represent the inclusion of the child component in its parent element, where the scope of an element is bounded by its start and end tags. The tree corresponding to an XML document is rooted at a virtual element, ROOT, which contains the document element. We will discuss XML documents in terms of their tree representation; D represents an XML document, and N_D and E_D denote its nodes and edges respectively.

For simplicity of exposition, we focus on elements in this paper, and ignore attributes, text nodes, etc. The tree, therefore, consists of the virtual root and the elements of the document. We refer to the nodes of the document tree as *elements* to avoid confusion with vertices of the tree representation of an XPath which we will discuss shortly. We assume that the following functions are defined on the elements of an XML document:

- ID$_D$: $N_D \rightarrow$ *Integer*: Returns a unique identifier for each element in a document. We will assume that ID$_D$ is a total order on the elements in D, such that the assignment of identifiers to elements corresponds to a depth-first preorder traversal of the tree (that is, *document order* in XML).
- TAG$_D$: $N_D \rightarrow$ *String*: Returns the tag name of the element.

We also assume functions, CHILD$_D$, DESC$_D$, SELF$_D$, FS$_D$, and FOLLOWING$_D$, each with the signature $N_D \times N_D \rightarrow \{true, false\}$. The semantics of these functions is straightforward, CHILD$_D(v_1, v_2)$ returns *true* if v_2 is a child of v_1 in D, and FS$_D(v_1, v_2)$ returns *true* if v_1 and v_2 share a common parent, and moreover, ID$_D(v_2) >$ ID$_D(v_1)$. FOLLOWING$_D(v_1, v2)$ returns true if ID$_D(v_2) >$ ID$_D(v_1)$ and v_2 is not a descendant of v_1. Finally, SELF$_D(v_1, v_2)$ returns true if $v_1 = v_2$.

3.2 XPath Subset

The grammar of XPath expressions accepted by our projection algorithm is provided below. In the grammar, the non-terminal *Axis* includes all axes defined in the XPath specification [12]. For simplicity, we will only consider elements and not consider the **namespace** and **attribute** axes.

$$
\begin{aligned}
AbsLocPath &:= '/'\ RelLocPath \\
RelLocPath &:= Step\ '/'\ RelLocPath\ \mid\ Step \\
Step &:= Axis :: NodeTest\ \mid Step\ '['\ PredExpr\ ']' \\
PredExpr &:= RelLocPath\ and\ PredExpr\ \mid AbsLocPath\ and\ PredExpr\ \mid \\
&\quad\ RelLocPath\ \mid\ AbsLocPath \\
NodeTest &:= String\mid *
\end{aligned}
$$

An *absolute* path expression corresponds to one that satisfies *AbsLocPath* and is evaluated with respect to the root node of the tree. A relative XPath expression corresponds to *RelLocPath* and is evaluated with respect to a provided set of elements in the tree.

3.3 XPath Expression Trees

An XPath expression can be represented as a rooted tree $T = (V_T, E_T)$ with labeled vertices and edges. The root of the tree is labeled ROOT. For every *NodeTest* in the expression, there is a vertex labeled with the *NodeTest*. Each vertex other than ROOT has a unique incoming edge labeled with the *Axis* specified before the *NodeTest*. The vertex corresponding to the rightmost *NodeTest* which is not contained in a *PredExpr* is designated to be the output vertex. There are functions, LABEL$_T$: $V_T \rightarrow$ *String*, and AXIS$_T$: $E_T \rightarrow$ *Axis* that return the labels associated with the vertices and edges respectively. Figure 4 provides an example of the tree representation of the XPath expression `//book[title and author]/ancestor::publisher`.[2]

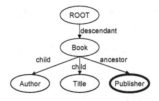

Fig. 4. Tree representation of the XPath expression `//Book[Title and Author]/ancestor::Publisher`. The output vertex has a thick border.

The semantics of an absolute XPath expression is defined in terms of *embeddings* [9].

---

[2] We will use the abbreviated XPath syntax in the paper for conciseness.

Definition 1. *A pair of elements* (n_1, n_2) *in a document,* D, $n_1, n_2 \in N_D$ *satisfies an edge constraint* (v_1, v_2) *in the tree representation* T *of an XPath expression if the relation between* n_1 *and* n_2 *in the document matches* $\text{AXIS}_T(v_1, v_2)$. *For example,* n_1, n_2 *satisfies* (v_1, v_2) *if* $\text{AXIS}_T(v_1, v_2) = child$ *and* $\text{CHILD}_D(n_1, n_2) = true$, *or, if* $\text{AXIS}_T(v_1, v_2) = ancestor$ *and* $\text{DESC}_D(n_2, n_1) = true$.

Definition 2. *An embedding of an absolute XPath expression* T *into a document* D *is a function* $\mathcal{E} : V_T \to N_D$ *such that:*

1. $\mathcal{E}$ *maps the* ROOT *vertex of the XPath expression to the* ROOT *element of the document.*
2. *Labels are* matched, *that is, for each* $v \in V_T$, $\text{LABEL}_T(v) = *$ *or* $\text{LABEL}_T(v) = \text{TAG}_D(\mathcal{E}(v))$.
3. *Edges are* satisfied, *that is, if* $(v_1, v_2) \in E_T$, *then* $(\mathcal{E}(v_1), \mathcal{E}(v_2))$ *satisfies* (v_1, v_2).

Let o be the output vertex of the tree representation of an absolute XPath expression. The output of an XPath expression is defined as all $n \in N_D$ such that there exists an embedding where $\mathcal{E}(o) = n$. The definition can be extended easily to relative XPaths by replacing the embedding of the ROOT element with the context node.

For example, an embedding of the XPath expression tree of Figure 4 into the XML document from Figure 5 is the following : $\mathcal{E}(ROOT) = \{1\}, \mathcal{E}(Book) = \{5\}$, $\mathcal{E}(Author) = \{6\}$, $\mathcal{E}(Title) = \{8\}$ and $\mathcal{E}(Publisher) = \{3\}$.

3.4   Projection

A projected document is defined by Marian and Siméon in terms of an input document D and a set of XPath expressions P, where some of the expressions may be marked with the special output flag $\#$ [8]. Each XPath expression in P is an absolute XPath expression (that is, it is evaluated with respect to the root of the document). Only uses of the `child` and `descendant` axes are allowed (predicates and backward axes are not allowed). Given P and D, the projected document D' is defined as follows: The projected document contains all elements that are in the result set of an XPath expression in P, as well as, their ancestors. All subtrees rooted at some result of an XPath expression marked $\#$ are materialized as well. The definition guarantees that the projected document D' satisfies the key property that the evaluation of any XPath expression in P on D' returns the same result as the evaluation of that XPath expression on D. As a result, one can substitute D' for D without changing the behavior of query evaluation with respect to P.

For example, consider the XPath expression, `//Title`, and assume that it is marked with a $\#$. Figure 5 depicts the elements that would be constructed in the projection of the document with respect to this XPath expression.

When XPath expressions with axes other than `child` and `descendant` are allowed in P, projection as defined in [8] can no longer be applied; the evaluation of an XPath expression on the projected document D' may differ from that on

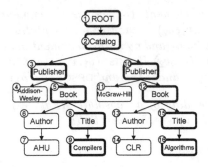

Fig. 5. Tree representation of an XML document. Highlighted nodes depict nodes selected by the algorithm of Marian and Siméon.

D. Consider the XPath expression, `//Author/ancestor::Publisher//Title` executed on the document in Figure 5. Only the elements highlighted in Figure 5 belong to the projected document D'. The result of the XPath expression on D' will be the empty set since it does not contain any `Author` elements.

The embeddings of XPath expressions into a document D can be used as the basis for a general definition of projection when complex axes such as `ancestor` are allowed. The definition we provide subsumes that of [8] and serves as the basis for the algorithm presented in Section 4.

Definition 3. *Let D be a document and P be a set of absolute XPath expressions, where some XPath expressions in P are marked with a special flag #. The projected document D' is composed of the set of all elements n in D that satisfy at least one of the following conditions:*

- *For some XPath expression p in P, there is an embedding $\mathcal{E}$ of p into D such that $\mathcal{E}(v) = n$, where v is some vertex in p, or*
- *For some XPath expression p in P, there is an embedding $\mathcal{E}$ of p into D such that $\mathcal{E}(v) = n'$, where v is some vertex in p, and n is an ancestor of n' in D, or*
- *For some XPath expression p in P marked with the symbol #, n is the descendant of an element in the result set of the evaluation of p on D.*

In other words, the projected document consists of all elements that participate in an embedding and their ancestors. Moreover, for each element in the result set of the evaluation of a specially marked XPath expression, that element and all its descendants belong to the projected document.

4   Inflatable Tree Construction

In this section, we present an algorithm for constructing an inflatable tree from a given set of XPath expressions while parsing the document. The challenge is in being able to handle complex XPath axes such as `ancestor` efficiently in a single pass over the input document. Our algorithm may be imprecise in that it may materialize some elements that do not satisfy any of the conditions of Definition 3. The algorithm is, however, careful in limiting the construction of these inessential nodes.

Our algorithm works in two stages. First, the set of input XPath expressions P is normalized into a canonical form. In the second stage, a document (or a subtree of the document) is traversed to build the inflatable tree. Our algorithm will not distinguish XPath expressions marked "#" from those that are not. Since the bytes corresponding to the document are readily available, there is no need to inflate the subtrees under output nodes, unless portions of these subtrees may participate in an embedding (that is, satisfy the first two conditions of Definition 3).

4.1   Normalizing XPath Expressions

The XPath axes `following`, `preceding`, `following-sibling` and `preceding-sibling` are order-based axes (the result set for these axes depends on the order between sibling tree nodes). The first step in our normalization is to rewrite instances of these axes in XPath expressions into order-blind axes (such as `parent` and `ancestor`). The rules for rewriting XPath expression trees are shown in Figure 6. In the figure, v_1 and v_2 are vertices in a given XPath expression tree, connected by an edge labeled with one of the order-based axes. The rewriting rules may introduce new vertices. The rules are ordered so that the rules of Figure 6a and Figure 6b are applied until there are no instances of `following` and `preceding` in the XPath expression tree. The rules of Figure 6c and Figure 6d are then applied to the XPath expression tree.

For example, for the `following-sibling` axes, we replace instances of the pattern v_1/`following-sibling::`v_2 with instances of v_1/`parent::*/`v_2. The rewritten XPath expression is an approximation of the original one — it chooses v_2 elements that both precede and follow v_1 elements. The rewritings guarantee that for any document, if an element n participates in an embedding of the original XPath expression tree into the document, n also participates in an embedding of the rewritten tree into the document.

4.2   Constructing an Inflatable Tree

The inflatable tree construction algorithm can be invoked by the client in one of two states. In the first case, the document is being processed for the first time and must be read from an external source. In the second case, an inflatable tree already exists for the document in question, and the inflatable tree must be modified to account for the new projection set of XPath expressions. In either of the two cases, the algorithm traverses the document in a depth-first manner and generates events similar to SAX [10]. A *start* element event is generated when the traversal first visits an element, and an *end* element event once the traversal of the subtree rooted at that element is finished. We will assume that an event contains all information about the relevant element, such as its tag and unique identifier (we will use the offset in the byte array for this purpose). At

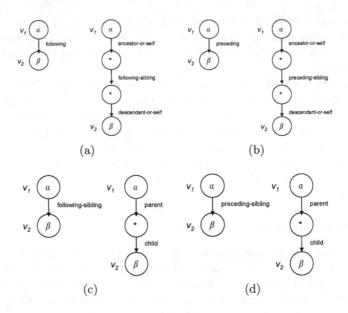

(a)   (b)

(c)   (d)

Fig. 6. (a) Rule for rewriting `following` edges. (b) Rule for rewriting `preceding` edges. (c) Rule for rewriting `following-sibling` edges. (d) Rule for rewriting `preceding-sibling` edges.

each of these events, an event handler is invoked to perform actions related to the construction of the tree.

In the case where a document is read for the first time from an external source, the traversal records the bytes corresponding to the XML document into an array. It simultaneously parses the document and generates appropriate events. In the other case, where an inflatable tree already exists, the document traverser walks over the inflatable tree and generates events. When it reaches an inflatable node, it parses the portion of the byte array corresponding to that node and generates appropriate events.

Definitions and Data Structures. The description of our algorithm will use the following definitions.

Definition 4. *The* backward vertex set, $\mathcal{B}(v)$, *of a vertex* $v \in V_T$ *in an XPath expression tree is defined as* $\{v'|(v,v') \in E_T, \text{AXIS}(v,v') \in \{$`parent, ancestor, ancestor-or-self, self` $\} \cup \{v''|(v'',v) \in E_T, \text{AXIS}(v'',v) \in \{$ `self, child, descendant, descendant-or-self`$\}$. *A* backward constraint *is an edge between* v *and a vertex in its backward vertex set.*

In other words, the *backward vertex set* with respect to a vertex v consists of those vertices to which an outgoing edge from v is labeled with a backward axis and those from which an incoming vertex into v is labeled with a forward axis. We have a dual definition for a *forward vertex set* with respect to a vertex v.

Definition 5. *The* forward vertex set, $\mathcal{F}(v)$, *of a vertex* $v \in V_T$ *in an XPath expression tree is defined as* $\{v'|(v,v') \in E_T, \text{AXIS}(v,v') \in\{ child,\ descendant,$ $descendant\text{-}or\text{-}self,\ self\ \} \cup\{v''|(v'',v) \in E_T, \text{AXIS}(v'',v) \in \{\ self,\ parent,$ $ancestor,\ ancestor\text{-}or\text{-}self\}.$ *A* forward constraint *is an edge between* v *and a vertex in its forward vertex set.*

Our algorithm maintains an *active stack*, which contains, at any time, the list of elements for which a start event has been received, but no end event has been received yet. For each element e in the stack we maintain and update the following information as we traverse the document:

- TAG(e) which corresponds to the tag of the element.
- Sets of vertices from the XPath expression tree: SELF(e), ANCESTORS(e), PARENT(e), CHILDREN(e), and DESCENDANTS(e). A vertex v is in SELF(e) if e may embed into v. v is in PARENT(e) if the parent element of e may embed into v. $v \in$ CHILDREN(e) implies that some child of e may embed into v; $v \in$ DESCENDANTS(e), if some descendant of e may embed into v, and finally, $v \in$ ANCESTORS(e) implies that some ancestor of e in the tree may embed into v.
- An ordered set SUBTREES(e) of inflatable trees. This set corresponds to the inflatable trees constructed for the children of e.

For each vertex v in the XPath expression, the algorithm maintains COUNT(v), which represents how many elements e in the active stack contain v in SELF(e).

Algorithm Overview. We first describe our algorithm with respect to a projection set that contains a single XPath expression, and then, discuss how to extend the algorithm for multiple XPath expressions. The essence of the algorithm is simple — materialize an element if it could participate in an embedding. As a tree is traversed and events are generated, for each vertex in the tree representation of the input XPath expression, the algorithm keeps track of the forward and backward constraints that have been satisfied. The following two conditions are used to determine whether a given element may participate in an embedding:

- Satisfaction of Backward Constraints: Let an element e belong to an embedding $\mathcal{E}$ of T into D such that for some vertex v, $\mathcal{E}(v) = e$. For each vertex v' in $\mathcal{B}(v)$, there must be some ancestor of e, e' such that $\mathcal{E}(v') = e'$, and the relation between e and e' satisfies the edge constraint between v and v'. This is a straightforward consequence of the definition of embeddings. At a start element event for an element, we verify that if the label of e matches some vertex v, then for each vertex $v' \in \mathcal{B}(v)$, one can find such a candidate e'. The vertex sets SELF(e), PARENT(e) and ANCESTORS(e) are used for this purpose. For example, if AXIS$(v,v') = $ ancestor, we require that ANCESTORS(e) contains v'. Otherwise, e cannot participate in an embedding for v. For ancestor-or-self constraints, we require that v' be present in the ANCESTORS(e) or SELF(e) vertex sets.
- Satisfaction of Forward Constraints : A similar statement can be made for forward vertex sets. Let an element e belong to an embedding $\mathcal{E}$ of T into D

such that for some vertex v, $\mathcal{E}(v) = e$. For each vertex v' in $\mathcal{F}(v)$, there must be some descendant of e, e' such that $\mathcal{E}(v') = e'$, and the relation between e and e' satisfies the edge constraint between v and v'. At the end element event, the algorithm can verify that if the label of e matches some vertex v, then such a candidate e' exists for all vertices $v' \in \mathcal{F}(v)$. The vertex sets SELF(e), CHILDREN(e) and DESCENDANTS(e) are used for this purpose in a similar manner to the use of the SELF(e), PARENT(e) and ANCESTORS(e) sets for backward constraints.

At an end element event, the algorithm determines (given the current information) whether the current element e or some node in its subtree is a possible candidate for an embedding. If so, the algorithm materializes the element; otherwise, it creates an inflatable node for the element. The COUNT data structure is used to prune information, as will be described shortly.

The handling of multiple XPath expressions is a straightforward extension to the handling of a single XPath expression — the algorithm evaluates each of them in parallel. An element is materialized if it is required by any of the XPath expressions.

Algorithm Details. The inflatable tree construction algorithm processes a given XPath expression $T = (V_T, E_T)$ and a document $D = (N_D, E_D)$ to construct the inflatable tree in a bottom-up manner — at each end element event for an element, the algorithm decides whether to build a materialized node or an inflatable node for that element based on decisions taken for its children.

- Initially, set the active stack to be empty.
- At a start element event for an element e, push e on to the active stack.
  1. Set ANCESTORS(e), CHILDREN(e), DESCENDANTS(e) to be empty.
  2. If e is the root of the document, set PARENT(e) to be empty, otherwise set PARENT(e) to equal SELF(e'), where e' is the parent of e in the tree.
  3. Set SELF(e) to be all vertices v in the XPath expression tree such that TAG(e) matches LABEL(v). For each vertex v in SELF(e) try to satisfy all the constraints in $\mathcal{B}(v)$ using SELF(e), PARENT(e) and ANCESTORS(e) as described previously. If all constraints for v cannot be satisfied, remove v from SELF(e). Continue this process until no further vertices can be removed from SELF(e). For each vertex v remaining in SELF(e), increment COUNT(v).
- At an end element event for an element e:
  1. If SELF(e) is non-empty, for each vertex v in SELF(e), check for the satisfaction of forward constraints using the SELF(e), CHILDREN(e) and DESCENDANTS(e) vertex sets. If the forward constraints cannot be satisfied for v, remove v from SELF(e) and decrement COUNT(v). If COUNT(v) becomes 0, we can prune DESCENDANTS(e). If DESCENDANTS(e) does not contain v, and COUNT(v) is 0, then all vertices v' that are descendants of v in the XPath expression tree can be removed from DESCENDANTS(e). Consider a v' that is in DESCENDANTS(e) such that v' is a descendant of v in the XPath expression. For an element e' in the subtree rooted at

e to be mapped to v' in some embedding, there must be an element e'' that is mapped to v in that embedding. Since v' is a descendant of v in the XPath expression tree, e'' must be an ancestor of e'. If COUNT(v) is 0 and DESCENDANTS(e) does not contain v, then observe that there can be no such e'' in the tree.

2. Repeat Step 1 for vertices in SELF(e) until no more vertices can be removed from SELF(e).

3. If SELF(e) and DESCENDANTS(e) are *both* empty, construct an inflatable node for e (and the subtree rooted under it), and discard the contents of SUBTREES(e).

4. If SELF(e) is not empty and DESCENDANTS(e) is empty, construct a materialized node for e. If SUBTREES(e) is not empty, construct a single inflatable node that represents all the children of e and insert this inflatable node as a child of the materialized node corresponding to e.

5. Otherwise, construct a materialized node for e and insert SUBTREES(e) as the children of this materialized node.

6. Let e' be the parent of e in D. Update CHILDREN(e') to CHILDREN(e') $\bigcup$ SELF(e). Set DESCENDANTS(e') to DESCENDANTS(e') $\bigcup$ DESCENDANTS(e) $\bigcup$ SELF(e). For each vertex v remaining in SELF(e), decrement COUNT(v).

In all cases, once the node for e is constructed, e is popped off the active stack and the node corresponding to e is appended to SUBTREES(e'), where e' is the current head of the stack (corresponds to e's parent in the document). If the node corresponding to e and the tail of SUBTREES(e') are both inflatable nodes, the two nodes are merged.

5   Implementation

We use a custom parser to generate the start and end element events corresponding to the depth-first traversal of the document. A key characteristic of the parser is the ability to support controlled parsing over a byte array — we can specify the start and end offsets of the byte array that the parser should use as the basis for parsing. This property is essential for the parsing of subtrees corresponding to inflatable nodes. Another feature of the parser is that at element event handlers, it provides offset information rather than materializing data as SAX does. For example, rather than constructing a string representation of the element tag's name, it returns an offset into the array and a length.

One challenge in the implementation of a projection algorithm is efficiency when complex axes are used. For example, Marian and Siméon report that document instance construction can degrade when XPath expressions involving **descendant** axes are used [8]. As we will demonstrate in Section 6, our algorithm scales well even in the presence of complex axes. The main reason for the efficiency of our implementation is a careful design of the data structures used to implement the algorithm of Section 4. We use bitmaps to represent much of the information that is necessary — set containment and union operations are encoded using efficient bitmask operations. As an optimization, our algorithm skips processing a subtree if it can detect that the subtree below the element cannot participate in any embedding. This happens if all the paths in the XPath set contain prefixes without any `ancestor` or `descendant` axes. For example, if the set of XPath prefixes is {/a/b/c, /a/d}, then if we encounter a start tag of a followed by an f, we can skip processing the subtree rooted at f.

Our system is implemented in Java. We use the Xerces [2] DOM representation as the underlying representation for the inflatable tree. Materialized nodes are represented as normal DOM nodes. Inflatable nodes have a special tag "_INFLATABLE_" and they contain two attributes indicating the start and end offsets in the byte representation of the document. The ability to use DOM as our underlying representation is a key advantage — we are able to run DOM-based XPath processors without modification on our inflatable trees; the semantics of projection guarantees that the inflatable nodes do not affect the result of evaluation of any XPath in the projection set!

6   Experiments

We used the queries of the XMark [11] benchmark set to evaluate the performance of our algorithm. In our experiment, the same benchmark code was used for both DOM and InflateX; the only difference being that for InflateX, the document was first projected with respect to a set of XPath expressions derived from the queries using the rules in [8]. In both cases, we used Xalan [1] as our XPath engine. We used a custom parser to generate appropriate events to construct both the inflatable tree, and in the DOM version, the full DOM data model instance. We used a custom parser rather than a standard XML parser such as Xerces [2] because our parser generates appropriate byte offset information in the events. We compared the performance of our parser for the construction of a full DOM instance with that of Xerces and found them comparable.[3] All experiments were run on a 1GHz IBM ThinkPad with 256MB of memory — the Java heap size was set at 128MB.

We will explore the efficiency of InflateX versus DOM in several dimensions: document construction time, query evaluation time, memory requirements, serialization, and dynamic projection. For both InflateX and DOM, the document is read from a file in the file system, the query is evaluated, and the results are serialized to a file. We will use the 20 original queries of the XMark benchmark. Since the XMark query set does not include queries that use axes such as `parent` and `following-sibling`, we have added two additional queries consisting of XPath expressions that use these axes. The projection sets corresponding to these two queries, which we refer to as Q21 and Q22 are provided in Table 1. All experiments were run on a 10 MB XMark file.

Construction Time. Figure 7 compares the time taken to construct the in-memory projection using InflateX with that for constructing a DOM instance.

---

[3] The cost of constructing a DOM instance from a 10MB XMark file using our parser was 1312ms compared to 1612ms for Xerces.

Table 1. Projection sets involving uses of axes other than `child` and `descendant`

Q21 {//item[ancestor::africa]/name[following-sibling::payment]//mailbox//from}
Q22 {/site/closed_auctions/closed_auction/itemref[preceding-sibling::buyer],
     /site/person/name[ancestor::people],
     /site/regions//item[parent::europe]/name}

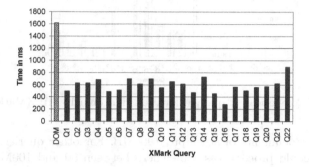

Fig. 7. Comparison of document construction time on a 10MB XMark file. The first column shows the cost of constructing a DOM in-memory instance. The remaining columns provide times for projection construction on the various queries.

As can be seen from the figure, our scheme is 2-3 times more efficient than DOM depending on the size of the projection. In Marian and Siméon, the document construction performance degrades with the presence of the `descendant` axis [8]. Our scheme is robust for descendant axes and performs well even when axes such as `ancestor` or `preceding-sibling` are used (as can be seen from the results for Q21 and Q22). The reason for the robustness is in the implementation of our algorithm. Our algorithm does not maintain much state apart from the projection tree that is being constructed; we encode much of the state using compact bitmaps.

Query Evaluation. As in Marian and Siméon, our projection scheme improves query evaluation because the queries are evaluated over a smaller document. Figure 8 compares the execution of the XMark queries with that of a similar evaluation over a full DOM instance. Most of the XMark queries contain only child axes. The performance of these queries improves marginally as such XPaths can be efficiently evaluated without having to search subtrees. In the presence of descendant axes (Q7, Q19), we obtain factors of improvement of 13 and 2.5. This is because the XPath processor searches entire subtrees to match descendant nodes.

Memory Requirements. In terms of the absolute memory sizes that can be handled, for DOM, the largest document that could be constructed in memory was 25 MB on our system (irrespective of the query). The amount of data that InflateX was able to handle depends on the projected set. For the projection path Q21 in Table 1, and for most other XMark queries, our projection scheme was

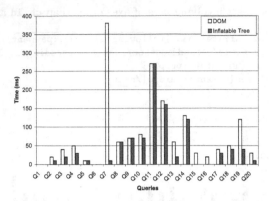

Fig. 8. Comparison of query evaluation time on a 10 MB XMark file

able to handle documents of size upto 100 MB. For other queries, the largest document we could process was somewhere between 50 and 100MB. The size of the projection is small relative to the overhead of storing the byte array in memory.

Figure 9 measures the number of nodes in the inflatable trees for each of the XMark queries. On average, we materialize about 10% of the nodes. The number of inflatable nodes that we construct is of the order of the projection, and therefore, does not add much overhead.

Serialization. Many queries return large result sets that need to be serialized out as a sequence of bytes to a client. The definition of projection by Marian and Siméon would construct all nodes that might have to be serialized. These nodes would be traversed to generate the bytes corresponding to the result. Our inflatable trees allow for efficient serialization directly from the byte array when

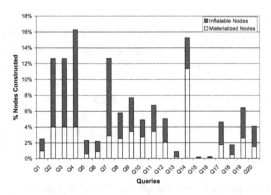

Fig. 9. Comparison of memory overhead on a 10MB XMark file. The total height of a column is the percentage of nodes in the original tree that are constructed (the tree contains 510946 nodes). Each column shows the breakdown in terms of materialized nodes and inflatable nodes constructed.

Table 2. Comparison of inflatable tree query execution time to the scheme that constructs the subtrees of all output nodes

	Inflatable Tree	Output Projection
Construction	470ms	680ms
Serialization	70ms	380ms
Number of Nodes	5119	78923

possible. Furthermore, we avoid the cost of having to construct all elements that are materialized solely because they are required for the output.

Table 2 compares the cost of query execution of the XPath expression `/site/regions/namerica/item` using different projections. The first uses our algorithm to build a projection based on inflatable trees. The second, *Output Projection*, constructs the subtrees of all output nodes in the document (as in Marian and Siméon).

The presence of the byte array corresponding to the document allows for a drastic reduction in the size of the projection, which in turn, reduces construction time. Furthermore, the cost of serialization reduces by a factor of four. The serialization of XML from a data model instance can be slow since the serializer must traverse the entire data model instance and output the appropriate XML constructs. The byte array allows our serialization mechanism to avoid this cost.

Dynamic Projection. One advantage of the inflatable tree representation over projection as defined by Marian and Siméon is that it allows clients to expand portions of the tree dynamically. For example, a client may choose to expand with respect to one set if an `if` branch is taken and another if the corresponding `else` branch is taken. Figure 10 explores the performance of dynamic projection in the common situation where a client first issues a query and then refines the query based on the results. In the experiment, the document is first projected with respect to the XPath expression `/site/regions/namerica`, and subsequently, the client refines the query with respect to XPath expression `/site/regions/namerica/item`. We compare the cost of dynamic projection over the inflatable tree to the cost of constructing a new projection (as would be done in Marian and Siméon). As can be seen, there can be a significant advantage to dynamic projection.

7   Conclusions

In this paper, we have proposed the inflatable tree data structure as a viable in-memory representation of XML. Our representation also supports dynamic projection of XML documents and efficient serialization of results to clients.

We have also developed a projection algorithm that can handle complex axes such as `ancestor` and `following-sibling`. Our experiments demonstrate that our algorithm constructs inflatable trees that are small compared to the full data instance, even when these complex axes are used. In addition to reducing

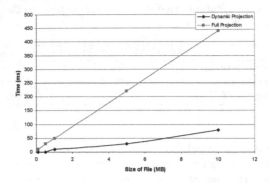

Fig. 10. Comparison of dynamically projecting a subtree of the document rather than projection over the entire document

the memory overhead of the in-memory representation of XML, our algorithm is efficient and can reduce the cost of constructing the instance significantly.

In the future, we plan to explore the use of schema information to drive the derivation of projections. Schema information in conjunction with the projection set of XPath expressions can be used to prune projections more precisely. Another area of interest is the exploration of automatically *deflating* trees, that is, determining from an XQuery expression, when a subtree in the XML document is no longer required.

References

1. Apache Software Foundation. *Xalan-Java.* http://xml.apache.org/xalan-j.
2. Apache Software Foundation. *Xerces2 Java Parser.* http://xml.apache.org/xerces2-j.
3. C. Barton, P. Charles, D. Goyal, M. Raghavachari, M. Fontoura, and V. Josifovski. Streaming XPath processing with forward and backward axes. In *Proceedings of the 19th IEEE International Conference on Data Engineering (ICDE)*, pages 455–466, March 2003.
4. P. Bohannon, S. Ganguly, H. F. Korth, P. P. S. Narayan, and P. Shenoy. Optimizing view queries in ROLEX to support navigable result trees. In *Proceedings of the 29th International Conference on Very Large Databases (VLDB)*, pages 119–130, 2002.
5. P. Buneman, M. Grohe, and C. Koch. Path queries on compressed XML. In *Proceedings of the 29th International Conference on Very Large Databases (VLDB)*, pages 141–152, 2003.
6. C.-Y. Chan, P. Felber, M. Garofalakis, and R. Rastogi. Efficient filtering of XML documents with XPath expressions. *The VLDB Journal*, 11(4):354–379, 2002.
7. Y. Diao, M. Altinel, M. J. Franklin, H. Zhang, and P. Fischer. Path sharing and predicate evaluation for high-performance XML filtering. *ACM Transactions on Database Systems*, 28(4):467–516, 2003.
8. A. Marian and J. Siméon. Projecting XML documents. In *Proceedings of the 29th International Conference on Very Large Databases (VLDB)*, pages 213–224, 2003.

9. G. Miklau and D. Suciu. Containment and equivalence for a fragment of XPath. *Journal of the ACM*, 51(1):2–45, 2004.
10. *Simple API for XML*. http://www.saxproject.org.
11. A. Schmidt, F. Waas, M. Kersten, M. Carey, I. Manolescu, and R. Busse. Xmark: A benchmark for XML data management. In *Proceedings of the 28th International Conference on Very Large Databases (VLDB)*, pages 974–985, 2002.
12. World Wide Web Consortium. *XML Path Language (XPath) Version 1.0*, November 1999.
13. World Wide Web Consortium. *Document Object Model Level 2 Core*, November 2000.
14. World Wide Web Consortium. *XQuery 1.0: An XML Query Language*, August 2003. W3C Working draft.

INDISS: Interoperable Discovery System for Networked Services

Yérom-David Bromberg and Valérie Issarny

INRIA-Rocquencourt,
Domaine de Voluceau, 78153 Le Chesnay, France
{David.Bromberg, Valerie.Issarny}@inria.fr

Abstract. The emergence of handheld devices associated with wireless technologies has introduced new challenges for middleware. First, mobility is becoming a key characteristic; mobile devices may move around different areas and have to interact with different types of networks and services, and may be exposed to new communication paradigms. Second, the increasing number and diversity of devices, as in particular witnessed in the home environment, lead to the advertisement of supported services according to different service discovery protocols as they come from various manufacturers. Thus, if networked services are advertised with protocols different than those supported by client devices, the latter are unable to discover their environment and are consequently isolated. This paper presents a system based on event-based parsing techniques to provide full service discovery interoperability to any existing middleware. Our system is transparent to applications, which are not aware of the existence of our interoperable system that adapts itself to both its environment across time and its host to offer interoperability anytime anywhere. A prototype implementation of our system is further presented, enabling us to demonstrate that our approach is both lightweight in terms of resource usage and efficient in terms of response time.

1 Introduction

The home environment now embeds networked devices, possibly wireless, from various application domains, i.e., home automation, consumer electronics, mobile and personal computing domains. The networked home shall then enable an open spontaneous network in which authorized devices are discovered and connected, as in particular investigated in the Amigo IST project [1].

Service discovery protocols enable finding and using networked services without any previous knowledge of their specific location. Several Service Discovery Protocols (SDP), like Jini [2], SLP [3], UPnP [4] and Salutation [5], are now available. With the advent of both mobility and wireless networking, SDPs are taking on a major role in networked environments, and are the source of a major heterogeneity issue across middleware. Furthermore, once services are discovered, applications need to use the same interaction protocol to allow unanticipated connections and interactions with them. Consequently, a second heterogeneity issue appears among middleware. Summarizing, middleware for the networked home environment must overcome two

G. Alonso (Ed.): Middleware 2005, LNCS 3790, pp. 164–183, 2005.

heterogeneity issues to provide interoperability, i.e.: (i) heterogeneity of service discovery protocols, and (ii) heterogeneity of interaction protocols between services. Interoperability is also difficult between devices made by different manufacturers, as they can implement differently a standardized protocol.

Distributed systems for the networked home must provide efficient mechanisms to detect and interpret protocols used by the networked devices, which are not known in advance. Furthermore, detection and interpretation must be achieved without increasing consumption of resources that are limited on a number of devices (e.g., handheld). New techniques must be used to both: (i) offer lightweight systems so that they can be supported by resource-constrained devices, and (ii) support system adaptation according to the dynamics of the open networked environment. Middleware solutions, designed to cope with the above issues, have been introduced, as surveyed in [6]. From this pool of existing middleware, more or less adapted to the constraints of the networked home, reflective middleware seem to be flexible enough to provide interoperability among networked services. However, solutions to interoperability based on reflective techniques, like ReMMoC [7,8], do not bring simultaneously interoperability and high performance, as discussed in [9]. SDP interoperability needs to be revisited to improve efficiency of SDP detection, interpretation and evolution. Moreover, to provide interoperability, we need a fine-grained control over protocols. Our approach is to decouple components from protocols with the use of concepts inherited from software architecture enhanced with event-based parsing techniques [10,11].

The originality of our approach comes from the trade offs achieved among efficiency, interoperability and flexibility. Our interoperability system, called INDISS (INteroperable DIscovery System for networked Services), may further be integrated with any existing middleware platform. Hosting INDISS enables the networked home system to discover and interpret all the services available in the home environment, independent of underlying middleware technologies. One key feature of INDISS is to provide efficient interoperability without altering the existing applications and services.

Based on conceptual similarities among SDPs, we are able to provide a generic mechanism supporting discovery protocol interoperability, as presented in Section 2. According to user activities, the networked home can become a highly dynamic network formed by the random arrival of devices based on different middleware. Whatever the networked home configuration/composition, interoperability must be maintained transparently without requiring to change the applications and/or services. In this context, INDISS must adapt itself to the evolution of the home environment across time. Section 3 discusses both the self-adaptation and context-awareness capabilities of INDISS. To validate the INDISS design, in particular in terms of efficiency, we have developed a first prototype, which is flexible enough to consider several use cases. Section 4 provides performance results, which demonstrate the efficiency of INDISS. Finally, Section 5 summarizes our contribution and discusses our future work on achieving middleware interoperability.

2 Service Discovery Protocol Interoperability

According to the architectural style of service-oriented computing systems, a majority of SDPs support the concepts of *client* and *service*. In order to find needed services, clients may perform two types of request: *unicast* or *multicast*. The former implies the use of a repository, equivalent to a centralized lookup service, which aggregates services information from service advertisements. The latter is used when either the repository's location is not known or there does not exist any repository in the environment. Similarly, services may announce themselves with either unicast or multicast advertisement, depending on whether a repository is present or not. From the aforementioned approaches, two SDP models are identified, irrespectively of the repository's existence: (i) the passive discovery model, and (ii) the active discovery model. When a repository exists in the network environment, the main challenge for clients and services is to discover the location of the repository, which acts as a mandatory intermediary between clients and services [3]. In this context, using the passive discovery model, clients and services are passively listening on a multicast group address specific to the SDP used and are waiting for multicast advertisements from a repository. On the contrary, with an active discovery model, clients and services send multicast requests to discover a repository that sends back a unicast response to the requester to indicate its presence. In a "repository-less" context, a passive discovery model means that the client is listening on a multicast group address, which is specific to the SDP that is used to discover services. Obviously, the latter periodically send out multicast announcement of their existence to the same multicast group address. In contrast, with a repository-less active discovery model, the roles are exchanged. Thereby, clients perform periodically multicast requests to discover needed services and the latter are listening to these requests. Furthermore, services send unicast responses directly to the requester only if they match the requested service. Summarizing, most SDPs support both passive and active discovery with either optional or mandatory centralization points. The following details our solution to SDPs interoperability, which is compatible with both the passive and active discovery models.

The following sections introduce the architectural principles of INDISS that builds on [9] and decomposes into mechanisms for: (i) SDP detection (§2.1) and (ii) SDP interoperability (§2.2). Specifically, SDP interoperability is achieved through translation of SDP functions in terms of events coordination (§2.3). This translation process is then outlined through a concrete example (§2.4).

2.1 SDP Detection

All SDPs use a multicast group address and a UDP/TCP port that must have been assigned by the Internet Assigned Numbers Authority (IANA). Thus, assigned ports and multicast group addresses are reserved, without any ambiguity, to only one type of use. Typically, SDPs are detected through the use of their assigned address and port. These two properties form a unique pair and may be interpreted as a permanent SDP identification tag. Furthermore, it is important to note that an entity may subscribe to several multicast groups simultaneously. These only two characteristics are sufficient to provide simple but efficient environmental SDP detection. We discover passively the environment by listening to the well-known SDP multicast groups. In fact, we learn the SDPs that are currently used from both services' multicast announcements and clients' multicast service requests. To achieve this feature, a component, called *monitor component*, embeds two major behaviours:

   – The ability to subscribe to several SDP multicast groups, and
   – The ability to listen to all their respective ports.

Figure 1 depicts the mechanism used to detect active and passive SDPs in a reposi-tory-less context. The *monitor component,* which may be deployed on the client side and/or service side, joins both the SDP1 and SDP2 multicast groups and listens to the corresponding registered UDP/TCP ports. We assume that SDP1 is based on an active discovery model. Hence, SDP1 clients perform multicast requests to the SDP1 multicast group to discover services in their vicinity. The *monitor component,* as a member of the SDP1 multicast group, receives client requests and thus is able to detect the existence of SDP1 in the environment as data arrival on the SDP1-dedicated UDP/TCP port identi-fies the discovery protocol. Assuming SDP2 is based on a passive discovery model, SDP2 services advertise themselves to the SDP2 multicast group to announce their exis-tence to their vicinity. Similarly to SDP1, as soon as data arrive at the SDP2-dedicated UDP/TCP port, the *monitor component* detects the SDP2 protocol. The *monitor compo-nent* is able to determine the current SDP(s) that is(are) used in the environment upon the arrival of the data at the monitored ports without doing any computation, data inter-pretation or data transformation. It does not matter what SDP model is used (i.e., active or passive) as the detection is not based on the data content but on the data existence at the specified UDP/TCP ports inside the corresponding groups.

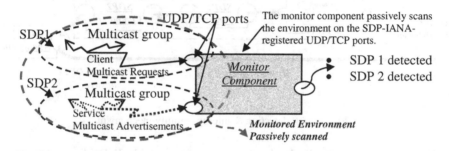

Fig. 1. Detection of active and passive SDPs through the monitor component

The monitor component is easy to implement, as both subscription and listening are solely IP features. Hence, any middleware based on IP support the *monitor component,* which simply maintains a static correspondence table between the IANA-registered permanent ports and their associated SDP. Hence, SDP detection only depends on which port raw data arrived. Therefore, the cost of SDP detection is reduced to a minimum.

2.2 SDP Interoperability

SDP detection is just a first step towards SDP interoperability. The main issue is still unresolved: the incoming raw data flow, which comes to the *monitor component,* needs to be correctly interpreted to deliver the service descriptions to the application components. To effectively support SDP interoperability, we reuse event-based pars-ing concepts.

Upon the arrival of raw data at monitored ports, the *monitor component* detects the SDP that is used (Figure 2, Step), and forwards the input data to the appropriate *parser* (Step), to successfully transform the raw data flow into a series of events. The *parser* extracts semantic concepts as events from syntactic details of the SDP detected. Then, the generated events are delivered to *composers* that are locally deployed (Step). Finally, the composer delivers a SDP message understood by the target application (Step). The communication between the *parser* and the *composer* does not depend on any syntactic detail of any protocol. They communicate at a semantic level through the use of events. Indeed, a fixed set of common events has been identified for all SDPs (see §2.3). And, a larger, specific set of events is defined for each SDP. For example, a subset of events generated by a UPnP parser are successfully understood by a SLP *composer,* whereas specific UPnP events, due to UPnP functionalities that SLP does not provide, are simply discarded from the SLP *composer,* as they are unknown.

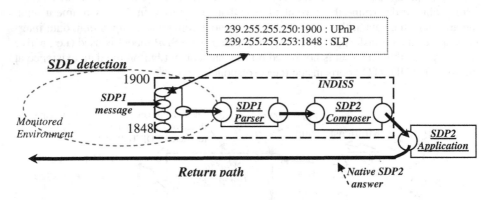

Fig. 2. SDP detection & interoperability mechanisms

Event streams are totally hidden to components outside INDISS, as they are assembled into SDP-specific messages through *composers.* Consequently, interoperability is guaranteed to existing applications tied to a specific SDP without requiring any change to applications. Similarly, future applications do not need to be developed with a specific middleware API to benefit from SDP interoperability. In general, application components continue to use their own native service discovery protocol; interoperability is achieved through a transparent integration of INDISS. It is further important to note that the system may be deployed on either the service provider or client application side. It may even be distributed among both parties or deployed on some intermediate (e.g., gateway) networked node (see §4.2).

Parsers and composers are dedicated to specific SDP protocols. Then, to support more than one SDP, several parsers and composers must be embedded into the system. Embedded parsers and composers are dynamically instantiated.

SDP interoperability comes from the composition of parsers and composers dedicated to different SDPs. As depicted in Figure 3, an incoming SDP1 message is successfully translated into an SDP2 message that is then forwarded to an SDP2-related application. According to several SDP specifications, an incoming message is often followed by a reply message. In this context, two cases may be considered: (i) the reply is directly sent by the native SDP (Figure 2, Step), which requires the receiver to translate the message into a message of the hosted SDP, (ii) the reply is translated into a message of the destination's SDP (Figure 3). The former solution leads to the sharing of the interoperability tasks among all participating nodes. However, this requires all the nodes to embed INDISS. As a result, nodes that do not integrate the necessary interoperability mechanisms are likely to be isolated. Therefore, this specific configuration must be considered as a special case but cannot be assumed nor enforced in general. Instead, we consider that a node embedding INDISS is able to take care of the complete interoperability process, i.e., both receiving and sending messages from/to non-native SDPs. Thus, interoperability among nodes is achieved without requiring all the participant nodes to embed INDISS. SDP interoperability is achieved if the proposed interoperability system is embedded in at least one of the following nodes: client, server or even gateway.

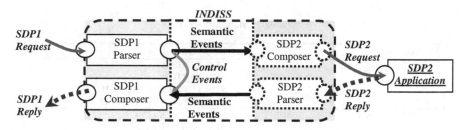

Fig. 3. Coupling of parser and composer

From the above, it follows that within INDISS, a parser is coupled with a composer that does the reverse translation process, in a way similar to the marshalling/unmarshalling functions of middleware stubs. Furthermore, depending on the SDP specification, the parser and composer may have to share one bi-directional session. Such a coupling occurs when, e.g., once the parser has received a request message, the composer has to send some acknowledgement or control message to simply maintain or validate a communication session with the requester. In general, SDP functions like service request, service registration or service advertisements, are complex distributed processes that require coordination between the actors of the specific service discovery function. It follows that the translation of SDP functions that is realised by INDISS is actually achieved in terms of translation of processes and not simply of exchanged messages, further requiring coordination between the parser and composer. This is realized by embedding the parser and composer within a *unit* that runs coordination processes associated with the functions of the supported SDP. The unit is further self-configurable in that it manages the evolution of its configuration, as needed by the SDP specifics and the evolution of the environment. The behaviour of the unit may easily be specified using finite state machines, as detailed in the next section.

2.3 Event-Based Interoperability

A unit implements event-based interoperability for a specific SDP by: (i) translating to and from semantic events associated with service discovery, messages of the specific SDP, and (ii) implementing coordination processes over the events according to the behaviour of the SDP functions.

The overall coordination process implemented by the SDP unit is specified using a Finite State Machine (FSM). A SDP state machine is a graph of states connected by transitions. A SDP state machine is a Deterministic Finite Automaton (DFA) and is, as usual, defined as a 5-tuple $(Q, \sum, C, T, q0, F)$, where Q is a finite set of states, $\sum$ is the alphabet defining the set of input events (or triggers) the automaton operates on, C is a finite set of conditions, $T: Q \times \sum \times C \to Q$ is the transition function, $q0 \in Q$ is the starting state and $F \subset Q$ is a set of accepting states. *States* keep track of the progress of the SDP coordination process. *Transitions* are labelled with events, conditions and actions.

Table 1. Mandatory events

Event set	Event type
SDP Control Events	SDP_C_START SDP_C_STOP SDP_C_PARSER_SWITCH SDP_C_SOCKET_SWITCH
SDP Network Events	SDP_NET_UNICAST SDP_NET_MULTICAST SDP_NET_SOURCE_ADDR SDP_NET_DEST_ADDR SDP_NET_TYPE
Service Events	SDP_SERVICE_REQUEST SDP_SERVICE_RESPONSE SDP_SERVICE_ALIVE SDP_SERVICE_BYEBYE SDP_SERVICE_TYPE SDP_SERVICE_ATTR
SDP Request Events	SDP_REQ_LANG
SDP Response Events	SDP_RES_OK SDP_RES_ERR SDP_RES_TTL, SDP_RES_SERV_URL

The occurrence of an event may cause a transition if the event matches both the event and the condition of the transition. When a transition is engaged, several actions may be executed, relating to translation of events to/from message data, coordination, and configuration management (see Section 3). A SDP DFA is dedicated to one protocol to account for the protocol's specifics and consequently realize some optimisation. Events are basic elements and consist of two parts: *event type* and *data*. Whatever their types, events are always considered as triggers for the unit components to react and eventually activate some coordination rule. We define the minimal/mandatory set of events that is common to all SDPs and sets of specialized events that are specific to SDPs. The set of mandatory events $\sum$ is defined as the union of a number of subsets (see Table 1):

$\sum_m =$ *"SDP Control Events"* $\cup$ *"SDP Network Events"* $\cup$ *"SDP Service Events"* $\cup$
"SDP Request Events" $\cup$ *"SDP Response Events"*.

The set *"SDP Control Events"* contains events that may be generated by components embedded in INDISS (See section 3) to notify their listeners of their internal states. For instance, it enables either the *unit* to control the coordination of its registered components (i.e., parsers, composers) or any other components, registered as a listener, eventually from an upper layer like the application layer, to trace, in real time, SDP internal mechanisms. This is a useful feature, not only for debugging purposes, but also for a dynamic representation of the run-time interoperability architecture. The set *"SDP Network Events"* is related to network properties and, for instance, defines events to determine if the SDP messages are either unicast or multicast, to indicate the SDP used and to specify the source or target address. Then, *"SDP Service Events"* enriches the above set with necessary events to describe the functions that are common to the different SDPs: service search request, service search response, service advertisements and the type of the service searched. Then, *"SDP Request Events"* and *"SDP Response Events"* contain events respectively dedicated to the description of SDP requests with richer descriptions, and to specific events to express possible common SDP answers (e.g., positive or negative acknowledgement, URL of the searched service etc).

All SDP parsers must at least generate the mandatory events. Conversely, all SDP composers must also understand them. The mandatory events result from the greatest common denominator of the different SDP functionalities. Nevertheless, a given SDP parser may generate additional events related to its advanced functionalities. Similarly, a SDP composer may manage these additional events. However, SDP composers are free to handle or ignore them. For instance, SLP does not manage UPnP advanced functionalities. Consequently, the SLP composer ignores UPnP-specific events generated by the UPnP parser. On the other hand, a JINI-related composer may support some of the UPnP-specific events. In fact, events added to the mandatory ones enable the richest SDPs to interact using their advanced features without being misunderstood by the poorest. The behaviour of the latter is unchanged as they discard unknown events and consider only the mandatory events. Moreover, INDISS is extensible and integration of future SDPs is rather direct. In particular, the possible introduction of new events to increase the quality of the translation process will not trigger a whole cascade of changes of SDP components. This is a direct consequence of building INDISS upon the event-based architectural style. We introduce three open, *extension sets* for the definition of additional events: *"Registration Events"*, *"Discovery Events"* and *"Advertisement Events"*. For instance, specific SDP messages involved in the registration of services are translated to events belonging to the *"Registering Events"* set, which enriches both *"SDP Requests Events"* and *"SDP Responses Events"*. The same applies for the *"Discovery Events"* set. On the other hand, *"Advertisement Events"* enriches only *"SDP Responses Events"* since an advertisement is a one-way message to spread service location.

States of the DFA (or coordination process) of a unit are activated according to triggers that define the event types that can cause transitions between states. Transitions imply that the unit executes some actions or coordination rules among its components (i.e., composer, parser). According to the unit's current state, incoming events are filtered and may be dispatched to different listeners (i.e., composer, parser or other units) until new incoming triggers cause a transition to a new state and so on. Reply messages generated through the composer may rely on data associated with events generated previously by its associated parser. Thus, events data from previous states are recorded using state variables. Conditions are written as Boolean expressions over incoming and/or recorded data and may test their properties, whereas actions are a sequence of operations that a unit can perform to: dispatch events to components, record events, or reconfigure the composition of its embedded components (e.g., changing dynamically the current parser or composer). Actions that may be performed by a unit are specific to the SDP that it manages. However, all units have to support mandatory actions.

2.4 Example

We illustrate our solution using a scenario where a SLP client is searching, e.q., a clock service. The clock service is based on UPnP and interoperability is enabled through the transparent use of INDISS (See Figure 3 with SDP1=SLP and SDP2=UPnP). Our aim, in this scenario, is to outline the different steps involved in the interoperability process and more particularly, to describe how messages are successfully transformed to events and vice-versa, during a search session initiated by a SLP client, to discover a service based on UPnP. However, for brevity, we describe only the most meaningful events that occur during this scenario.

First, the client broadcasts a SLP search request to discover its environment in order to find a clock service. As presented in Sections 2.1 and 2.2, INDISS catches the request as a raw data stream and forwards it to the parser of the SLP unit that generates a stream of events, which is dispatched to the composer of the UPnP unit as depicted in Figure 4, step . The event stream always starts with a *SDP_C_START* event and ends with a *SDP_C_STOP* event to specify the events belonging to a same message. On the other hand, the *SDP_NET_MULTICAST, SDP_SERVICE_REQUEST, SDP_SERVICE_TYPE* events are used to generate a corresponding UPnP search request. *SDP_REQ_VERSION, SDP_REQ_SCOPE, SDP_REQ_PREDICATE* and *SDP_REQ_ID* are events specific to SLP and are thus discarded by the UPnP unit's composer. The *SDP_NET_SOURCE_ADDR* is directly forwarded to the SLP composer embedded into the SLP unit to prepare the reply. The routing of events and related actions are specified by the DFA of the units as presented in §2.3.

Once the UPnP service has received the UPnP search request from INDISS, it responds to it with a corresponding UPNP search answer (Figure 4, step), which is then parsed by the UPnP unit. An event stream is generated and dispatched to the SLP unit's composer. However, thanks to its DFA, the UPnP unit detects that it does not get enough events from the UPnP service. The *SDP_RES_SERV_URL* event, which indicates the URL of the searched service, has never been generated. Therefore, the UPnP unit needs to recursively generate additional requests to the remote service until it receives the expected event. To achieve this task, the UPnP-specific events generated by the UPnP unit are consumed internally by the composer to generate other UPnP requests. For instance, the *SDP_DEVICE_URL_DESC* event gives the URL of the description of the remote service that contains the URL of the remote service endpoint. Therefore, once the composer of the UPnP unit receives this event, it generates a corresponding request to get the description. As previously, the next answer from the service is parsed (Figure 4, step) but the reply contains a XML body that the current UPnP parser, which is dedicated to the SSDP protocol, does not understand. Therefore, the current parser generates a *SDP_C_PARSER_SWITCH* event to ask its unit to switch to a XML parser to continue the parsing to get finally the expected *SDP_RES_SERV_URL* event. The XML description is converted to several *SDP_RES_ ATTR* events. As soon as the composer of the SLP unit has received all of them (as indicated by *SDP_C_STOP*), a SLP answer is generated (the *SDP_RES_ ATTR* are translated to traditional SLP attributes) and received by the SLP client.

Step	Request	Generated Events	Composed request
	SLP Search	SDP_C_START .... **SDP_NET_MULTICAST** SDP_NET_SOURCE_ADDR **SDP_SERVICE_REQUEST** SDP_REQ_VERSION SDP_REQ_SCOPE SDP_REQ_PREDICATE SDP_REQ_ID **SDP_ SERVICE_TYPE:** SDP_C_STOP	*From the previous events, the UPnP unit multicasts a UPnP search request to discover UPnP services in its vicinity:* M-SEARCH * HTTP/1.1 SERVER: 239.255.255.250:1900 ST: urn:schemas-upnp org:device:clock MAN: ssdp:discover MX: 0

Step	Reply Parsing	Generated Events	Composed request
	HTTP/1.1 200 OK **CONTENT-TYPE:** text/html; **SERVER**: UPnP/1.0 CyberLink/1.3.2 **CONTENT-LENGTH**: 0 .... ST: upnp:clock USN: uuid: ClockDevice::upnp:clock **LOCATION:** http://128.93.8.112:4004/description.xml	SDP_C_START SDP_NET_TYPE SDP_SERVICE_TYPE **SDP_DEVICE_URL_DESC**	*As the UPnP unit did not get the location of the remote service it must generate additional UPnP requests:* GET /description.xml HTTP/1.1

Step	Reply	Generated Events	Composed reply
	Service answer to the GET request: **HTPP Reply**	*Events generated from the HTPP reply:* SDP_C_PARSER_SWITCH SDP_RES_ATTR SDP_RES_ATTR ..... **SDP_RES_SERV_URL** SDP_C_STOP	<u>SrvRply</u>: **sevice:clock:soap://128.93.8.112:4005/** **service/timer/control** ;**major**:"1";**minor**:"0";**friendlyName**:"CyberGarage Clock Device"; **modelDescription**:"CyberGarage"; **manufacturerURL**:"http://www.cybergarage.org"; **modelDescription**:"CyberUPnP Clock Device"; **modeName**:"Clock";**modelNumber**:"1.0"; **modelURL**:"http://www.cybergarage.org";

Fig. 4. SLP-UPnP interoperability in action

3   Context-Aware, Self-adaptive Interoperability

INDISS is based on a specialization of the event-based architectural style. Advantages of using an event-based architecture are: increasing the degree of decoupling among components and of interoperability, and providing a dynamic and extensible architecture. Since interactions among components are based on events, components operate without being aware of the existence of other components and consequently parsers, composers and units may change dynamically at runtime without altering the system (see Figure 5). INDISS is consequently defined as a set of event-based components. We distinguish between these components that are inside the system, and other components that are outside INDISS and are therefore considered as application components.

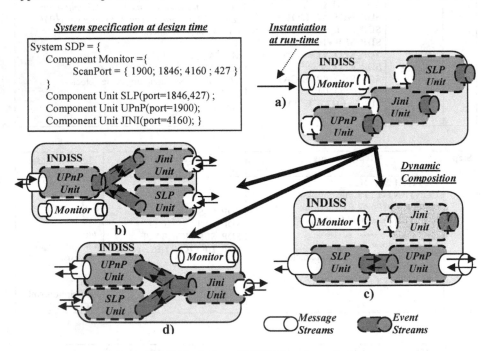

Fig. 5. Evolution of INDISS configuration

The INDISS internal architecture has to evolve across time due to two main reasons. First, as devices joining the network, whether mobile or stationary, evolve over time, the current SDP that is used and/or the SDPs with which interoperability is required may change accordingly. Second, some SDPs are actually based on a combination of protocols. For instance, UPnP uses alternatively SSDP, HTTP, and SOAP. To support these two types of changes, we need to define rigorous composition rules to describe the specific architecture of a given instance of INDISS. Configuration of a INDISS instance is initially defined in terms of supported SDPs and the corresponding units that need be instantiated. As illustrated in Figure 5.a, specification of the system configuration does not describe when and how to compose units. Indeed, unit composition is achieved dynamically according to both the context and the hosted application components. The context is discovered with the help of the monitor component, as presented in Section 2.1. At run-time, embedded units of different types are instantiated and dynamically composed depending on the environment and the applications used. Thus, several configurations may occur (e.g., see Figure 5.b, c, d).

At the system level, SDP interoperability is achieved through the correct composition of some units. As depicted in Figure 5.c, the translation from SLP to UPnP discovery corresponds to the composition of a SLP unit with a UPnP unit. At this level, a unit is only considered as a computational element that transforms messages to events and vice versa. The unit's internal mechanisms are totally hidden. Referring to event-based architectures, components can be either event listeners or event generators or both. The same applies for units; they are both event generator and listener. Units are composed and communicate together through events, whereas they use messages to interact with components that are outside INDISS. Therefore, the use of events is internal to INDISS.

At the unit level, coordination and composition rules among embedded SDP components are specialized with respect to a given SDP, according to the unit's state-machine. The unit is then in charge of dispatching event notifications to its registered listeners. However, there are some variations applied to the traditional event-based style. First, the unit does not systematically forward incoming events to all subscribers. The unit filters events, and may additionally react to them through actions to modify its current configuration. Events delivery and executed actions are dependent upon the unit's state machine described earlier. A notable feature of our solution is that SDP interoperability components that are developed are not necessarily specific to a SDP. Customization of a unit with respect to a SDP results from the specific configuration and in particular the embedded FSM.

As a result, interoperability components may be reused in various units, even if not related to the same SDP. For instance, at the implementation level, HTTP or XML parsers developed for one SDP may be reused for another. Definition of a unit then relies upon specifying embedded components, as exemplified below for a UPnP unit:

```
Component Unit UPnP = {
    setFSM(fsm, UPNP);
    AddParser(component, SSDP);
    AddComposer(component, SSDP);
    ...}
```

The state machine's description is itself considered as a part of the system specification. Hence, a new operator is introduced to define state machines:

```
Component UPnP-FSM ={
    AddTuple(CurrentState,triggers,condition-guards,NewState,actions)
    ...}
```

In the above tuple, *CurrentState* and *NewState* are labels to name different states, *triggers* are taken from the set of previously defined events, *condition-guards* are Boolean expression on events and *actions* are those provided by the unit's interface.

4 Prototype Implementation and Performance

We have implemented a first prototype of INDISS. Currently, it includes a UPnP unit and a SLP unit. Although our prototype is not yet optimised, it is robust enough to assess the performance of our approach in different use cases. The following discusses key elements of the prototype. We first outline its small size requirements compared to existing solutions (§4.1). We then discuss how it improves interoperability within the networked home according to the nodes on which it is deployed and the usage context (§4.2). Finally, we evaluate INDISS performance by comparing response times with native service discovery (§4.3).

4.1 Prototype Implementation

The prototype is implemented in Java to take advantage of cross platform portability. We are, in particular, able to deploy our solution on any mobile device that embeds J2ME [12], which provides a Java virtual machine customized for devices with limited resources. However, INDISS is not constrained to be written in Java, and may be developed as well in C or in any other programming language closer to the embedded operating system, to get a smaller code-size foot print and better execution speeds. Nevertheless, in Java, we get already very encouraging results. We compare the size required by INDISS with common open-source library like *OpenSlp*[1] and *Cyberlink* for Java[2].

As depicted in Table 2, currently, the overall INDISS system consists of 39 Java classes, and 2910 lines of Non Commented Source Statements Classes (NCSS). The overall system size is 218 Kbytes. This includes 125Kbytes for the UPnP Unit and 49Kbytes for the SLP one. To be interoperable, nodes running UPnP (resp. SLP) applications need to host native UPnP (resp. SLP) library plus INDISS. This is to be contrasted with a device that is not equipped with our interoperable system, which needs: (i) to host both the full UPnP stack and the SLP library and, (ii) some engineering effort to develop and host an additional SLP (resp. UPNP) client that is equivalent in terms of functionalities to the UPnP (resp. SLP) client.

Still in Table 2, without INDISS, the size requirements of a middleware that needs to be interoperable for hosting one simple service is 514Kbytes. Conversely, the size requirement for a middleware dedicated to UPnP (resp. SLP) equipped with INDISS is 598Kbytes (resp. 352Kbytes). Moreover, the size requirements increase proportionally with the number of hosted services. Therefore, according to the number of hosted services, the size requirements of an interoperable middleware without INDISS increases faster than the one equipped with INDISS simply because, for the former, each time we add a service we are multiplying its size by two (e.g., SLP service size + UPnP service size).

Thus, the small size overhead introduced by INDISS with UPnP applications disappears with the number of hosted services. Last but not least, a middleware that needs to host different services, in terms of both functionalities and SDP used,

---

[1] http://www.openslp.org/
[2] http://www.cybergarage.org/net/upnp/java/

Table 2. Size requirements in KBytes for known libraries and INDISS

INDISS size requirements			
	Size (KB)	Classes	NCSS	Overhead
Core framework	44	15	789	-
UPnP Unit	125	18	1515	-
SLP Unit	49	6	606	-
Total	218	39	2910	-
SDP library size requirements			
OpenSlp Library	126	21	1361	-
Cyberlink UPnP	372	107	5887	-
Total	498	128	7248	-
Size requirements to provide interoperability with and without INDISS			
SLP &UPNP Library + SLP & UPnP clients	514	-	-	-
UPnP client & Library + INDISS	598	-	-	14%
SLP client & Library + INDISS	352	-	-	-31.5%

must have all the corresponding native libraries irrespectively of the use of INDISS. How ever, in this case, the latter still provides efficient interoperability: it reduces drastically both the number of hosted services and, in the long term, the overall middleware size since you do not have to develop and deploy services for each existing SDP.

4.2 Interoperability Scenarios

One of our objectives is to provide service discovery interoperability to applications without altering them. Hence, applications are not aware of interoperability mechanisms and actually have the illusion that the remote applications that they discover (and/or discover them) use the same SDP. In this context, several use cases may be considered, according to both the nature of the SDPs that are used and the location of INDISS, which can be localized on the client, server, both or gateway.

Another of our other objectives is to save resources on resource-constrained devices and the bandwidth that is shared among devices in the network. It is thus important to examine the impact of INDISS on resource consumption. This may in particular vary according to the system's location (i.e., where it is deployed) and usage context. The usage context of the system depends on the SDP model used by the clients and services. Referring to Section 2, there exist two SDP models: passive and active. We need thus to distinguish cases where the client (resp. service provider) acts as listener and as a requester. Moreover, we obviously assume that either the client or service node hosts INDISS. As a result, for each possible scenario, two uses cases are possible, according to the location of INDISS.

Consider first that both clients and services are based on the passive discovery model (see Figure 6). In this context, clients are listeners and services are requesters. The most optimised location for INDISS is to be hosted on the client side. Thereby, clients are able to intercept all messages generated by the remote service whatever its specific multicast group or message format (see left-top of Figure 6). In contrast, if as, INDISS is localized on the service side, it will never intercept messages from clients INDISS is localized on the service side, it will never intercept messages from clients by definition of the passive discovery model, clients are listeners and never generate messages. We get a blocked situation as depicted in the right top of Figure 6.

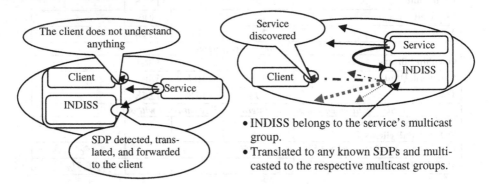

Fig. 6. SDP interoperability and passive service discovery

Consequently, we must define a *network traffic threshold* below which INDISS, hosted on the service host, must become active so as to intercept messages generated from the local services in order to translate them to any known SDPs according to the embedded units (see bottom of Figure 6). Although this specific use case illustrates the high flexibility of INDISS to adapt itself to the context, it has non-negligible impact on resource consumption. Indeed, dynamic reconfiguration of the system has a processing cost and service advertisements following the enactment of the active model increases bandwidth usage. However, interoperability is enforced without really saturating the bandwidth, as INDISS is switched to the active model only when the network traffic is low.

Consider now the case where both clients and services are based on the active discovery model, i.e., clients are requesters and services are listeners. In order to optimise the bandwidth usage and computational resources, the most suitable location for INDISS is to be on the service side. Otherwise, in a way similar to the previous scenario, ineffective SDP interoperability may arise when INDISS is located on the requester side. In general, when the clients and services are based on the same discovery model, the most convenient location for INDISS is on the listener side.

It may be the case that the clients and services are based on different discovery models. If the clients are based on the active model and services are based on the passive model, then both clients and services generate SDP messages. Interoperability is guaranteed without additional resources cost. Nevertheless, some subtleties arise. Hosting INDISS on the client side means that the client benefits from the advertisements of remote services. But, the client's requests will not reach remote services that are based on different SDPs if they are not interoperable (i.e., they do not host our interoperability system). On the contrary, if services embed INDISS and not the clients, requests from the latter will be taken into consideration from services, whereas clients will not be aware of services' advertisements originating from SDPs different than the one hosted on the clients. Although, in this case, interoperability is not as effective as expected, clients and services do interact. Furthermore, interoperability effectiveness may be improved if the bandwidth is under-utilized, thanks to INDISS reconfigurability

Conversely, when clients are based on the passive model and services are based on the active model, both clients and services are listeners. Once again, we are faced with the recurrent ineffective discovery interoperability. However, in this particular case, dynamic reconfiguration of INDISS does not resolve the clients' inability to discover services, since there is no node initiating SDP-related communication. There is no way to resolve this issue, considering our constraint to not alter the behaviour of SDPs, clients and services. On the other hand, this specific case is unlikely to happen. Nowadays, in practice, clients are always able to generate requests.

Summarizing, irrespective of the service discovery model used by clients and services, we are able to guarantee a minimum level of interoperability. Depending on the environment, the bandwidth usage may be increased to enable interoperability. The basic idea is to provide a quasi-full interoperability as long as the bandwidth-usage enables it. Then, interoperability degradation may occur according to the traffic. Furthermore, by design, INDISS is independent of its host. Thus, it is not mandatory for INDISS to be deployed on the client or service host. INDISS may be deployed on a dedicated networked node, depending on the specific network environment. Such a dedicated node may in particular translate messages generated in one environment from any SDP to messages handled by any other SDP, according to the traffic condition. Obviously, this specific configuration generates additional traffic and is only valid as long as there is enough bandwidth.

4.3 Experimental Results

We evaluate the performance of our interoperability mechanisms by investigating the response time of INDISS when enabling a client dedicated to one SDP to discover a service based on another SDP. Specifically, the experiments consider the case where a SLP (resp. UPnP) client searches a SLP (resp. UPnP) service. We then compare the native client waiting time to get an answer from a native service, with its waiting time to get an answer from an INDISS-translated service. The impact of INDISS on performance varies according to its location, on either the client or the service side. Thus in the following, we consider the two cases. In addition, as interoperability is achieved without generating additional traffic, we have not evaluated the network bandwidth consumption. Indeed, the generated traffic is well known since we are neither providing a new service discovery protocol nor altering native protocols.

Although our solution is dedicated to various devices, including resources constrained ones, all tests are performed on workstations equipped with 256Mbytes RAM on Intel PIV processor rated at 1.8GHz. In fact, currently, to the best of our knowledge, there does not exist any UPnP profile for J2ME devices in the open source community. Thus, the operating system, the Java virtual machine and the performance tools platform used are respectively Linux from Redhat Fedora Core 2, JDK1.4.2 from SUN and the Hyades platform from Eclipse Foundation. Moreover, the SLP (resp. UPnP) client and SLP (resp. UPnP) service are hosted on different hosts connected to a LAN at 10Mb/s. The SLP client and service are based on OpenSlp whereas UPnP client and service use Cyberlink for Java. The given measurements are in ms and are the median of 30 successful tests to avoid a mean skewed by a single high or low value.

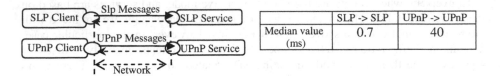

	SLP -> SLP	UPnP -> UPnP
Median value (ms)	0.7	40

Fig. 7. Native clients & services

In Figure 7, we first give the response time of a search request generated by a native client to get a successful answer from a native service: for SLP, we get 0.7 ms, whereas for UPnP, we get 40ms. It is clear that using SLP is much more efficient than UPnP, which is a higher-level protocol than SLP. These results are considered as references values to enable us to interpret the following results.

Consider now the case where INDISS is located on the service side to enable the latter to be interoperable with any client independently of its SDP (Figure 8). In the context where the client is SLP and the service is UPnP, the client gets an answer in 65 ms. The translation between SLP and UPnP is not direct. For instance, UPnP and SLP search responses are semantically different: a SLP client expects a direct reference to interact with the service discovered whereas a UPnP client expects a reference to a description file corresponding to the service found. Consequently, INDISS has translated the SLP request into two local UPnP requests to get the information that is necessary to generate on the network the corresponding SLP response. This means that INDISS has waited and parsed successively two UPnP responses increasing thus the SLP responsiveness latency. On the service side, it is clear that INDISS simulates a UPnP client and therefore we cannot interfere on the native time taken to get UPnP response from the service. In this context, the INDISS result is pretty good.

Still in Figure 8, when the client is UPnP and the service is SLP, the response time to get an answer is 40ms. In fact, it corresponds exactly to a search request generated

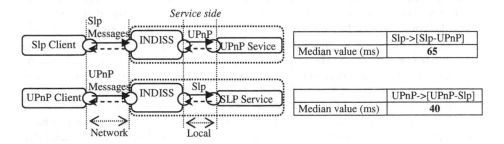

	Slp->[Slp-UPnP]
Median value (ms)	65

	UPnP->[UPnP-Slp]
Median value (ms)	40

Fig. 8. Performance with INDISS located on the service side

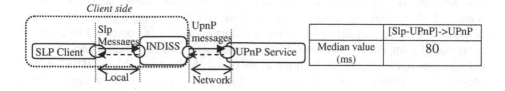

a) SLP search request to a UPnP service

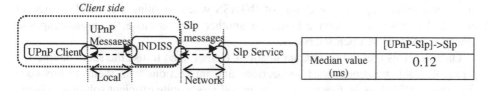

b) UPnP search request to a SLP service

Fig. 9. Performance with INDISS located on the client side

on the network from a native UPnP client to a native UPnP service. On the service side, the response time to a SLP request is negligible as the latter is generated locally.

When INDISS is located on the client side (Figure 9a), the latter becomes interoperable and can discover any service whatever its SDP. If the client is SLP and the service is UPnP the SLP client gets the answer to its search request in 80ms. It corresponds globally to two native UPnP responses from a native UPnP service. It is obvious since, as previously, INDISS has translated the SLP request into two network UPnP requests to get the necessary information to generate locally the corresponding SLP response. Once again, INDISS result is encouraging. It is important to note that compared to the case depicted in Figure 8, the response time is higher than previously simply because the UPnP traffic goes across the network between INDISS and the UPnP service, increasing by 15 ms the response time. In the same context, the lack of speed inherent to the UPnP protocol is confirmed as a UPnP client gets a response from a SLP service in only 0.12ms (Figure 9b). This is due to the fact that first the UPnP traffic is local and then the only traffic that goes across the network is SLP, which is particularly fast. In addition, the necessary information to generate a search response for UPnP is tiny. We can consider this case as the best case.

From the above results, we have shown that INDISS is particularly efficient in providing interoperability in all possible context use.

5 Conclusion

INDISS overcomes the heterogeneity of service discovery in the networked home and decomposes into two mechanisms: SDP detection and SDP interoperability, allowing therefore any networked home system to discover and interpret all the services available in the home environment, independent of underlying middleware technologies.

Our solution is specifically designed for highly dynamic home networks, which requires both minimizing resource consumption, and introducing lightweight mechanisms that may be adapted easily to any platform. INDISS is composed of a set of event-based components and their composition/configuration is performed dynamically at run-time according to both the context and the host on which INDISS is deployed. As a result, service discovery interoperability is provided to applications without altering them: applications are not aware of the existence of INDISS, which adapts itself to the context. In particular, INDISS may be deployed on a client, a service or a gateway. As demonstrated by the first INDISS prototype, experiment results are encouraging. The response time of INDISS when enabling a client dedicated to one SDP to discover a service based on another SDP is close to request/response among related native clients/services.

Once services are discovered, applications further need to use the same interaction protocol to allow unanticipated connections and interactions with them. In this context, the ReMMoC reflective middleware introduces a quite efficient solution to interaction protocol interoperability. The plug-in architecture associated with reflection features allows mobile devices to adapt dynamically their interaction protocols (i.e., publish/subscribe, RPC etc.). Furthermore, [13] proposes to use ReMMoC together with WSDL [14] for providing an abstract definition of the remote component's functionalities. Client applications may then be developed against this abstract interface without worrying about service implementation's details. However, the solution discussed in [13] suffers from a major constraint: service and client must agree on a unique WSDL description. But, once again, in a dynamic network, the client does not know the execution context. Therefore, it is not guaranteed to find exactly the expected service. Client applications have to find the most appropriate service instance that matches the abstract requested service. In addition, this leads to the dynamic composition of services. This issue is addressed by the WSAMI middleware developed in the context of the Ozone project [15], which introduces enhanced WSDL specification for mobile services and a dedicated middleware to allow a service instance to be *automatically selected and composed upon a user request, according to the services that may be retrieved in the environment*. However, if WSAMI provides interoperability to Web services in the mobile environment, it is still a SOAP based middleware, and hence does not deal with interoperability among components using heterogeneous interaction protocols. We are currently investigating solutions to this issue to complement our solution to SDP interoperability and thus support middleware interoperability, as required by today's network environments [1].

Acknowledgements

This work has received the support at the European Commission through the IST program, as part of the AMIGO project (http://www.amigo-project.org). The authors would like to thank Daniele Sacchetti for helping us make performance measurements. The authors are further grateful to anonymous reviewers for useful comments.

References

[1] Amigo Consortium. Specification of the Amigo abstract middleware architecture. http://www.hitech-projects.com/euprojects/amigo/.

[2] Sun. Technical White Paper: Jini Architectural Overview. 1999.

[3] C. Bettstetter and C. Renner. A comparison of service discovery protocols and implementation of the service location protocol. In Proceedings of the 6th EUNICE Open European Summer School: Innovative Internet Applications, 2000.

[4] Universal Plug and Play Forum. Universal Plug And Play Device Architecture. 2000.

[5] Salutation Consortium. White paper: Salutation Architecture. 1998.

[6] C. Mascolo, L. Capra, W. Emmerich. Middleware for mobile computing (A survey). In Advanced Lectures in Networking. Editors E. Gregori, G. Anastasi, S. Basagni. Springer. LNCS 2497. 2002.

[7] G. Coulson, G. Blair, M. Clarke and N. Parlavantzas. The design of a configurable and reconfigurable middleware platform. In Distributed Computing. April 2002.

[8] P. Grace, G. Blair and S. Samuel. Middleware awareness in mobile computing. In Proceedings of the 1st international ICDCS Workshop on Mobile Computing Middleware, May 2003.

[9] Y.-D. Bromberg, V. Issarny. Service Discovery Protocols Interoperability in the Mobile Environment. In Proceedings of the International Workshop Software Engineering and Middleware (SEM). September 2004.

[10] N. Ryan and A. Wolf. Using event-based parsing to support dynamic protocol evolution. In Proceedings of the 26th International Conference on Software Engineering (ICSE'04).2004

[11] D. Garlan. Formal modeling and analysis of software architecture: Components, connectors, and events. In Third International School on Formal Methods for the Design of Computer, Communication and Software Systems. September 2003.

[12] The Micro Edition of the Java 2 Platform, http://java.sun.com/j2me/

[13] P. Grace, G. Blair and S. Samuel. A marriage of Web services and reflective middleware to solve the problem of mobile client interoperability. In Proceedings of Workshop on Middleware Interoperability of Enterprise Applications. September 2003.

[14] W3C."Web Services Description Language (WSDL)", W3C Working Draft. 2003

[15] V. Issarny, D. Sacchetti, F. Tartanoglu, F. Sailhan, R. Chibout, N. Levy, and A. Taloma. Developing ambient intelligence systems: A solution based on Web services. Journal of Automated Software Engineering, 2005.

Dual-Quorum Replication for Edge Services

Lei Gao[1], Mike Dahlin[1], Jiandan Zheng[1], Lorenzo Alvisi[1], and Arun Iyengar[2]

[1] University of Texas at Austin, Austin TX 78712, USA
{lgao, dahlin, zjiandan, lorenzo}@cs.utexas.edu
[2] IBM TJ Watson Research Center, Yorktown Heights, NY 10598, USA
aruni@us.ibm.com

Abstract. This paper introduces dual-quorum replication, a novel data replication algorithm designed to support Internet edge services. Dual-quorum replication combines volume leases and quorum based techniques in order to achieve excellent availability, response time, and consistency the references to each object (a) tend not to exhibit high concurrency across multiple nodes and (b) tend to exhibit bursts of read-dominated or write-dominated behavior. Through both analytical and experimental evaluation of a prototype, we show that the dual-quorum protocol can (for the workloads of interest) approach the excellent performance and availability of Read-One/Write-All-Async (ROWA-A) epidemic algorithms without suffering the weak consistency guarantees and resulting design complexity inherent in ROWA-Async systems.

1 Introduction

This paper introduces dual-quorum replication, a novel data replication algorithm motivated by the desire to support data replication for edge services [1,3,10,29]. As Figure 1 illustrates, the Internet edge service model attempts to improve service availability and latency by allowing clients to access the closest available edge servers rather than a centralized server (or a centralized server cluster). But as Figure 1 also indicates, in order to provide a single service from multiple locations, service logic (code) replicated on all edge servers must access a collection of shared data. Thus, support for data replication is a key problem in realizing the promise of Internet edge services.

By exploiting object-specific workload characteristics, we seek to design a replication system for edge services that offers optimized trade-offs among availability, consistency, and response time. Although it is impossible to simultaneously provide optimal consistency, availability, and performance for *general-case* wide-area-network replication [5,17], we, perhaps, provide nearly optimal behavior for *specific objects* by taking advantage of a given application's workload characteristics. For example, our previous studies show how to provide nearly optimal replication for *information dissemination* applications such as news [22] and *e-commerce* applications such as TPC-W [10]. In particular, we developed customized consistency protocols for three categories of objects: (1)

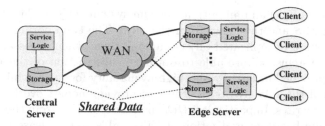

Fig. 1. Internet edge service architecture

single-writer, multi-reader objects like product descriptions and prices; (2) multi-writer, single-reader objects like customer orders; and (3) commutative-write, approximate-read objects like the inventory count of each product.

However, a key limitation of our previous efforts to support edge services was our decision to use weak consistency—and thereby introduce undesirable complexity—for a fourth category of objects: multi-writer, multi-reader objects such as TPC-W's per-customer *profile* information (e.g., name, account number, recent orders, credit card number, and address.) We, like several other systems [24,26,33], made use of a Read-One, Write-All-Asynchronously (ROWA-Async) protocol based on local reads and asynchronous epidemic propagation of writes. ROWA-Async protocols provide excellent read performance and availability; and although ROWA-Async protocols allow applications to observe inconsistencies between reads and writes, such inconsistencies should be rare because multi-reader, multi-writer shared objects often have workloads with low concurrency to any given object. For example, in our edge-server TPC-W application, reads and writes to a given customer's profile typically come from just one edge server for some interval of time, until the customer is redirected to a different server. Unfortunately, although inconsistencies are rare for the workloads of interest, these rare cases introduce considerable complexity into the system design, because all cases must be handled no matter how rare they are and because reasoning about corner cases in consistency protocols is complex. Furthermore, because reads can always complete locally, these protocols provide no worst-case bound on staleness (i.e., it is possible for a read to return stale data arbitrarily long after a write) which can be unacceptable for some applications.

By introducing dual-quorum replication, this paper provides the key missing piece to achieve highly-available, low-latency, and consistent data replication for a range of edge services. In particular, dual-quorum replication optimizes these properties for data elements that can be both read and written from many locations, but whose reads and writes exhibit locality in two dimensions: (1) at any given time access to a given element tends to come from a single node and (2) reads tend to be followed by other reads and writes tend to be followed by other writes. For other workloads, our algorithm continues to provide regular consistency semantics [16], but its performance and availability may degrade.

Our dual-quorum replication protocol combines ideas from volume leases [30] and quorums [11,12]. The protocol employs two quorum systems, an input quorum system (IQS) and an output quorum system (OQS). Clients send their writes to the IQS and they read from the OQS. The two quorum systems synchronize the state of replicated objects among them when necessary. By using two quorum systems, we are able to optimize construction of the OQS's read quorums to provide low latency and high availability for reads while optimizing construction of the IQS's write quorums to provide modest overhead and high availability for writes. In particular, OQS nodes cache data from the IQS servers using a quorum-based generalization of Yin et al.'s volume lease protocol [30], which invalidates individual cached objects as they are updated. The protocol uses short-duration volume leases to allow writes to complete despite network partitions and aggregates these leases across large numbers of objects in a volume to amortize the cost of renewing short leases. Using our dual-quorum protocol, workloads with large numbers of repeated reads (or writes) perform well because reads (or writes) can often be supplied by a read-optimized OQS read quorum (or write-optimized IQS write quorum) without requiring communication with the IQS (or OQS).

Through both analytical and experimental evaluations, we compare the availability, response time, communication overhead, and consistency guarantees of the dual-quorum protocol against other popular replication protocols: the synchronous and asynchronous Read-One/Write-All (ROWA) protocol family,[1] majority quorums, and grid quorums [7]. For the important special configuration of single-node OQS read quorums, average read response time can approach a node's local read time, making the read performance of this approach competitive with ROWA-Async epidemic algorithms such as Bayou [26]. But, the dual quorum approach avoids suffering the weak consistency guarantees and resulting complexity inherent in ROWA-Async designs. Additionally, the overall availability of the dual-quorum protocol is competitive with the optimal majority quorum protocol for the targeted workloads. Finally, for the targeted workloads, the communication overheads of this approach are comparable with existing approaches. However, in the worst-case scenario in which the workload consists of only interleaved reads and writes, the dual-quorum protocol requires significantly more message exchanges than traditional quorum protocols to coordinate internal nodes.

The main contribution of this paper is to introduce the dual-quorum algorithm, a novel data replication algorithm targeted at a key workload for Internet edge service environments. Note that although our work is motivated by a specific replication scenario, we speculate that it will be more generally useful. In particular, we believe that it may not be uncommon for systems that can, in principle, have any node read or write any item of data to, in practice, experience sufficient locality to benefit from our approach.

Our paper is organized as follows. Section 2 presents our system model and a set of assumptions on which our system is built. In Section 3, we present our system's design. We compare our system with existing ones in Section 4 with

---

[1] Note that ROWA protocols are, in fact, a special case of quorum protocols, but they are often treated separately in the literature.

both analytical and experimental evaluations. In Section 5, we discuss related work. Concluding remarks are presented in Section 6.

2 System Model and Definitions

Our edge service environment consists of a collection of edge server nodes that each play one or more of the following three roles: (a) *front end* nodes that handle *application client* requests from across the Internet, execute application-specific processing, and act as *service clients* to the dual-quorum storage system; (b) *Output Quorum System* (*OQS*) nodes that process read requests; and (c) *Input Quorum System* (*IQS*) nodes that process write requests. We assume a *request redirection architecture* that directs application clients to a good (e.g., nearby, lightly loaded, or available) front end edge server; a number of suitable redirection systems are discussed in the literature [15,31]. Note that application clients are unaware of the underlying data storage system and never contact the *OQS* or *IQS* interfaces directly.

In an edge service environment, servers typically process sensitive or valuable information, so they must run on trusted machines such as dedicated servers in a hosting center. We therefore assume a fail-stop model in which servers may crash but cannot issue incorrect requests or replies. The network may delay, duplicate, or reorder messages. We assume secure communication among nodes and that if the network corrupts a message, this corruption is detected by low-level checksums and the message is silently discarded. Each node can read a local real-time clock and there exists a maximum drift rate *maxDrift* between any pair of clocks.

For performance, our system assumes that concurrent reads and writes to a given object by different nodes are rare. But, for correctness, we must define the system's consistency semantics in the presence of concurrent reads and writes to the same object. The dual quorum design provides *regular* semantics [16]: a read r that is not concurrent with any write returns the value of the latest write that completed before r began and a read r that is concurrent with one or more writes returns one of (a) the value of the last write that completed before r began, or (b) the value of one of the writes concurrent with r.

For convenience of exposition, we describe interactions with a quorum system in terms of a QRPC (quorum-based remote procedure call) operation [18]. $replies = QRPC(system, READ/WRITE, request)$ sends *request* to a collection of nodes in the specified quorum *system* (e.g., the *IQS* or *OQS*). The QRPC call then blocks until a set of *replies* constituting the specified quorum (*READ* or *WRITE*) on the specified *system* have been gathered. The call then returns the set of *replies* that it received. The QRPC operator abstracts away details of selecting a quorum, retransmissions, and timeouts, but our protocol does not depend on any specific QRPC implementation. In particular, different implementations may choose different ways to select which nodes from *system* to send requests to, and they may select different retransmission strategies: our simple prototype implementation always transmits requests to the local node if the local node is a member of *system*; it then randomly selects a sufficient number of additional nodes to form a *READ* or *WRITE* quorum and transmits the request to them; retransmissions are each to a new randomly selected quorum using an exponentially-increasing retransmission interval. A more aggressive implementation might send to all nodes in *system* and return when the fastest quorum has responded or might track which nodes have responded quickly in the past and first try sending to them.

3   Dual Quorum Protocol Design

This section describes the design of the dual-quorum replication system and the key ideas for achieving our design goals. The basic idea is to separate the read and write quorum into two quorum systems so that they can be optimized individually to improve response time and availability for read-dominated or write-dominated workloads. The read and write quorums of the *OQS* and *IQS* can be separately configured in any way desired, but we would expect one common configuration to be to optimize read performance by having the *OQS* span all nodes in the system with a read quorum size of 1 and to get good write availability by having the *IQS* span a modest number of nodes with any majority of the *IQS* nodes forming a write quorum. As Figure 2 illustrates, in the dual quorum system service clients retrieve objects from a read quorum in *OQS* and send object updates to a write quorum in *IQS*. The two quorum systems conditionally synchronize with each other to maintain the consistency of data replicated on them when processing both reads and writes.

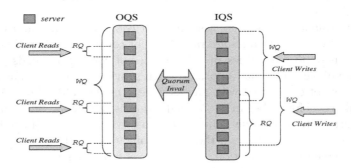

Fig. 2. Dual quorum architecture overview. Note that client reads and writes are issued by the service clients, not the application clients.

To simplify the discussion, we present the protocol in two steps. First, we will discuss the basic dual-quorum protocol, a simplified asynchronous protocol, in Section 3.1. This protocol allows separate optimizations of read and write quorums, but because it assumes an asynchronous system model, a write can block for an arbitrarily long period of time. Then, in Section 3.2 we describe how we introduce volume leases to improve write availability while retaining good read performance.

3.1   Dual Quorum Protocol

High level overview. The basic idea of the dual quorum protocol is to process reads and writes in two different quorum systems, *IQS* and *OQS* , and use a cache invalidation strategy to synchronize the state of objects replicated in *IQS* nodes and cached in *OQS* nodes.

Clients perform similar tasks for reading and writing data as in the conventional quorum based protocols. When a client read arrives in *OQS* , two possible scenarios can happen, as illustrated in Figure 3 (a) and (b). In a *read hit* case, the *OQS* read quorum contains a valid cache copy of the requested object, which is immediately sent back to the client. When there is a *read miss*, i.e. the cache copy on the *OQS* read quorum is invalid, the *OQS* read quorum validates the cache copy by querying an *IQS* read quorum for the latest update. Once the cache copy of the *OQS* read quorum is validated, the *OQS* read quorum sends the updated value to the client. There are also two scenarios when processing client writes, as illustrated in Figure 3 (c) and (d). In a *write suppress* case, the cache copy in an *OQS* write quorum is already invalid. The *IQS* write quorum can just apply the write to the local object and send the completion acknowledgment to the client. In the case of a *write through*, an *OQS* write quorum may hold a valid cache copy. Therefore, the *IQS* write quorum that receives the client write has to invalidate the cache copy on one *OQS* write quorum before the write can complete.

For workloads consisting of read bursts, the first read forces all *OQS* nodes of the read quorum to validate their cached copies. Therefore, all subsequent reads via that quorum are *read hits*. If we configure the *OQS* read quorum to contain only one node, reads becomes local, and the protocol can yield near optimal read response time and availability for read-dominated workloads. For workloads consisting of write bursts of the same data, the first write invalidates cached copies in an *OQS* write quorum, making all subsequent writes *write suppresses*. Naturally, we can configure *IQS* as a majority quorum system to provide near optimal write availability for such workloads.

Protocol details. The following paragraphs provide the details of the basic dual-quorum protocol by describing the actions taken at individual nodes.

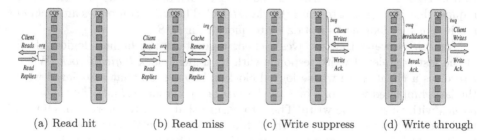

(a) Read hit   (b) Read miss   (c) Write suppress   (d) Write through

Fig. 3. Request processing scenarios

Data structures. Each *IQS* node maintains the following state for each object o: $lastWriteLC_o$ stores the logical clock of the last write to o, $lastReadLC_o$ stores the value of $lastWriteLC_o$ from the time of the last read of o, $lastAckLC_{o,j}$ stores the logical clock contained in the highest invalidation reply from OQS node j for o, and $value_o$ stores the value of o. Each node in IQS maintains a logical clock $logicalClock$ whose value is always at least as large as the node's largest $lastWriteLC_o$ for any object o. Each node in OQS maintains the following per-object o per-IQS-node i state: $logicalClock_{o,i}$ indicates the highest version number (logical clock) of o for which an invalidation or update has been received from i, and $valid_{o,i}$ is true if $logicalClock_{o,i}$ corresponds to an update (false if it corresponds to an invalidate). Finally $value_o$ stores the update body for the highest logical clock received in any update message for o from any node.

Object validity. The system maintains the following key invariant: If node j in OQS has from node i in IQS a valid object o ($j.valid_{o,i}$) then node i in IQS knows node j in OQS has a valid object callback ($i.lastReadLC_o > i.lastAckLC_{o,j}$).

Client read. From the client's point of view, a dual-quorum read is the same as a standard quorum read [11,12]. *client* sends a read request to the OQS via $QRPC$. After receiving replies from a read quorum in OQS, *client* selects the value with the highest logical clock.

A node j in OQS that receives a client read request first checks whether the object o is valid. This check is done by first finding the IQS nodes i that sends the highest $logicalClock_{o,i}$ to j. Object o is valid if $valid_{o,i} = TRUE$, invalid otherwise. If o is valid, j returns the object's locally-stored logical clock and value. If not, j renews the object by sending object renewal messages to IQS using $QRPC$. After receiving replies R from a read quorum in IQS, j updates its local state ($\forall i$, $s.t. i \in R$: if $R.r_{o,i}.lc \geq logicalClock_{o,i}$, then $logicalClock_{o,i} := R.r_{o,i}.lc$ and $valid_{o,i} := true$). Then, j updates $value_o$ with the value in the reply with the highest logical clock and returns both the value $value_o$ and the highest logical clock to the client. Each IQS server that receives an object renewal message returns to the OQS server $value_o$ and $lastWriteLC_o$ and then updates $lastReadLC_o = max(lastReadLC_o, lastWriteLC_o)$.

Client write. Just like the standard quorum write protocol [11,12], *client* first queries IQS using $QRPC$ to retrieve the highest logical clock from a read quorum in IQS. Next, *client* advances the logical clock and embeds it in the write request that is then sent to the IQS via $QRPC$. The write completes after *client* receives acknowledgments from a write quorum in IQS.

An IQS server i that receives a client request for the highest logical clock of the last completed write responds with its logical clock $logicalClock$. When i receives a client write whose logical clock is larger than that associated with the last completed write of o on i ($lastWriteLC_o$), i updates $lastWriteLC_o$ and $value_o$ with those in the write. Then, to ensure that a write quorum in OQS is unable to read the old version of the data, i performs one of the following tasks: (a) if no OQS server has renewed since the completion of the last write, (e.g. $\forall j$, $s.t. j \in OQS$, $lastReadLC_o < lastAckLC_{o,j}$), i suppresses invalidations to

OQS; (b) otherwise, i sends invalidations with the logical clock of the write to OQS using $QRPC$. The write completes after receiving invalidation replies from a write quorum in OQS, at which point i updates $lastAckLC_{o,j}$ for all j in the $QRPC$ reply and returns to the client.

An OQS server j that receives from node i in IQS an invalidation with a logical clock $lc_{o,i}$ compares $lc_{o,i}$ with $logicalClock_{o,i}$. If the invalidation has the higher logical clock, j updates the local state ($logicalClock_{o,i} = lc_{o,i}$ and $valid_{o,i} = false$). Finally, j sends an invalidation acknowledgment back to i.

3.2   Dual Quorum with Volume Leases (DQVL)

The basic protocol just described allows one to vary read and write quorum sizes independently. However, our application would benefit from using a read quorum size of 1 so that reads can be serviced locally; any larger read quorum size introduces a network delay to every read and provides qualitatively worse read response time. However, a read quorum size of 1 could lead to unacceptable write availability because it could require a write to contact all nodes in the OQS to invalidate cached data. We therefore adapt Yin et al.'s volume lease protocol [30] to support very small read quorums in OQS while retaining acceptable availability on writes.

High level overview. We group objects into collections called volumes. To process a read, a read quorum in OQS must hold both a valid *volume lease* and a valid *object lease* for some read quorum in IQS. A lease represents permission to access some object that expires at some specified time [13]. Similar to the basic dual quorum protocol described in the previous section, when an OQS read quorum holds both valid leases, all client reads processed by this read quorum are *read hit*. A *read miss* implies that either or both leases are invalid - they can be renewed by querying from an IQS read quorum. Similarly, a *write suppress* occurs when either or both leases are invalid in at least one OQS write quorum. To process a write in the *write through* scenario, the IQS write quorum can (a) invalidate the object lease in an OQS write quorum or (b) wait for the lease to expire on the volume containing the requested object in an OQS write quorum.

The key challenge in introducing volume leases is to manage the callback state when invalidations are suppressed at IQS when the volume lease expires in an OQS write quorum. When an IQS write quorum processes a write to o while the lease expires for the volume v containing o in an OQS write quorum, i.e. a *write suppress* scenario, the IQS write quorum has to enqueue the invalidation of o as a *delayed invalidation* [30]. All delayed invalidations of objects under v must be processed by the OQS write quorum before v's lease can be renewed so that all required callbacks to IQS are installed on OQS. Those callbacks ensure that OQS queries IQS to retrieve possible updates suppressed at IQS.

A final implementation detail we take from Yin et al. [30] is to bound the size of the list of delayed invalidations for OQS using *epochs*. Volume lease renewals are marked with an epoch number, and when this epoch number changes, OQS conservatively assumes all object callbacks have been revoked by IQS.

In this case, OQS suspects that all objects under this volume are updated at IQS and OQS needs to query an IQS read quorum to validate the cache copy before sending any object to a client.

The key benefit of volume leases is that they can be of short duration while object leases are of long duration.[2] This combination yields good read response time; nodes in OQS can cache objects locally for a long time, and although they must frequently renew volume leases, this cost is amortized across many objects in a volume. This combination also yields good write responsiveness and availability: a write can complete by invalidating nodes caching data *or* waiting for a (short) volume lease to expire.

Protocol details. The protocol details at the node level are similar to the basic dual quorum protocol except that each IQS node tracks the volume lease and callback state on all OQS nodes. The pseudo-code describing actions at an IQS and an OQS node is shown in Figures 4 and 5.

Data structures. Each node in IQS maintains a real time clock $currentTime$ (with bounded drift with respect to the other clocks as described in Section 2) and a logical clock $logicalClock$. Each IQS node also maintains the following per-volume v, per-OQS-node j state: $expires_{v,j}$ which indicates when v expires at j, $delayed_{v,j}$ which contains a list of delayed invalidations that must be delivered to j before v is renewed, and $epoch_{v,j}$ which indicates j's current epoch number for v. Finally, each IQS node maintains the following per-object o state: $lastWriteLC_o$ stores the logical clock of the last write to o, $lastReadLC_o$ stores the value of $lastWriteLC_o$ from the time of the last read of o, $lastAckLC_{o,j}$ stores the logical clock contained in the highest invalidation reply from node j for o, and $value_o$ stores the value of o.

Each node in OQS maintains a bounded-drift real time clock $currentTime$. In addition, it maintains the following per-volume v per-IQS-node i state: $epoch_{v,i}$ is the highest epoch number for which a valid volume lease from i was held on v and $expires_{v,i}$ is the time when the lease on v from i will expire. And, it maintains the following per-object o per-IQS-node i state: $epoch_{o,i}$ indicates the last epoch for which a valid object lease on o from i was held, $logicalClock_{o,i}$ indicates the highest version number (logical clock) of o for which an invalidation or update has been received from i, and $valid_{o,i}$ is true if $logicalClock_{o,i}$ corresponds to an update (false if it corresponds to an invalidate). Finally $value_o$ stores the update body for the highest logical clock received in any update message for o from any node.

Volume and object validity. The system maintains the following key invariant: If node j in OQS has from node i in IQS both a valid volume v ($expires_{v,i} > currentTime$) and a valid object o ($epoch_{v,i} = epoch_{o,i}$ && $valid_{o,i}$) then node i in IQS knows node j in OQS has a valid volume lease ($expires_{v,j} > currentTime$) and valid object callback ($lastReadLC_o > lastAckLC_{o,j}$).

---

[2] For simplicity, we will assume infinite-length object leases or *callbacks* [14]. Generalizing to finite-length object leases is straightforward and can help optimize space and network costs [9].

```
 1   processLCReadRequest(){                        24   processVLRenewal(Volume  v ,  Sender  j ,
 2     sendMsg(CLIENT_LC_READ_REPLY, logicalClock); 25                                 RequestorTime  t_{v,0} ){
 3   }                                              26    expires_{v,j} := L + currentTime;
 4                                                  27    sendMsg(VOLUME_RENEW_REPLY, delayed_{v,j} ,
 5   processWriteRequest(Object  o ,  Value  v ,    28                    L , epoch_{v,j} , t_{v,0} );
 6                       LogicalClock  lc ){        29   }
 7     if (lc > lastWriteLC_O ){                    30
 8       value_O := v ;                             31   processVLRenewalAck(Volume  v ,  Sender  j ,
 9       lastWriteLC_O := lc ;                      32                             LogicalC  lc ){
10       //ensure an invalid OQS write quorum       33    //remove delayed invals already
11       while (!isOWQInvalid(o , lc )){            34    //applied at the sender
12         invalidateOWQ(o , lc );                  35    ∀k, s.t. inval_{k,j} ∈ delayed_{v,j} {
13         //see text for descriptions              36      if (lc ≥ inval_{k,j}.lc ){
14       }                                          37        delete inval_{k,j} ;
15     }                                            38      }
16     sendMsg(CLIENT_WRITE_ACK, o , lc );          39    }
17   }                                              40   }
18                                                  41
19   processInvalAck(Object  o ,  Sender  j ,       42   processObjRenewal(Object  o ){
20                   LogicalClock  lc ){            43    //update last−read logical clock
21     //update the last inval ack in               44    lastReadLC_O := lastWriteLC_O ;
22     //the record for the sender                   45    sendMsg(OBJECT_RENEW_REPLY, value_O ,
23     lastAckLC_{O,j} := MAX(lastAckLC_{O,j}, lc ); 46                  lastWriteLC_O );
24   }                                              47   }
```

Fig. 4. IQS server operations (pseudocode) – Dual quorum with volume leases

Client read. As detailed by **processReadRequest** in the pseudo-code, a node j in OQS processes a client read of object o by ensuring Condition C: there exists a read quorum irq in IQS such that j holds both a valid volume lease and valid object lease from irq. If C is already true, then j can immediately return the value $value_o$ and the associated logical clock $MAX_{\forall i, s.t. i \in IQS}(logicalClock_{o,i})$.

If C is not true, then j performs a variation on QRPC. QRPC as defined in Section 2 sends and resends a request to different nodes until it receives a quorum of replies. This variation sends *different* requests to different nodes and processes replies until condition C becomes true. In particular, for each target node i selected, j sends one of three things: (a) if the volume from i has expired and the object from i is invalid, it sends a combined volume renewal and object read; (b) if just the volume has expired, it sends a volume renewal; or (c) if just the object is invalid, it sends an object read. As detailed in the pseudo-code **processVLRenewReply**, j processes replies to volume renewal requests from IQS node i by applying the delayed invalidations included in the reply (in the same way as applying normal invalidations as described below) and updating $expires_{v,i}$ as well as $epoch_{v,i}$. To account for worst-case clock drift, j conservatively sets $expires_{v,i} = t_o + L * (1 - maxDrift)$ where t_o is the time that j *sent* the volume lease renewal request, L is the volume lease length granted in the reply, and $maxDrift$ is as defined in Section 2. Finally, j sends i a volume lease renewal acknowledgment (which i uses to clear its delayed invalidation queue.) As detailed in the pseudo-code **processRenewReply**, j processes object renewal replies from i by updating $epoch_{o,i}$, $logicalClock_{o,i}$, and $valid_{o,i}$; furthermore, if $valid_{o,i}$ is true and $logicalClock_{o,i}$ exceeds the logical clock of any other *valid* logical clock for this object, j updates $value_o$. The repeated sends and the processing of replies in this QRPC variation ensure that C eventually becomes true, at which point j returns $value_o$ and the associated logical clock ($logicalClock_{o,i_{max}}$) as the result of the read.

On the IQS side, node i in IQS processes volume renewal messages for volume v from node j as described in the pseudo-code **processVLRenewal**: i

```
1   processVLRenewReply(Volume v, Sender i,
2                       Lease L, Epoch e, DI di,    27   processReadRequest(Object o){
3                       RequestorTime t_{v,0}){     28   //ensure valid local object and volume
4   expires_{v,i} := MAX(expires_{v,i}, t_{v,0} + L*(1-maxDri|p|))  29   while(!isLocalValid(o)){
5   ;                                               30   //renew invalid volume and object
6   epoch_{v,i} := MAX(epoch_{v,i}, e);            31   validateLocal(o);
7   //apply delayed invals in the reply           32   }
8   ∀k, s.t. inval_{k,i} ∈ di {                    33   //send reply to client
9     if(inval_{k,i}.lc > logicalClock_{k,i}){     34   lc := MAX_{∀i, s.t. value_{o,i}=true}(logicalClock_{o,i});
10      logicalClock_{k,i} := inval_{k,i}.lc;      35   sendMsg(CLIENT_READ_REPLY, value_o, lc);
11      valid_{k,i} := false;                      36   }
12    }                                            37
13  }                                              38   processRenewReply(Object o, Sender i,
14  sendMsg(VOLUME_RENEW_REPLY_ACK,                39                     Epoch epoch, LogicalClock lc,
15          v, MAX(di.lc));                        40                     ObjectValue value){
16  }                                              41   epoch_{o,i} := MAX(epoch_{o,i}, epoch);
17                                                 42   if(logicalClock_{o,i} ≤ lc){
18  processInval(Object o, Sender i,               43     logicalClock_{o,i} := lc;
19               LogicalClock lc){                 44     valid_{o,i} := true;
20  //update the local logic clock                 45   }
21  //and object status                           46   if(valid_{o,i} = true &&
22  if(logicalClock_{o,i} < lc){                        logicalClock_{o,i} ≥ MAX_{∀k,k∈IQS}(logicalClock_{o,k})
23    logicalClock_{o,i} := lc;                    47   ){
24    valid_{o,i} := false                         48     value_o := value;
25  }                                              49   }
26  sendMsg(INVAL_ACK, lc);                        50   }
27  }
```

Fig. 5. OQS server operations (pseudocode) – Dual quorum with volume leases

sends the delayed invalidations $delayed_{v,j}$ and the volume renewal, containing the epoch number $epoch_{v,n}$ and lease length L. i then records the volume expiration time $(expires_{v,j} = L + currentTime)$. When i receives a volume lease renewal acknowledgment for volume v and logical clock lc from j, as detailed in the pseudo-code **processVLRenewalAck**, i clears all delayed invalidations with logical clocks up to lc from $delayed_{v,j}$. As **processObjRenewal** indicates, when i in IQS processes a read of object o from OQS node j, it replies with $value_o$ and $lastWriteLC_o$ and updates $lastReadLC_o = lastWriteLC_o$. Note that $lastReadLC_o$, $lastAckLC_{o,j}$, and $lastWriteLC_o$ allow i in IQS to track which nodes j in OQS may hold valid object callbacks. Finally, if an IQS server i wishes to garbage collect delayed invalidation state for j, i advances $epoch_{v,j}$ and deletes the delayed invalidations $delayed_{v,j}$. Note that if j receives from i a volume lease with a new epoch, then $epoch_{v,i} \neq epoch_{o,i}$ for all o. So all previously valid object leases from i immediately become invalid. Thus, if j misses some object invalidations from i when its volume lease from i has expired, a volume lease renewal from i can resynchronize j's state by either (a) updating $valid_{o,i}$ with the missing delayed invalidations or (b) advancing $epoch_{v,i}$ by sending a volume renewal with a new epoch number.

Client write. A client first determines the highest logical clock of any completed write by calling IQS's **processLCReadRequest**. A node i in IQS responds to such a call for object o by returning the node's *global* logical clock $logicalClock$. A client then issues the actual write of object o. As detailed in **processWriteRequest** in the pseudo-code, if the write's logical clock exceeds that of the highest write seen so far $(lastWriteLC_o)$, node i stores the write's logical clock and value. i then ensures that a write quorum in OQS is unable to read the old version of the data by performing a variation on QRPC that "sends" differently to different nodes depending on whether their volume and object leases are valid. There are three cases for i to consider for node j, object o, and volume v: (a) if i knows o is invalid at j (e.g., $lastReadLC_o < lastAckLC_{o,j}$) then i need take no action for j; (b) otherwise if o is valid at j but v is invalid at j (e.g., $expires_{v,j} < currentTime$) then i enqueues an invalidation in $delayed_{v,j}$ which will be processed at j when it renews its volume; or (c) both the object and volume are valid (e.g., $lastReadLC_o > lastInvalLC_{o,j}$) then j sends an object invalidation containing the write's logical clock ($lastWriteLC_o$) to j. In this last case, if j receives an invalidation from i for object o with logical clock lc, then as the pseudo-code in **processInval** describes, j applies the invalidation: if the invalidation is the newest information about o from i (e.g., $lc > logicalClock_{o,i}$) then j updates the logical clock and validity information ($\{logicalClock_{o,i} = lc; valid_i = false\}$). Finally, if i receives an invalidation-acknowledgment from j for logical clock lc, then as the pseudo-code in **process-ClientInvalAck** describes, i updates $lastAckLC_{o,j} = max(lastAckLC_{o,j}, lc)$.

3.3 DQVL Correctness

Because of space constraints, we omit the proof [3] that the system has regular semantics [16]. In particular, the proof shows (1) a read of o that is not concurrent with any writes of o can return only the value and logical clock from the completed write of o with the highest logical clock and (2) a read of o that is concurrent with one or more writes of o can return only (a) the value and logical clock from the completed write of o with the highest logical clock or (b) the value and logical clock from some concurrent write of o.

To give intuition for why DQVL provides *regular semantics*, consider the invariant: If node j in OQS has from node i in IQS both a valid volume v ($expires_{v,i} > currentTime$) and a valid object o ($epoch_{v,i} = epoch_{o,i}$ && $valid_{o,i}$) then node i in IQS knows node j in OQS has a valid volume lease ($expires_{v,j} > currentTime$) and valid object callback ($lastReadLC_o > lastAckLC_{o,j}$).

For a read that is not concurrent with any writes: This invariant is established by having j renew its volume v and (or) object o from i. Therefore, j contains the last completed write $value_o$ on node i when j has both a valid volume v and a valid object o from node i. Furthermore, j will contain the last completed write $value_o$ on a write quorum in IQS (iwq) when j has both a valid volume v and a valid object o from a read quorum in IQS (irq) (because an OQS read quorum (orq) and an OQS write quorum (owq) intersect by at lease one node). Because a client write is performed on an iwq, $value_o$ held on j is actually the last completed client write in the system. Because j can not process any client read unless it holds both a valid volume v and a valid object o from a read quorum irq, j guarantees to always return the value $value_o$ of the last completed write in the system.

For a read that is concurrent with some writes: Assume that the last completed write has logical clock lc_0 and a read r that is concurrent with some writes with logical clock $lc_1...lc_n$ ($lc_t > lc_0$) is sent to an orq. If the invariant is

---

[3] The details are presented in Chapter 4 of Lei Gao's dissertation available at www.cs.utexas.edu/users/lgao/papers/dissertation.pdf.

established in the orq, r returns the value associated with lc_0. Otherwise, the orq will try to establish the invariant by querying an irq. Because some writes are being processed in IQS, the irq may return to the orq the value associated with any of the logical clock $o.lc_0...o.lc_n$. Meanwhile, some iwq may send invalidations with logical clock $inval.lc_0...inval.lc_n$ to the orq as the result of the concurrent writes. When the maximum logical clock received in the renew replies is less than that of any invalidations on any server j of the orq, this server keeps renewing from some irq. As long as those concurrent writes terminate, j will eventually receive $o.lc_n$ (the highest logical clock among all concurrent writes) from some irq. Therefore, r may return the value associated with any of the logical clock $lc_0...lc_n$.

4   Evaluation

Through both analytical and experimental evaluations, we compare the availability, performance, and communication overhead of DQVL against other popular replication protocols. We show that DQVL yields a read performance competitive with ROWA epidemic algorithms and overall availability competitive with the majority quorum protocol.

4.1   Response Time

A prototype has been implemented by using DQVL and other popular replication protocols, such as primary/backup, majority quorum, ROWA-Async and ROWA, to compare their response times. The prototype is similar to a read/write register in that it allows clients to read and write the value of a *single* object. But our prototype supports reads and writes on *multiple* objects and ensures a consistent view of all objects on every server.

All the prototypes are built in Java. In our prototype experiment, we set the "LAN" delay between an application client and its closest edge server to 8 ms. The "WAN" delay between the application client and other edge servers is 86 ms. And the network delay among edge servers is 80 ms. Because the experiments focus on how various protocols can minimize WAN delays by taking advantage of having an edge server near every application client, we assume a constant processing delay on every edge server for both reads and writes. An application client sends requests to the system with a specified write ratio. The application client sends the next request only after it receives the response of the current request. We run up to nine edge servers and three application clients in the experiment.

This section compares the response time of five protocols under our target workloads. We show that DQVL yields better response time than protocols providing strong consistency guarantees and competitive response time to protocols with relaxed consistency guarantees.

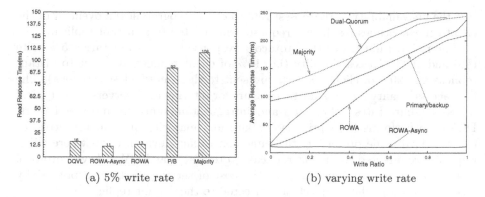

(a) 5% write rate   (b) varying write rate

Fig. 6. Response time vs. write rate

Write ratio. We first evaluate the response time by fixing the write rate to 5%, which is the update rate for TPC-W[4] profile object, i.e. a workload with a low update rate and strong access locality. Accesses to the profile object consist of 95% reads on a customer's purchase history, credit information, and addresses and 5% writes on a customer's shipping address when processing an online purchase. When the profile is replicated on edge servers, a customer is routed to the closest edge server to access its profile information.

As illustrated in Figure 6 (a), DQVL provides at least a six times read response time improvement over primary/backup and majority quorum protocols that are used to provide strong consistency guarantees. DQVL yields comparable read response time to ROWA and ROWA-Async protocols because it allows most client reads to be processed locally at the client's closest edge server while maintaining the same level of consistency guarantees as both primary/backup and majority quorum protocols by running the dual-quorum protocol between the closest replica and the rest of the replicas in the system.

Figure 6 (b) is the sensitivity graph illustrating the response time as we vary the write rate. As writes dominate the workload, DQVL's response time approximates that of the majority quorum protocol and becomes higher than those of primary/backup and ROWA. The main reason is that DQVL clients, following the same procedure as the majority quorum protocol, need to obtain the latest timestamp from a read quorum before sending the write to a write quorum in *IQS*. Two round trips are required for both the majority quorum protocol and DQVL while only one round trip is needed for primary/backup and ROWA protocols. For this reason, the average response times of both DQVL and the majority quorum protocol are worse than that of ROWA although both protocols do not require every write to be processed by all nodes.

Access locality. In this subsection, we evaluate response time when some portion of client requests are routed to replicas other than the client's closest one. Under normal circumstances, requests are routed to the client's closest server.

---

[4] TPC-W is a transaction processing benchmark for the web [8].

But the unavailability of the closest replica or the geographical movement of the client can sometimes result in a request being routed to a distant replica.

Figure 7 (a) illustrates the protocols' response times at our target 5% write rate and at 90% access locality (i.e. 10% of client requests are sent to distant replicas and 90% of client requests are sent to the client's closest replica). The 90% access locality is a pessimistic measure for Internet edge servers given typical network failure rates below 10% and infrequent mobility by most end users. DQVL outperforms both primary/backup and majority quorum protocols for the workload while preserving the same consistency level in cases where client requests are directed to distant replicas. Note that that ROWA-Async protocol yields the optimal response time at the cost of serving reads with potentially inconsistent data when requests are directed to the distant replicas.

In the DQVL protocol, the response time of reads at distant replicas is higher than the normal response time experienced when reading from the closest one. As the access locality varies, the overall response time changes accordingly. Figure 7 (b) indicates the relationship between the access locality and the overall response time of five protocols. DQVL suffers when access locality is low because both reads and writes need to contact replicas in both input and output quorum systems. But DQVL's response time keeps improving as the access locality becomes higher. The majority quorum and primary/backup protocols are not affected by the access locality because neither protocol is designed to take advantage of the access locality in the edge service environment. This graph suggests that when the access locality is 70% or higher, DQVL should be preferred over primary/backup or majority quorum protocols for replication systems requiring low response time and strong consistency guarantees.

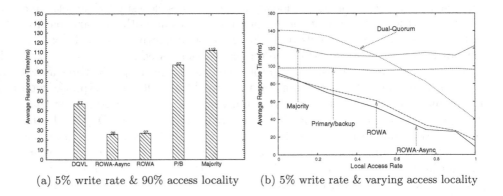

(a) 5% write rate & 90% access locality   (b) 5% write rate & varying access locality

Fig. 7. Average response time vs. access locality

4.2   Availability

In this section, we provide analytical models to evaluate the availability of the dual quorum protocol in comparison with other popular replication protocols.

We define the availability (av) as the number of client requests successfully processed by the system over the total number of requests submitted to the system during a given time period. A request is rejected by the system when target consistency semantics can not be satisfied. In the context of this paper, systems are required to provide regular semantics [16]. For example, if more than half of the nodes are unavailable in the *IQS* of a dual quorum system or in a majority quorum system, a client write will be rejected because the system can no longer guarantee that a later read can always retrieve the value of this write. Because the ROWA-Async protocol allows reads to return stale data from nodes without the latest update, it does not provide regular semantics. Therefore, to make the comparison fair [32], our analysis of the system implementing ROWA-Async protocol assumes that the system rejects client reads that would return stale data.

Figure 8 illustrates the unavailability of DQVL in comparison with other protocols in log scale. The unavailability is computed as $1 - av$. An unavailability of 10^{-i} corresponds to the availability of i 9's. Our simple model assumes a per node unavailability $p = 0.01$ and that node failures (including server crashes and network failures) are independent. Read and write rates are defined as $1 - w$ and w.

For DQVL, the availability of both *read hit* and *read miss* are $\min(av_{orq}, av_{irq})$. The availability of both *write through* and *write suppress* are $\min(av_{irq}, av_{iwq})$. Therefore, the availability of DQVL is $av_{DQVL} = (1 - w) * \min(av_{orq}, av_{irq}) + w * \min(av_{iwq}, av_{irq})$.[5]

Figure 8 (a) illustrates the unavailability of our target protocols as we vary the write ratio and fix the number of replicas to 15 (in both *IQS* and *OQS*). The key result is that DQVL's availability tracks that of the majority quorum. Note that the DQVL's availability measurement is pessimistic because a read can proceed without contacting any read quorum in IQS if the read quorum in OQS holds valid volume and object leases; this effect may mask some failures that are shorter than the volume lease duration. Note that ROWA-Async protocol provides excellent availability by allowing reads to return arbitrary stale data to clients. But if we allow no stale reads by the ROWA-Async protocol, its availability decreases to several orders of magnitude worse than other quorum based protocols and our DQVL protocol.

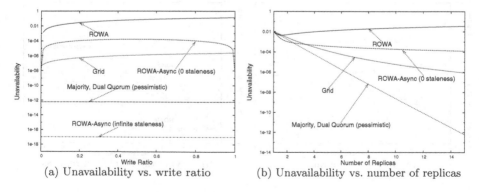

(a) Unavailability vs. write ratio   (b) Unavailability vs. number of replicas

Fig. 8. System unavailability

Figure 8 (b) illustrates unavailability as we vary the number of replicas and fix the write ratio at 25%. The unavailability of DQVL is similar to that of the majority quorum system. The availability of quorum based protocols, including DQVL, improves as the total number of nodes increases. The availability of ROWA and ROWA-Async with no stale reads is insensitive to the number of nodes in the system.

4.3   Communication Overhead

This section analyzes DQVL's communication overhead in terms of the number of message exchanges required in processing a client request. To simplify the model, the study assumes the weights of all message types are equal. Because of space constraints, we omit a detailed discussion of the communication overhead model.[5] Figure 9 shows the average number of messages required to process a client request in log scale. As illustrated in Figure 9 (a), in the worst case where the write ratio is 50%, DQVL can have high communication overhead as reads and writes interleave with each other. In this case, most reads are *read misses* and most writes are *write throughs* which involve both *IQS* and *OQS* in processing requests. However, DQVL's overhead should be comparable to other approaches in practice. First, workloads that DQVL is designed to face are dominated by reads. Consecutive reads are likely to benefit from having objects cached on OQS servers, i.e. the target workloads have a large number of *read hits*. Second, the design of DQVL allows us to vary the OQS size to meet read performance goals while varying the IQS size to balance overhead vs. availability goals. As shown in Figure 9 (b), once we fix IQS at a moderate size while letting the OQS size grow, the communication overhead yielded by DQVL is comparable to that of the majority quorum protocol without requiring many *read hits* in the workload.

Note that although the dual quorum protocol is described in terms of two quorum systems, *IQS* and *OQS*, an *IQS* server could physically be on the same node as an *OQS* server, reducing the overall communication overhead.

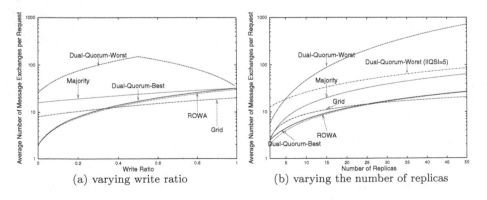

(a) varying write ratio   (b) varying the number of replicas

Fig. 9. Communication overhead

5   Related Work

In read-one/write-all (ROWA) protocol the "read-one" property yields excellent read availability and response time. But this protocol has limited write availability and response time because writes can not complete if any of the replicas are unavailable. Protocols with the read-one/write-all-async property (ROWA-Async) [21,24,25] yield better write availability and response time by allowing writes to be propagated to other replicas asynchronously, but they are only suitable for weakly consistent replication because they can not guarantee that reads will always return the data modified by the latest completed write. A variation of ROWA [4] performs writes synchronously on the available replicas to provide better consistency, but it requires membership protocols to maintain a consistent view of active members.

The primary-backup (or primary-copy) model [2] tolerates network partitions by only allowing the partition with the primary server to perform writes. However, the primary server becomes the bottleneck when it can not meet required levels of availability and performance. Group-communication based techniques, such as extended virtual synchrony [19,20], enable the election of a new primary by actively propagating updates to all group members and constantly running membership protocols to maintain the correct memberships. The new primary can be selected from active members and the change of the primary is also broadcast to all active members as well. This class of techniques has degraded performance in WANs because the membership protocol may always need to run to constantly include/exclude certain replicas when they are mistakenly considered as crashed/recovered due to slow WAN links. In addition, all primary-server based protocols are inflexibly in favor of reads' availability and performance.

Quorum based protocols [11,12,23,27] tolerate network partitions as long as connected replicas can form a quorum to process requests. However, the reads' response time and availability of most quorum systems are worse than those of ROWAA or primary-backup based protocols because reads usually need to query a larger set of servers. Quorum based protocols may not be desirable to handle a read-dominated workload, e.g. a workload from interactive online applications.

Some quorum based techniques use light-weight nodes, such as ghosts [28] to help form quorums for processing requests. When propagating a write, a replica only sends to these nodes the timestamp and object ID of the write. Our dual-quorum invalidation protocol shares the idea of replacing writes with invalidations when propagating to some replicas. But our use of invalidations also allows us to reduce the future message propagation to other replicas.

The traditional cache invalidation protocols [13,30] are primarily used in the client-server model where the server hosts the objects and clients keep cached copies. Those protocols assume that an object has a home location that can grant leases to cached copies, but this single centralized server may hurt availability.

6 Conclusion

This paper presents dual-quorum replication, a novel replication algorithm designed to support Internet edge services. Through both analytical and experimental evaluations, we demonstrate that the protocol offers nearly ideal trade-offs among high availability, good performance, and strong consistency for some workloads of interest.

Several important issues will be addressed in our future work. It will be interesting to configure both IQS and OQS to optimize other metrics. For example, we can configure the read quorum size in OQS to be larger than one to avoid timeouts on invalidations. We can also configure IQS as a grid quorum system [6] to reduce the overall system load. We are also interested in modifying DQVL to provide different consistency semantics (e.g. atomic semantics [16]) and comparing the cost difference.

References

1. Inc. Akamai Technologies. AkamaiThe Business Internet A Predictable Platform for Profitable EBusiness. http://www.akamai.com/BusinessInternet/whitepaper_business_internet.pdf, 2004.
2. P. Alsberg and J. Day. A Principle for Resilient Sharing of Distributed Resources. In *the 2nd Intl. Conference on Software Engineering*, 1976.
3. A. Awadallah and M. Rosenblum. The vMatrix: A Network of Virtual Machine Monitors for Dynamic Content Distribution. In *7th International Workshop on Web Content Caching and Distribution*, August 2002.
4. P. Bernstein, V. Hadzilacos, and N. Goodman. *Concurrency Control adn Receivery in Database Systems*. Addison Wesley, 1987.
5. E. Brewer. Lessons from giant-scale services. In *IEEE Internet Computing*, July/August 2001.
6. S. Cheung, M. Ahamad, and M. Ammar. The grid protocol: a high performance scheme for maintaining replicated data. In *Proceedings of the Sixth International Conference on Data Engineering*, pages 438–445, 1990.
7. S. Cheung, M. Ahamad, and M. H. Ammar. Optimizing Vote and Quorum Assignments for Reading and Writing Replicated Data. *IEEE Transactions on Knowlegde and Data Engineering*, 1(3):387–397, September 1989.
8. Transaction Processing Performance Council. TPC BENCHMARK W. http://www.tpc.org/tpcw/spec/-tpcw_V1.8.pdf, 2002.
9. V. Duvvuri, P. Shenoy, and R. Tewari. Adaptive Lease: A Strong Consistency Mechanism for the World Wide Web. In *Proceedings of IEEE Infocom*, March 2000.
10. L. Gao, M. Dahlin, A. Nayate, J. Zheng, and A. Iyengar. Improving Availability and Performance with Application-Specific Data Replication. *IEEE Transactions on Knowledge and Data Engineering*, March 2005.
11. H. Garcia-Molina and D. Barbara. How to Assign Votes in a Distributed System. In *Journal of the ACM 32 (4)*, 1985.
12. D. Gifford. Weighted voting for replicated data. In *Proceedings of the Seventh ACM Symposium on Operating Systems Principles*, December 1979.

13. C. Gray and D. Cheriton. Leases: An Efficient Fault-Tolerant Mechanism for Distributed File Cache Consistency. In *Proceedings of the Twelfth ACM Symposium on Operating Systems Principles*, pages 202–210, 1989.

14. J. Howard, M. Kazar, S. Menees, D. Nichols, M. Satyanarayanan, R. Sidebotham, and M. West. Scale and Performance in a Distributed File System. *ACM Transactions on Computer Systems*, 6(1):51–81, February 1988.

15. D. Karger, E. Lehman, T. Leighton, M. Levine, D. Lewin, and R. Panigrahy. Consistent Hashing and Random Trees: Distributed Caching Protocols for Relieving Hot Spots on the World Wide Web. In *Proceedings of the Twenty-ninth ACM Symposium on Theory of Computing*, 1997.

16. L. Lamport. On interprocess communications. *Distributed Computing*, pages 77–101, 1986.

17. R. Lipton and J. Sandberg. PRAM: A Scalable Shared Memory. Technical Report CS-TR-180-88, Princeton, 1988.

18. D. Malkhi and M. Reiter. An Architecture for Survivable Coordination in Large Distributed Systems. *IEEE Transactions on Knowledge and Data Engineering*, pages 187–202, March 2000.

19. D. Malki, K. Birman, A. Schiper, and A. Ricciardi. Uniform Actions in Asynchronous Distributed Systems. In *ACM SIGOPS-SIGACT*, August 1994.

20. D L. Moser, Y. Amir, P. Melliar-Smith, and D. Agarwal. Extended virtual synchrony. In *Proceedings of the Fourteenth International Conference on Distributed Computing Systems*, June 1994.

21. A. Muthitacharoen, R. Morris, T. Gil, and B. Chen. Ivy: A read/write peer-to-peer file system. In *Proceedings of the Fifth Symposium on Operating Systems Design and Implementation*, December 2002.

22. A. Nayate, M. Dahlin, and A. Iyengar. Transparent Information Dissemination. In *ACM/IFIP/USENIX 5th International Middleware Conference*, October 2004.

23. J. Paris and D. Long. Efficient Dynamic Voting Algorithms. In *Int'l Conference on Data Engineering*, 1988.

24. K. Petersen, M. Spreitzer, D. Terry, M. Theimer, and A. Demers. Flexible Update Propagation for Weakly Consistent Replication. In *Proceedings of the Sixteenth ACM Symposium on Operating Systems Principles*, October 1997.

25. Y. Saito, C. Karamanolis, M. Karlsson, and M. Mahalingam. Taming aggressive replication in the pangaea wide-area file system. In *Proceedings of the Fifth Symposium on Operating Systems Design and Implementation*, December 2002.

26. D. Terry, M. Theimer, K. Petersen, A. Demers, M. Spreitzer, and C. Hauser. Managing Update Conflicts in Bayou, a Weakly Connected Replicated Storage System. In *Proceedings of the Fifteenth ACMSymposium on Operating Systems Principles*, pages 172–183, December 1995.

27. R. Thomas. A Majority Consensus Approach to Concurrency Control for Multiple Copy Database. In *ACM Transactions on Database Systems*, pages 180–209, June 1979.

28. R. van Renesse and A. Tanenbaum. Voting with Ghosts. In *Proceedings of the Eighth International Conference on Distributed Computing Systems*, pages 456–462, 1988.

29. A. Whitaker, M. Shaw, and S. Gribble. Scale and Performance in the Denali Isolation Kernel. In *OSDI02*, December 2002.

30. J. Yin, L. Alvisi, M. Dahlin, and C. Lin. Volume Leases to Support Consistency in Large-Scale Systems. *IEEE Transactions on Knowledge and Data Engineering*, February 1999.

31. C. Yoshikawa, B. Chun, P. Eastham, A. Vahdat, T. Anderson, and D. Culler. Using Smart Clients to Build Scalable Services. In *Proceedings of the 1997 USENIX Technical Conference*, January 1997.

32. H. Yu and A. Vahdat. The Costs and Limits of Availability for Replicated Services. In *Proceedings of the Eightteenth ACM Symposium on Operating Systems Principles*, 2001.

33. H. Yu and A. Vahdat. Design and evaluation of a conit-based continuous consistency model for replicated services. *ACM Transactions on Computer Systems*, pages 239–282, August 2002.

Frugal Event Dissemination in a Mobile Environment*

Sébastien Baehni, Chirdeep Singh Chhabra, and Rachid Guerraoui

School of Computer and Communication Sciences, EPFL

Abstract. This paper describes an event dissemination algorithm that implements a topic-based publish/subscribe interaction abstraction in mobile ad-hoc networks (MANETs). Our algorithm is frugal in two senses. First, it reduces the total number of duplicates and parasite events received by the subscribers. Second, both the mobility of the publishers and the subscribers, as well as the validity periods of the events, are exploited to achieve a high level of dissemination reliability with a thrifty usage of the memory and bandwidth. Besides, our algorithm is inherently portable and does not assume any underlying routing protocol. We give simulation results of our algorithms in the two most popular mobility models: city section and random waypoint. We highlight interesting empirical lower bounds on the minimal validity period of any given event to ensure its reliable dissemination.

1   Introduction

The publish/subscribe (pub/sub) communication abstraction is a very appealing candidate for disseminating events in mobile ad-hoc networks (MANETs) [1]. In such networks, devices are mobile, they may not know each other and might not always be up and running. With a pub/sub abstraction, remote devices can communicate by playing two roles: the *publishers* produce events that are disseminated in the network and *subscribers* receive events they are interested in. Publishers and subscribers are decoupled in time, space and flow [2]. This makes the pub/sub abstraction appropriate for loosely coupled MANET applications.

Whereas the writing of MANET applications is appealing with a pub/sub abstraction, the effective implementation of such abstraction is not an easy task. In particular, ensuring a reasonable level of reliability of the dissemination is challenging without flooding the entire network. Indeed, devices in a MANET can directly broadcast information in their geographical neighborhood but need multiple indirections to reach far away devices. In addition, the devices typically run with a limited amount of memory and the dissemination algorithm cannot use a large portion of it just for buffering events. Similarly, the battery power of a device is (dynamically) limited and cannot anyway entirely be devoted to receiving and forwarding events, especially if those are duplicates or of no interest (i.e., *parasite* events).

---

* The work presented in this paper was sponsored both by the European IST PALCOM project (OFES No 03.0495-1), as well as by the National Competence Center in Research on Mobile Information and Communication Systems (NCCR-MICS), a center supported by the Swiss National Science Foundation under grant number 5005-67322.

G. Alonso (Ed.): Middleware 2005, LNCS 3790, pp. 205–224, 2005.

This paper presents an event dissemination algorithm that implements a topic-based pub/sub abstraction in MANETs. Our algorithm is inherently portable and does not assume any specific multicast routing protocol: we only rely on a standard Media Access Control (MAC) layer (e.g., Bluetooth [3] or 802.11 [4]). Events are (1) assumed to have a validity period that represents the time interval after which they are of no use and (2) are arranged according to a topic-hierarchy. The originality of our algorithm lies in its frugality, and this covers two aspects: first, despite the broadcast nature of the communication medium, we ensure that the subscribers receive a minimal number of duplicates and parasite events; second, both the mobility and validity periods of the events are used to enforce the reliability of the dissemination with a thrifty usage of the memory and bandwidth.

Our algorithm goes through three phases: (1) neighborhood detection based on exchanges of heartbeats in surrounding environments; (2) events dissemination after back-off periods calculated as functions of the frequency of the heartbeats and the number of events to send; and (3) garbage collection using the validity periods of the events as well as the number of times they have been propagated (a logical notion of "age").

We give simulations that highlight empirical lower bounds on the validity period needed to achieve a certain level of reliability. Interestingly, the lower bounds depend on the number of devices (publishers/subscribers), their speed, their interests (subscriptions), and the considered mobility models (i.e., random waypoint [5] or city section [6]). For instance, in the random waypoint model, an event with a validity period of 180 seconds is received by 95% of the 120 devices which move at 10 meters per second in an area of $25[km^2]$.

We compare our algorithm with three different flooding variants and show that, for the same reliability, our algorithm outperforms the alternatives in terms of bandwidth, duplicates and parasite events. For instance, for disseminating one event of 400 bytes in the very same previously described environment, we save between 300% and 450% of the bandwidth and each subscriber receives between 70 and 100 times less duplicates and between 50 and 90 times less parasite events.

The rest of the paper is structured as follows: Section 2 describes the MANET environment we consider. Section 3 gives an overview of the algorithm. Section 4 details the main elements of our algorithm. Section 5 gives various simulation results. Section 6 discusses related work and concludes our paper.[1]

2   Model

In this section we present some basic elements of the underlying MANET we consider. We discuss the communication medium, the network topology and the processes involved in the pub/sub interaction.

Overview. What we call a process in this paper is the piece of software of a mobile device that is responsible of disseminating/forwarding the events subscribed to by the

---

[1] An implementation of our algorithm for a parking application is given in [7]. The cars leaving the car parks act as publishers and propagate the information of free parking spots. When receiving such information, other cars, acting as subscribers, are able to locate the free place that is closest to their destination.

application running on the device. We assume the processes to be mobile (they move with their host device) and to communicate directly with their immediate neighborhood (i.e., one-hop neighbors). A process can represent a publisher, a subscriber or both. All processes run our algorithm directly on top of the MAC layer (e.g., Bluetooth [3] or 802.11 [4]), without relying on any routing algorithm.

Communication Medium. The range of a process is the geographical zone within which it can directly reach other processes using a simple send communication primitive of the underlying MAC layer (one-hop). The set of processes in the range of a process p_i is called the neighborhood of p_i. A process cannot send a message to only one of its neighboring processes nor directly send a message to processes multiple hops away (i.e., no underlying unicast/multicast routing algorithm is assumed).

Network Topology. We assume that the network is completely ad-hoc and no fixed infrastructure is present. We do not make any assumption on the size of the network (number of processes), nor on the connection graph of the processes. In particular, the graph does not need to be fully connected at any given point in time. The processes are assumed to be mobile. When analyzing our algorithm, we will study the two most popular mobility models: (1) random waypoint [5] and (2) city section [6], which we recall below.

- In the random waypoint model, a process moves from its current location to a new location by randomly choosing a direction and a speed. The speed and direction are chosen from pre-defined ranges, [*speedmin, speedmax*] and $[0, 2\pi]$ respectively. This model includes pause times between changes in direction and/or speed.
- In the city section model, the mobility area is a street network that typically represents a section of a city. In this model, the processes follow predefined guidelines like speed limits, one way lanes, and other traffic laws. Each process begins the simulation at a predefined point on some street, and randomly chooses a destination. It is common to consider specific characteristics like pause times, acceleration and deceleration in certain intersections.

Processes, Topics and Events. Each process p_i has a unique identifier i. All processes have to deal with limited bandwidth, energy and memory. A process can move in and out of the range of other processes, or crash (or recover), at any time.

Each event $e_j^{T_k}$ published by a process p_i: (1) has a unique identifier j,[2] (2) a validity period, i.e., $val(e_j^{T_k}) = t$, after which the information carried by the event is of no use in the system, and (3) is associated to a specific topic, e.g., T_k. Topics are arranged in a hierarchy (e.g., *.grenoble.conferences.middleware*) and a subscriber that subscribes to a specific topic (e.g., *.grenoble.conferences*) is expected to receive events of this topic and all its subtopics (e.g., *.grenoble.conferences.middleware*). The root topic of the topic tree is denoted by the *dot (.)* sign. An event of a topic, which a process has not subscribed to, is called a *parasite* event for that process.

---

[2] In the paper, we assume, without loss of generality, that the size of the event identifier is smaller than the size of the data carried by the event.

3   Algorithm Overview

We give here an overview of our algorithm before detailing it in subsequent sections. Our algorithm goes through three phases: (1) neighborhood detection, (2) event dissemination and (3) garbage collection. We first introduce these phases and then give a short example to illustrate their execution.

Phase 1: Neighborhood detection. The processes periodically exchange heartbeat messages, each contains the following elements: (1) the identifier of the process, (2) a list of its current subscriptions (i.e., a list of topics $T_i, T_j, ..., T_n$)[3] and, (3) its current speed (this information is only useful for optimization purpose and is not mandatory). Each process p_i uses the heartbeat messages it receives to construct a dynamic one-hop neighborhood table, containing the identifiers of the processes in the neighborhood along with their subscriptions and their current speed (if available). Only the processes whose subscriptions match with the ones of p_i, are kept in p_i's table. Other one-hop neighbors are of *no interest* to p_i. The neighborhood table is continuously garbage collected and updated (depending on the periodicity of the heartbeats). If the speed information of the processes is available (for example with the help of a tachometer), the process can adjust the periodicity of the heartbeats to match to the dynamicity of its environment. Otherwise, this periodicity is set to a static value (see Section 4.2).

When processes detect each other, they exchange a list of identifiers of the events they have kept after receiving them and which are still valid. When receiving event identifiers, each process checks if its neighbor is interested in an event it has not already received (i.e., needs the event). In this case, the processes proceed to the dissemination phase (see below). Sending the events identifiers instead of the events themselves preserves network bandwidth and CPU processing power. Indeed, it might happen that a process p_i has already received the same events as process p_j. Consequently, it makes no sense for p_j to send these events to p_i again.

Phase 2: Dissemination. When a process detects that one of its neighbor needs an event (when comparing the list of events identifiers it receives with its own list of events), it broadcasts the required event to its neighborhood together with the list of its interested neighbors, after a back-off period (see Section 4.2).

After receiving the event, the neighboring processes of the sender might decide to propagate the event if they know other processes, in their neighborhood, that have not yet received it and that are interested in it (see Section 4.3). If the processes that receive the event have subscribed to the topic of this event and have not received it yet, they deliver it to the application and store it, until it is garbage collected. A process that receives an event it is not interested in (parasite event), simply drops it. This way, we minimize the burden induced by parasite events and save valuable memory.

Phase 3: Garbage collection. Throughout the two previous phases of our algorithm, we mainly use two main data structures (see Section 4.1) at every process.[4] The first one is used for storing the list of neighbors that shares the same subscriptions as the process itself (neighborhood table). The second one is used for storing the events. The

---

[3] This list can change at any point in time with respect to the interests of the process.
[4] Other data structures are involved in the algorithm, but those cannot induce memory problems.

neighborhood table is constantly updated (based on the periodicity of the heartbeats) and its size is bounded.[5]

The data structure used to store the events can grow rapidly. This is because the total number of events published in the system is unbounded and the processes have to store them until their validity period expires. It can thus happen that a process receives an event and cannot store it because its memory is full. Our garbage collection scheme collects, every time a new event has to be stored and if the memory is full, the events according to their validity period and the number of times they have been propagated (sent/forwarded) by the processes.

Illustration. Figure 1 depicts a simple scenario illustrating the three phases of our algorithm. We consider a hierarchy made of three topics: T_0, T_1 and T_2; T_1 is a subtopic of T_0 whereas T_2 is a subtopic of T_1. Three processes, p_1, p_2 and p_3 are involved: p_1 has subscribed to T_1, p_2 has subscribed to T_2 and p_3 has subscribed to T_0. Three events are published in the system: $e_3^{T_1}$, $e_4^{T_2}$ and $e_5^{T_2}$. We assume that p_1 has already received $e_3^{T_1}$ and p_2 has already received $e_4^{T_2}$ and $e_5^{T_2}$.

In part I of Figure 1, processes p_1 and p_2 become neighbors and hence know their common subscriptions. They then exchange the identifiers of the events corresponding to the topics they have commonly subscribed to. As a consequence, p_2 sends to p_1 events $e_4^{T_2}$ and $e_5^{T_2}$ (as T_1 is a super-topic of T_2).

In part II of Figure 1, all three processes become neighbors, and exchange their event identifiers: p_1 and p_2 realize that p_3 misses events, $e_3^{T_1}$, $e_4^{T_2}$ and $e_5^{T_2}$. As both p_1 and p_2 have events to send, they both send them after a back-off period. It is important to notice that, because p_1 has more events to send than p_2, p_1 has a smaller back-off period than p_2 (see Section 4.3).

In part III of Figure 1, p_1 moves on, but p_2 and p_3 still remain in range. As p_2 was in the range of p_1 when it sent the events list, p_2 heard the events that p_1 sent for p_3. Now, p_2 and p_3 know that they do not have to exchange events anymore.

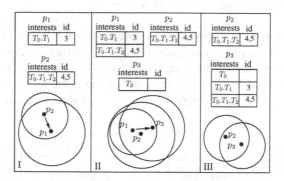

Fig. 1. Illustration of our algorithm

---

[5] The upper bound corresponds to the maximum number of neighbors a process can handle. This bound depends on the structure of the network and on the amount of memory of the processes.

4 Algorithm Description

In this section we first detail the data structures involved in the algorithm. Then we describe the neighborhood detection, the dissemination and finally the garbage collection.

4.1 Data Structures

As illustrated in Figure 4, we consider a list of *subscriptions* for every process p_i (*p_i.subscriptions*), a *neighborhood table* (*neighborhoodTable*) and an *event table* (*eventsTable*). These two tables are detailed below. There is also the list containing the *events to send* (*eventsToSend*). The different parameters used, as listed in Figure 4, are: the heartbeat delay (*HBDelay*), the neighborhood garbage collection delay (*NGCDelay*) and the back-off delay (*BODelay*).

Subscriptions of a process. The different subscriptions of every process p_i are stored in the list p_i.*subscriptions*. We assume, without loss of generality, that the size of this list is bounded as the number of subscriptions of a process is usually limited in the topic-based scheme. In this scheme, a process only has to subscribe to a topic to receive all the events regarding this topic and all its subtopics. A process can change the list of its subscriptions at any time.

Neighborhood Table. Figure 2 illustrates the neighborhood table of a process. The first column of this table stores the identifiers of the neighbors of a process. The second column stores the topics those processes have subscribed to. The third column stores the identifiers of the events the neighbors have received, the fourth column contains the speed of the neighbors (this column is not mandatory and the speed of the processes is only used for optimization purpose) and the last column contains the time when the entry has been stored/updated into the table. This last entry is used for garbage collection purpose. We discuss in more detail the use of the neighborhood table in Section 4.3 and present its garbage collection algorithm in Section 4.4.

Event Table. Each process stores an event table as shown in Figure 3. This table contains a list of topics the process has subscribed to, together with the list of events this process has received and/or published. These events are stored according to the topic hierarchy (from the partial topic tree information the process has). Each event has a unique identifier (*id*), a validity period (*validity*), a counter (*counter*), a topic (*topic*)

Neighbors	Topics	Events ID	Speed	Store Time
1	T_0	1, 2	1 [mps]	07:45:23
32	$T_0.T_1.T_2$	10	– [mps]	07:43:20
542	$T_0.T_4$	210	20 [mps]	07:44:45

Fig. 2. Neighborhood table

Topic Hierarchy

T_0

T_1 T_4

T_2 T_3

Topics	Events	Validity	Counter
$T_0.T_1.T_2$	$e_{10}^{T_2}$	100 [s]	5
	$e_5^{T_2}$	60 [s]	1
$T_0.T_1.T_3$	$e_3^{T_3}$	20 [s]	2
	$e_{143}^{T_3}$	120 [s]	12

Fig. 3. Event table

and its internal data information (*data*: this information is not shown in Figure 3). The validity period expresses the time interval after which the event can be removed from the system. The counter represents the number of times an event has been forwarded; it is used, together with the validity period, in the garbage collection phase (see Section 4.4).

The events to send. This structure contains the events a process sends to its neighbors. This structure can be, at most, as big as the event table (if a process has to send all its events to its neighbors). The structure is reset each time the events are sent (i.e., after each back-off).

4.2 Neighborhood Detection

Before detecting neighbors, the processes have to subscribe to topics they are interested in. The subscription/unsubscription sub-protocol is depicted in Figure 5. Basically, when a process wants to subscribe to a specific topic, it adds this topic to its list of subscriptions and starts the *heartbeat* and *neighborhoodGC*[6] tasks. A process that wants to unsubscribe to a topic, removes this topic from its list of subscriptions. When the list of subscriptions is empty, the *heartbeat* and *neighborhoodGC* tasks are stopped.

For each process p_i

```
1: {The subscriptions of the process}
2: p_i.subscriptions = ∅;
3: {The neighborhood table }
4: neighborhoodTable = ∅;
5: {The event table}
6: eventsTable = ∅;
7: {The structure containing the events to
    send}
8: eventsToSend = ∅;
9: {The default heartbeat delay}
10: HBDelay = 15000;
11: {The default neighborhood garbage col-
    lection delay}
12: NGCDelay = HBDelay*HB2NGC;
13: {The default back-off delay}
14: BODelay = HBDelay/HB2BO;
```

For each process p_i

```
1: {The subscription algorithm}
2: upon SUBSCRIBE(T_k) do
3:    p_i.subscriptions = p_i.subscriptions ∪ T_k;
4:    if (HEARTBEAT not started) then
5:        start HEARTBEAT;
6:    end if
7:    if (NEIGHBORHOODGC not started) then
8:        start NEIGHBORHOODGC;
9:    end if
10: end upon

11: {The unsubscription algorithm}
12: upon UNSUBSCRIBE(T_k) do
13:    p_i.subscriptions = p_i.subscriptions \ T_k;
14:    if (p_i.subscriptions == ∅) then
15:        stop HEARTBEAT; stop NEIGHBORHOODGC;
16:    end if
17: end upon
```

Fig. 4. Data structures

Fig. 5. Subscription, unsubscription

The heartbeats of a process carry the list of subscriptions of the process (e.g., "T_0, T_1,..., T_n") along with its process identifier and its current speed. As we pointed, the information about the speed of the processes is not mandatory and is only used as an optimization. For instance, this information can be used to tune the number of heartbeat messages according to the speed of the process and the speed of its neighbors. In a

---

[6] The *neighborhoodGC* task is used for garbage collecting the entries of the neighbors' identities from the neighborhood table; it is presented in Section 4.4.

dynamic environment, the delay between two heartbeats could be set to a shorter period than in a more static one.

After receiving the heartbeat messages, each process builds a view of its neighborhood, together with a list of their subscriptions. If two neighboring processes do not share any common topics, these topics are not stored in their respective neighborhood table. The neighborhood information of a process is stored in a specific table (Figure 2) and updated accordingly (using the UPDATENEIGHBORINFO() method[7]).

For each process p_i

1: {*The heartbeat task*}
2: **task** HEARTBEAT
3:   SEND(i,p_i.subscriptions, [currentSpeed]);
4: **end**

5: {*When receiving a heartbeat message*}
6: **upon** RECEIVE(j,subscriptions,[speed]) **do**
7:   **if** subscriptions $\in p_i$.subscriptions **then**
8:     RAISE new neighborEvent(j,subscriptions);
9:     **if** (j $\notin$ neighborhoodTable) **then**
10:       neighborhoodTable $\cup$
          (j,subscriptions,[speed],currentTime);
11:     **else**
12:       UPDATENEIGHBORINFO(j,
          subscriptions,[speed],currentTime);
13:     **end if**
14:   **end if**
15:   COMPUTEHBDELAY(neighborhoodTable);
16:   COMPUTENGCDELAY();
17: **end upon**

For each process p_i

18: {*A new neighbor has been detected*}
19: **upon** new neighborEvent(j,subscriptions) **do**
20:   **if** subscriptions $\in p_i$.subscriptions **then**
21:     SEND(i,GETEVENTSIDS(subscriptions,
          eventsTable));
22:   **end if**
23: **end upon**

24: {*Reception of a list of events identifiers*}
25: **upon** RECEIVE(j, eventsIDs) **do**
26:   **if** j $\in$ neighborhoodTable **then**
27:     **for all** eventID $\in$ eventsIDs **do**
28:       UPDATENEIGHBOREVENTINFO(j, eventID,
          currentTime);
29:     **end for**
30:     RETRIEVEEVENTSTOSEND();
31:   **end if**
32: **end upon**

Fig. 6. Neighborhood detection

If the subscriptions of a process match the ones of its neighbor, they then exchange the event identifiers they have subscribed to (the event identifiers are retrieved via the GETEVENTSIDS() method[8]). Once those event identifiers are received, the process updates its neighborhood table with those and checks if it has to send events to its neighbors (via the RETRIEVEEVENTSTOSEND() method, described in Section 4.3). The identifiers of the events are exchanged instead of the actual events to minimize the duplicate messages. It may happen that a process and its neighbors have the same set of events; in this case, there is no need for them to exchange the events.

The computation of the time intervals for (1) the heartbeat messages, (2) the neighborhood garbage collection and (3) the back-off period are determined at the reception of the heartbeat messages, using respectively the following methods: (1) COMPUTE-HBDELAY(), (2) COMPUTENGCDELAY() and (3) COMPUTEBODELAY(). Figure 8 describes an implementation of these methods. Parameter x represents a variable the

---

[7] This method is omitted for space limitations. It simply consists of updating the information (i.e., subscriptions, speed and store time) corresponding to the right neighbor.

[8] Again, this method is omitted for space limitations. It consists in retrieving, from the *eventsTable*, the event identifiers of the received events corresponding to a certain topic.

For each process p_i

```
1: {Computation of the events to send}
2: function RETRIEVEEVENTSTOSEND()
3:    eventsToSend = ∅;
4:    for all neighbor ∈ neighborhoodTable do
5:       if neighbor.subscriptions ∈ p_i.subscriptions then
6:          for all e_k^{T_j} ∈ eventsTable do
7:             if T_j ∈ neighbor.subscriptions &&
                   k ∉ neighbor.eventsIDs &&
                   val(e_k^{T_j}) < currentTime then
8:                eventsToSend ∪ e_k^{T_j};
9:          end if
10:         end for
11:      end if
12:      if eventsToSend ≠ ∅ then
13:         COMPUTEBODELAY();
14:         if backOff not started &&
                BODelay != null then
15:            start backOff with computed BODelay;
16:         end if
17:      end if
18:   end for
19: end
```

Fig. 7. Event retrieval

For each process p_i

```
1: {Computation of the hearbeat delay}
2: function COMPUTEHBDELAY(neighborhoodTable)
3:    averageSpeed =
         AVERAGESPEED(neighborhoodTable);
4:    if averageSpeed ≠ null then
5:       HBDelay = x/averageSpeed;
6:    end if
7:    HBDelay = MIN(HBDelay, heartbeat upper bound);

8:    HBDelay = MAX(HBDelay, heartbeat lower bound);
9: end

10: {Computation    of    the    neighborhood
       garbage collection delay}
11: function COMPUTENGCDELAY()
12:    NGCDelay = HBDelay*HB2NGC;
13: end

14: {Computation of the back-off delay}
15: function COMPUTEBODELAY()
16:    if BODelay == null then
17:       BODelay =
             HBDelay/(HB2BO*sizeof(eventsToSend));
18:    else
19:       BODelay = MIN(BODelay,
             HBDelay/(HB2BO*sizeof(eventsToSend)));
20:    end if
21: end
```

Fig. 8. Computing delays

programmer can use to tune the heartbeat delay with respect to the average speed of the processes (for instance, x can represent the propagation radius of the wireless device). Parameters *HB2BO*, respectively *HB2NGC*, represent the factors by which the heartbeat delay is divided, respectively multiplied, in order to set the periodicity of the back-off delay, respectively the neighborhood garbage collection delay.

4.3 Dissemination

Our dissemination scheme algorithm is described in Figure 9. Basically the process uses the PUBLISH() method to send the event to the neighboring processes if at least one of those has subscribed to the topic of the event. In calling this method, the process updates the neighbor information in its neighborhood table (via the UPDATENEIGH-BOREVENTINFO() method[9]).

As soon as a process receives an event, it updates its neighborhood table (using the UPDATENEIGHBOREVENTINFO() method) with the list of neighbor identifiers it received with the events. The process then checks if it has subscribed to the topic of that event and if so, it delivers it to the application and adds it to its event table (after checking that the event table is not full, otherwise it calls the GARBAGECOLLECT()

---

[9] For space limitation, this method is not shown in the algorithm; it basically consists in updating the list of the presumed received events of a neighbor with the event identifier given as a parameter.

method). If the process has not subscribed to the topic of the event, it simply drops it. Once it has delivered the event to the application, the process checks if it has to forward its events to its neighbors (i.e., RETRIEVEEVENTSTOSEND() method, Figure 7).

If a process p_i finds out that some of its neighbors have subscribed to the topic of the still valid events p_i owns, p_i starts a back-off period (the back-off delay is determined by the function COMPUTEBODELAY()[10]). Taking into account the events that have been received by the processes reduces the number of useless retransmissions and hence prevents duplicates and saves bandwidth.

Once the back-off delay expires, the events to send are recomputed (in case the neighborhood of the process has changed between the beginning and the end of the back-off or if the validity period of an event expires) and the new events are sent, together with a list of its neighbor identifiers. The sending process then updates its neighborhood table and increments the counter of each event that has just been sent.

4.4 Garbage Collection

We present here how the different data structures are garbage collected in order to conserve the sparse memory optimally.

Subscription list of a process. As stated in Section 4.1, we can assume that the size of this data structure is limited and the information it contains is constantly updated when the process decides to subscribe or unsubscribe to specific topics.

Neighborhood table. Each time the *neighborhood garbage collection delay* expires, the process identities whose store times have expired are collected from the neighborhood table (see Figure 10). As this task is executed periodically and as we assume that the total number of neighbors is limited, the size of the table is bounded.

Event table. Each time a new event has to be stored in the *eventsTable*, a check to test if the memory is full is done. If the check succeeds, one event, whose validity period has expired, is garbage collected. If all the events in the *eventsTable* are still valid, we run a garbage collection algorithm based on the notion of validity period and on the number of times an event was propagated. This algorithm ensures that events with high validity periods that have been propagated several times are garbage collected before events with short validity periods that have never been forwarded. Equation 1 captures the way we collect the events, based on: (1) their validity period (i.e., $val(e_k^{T_j})$) and (2) the number of times an event has been forwarded (i.e., $fwd(e_k^{T_j})$). The garbage collection function for an event $e_k^{T_j}$ is given as ($\forall val(e_k^{T_j}), fwd(e_k^{T_j}) \in \mathbb{N}^*$):

$$gc(e_k^{T_j}) = \frac{val(e_k^{T_j})}{(fwd(e_k^{T_j}) + val(e_k^{T_j}))} \tag{1}$$

For instance, an event with a validity period of 2[min] that has been forwarded less than 2 times, will be collected after an event with a validity period of 5[min] that has been forwarded 5 times.

---

[10] An implementation is given in Figure 8. In this implementation, the back-off delay depends on the heartbeat delay and the total number of events to send.

For each process p_i

```
1:  {Executed when the back-off expires}
2:  upon backOff expiration do
3:     BODelay = null;
4:     if eventsToSend ≠ ∅ then
5:        SEND(i, eventsToSend, neighborsIDs);
6:        eventsIDs = GETEVENTSIDS(eventsToSend);
7:        for all neighborID ∈ neighborhoodTable do
8:           for all id ∈ eventsIDs do
9:              UPDATENEIGHBOREVENTINFO(neighborID,
                    id);
10:          end for
11:       end for
12:       INCREMENT(eventsToSend, eventsTable);
13:    end if
14: end upon
```

```
15: {Reception of a list of events}
16: upon RECEIVE(j, events, neighborsIDs) do
```
17:      **for all** $e_k^{T_j} \in$ events **do**
18:        **for all** neighborID $\in$ neighborsIDs **do**
19:          UPDATENEIGHBOREVENTINFO(neighborID, k);
20:        **end for**
21:      **if** $T_j \in p_i$.subscriptions && $e_k^{T_j} \notin$ eventsTable **then**
22:        interested = true; STOP backOff timer;
23:        **if** eventsTable is full **then**
24:          garbageCollect(eventsTable);
25:        **end if**
26:        eventsTable $\cup\ e_k^{T_j}$;DELIVER($e_k^{T_j}$);
27:      **end if**
28:      **end for**
29:      **if** interested **then**
30:        RETRIEVEEVENTSTOSEND();
31:      **end if**
32: **end upon**

For each process p_i

33:   {*Publication of a new event* $e_k^{T_j}$ }
34: **function** PUBLISH(i, $e_k^{T_j}$, neighborsIDs)
35:      **for all** neighbor $\in$ neighborhoodTable **do**
36:        **if** neighbor.subscriptions $\in$
         p_i.subscriptions **then**
37:          interested = true; break;
38:        **end if**
39:      **end for**
40:      **if** interested **then**
41:        SEND(i, $e_k^{T_j}$, neighborsIDs);
42:        **for all** neighborID $\in$ neighborhoodTable **do**
43:          UPDATENEIGHBOREVENTINFO(neighborID, k);
44:        **end for**
45:      **end if**
46:      **if** eventsTable is full **then**
47:        garbageCollect(eventsTable);
48:      **end if**
49:      eventsTable $\cup\ e_k^{T_j}$; DELIVER($e_k^{T_j}$);
50:      **if** (NEIGHBORHOODGC not started) **then**
51:        start NEIGHBORHOODGC;
52:      **end if**
53: **end**

Fig. 9. Dissemination

For each process p_i

1:   {*Garbage collection of the neighborhood table*}
2: **task** neighborhoodGC
3:      **for all** neighbor $\in$ neighborhoodTable **do**
4:        **if** currentTime - NGCDelay > neighbor.storeTime **then**
5:          REMOVE(neighbor,neighborhoodTable);
6:        **end if**
7:      **end for**
8: **end**

For each process p_i

9:   {*Garbage collection of the events table*}
10: **function** garbageCollect(eventsTable)
11:      gc = null;
12:      **for all** $e_k^{T_j} \in$ eventsTable **do**
13:        **if** $val(e_k^{T_j})$ > currentime **then**
14:          gc = $e_k^{T_j}$; break;
15:        **end if**
16:        **if** $\dfrac{val(e_k^{T_j})}{(fwd(e_k^{T_j})+val(e_k^{T_j}))} \leq \dfrac{val(gc)}{(fwd(gc)+val(gc))}$ **then**
17:          gc = $e_k^{T_j}$;
18:        **end if**
19:      **end for**
20:      REMOVE(gc,eventsTable);
21: **end**

Fig. 10. Garbage collection

The events to send. As discussed in Section 4.1, the data structure capturing the events to be sent does not need to be garbage collected as it is reset every back-off period. Moreover, its size depends on the size of the event table, but as this data structure is efficiently garbage collected, the size of the *events to send* list cannot grow indefinitely.

5 Performance

We present here performance results obtained from simulating our algorithm, according to the two popular mobility models. We first describe the simulation setting and then give the actual performance measurements.

5.1 Environment

Our algorithm was simulated using *Qualnet 3.7* [8], directly on the 802.11b MAC layer, in the two different mobility models: (1) random waypoint [5] and (2) city section [6].

Configuration Parameters. The size of the events is set to 400 bytes, x to 40, *HB2BO* to 2 and *HB2NGC* to 2.5. The heartbeat upper bound period is set to 1[s] for the random waypoint model and varies in the city section model. The mobility of the processes and the validity periods of the events vary (see the following performance measurement configuration). The choice of these values (i.e., x, *HB2BO* and *HB2NGC*) reflects a trade off between the overall number of messages sent (heartbeats, events identifiers, and actual events) and the reliability of the dissemination. For the random waypoint model, the data were gathered after the first 600 seconds of the simulation time (due to the high variability in the neighborhood percentage during these first seconds [9]).

Random Waypoint in Qualnet. In our experiments, the pause time is always set to 1[s]. The maximum and minimum speed vary during the entire set of experiments, see Section 5.2. Moreover, in this model, we have conducted our experiments on a virtual area of $25[km^2]$, populated randomly with 150 processes. Regarding the overall settings of the simulator, a "standard" 802.11b ad-hoc network was used. The transmission power is 15[db] for all the rates 1,2,6 and 11[Mbps], whereas the reception sensitivity is -93[db], -89[db], -87[db] and -83[db] for 1,2,6 and 11[Mbps] respectively.[11] The channel frequency is 2.4[Ghz] and uses a statistical propagation model, with a limit of -111[dbm] and a two ray path loss model. Each process has an omni-directional antenna with an efficiency of 0.8.

City Section in Qualnet. For this model, the map of our campus at EPFL was chosen and a specific mobility model for 15 processes was created. The EPFL campus covers $1200x900[m^2]$. The processes do not walk/drive randomly on each of the roads. The real traffic conditions were considered (e.g., some roads are more often used than others). The overall settings of the simulator are the same as for the random waypoint, except for the reception sensitivity which is -65[db] for all rates (1,2,6 and 11[Mbps])[12]. We have adapted these values to simulate the real radio range of a city.

---

[11] This corresponds to a radio range of a sphere which radius is 442[m], 339[m], 321[m] and 273[m] respectively.

[12] This corresponds to a radio range of a sphere which radius is 44[m].

5.2 Results

Random Waypoint Model. We conducted the simulation for different speeds: 0[mps], 1[mps], 5[mps], 10[mps], 20[mps], 30[mps] and 40[mps]. All the simulations were run 30 times with different initialization (i.e., seed) values and the results presented in each case were averaged over the 30 obtained values. One event is published in each case.

In the first experiment, the validity period of the events and the speed of the processes were considered. The plain and dashed graphs of Figure 11 represent reliability values obtained when only 20% and 80%, of the processes, have respectively subscribed to the topic of the event. We can see that, when few processes have subscribed to that topic (20%), it is very difficult to achieve high reliability, unless if the processes move at high speed. We can explain this by the fact that the area is far too big with respect to the number of subscribers. If only 20% of them have subscribed to the topic of the event, we end up with only 30 processes for a region of $25[km^2]$; the network is too sparse. However, when more processes have subscribed to the topic (80%), we can achieve a fairly high reliability with different validity periods and different speeds of the processes. For example, processes moving at 10[mps] and publishing events with a validity period of 180[s] have the same 95% reliability than processes moving at 30[mps] and publishing events with a validity period of 90[s]. Interestingly, under some lower bounds of validity period, it is possible, to achieve a specific reliability given different mobility models and speeds of the processes.

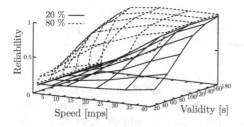

Fig. 11. Probability of event reception as a function of the validity period, the speed of the processes and the number of subscribers

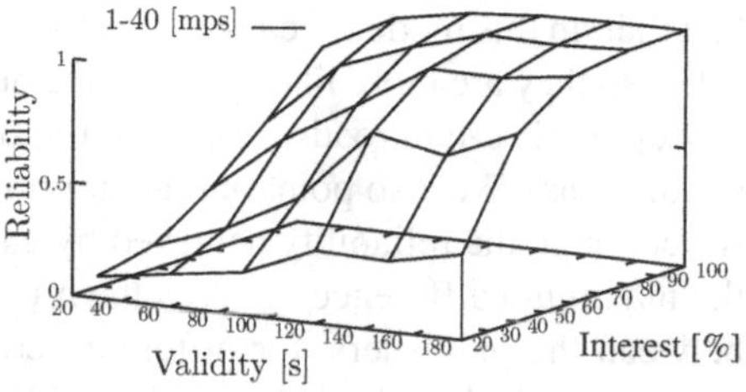

Fig. 12. Probability of event reception as a function of the validity period and the number of subscribers, in a heterogeneous mobile environment

In Figure 12, we depict the same experiments as before, except that now we have a more heterogeneous mobile network, in which the processes randomly move between 1[mps] and 40[mps]. With a low number of subscribers, the reliability is low also. However, even if only 60% of the processes have subscribed to the topic of an event with a validity period of 120[s], all of them receive the event. We can relate these results to the ones of a network in which all processes move at a speed of 20[mps]. Indeed, according to our results, the overall reliability depends on the validity period and the average speed of the processes in the network, rather than on the specific speed of each process.

City Section Model. In this model, all 15 processes drive at a given speed which is the speed limit of the road they are currently driving on (which is between 8[mps] and 13[mps]) and it may happen that they stop for a while for several reasons (red light, parking etc.). In all experiments, all processes, in turn, become the original publisher. This basically means that the original publisher is not always the same process but changes for each experiment. Again, all experiments were conducted 30 times and the results we present are an average over these 30 times for the 15 publishers.

In the first set of experiments, the importance of the heartbeat period over the overall reliability was measured. In such a network, with no upper bound set, the processes send heartbeats every 4[s] (which is the fraction of x over the average speed of 10[mps]). Figure 13 depicts the different results obtained when varying the heartbeat upper bound period from 1[s] to 5[s], where all the processes have subscribed to the topic of the event and where the validity period of this event is 150[s].

We can notice that there is no real difference in reliability between the heartbeats sent every 1[s] or 2[s]. However, between 1[s]-2[s] and 5[s], we have a loss of 22% reliability. Interestingly, having heartbeats every 4[s] is better than having them every 3[s]. This surprising result is explained by the fact that, with this heartbeat period of 3[s], the messages sent by the processes are more likely to collide.

In the second set of experiments, the heartbeat upper bound period was set to 1[s] and the number of subscribers varied from 20% to 100%. Interestingly, these results are not comparable with the ones obtained in the random waypoint model. Indeed, even if only 20% of the processes have subscribed to the topic of the event, almost 60% of them receive the event which is better than the previous model. This can be explained by the fact that, in this model, the processes follow specific paths defined according to specific rules, so they are more likely to become neighbors than in the random waypoint model, especially if certain roads have more importance than others (which was the case in our simulations). We also point out the importance of the path taken by the processes when we compare the reliability achieved by each of the publishers. In Figure 15, we depict the maximum difference between the minimum reliability and the maximum reliability between the publishers, for different percentage of subscribers. There can be a huge difference of reliability between the publishers that originally publish the event and this difference is due to the path taken by the publisher.

In the third set of experiments, the heartbeat upper bound period was set to 1[s] and the validity period of the events varied between 20[s] and 150[s]. In Figure 16, we can see that the validity period of the event has a crucial importance on the overall reliability. This comes from the fact that, in this specific model, we cannot distinguish *where* and *when* the processes become neighbors. In the random waypoint model, the processes exchange information uniformly during the simulation: there is no real hot-

Heartbeat upper bound period [s]				
1	2	3	4	5
76.9%	75.1%	65.5%	69.9%	54.0%

Fig. 13. Probability of event reception as a function of the heartbeat period

Subscribers [%]				
20%	40%	60%	80%	100%
58.1%	59.7%	62.5%	68.6%	76.9%

Fig. 14. Probability of event reception as a function of the number of subscribers

Subscribers [%]				
20%	40%	60%	80%	100%
40.9%	44.7%	47.9%	53.9%	60.0%

Event Validity Period[s]					
25	50	75	100	125	150
11%	27%	44%	52%	69%	77%

Fig. 15. Difference of reliability between the processes

Fig. 16. Probability of event reception as a function of the event validity period

spot where the processes meet. On the contrary, in the city section model, the processes are more likely to meet and exchange their information at social meeting points, hence the huge differences in reliability.

Frugality. To quantify the frugality of our algorithm, it was compared with three alternative approaches: (1) simple flooding, (2) simple flooding while taking into account the interests of the subscriber (interests-aware flooding) and (3) simple flooding in taking into account the interests of both the subscriber and its neighbors (neighbors' interests flooding). In (1), an event is sent every second by a process to all its neighbors which in turn, irrespective of their interests, propagates it with the same technique. In (2), the processes, at every one second interval, propagate only the events they are interested in. In (3), a process propagates an event to its neighbors only if the process itself and its neighbors are interested in the event. We compared four different measurements: (1) the bandwidth used per process, (2) the number of events sent per process, (3) the number of duplicates received per process and (4) the number of parasite events received per process.

All of the following measurements were averaged over 30 experiments and have been done using the random waypoint model described above with the speed of the processes set to 10[mps] (in order to compare the approaches with the same reliability degree)[13]. The size of one heartbeat was set to 50 bytes and the size of one event identifier to 128 bits. We varied the number of subscribers from 20% to 100% as well as the number of events from 1 to 20 (the size of one event has been set to 400 bytes).

Figure 17 shows the bandwidth used per process during a simulation of 180[s].[14] Our algorithm consumes less bandwidth than the other approaches in every cases, except if the sum of the events' sizes is lower than 1,5[kB] and the number of interested processes is less or equal to 20%. In this very special case, the second alternative is better. However, our algorithm is much less sensitive to the size of the events as we send very few of them (see Figure 18). Our algorithm sends between 50 to 100 times lesser events compared to the other alternative approaches. Consequently, if one event is of size 1.6[kB] instead of 400 bytes, we outperform every other alternatives, even for a small number of events published and a small number of subscribers.

Figure 19 depicts the number of duplicates received per process during the 180[s].[15] Our algorithm outperforms approach (2) by a factor varying from 50 up to 80 and approaches (1) and (3) by a factor between 80 to 700. On the worst case, when all the

---

[13] Please note that approach (1) as always 100% reliability, due to its inherent behavior.

[14] Approach (3) is not shown in this figure because of the high bandwidth it consumes per process (more than 1[MB]).

[15] Again, in Figure 19, we do not show approach (1) and (3) in order to clearly depict the distinction between our algorithm and the best alternative approach (2).

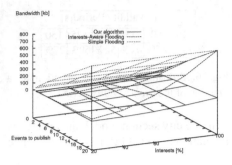

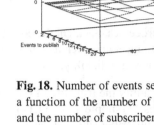

Fig. 17. Bandwidth usage per process as a function of the number of events to publish and the number of subscribers

Fig. 18. Number of events sent per process as a function of the number of events to publish and the number of subscribers

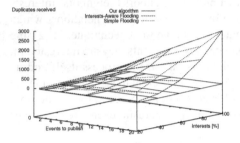

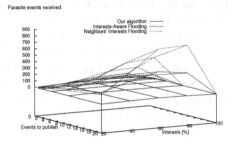

Fig. 19. Number of duplicates received as a function of the number of events to publish and the number of subscribers

Fig. 20. Number of parasite events received as a function of the number of events to publish and the number of subscribers

processes are interested in receiving the events, they will at most receive them 4 times during 180[s]. This corresponds to 1 duplicate per minute, which is very few.

Figure 20 depicts the number of parasite events received per process.[16] Our algorithm does not induce a lot of parasite events unlike the other two depicted alternatives. Not surprisingly, the more the subscribers, the lesser the parasite events (because more and more subscribers are interested in receiving the events). The greatest number of parasite events received per process is reached when 60% of the processes are interested in receiving such events. In this case, we outperform the other approaches by a factor of 20 to 50 depending on the number of events.

6 Concluding Remarks

Many algorithms [10,11,12,13,14,15,16,17,18] have tackled the issue of disseminating events in a MANET. In [10], the *broadcast storm* problem is introduced. This problem

---

[16] Again, Figure 20 does not contain approach (1), because our algorithm outperforms it by a factor of up to 800 times.

is raised when flooding is used for broadcasting an event in a wireless network. Different schemes are compared: (1) a probabilistic scheme, (2) a counter-based scheme, (3) a distance-based scheme, (4) a location-based scheme and (5) a cluster-based scheme. The last two schemes (i.e., (4) and (5)) rely on a GPS device and cluster heads respectively: assumptions that we do not make in our algorithm. It has been shown in [10] that the first scheme is outperformed by the others. The second and third schemes have been revisited in [19] and feature very interesting characteristics. In our algorithm, we did not explore any distance-based techniques as this would imply more calculation for the mobile devices and require more computing power. In addition, the distance-based scheme together with the counter-based one have been proved to be outperformed by the neighborhood scheme [20]. Our algorithm is close to the latter with certain specificities that we discuss below.

The neighborhood scheme has often been studied in the literature [13,14,15,16,17,18,19]. The corresponding algorithms follow roughly one of two different patterns: (1) one-hop neighbor information and (2) multi-hops neighbors information. The first pattern is called self-pruning and the decision of rebroadcasting an event depends on the one-hop knowledge of the neighbors of the processes [18,13,19]. This approach achieves fairly good performance without involving too much processing time, which is not the case with the second approach [13,15,16,17], where the processes rebroadcast either according to their two-hops neighborhood knowledge [15,16,17] or according to the decisions of other processes [13]. As the decision of rebroadcasting is often based on a greedy algorithm [21], this consumes a large amount of processing time and is not suited to highly mobile networks. To limit the number of duplicates messages, the neighborhood schemes can be used with a back-off mechanism (like in [14]). In the model we consider, the processes are mobile and only have information about their one-hop neighbors. In this sense, our algorithm belongs to the one-hop category. In our approach however, a process p_i disseminates an event according to: (1) the validity period of the events of p_i, (2) the subscriptions of the neighbors of p_i and (3) the events those neighbors have received.

The algorithms presented in [11,12] make specific assumptions on the stabilization of the network, use cluster heads, and switch to flooding when network partitions are frequent. We make no assumption on the topology or stabilization of the network and do not rely on any cluster heads or routing algorithms.

Topic-based pub/sub algorithms for MANETs were also presented in [22,23,24]. The algorithm relies on brokers which are responsible for buffering the events the subscribers are interested in. When the subscribers connect again to one of the brokers, they ask for the events they have not yet received and the brokers are responsible for providing them with these. Speeding up the bootstrapping latency has been tackled in [25,26], where client proxies are responsible for collecting events and dispatching them to the real clients when those connect back to the brokers. All these schemes are based on brokers. Our algorithm is completely decentralized.

The approaches described in [27,28,29,30,31,32,33] do not rely on brokers. In [27] a direct acyclic graph is maintained between the subscribers and the publishers. To maintain this graph, the network is supposed to remain unpartitioned for some period of time: we do not make this assumption. Moreover, unlike in our algorithm, there can be a huge latency in [27] before a publisher is allowed to publish an event.

A generic way to store data at the most interested mobile processes is described in [28]. The dissemination scheme is not detailed and it is not clear how flooding is avoided when different subscribers have subscribed to the same topic. A specific kind of validity is considered in the sense that each data is associated with a counter which is kept up to date only when the data is used, but the limited memory of the processes is not addressed. In our approach, each event is associated with a timeout that never changes during the entire lifetime of the publication, and after which the event is garbage collected. Like [28], the algorithm presented in [29] implements a distributed hashtable in a MANET. The algorithm of [29] uses dynamic source routing [5] (DSR) to create the routes between publishers and subscribers and consequently floods the network with request and reply messages, which is not the case of our algorithm. Unlike our algorithm, the algorithm of [29] does not consider any validity period for the events and mobile processes must route events they are not interested in. In [30], events are split into several pieces and dispatched on the network. When a process wants to recover the full event, it moves in the network, gathers the different pieces and re-conciliates them. Though this algorithm does not make use of brokers, several processes receive pieces of information they are not interested in, and no notion of validity period is considered.

A pub/sub implementation based on a weakly connected multicast tree is given in [32]. The root of the multicast tree is responsible for publishing the events. This scheme has two drawbacks: the maintenance is time consuming in a high mobile environment and the processes located at the root of the multicast tree have more work to perform than the ones at the leaves. Our algorithm does not need to create or maintain a multicast tree, and processes that have not subscribed to a topic do not need to care about events of that topic.

In the content-based pub/sub algorithm of [33], event dispatchers are responsible for forwarding the events to the interested subscribers and need to store subscriber information located multiple hops away. Our algorithm relies only on one-hop information and events are only forwarded by mobile processes that are interested in those.

In the proximity-based algorithm of [31], the subscribers only receive events associated to a certain geographical region. Filtering techniques are used to minimize the burden at publishers and subscribers. In comparison, our algorithm is not limited to a specific location, it supports the dynamic inclusion of topics and exploits the mobility of the processes to disseminate events.

References

1. Cugola, G., Jacobsen, H.A.: Using publish/subscribe middleware for mobile systems. In: Proceedings of the ACM SIGMOBILE Mobile Computing and Communications Review. Volume 6. (2002) 25–33
2. Eugster, P., Felber, P., Guerraoui, R., Kermarrec, A.M.: The many faces of publish/subscribe. ACM Computing Surveys **35** (2003) 114–131
3. (Bluetooth web site: http://www.bluetooth.com/)
4. (IEEE organisation, 802.11 web site: http://grouper.ieee.org/groups/802/11/)

5. Johnson, D., Maltz, D.: Dynamic source routing in ad hoc wireless networks. In Imielinski, Korth, eds.: Mobile Computing. Volume 353. Kluwer Academic Publishers (1996) 153–181
6. Davies, V.: Evaluating mobility models within an ad hoc network. Master's thesis, Colorado School of Mines (2000)
7. Flury, R., Baehni, S.: EPFL Free Car Parks Application, http://lpdwww.epfl.ch/sbaehni/work/carPark/carPark.html. (2004)
8. Zeng, X., Bagrodia, R., Gerla, M.: Glomosim: a library for parallel simulation of large-scale wireless networks. In: Proceedings of the 12th Workshop on Parallel and Distributed Simulations. (1998)
9. T. Camp, J. Boleng, V.D.: A survey of mobility models for ad hoc network research. In: Proceedings of Wireless Communication and Mobile Computing: Special issue on Mobile Ad Hoc Networking: Research, Trends and Applications. Volume 2. (2002) 483–502
10. Ni, S.Y., Tseng, Y.C., Chen, Y.S., Sheu, J.P.: The broadcast storm problem in a mobile ad hoc network. In: Proceedings of the 5th ACM International Conference on Mobile Computing and Networking. (1999) 151–162
11. Pagani, E., Rossi, G.P.: Providing reliable and fault tolerant broadcast delivery in mobile ad-hoc networks. Journal of Mobile Networks and Applications **4** (1999) 175–192
12. Gupta, S.K.S., Srimani, P.K.: An adaptive protocol for reliable multicast in mobile multi-hop radio networks. In: Proceedings of the 2nd IEEE Workshop on Mobile Computer Systems and Applications. (1999) 111–122
13. H. Lim, C.K.: Multicast tree construction and flooding in wireless ad hoc networks. In: Proceedings of the ACM International Workshop on Modeling, Analysis and Simulation of Wireless and Mobile Systems. (2000) 61–68
14. Peng, W., Lu, X.C.: On the reduction of broadcast redundancy in mobile ad hoc networks. In: Proceedings of the 1st ACM International Symposium on Mobile Ad Hoc Networking and Computing. (2000) 129–130
15. Peng, W., Lu, X.C.: AHBP: An efficient broadcast protocol for mobile ad hoc networks. Journal of Science and Technology (2002)
16. Sucec, J., Marsic, I.: An efficient distributed network-wide broadcast algorithm for mobile ad-hoc networks. Technical Report 248, Rutgers University (2000)
17. Qayyum, A., Viennot, L., Laouiti, A.: Multipoint relaying for flooding broadcast messages in mobile wireless networks. In: Proceedings of the 35th Annual Hawaii International Conference on System Sciences. (2002) 298–308
18. Cartigny, J., Simplot, D., Carle, J.: Stochastic flooding broadcast protocols in mobile wireless networks. Technical report, LIFL Univ. Lille 1 (2002)
19. Tseng, Y.C., Ni, S.Y., Shih, E.Y.: Adaptive approaches to relieving broadcast storms in a wireless multihop mobile ad hoc network. IEEE Transactions on Computers **52** (2003) 545–557
20. Williams, B., Camp, T.: Comparison of broadcasting techniques for mobile ad hoc networks. In: Proceedings of the 3rd ACM International Symposium on Mobile Ad Hoc Networking and Computing. (2002) 194–205
21. Lovasz, L.: On the ratio of optimal integral and fractional covers. In: Discrete Mathematics. Volume 13. (1975) 383–390
22. Huang, Y., Garcia-Molina, H.: Publish/subscribe in a mobile environment. In: Proceedings of the 2nd ACM international workshop on Data engineering for wireless and mobile access. (2001) 27–34
23. Cugola, G., Nitto, E.D., Fuggetta, A.: The jedi event-based infrastructure and its application to the devlopment of the opss wfms. IEEE Transactions on Software Engineering **27** (2001) 827–850

24. Caporuscio, M., Inverardi, P., Pelliccione, P.: Formal analysis of clients mobility in the siena publish/subscribe middleware. Technical report, Department of Computer Science, University of L'Aquila (2002)
25. Cicila, M., Fiege, L., Haul, C., Zeidler, A., Buchmann, A.P.: Looking into the past: enhancing mobile publish/subscribe middleware. In: Proceedings of the 2nd international workshop on Distributed event-based systems. (2003) 1–8
26. Caporuscio, M., Carzaniga, A., Wolf, A.L.: Design and evaluation of a support service for mobile, wireless publish/subscribe applications. IEEE Transactions on Software Engineering **29** (2003) 1059–1071
27. Anceaume, E., Datta, A.K., Gradinariu, M., Simon, G.: Publish/subscribe scheme for mobile networks. In: Proceedings of the second ACM international workshop on Principles of mobile computing. (2002) 74–81
28. Datta, A., Quarteroni, S., Aberer, K.: Autonomous gossiping: A self-organizing epidemic algorithm for selective information dissemination in wireless mobile ad-hoc networks. In: Proceedings of the International Conference on Semantics of a Networked World. (2004)
29. Pucha, H., Das, S.M., Hu, Y.C.: Ekta: An efficient dht substrate for distributed applications in mobile ad hoc networks. In: Proceedings of the 6th Workshop on Mobile Computing Systems and Applications. (2004)
30. Li, Z., Li, B., Xu, D., Zhou, X.: iFlow: middleware-assisted rendezvous-based information access for mobile ad-hoc application. In: Proceedings of the 2st ACM International Conference on Mobile Systems, Applications and Services. (2003) 71–84
31. Meier, R., Cahill, V.: Steam: Event-based middleware for wireless ad hoc networks. In: Proceedings of the 22nd International Conference on Distributed Computing Systems Workshops. (2002) 639–644
32. Huang, Y., Garcia-Molina, H.: Publish/subscribe tree construction in wireless ad-hoc networks. In: Proceedings of the 4th International Conference on Mobile Data Management. (2003) 122–140
33. Costa, P., Picco, G.P.: Semi-probabilistic Content-Based Publish-Subscribe. In: Proceedings of the 25th IEEE International Conference on Distributed Computing Systems. (2005)

RTZen: Highly Predictable, Real-Time Java Middleware for Distributed and Embedded Systems*,**

Krishna Raman, Yue Zhang, Mark Panahi, Juan A. Colmenares***,
Raymond Klefstad, and Trevor Harmon

Department of Electrical Engineering and Computer Science,
University of California, Irvine, CA 92697, USA
{kraman, yuez, mpanahi, jcolmena, klefstad, tharmon}@uci.edu

Abstract. Distributed real-time and embedded (DRE) applications possess stringent quality of service (QoS) requirements, such as predictability, latency, and throughput constraints. Real-Time CORBA, an open middleware standard, allows DRE applications to allocate, schedule, and control resources to ensure predictable end-to-end QoS. The Real-Time Specification for Java (RTSJ) has been developed to provide extensions to Java so that it can be used for real-time systems, in order to bring Java's advantages, such as portability and ease of use, to real-time applications.

In this paper, we describe RTZen, an implementation of a Real-Time CORBA Object Request Broker (ORB), designed to comply with the restrictions imposed by RTSJ. RTZen is designed to eliminate the unpredictability caused by garbage collection and improper support for thread scheduling through the use of appropriate data structures, threading models, and memory scopes. RTZen's architecture is also designed to hide the complexities of RTSJ related to distributed programming from the application developer. Empirical results show that RTZen is highly predictable and has acceptable performance. RTZen therefore demonstrates that Real-Time CORBA middleware implemented in real-time Java can meet stringent QoS requirements of DRE applications, while supporting safer, easier, cheaper, and faster development in real-time Java.

Keywords: RTSJ, Real-Time CORBA, Design Patterns, Middleware, DRE.

* This material is based upon work supported by the National Science Foundation under Grant No. 0410218, Boeing DARPA contract Z20402, and AFOSR grant F49620-00-1-0330.
** Any opinions, findings, and conclusions or recommendations expressed in this material are those of the authors and do not necessarily reflect the views of the National Science Foundation.
*** Also with the Applied Computing Institute, College of Engineering, University of Zulia.

G. Alonso (Ed.): Middleware 2005, LNCS 3790, pp. 225–248, 2005.
© IFIP International Federation for Information Processing 2005

1 Introduction

For as long as computers have been able to talk to one another, software engineers have struggled with the task of building distributed applications. Over the years, various technologies have been created to deal with the problem, culminating in the "golden age of networking" of the early 1980s, which saw the advent of remote procedure calls and the socket metaphor. More recently, object-oriented architectures such as CORBA have become popular for making computer communication easier to implement.

Traditionally, the overhead of CORBA-based middleware has limited its deployment to large enterprise-class servers and workstations. Developers of distributed, real-time, and embedded (DRE) systems, who must contend with far more limited resources, often seek lighter-weight alternatives, such as socket libraries, but these solutions are nearly as tedious and error-prone as they were following their invention a quarter-century ago.

In the last few years, however, research has shown that intelligent design and careful implementation of CORBA can produce middleware that meets the needs of today's DRE developers [1]. By bringing the CORBA model to the DRE domain, the low-level details of the network are abstracted away to the middleware layer, which shortens and simplifies the development cycle for distributed applications. Thus, DRE developers can enjoy the same benefits of CORBA that enterprise developers have enjoyed for many years, such as interoperability across varying hardware, languages, and operating systems.

CORBA middleware for DRE developers offers more benefits than just simplicity and portability. The recent Real-Time CORBA Specification [2] provides stringent quality of service (QoS) constraints on memory, performance, and dependability. CORBA middleware that conforms to this specification improves predictability by bounding priority inversions and managing system resources end-to-end. Such features are vital for DRE systems.

One key challenge in adopting CORBA, however, has been the steep learning curve for C++ middleware implementations, primarily due to the complexity of the CORBA-C++ mapping [3,4,5]. Simpler, easier-to-use languages, particularly Java, have been applied successfully to address this problem [6]. Java offers less "accidental complexity" than C++, a higher degree of portability, native support for concurrency and synchronization, a comprehensive class library, and other features that make it attractive to application developers.

In the DRE domain, however, Java middleware has previously been unable to offer the necessary QoS guarantees of predictability for two primary reasons: i) the under-specified scheduling semantics of Java threads can lead to the most eligible thread not always being run; and ii) the Java garbage collector can preempt any other Java thread, thus yielding unpredictably long preemption latencies.

The need to allocate or reclaim memory can potentially be a major source of unpredictability if such operations are allowed to occur *on demand* in unexpected circumstances (e.g., reallocating a buffer to handle a larger-than-expected amount of data, or having a garbage collector run to reclaim memory). To address this concern, the Real-Time Java Experts Group has defined the Real-Time Specification for Java [7]. RTSJ brings a simpler, more portable, and easier-to-use language to the world of DRE systems. It provides stronger guarantees on thread semantics than conventional Java and defines a new memory management model that allows allocation of objects not subject to garbage collection.

By using these newly-defined real-time Java features, CORBA middleware implemented in Java can provide the best of both worlds: a portable, developer-friendly language and the guarantee of predictability required by DRE systems. Implementing such middleware is not simply a feat of engineering, however. It remains to be seen, for instance, if the developer community will accept the strict scoped memory model of RTSJ, or whether ongoing research into real-time garbage collection will make such memory models obsolete.

Real-time systems are inherently more complex to develop and maintain than conventional systems. Thus, designing and implementing a software system as powerful as CORBA middleware, using the new RTSJ features for real-time memory management, is necessarily more complex than developing systems in conventional Java. However, RTSJ still retains many of Java's advantages compared to C++, such as superior portability and native thread support. Furthermore, RTSJ's memory model may be easier to manage than that of C++, which requires programmers to handle the memory management of each individual object. RTSJ addresses this problem with the concept of *scoped memory*, allowing the system to reclaim the memory of multiple objects automatically. Maintaining entire blocks of memory as scopes can be less complex and error-prone than managing each object manually, as in C++.

Mapping Real-Time CORBA object lifetime models into this RTSJ memory model is a challenging task. The system must be designed carefully to ensure predictability through RTSJ features, while simultaneously complying with the Real-Time CORBA Specification, all the while shielding these complexities from the middleware user and maintaining Java's key advantage: ease of use.

In this paper, we show how we achieved these goals in designing and implementing the first open-source real-time Java, Real-Time CORBA middleware, which we call *RTZen*.[1] The largest known open-source RTSJ project, RTZen demonstrates that real-time Java and Real-Time CORBA are maturing into viable technologies for DRE system development. More importantly, our work proves that these specifications can be integrated into a single middleware architecture that combines the advantages of each. The result is a predictable, efficient, customizable, and embeddable RTSJ implementation of CORBA.

The remainder of this paper is organized as follows: Section 2 explains the RTSJ features used in RTZen to ensure predictability, with special focus on memory scoping; Section 3 describes the RTSJ-specific design patterns that we adopted in RTZen's implementation; Section 4 describes the architecture of RTZen; Section 5 presents empirical results that demonstrate RTZen's ability to accommodate real-time requirements; Section 6 describes related work; and in Section 7 we provide concluding remarks.

---

[1] Available at http://doc.ece.uci.edu

2   Overview of RTSJ

Java offers developers significant advantages, with features like object-oriented programming, platform independence, dynamic class loading, simplified memory management, exception handling, and run-time consistency checks. However, the Java VM mechanism that enables simplified memory management—the garbage collector—introduces challenges for real-time systems by potentially causing unbounded priority inversions, thus reducing predictability. To address this challenge, RTSJ reduces the need for garbage collection by introducing new types of memory regions and real-time threads.

2.1   RTSJ Memory Areas and Switching

In addition to heap memory in standard Java, RTSJ introduces two new memory regions with restrictions aimed at making memory management more predictable. RTSJ specifies three memory regions: heap memory, immortal memory, and scoped memory. Each memory region has an associated life-span, and objects may be allocated within these regions by setting the allocation context before making allocations.

- **Heap memory** is the same as the original Java heap. Objects can be allocated in heap memory, and are alive until the last reference to them is removed, when the object becomes "garbage." Garbage objects may be collected automatically by the garbage collector. The running of a garbage collector is undesirable for real-time systems, because it may be invoked at a time which causes higher-priority tasks to be interrupted from accomplishing their time-critical task.[2] The lifespan of heap memory is the same as that of the JVM; i.e., objects created in heap memory can stay alive as long as the JVM exists or until they become garbage.
- **Immortal memory** is a fixed-sized area whose lifetime is the same as that of the JVM. Objects allocated in immortal memory, however, will never be garbage collected. Therefore, if not managed carefully, the memory in this region could easily become exhausted which will cause an `OutOfMemory Exception`. As a consequence, this region must be used sparingly and managed carefully. In particular, memory allocations from the immortal region should generally occur at application initialization.
- **Scoped memory** is a memory region with a limited lifetime. The end of this lifetime occurs when there are no more threads executing in the region. Scoped memory is ideal for temporary allocations that follow the lifetimes of specific threads of control. The benefit of using scoped memory is that it is both allocated and reclaimed as a single (not necessarily contiguous) block,[3] which are predictable operations.

---

[2] This is assuming that real-time garbage collection is not used.

[3] While RTSJ supports both linear- and variable-time allocation of scoped memory regions, we strictly use the linear-time allocation mechanism in this work.

RTSJ also introduces two new thread types which can be used to execute in memory regions and are used to determine the lifetime of scoped regions. The most important feature of these new threads is that they are scheduled preemptively so that the highest priority thread is always running.

- `RealtimeThreads` (RTTs) are used to enter scoped, immortal, and heap regions. Also, memory located in the heap can be referenced from any other region, following the rules imposed by RTSJ (see Sect. 2.2).
- `NoHeapRealtimeThreads` (NHRTTs) are similarly used to enter scoped and immortal regions, but possess one important distinction: no heap access is allowed. According to normal memory access rules, any region can access the heap. However, if there is code executing in a NHRTT, that code cannot access the heap. The important consequence of this restriction is that NHRTTs can never be preempted by the garbage collector, whereas RTTs can. Therefore, NHRTTs should be used whenever possible to ensure predictability, even if heap memory will also be used in the application.

2.2   Nested Scopes

Scoped memory may be nested, producing a scoping structure called a scope stack. Since multiple memory areas can be entered from an existing memory area, this scope stack can form a tree-like structure. One key relationship is as follows: if region B is entered from region A, then A is considered the *parent* of B (see Fig. 1(a)). Certain rules govern memory access among scopes. Code within a given memory scope A can reference memory in another region B only if the lifetime of the memory in the region B is at least as long as that of the first region A. This lifetime can be guaranteed only if the requested object resides in an ancestor region (i.e., a parent or grandparent, etc.), immortal, or heap memory. A violation of this rule results in an `IllegalAssignmentError` or `IllegalAccessError`.

One important constraint is that a memory region can have only one parent, thereby preventing cycles in the scope stack. Consequently, a single scope cannot have two or more threads from different parent scopes enter it. If one thread takes a particular path to get to a memory region and forms a scoped memory

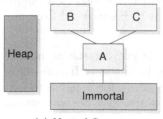

	to Heap	to Immortal	to A	to B	to C
from Heap	yes	yes	no	no	no
from Immortal	yes	yes	no	no	no
from A	yes	yes	yes	no	no
from B	yes	yes	yes	yes	no
from C	yes	yes	yes	no	yes

(a) Nested Scopes

(b) Access rules for (a)

Fig. 1. RTSJ Access Rules

hierarchy, a second thread will have to follow the same hierarchy to reach the same memory region, otherwise a `ScopedCycleException` is thrown. For example, if a thread enters scope B from A, then another thread that enters B must also be entered from A. An important implication of this restriction on scoping structure is that a given region cannot access memory residing in its "sibling" region. In the event that these two regions need to coordinate to perform some task, they will need to do so through memory stored in a common ancestor region. For example, in Fig. 1(a), scope C cannot access scope B. These regions can coordinate only via objects stored in A or immortal memory. Table 1(b) depicts the complete access rules among scopes in Fig. 1(a).[4]

The new memory regions introduced in RTSJ and described above provide memory that will not be managed by the garbage collector, but the restrictions imposed on these memory regions pose challenges for designing real-time middleware such as RTZen.

3   RTZen's Design Patterns

Traditional design patterns [8,9] are used to simplify the development process of large software systems. Using design patterns leads to better modularity and maintainability of code. RTZen is based on such design patterns, especially those used in the development of networked and concurrent object-oriented middleware systems such as *Acceptor-Connector*, *Half-sync/Half-async* and *Interceptor*.

Design patterns have the potential to mitigate the complexity of RTSJ to a large degree. Consequently, some RTSJ design patterns have been proposed in the literature [10,11,12]. Also, additional RTSJ design patterns have been discovered in the course of developing RTZen, and the main goal of this section is to describe them.

3.1   Summary of Existing RTSJ Patterns

The patterns below alleviate some of the most common difficulties that an RTSJ programmer is likely to encounter. These difficulties mostly pertain to properly handling scoped memory hierarchies and obeying memory access rules.

Immortal Singleton. The Immortal Singleton pattern [12] is a simple adaptation of the classical *Singleton* pattern [8]. It allows the creation of a unique instance of a class from immortal memory, allowing it to be accessed from any memory area.

Wedge Thread. A Wedge Thread [10,11] is used to prevent the premature reclamation of a scoped memory area by controlling its lifetime. It consists of a real-time thread that enters a scope and blocks, waiting for a signal to exit the area. Wedge threads should be used sparingly since they occupy system resources.

---

[4] Table 1(b) assumes that real-time threads are used. Note that if no-heap real-time threads are used, no references to the heap are permitted.

Memory Pool. The Memory Pool pattern [10] is a set of instances of a given class preallocated in a specific memory area (e.g., immortal memory). When an instance of this class is requested, an object is taken from the pool and when the instance is no longer needed, it is returned to the pool. Depending on the implementation, the pool size may vary (e.g., if the pool is empty, a new instance may be created and returned). In general, pooled objects must be mutable, so they can be reconfigured and reused.

Encapsulated Method. The Encapsulated Method pattern [11] allows the allocation of objects that represent intermediate results of an algorithm in a *temporary scope*. After the final result is obtained, the temporary scope is discarded, thereby avoiding unnecessary allocations in the original scope.

Multi-scoped Object. The Multi-scoped Object pattern allows transparent access of an object regardless of the originating region of the callee. This pattern ensures that the necessary steps are taken to guarantee that a given method is called from the correct scope by performing the proper memory scope traversals on behalf of the callee. Pizlo et al. [11] attempt to generalize the idea, but they cover only the case of a multi-scoped object performing allocations in its own scope from a child scope, among other simpler cases.

Memory Block. The Memory Block pattern [10] allows the pooling, via serialization, of objects of varying sizes in a byte array block allocated from immortal memory, thus allowing read and write access from any memory scope and any thread type. When an object is discarded, the memory block makes those bytes available for further use. This pattern can be used to communicate information between scopes and threads otherwise forbidden by RTSJ access rules. However, it has important disadvantages: i) it requires explicit memory management, and ii) (de)serialization incurs additional overhead.

3.2   New RTSJ Patterns

In developing one of the largest and most complex open-source RTSJ software projects, we have encountered more situations that warrant the use of four new design patterns.

Separation of Creation and Initialization

Context. To use memory efficiently, RTSJ applications typically create some pools of recyclable objects, preallocated in specific memory areas such as immortal memory [10].

Problem. Creation of objects in another memory area requires the use of Java reflection. But reflection can become memory inefficient when creating objects with parameters because the parameters for the reflection call must be objects themselves.

Solution. To solve this issue, the Separation of Creation and Initialization pattern is used. It defines classes with the default constructor that creates uninitialized instances, as well as accessor methods that allow the modification of the

```
public class
    ExecuteInRunnable
    implements Runnable{
  private Runnable r;
  private MemoryArea a;
  public void init(
    Runnable r,MemoryArea a){
    this.r = r; this.a = a;
  }
    public void run(){
    try { a.enter(r);}
    catch(Throwable ex){...}
}}
```

Fig. 2. The Execute-InRunnable class

```
MemoryArea parent;
ScopedMemory sibling;
Runnable logic;
...
ExecuteInRunnable eir =
    EIRPool.getEIR();
eir.init(logic, sibling);
...
try { parent.executeInArea(
      eir);}
catch (Throwable t) { ... }
finally { EIRPool.freeEIR(eir
      );}
...
```

Fig. 3. Using Execute-InRunnable

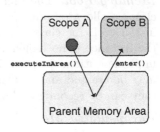

Fig. 4. Invocation between sibling scopes

object's internal state (i.e., the configuration) just before they are going to be used. RTZen uses this pattern to (de)marshal requests, as well as to create ORB and POA façades in memory pools.

Cross-scope Invocation

Context. RTSJ programmers often encounter situations in which the calling object needs to invoke an operation on an object allocated in an different scope, such as in a sibling scope.

Problem. However, the memory access rules of RTSJ dictate that a given object can be accessed *directly* only if it is residing in the calling object's scope stack (an ancestor scope). Therefore, for *indirect* access to occur, elaborate memory traversal must be performed, in which the control thread must first jump to a scope that is a common ancestor of both objects, then enter the callee object's region (possibly traversing intermediate regions along the way), and finally invoke the operation.

Solution. By using the `ExecuteInRunnable` class (see Fig. 2), the Cross-scope Invocation pattern can simplify the indirect access process. If necessary, this `ExecuteInRunnable` class can be used repeatedly to perform such a memory traversal.

Figures 3 and 4 show the use of this pattern. Assume the simplest case in which B and C are sibling scopes and A is their parent memory region, with B being the current scope (Fig. 4). After being instantiated using the default constructor or obtained from a pool, the `ExecuteInRunnable` object is initialized within the sibling scope C and a `Runnable` object that contains the logic to be executed in B. Once the `executeInArea` method of the `MemoryArea` class is called by B, the `ExecuteInRunnable` object starts to run in A, making the current thread enter C and finally execute the logic provided in the `Runnable` object.

As is common in RTSJ programming, the allocation of arguments and returned values of the requested method require special care to avoid illegal access errors: arguments must be accessible from the callee scope, and returned values must be accessible from the caller scope. This requirement may add significant code complexity, but this complexity can be alleviated by the adoption of the Memory Pool and Memory Block patterns [10].

Immortal Exception

Context. In RTSJ applications, exceptions may need to be thrown and handled in different memory areas.

Problem. However, in RTSJ, the propagation of exceptions is restricted by memory access rules. A given exception object must be handled in a memory area that can legally reference that exception. If not, a `ThrowBoundaryError` is returned and the original exception is lost.

RTSJ's memory area rules introduce accidental complexity into exception handling. The CORBA specification requires exceptions to be thrown in many scope regions. However, some of those exception objects cannot be handled in their local scopes, yet cannot be legally accessed from the region that can handle them either. For example, an exception raised in the *Thread Pool Scope* may need to be handled in *ORB Memory Scope*, but this access is prohibited by RTSJ memory access rules.

Corsaro et al. [12] proposed that exceptions can be initially handled in the local scope. With this approach, the notification of the exceptional condition is encapsulated in a status variable or object and then transferred to an outer scope, where the condition is finally handled, or propagated again to an outer scope. Although effective, this approach has the following drawbacks: 1) the code complexity is increased; 2) the exception propagation mechanism is tightly coupled with the system's memory structure; 3) the actual exceptional condition may not be reported correctly because of an inappropriate mapping between the exception type and the status variable or object (e.g., exceptions are commonly handled using general types); and 4) system performance may be affected since the exception must be re-instantiated several times as it is propagated from scope to scope.

Solution. Consequently, we have designed the Immortal Exception pattern, an efficient and flexible solution that allows exceptions to be handled independently of the memory area in which they are thrown, without violating RTSJ referencing rules. In this pattern, a factory class that creates exception objects of specified types resides in immortal memory. The Immortal Singleton pattern [12] is used to cache the exception objects in the factory so that they can be reused (i.e., re-thrown). Distinct families of exceptions, such as CORBA system exceptions and application exceptions, are organized into different factories.

This pattern offers important advantages and a minor disadvantage. Since all exceptions are allocated in immortal memory, they can be accessed from anywhere, thereby avoiding the boundary problem. This design is particularly useful when the system must handle a large number of exceptions, such as the 400 instances of CORBA system exceptions handled by RTZen. A limitation of this pattern, however, is that since exception objects are preallocated, no message that explains the cause of the run-time exception can be associated with the exception objects. However, good documentation can alleviate this inconvenience.

Immortal Façade

Context. A consequence of RTSJ's scoping rules is that large RTSJ applications, such as RTZen, often have complex scoping structures.

Problem. Scoping structures introduce more development complexity to application users. In general, when objects in different scopes interact using method calls, the complexity of traversing the memory structure is exposed to both the caller object and callee object. Furthermore, the caller is typically tightly coupled with the system's memory structure, in particular with the callee object's locality. This exposed complexity makes development and system maintenance more difficult and therefore compromises one of RTZen's design goals.

Solution. To hide complexity from the application developer, as well as to minimize the dependencies of the caller object on the callee object's memory locality, we used the Immortal Façade pattern based on the Gang of Four's Façade design pattern [8]. The Immortal Façade consists of a *façade class* and an *implementation class*. The façade class acts as a surrogate for and typically implements the same interface as the actual implementation class. It encapsulates the logic that handles the cross-scope invocation. The façade objects need to be accessible from scopes of interest, so they are frequently allocated in immortal memory and managed by a pool. The *implementation class* implements the actual business logic behind the façade. An instance of it is allocated in a specific scoped memory.

In RTZen, two key patterns, Cross-scope Invocation and Immortal Façade, have been used to hide the complex scoping structures between callers and callees. One example of the combined use of these two patterns is the ORB façade. RTZen maintains a pool of ORB façade objects in immortal memory. These façades do not implement any business logic. All the logic is contained in the ORB implementation object hosted in the ORB scope. Since the ORB façade is in immortal memory, the user can access it with ease and make invocations on it. The Cross-scope Invocation pattern is used when the invocation thread needs to laterally traverse scoped regions.

4   Architecture

This section explains the rationale behind the design of RTZen. First, we outline the goals for RTZen and the CORBA features influenced by the memory and thread constructs of RTSJ. Next, we describe the design of RTZen, emphasizing its scoped memory structure and illustrating the processing of an invocation on a remote object. Finally, we present an overview of RTZen's customization features.

4.1 RTZen Design Goals

The design of RTZen has been driven by the following requirements.

- **Predictability.** Real-time middleware must provide a high degree of predictability. As a result, a Real-Time CORBA implementation requires eliminating priority inversions and bounding the size of critical sections.
- **Specification Compliance.** An ORB must be compliant to the CORBA specification to ensure application portability across ORB implementations. However, proprietary features and optimizations should still be available if they prove to be advantageous in certain cases.
- **Performance.** Even though real-time applications tend to favor predictability over performance, it is the goal of RTZen not to compromise on this requirement. RTZen aims to provide both a predictable and high performance CORBA implementation.
- **Minimize User Complexity.** One of the key aspects of middleware is that it offloads the complexities of distributed programming from the application developer to the middleware developer. In the case of RTSJ middleware, complexities related to distributed programming brought on by the addition of memory and thread constructs are offloaded as well.
- **Efficient Use of Memory.** RTSJ memory constructs must be used efficiently. Allocations must be made in the context of memory scopes or managed carefully in pools or caches located in immortal memory. Memory leaks must be completely avoided to ensure continuous system operation. If possible, use of heap memory should be avoided to ensure that the garbage collector always remains idle.
- **Customizability.** Finally, middleware should be customizable and support minimization of footprint for embedded applications while maintaining all the advantages of using middleware.

Our earlier work with ZEN [13] focused on each of these goals except for the efficient use of memory, as RTSJ implementations have only recently become available. Maturing RTSJ implementations, such as jRate [14], have provided the real-time JVM layer necessary to ensure predictability and make the memory model of RTZen possible.

4.2 Mapping Real-Time CORBA to RTSJ

Primary features of RTZen are heavily influenced by the constraints imposed by the added memory and thread constructs of RTSJ. To understand the architecture of RTZen we must first examine them.

The feature that influences the architecture of RTZen the most is the CORBA requirement that an application developer must be able to control the lifetimes of various components, including ORB instances, POA instances, and CORBA objects. As a result of this requirement, each of these components is mapped onto a scoped memory region (Section 4.3). Furthermore, the CORBA specification defines the API that must be exposed to application programmers. Since RTZen will use scoped memory regions, the traversal of its internal scoped memory structure must not be exposed to the user.

The final issue is the selection of priorities of RTSJ threads. Recall that RTSJ introduces two new types of threads: `RealtimeThread` (RTT) and `NoHeapRealtimeThread` (NHRTT). The RTSJ platform was designed under the assumption that any NHRTT will possess a higher priority than any RTT, so that NHRTTs will never block for garbage collection [15]. If the application developer chooses to use both RTTs (to access heap memory) and NHRTTs, the priority mappings can ensure that NHRTTs are always mapped to higher priorities than are RTTs.

4.3   RTZen Design

To meet all of the goals and successfully implement the Real-Time CORBA specification, RTZen was designed with a unique memory hierarchy (Fig. 5). The main purpose of this hierarchy is to enable objects to be independently allocated and freed to follow the Real-Time CORBA specification. As a side effect, this design also allows for pluggable and customizable architecture that does not use the heap.

The idea of lifetime – the length of time for which an object is valid – is central to understand the rationale behind the design of RTZen. CORBA exposes to the application the ability to both create and destroy various CORBA components (e.g., ORBs and POAs). RTZen enables this by assigning memory scopes to these components. When the user creates one of these components, the associated memory scope is created, along with a wedge thread if required. Recall that wedge threads occupy system resources; therefore they are only used in scopes where there is not already an active thread keeping that scope alive. When the component is destroyed, the associated memory scope is freed by signaling all active threads in that region to terminate (including wedge threads).

RTZen is organized as a scoped hierarchy: Fig. 5 shows the memory layout of the RTZen components. Each component with a defined lifetime is allocated in its own scope and maintains its state within the scope. Moreover, some components have child scopes for dependent components with smaller lifetimes, thus creating a tree-like scoped memory structure.

In RTZen the application initially starts in immortal memory. The first application scope region is above the initial immortal region and holds references to the ORB façade and POA façade objects which are allocated from immortal memory and cached. The ORB and POA façades internally hold a reference to the ORB and POA scoped memory region respectively, not to the corresponding implementation object itself. In both cases the implementation object is the portal of the scope. Under the ORB scope, there are various other scoped regions for transport, acceptor, POAs, thread pools, and temporary request processing. Each region has at least one thread object inside to keep the region alive. Wedge threads keep the ORB and POA regions alive, whereas threads in the other regions perform an active role for request processing.

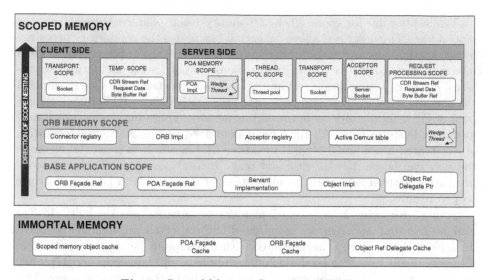

Fig. 5. Scoped Memory Structure of RTZen

The scoped memory structure combined with object-oriented concepts like inheritance and polymorphism enables the development of customizable and adaptable systems [16,13]. Each component can inherit its interface from a base class and implement different features. And since each component is maintained in an individual scoped region, it can be easily plugged in and out of the run-time memory structure of the program. RTZen's protocol and transportation framework is built using this technique. Thus transports and protocols can be configured, added, and removed in a pluggable manner without affecting the other components of the ORB.

This scoped hierarchy also allows RTZen to avoid any heap allocation. However, since RTSJ scoped regions are not garbage collected, RTSJ developers have to be very careful about allocating and maintaining references to objects in these scoped regions. In RTZen, this issue has been resolved using memory pools and the immortal singleton pattern. Memory pools are used for any object that stores state and is simultaneously accessed by multiple request threads, while an immortal singleton is maintained for those objects which require only a global state and are accessed in a synchronous manner.

On the other hand, the scoped hierarchy introduces two accidental complexities into the design of RTZen. The first one is exception handling. Exceptions in RTSJ are not propagated beyond the scope in which they were thrown. However, the CORBA specification requires that the ORB throw exception in many locations. To solve this issue, RTZen uses a combination of local exception handling and the Immortal Exception pattern (Section 3). The second issue that may occur is creation of objects and references across scopes. RTSJ does allow creation of objects across scopes using reflection. However, if the constructor requires any arguments, then reflection causes wasteful allocation of memory for the arguments. To solve this issue, RTZen separates the creation and initialization of objects.

While allowing for more efficient memory usage and customizability, the scoped hierarchy described above potentially increases the complexity perceived by application developers – since it requires traversing the application and ORB internal scoped hierarchy to make invocations – if not for the use of two key patterns: cross-scope invocation and immortal façade (Section 3.2). One example of the combined use of these two patterns is the ORB façade. RTZen maintains a pool of ORB façade objects in immortal memory. These façades do not implement any business logic. All the logic is contained in the ORB implementation object hosted in the ORB scope. Since the ORB façade is in immortal memory, the user can access it with ease and make invocations on it. The cross-scope invocation pattern is used if this invocation's thread needs to laterally traverse scoped regions.

Along with using RTSJ scoped memory to enhance predictability, RTZen also ensures that priorities are maintained and respected throughout the ORB. To achieve this, RTZen is implemented with an endpoint-per-priority paradigm: for every distinct priority level, RTZen maintains a separate endpoint [17]. Each endpoint executes at the highest priority of requests that it may process. This ensures that i) high priority requests are not queued behind low priority requests, and ii) incoming requests are guaranteed that the thread reading the request data from the socket will run at an equal or higher priority.

RTZen also includes many of the performance and predictability enhancing techniques pioneered in ZEN [18,19,20] and TAO [21,22,23,24]. For example, RTZen's thread pool implements the Half-Sync/Half-Async pattern [9] to minimize complexity and allow high throughput, and the POA uses active-demux tables to allow $O(1)$ demultiplexing of server-side objects.

4.4   Sample Invocation Using RTZen

This section traces through an invocation on the client and server side to illustrate the traversing of the scoped memory structure of RTZen during a remote method call. We assume that priorities are propagated with each request from the client to the server and that the server is using a thread-pool with lanes.

The server object is created on the remote end with the appropriate policies, and the corresponding Interoperable Object Reference (IOR) is generated. The IOR informs the client about the remote object's location and some supported policies. When the server object is registered on the server side, RTZen creates a separate endpoint for each supported request priority. This allows requests of varying priorities to be handled independently of each other. This information is also propagated to the client in the IOR.

After obtaining the IOR (e.g., from a Naming Service), the client application reads it and uses the client-side ORB to create a stub of the remote object. The stub acts as a placeholder for the remote object: local invocations made on the stub are translated to remote invocations on the server object by the ORB. RTZen creates the stub objects in the application scope so that the client application may invoke requests on them directly without having to traverse any scopes.

The invocation starts when the client application sets the priority of the request and invokes a method on the stub. Based on the priority, the stub locates the appropriate endpoint on the remote ORB to contact, sends the request message and then waits for the return value. Within the ORB, this translates to using the Cross-Scope Invocation pattern to jump to the ORB scope and then to the transport scope. At this point, the message is sent and the active thread jumps back to the ORB scope and then enters to a temporary scope where it waits for the reply.

After the request message is received by the server transport, the transport thread reads the request header to locate the POA that the remote object is registered with. Then the transport thread uses cross-scope invocation to jump from the transport scope to the POA scope where it locates the reference to the target remote object. At this point, the transport thread jumps to the thread pool region and locates a thread which supports the priority of the request. The request is passed to a thread from the thread pool, and the transport thread returns to its initial scope (i.e., the transport scope) and listens for more incoming requests (Half-Sync/Half-Async pattern [9]). The thread-pool thread now processing the request uses cross-scope invocation to jump to a temporary memory scope where the request is processed. At this point, the invocation is made on the actual remote object and once the invocation is complete, the thread jumps to the transport thread and sends back the reply message.

Finally, on the client side, the client transport thread receives the reply message and jumps to the temporary scope where the thread that made the request is waiting. The client transport thread hands the reply back to the waiting thread which exits back to the client scope and returns from the invocation on the stub.

4.5   Customization Features

Over and above the Real-Time CORBA specification, RTZen also implements some additional features which allow for greater customizability. First, RTZen allows the server-side object to be hosted on thread pools which can be based on either RTTs or NHRTTs. This feature allows the application developer to choose the tradeoff between being able to use the heap or having a more predictable environment.

Second, RTZen includes the implementation of a pluggable transport and protocol framework [25,13] that allows the application developer to plug in custom transport layers or protocols to the ORB. This is specially useful in embedded environments where standard TCP/GIOP functionality may be unnecessary or wasteful. Currently, RTZen includes a very compact version of GIOP with reduced functionality as well as a pluggable serial transport that enables the use of the serial port for CORBA invocations.

Third, RTZen also includes a set of Mock RTSJ classes[5] which enable it to run on standard (non-RTSJ) Java VMs. This feature also allows Java developers to use a standard Java VM to prototype RTSJ applications.

---

[5] Currently, the Mock RTSJ classes expose a reduced set of the RTSJ API and do not perform allocation of access checks.

Finally, we have also developed ZEN-kit [26], a user-friendly graphical tool for customizing RTZen. ZEN-kit implements a customization strategy based on conditional compilation that takes advantage of the RTZen's modular architecture. Using this tool, developers can selectively include Core and Real-Time CORBA features into the ORB in order to meet specific requirements of DRE applications, in particular those related to memory footprint.

5   Empirical Results

5.1   Testing Environment

All experiments were run on 865 MHz Pentium III (Coppermine, 256KB Cache) processors with 512MB PC133 ECC SDRAM, for both server side and client side, connected via 10 Mbps Ethernet on a closed subnet. The operating system was TimeSys Linux GPL 4.1 based on the Linux kernel 2.4.21, which supports the Native POSIX Thread Library (NPTL) [27]. The non-real-time Java Virtual Machine (JVM) used for comparison was the Sun JDK 1.4 JVM. The real-time Java platform was jRate [14], a real-time Java ahead-of-time compiler.

5.2   Performance Measurements

For all tests, measurements were based on *steady state* observations, where the system is run until the transitory effects of cold starts are eliminated before collecting the measured observations.
Measuring typical performance. We used the median as a measure of typical performance because, as so often is true in real-time systems, distributions were typically highly skewed toward the minimum observation, with a large spike near the typical observation, and with a long, low-probability tail toward the maximum.
Measuring worst-case performance. We used the maximum as an estimate of a system's "worst case." The worst case is an important measurement for real-time systems because real-time systems must be designed with the assumption that the system will always deliver the worst possible performance, even though designing to that assumption is wasteful since typical times are usually near the best case [15].

For these experiments, the observed maximum in a sample size of 10,000 observations was used to estimate the worst case for each message size. A sample size at least this large was necessary to observe a reasonable estimate for the maximum latency because the maximum values tended to be extremely low-probability events. The range of the observations ($maximum - minimum$), or jitter was also used as another measure of a system's predictability.

5.3   Typical Performance: Comparison of RTZen on jRate; TAO, JacORB on Sun JVM; and RTZen on Sun JVM

The test case used here has a single thread running on the client side, sending variable-size `octet` sequences to the server side. The size ranged from 32 bytes to 1024 bytes.

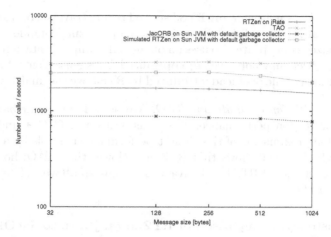

Fig. 6. Typical Performance: Comparison of RTZen on jRate; TAO, JacORB on Sun JVM; and RTZen on Sun JVM

Comparison of RTZen on Sun JVM to JacORB on Sun JVM. Java developers in non-real-time domains can afford to be careless about memory management because of the existence of the garbage collector. The process of memory house-keeping — allocating memory and cleaning it after it is used — creates overhead that can slow an application substantially. RTSJ developers, on the other hand, do not have the luxury of depending on a garbage collector for memory reuse, and must instead be more heedful of memory usage. Section 4 described the careful memory management design in RTZen. Along with the obvious effect of improved predictability, yet another consequence of careful memory management is improved performance. This would be shown by the fact that the typical performance of RTZen is better than JacORB's.

To measure this performance improvement, we compared RTZen with JacORB [6], a widely used Java-based ORB. Both ORBs were tested on the standard Sun non-real-time JVM detailed above. In this case, RTZen used its Mock RTSJ classes (Section 4.5), so all scopes and immortal memory regions were therefore simulated as heap memory, and all allocations in those regions were subject to garbage collection.

The performance of JacORB was measured using the four types of garbage collectors (default, throughput, concurrent low pause, and incremental) supported by the JVM [28]. JacORB obtained its highest throughput with the throughput garbage collector, shown in Fig. 6. Note that, in the same conditions, RTZen significantly outperforms JacORB. Thus, the test shows the performance improvement gained from the extensive memory reuse (memory pools) and other performance enhancing techniques in RTZen (Section 4.3).

Comparison of RTZen on Sun JVM and RTZen on jRate. Figure 6 shows that RTZen on jRate performs about 30% slower than RTZen on Sun JVM. On the Sun JVM, RTZen uses the heap instead of the scoped memory and immortal memory regions; thus it does not incur any RTSJ scoped region traversal or access/allocation check penalties. In addition, jRate is not an optimizing compiler, so it generates unoptimized code; jRate also uses an open-source implementation of the Java API libraries which may not have been optimized. This measurement provides an approximate idea of the overhead introduced by RTSJ over normal Java.

Comparison of RTZen on jRate and TAO. We used TAO as our baseline measurements for RTZen performance. TAO was written in C/C++ and thus provides a good approximation of the highest performance possible by a Real-Time CORBA ORB. Figure 6 shows that RTZen is slower than TAO; however, considering the overhead of RTSJ and Java VMs discussed above, RTZen compares favorably to TAO.

5.4   Consistency: Comparison of RTZen on jRate to JacORB on Sun JVM

We next compared the round-trip latency jitter of RTZen and JacORB. JacORB was run on the Sun JVM with the default garbage collector, on which JacORB obtained its narrowest jitter; RTZen was run on jRate. Although the platforms were different, the measurements show the performance that can be expected from these ORBs on the platforms for which they were designed. Since performance was more or less equivalent across different message sizes, as shown in Fig. 6, we compared the two ORBs for a message size of 128 bytes. Figure 7 shows the distribution of the round-trip latency values with the maximum and minimum bound indicated, as well as the circle to represent the median value. From Fig. 7 we can see RTZen is highly predictable compared to JacORB, with the jitter value of 90 μs and 9770 μs respectively; RTZen's maximum value is close to its median. Also, RTZen has not achieved this predictability by unduly degrading performance. Notably, RTZen's typical performance and predictability, as measured by the worst case observed, are within the range of time units typically used for distributed real-time systems (10 ms) [15]. These jitter values were expected and highlight the predictability gained by developing in RTSJ.

5.5   Typical Performance and Consistency: RTZen on jRate with Variable Message Size

Figure 8 shows that RTZen is predictable across varying message sizes. RTZen performs within round-trip latency jitter of around 200 μs in all cases, which is better than the distributed real-time application requirements of 10 ms [15].

While satisfying the jitter requirement, RTZen's typical performance stays roughly constant even when message size increases. Throughput increases minimally (about 20 μs) as the message size increases from 32 bytes to 1024 bytes. Once the message size exceeds the allocated buffer limit (1024 bytes), the round-trip latencies increase slightly (about 50 μs, about 8%). RTZen allows application developers to configure the message buffer size to customize performance and predictability as required.

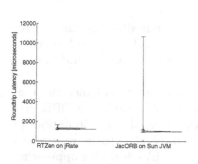

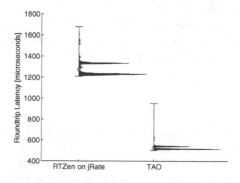

Fig. 7. Consistency: Comparison of RTZen on jRate and JacORB on Sun JVM

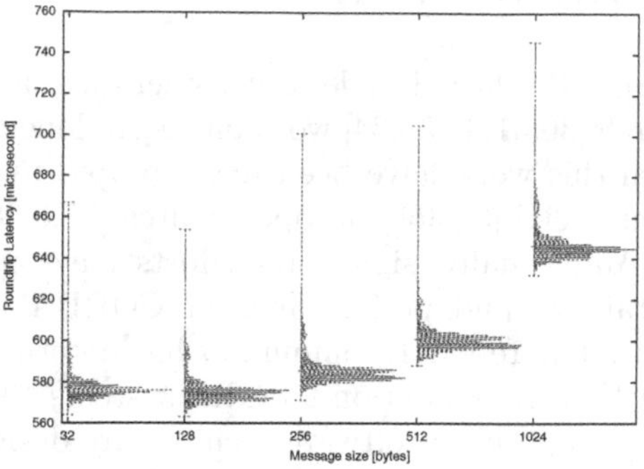

Fig. 8. Consistency: RTZen on jRate with variable message sizes

5.6   Consistency: Comparison of RTZen on jRate and TAO

To compare the round-trip latency jitter of RTZen and TAO, we set up a test case running two client threads. The purpose of this experiment was to test the jitter bounds of both ORBs and to show that RTZen can be set up with NHRTTs that are not interrupted by the garbage collector. The first thread was run at the highest CORBA priority, while the second thread was run at the lowest CORBA priority. The low priority thread performed a long operation; the high priority thread performed a short action which would interrupt the lower priority thread. In RTZen, the high priority was a NHRTT, and the low priority thread was a RTT. The RTT was also set up to allocate data on the heap to generate some garbage data which would be reclaimed by the garbage collector.

Figure 9 shows a comparison of jitter measurements on the high priority thread with RTZen and TAO running. Although RTZen is still slower than TAO, the jitter of the high-priority task in RTZen is similar to TAO's. These performance and jitter measurements demonstrate RTZen's ability to accommodate real-time requirements.

Fig. 9. Consistency: Comparison of RTZen on jRate and TAO

6   Related Work

During the last decade, a considerable amount of standardization [29] and research [30,31,32,33,34] work has been done on CORBA, and some results derived from this work have been incorporated in various ORBs available today, both commercial [35,36] and open-source [37,6,38].

Additionally, significant efforts have been carried out to enhance the predictability and performance of CORBA and make it suitable for DRE systems. The research community has determined the strengths and limitations of CORBA as foundation for DRE systems [39,40], and based on them, researchers have proposed i) software architecture designs [25,23], ii) scheduling approaches and mechanisms [41,42,43], iii) techniques for improving quality of service [44,24], iv) extensions for real-time network protocols [25,45,46,47], v) the adaptation of CORBA services [48,49], vi) techniques for tailoring CORBA ORBs to computational platforms under stringent resource constraints [50,51,13], and vii) modeling and verification methods [52]. Meanwhile, the Object Management Group has produced the Real-Time CORBA specifications [53,17].

Several Real-Time CORBA implementations exist as of this writing. Perhaps the most well-known is TAO [21,54], a popular open-source ORB compliant with most of the features and services defined in CORBA 3.x [55]. Built on top of TAO is CIAO [56], a CORBA Component Model (CCM) implementation for developing component-oriented DRE systems. ROFES [57] is a minimal memory footprint prototype of Real-Time CORBA. It has been adapted to work with several different hard real-time networks, including SCI [45], CAN, ATM, and an Ethernet-based time-triggered protocol [46]. Commercial Real-Time CORBA implementations are also available: OpenFusion e*ORB C Edition for Real-time [58] from PrismTech, ORBexpress RT [59] from Objective Interface Systems, and VisiBroker-RT [60] from Borland Software Corporation. Very recently, PrismTechnologies and Objective Interface Systems announced Real-Time CORBA compliant ORBs for RTSJ: OpenFusion RT for Java and ORBexpress RT for Java, respectively.

Java Remote Method Invocation (RMI) [61] is a mechanism for developing object-oriented distributed systems in Java, and there is some progress adapting RMI so that RTSJ supports timely invocation of remote objects [62]. Standard Java RMI has become more compatible with CORBA, in particular due to RMI/IIOP, a form of RMI that uses IIOP as the underlying protocol. RMI/IIOP holds promise to evolve into a bridge to RT-CORBA.

7   Conclusion

Memory management is a vital part of any RTSJ application. The RTZen architecture addresses the memory allocation and scoping issues related to implementing a Real-Time CORBA ORB using RTSJ. It provides a solid foundation for further research into implementations of Real-Time CORBA services and applications based on Java. Such research would incorporate RTSJ scheduling features into the RTZen scheduling service and provide support for custom configuration of RTZen to minimize its memory footprint for smaller embedded applications. Further research is also needed for adapting RTZen to Java virtual machines that support a real-time garbage collector.

In its current state, however, RTZen fulfills the essential goals of real-time distributed systems: predictability, specification compliance, high performance, minimal user complexity, customizability, and efficient use of memory. Our work proves that the RTSJ and Real-Time CORBA specifications can be integrated into a single middleware architecture that combines the advantages of each.

Acknowledgments

The authors thank Susan Anderson Klefstad for significant revision work and suggestions and Morgan Deters for timely jRate bug fixes. Juan A. Colmenares thanks the University of Zulia (LUZ) for supporting his participation in this research.

References

1. Schmidt, D.C.: R&D Advances in Middleware for Distributed, Real-time, and Embedded Systems. Communications of the ACM. Special Issue on Middleware **45** (2002) 43–48
2. Object Management Group: Real-time CORBA Specification. OMG Document formal/02-08-02 edn. (2002)
3. Schmidt, D.C., Vinoski, S.: The History of the OMG C++ Mapping. C/C++ Users Journal (2000)
4. Schmidt, D.C., Vinoski, S.: Standard C++ and the OMG C++ Mapping. C/C++ Users Journal (2001)
5. ZeroC, I.: The Internet Communications Engine^{TM}. www.zeroc.com/ice.html (2003)
6. Gerald Brose and André Spiegel and Reimo Tiedemann et al.: Jacorb. http://www.jacorb.org/ (2004)
7. Bollella, Gosling, Brosgol, Dibble, Furr, Hardin, Turnbull: The Real-Time Specification for Java. Addison-Wesley (2000)
8. Gamma, E., Helm, R., Johnson, R., Vlissides, J.: Design Patterns: Elements of Reusable Object-Oriented Software. Addison-Wesley, Reading, MA (1995)
9. Schmidt, D.C., Stal, M., Rohnert, H., Buschmann, F.: Pattern-Oriented Software Architecture: Patterns for Concurrent and Networked Objects, Volume 2. Wiley & Sons, New York (2000)
10. Benowitz, E.G., Niessner, A.F.: A patterns catalog for RTSJ software designs. In: Lecture Notes in Computer Science. Volume 2889., OTM 2003 Workshops (2003) 497–507
11. Pizlo, F., Fox, J.M., Holmes, D., Vitek, J.: Real-time java scoped memory: Design patterns and semantics. In: 7th IEEE Int'l Symposium on Object-Oriented Real-Time Distributed Computing (ISORC 2004). (2004) 101–110
12. Corsaro, A., Santoro, C.: Design patterns for RTSJ application development. In: Lecture Notes in Computer Science. Volume 3292., OTM 2004 Workshops (2004) 394–405

13. Klefstad, R., Rao, S., Schmidt, D.C.: Design and Performance of a Dynamically Configurable, Messaging Protocols Framework for Real-time CORBA. In: Proceedings of the 36th Annual Hawaii Int'l Conference on System Sciences. (2003)
14. Corsaro, A., Schmidt, D.C.: The Design and Performance of the jRate Real-Time Java Implementation. In Meersman, R., Tari, Z., eds.: On the Move to Meaningful Internet Systems 2002: CoopIS, DOA, and ODBASE, Berlin, Lecture Notes in Computer Science 2519, Springer Verlag (2002) 900–921
15. Dibble, P.C.: Real-Time Java Platform Programming. Prentice Hall (2002)
16. Klefstad, R., Schmidt, D.C., O'Ryan, C.: Towards highly configurable real-time object request brokers. In: Proceedings of the 5th IEEE Int'l Symposium on Object-Oriented Real-Time Distributed Computing (ISORC 2002). (2002) 437–447
17. Object Management Group: Real-Time CORBA (Dynamic Scheduling). 2.0 edn. (2003)
18. Klefstad, R., Krishna, A.S., Schmidt, D.C.: Design and Performance of a Modular Portable Object Adapter for Distributed, Real-Time, and Embedded CORBA Applications. In: Proceedings of the 4th Int'l Symposium on Distributed Objects and Applications. (2002)
19. Krishna, A., Klefstad, R., Schmidt, D.C., Corsaro, A.: Towards predictable real-time Java object request brokers. In: Proceedings of the 9th IEEE Real-Time and Embedded Technology and Applications Symposium (RTTAS 2003). (2003) 49–56
20. Krishna, A., Schmidt, D.C., Klefstad, R.: Enhancing real-time CORBA via real-time java features. In: Proceedings of the 24th Int'l Conference on Distributed Computing Systems (ICDCS 2004). (2004) 66–73
21. Schmidt, D.C., Levine, D.L., Mungee, S.: The design of the TAO real-time object request broker. Computer Communications **21** (1998) 294–324
22. Gokhale, A., Schmidt, D.C.: Techniques for optimizing CORBA middleware for distributed embedded systems. In: Proceedings of the 18th Annual Joint Conference of the IEEE Computer and Communications Societies (INFOCOM '99). Volume 2. (1999) 513–521
23. Pyarali, I., Spivak, M., Cytron, R., Schmidt, D.C.: Evaluating and optimizing thread pool strategies for real-time CORBA. In: Proceedings of the ACM SIGPLAN Workshop on Languages, Compilers and Tools for Embedded Systems (LCTES '01). (2001) 214–222
24. Pyarali, I., Schmidt, D.C., Cytron, R.: Techniques for Enhancing Real-time CORBA Quality of Service. Proceedings of the IEEE **91** (2003) 1070–1085
25. O'Ryan, C., Kuhns, F., Schmidt, D.C., Othman, O., Parsons, J.: The design and performance of a pluggable protocols framework for real-time distributed object computing middleware. In: IFIP/ACM Int'l Conference on Distributed Systems Platforms (Middleware '00). (2000) 372–395
26. Gorappa, S., Colmenares, J.A., Jafarpour, H., Klefstad, R.: Tool-based configuration of real-time corba middleware for embedded systems. In: Proceedings of the 8th IEEE Int'l Symposium on Object-Oriented Real-Time Distributed Computing (ISORC 2005). (2005)
27. Corp., T.: TimeSys Linux GPL 4.1. www.timesys.com (2004)
28. Sun Microsystems, I.: Tuning garbage collection with the 1.4.2 java[tm] virtual machine. (2003)
29. Object Management Group: Catalog of OMG Specifications. http://www.omg.org/technology/documents/spec_catalog.htm (2005)
30. Gokhale, A., Schmidt, D.C.: Principles for Optimizing CORBA Internet Inter-ORB Protocol Performance. In: Proceedings of the 31st Annual Hawaii Int'l Conference on System Sciences. Volume 7. (1998) 376–385

31. Arulanthu, A.B., O'Ryan, C., Schmidt, D.C., Kircher, M., Parsons, J.: The Design and Performance of a Scable ORB Architecture for CORBA Asynchronous Messaging. In: Proceedings of the IFIP/ACM Int'l Conference on Distributed Systems Platforms (Middleware 2000). (2000) 208–230

32. Mishra, S., Shi, N.: Improving the Performance of Distributed CORBA Applications. In: Proceedings of the Int'l Parallel and Distributed Processing Symposium (IPDPS 2002). (2002) 36–41

33. Alberto Coen Porisini, Matteo Pradella, Matteo Rossi, Dino Mandrioli: A formal approach for designing CORBA-based applications. ACM Transaction on Software Engineering and Methodology 12 (2003) 107–151

34. Majumdar, S., Shen, E.K., Abdul-Fatah, I.: Performance of adaptive CORBA middleware. Journal of Parallel and Distributed Computing 64 (2004) 201–218

35. Borland Software Corporation: Borland Enterprise Server, VisiBroker Edition. http://www.borland.com/visibroker/ (2005)

36. IONA Technologies: Orbix 6.2. http://www.iona.com/products/orbix/ (2005)

37. McConnell, S., Pedersen, J., Evans, J.S., Kühne, L., Rumpf, M., Boyce, S., Wood, C.: Openorb community project. http://sourceforge.net/projects/openorb/ (2004)

38. Puder, A.: Mico: An open source corba implementation. IEEE Software 21 (2004) http://www.mico.org/.

39. Gokhale, A., Schmidt, D.C.: Evaluating CORBA latency and scalability over high-speed ATM networks. In: Proceedings of the 17th Int'l Conference on Distributed Computing Systems (ICDCS '97). (1997) 401–410

40. O'Ryan, C., Schmidt, D.C., Kuhns, F., Spivak, M., Parsons, J., Pyarali, I., Levine, D.L.: Evaluating policies and mechanisms for supporting embedded, real-time applications with CORBA 3.0. In: Proceedings of the 6th IEEE Real-Time Technology and Applications Symposium (RTAS 2000). (2000) 188–197

41. Gill, C.D., Levine, D.L., Schmidt, D.C.: The Design and Performance of a Real-Time CORBA Scheduling Service. Real-Time Systems 20 (2001)

42. Dipippo, L.C., Wolfe, V.F., Esibov, L., Cooper, G., Bethmangalkar, R., Johnston, R., Thuraisingham, B., Mauer, J.: Scheduling and priority mapping for static real-time middleware. Real-Time Systems 20 (2001) 155–182

43. Hao, T., Zhigang, L., Jinde, L.: An end-to-end scheduling approach for real-time CORBA. In: Proceedings of the 2002 IEEE Region 10 Conference on Computers, Communications, Control and Power Engineering (TENCON '02). Volume 1. (2002) 318–322

44. Zinky, J.A., Bakken, D.E., Schantz, R.: Architectural Support for Quality of Service for CORBA Objects. Theory and Practice of Object Systems 3 (1997) 1–20

45. Lankes, S., Pfeiffer, M., Bemmerl, T.: Design and Implementation of a SCI-based Real-Time CORBA. In: Proceedings of the 4th IEEE Int'l Symposium on Object-Oriented Real-Time Distributed Computing (ISORC 2001). (2001) 23–30

46. Lankes, S., Jabs, A., Reke, M.: A time-triggered ethernet protocol for real-time corba. In: Proceedings of the 5th IEEE Int'l Symposium on Object-Oriented Real-Time Distributed Computing (ISORC 2002). (2002) 215–222

47. Lankes, S., Jabs, A., Bemmerl, T.: Design and performance of a CAN-based connection-oriented protocol for Real-Time CORBA. Journal of Systems and Software 77 (2005) 37–45

48. Harrison, T.H., Levine, D.L., Schmidt, D.C.: The design and performance of a real-time CORBA event service. In: Proceedings of the 12th ACM SIGPLAN Conference on Object-oriented Programming, Systems, Languages, and Applications (OOPSLA '97). (1997) 184–200

49. Hong, S., Kim, Y., Kweon, M., Min, D., Han, S.: Object-oriented real-time CORBA naming service on distributed environment. In: Proceedings of the 12th Int'l Conference on Information Networking (ICOIN-12). (1998) 637–640

50. Gokhale, A., Schmidt, D.C.: Optimizing a CORBA IIOP Protocol Engine for Minimal Footprint Multimedia Systems. Journal on Selected Areas in Communications - Special issue on Service Enabling Platforms for Networked Multimedia Systems **17** (1999)

51. Kim, K., Geon, G., Hong, S., Kim, S., Kim, T.: Resource-conscious customization of CORBA for CAN-based distributed embedded systems. In: Proceedings of the 3rd IEEE Int'l Symposium on Object-Oriented Real-Time Distributed Computing (ISORC 2000). (2000) 34–41

52. Rossi, M., Mandrioli, D.: A formal approach for modeling and verification of rtcorba-based applications. In: Proceedings of the 2004 ACM SIGSOFT Int'l Symposium on Software Testing and Analysis (ISSTA '04). (2004) 263–273

53. Object Management Group: Real-Time CORBA (Static Scheduling). 1.2 edn. (2005)

54. Schmidt, D.C.:   TAO. Real-time CORBA with TAO (The ACE ORB). http://www.cs.wustl.edu/ schmidt/TAO.html (2004)

55. Object Management Group: Common Object Request Broker Architecture: Core Specification. 3.0.3 edn. (2004)

56. Schmidt, D.C.: CIAO. Real-time CCM with CIAO (Component Integrated ACE ORB). http://www.cs.wustl.edu/ schmidt/CIAO.html (2004)

57. RWTH Aachen: ROFES. http://www.rofes.de (2005)

58. PrismTech Corporation: OpenFusion e*ORB C Edition for Real-time. http://www.prismtechnologies.com (2005)

59. Objective Interface Systems, Inc.: ORBexpress RT. http://www.ois.com (2005)

60. Borland Software Corporation: VisiBroker-RT.   http://www.borland.com/ visibroker/ (2005)

61. Sun Microsystems Inc.: Java Remote Method Invocation (Java RMI). http://java.sun.com/products/jdk/rmi/ (2004)

62. Borg, A., Wellings, A.: A real-time RMI framework for the RTSJ. In: Proceedings of the 15th Euromicro Conference on Real Time Systems. (2003)

Composite Subscriptions in Content-Based Publish/Subscribe Systems

Guoli Li and Hans-Arno Jacobsen

Middleware Systems Research Group, University of Toronto,
Toronto, ON, Canada

Abstract. Distributed publish/subscribe systems are naturally suited for processing events in distributed systems. However, support for expressing patterns about distributed events and algorithms for detecting correlations among these events are still largely unexplored. Inspired from the requirements of decentralized, event-driven workflow processing, we design a subscription language for expressing correlations among distributed events. We illustrate the potential of our approach with a workflow management case study. The language is validated and implemented in PADRES. In this paper we present an overview of PADRES, highlighting some of its novel features, including the composite subscription language, the coordination patterns, the composite event detection algorithms, the rule-based router design, and a detailed case study illustrating the decentralized processing of workflows. Our experimental evaluation shows that rule-based brokers are a viable and powerful alternative to existing, special-purpose, content-based routing algorithms. The experiments also show that the use of composite subscriptions in PADRES significantly reduces the load on the network. Complex workflows can be processed in a decentralized fashion with a gain of 40% in message dissemination cost. All processing is realized entirely in the publish/subscribe paradigm.

1 Introduction

In distributed applications large numbers of events occur. In isolation these events are often not too interesting or useful. However, as correlations over time, for example, these events may represent interesting and useful information. This information is important for coordinating activities in a distributed system. Workflow processing and business process execution, where different stages of the flow or process execute on distributed nodes, are examples of distributed applications generating potentially huge numbers of events. The efficient correlation of these events reveals information about the status of the workflow. Events in a workflow could be the initiation, the termination, or the status of a task.

Distributed publish/subscribe systems are well-suited to handle large numbers of events. A publish/subscribe system is comprised of information producers who publish and information consumers who subscribe to information. The key benefit of publish/subscribe for distributed event-based processing is the natural decoupling of publishing and subscribing clients. This decoupling can enable the

G. Alonso (Ed.): Middleware 2005, LNCS 3790, pp. 249–269, 2005.

design of large, distributed, loosely coupled systems that interoperate through simple publish and subscribe-style operations.

However, current publish/subscribe approaches lack the ability to address event correlation and enable the coordination of activities associated with disparate clients in the content-based network. In order to allow publish/subscribe to support such distributed applications, first, an appropriate subscription language needs to be designed which offers a suitable view over available events to enable coordination. Second, event correlation requires the detection of distributed events. In publish/subscribe this is based on routing subscriptions and publications throughout the broker network and on efficient composite event detection algorithms realized on a single publish/subscribe broker.

Some work on detecting composite events in distributed publish/subscribe systems is starting to appear [21,22,5]. However, these approaches are mainly focusing on the design of the subscription language and do not address the event correlation problem central to our approach. We have developed an expressive content-based subscription language that is derived from the requirements of event-driven, decentralized workflow management and business process execution scenarios. To validate our approach we have implemented the language in PADRES (Publish/subscribe Applied to Distributed REsource Scheduling), a novel distributed, content-based publish/subscribe messaging system, and have built all the necessary infrastructure to support the deployment, monitoring, and execution of workflows and business processes. In essence, we have realized a decentralized workflow management and execution environment that builds directly on top of a standard publish/subscribe interface.

PADRES's subscription language is fully content-based, includes notions to express time, supports variable bindings, coordination patterns, and composite subscriptions. *Composite subscriptions* offer a higher level view for subscribers by enriching the expressiveness of the subscription language. A composite subscription consists of several *atomic subscriptions* linked by logical or temporal operators. An atomic subscription refers to the traditional notion of a subscription in publish/subscribe and is matched by a single publication event; a composite subscription is matched by a set of independent events potentially occurring at different locations and times. PADRES is based on a rule-based broker that implements composite event detection and introduces a novel distributed algorithm for composite subscription routing.

Support for composite subscriptions is essential for applications where it is impossible to detect a particular condition from isolated atomic events. For example, in workflow management systems, tasks can only be executed if certain conditions are met. A given task may require that two other tasks have successfully completed and a certain timing constraint is met. We will show experimentally that supporting composite subscriptions in content-based publish/subscribe systems has two key advantages. First, subscribers receive fewer messages and network traffic is reduced. Without composite subscriptions, the subscriber must subscribe to all the corresponding atomic events in order to receive the necessary information. The subscriber would be overwhelmed by an excessive amount of atomic events, most of which may be irrelevant and could be filtered out before reaching the subscriber. Second, the overall performance of the publish/subscribe system is improved by detecting composite events in the network, rather than at the edge of the network. Moreover, composite subscriptions reduce the complexity of subscriber components.

The rest of this paper is organized as follows. Section 2 presents background material and related work. An overview of PADRES is given in Section 3. Section 4 presents the PADRES subscription language, composite subscription routing and composite event detection in detail. A workflow management system case study built on PADRES is discussed Section 5. An experimental evaluation of PADRES and its potential for workflow management is presented in Section 6.

2 Background and Related Work

Content-based Routing. Content-based publish/subscribe systems typically utilize *content-based routing* in lieu of the standard address-based routing. Since publishers and subscribers are decoupled, a publication is routed towards the interested subscribers without knowing specifically where subscribers are and how many subscribers exist. The *content-based address* of a subscriber is the set of subscriptions issued by the subscriber. There are several interesting projects dealing with content-based routing, such as SIENA [3], REBECA [18], JEDI [6], Hermes [20] and Gryphon [19]. Covering and merging-based routing, which are optimizations for content-based routing, are discussed in SIENA [3], JEDI [6], REBECA [18], and PADRES [15]. In addition to publications and subscriptions, content-based routing can use *advertisements* [18,3], which are indications of the data that publishers will publish in the future. Advertisements are used to form routing paths along which subscriptions are propagated. Without advertisements, subscriptions must be flooded throughout the network. PADRES adopts the publication-subscription-advertisement model for content-based routing and suggests several novel features not realized in existing approaches. The novel features of PADRES discussed in this paper include a rule-based router design, algorithms to support composite subscription routing, composite event detection, coordination patterns for expressing workflows and business processes, and support for the decentralized deployment and execution of workflows and business processes.

Composite Events. An *event* is defined as a state transition. In the publish/subscribe literature, events describe state transitions of interest to subscribers. Events are often synonymously referred to as *publications*[1]. A *subscription* captures the interest of a subscriber to be informed about possible events. We generically refer to subscriptions, publications, and advertisement as *messages*, if no distinction is required.

A *composite event* refers to a pattern of event occurrences of interest to a subscriber. These patterns may express temporal or causal relationships between

---

[1] One could further distinguish between the state transition (i.e., event) and the published information that reports on the transition (i.e., the *publication*).

different events. A pattern is matched, if the specified events have occurred, subject to optional timing constraints. Since several events are involved in the matching of a single subscription pattern the matching engine has to store partial matching states. In the literature, the term *composite event* has been used to refer to a subscription that expresses the pattern defining a composite event. To make the difference between the state transitions (i.e., the events) and the actual interest specification clearer, when discussing our work, we use the term *composite subscription* to refer to the pattern and use *composite event* to mean the distributed state transitions of relevance for the subscriber of the composite subscription. Also to distinguish composite subscriptions from traditional, non-composite subscriptions, we refer to the latter as *atomic subscriptions*.

The earliest approaches for enabling the processing of composite events were rule-based production systems established in artificial intelligence. One of the most widely used matching algorithms, the Rete algorithm is used in many expert systems today [9]. Rete compiles rules into a network. The design of Rete trades off space for processing efficiency. The Java Expert System Shell (*Jess*) [10] is a rule-based matching engine based on the Rete algorithm. Our PADRES broker is based on *Jess*. The Publication Routing Table (PRT) and Subscription Routing Table (SRT) are two *Jess* engines. We show how content-based publish/subscribe messages (i.e., subscriptions, composite subscriptions, publications, and advertisements) can be mapped to rules and facts processed by Rete-type rule engines.

Many early approaches for composite event processing relate to active databases and are based on centralized evaluation schemes [12,11,16,13,17,4]. These projects differ primarily in the mechanism used for event detection. Ode [12] uses a finite automaton and SAMOS [11] uses a Petri Net. Other approaches use trees as the data structure for representing and detecting composite events. The main reason for adopting trees is that they are simple and intuitive for representing composition. The traversal and manipulation of trees have been thoroughly studied in the past, and a large number of efficient algorithms have been developed [16,13,1,17]. GEM [16] and READY [13] are projects using tree-based approaches to process incoming events. Atomic events are leaf nodes and operators are inner nodes in the tree structure. The composite event is represented by the root of the tree. The main limitation of GEM is each composite event has its own tree, and identical subtrees cannot be shared among composite event trees. Similar to GEM and READY, EPS (Event Processing Service) [17] provides a tree-based event specification language. EPS alleviates the limitation of GEM by using a shared subscription tree to process incoming events. Snoop [4], also a tree-based approach, provides an expressive composite event specification language with temporal support. Snoop introduces the notion of consumption policies called *contexts*. They are used to capture application semantics by resolving which events are consumed from the event history for composite event detection in case of ambiguity. Composite subscriptions in PADRES are also represented by trees. Unique to PADRES is the mapping of atomic and composite subscriptions to rules and the support of full content-based, composite subscriptions. The rule-based processing has been thoroughly studied, leading to a large number of efficient algorithms for rule/fact matching. The rule-based approach employed in PADRES takes advantage of the existing research for the PADRES broker design. PADRES also supports a tree decomposition algorithm for composite subscription routing.

The specification and detection of composite events in the context of publish/subscribe systems has recently become an important research area [21,22,5]. Hermes [20] and Gryphon [19] provide parameterized atomic events to enrich the expressiveness of subscriptions. Courtenage [5] specifies composite events based on the λ-calculus. The approach lacks support for temporal constraints. CEA [21] proposes a Core Composite Event Language to express event patterns that occur concurrently. CEA constitutes a composite event detection framework built as an extension of an existing publish/subscribe middleware platform. The CEA language is compiled into automata for distributed event detection supporting regular expression-type patterns. CEA employs policies to ensure that mobile event detectors perform distributed event detection at favorable locations, such as close to event sources. REBECA [22] describes composite events using composite event filter expressions, which can be mapped to expressions of the Core Composite Event Language [21]. The subscription language design of PADRES has been inspired from requirements set forth by workflow and business process description languages and the requirements of distributed execution of these processes. Unique to PADRES is the use of variables in subscriptions to join atomic events. PADRES also supports language elements to express dependencies and condition-based repetition relationships of activities (i.e., while loops). Architecturally different from existing approaches, PADRES builds the composite subscription processing and composite event detection capability into the publish/subscribe layer.

3 PADRES System Description

The PADRES system consists of a set of brokers connected by a peer-to-peer overlay network. Clients connect to brokers using various binding interfaces such as Java Remote Method Invocation (RMI) and Java Messaging Service (JMS). Each PADRES broker employs a rule-based engine to route and match publish/subscribe messages, and is used for composite event detection. An overview of PADRES is provided in [8]. This paper focuses on the specification, detection, and use of composite events. PADRES provides four other novel features as well: monitoring support, historic query capability, fault detection and repair, and load balancing. A monitor module, which is an administrative client in PADRES, could display the broker network topology, trace messages, and measure the performance of the broker network. The historic data access module allows clients to subscribe to both future and historic publications. The fault tolerance module detects failures in the publish/subscribe layer and initiates failure recovery. The load balancing module handles the scenarios in which a broker is overloaded by a large number of publishers or subscribers. The detail

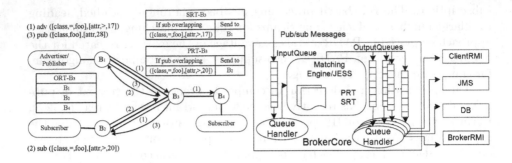

Fig. 1. Broker Network   **Fig. 2.** Broker Architecture

of these features goes beyond the scope of this paper. Fig. 10 shows the protocol stack of PADRES. This section discusses the architecture of PADRES for processing of atomic subscriptions. The extension of PADRES to process composite subscription and the case study applying composite subscription processing to workflow management are discussed later.

3.1 Message Format

The PADRES subscription language is based on the traditional [attribute, operator, value] predicates used in several existing content-based publish/subscribe systems [3,18,19,7]. An atomic subscription is a conjunction of predicates. For example, an atomic subscription in workflow management may be ([class, =, job-status], [appl, =, payroll], [job-name, isPresent, *]). The comma between predicates indicates the conjunction relation. This subscription is matched by publications of all jobs involved in application *payroll*. We support operators, such as =, >, <, ≥, ≤, and *isPresent*. The special operator *isPresent* means an attribute could be any value in a given range. Each subscription message has a *mandatory* tuple describing the *class* of the message. The *class* attribute provides a guaranteed selective predicate for matching, similar to the *topic* in topic-based publish/subscribe systems[2]. Other predicates are constraints on particular attributes. Advertisements have the same format as atomic subscriptions. Publications are sets of [attribute, value] pairs. There is a match between a subscription and a publication if each predicate in the subscription is satisfied by a corresponding [attribute, value] pair in the publication. A match between a subscription and a advertisement means the sets of publications matching the advertisement and the subscription are overlap.

3.2 Network Architecture

The overlay network connecting the brokers is a set of connections that form the basis for message routing. The overlay routing data is stored in Overlay

---

[2] The PADRES language is fully content-based based on a rich predicate language.

Routing Tables (ORT) at each broker. Specifically, each broker knows its neighbors from the ORT. Message routing in PADRES is based on the publication-subscription-advertisement model established by the SIENA project [3]. We assume that publications are the most common messages, and advertisements are the least common ones. A publisher issues an advertisement before it publishes. An advertisement allows the publisher to publish a set of publications matching this advertisement. Advertisements are effectively flooded to all brokers along the overlay network. A subscriber may subscribe at any time. The subscriptions are routed according to the Subscription Routing Table (SRT), which is built based on the knowledge of advertisements. The SRT is essentially a list of [advertisement,last hop] tuples. If a subscription overlaps an advertisement in the SRT, it will be forwarded to the last hop broker the advertisement came from. Subscriptions are routed hop by hop to the publisher, who advertises information of interest to the subscriber. Meanwhile, the subscription will be used to construct the Publication Routing Table (PRT). Like the SRT, the PRT is logically a list of [subscription,last hop] tuples, which is used to route publications. If a publication matches a subscription in the PRT, it will be forwarded to the last hop broker of that subscription until it reaches the subscriber. A diagram showing the overlay network, SRT and PRT is provided in Fig. 1. In this figure, step *1)* an advertisement is propagated from B_1. Step *2)* a matching subscription enters from B_2. Since the subscription overlaps the advertisement at broker B_3, it is sent to B_1. Step *3)* a publication is routed along the path established by the subscription to B_2. A subscription/advertisement covering and merging scheme [15] is used to optimize content-based routing by reducing network traffic and routing table size, especially for applications with highly clustered data.

3.3   Broker Architecture

The PADRES brokers are modular software components built on a set of queues: one input queue and multiple output queues. Each output queue represents a unique message destination. A diagram of the broker architecture is provided in Fig. 2. The matching engine between the input queue and output queues is built using *Jess*. It maintains the SRT and PRT, which are Rete trees [9]. For example, in the PRT, subscriptions are mapped to rules, and publications are mapped to facts, as shown in Fig. 3. An atomic subscription message is mapped to the antecedent of a rule; the actions to be taken if the subscription is matched are mapped to the consequent of the rule. The antecedent encodes the message filter condition and the consequent encodes the notification semantic.

The matching between subscriptions and publications is transformed to the matching between rules and facts, which is performed by the rule-based broker. When a new message is received by the broker, it is placed in the input queue. The matching engine takes the message from the input queue. If the message is a publication, it is inserted into the PRT as a fact. When a publication matches a subscription in the PRT, its next hop destination is set to the last hop of the subscription, and it is placed into the corresponding output queue(s). If the message

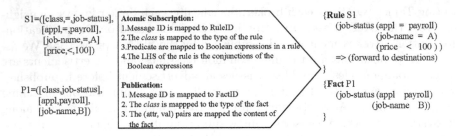

Fig. 3. Mapping Subscriptions/Publications to Rules/Facts

is a subscription, the matching engine first routes it according to the SRT, and, if there is an advertisement overlapping the subscription, the subscription will be inserted into the PRT as a rule. Essentially, the rule-based broker performs matching and decides the next hop destinations of the messages as a router. This novel rule-based approach allows for powerful subscription language and notification semantics and naturally enables composites subscriptions.

4 Composite Subscription Processing

4.1 Composite Subscription Language

The composite subscription language is inspired by the requirements of workflow management and business process execution. The language should be powerful enough to eventually describe workflows defined using the Business Process Execution Langauge (BPEL4WS) [14], which is a standard language for business processes. PADRES supports *parallelization, alternation, sequence* and *repetition* compositions. PADRES also supports *variable bindings* that serve to correlate and aggregate publications by specifying constraints on attribute values between different atomic subscriptions. A composite subscription is represented by a subscription tree, where the internal nodes are operators and leaf nodes are atomic subscriptions, as shown in Figure 4 (b).

The operator to represent the *parallelization* pattern is AND, denoted by the symbol (&). The composite subscription (s_1 & s_2) is matched when both s_1 and s_2 are matched, irrespective of their matching order. The operator & is to connect two or more subscriptions, and it is different from the conjunction operator between predicates in an atomic subscription that requires to be matched by one publication. The *alternation* pattern represents the matching of any of two specified subscriptions using operator OR, denoted as (∥). The composite subscription (s_1 ∥ s_2) is satisfied when either s_1 or s_2 is matched by a publication. Furthermore, composite subscriptions in PADRES can have variables bound to values in the publications. Variables are represented by $ in subscription predicates. Parenthesis are used to specify the priority of operators. In the example below, the composite subscription consists of three atomic subscriptions, linked using & and ||, and requires the values of the attribute *appl* in the matching publications to be equal. This is expressed using the variable symbol $X.

```
{Rule (((job-status (appl = $X) (job-name = A)(state = succ)) &
        (job-status (appl = $X) (job-name = B)(state = succ)))||
        (job-status (appl = $X) (job-name = C)(state = succ)))
  => (forward a notification to proper destinations)}
```

Events in applications may have sequential relations, that is, one event happens before the occurrence of another event. The *sequence* pattern describes this kind of event relation. The composite subscription $(s_1;_{[timespan:ts]} s_2)_{[within:wi]}$ is matched when a publication p_2 matching s_2 occurs provided publication p_1 matching s_1 has already occurred. The *timespan* parameter specifies the minimum time step of the two publications; the *within* parameter limits the maximum time span between them. In the *sequence* pattern, a *time* predicate is added to standard subscriptions. Suppose s_1 and s_2 subscribe to job A and job B respectively, as in the previous example. The composite subscription is mapped to a rule as described below. This pattern requires that the time p_2 is published is greater than that of p_1.

```
{Rule ((job-status ...(job-name = A)(time = $Y)...) &
        (job-status ...(job-name = B)(time > $Y+ts)(time < $Y+wi)))
  => (forward a notification to proper destinations)}
```

The *repetition* pattern describes an aperiodic or periodic event. PADRES can describe the repetition events as Repetition(S, n, attr, v). It means publications matching S happen n times and attribute *attr* increases by step v, or decreases if v is negative. The iteration is controlled the value of *attr* with step v. A *repetition* pattern can be mapped to a rule as below.

```
{Rule ((job-status ...(job-name = A)(attr = $Z)...) &
        (job-status ...(job-name = A)(attr = $Z+v)...)&
                     ...                               &
        (job-status ...(job-name = A)(attr = $Z+(n-1)v)...))
  => (forward a notification to proper destinations)}
```

Composite subscriptions can be composed in a nested fashion using the above operators to create more complex composite subscriptions. Mapping composite subscriptions to rules consists of three steps: first, each atomic subscription is mapped to part of the antecedent. Second, connect each part of the antecedent using logical operators and variables. Third, activites to be taken after matching are mapped to the consequent of the rule. In the PADRES broker, both atomic and composite subscriptions are mapped to rules. That is, extending this subscription language does not require significant changes in the matching engine.

4.2   Composite Subscription Routing

In a large-scale publish/subscribe system, publications are issued at geographically dispersed sites. A centralized composite event detection scheme constitutes a potential bottleneck and consists of a single point of failure. All atomic publications have to be centrally collected in order to detect an occurrence of a

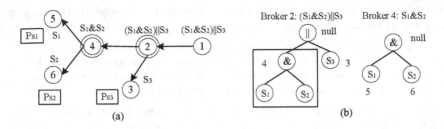

Fig. 4. Composite Subscription Routing

composite event. Our distributed solution consists in detecting parts of an event pattern and aggregating the parts. A notification message signifying the occurrence of the composite event is sent to the subscriber only after all the parts are detected. The main difficulties of distributed event detection are routing composite subscriptions, including where and how to decompose a composite subscription, and routing the individual parts of the subscription. The location of detection should be as close to publishers as possible to ensure that the publications contributing to a given composite subscription are not unnecessarily disseminated throughout the broker network. In other words, the composite subscription should be forwarded to the publishers within the broker network as far as possible before it is decomposed. As a result, bandwidth usage is reduced. Following the example in Fig. 4 (a), suppose a composite subscription $((s_1$ & $s_2)$ ‖ $s_3)$ arrives from broker 1, and its matching publications arrive from broker 3, 5, and 6. The composite subscription is split into parts along the routing path, since the matching publications may arrive from different brokers. Atomic subscriptions s_1 and s_2 are detected at broker 5 and 6 respectively and the detection results are combined at broker 4 for $(s_1$ & $s_2)$. Moreover, the detection results could be shared among subscribers that have common subexpressions of composite subscriptions in order to save bandwidth and computational effort.

Each atomic subscription in a composite subscription could find its destination(s) from SRT. If all atomic subscriptions have the same next hop destination, a broker should forward the composite subscription as a whole to the destination; otherwise the composite subscription should be split into parts according to different destinations, and each part should be forwarded to its own destination. In Fig. 4 (b), since all matching publications are coming from broker 2, broker 1 routes the composite subscription as a whole. At broker 2 publications matching s_1 and s_2 arrive from broker 4 according to the SRT, while s_3's publications will arrive from broker 3. As a result, the composite subscription is split into two parts: $(s_1$ & $s_2)$ and s_3. The first part is sent to broker 4, where it is split into s_1 and s_2, and sent to broker 5 and 6 respectively. The second part s_3 is routed to broker 3. The routing scheme is to detect the event pattern matching a composite subscription at a location which is as close as possible to the data sources. A composite subscription is mapped to a rule, and a publication is mapped to a fact at a single broker. The rule-based broker matches facts against rules and decides where to route the notification if there is a match. Therefore, the broker acts as both a message router and a composite event detector. The advantage of using a rule-based matching engine is that it enables composite subscriptions naturally without significant changes to the broker.

Composite subscriptions in PADRES are represented by a tree structure. When a broker receives a composite subscription, it performs the following steps. First, a destination tree is built bottom-up for the composite subscription according to the SRT, which knows where all the atomic subscriptions came from. Leaf nodes of the tree are destinations of atomic subscriptions; an internal node is the destination of its child nodes if the two child nodes have the same destination, or *null* otherwise. If a node is *null*, all its parent nodes are *null*. Each node in the composite subscription tree has a corresponding node in the destination tree. The recursive algorithm for building such a tree is presented in Fig. 5. The average time complexity of this algorithm is $O(N)$ and the average space complexity is $O(N+logN)$, where N is the number of atomic subscriptions in a composite subscription. Second, the composite subscription tree is split according to its destination tree. The decomposition process of a composite subscription tree is top-down. If the destination of a node in the composite subscription tree is *null*, the subscription represented by the node is split into two parts, one for each child node. Otherwise the node and its subtree are kept as a whole unit. The algorithm is given in Fig. 6. The time and space complexity of this algorithm is the same as algorithm *buildDestinationTree(cs)*. Last, each part resulted from the decomposition is routed to its destination, and the composite subscription is mapped to a rule and inserted into the PRT for later event detection. The process happens at each broker on the routing path. As a result, all the atomic subscriptions are routed to their destinations as specified by the destination tree and the broker network is ready to detect composite events in a distributed mode. Moreover, after composite subscriptions are split into atomic subscriptions, the covering-based and merging-based routing techniques can be applied to create compacted PRTs/SRTs at brokers and further reduce the network traffic [18,15].

```
buildDestinationTrees(cs):
Input: composite subscription cs
Output: a destination tree T

Initialize T according to cs
If (cs.root is leaf node) {
      T.destination = cs.root.destination
}Else{
      T.left = buildDestinationTree(cs.root.left)
      T.right = buildDestinationTree(cs.root.right)
      If (T.left.destination == T.right.destination) {
            T.destination = T.left.destination
      }Else{
            T.destination = null
      }
}
Return T
```

Fig. 5. Algorithm for Building a Destination Tree

```
decomposition(cs, T):
Input: composite subscription cs; destination tree T
Output: a set of subscriptions S

Initialize S = empty
If (T.destination == null){
      S = S ∪ decomposition(cs.root.left, T.left) ∪
            decomposition(cs.root.right, T.right)
}Else{
      S = S ∪ cs
}
Return S
```

Fig. 6. Algorithm of Decomposing a Composite Subscription

There are several advantages of using distributed composite event detection. Redundant detection is eliminated by sharing the detection results among subscribers. For the overlapping expressions of composite subscriptions issued by clients, the detection is executed once, and subscribers close to each other can reuse the detection results. Distributed detection also reduces network traffic. A composite subscription is forwarded into the network as far as possible before it is split. As a result, the number of subscriptions injected into the network does not increase significantly for composite subscriptions. Furthermore, composite events are detected close to their data sources in the network and are not widely disseminated. A single notification is sent after a match, instead of a set of individual notifications for each matching publication, reducing the number of publications routed in the federation.

4.3   Distributed Composite Event Detection

Each broker is an atomic/composite event detector. It processes a large number of publications/subscriptions and maintains them as rules/facts in its matching engine. The broker matches the rules against the facts. The occurrence of a composite event is marked by the occurrence of the last event that completes the composite event. When a publication is received, it is inserted as a fact. The fact may match part of a rule, or several rules. Then the rule(s) are maintained in the engine in a partial match state. If the fact does not fire a rule, the matching engine updates the partial match state with the new fact. If the fact fires a rule, that is, the fact makes a partially matched rule a full match then associated composite subscription is satisfied. A notification message with a set of matching publications, called a detection set, as its payload is issued as result. The main problem in composite event detection is consuming the publications received by the brokers, e.g. among all the matching publications what should go to the detection set. To be more flexible, our matching engine provides all the possible combinations of matching publications. Consider the composite subscription $((s_1 \ \& \ s_2) \ \& \ s_3)$, where s_i matches publication type e_{ij}, $i=1 \sim 3$ and j is the instance number of e_i. Subscription is issued after e_{22}. Our composite event detection semantic is based on the constraint that at least one of the events in the detection set must be issued after the composite subscription. This is to remain compatible with standard publish/subscribe approaches, where subscriptions refer to information published in the future. The subscription is inserted into the PRT as a rule. The matching engine filters out the solution set $< e_{11}, e_{21}, e_{31},$ which is older than the subscription. The rule is partially matched in the matching engine. Four possible composite event patterns matching the subscription are given in Fig. 7 when e_{32} arrives.

4.4   Unsubscription of Composite Subscriptions

In PADRES, if a client wants to revoke a subscription, it issues an unsubscription message. To maintain the consistency of routing tables in the broker network, *ack* messages are used to ensure the unsubscription process is successful. An

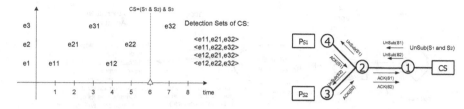

Fig. 7. Event Consuming   **Fig. 8.** Unsubscription

ack message is sent if a broker removes a subscription from its matching engine. The unsubscription message is sent periodically every t_1 *ms* until its *ack* is received.[3] When a broker receives an unsubscription, the following three steps are performed: first, it checks the SRT to find the list of neighbor brokers to which it previously routed the subscription (or part of the subscription). Second, if the list is empty, it removes the subscription from its routing table, and sends back an *ack* message. Otherwise, it splits the unsubscription if necessary, forwards the unsubscription(s) to the brokers in the list, and waits for *ack* messages from them. Last, the broker cannot safely delete the subscription until it collects all the *ack* messages back from its neighbors. An *ack* message is sent back to the broker/client who forwards the unsubscription. Fig. 8 shows an example of the unsubscription process.

5   Case Study: Event-Based Workflow Management

A workflow management system performs coordinated execution of workflows. A *workflow*, also called an *application*, is a set of business-related activities that are invoked in a specific sequence to achieve a business goal. An *activity* is a computer *job*, such as a Unix job, a Windows NT job or a database job, which is executed by a *job execution agent*. The agents are distributed in the network, working in coordination with each other. The workflow manager starts an execution *instance* of a workflow by issuing a *workflow trigger*, a message starting the execution of a workflow.

The publish/subscribe messaging paradigm efficiently supports the decentralized execution of event-driven, loosely coupled applications, such as workflows and business processes. Since routing is content-based, the workflow manager does not need to maintain the address information of each job execution agent and route the messages to and from agents, as those messages are automatically delivered using content-based routing. Moreover, no centrical workflow manager is required, as workflow processing is fully decentralized. Job execution agents are lightweight components without special logic for workflow management. They only need the capability to send and receive messages and execute jobs. The

---

[3] If the *ack* does not arrive in t_2 *ms*, we assume the neighbor broker has failed. A fault tolerant module is called to recover SRTs/PRTs. The details are beyond the scope of this paper.

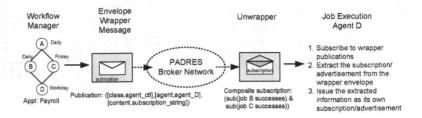

Fig. 9. Envelope Wrapper Message

agents are publish/subscribe clients, who subscribe and publish to exchange information using the publish/subscribe network. PADRES, which introduces composite subscriptions in addition to the standard publish/subscribe features, illustrates the successful application of the publish/subscribe paradigm to workflow management. The overall architecture for supporting workflow processing is shown in Fig. 10. The publish/subscribe-based workflow management system includes four components: workflow transformation, workflow deployment, workflow execution and workflow monitoring.

Workflow Transformation. Workflows are specified as XML documents detailing the job execution information and the various dependencies between jobs. The XML documents are converted into a set of subscriptions and advertisements. Fig. 9 shows an example of a workflow consisting of four jobs. Job D depends on job B and job C, respectively, subject to certain constraints, such as time and resources. Composite subscriptions are used to express all job dependencies and constraints. A job can be run only when its job dependency subscription is matched. Advertisements enable job execution agents to publish job status information after completing a job. In a workflow, the jobs that have no predecessors are called *start jobs*, for instance, job A is a start job in *payroll*. Start jobs subscribe to a *workflow trigger*.

Workflow Deployment. The goal of workflow deployment is to send the subscriptions and advertisements generated from the workflow definition file to the corresponding *job execution agents*. For example, the agent for job D should subscribe to execution status information of job B and job C. To send job dependency subscriptions to job execution agents, the workflow manager uses an *envelope wrapper*[4] message pattern to wrap the subscription inside an envelope message that is complies with the publish/subscribe messaging paradigm. Each envelope wrapper is a publication which indicates its destination agent. Agents receive the wrapper messages by subscribing to the wrapper. For instance, agent D subscribes to ([class,=,agent_ctl],[agent,=,agent_D]) in Fig. 9. As a result, agent D receives the wrapper with a composite subscription embedded in the message. Agents unwrap envelope messages by extracting the subscriptions from the envelopes, and issue them as their own subscriptions. The same process applies for advertisements. As a result, the agents are ready to receive and publish work-

---

[4] The class of the envelope wrapper message is *agent_ctl*.

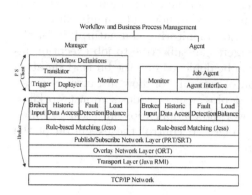

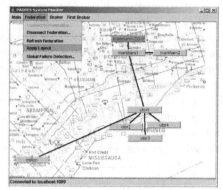

Fig. 10. PADRES Protocol Stack   **Fig. 11.** PADRES System Monitor

flow execution information. This deployment process is performed entirely using publish/subscribe interactions.

Workflow Execution. The job execution agents are both subscribers and publishers. The dual roles enable them to exchange messages within the publish/subscribe messaging system, enabling a coordinated execution of the workflow. A particular instance of a workflow is started by a *trigger*. It fires all start jobs. When these start jobs are finished, they trigger their subsequent jobs. Execution continues until all the jobs defined in the workflow are finished. The key to workflow execution is job dependency subscriptions, which determine the order of execution of jobs. All the message routing is automatic and transparent to the workflow management layer.

Workflow Monitoring. A workflow management system maintains a trace of job executions and provides a control and monitoring interface. The monitor may be a separate publish/subscribe client in Fig. 10. An important function of a workflow management system is monitoring. Real-time monitoring fits directly in the content-based publish/subscribe paradigm. The monitor simply subscribes to job execution status information publications of a particular set of jobs. As a result, when the job is completed, the monitor knows the execution status information. PADRES also provides a graphical interface which allows the monitor to visualize the network topology and message routing in order to gain an intuitive picture of the workflow execution as shown in Fig. 11. All the monitoring functions are entirely based on the publish/subscribe layer's primitives.

There are several advantages to use a publish/subscribe system for workflow management. First, workflows are by nature event-driven. A workflow is started by a trigger and is driven by publication messages of finished jobs. Control messages are automatically and transparently routed to the appropriate agents in the publish/subscribe layer. Second, workflows are easily scalable to multiple platforms, as the publish/subscribe architecture supports cross-platform applications in a distributed environment. Moreover, large-scale applications can be supported easily. Third, the management of workflow definitions is flexible. It is easy to add, modify or delete jobs from a workflow. The modification can be performed dynamically. Furthermore, job monitoring is a natural fit for the publish/subscribe paradigm, since managers can subscribe to job execution information. Fourth, multiple workflows can be deployed into the broker federation at the same time. Concurrent execution of several workflow instances is possible. Finally, the distributed application deployment provides a robust workflow management mechanism. Deploying a workflow application into a distributed network, instead of using a central manager to control the execution of the workflow, avoids a single point of failure.

6   Evaluation

We implement PADRES in Java with JDK1.4.2 using *Jess* as a matching engine and RMI as the native transport protocol. All our experiments are performed on a computer with an Intel Xeon 3GHz processor and 2GB RAM, of which 1GB is allocated to the JVM. Due to lack of benchmarks or real application data, we generate the subscriptions and publications using a workload generator which produces the data by selecting between 3 and 6 attributes from a list of twenty attributes $\{a_i, i = 1...20\}$ and selecting values from given value ranges, [1..100] by default. We generate two kinds of data sets. Attributes and values in the first data set are selected randomly following a uniform distribution. The second data set follows a Zipf distribution, in which attributes are chosen from the attribute set $\{a_i, i = 1...20\}$, where the probability of selecting a_i is $\frac{1}{i}$, and value v_i is chosen with the probability of $\frac{1}{v_i}$. For evaluating the distributed workflow management system, we deployed a distributed network of 5 overlay brokers, one with 10 job agents and one with 30 job agents, each representing a separate workflow. In our experimental evaluation we focus on proving the viability of composite subscriptions to encode workflows and business processes and the use of publish/subscribe for the decentralized execution of these workflows. Furthermore, we aim to evaluate the performance and overhead associated with composite event detection and the effect of composite subscriptions on network traffic for the execution of workflows. A small network is fully sufficient for this purpose. The evaluation of large-scale broker networks comprising hundreds of nodes is deferred to future work.

Publication Matching Time. We generate 200,000 subscriptions and 5,000 publications for both uniform distribution and Zipf distribution to evaluate the publication matching time of PADRES brokers. Fig. 12 shows the average matching time of publications against atomic subscriptions. The matching time is given using a logarithmic scale. Each data point is obtained by averaging the time taken to process 5,000 publications. We compare our broker based on the *Jess* rule-based matching engine with two other methods. One is a naive matching algorithm which linearly scans the routing table to find the matched subscriptions. The other is a matching algorithm that is similar to the predicate counting algorithm [2]. This algorithm calculates distinct predicates only once. Our exper-

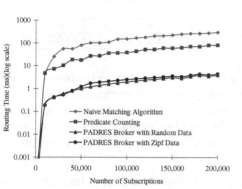
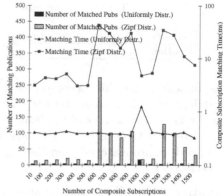

Fig. 12. Publication Matching Time   **Fig. 13.** Composite Event Detection

iments show that the rule-based matching engine using a Rete network is very efficient. It takes only $4.52\,ms$ to route a publication against 200,000 subscriptions for both sets. The well-known Rete algorithm trades space for time. (Matching a publication against 200,000 subscriptions, the PADRES broker uses 644MB of memory while the predicate counting algorithm uses about 38MB memory space.)[5] The matching time does not increase significantly with an increase in the number of subscriptions for both data sets. This indicates that the Rete-based approach is suitable for large scale publish/subscribe systems and can process a large number of publication and subscription messages efficiently.

Composite Subscription Matching Time. The performance of composite subscription matching is shown in Fig. 13. We first inject 1,000 publications into the broker, and then insert 2,000 composite subscriptions, each of which consists of 3 atomic subscriptions. Fig. 13 shows the average detection time per composite subscription against the publications and the number of matched publications. Each data point in Fig. 13 represents the average detection time for 50 composite subscriptions. In the uniformly distributed data set, the number of matched publications per composite subscription[6] does not change significantly, as a result, the composite subscription matching time is stable. In the Zipf data set, more publications are matched and the composite subscription matching time varies according to the number of matched publications. The results show that, given the publication set, the detection time does not increase with the number of composite subscriptions in the matching engine for both data sets. The matching time is effected by the number of matched publications. That is, the more publications match a subscription, the longer it takes the matching engine to process the subscription. From the experiment, we notice that if there is

---

[5] We maintain two *Jess* Retes in the matching engine as SRT and PRT. To support composite subscription, publications are maintained in PRT as facts which consume the space.

[6] The matched publications maybe count multiple times in different detection sets.

Table 1. Composite Subscription Routing Delay

Number of Atomic Subscriptions	2	3	4	5	6
Routing Delay (ms)	3.210	5.367	9.287	11.437	12.074

no publication matching a composite subscription, the matching engine stops the matching in $0.01ms$ no matter how many composite subscriptions are resident in the broker. The number of publications resident in the matching engine affects the detection time as well. The larger the number of publications, the more publications are matched, and the longer matching time it takes per composite subscription.

Routing Delay. We route a composite subscription according to its destination tree. The routing delay for a composite subscription at a broker includes the time to build the destination tree and to split the composite subscription. Table. 1 shows that the routing delay increases with the number of atomic subscriptions included in a composite subscription. This substantiates the time complexity of the two algorithms we discussed in Section 4.2 are $O(N)$, where N is the number of atomic subscriptions in a composite subscription. The more complex a composite subscription is, the longer it takes to route the subscription.

Network Traffic Overhead. Detecting composite events in the broker network reduces the message traffic received by clients. We compare two scenarios. In the first scenario, a client issues 200 composite subscriptions, each consisting of 5 atomic subscriptions. In the second scenario, instead of composite subscriptions, the client issues the 1000 atomic subscriptions that make up the original 200 composite subscriptions. After 40,000 publications are injected into the broker network, we measure the number of notifications received by the client in the different scenarios, as shown in Fig. 14. The result shows that the number of notifications sent to the client is greatly reduced by the composite subscriptions, yielding an overall reduced message traffic. For this scenario, the reduction is up to 65%.

Distributed Workflow Deployment and Execution. We measure the network traffic overhead of a workflow deployment and execution to show the effect

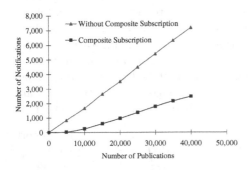

Fig. 14. Number of Notifications

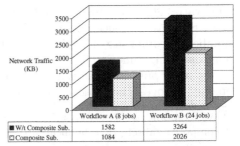

Fig. 15. Workflow Traffic

of composite subscriptions for workflow processing. We design two workflows: workflow A is a workflow with 8 jobs which includes the *payroll* example, a diamond workflow shown in Fig. 9, twice in sequence. Workflow B is a workflow with 24 jobs, which is workflow A followed by 4 concurrent diamond workflows. The manager dispatches the workflow to agents[7]., and the agents submit advertisements and subscriptions, which represent the job dependencies. Without composite subscriptions, agents have to subscribe to several atomic subscriptions instead of a single composite one. When a composite subscription issued by an agent is matched, only one notification message is sent back to the agent, as opposed to several individual atomic notifications. So more messages are disseminated in the broker network. To simplify the measurements, we assume each publication and subscription message is 1KB. We measure the traffic overhead of the workflow deployment and 10 execution instances in Fig. 15. The results show that composite subscriptions reduce the network bandwidth by about 40% for both workflows.

7   Conclusions

In this paper, we introduce the PADRES project. PADRES is a distributed publish/subscribe system building on and extending existing content-based routing approaches. PADRES offers an expressive subscription language, including unique features such as composite subscriptions, various coordination patterns, a notion of time and time-based subscriptions, and variable bindings. PADRES fully integrates these features in a standard content-based subscription language. The choice of language features has been derived from the requirements of workflow management and business process execution use cases. For example, structured coordination activities, such as `sequence` and `while loops`, today available in BPEL4WS, are expressible.

The PADRES brokers build on a rule-based approach to perform content-based event matching and composite event detection. We present two algorithms for composite subscription routing and distributed composite event detection. The experimental evaluation of PADRES shows that the rule-based broker design is an efficient alternative to existing content-based message routing, matching, and distributed event detection algorithms. For example, the routing overhead is on the order of a few milliseconds for hundreds of thousands of subscriptions.

A distributed, decentralized workflow management system based on PADRES is presented to validate the approach. The case study proves the viability of the approach and introduces the concepts of decentralized deployment, execution, and monitoring of workflows entirely in the publish/subscribe layer. Our experiments show that through the use of composite subscriptions, subscribers receive less notification messages. As a result, the overall network traffic overhead is reduced. The experiments for workflow management further substantiate this conclusion by showing that more benefits are gained from composite

---

[7] This is done through the publish/subscribe based injection mechanism described in Section 5.

subscriptions, for both workflow deployment and execution, leading to about 40% fewer messages overall.

Acknowledgements

We would like to thank the PADRES team for their help and feedback in carrying out this research. The team is currently comprised of Eli Fidler, Vinod Muthusamy, Pengcheng Wan, Alex Cheung, and Serge Mankovski (Cybermation, Inc.) Between May 2003 and April 2005, the PADRES project was supported by Cybermation, Inc., CITO, and NSERC.

References

1. A. Aho, J. Hopcroft, and J. Ullman. Data structures and algorithms. *Reading, MA: Addison-Wesley; 1983*, 1983.
2. G. Ashayer, H. Leung, and H.-A. Jacobsen. Predicate matching and subscription matching in publish/subscribe systems. In *DEBS'02 Workshop at ICDCS'02*, Vienna, Austria, 2002.
3. A. Carzaniga, D. S. Rosenblum, and A. L. Wolf. Design and evaluation of a wide-area event notification service. *ACM Transactions on Computer Systems*, 19(3):332–383, 2001.
4. S. Chakravarthy and D. Mishra. Snoop: An expressive event specification language for active databases. *Data and Knowledge Engineering*, 14(1):1–26, 1994.
5. S. Courtenage. Specifying and detecting composite events in content-based publish/subscribe systems. In *Proceedings of the 1st International Workshop on Distributed Event-Based Systems(DEBS'02)*, 2002.
6. G. Cugola, E. D. Nitto, and A. Fuggetta. The JEDI event-based infrastructure and its application to the development of the OPSS WFMS. *IEEE Transactions on Software Engineering*, 27(9), 2001.
7. F. Fabret, H.-A. Jacobsen, F. Llirbat, J. Pereira, K. A. Ross, and D. Shasha. Filtering algorithms and implementation for very fast publish/subscribe systems. *SIGMOD Rec.*, 30(2):115–126, 2001.
8. E. Fidler, H.-A. Jacobsen, G. Li, , and S. Mankovski. Distributed publish/subscribe for workflow management. *International Conference on Feature Interactions in Telecommunications and Software Systems (ICFI'05), Leisester, UK*, 2005.
9. C. L. Forgy. Rete: A fast algorithm for the many pattern/many object pattern match problem. *Artificial Intelligence*, 19(1):17–37, 1982.
10. E. J. Friedman-Hill. Jess, The Rule Engine for the Java Platform. http://herzberg.ca.sandia.gov/jess/.
11. S. Gatziu and K. R. Dittrich. Detecting composite events in active database systems using petri nets. In *Proceedings of the 4th Intl. Workshop on Research Issues in Data Engineering (RIDE): Active Database Systems, Houston, Texas*, 1994.
12. N. H. Gehani, H. V. Jagadish, and O. Shmueli. Composite event specification in active databases: Model & implementation. In *Proceedings of the 18th International Conference on Very Large Data Bases*, pages 327–338, 1992.
13. R. E. Gruber, B. Krishnamurthy, and E. Panagos. The architecture of the ready event notification service. *In 19th IEEE International Conference on Distributed Computing Systems Middleware Workshop*, 1999.

14. IBM and Microsoft. Business process execution language for web services version 1.0. http://dev2dev.bea.com/techtrack/BPEL4WS.jsp.
15. G. Li, S. Hou, and H.-A. Jacobsen. A unified approach to routing, covering and merging in publish/subscribe systems based on modified binary decision diagrams. *International Conference on Distributed Computing Systems (ICDCS'05), Columbus, Ohio, USA*, 2005.
16. M. Mansouri-Samani and M. Sloman. GEM: A generalized event monitoring language for distributed systems. *IEE/IOP/BCS Distributed Systems Engineering Journal*, 4(2), June 1997.
17. D. Moreto and M. Endler. Evaluating composite events using shared trees. *IEE Proceedings - Software*, 148(1):1–10, 2001.
18. G. Mühl. *Large-scale content-based publish/subscribe systems*. PhD thesis, Department of Computer Science, Darmstadt University of Technology, 2002.
19. L. Opyrchal, M. Astley, J. Auerbach, G. Banavar, R. Strom, and D. Sturman. Exploiting IP multicast in content-based publish-subscribe systems. In *IFIP/ACM International Conference on Distributed systems platforms*, pages 185–207, 2000.
20. P. R. Pietzuch and J. Bacon. Hermes: A distributed event-based middleware architecture. In *Proceedings of the 22nd International Conference on Distributed Computing Systems*, pages 611–618. IEEE Computer Society, 2002.
21. P. R. Pietzuch, B. Shand, and J. Bacon. Composite event detection as a generic middleware extension. *IEEE Network Magazine, Special Issue on Middleware Technologies for Future Communication Networks*, January/February 2004.
22. A. Ulbrich, G. Mühl, T. Weis, and K. Geihs. Programming abstractions for content-based publish/subscribe in object-oriented languages. In *CoopIS/DOA/ODBASE (2)*, pages 1538–1557, 2004.

Scrivener: Providing Incentives in Cooperative Content Distribution Systems*

Animesh Nandi[1], Tsuen-Wan "Johnny" Ngan[1], Atul Singh[1],
Peter Druschel[2], and Dan S. Wallach[1]

[1] Department of Computer Science, Rice University
[2] Max Planck Institute for Software Systems

Abstract. Cooperative peer-to-peer (p2p) applications are designed to share the resources of participating computers for the common good of all users. However, users do not necessarily have an incentive to donate resources to the system if they can use the system's services for free. In this paper, we describe Scrivener, a fully decentralized system that ensures fair sharing of bandwidth in cooperative content distribution networks. We show how participating nodes, tracking only first-hand observed behavior of their peers, can detect when their peers are behaving selfishly and refuse to provide them service. Simulation results show that our mechanisms effectively limit the quality of service received by a user to a level that is proportional to the amount of resources contributed by that user, while incurring modest overhead.

1 Introduction

This paper concerns itself with the fair sharing of resources in cooperative peer-to-peer (p2p) systems. In such a system, participating nodes are expected to contribute a fraction of their resources in exchange for access to a service provided by the system. Clearly, if participants fail to contribute enough resources to offset the load imposed by all users, then the system's stability and usability may be in danger.

Experience with file-sharing systems like Gnutella and KaZaA shows that many users may choose to consume the system's services without providing any of their own resources for the use of others [2]. The problem is that participants have no natural *incentive* to provide services to their peers if it is not somehow required of them. Users more closely resemble economically "rational" agents who are willing to follow the protocol only if that behavior maximizes the node's "utility" from the p2p network. If there is no immediate penalty for selfish behavior, then nodes will behave selfishly, and the p2p system will fail. Economic theory calls these users "free riders" or "freeloaders," and the resulting scenario "the tragedy of the commons" [21].

Ideally, we would like to design a system where nodes, acting in their own best interest, behave collectively to maximize the common welfare. Designing such a system without a centralized authority that has complete knowledge of the system becomes

---

* This research was supported in part by Texas ATP (003604-0079-2001), by NSF (ANI-0225660, http://project-iris.net) and by gifts from Microsoft Research and from Intel Research.

G. Alonso (Ed.): Middleware 2005, LNCS 3790, pp. 270–291, 2005.

a distributed algorithmic mechanism design (DAMD) problem [12]. DAMD is a current area of study that combines computational tractability in theoretical computer science with incentive-compatible mechanism design in the economics literature. It provides a useful framework for considering p2p systems [33, 27, 28]. This paper considers incentives-based mechanisms that ensure fair sharing, focusing on cooperative systems where network bandwidth is the contented resource.

One way to enforce fairness is to have, for each node in the system, a set of other nodes account for that node's actions and approve requests according to the system's policy. KARMA [36] is an example of such a system. However, coordinating the actions of this auditor set requires both cryptographic operations and additional communication *every* time a peer issues or responds to a request. This can add substantial overhead and latency to the system. Moreover, this approach introduces the additional problem of how to incentivize the auditor set to perform its function correctly [36].

Instead, we hypothesize that a normal p2p node, monitoring the behavior of its overlay neighbors, will have sufficient information to locally identify and discourage selfish behavior. When nodes give preferential service to peers who follow the rules, rational agents will choose to follow the rules to receive better services. An early example of a p2p system built in this fashion is BitTorrent [7], where nodes employ a "tit-for-tat" policy, preferring to transmit content to other nodes who are willing to return the favor. BitTorrent focuses on the case where all peers are interested in the same content, e.g., different blocks of a large software distribution. Thus, it is common that two peers simultaneously have a block that is of interest to the other, enabling a "clean swap."

In this paper, we are attempting to solve the more general problem of a content distribution system where peers are interested in obtaining objects from a large collection, consisting of both popular and unpopular objects. In this setting, a simultaneous swap of content is rarely possible. Instead, it is necessary to maintain a history of interactions (in terms of credit and debt) with a peer to make decisions concerning the peer in the future. Moreover, the good will accumulated by a BitTorrent node is lost when that node completes downloading the object and leaves the system. BitTorrent nodes have no incentive to stay around and help their peers. In our system, we wish to encourage such behavior by allowing peers to accumulate credit that can be redeemed at a later time, for possibly unrelated content.

The remainder of this paper is structured as follows. Section 2 describes the model and the goals of our system. In Section 3, we present the design of Scrivener, a system that enforces fair bandwidth sharing in a cooperative content distribution system. Section 4 describes the implementation of Scrivener in the context of an existing content distribution system. We present simulation results in Section 5. Finally, Section 6 discusses related work and Section 7 concludes.

2   System Model and Goals

We consider cooperative content distribution systems where participants wish to obtain content stored on other participants' computers. Content is assumed to be published by its owner and disseminated into the system for distribution. We assume that, at least for popular objects, the owner has insufficient bandwidth to service every possible request and wishes to leverage the bandwidth available among other nodes in the system.

The set of participating nodes is assumed to form an overlay network. Scrivener is based on mechanisms that in principle can be applied to both unstructured [23, 17] and structured overlay networks [34, 30], as long as they meet the following minimal requirements: (1) Each node in the overlay communicates directly with only a bounded (i.e., constant or logarithmic in the size of the overlay) number of overlay *neighbors*; (2) the overlay has a mechanism to discover new overlay neighbors; and, (3) the overlay supports a search primitive that discovers, when given a valid content identifier, one or more overlay paths to a node that stores content associated with that identifier.

We further assume that node identifiers cannot be created and discarded freely. The mechanisms we will describe are all based on observing which nodes have behaved properly and which have not. If nodes could misbehave under one identity, only to discard it and assume another identity, then there would be no incentive for proper behavior. Such "Sybil attacks" [11] are a fundamental issue in overlay networks and a host of different attacks become possible unless nodeIds are somehow controlled. For the purposes of our research, we require an external solution to Sybil attacks. For example, Castro et al. [6] address this by requiring a trusted authority to issue certificates that bind a nodeId to a public key; they also describe a weaker, decentralized approach to issuing such certificates. Since we are primarily interested in supporting systems for the distribution of legal content, maintaining user anonymity is not a design goal of Scrivener. If, however, an anonymity-preserving defense against Sybil attacks was available, Scrivener might still be applicable.

2.1   Attack Model

The adversarial model assumed by Scrivener is limited to simple *freeloading* behavior, whose only objective is to obtain service without contributing an equivalent fair share of bandwidth to the system. This is in contrast to more general *malicious* behavior, where the objective of the attacker may include obtaining unauthorized access to content, corrupting or censoring content, or denying or degrading service to other users. Mechanisms to prevent or mitigate such behavior (e.g., sealed and self-certifying content [15], content entanglement [37], Castro et al. [6]'s secure routing primitive) may be employed to complement Scrivener. Most p2p systems are already engineered to be robust against traffic loss due to network failures. In the extreme case of a node refusing to properly forward low-level traffic, that nodes' neighbors could flag the node as unresponsive and would likely remove the node from the network. As such, we are primarily concerned with *application layer* freeloading, where the application's goal is the sharing and distribution of content of varying size and popularity.

It is useful to consider freeloading separately from more general malicious behavior, particularly when in many systems it is much easier to freeload than to mount a malicious attack. In KaZaA [23], for example, a client configured to have minimum upload bandwidth and turning off the super-peer flag suffices to freeload. A malicious attack, on the other hand, would require considerable technical expertise. Thus, the fraction of users who have the motivation and ability to freeload is likely to far exceed the fraction of users that are intent and able to mount a malicious attack.

Accordingly, the two threats call for different mechanisms. A defense against free-loading must be effective and efficient even when a large fraction of participants attempt to freeload. A defense against malicious behavior can, and often must, assume that malicious behavior is limited to a small minority of users. We expect that a production content distribution system would include both types of mechanisms. For the remainder of this paper, we will focus exclusively on detecting and preventing freeloading.

2.2 Goals

Scrivener's goal is to achieve fair sharing of bandwidth in content distribution systems. The key aspects of this goal are summarized below.

- *Fairness*. The system must ensure that participants receive a quality of service that is proportional to the amount of bandwidth they are actually contributing to the system. Furthermore, no participant should be permitted to perpetually consume resources in excess of their contributions at the expense of another participant. This provides an incentive for nodes not to freeload.
- *Low overhead*. The overhead imposed by the mechanisms used should be modest. Moreover, the marginal cost related to ensuring fairness when downloading an object should be low, to ensure efficiency despite small object sizes.
- *Robustness*. The system should retain the above properties even in the presence of large numbers of freeloaders and in the presence of modest churn.

3 Design

Fundamentally, Scrivener is based on the idea of a pairwise exchange of content between overlay participants. This is similar in spirit to BitTorrent, where participants exchange content fragments "tit-for-tat." However, unlike BitTorrent, Scrivener considers the general case of a content distribution system where participants with different interests choose from a large set of content objects. In such a system, it is unlikely that two overlay neighbors are simultaneously interested in each other's content, which would enable a "clean swap." Making pairwise exchange work in a general content distribution network presents several challenges. The basic concepts of Scrivener include:

Relationships: A Scrivener node maintains a relationship with each of its overlay neighbors. Each of the two nodes involved in a relationship maintains a credit and a confidence value for the other node, defined below. These values are maintained in persistent storage and are remembered even as a node departs and subsequently rejoins the overlay. The values are maintained and used only locally to a given node.

Credit: Credit is the difference between the amount of data sent to and the amount of data received from the peer.[1] Negative values of credit are called *debt*.

---

[1] We assume here that the cost of transferring an object is equal to the size of the object in bytes. It is equally possible to define certain objects as more valuable than others.

Confidence: The positive confidence value for the neighbor is calculated according to an additive increase, multiplicative decrease policy, based on the success or failure of content requests that were forwarded to the neighbor. The confidence value is used in deciding how to forward requests during content search and it is used to compute the credit limit (defined below) granted to the neighbor node.

Building on these core ideas, easily applicable to any p2p content distribution system, we can invent a number of mechanisms:

Maintaining credit / debt: To enable non-simultaneous pairwise swapping, each Scrivener node maintains a record of credit / debt with each of its overlay neighbors. We wish to enable a node A to obtain content from another node B, even when A may not currently have any content of interest to B. A can repay the resulting debt to B at a future time, when B happens to be interested in some content held by A. A node honors requests from a peer if and only if that peer is in good standing, i.e., the peer's debt is below a certain limit.

Limiting generosity: To bootstrap the system, one node must be willing to extend a loan to another node with which it has had no prior relationship. However, such loans must not enable freeloading. A Scrivener node A grants a small initial credit to each node B that A has chosen to initiate a relationship with. However, node B does not necessarily grant A any credit in return. As A and B interact and respond to each other's requests, the confidence among the peers, and thus the amount of credit granted, can increase over time.

Limiting relationships: Each node initiates relationships with only a limited number of peers, typically the neighbors chosen by the overlay network. This limits the amount of state maintained by each node and it limits the total credit a node grants its peers.

Transitive trading: What if a node wishes to obtain a content object not held by any of its overlay neighbors? We need a mechanism that allows a node to use the credit it has with its neighbors to obtain content from a more distant node that has the desired content, but with which it does not have a pre-existing relationship. Transitive trading is such a mechanism. Performing a transitive trade involves finding a path from the requester to a content holder such that each node along the path is in good standing with the subsequent node. Then, the content holder sends the content to the requester, and each node along the path credits the subsequent node.

3.1   Relationships

Each Scrivener node maintains relationships with a small number of other nodes, typically its overlay neighbors, as selected by the overlay protocol. More precisely, any two nodes in the overlay network form a relationship if and only if at least one of them has the other in its overlay neighbor table. A Scrivener node A grants a small initial confidence value (and thus a small credit limit) to any node that A has chosen as a neighbor, but it assigns an initial confidence of zero (and thus no credit) to any node that has invited A to be a neighbor. This prevents freeloaders from obtaining a large credit limit by initiating many relationships with many nodes, perhaps pretending that its normal neighbors have failed.[2]

The small initial credit limit allows neighbors chosen by A to request content from A, and it allows A to request content from legitimate nodes who have chosen A as a neighbor. As content is exchanged, the parties gain more confidence in each other and gradually grant each other larger credit limits. Our scheme puts newcomers at a disadvantage; they need to initiate relationships, forcing them to grant credit and offer service while receiving little in return initially. This is the price for defending against freeloaders in any reputation-based system. However, as we will show, the initial sacrifice is rewarded quickly as the node establishes confidence and gains credit with its neighbors.

When a Scrivener node A finds that one of its neighbors B has accumulated debt in excess of its credit limit, it ceases to accept requests from B. Regardless, A continues to make requests to B in order to give B the opportunity to pay back its debt. Likewise, A may find that the confidence value of one of its neighbors B goes to zero, perhaps because B has repeatedly failed to fulfill requests from A even though A is in good standing with B. In this case, A ceases to make requests via B or to accept requests from B. From A's perspective, B might as well not be a part of the overlay network. A then uses existing mechanisms provided by the overlay network to replace B with a different, and hopefully more cooperative, neighbor.

In principle, a Scrivener node must maintain a record of its past overlay neighbors indefinitely. Erasing a negative record would amount to forgiving debt, and would enable freeloading. In practice, it is acceptable to delete records of nodes that have been offline for long periods, perhaps a year, thus seriously inconveniencing freeloaders who wish to exploit the resulting loophole. Storing a year's worth of records is reasonable as these records are very compact: only a nodeId and two integer values, the credit and confidence values, are required. Such concise records could easily scale to track the millions of neighbors that a node might see in a year's time.

Note also that due to the pairwise relationships, freeloader cannot benefit from collusion. While colluding freeloaders may be able to convince legitimate nodes to shift credit from one freeloader to another, the total credit will be unchanged.

3.2 Confidence

Scrivener nodes keep a confidence estimate for each of their overlay neighbors. The confidence value serves two purposes: (1) it determines the magnitude of the credit limit granted to a neighbor and (2) it can be used to bias overlay routing decisions towards cooperative neighbors.

The confidence assigned by a node to its neighbor is based on the history of their relationship. The confidence estimate has the following properties: (1) As nodes exchange content, the confidence increases slowly; (2) The confidence drops rapidly once a neighbor starts to misbehave; (3) The confidence is bounded to limit the damage caused by a

---

[2] Overlay network systems are generally engineered to assume a high rate of node failure and include elaborate mechanisms to locate previously unknown nodes and form new relationships in order to preserve important invariants, including the degree of node-to-node connectivity and of file replication. As a result, we need to limit the benefits automatically granted to a node solely because it happens to be a peer.

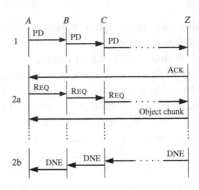

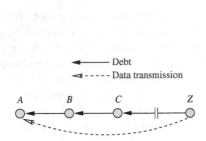

Fig. 1. Using a credit path to leverage a chain of credit to obtain content directly from a non-neighbor node

Fig. 2. The stages in the transitive trade protocol

node that plays by the rules for an extended period and then starts to freeload. An additive increase, multiplicative decrease (AIMD) strategy offers a simple implementation of these properties.

3.3 Transitive Trade

In p2p content distribution systems with a large content set, the odds are small that a desired object can be found on an immediate overlay neighbor of the node wishing to fetch that object. We need a way for nodes to trade their credits and debts with one another, and we would like to avoid the overhead of digital cash or other cryptographic schemes. Instead, we designed an incremental trading strategy we call *transitive trade*, which works by identifying a *credit path* from a source node to a node that has the desired object. In a credit path, each node in the path either has credit with the next node, or its debt is below the next node's credit limit. We describe a scheme to locate such paths in Section 4.3.

Conceivably, once we have identified a credit path, we could rearrange all the credits in the path such that the destination node now owes something not to its predecessor in the route, but instead to the source of the route. This is illustrated in Figure 1. A series of debts, where *B* owes *A*, *C* owes *B*, and so forth until *Z* owes its predecessor could all be replaced with a direct debt from *Z* to *A*. *Z* can now cancel this debt by providing *A* with the desired content.

To make debt swapping work, we need a protocol that is robust against any node in the trading chain cheating. For example, a node could attempt to cancel a debt that it owes without giving up the debt owed to it by the successor in the trading chain. Rather than resorting to a complex cryptographic commitment protocol, we take a straightforward, incremental approach. The protocol is depicted in Figure 2.

1: Credit path discovery: *A* first routes a "path discovery" message (PD) towards *Z*. As a side effect, *A* "pays" *B* for this message, *B* pays *C*, and so forth until *Z* is paid. At the same time, each node reduces its confidence in its successor as if the request had failed (even though it may be working perfectly well). This design avoids the need to maintain timeouts to detect and react to failures. The credit path discovery might fail for a number of reasons, ranging from a freeloader dropping the message to network failures (see Section 4.3). The effect is that every node that forwarded the request will have reduced confidence in its successor. Furthermore, the last node in the chain effectively keeps the credit originally transfered from A.

2a: Object exists: Upon receiving the request, Z transmits a confirmation message (ACK) directly to A. A now routes a request message (REQ) for a chunk of the content object along the existing credit path, paying for the chunk as a side-effect of the message transmission. Z transmits the requested object chunk directly to A. A repeats this step until it has obtained the last chunk of the object. A final message, announcing A's success, causes each node to adjust the confidence value of its successor to compensate for the reduction in step (1), plus an additional confidence gained as a result of the trade.

2b: Object does not exist: Upon receiving the request, Z routes a "does not exist" message (DNE) along the reverse credit path. The message contains the addresses of the complete set of nodes that would store replicas of the content if it existed. Intermediate nodes can contact a member of this set to verify that the object does not exist. If they are convinced that the object really does not exist, they restore the confidence of the successor node to compensate for the reduction taken in step (1).

Each participating node has an incentive to follow each of the protocol steps: Node A wants to receive all the chunks, node Z wants to be credited for transmitting all the chunks, and all nodes wish to maintain the confidence of their predecessors along the credit path. When a node *defects* from the protocol at some stage, it can collect credit without providing the corresponding service. However, the price is a drop in the confidence of the node's predecessor. Also, the damage is limited to the size of a single chunk, which can be made appropriately small.

In general, for any failure, the client A is charged for at most a single chunk – a modest loss. The charge can be interpreted as the price for imposing load on the overlay by issuing a request that could not be satisfied. Such a charge also discourages flooding requests into the system; the client must pay for each and every request it makes. The client can minimize the loss associated with a failure when it begins with a small chunk and gradually increases the request size as its confidence in the path increases.

Over the long term, transitive trading tends to balance credit and debt among a node's overlay neighbors, maximizing the chances that the node will be able to obtain content in the future. Moreover, participation in a transitive trade is beneficial because it increases the confidence of each node along the path in its successor.

At the same time, nodes have a disincentive to refuse participation in a transitive trade. Such a refusal leads the predecessor along the credit path to reduce its confidence in the node. While the failure of a neighbor adversely affects a node, if it happens repeatedly, the node quickly reduces its confidence in that neighbor, and avoids routing messages through that neighbor in the future. As a result, failing nodes are avoided by the neighbors and become isolated.

It is important that nodes are not penalized for being off-line. When a node is off-line, other nodes merely suspend their relationship with the node until it returns. A related question is whether a node has an incentive to swap credit from an established neighbor to a newcomer as part of a transitive trade. In practice, having credit with a large and diverse set of neighbors maximizes the chances that a node will be able to successfully locate a credit path for a future request.

3.4 Caching

In general, objects in a content distribution system have a highly skewed popularity distribution [20][3]. To avoid load imbalances as a result of such skew, caching is used in these systems to dynamically adjust the number of nodes serving a content object according to its popularity. Typically, once a node has obtained some content for itself, it serves the content to other interested clients from its local cache. Thus, popular objects tend to be replicated widely.

In Scrivener, dynamic caching is required to address an additional form of imbalance caused by skewed popularity. Without caching, nodes serving popular objects would tend to accumulate a huge amount of credit. Nodes that serve less popular objects would tend to accumulate debt and lack the "earning potential" to ever repay the debt. Our simulations (see Section 5) will demonstrate this effect in action and show how caching addresses the problem. Moreover, nodes have an incentive to cache objects, because it increases their earning potential. Caching popular objects allows a node to earn the credit needed to satisfy its own future needs.

4 Implementation

In this section, we describe an implementation of our Scrivener prototype. We chose to implement our prototype using FreePastry, a structured overlay network with a distributed hash table service called PAST [13, 30, 31]. Scrivener uses only the key-based routing (KBR) API [9] exported by FreePastry [13]. Thus, our implementation will also work with any structured overlay that supports this interface, e.g., Chord [34].

4.1 Background

Pastry is a structured p2p overlay network that provides a KBR service. In such overlays, every node and every object is assigned a unique identifier randomly chosen from a large id space, referred to as a *nodeId* and *key*, respectively. Given a message and a key, Pastry can route the message to the live node whose nodeId is numerically closest to the key in less than $\log_{2b} N$ hops, where N is the number of nodes in the network and b is the routing base, usually set to 4. Castro et al. [6] describe techniques that make Pastry robust to collusions of a minority of malicious nodes in the overlay who attempt to compromise the overlay. These techniques are complementary to the techniques described in this paper and can be used in conjunction with Scrivener if malicious participants (rather than mere freeloaders) are a threat.

PAST provides a distributed hash table (DHT) abstraction on top of Pastry. Each stored item in PAST is given a key (hereafter referred to as the *handle*), and replicas

---

[3] This is not a problem for BitTorrent, since every user attempts to get the same object, and the popularity of each block is identical.

of an object are stored at the k live nodes whose nodeIds are the numerically closest to the object's handle (these nodes are called a *replica set*). PAST maintains the invariant that the object is replicated on k nodes, regardless of node addition or failure. If a node in the replica set is out of space, the object will be diverted to a node close in nodeId space but not in the replica set, and stored there temporarily. The handle is built from a cryptographically secure hash (e.g., SHA-1) applied to the data being stored. As such, the handle has sufficient information for the holder of the handle to verify that the content obtained from PAST is authentic.

4.2 Node Bootstrapping

Recall that when a new node joins the system, it has no credit or debt. To earn credit, it needs to obtain some initial content that it can then serve to other nodes. In our prototype implementation, PAST's normal content placement and replication policy provides a node with its initial set of content objects.

When a PAST node joins the system, it is *required* to store a set of objects based on its position in the identifier space. The node obtains these initial objects from its neighbors in the id space for free; they form the new node's initial content offering and allow it to acquire credit with its overlay neighbors, which forward requests for these objects to the node as part of PAST's normal lookup operation. Our simulation results show that this simple mechanism suffices for a node to quickly bootstrap itself.

4.3 Finding Credit Paths

A key implementation issue is how to efficiently discover credit paths. The Pastry routing primitive finds an overlay path to a node that stores the requested content object, given the object's identifier. Finding a credit path introduces the additional constraint that each node along the path must be in good standing with its successor.

Our prototype uses a randomized, greedy algorithm to discover credit paths. To determine the next hop, a Scrivener node first selects the set of neighbors that satisfy the Pastry routing constraint. These nodes either have identifiers that match the requested object handle in a longer prefix than the present node's id, or their id matches as long a prefix as the present node's id but is numerically closer to the object handle. Forwarding the request to a node in this set guarantees that the route is loop-free and will end at a node that has the desired content, assuming the content exists in the overlay.

Next, we subtract from the candidate set any neighboring nodes where the present node is not in good standing. These neighbors would refuse requests from the present node because it had exceeded its credit limit. Because all of the information used by nodes to rate their neighbors is available equally to both parties, nodes can easily track their standing with their neighbors.

Among the set of remaining candidate nodes, we make a biased random choice, based on the following criteria:

– *Length of the neighbor's prefix match with the object handle.* Choosing a neighbor with higher prefix match than the present node reduces the latency and path length, and therefore also increases the chance to find a working path.

- *Confidence in the neighbor.* Neighbors with higher confidence values have been more helpful in the past, and are thus more likely to be helpful this time.
- *Amount of credit with the neighbor.* Choosing neighbors with higher credit helps the present node to balance credit and debt and therefore increases flexibility in handling future requests.

Scrivener strongly biases the forwarding choice toward neighbors with a prefix match (minimizing the number of overlay routing hops), while also trying to balance credit and debt, and gives preference to neighbors with high confidence values. More precisely, let $\mathcal{R}$ denote the remaining set of candidate nodes. Scrivener assigns a *score* to each node x in set $\mathcal{R}$, which is calculated as $score(x) = e^{\ell(x)} \cdot t(x) \cdot [c(x) - c_{min} + 1]$, where $\ell(x) \geq 0$ is the number of additional digits that the neighbor x shares with the object handle relative to the present node, $c(x)$ and $t(x)$ are the credit and confidence value of neighbor x, and $c_{min} = \min_{i \in \mathcal{R}} c(i)$. Then the probability that peer x is chosen is its score divided by the total score of all candidate peers, i.e., $score(x) / \sum_{i \in \mathcal{R}} score(i)$. The quality of a node's prefix match figures exponentially in its score to give a significantly greater weight to shorter routes. Note also that both confidence and credit/debt are measured in the same units, i.e., the number of objects or bytes transferred.

Our randomized, greedy algorithm is not guaranteed to discover a credit path even if one exists. A request could end up at a node that has no neighbor that satisfies the Pastry routing constraints and with which the node is in good standing. In such cases, the request cannot be forwarded on and the client will need to retry the request through a different neighbor.

Our simulations shows that the success rate is very high and the number of retries typically necessary to discover a credit path is very low in practice. There are several reasons for this. First, the Pastry overlay is richly connected and many redundant paths exist between a client and a node holding the required content. Second, dynamic caching effectively balances the "earning power" of nodes, avoiding strong imbalances in the credit available to different nodes. Third, the bias in the forwarding policy against nodes with low confidence tends to isolate freeloaders, causing requests to be effectively routed around such nodes. Lastly, the bias in the forwarding policy based on credit tends to balance the available credit a node has with its different neighbors. These various self-stabilizing forces reduce the probability that a credit path search might fail, either due to lack of credit or because a freeloader refuses to honor it.

4.4   Bounding Lengths of Credit Paths

Unlike the native Pastry routing policy, Scrivener does not always choose a neighbor with a longer prefix match, even if such a neighbor exists. As a result, Pastry's logarithmic bound on the expected path lengths does not strictly hold. Note that shorter path lengths are desirable for two important reasons: (1) shorter path lengths ensure low delay and network utilization, and (2) shorter paths are more robust against node failures. Since the routing policy of Scrivener may occasionally lead to long paths, we resort to another mechanism to bound the path length.

In the prototype implementation, Scrivener artificially bounds the credit path length to be logarithmic in the overlay size. When the search for a credit path has reached this bound, the request is dropped. A rough estimate of the size of the overlay N suffices to determine the bound. Since nodeIds are assigned at random, the overlay size can be extrapolated from the local density of nodeIds with sufficient accuracy. When a search exceeds this boundary, the request is dropped. Our simulation results, presented in Section 5, show that the impact of this restriction on the ability to locate credit paths is minimal, while it ensures deterministic bounds on the system's resource consumption.

5 Experimental Results

In this section, we present simulation results to evaluate our prototype implementation. We simulate a system where network messages are delivered instantaneously. Objects are replicated using PAST's replication strategy, storing an object on the k nodes with nodeIds closest to the identifier for that object. When requesting an object, client nodes perform at most 10 queries, each time attempting to discover a credit path using the randomized greedy algorithm. The initial credit limit is set to 1 object, and increases linearly with the confidence the node has in its peer. The credit paths are limited to $\lceil 3 \log N \rceil$ hops. Each node also has a fixed sized, 1024-object soft cache to retain objects it has previously obtained to satisfy future requests. We implement an LRU cache replacement policy to replace entries from the cache when it is full.

A node's peers maintain their credit and confidence values for a node that is temporarily off-line. Also, the Pastry routing tables are persistent, i.e., a node remembers its table while it is off-line. Inappropriate entries are simply replaced by the existing overlay maintenance mechanisms, but biased towards peers with which the node already has a relationship. As a last resort, the node initiates a new relationship. Also, for each entry in the routing table, a node maintains at most three neighbors but uses only the one with the highest confidence value. (Confidence estimation is described in Section 3.2.)

5.1 Workload Model

We use the model described by Gummadi et al. [20] to generate workloads. This model, derived from KaZaA traffic observations, captures the fetch-at-most-once behavior and the importance of new object arrivals in typical p2p file sharing applications. Based on this model, we chose the following parameters: number of nodes online $C = 800$, number of objects $O = 40,000$, request rate per node $\lambda_R = 50$, object arrival rate $\lambda_O = 12$, and node arrival rate $\lambda_C = 5$ (the units are nodes or objects per simulation time unit). The node departure rate is the same as the arrival rate, keeping the number of active nodes constant. Each object is initially replicated to $k = 3$ nodes. We assume that there is a fixed pool of 1,000 distinct nodes, out of which 800 are online at any time. As a result, during the first 40 time units all arriving nodes are fresh, but after time 40 all arriving nodes are those that were online once before. Nodes that go offline are chosen randomly from the currently live nodes.

5.2 System Performance

First, we study how our mechanisms affect the performance of the underlying cooperative content distribution system in the absence of freeloaders. In particular, we want to see how much overhead has been added to the system.

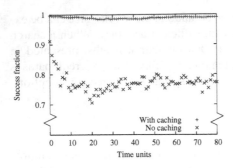

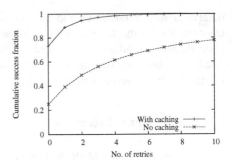

Fig. 3. Success rate with only obedient nodes

Fig. 4. Cumulative distribution of the number of retries to find a debt-based path

Success rate. Figure 3 shows the fraction of successful requests, both with and without caching. Without caching, the success rate stabilizes around 80%. This is because object popularity is so uneven that nodes around the replicas of popular objects become indebted to the replica holders, making it sometimes impossible for a node to find a credit path to the replicas. Many requests to popular objects fail despite retries. However, allowing nodes to serve cached objects eliminates this problem and the success rate approaches 100%. The stability of the success rate suggests that the system balances out nicely and obedient nodes do not build up debt over time[4].

Figure 4 shows the number of retries required to successfully find a credit path. When caching is enabled, over 73% of queries succeed on the first attempt, and three attempts are sufficient to achieve over 95% success rate. We conclude that the policy enforcement in Scrivener with bounded paths does not seriously affect object fetch reliability in the absence of freeloaders.

Path efficiency. Scrivener's randomized greedy routing strategy attempts to use Pastry's routing mechanism to achieve logarithmic-length paths, when possible, and falls back to less efficient mechanisms, when necessary, that are artificially capped to preserve an $O(\log N)$ expected path length (see Section 4.4). A cumulative distribution of path lengths at different overlay sizes is shown in Figure 5. By observing horizontal slices through this graph, we see that the growth in path length follows roughly the log of the number of nodes. Our simulations show that common case routes are quite efficient and the worst case routes are only twice as long as common-case routes.

Due to limitations of our simulation environment, we were unable to run simulations for overlay sizes larger than 2000. In order to emulate the effect of larger overlay sizes, we ran simulations with 1000 nodes, but with Pastry's routing base set to $b = 2$ instead of 4. The results show that the median Scrivener path lengths is around 5, close to the expected Pastry path length ($\log_{2^2} 1000 \approx 4.98$). Note that 5 is the expected path length for a Pastry overlay with one million nodes when $b = 4$. This result suggests that

---

[4] We have also implemented *speculative caching*, where nodes observe the requests they have forwarded and actively fetch objects that they consider popular. However, the improvements we observed in terms of success rate were insignificant.

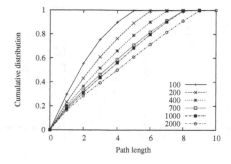

Fig. 5. Cumulative distribution of debt-based path lengths for different system sizes

Scrivener's greedy routing strategy easily scales to much larger overlay sizes than we were able to simulate.

Still, these longer paths, which would also occur as the number of nodes in the overlay increases, raise concerns about path usability, particularly if the system is experiencing high node churn. More nodes in a path increase the odds that one of those nodes will fail while a transitive trade is in progress. However, the system provides incentives for nodes to stay online until a transitive trade in which they are involved completes (see Section 3.3). If a path fails, the original requesting node can restart the trading protocol, find a new path to the source of the data (or a replica), and resume downloading the missing data.

The total overhead for Scrivener to fetch an object is the product of the average number of attempts to discover a credit path (≈ 2) and the average credit path length ($< \lceil 3 \log N \rceil$). Among competing systems that use auditor sets, KARMA [36] is the most efficient system we are aware of. KARMA's asymptotic message overhead is comparable to Scrivener's, but requires expensive public-key cryptographic operations and additional means of incentivizing auditors [36].

5.3   Introducing Freeloaders

Next, we introduce freeloaders into our simulation. Freeloaders issue requests like obedient nodes, but they may refuse to serve objects. In a deployed system, freeloaders can be expected to attempt a variety of strategies. In the following experiments, we consider a number of freeloading strategies, and show that in all cases there are no sustainable benefits to freeloading. We simulate 800 nodes, but now with 5% freeloaders. We assume that freeloaders forward requests and participate in transitive trades, as this allows them to earn confidence with minimal traffic overhead. While obedient nodes undergo churn as specified in the model, freeloaders are always online throughout the entire simulation period. Recall that routing tables are persistent, ensuring that freeloaders cannot neither escape a bad reputation by periodically departing from the system nor by repeatedly exploiting the limited credit granted by obedient nodes looking to establish relationships.

Freeloaders that never serve.   First we consider freeloaders that never serve any object. Figure 6 shows that their success rate drops to below 5% within a few time units,

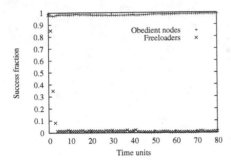

Fig. 6. Success rate with 5% freeloaders that do not serve objects

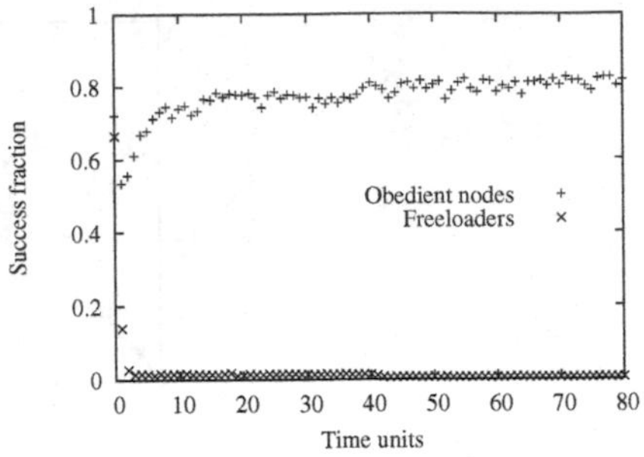

Fig. 7. Success rate with 50% freeloaders that do not serve objects

yet that of obedient nodes is unaffected. Note that the success rate for freeloaders never goes to zero. This is because freeloaders can still get the objects that they themselves are storing "for free."

To determine Scrivener's sensitivity to the size of the soft cache, we vary the cache size. The success rate remains virtually constant down to a cache size of 320 objects, and gradually decreases to 91% at 128 objects. This shows that Scrivener does not require a large soft cache to work efficiently.

We increased the fraction of freeloaders to 50%, with results shown in Figure 7. The success rate of freeloaders again drops quickly to near zero, while that for obedient nodes starts below 60% and plateaus at 80%. Note that with 50% freeloaders and a replication factor $k = 3$, it is expected that 12.5% of the objects are only stored by freeloaders and will thus never be served. This suggests that a more expensive search may increase the success rate somewhat, but with diminishing returns.

To test the system under extreme conditions, we increase the fraction of freeloaders to 80%. At this point, more than half of the objects are stored only by freeloaders and, unsurprisingly, the success rate for obedient nodes is only 30%. Also, as a result of more transitive trading failures, it takes longer for the success rate of obedient nodes to stabilize. Scrivener does continue to function remarkably well, despite the extreme freeloading rate. Given that these freeloaders receive no benefit from being present in the network, one would expect them to depart, allowing the remaining obedient nodes to operate more efficiently.

Since it takes time for obedient nodes to recognize freeloaders, one concern is that a high churn rate might enable freeloaders to get a satisfactory success rate by exploiting new node arrivals. We simulated a system with 800 nodes, but a churn rate λ_C of 50 nodes per time unit and with fresh nodes arriving for the first 100 time units. After time 100, the arriving nodes have all previously been part of the network and gone offline. Figure 8 clearly shows that with this higher churn of fresh nodes, the success rate for freeloaders stabilizes at around 15%, dropping after time 100 when the returning nodes remember previous freeloaders. Thus, while freeloaders can exploit newcomers, the benefit is limited. More importantly, the success rate for obedient nodes is unaffected. While obedient nodes waste some effort handling requests from freeloaders, they give clear priority to serving each other.

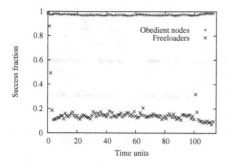

Fig. 8. Success rate with a higher churn rate

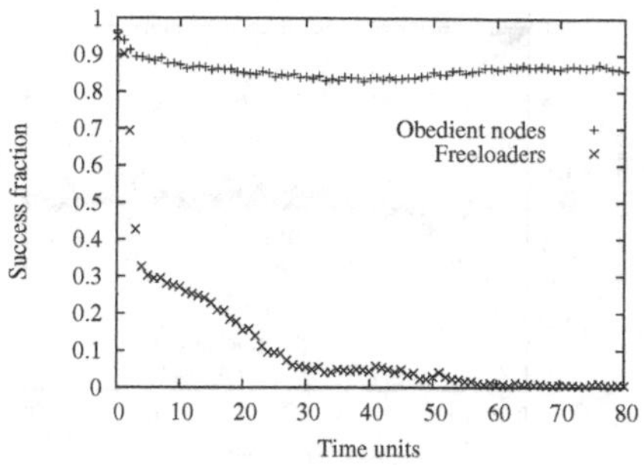

Fig. 9. Success rate with the worst-case scenario where every obedient node gives a high initial confidence to all freeloaders

Recall that a Scrivener node grants an initial credit to its chosen neighbors. We next consider an attack where a freeloader somehow convinces an obedient node to choose it as a neighbor, thus granting it an initial credit. We consider a worst-case scenario where freeloaders can always manipulate obedient nodes into choosing them as neighbors. With such an attack, freeloaders could now exploit the initial credit from each obedient node. Figure 9 shows that, indeed, freeloaders get a better success rate initially. However, the success rate drops to 30% quickly and gradually goes down as obedient nodes refuse to serve freeloaders after their debts build up. Our simulations show that, even with such a hypothetical attack, freeloaders would have little benefit and obedient nodes would observe no significant change in their own success rate.

Short-term cooperation. Participation in transitive trades, alone, can earn confidence and increase credit limits without actually serving any object. An interesting question is whether it is possible for freeloaders to build up confidence simply by participating in transitive trades, and then exploit that confidence. In Figure 10, we simulate freeloaders that participate in transitive trades for 20 time units before fetching any object. The

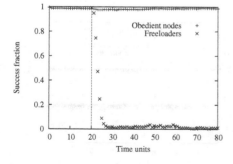

Fig. 10. Success rate with freeloaders that participates in transitive trades but do not fetch objects for the first 20 time units

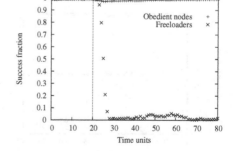

Fig. 11. Success rate with freeloaders that serve objects only for the first 20 time units

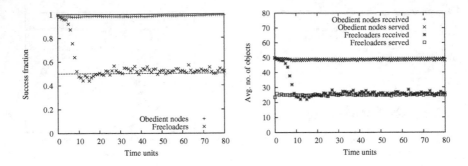

Fig. 12. Success rate and number of objects served and fetched with freeloaders that serve half of the object requests

success rate for freeloaders drops to below 0.1 within ten time units. Thus, participation in transitive trades does have a benefit, but only a small one.

We also simulated nodes that were obedient for 20 time units and then began freeloading. As shown in Figure 11, the freeloader's success rate now takes seven time units to drop below 0.1. The freeloader does benefit from its earlier obedience. However, once freeloading behavior begins, the success rate remains high for only two time units, then falls quickly.

These experiments demonstrate that short-term cooperation is not an effective strategy for freeloaders to exploit the system; once they start to freeload, obedient nodes will quickly refuse to serve them.

Providing partial service.   Another possible freeloading behavior is to serve objects at a reduced rate. We first consider freeloaders that arbitrarily serve half of their requests. Figure 12 shows that the success rate for freeloaders drops to and remains at roughly 50% — the same rate at which they are providing service. Note also that the number of objects received by freeloaders also approaches and stabilizes at the same level as the number they serve.

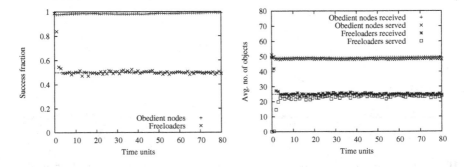

Fig. 13. Success rate and number of objects served and fetched with freeloaders that aim at 50% success rate

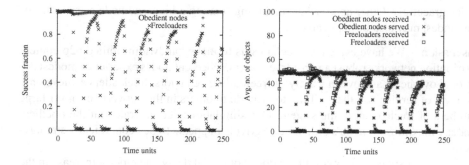

Fig. 14. Success rate and number of objects served and fetched with freeloaders that switch between cooperation and freeloading every 20 time units

Another potential strategy is to have a target quality of service. This freeloading behavior serves only enough requests to maintain a desired success ratio. We simulate freeloaders that target a 50% success rate. Figure 13 shows that the resulting success rate oscillates around 50%. As before, the number of objects served by the freeloader quickly dictates the number of objects the freeloader is allowed to consume.

We finally consider a strategy that alternates between obedience and freeloading, changing behaviors every 20 time units. Figure 14 shows that the success ratio quickly tends toward 1 and 0 whenever these nodes switch to cooperation and to freeloading, respectively, with the peak success ratio dropping over time. Also, during the cooperation periods, the former freeloaders service more requests, effectively making up for the debts they previously accumulated. On average, this alternation strategy performs worse, from the freeloader's perspective, than the previous 50% service strategy.

Other experiments. In our simulation, a node requests 50 objects per time unit. If each object is 64 Kbytes, this translates into roughly 3MB of data per time unit — about the size of a typical MP3 file or digital photograph. If we consider users that attempt to download 100MB of data per day, their success rate would drop to zero in about an hour. Increasing the download rate does not help, since its merely accelerates the decline in success rate.

To test Scrivener's sensitivity to the size of the downloaded content, we ran simulations where we divided large objects into smaller chunks that were stored and downloaded separately. The success rate of obedient nodes improved relative to our earlier experiments. When downloading smaller chunks, smaller credits were necessary, increasing the success rate of transitive trading. Also of note, freeloaders experienced an even lower success rate. Because a desired object may now be spread over several chunks, the odds successfully obtaining all of a file's chunks diminished. Of course, breaking a file into chunks will increase the overhead rate, as each chunk will need to be separately located and fetched.

We have also simulated scenarios with obedient nodes with diverse bandwidth capacities. The success rate for both types of nodes are very close to 100%, although the success rate for high-end nodes drops slightly. This shows that Scrivener can accommodate modest imbalances in the demands and "earning potentials" of participating nodes gracefully. Other approaches, including treating a high-end node as several virtual nodes, may also be applicable.

Discussion.   We have evaluated mechanisms to make bandwidth-limited p2p content distribution networks robust against freeloaders. Obedient nodes experience modest additional overhead, and over a variety of freeloading behaviors, freeloaders achieve only the level of service that they willing to provide to others in the network, even for large numbers of freeloaders in the system. Our simulations demonstrate that the obedient strategy maximizes a node's utility, i.e., Scrivener appears to be economically strategy-proof.

While our simulation environment does not model delay, the modest increase in the path length of content requests, combined with the fact that most p2p content downloads are bandwidth-limited, strongly suggests that download delay is not significantly affected by Scrivener.

We note that freeloaders still get some benefit during the first few time units after they join the system. If a freeloader can create new identities without restriction, such "Sybil attacks" [11] would be able to defeat our mechanisms. As discussed in Section 2, we require that the p2p overlay has security features to prevent such attacks. Alternatively, Scrivener could adopt a policy where all nodes receive degraded service quality when they join the p2p network, with the quality improving only after the new node has proven its worth.

6   Related work

There has been much work on providing incentives for cooperation in distributed systems. We roughly categorize the related works as follows.

Bandwidth-sharing networks.   SLIC [35] considers the query nature of unstructured p2p systems like Gnutella [17]. It proposes giving nodes service levels proportional to their contribution, so as to provide nodes incentives to share more data and handle more traffic. BitTorrent [7] facilitates large numbers of nodes all trying to acquire exactly the same file, with an emphasis on very large files (e.g., software distributions, digital movies, and so forth). Every BitTorrent node will have acquired some subset of the file and will trade blocks with other nodes until it has the whole file. In order to bootstrap new nodes, nodes reserve $1/4$ of their bandwidth for altruistic service. Nodes that fairly trade their bandwidth will experience a higher quality of service. Anagnostakis and Greenwald [3] suggested that performance can be improved if exchanges are extended to allow involving multiple parties. Scrivener solves the more general problem, where nodes are interested in content from a large set, of potentially much smaller size. We allow nodes to acquire credits from the files they serve to obtain any other files they desire in the future. Thus, they have an incentive to serve, even when they themselves do not require any content at the moment.

GNUnet [19] uses the idea of locally-maintained debit/credit relations in a similar fashion to our own work. It also uses debt relationships across nodes, comparable to our debt-based routing. As GNUnet is more concerned with anonymity than network efficiency, it does not support transmitting objects directly across the network. All traffic goes through the overlay, forcing intermediate nodes to carry the bulk traffic of the object transfer while giving them no particular incentive to do this, save for maintaining their own anonymity. For a path with n nodes, GNUnet transfers the object $O(n)$ times. Scrivener, on the other hand, finds efficient routes and transmits bulk data directly over the Internet, yielding higher performance, but lacking GNUnet's anonymity features. Scrivener also provides mechanism to locate and fetch objects, leveraging its existing credit/debit framework.

Storage networks. In a storage network, nodes share spare disk capacity for applications such as distributed backup systems. Ngan et al. [27] propose an auditing mechanism, which allows cheaters to be discovered and evicted from the system. Samsara [8] enforces fairness by requiring an equal exchange of storage space between peers and by challenging peers periodically to prove that they are actually storing the data. Storage incentivicing systems are solving a fundamentally different problem than bandwidth incentivicing systems. Storage is a commitment, over a long time period, to provide a stable service. If misbehavior is detected, a node can punish another by simply deleting its files. Bandwidth, on the other hand, is an ephemeral service. Bits transmitted cannot be taken back. Retribution can only be taken by refusing future requests.

Reputation. Resource allocation and accountability problems are fundamental to p2p systems. Dingledine et al. [10] surveys many schemes for tracking nodes' reputations. In particular, if obtaining a new identity is cheap and positive reputations have value, negative reputation could be shed easily by leaving the system and rejoining with a new identity. Friedman and Resnick [14] also study the case of cheap pseudonyms, and argue that suspicion of strangers is costly. There have been attempts to build a distributed trust management system [22, 1]. Blanc et al. suggest a reputation system for incentivicing routing in peer to peer networks that uses a trusted authority to manage the reputation values for all peers [4]. Unlike those efforts, our design relies solely on locally observable (and thus more trustworthy) information.

Trading and payments. SHARP [16] is a framework for distributed resource management, where users can trade resources like bandwidth with trusted peers. KARMA [36] and SeAl [29] rely on auditor sets to keep track of the resource usage of each participant in the network, similar to Ngan et al.'s quota manager approach [27]. MojoNation [26] similarly allowed peers to exchange certificates for resources. Golle et al. [18] considered centralized p2p systems with micro-payments, analyzing how various user strategies reach equilibrium within a game theoretic model.

Trading and payments architectures may be too expensive for many content distribution systems, as each download would incur cryptographic operations and additional communication. Moreover, implementing micro-payments either requires a centralized authority to issue currencies, or uses distributed trust and currency, which is still an active research area.

Mobile ad hoc networks. Since nodes in mobile ad hoc networks rely on each other to forward traffic, incentives are as important in these networks as they are in p2p content distribution systems. Marti et al. [25] consider monitoring the performance of other nodes and routing around uncooperative nodes. CONFIDANT [5] is a distributed reputation system to detect and isolate misbehaving nodes. Salem et al. [32] propose a micro-payment architecture for multi-hop cellular networks. Catch [24] is a mechanism to identify and punish selfish nodes who do not forward packets in a multi-hop wireless setting based on an anonymous challenge-response protocol. In general, mobile ad hoc networks may require different incentive mechanisms than p2p systems due to their limited computational resources and peer connectivity.

7 Conclusions

This paper presents Scrivener, a decentralized system that provides nodes in a cooperative content distribution network with incentives to share their bandwidth resources. Scrivener only requires nodes to track their neighbor's behavior. It uses a greedy randomized routing algorithm to find a credit path, allowing a node to leverage credit is has with its overlay neighbors to obtain content from an unrelated node that holds the desired content. At the same time, Scrivener effectively prevents freeloaders from exploiting obedient nodes. Our results show that Scrivener is scalable and effective at deterring freeloading behavior while incurring modest overhead.

References

1. K. Aberer and Z. Despotovic. Managing trust in a peer-2-peer information system. In *Proc. of the 10th Int'l Conf. of Information and Knowledge Management*, Atlanta, GA, 2001.
2. E. Adar and B. Huberman. Free riding on Gnutella. *First Monday*, 5(10), Oct. 2000.
3. K. G. Anagnostakis and M. B. Greenwald. Exchange-based incentive mechanisms for peer-to-peer file sharing. In *Proc. 24nd Int'l Conf. on Distributed Computing Systems*, Washington, DC, Mar. 2004.
4. A. Blanc, Y.-K. Liu, and A. Vahdat. Designing Incentives for Peer-to-Peer Routing. In *Proc. 24th IEEE Infocom*, Miami, FL, Mar. 2005.
5. S. Buchegger and J.-Y. Le Boudec. Performance analysis of the CONFIDANT protocol. In *Proc. MobiHoc'02*, Lausanne, Switzerland, June 2002.
6. M. Castro, P. Druschel, A. Ganesh, A. Rowstron, and D. S. Wallach. Security for structured peer-to-peer overlay networks. In *Proc. OSDI'02*, Boston, MA, Dec. 2002.
7. B. Cohen. Incentives build robustness in BitTorrent. In *Workshop on Econ. of Peer-to-Peer Systems*, Berkeley, CA, June 2003.
8. L. P. Cox and B. D. Noble. Samsara: Honor among thieves in peer-to-peer storage. In *Proc. SOSP'03*, Bolton Landing, NY, Oct. 2003.
9. F. Dabek, B. Zhao, P. Druschel, J. Kubiatowicz, and I. Stoica. Towards a common API for structured peer-to-peer overlays. In *Proc. IPTPS'03*, Berkeley, CA, Feb. 2003.
10. R. Dingledine, M. J. Freedman, and D. Molnar. Accountability. In A. Oram, editor, *Peer-to-Peer: Harnessing the Power of Disruptive Technologies*. O'Reilly & Associates, 2001.
11. J. R. Douceur. The Sybil attack. In *Proc. IPTPS'02*, Cambridge, MA, Mar. 2002.
12. J. Feigenbaum and S. Shenker. Distributed algorithmic mechanism design: Recent results and future directions. In *Proc. 6th Int'l Workshop on Discrete Algorithms and Methods for Mobile Computing and Communications*, Atlanta, GA, Sept. 2002.
13. FreePastry. Open source implementation of Pastry. http://freepastry.rice.edu/.
14. E. Friedman and P. Resnick. The social cost of cheap pseudonym. *Journal of Economics and Management Strategy*, 10(2):173–199, 2001.

15. K. Fu, M. F. Kaashoek, and D. Mazières. Fast and secure distributed read-only file system. *ACM Transactions on Computer Systems*, 20(1), Feb. 2002.

16. Y. Fu, J. S. Chase, B. N. Chun, S. Schwab, and A. Vahdat. SHARP: An architecture for secure resource peering. In *Proc. SOSP'03*, Bolton Landing, NY, Oct. 2003.

17. Gnutella. http://www.gnutella.com/.

18. P. Golle, K. Leyton-Brown, I. Mironov, and M. Lillibridge. Incentives for sharing in peer-to-peer networks. In *Proc. 3rd ACM Conf. on Electronic Commerce*, Tampa, FL, Oct. 2001.

19. C. Grothoff. An excess-based economic model for resource allocation in peer-to-peer networks. *Wirtschaftsinformatik*, June 2003.

20. K. P. Gummadi, R. J. Dunn, S. Saroiu, S. D. Gribble, H. M. Levy, and J. Zahorjan. Measurement, modeling, and analysis of a peer-to-peer file-sharing workload. In *Proc. SOSP'03*, Bolton Landing, NY, Oct. 2003.

21. G. Hardin. The tragedy of the commons. *Science*, 162:1243–1248, 1968.

22. S. D. Kamvar, M. T. Schlosser, and H. Garcia-Molina. The EigenTrust algorithm for reputation management in p2p networks. In *Proc. WWW 2003*, Budapest, Hungary, May 2003.

23. KaZaA. http://www.kazaa.com/.

24. R. Mahajan, M. Rodrig, D. Wetherall, and J. Zahorjan. Sustaining Cooperation in Multi-hop Wireless Networks. In *Proc. NSDI'05*, May 2005.

25. S. Marti, T. Giuli, K. Lai, and M. Baker. Mitigating routing misbehavior in mobile ad hoc networks. In *Proc. MobiCom'00*, Boston, MA, Aug. 2000.

26. MojoNation.   http://en.wikipedia.org/wiki/MojoNation/, see also Mnet http://mnetproject.org.

27. T.-W. J. Ngan, D. S. Wallach, and P. Druschel. Enforcing fair sharing of peer-to-peer resources. In *Proc. IPTPS'03*, Berkeley, CA, Feb. 2003.

28. T.-W. J. Ngan, D. S. Wallach, and P. Druschel. Incentives-compatible peer-to-peer multicast. In *2nd Workshop on the Economics of Peer-to-Peer Systems*, Cambridge, MA, June 2004.

29. N. Ntarmos and P. Triantafillou. SeAl: Managing accesses and data in peer-to-peer sharing networks. In *Proc. of the 4th IEEE Int'l Conf. on P2P Computing*, Zurich, Switzerland, 2004.

30. A. Rowstron and P. Druschel. Pastry: Scalable, distributed object address and routing for large-scale peer-to-peer systems. In *Proc. Middleware*, Heidelberg, Germany, Nov. 2001.

31. A. Rowstron and P. Druschel. Storage management and caching in PAST, a large-scale, persistent peer-to-peer storage utility. In *Proc. SOSP'01*, Oct. 2001.

32. N. B. Salem, L. Buttyan, J.-P. Hubaux, and M. Jakobsson. Node cooperation in hybrid ad hoc networks. *IEEE Transactions on Mobile Computing*, 2005. To appear.

33. J. Shneidman and D. Parkes. Rationality and self-interest in peer to peer networks. In *Proc. IPTPS'03*, Berkeley, CA, Feb. 2003.

34. I. Stoica, R. Morris, D. Karger, M. F. Kaashoek, and H. Balakrishnan. Chord: A scalable peer-to-peer lookup service for Internet applications. In *Proc. SIGCOMM'01*, San Diego, CA, Aug. 2001.

35. Q. Sun and H. Garcia-Molina. SLIC: A selfish link-based incentive mechanism for unstructured peer-to-peer networks. In *Proc. 24nd Int'l Conf. on Distributed Computing Systems*, Washington, DC, Mar. 2004.

36. V. Vishnumurthy, S. Chandrakumar, and E. G. Sirer. KARMA: A secure economic framework for p2p resource sharing. In *Workshop on Econ. of Peer-to-Peer Systems*, Berkeley, CA, June 2003.

37. M. Waldman and D. Mazières. Tangler: A censorship-resistant publishing system based on document entanglements. In *Proc. ACM CCS*, Philadelphia, PA, Nov. 2001.

MEDYM: Match-Early with Dynamic Multicast for Content-Based Publish-Subscribe Networks

Fengyun Cao and Jaswinder Pal Singh

Computer Science Department, Princeton University,
Princeton, New Jersey 08540, USA
{fcao, jps}@cs.princeton.edu

Abstract. Design of distributed architectures for content-based publish-subscribe (pub-sub) service networks has been a challenging problem. To best support the highly dynamic and diversified content-based pub-sub communication, we propose a new architectural design called MEDYM - Match-Early with DYnamic Multicast. MEDYM follows the End-to-End distributed system design principle. It decouples a pub-sub service into two functionalities: complex, application-specific matching at network edge, and simple, generic multicast routing in the network. This architecture achieves low computation cost in event matching and high network efficiency and flexibility in event routing. For higher scalability, we describe a novel approach to extend MEDYM to a hierarchy structure called H-MEDYM, which effectively balances the trade-off between event delivery efficiency and server states maintenance. We evaluate MEDYM and H-MEDYM using detailed simulations and real-world experiments, and compare them with major existing design approaches. Results show that MEDYM and H-MEDYM achieve high event delivery efficiency and system scalability, and their advantages are most prominent when user subscriptions are highly selective and diversified.

Keywords: Content-based publish-subscribe network, multicast.

1 Introduction

Content-based publish-subscribe (*pub-sub* for short) is an important paradigm for asynchronous communication among entities in a distributed network. In such systems, users *subscribe* to future *events* that are of their interest by specifying complex conditions on event content, and are *notified* when events satisfying the conditions are *published* into the system. For example, a user who subscribes to stock ticker events with condition "*PriceChange* > 10% AND *Volume* > 100m" is notified when a stock has price movement of above 10% or transaction volume of more than 100 million shares. Such timely delivery of customized information is of great value to many distributed applications, and has become an interesting and important research topic.

For scalability and reliability reasons, a large-scale pub-sub system often takes the form of a distributed service network: as shown in Fig. 1, a set of pub-sub servers is distributed over the Internet; clients access the service, either to publish events

G. Alonso (Ed.): Middleware 2005, LNCS 3790, pp. 292–313, 2005.

or to register subscriptions, through servers that are close to them or in the same administrative domains. In this paper, we study the problem of efficient event delivery in the service network, i.e. from servers where the events are published to servers with matching subscriptions. We do not address the "last-mile" event delivery from servers to local clients in this paper.

Efficient event delivery is challenging for two reasons: first, published events do not carry destination address information. Rather, it is the system's responsibility to *match* each event with user subscriptions to identify the servers that are interested in it. Second, even if the destinations are known, it is not clear how to *route* the events to the destination servers. This is because of the highly diversified user interests in a content-based pub-sub system: every event can match the interest of a different set of servers, and in the worst case, there can be $2^{\#servers}$ such destination sets. How to achieve efficient delivery to so many destination sets is yet an open question.

Existing architecture designs for content-based pub-sub networks typically connect servers into pre-configured overlay networks. Events are routed along the overlay network topology, choosing which connections to follow based on matching results. Because event delivery routes are constrained by the overlay topology, it is inevitable that events are sent to/through servers that are not interested in them, generating extra processing and network load. As analyzed in the paper, such overhead can be especially high when user interests are highly selective and diversified.

In this paper, we explore the possibility of a very different approach. Corresponding to the dynamic communication patterns in pub-sub networks, we propose an architecture called *MEDYM: Match-Early with DYnamic Multicast*. In MEDYM, events are first matched with subscriptions to identify destination servers, and then delivered to destinations along multicast routes computed and constructed on the fly. In this way, MEDYM allows fine-grained optimization for delivery of each individual event. For example, it is able to send events only to the servers that are interested in them, minimizing event traffic load on pub-sub servers. Using configured overlay networks, no existing solution achieves this highly desirable property. MEDYM network is also easy to deploy, and highly flexible to support various matching and routing policies.

The basic form of MEDYM is well-suited to service networks with up to thousands of servers. Given that each pub-sub server can support a large number of end users, this scale is adequate for many interesting pub-sub applications in the foreseeable future. For even further scalability, we propose a hierarchy structure called H-MEDYM. Different from existing hierarchal pub-sub network designs, H-MEDYM partitions the server network as well as the content space of a pub-sub system, to effectively reduce server states without introducing skewed load distribution.

The rest of the paper is organized as follows: in Section 2, we briefly review existing pub-sub network design approaches. We present design and efficient implementation techniques of MEDYM in Section 3, and the hierarchy extension to H-MEDYM in Section 4. In Section 5, we present simulation and experimental evaluation results of MEDYM and H-MEDYM, in comparison with the major existing approaches. In Section 5.8, we conclude the paper with directions for future work.

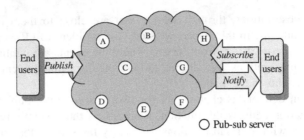

Fig. 1. Example of a publish-subscribe service network

2 Existing Solutions

Existing distributed content-based pub-sub architecture design can be largely categorized into two classes, which we call the *Content-based Forwarding* (CBF) approach [1][6][7][8][9][21][26] and the *Channelization* approach [11][18][19][25]. They balance the tradeoff between event matching complexity and routing accuracy differently.

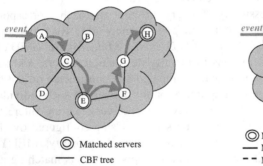

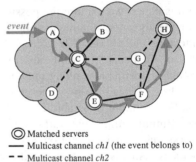

Fig. 2. Event delivery in a CBF tree

Fig. 3. Event delivery in Channelization

2.1 Content-Based Forwarding (CBF)

CBF proposes an elegant intelligent-network architecture. CBF servers are organized into an overlay network, on top of which one or more *CBF trees* are extracted. For simplicity, we use the single-tree case to illustrate the idea in Fig. 2. Each CBF server maintains a *forwarding table* that keeps track of the sum of subscriptions from servers in each direction of the tree. A published event is broadcast on the tree, matched against the forwarding tables at every step, and forwarded only in directions with matching subscriptions.

Through per-step filtering, CBF achieves highly accurate event routing. Its major challenges are the computation and maintenance cost introduced. First, the per-step content-based event matching is a computationally expensive operation; furthermore, many of the operations may be redundant, as an event may be repeatedly matched with the same subscriptions before reaching the destination servers. Second, events are often routed through uninterested intermediate servers, generating extra network as well as processing load. Servers and network links close to the center of the network are especially likely to carry irrelevant event traffic and become system bottlenecks. Finally, the forwarding tables can be expensive to maintain. When the overlay topology changes, e.g. to adapt to network environment changes, the relative positions of servers in the CBF tree(s) also change. Since subscriptions from each direction on the old tree have been aggregated together in the forwarding tables, there is no easy way to adjust the forwarding tables to reflect the new topology, except by transferring large amount of subscriptions along the new topology and re-computing forwarding tables, generating high network traffic and processing load.

In this paper, we use the work by the Siena group in [6] and [7] as representatives for the CBF approach, as they are perhaps the most prominent and complete works in this direction. They have also designed efficient event forwarding algorithms in [8]. Many other distributed pub-sub systems follow the CBF approach. In JEDI [9], a hierarchical event routing network was proposed, but was found to perform worse than the peer-to-peer topology in [6]. The Gryphon group [1][26] designed efficient content-based matching algorithms used in forwarding, and proposed using virtual time vectors to convey temporal consistency of subscription propagation. The Elvin system [21] proposed the concept of *quenching*, in which publishers are aware of the sum of all subscriptions in the system, so that they only publish events that have at least some interested subscribers.

2.2 Channelization

The central idea in the Channelization approach is to utilize existing group-based multicast techniques, such as IP multicast or application-level multicast, for event delivery. As shown in Fig. 3, offline, the event space is partitioned into a small number of disjoint event channels. For each channel, a multicast group is built that spans all servers whose subscriptions may match any event in that channel. When an event is published, the server first determines if any server wants the event. If so, it identifies the channel it belongs to, and then sends it to the multicast group for that channel.

The group-based multicast event routing in Channelization is very simple and fast. The main challenge for the approach is its routing accuracy. As discussed in Section 1, event traffic pattern in a content-based pub-sub system is highly diversified. The number of multicast groups a system can build is often much smaller than the total number of different event destination sets. As a result, the same event channel often has to accommodate events with different destination sets, and servers can receive many events that they are not interested in. To reduce such extraneous traffic, intelligent algorithms are used to cluster events with similar destination sets into the same channels. However, the effectiveness of clustering heavily depends on the event and subscription distribution. Unless the distribution offers promising clustering opportunity, as [18] pointed out, it is usually difficult to accurately support diversified user interests with only a small number of groups. Furthermore, the data distribution can be difficult to estimate and change over time.

In this paper, we use [18] as a representative for the Channelization approach. As a companion paper, [19] proposed optimization techniques for [18] and more extensive evaluation results. Although the techniques are proven to be effective, we expect them to be potentially applicable in other approaches as well, and therefore do not consider them as part of Channelization design in this paper. [11] studied the Channelization problem from a theoretical perspective. [25] experimented with different methods of clustering for different data distributions.

3   MEDYM

We propose a pub-sub network architecture called *MEDYM*, for *Match-Early with Dynamic Multicast*. Fig. 4 illustrates the event delivery process in MEDYM: a published event is first matched against subscriptions from remote servers, to obtain a *destination list* of successfully matched servers. Then, the event is routed to these servers through *dynamic multicast*: a transient, stateless multicast tree is computed and constructed on the fly, based on the destination lists carried in event message headers.

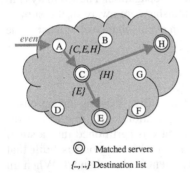

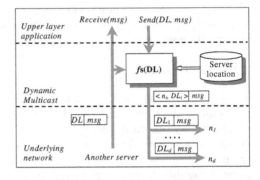

Fig. 4. Event delivery in MEDYM   **Fig. 5.** Dynamic multicast routing

MEDYM can be seen as following the *End-to-End* distributed system design principle [20]. It decouples the content-based pub-sub service into two functionalities: complex, application-specific matching at network edge, and simple, generic address-based routing in the network core. Such architecture offers several advantages:

- Low computation cost. Each event is matched with subscriptions for only once; the rest of the delivery process is through simple address-based routing.
- Minimum event traffic. Events are sent only to the servers with matching subscriptions. This not only minimizes the total event traffic on pub-sub servers, but also distributes the traffic consistently with servers' self-interests. Given the heterogeneous user interests in content-based pub-sub networks, this can be an important incentive for servers to join a network.
- Fine-grained routing optimization. Dynamic multicast allows network-efficient routing decisions be made based on individual event traffic patterns.

- Easy deployment and management. Servers are loosely coupled by soft states rather than configured overlay topology. This makes the network easy to deploy and adapt to changes and failures. Content-independent dynamic multicast can also support seamless integration of servers or networks running different pub-sub applications, and upgrade to different data types or matching semantics.

In this paper, we treat the relatively well-studied event matching problem ([1][8]) as an independent plug-in module and do not discuss it further. Next, we present design and implementation of dynamic multicast, and MEDYM server states maintenance. Due to space limitation, we omit the bootstrapping and self-organization of the MEDYM network, which are described in detail in [5].

3.1 Dynamic Multicast

Dynamic multicast is a generic scheme for routing messages to dynamic destination sets. As shown in Fig. 5, it serves a simple interface to the upper layer application: *send (DestinationList, message)*, and delivers received messages to the application through a callback function *Receive(message)*. Upon receiving a message with destination list DL, from either upper layer application or a remote server, a routing algorithm f_s runs as follows:

$$< n_i, DL_i > = f_s (DL) \qquad i = 1 \dots d$$

The algorithm computes a list of $d < n_i, DL_i >$ pairs, where n_i is the ith next-hop server, and DL_i is the new destination list for n_i. Different routing algorithms can be designed to suit different optimization goals, but the input and output of f_s should always satisfy the following *routing invariants*:

(a) $\bigcup\limits_{i=1}^{d} DL_i = DL - \{s\}$

(b) $DL_i \cap DL_j = \phi, i \neq j$

(c) $n_i \in DL_i$

These invariants guarantee that step by step, the message is sent to all its destination servers and to each server only once. Routing loops and redundant paths are naturally prevented. A multicast tree is thus resolved in a recursive way.

One of the major advantages of dynamic multicast is that because no routing states or pre-defined "groups" are maintained, there is no scalability limit on the number of destination sets it can support.

3.1.1 Distributed Dynamic Multicast

To avoid the fragility of centralized decision-making, in this paper, we focus on *distributed dynamic multicast*: each server accurately computes its local part of the multicast tree – its next-hop servers; it resolves the remote part of the tree only on a coarse-grain level, by assigning destinations to the destination lists for the next-hop servers. How the message will be routed beyond the next-hops is transparent and of no concern to the current server. This strategy suits well the fact that servers in a distributed network often have more accurate or up-to-date knowledge about their local environment than distant areas. In the event delivery process, servers improve routing decisions on a finer-grained level, and can easily adapt to network changes or failures. For example, when a server fails to deliver a message to a next-hop server n_i, it simply re-runs $f_s(DL_i - \{n_i\})$ so that the message is still delivered to other servers in DL_i. It also inserts n_i into the destination lists for one of the new next-hops, so that some other server will try to contact n_i, to bypass the possible network failure between the current server and n_i. After three such attempts, n_i is concluded to have failed.

3.1.2 Routing Algorithms

In this paper, we measure communication cost by network latency. Each MEDYM server maintains a *DistanceMatrix,* which contains the latency between every pair of servers in the system. Maintenance of the *DistanceMatrix* will be described in Section 3.2.

To minimize total network cost, we first experimented with routing algorithm that computes the multicast tree as a minimum spanning tree (*MST*) across destination servers. The major drawback of the MST algorithm is its high computation complexity, $O(D^2 \log D)$ where D is the number of destination servers. As the routing algorithm is run in real-time for every event message received, it is important that it can run fast enough to support high event routing throughput.

We then developed algorithm *SPMST,* for *Short-Path-MST*, which computes an *approximate* minimum spanning tree among the destination servers in a fast and distributed way. This algorithm is as shown in Fig. 6. Offline, an array called *Shadow-BitVectors* is maintained to help quickly identify next-hop servers. We say that server s_i is *shadowed* by server s_j, if s_i is closer to s_j than to current server s, and s is closer to s_j than to s_i. Under this condition, s_j would forward the message to s_i at lower (latency) cost than s does. Therefore, a server is a next-hop server if and only if it is not shadowed by any other destination. This can be quickly determined by the intersection of its *ShadowBitVector* and *DLBitVector*, the bit vector for *DL*. After choosing next-hops, the rest destinations are assigned to the destination lists of the next-hop servers closest to them.

```
computeShadowBitVectors_s() {          // offline
    foreach server s_i {
        foreach server s_j
            if (DistanceMatrix[i][j]<DistanceMatrix[s][i] &&
            DistanceMatrix[s][j]<DistanceMatrix[s][i])
            Set_jth_bit_in_ShadowBitVector[i]; }}

SPMSTRouting_s(DL) {                    // online
    Nexthops = DL;
    foreach server s_i in DL
        if (ShadowBitVector[i] & DLBitVector !=0)
            Nexthops_remove(s_i);
        if (|Nexthops|>maxNextHops))
            Nexthops = closest_nexthops(maxNextHops);
        foreach server s_j in (DL-Nexthops) {
            n_i = closest_nexthop_to(s_j);
            DL_i +={s_j}; }
        return(<n_i, DL_i>); }
```

Fig. 6. SPMST routing algorithm

Table 1 shows the computation time of MST and SPMST algorithm. The algorithms are written in Java and run with 2.0 GHz Pentium-III CPU and 512MB memory. Results show that SPMST runs much faster than MST, and can support routing of more than thousands of events per second. Furthermore, note that the *average* destination list size in a dynamic multicast message, as analyzed in Section 3.1.3, is much shorter than the IDLI sizes in the table. Therefore, compared to the results on content-based matching [1][8], we expect the computation cost of dynamic multicast routing to be lower and the process faster.

Table 1. Computation time of d-cast routing algorithms, with destination list size IDLI

Routing algorithm	Computation time (ms)		
	IDLI=100	IDLI=500	IDLI=1,000
MST	1.8	9	34
SPMST	0.08	0.29	0.62

Route Caching. An interesting question is whether dynamic multicast routes can/should be cached, so that future routing decisions can be made by cache look-up rather than real-time computation. The effectiveness of caching highly depends on the temporal locality of the pub-sub communication. We plan to study it in the context of specific pub-sub workload in the future, and do not assume caching as a general solution here. This results in a conservative estimation of the dynamic multicast routing computation overhead.

Routing on Mesh. Routing algorithms described above assume that every pair of servers may directly connect, which we expect is the normal scenario in a large-scale dedicated service network. When this is not the case, e.g. due to configurations or network failures, it may be inevitable that event messages be sent through non-destination servers. Our experiments show that the better connected the servers are, the more routing flexibility dynamic multicast can exploit, and the better performance it achieves. As this does not affect the overall MEDYM design, due to space limitation, we do not discuss such scenarios further in this paper.

3.1.3 Destination List Overhead
Destination lists carried in event messages introduce traffic overhead in MEDYM. Fig. 7 gives an informal analysis of the average destination list size in the process of delivery of one event: in a dynamic multicast tree, the destination lists are reduced at every step by a factor of the fan-out of the server in the tree. Therefore, the average list size is about equal to the diameter of the tree. This is confirmed by Fig. 8, which shows that as the diameters of the SPMST multicast trees are short and grow slowly with total number of destinations, so do the average destination list sizes. For example, to route an event to 1000 servers, an average message carries only 8 server IDs in its destination list. Such overhead is quite acceptable, especially considering that event messages in content-based pub-sub networks often carry rich content, such as attribute-value pairs, full-text or XML documents.

Although the destination lists are short on average, the overhead may not be well balanced, as the lists are longer at locations closer to the publisher. Instead of considering destination lists alone, we developed a routing algorithm to balance server routing load as a whole, as described in [5]. In Section 5, we examine through simulations the destination list overhead in various scenarios.

Note that the low destination list overhead is of critical importance to the scalability of dynamic multicast. [2] and [13] also proposed routing messages based on the destination information carried in message headers. However, as these approaches route messages on top of off-line maintained unicast routes, messages are inevitably sent through non-destination nodes. Traversing such nodes cannot reduce the destination information in the messages. Therefore, the average destination information in the messages is about linear to the number of destinations (rather than about logarithmic in dynamic multicast), and both approaches were developed on the assumption of a very small number (tens of) of receivers.

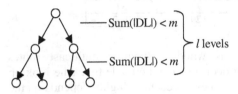

In total: $< ml$ destinations. $(m-1)$ messages.
On average: l destinations/message

Fig. 7. Intuitive analysis of average destination list size in a dynamic multicast tree

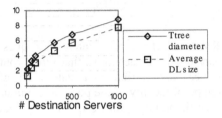

Destination Servers

Fig. 8. Simulation results for SPMST multicast tree diameters and average destination list sizes

3.2 Server States

MEDYM servers maintain two data structures: *routing tables* to support dynamic multicast routing, and *matching tables* for early event matching.

Routing Table. A routing table includes a *server list* of (*serverID, IPaddress, status*) for all servers in the system, and a *distance matrix M*, where $M_{i,j}$ represents communication cost between server i and j. In MEDYM, servers periodically broadcast *Refresh* messages using dynamic multicast. A refresh message contains the server's ID, IP address, network location and status (e.g. load condition). Servers receiving the Refresh message update their routing tables accordingly.

Server network location can be measured in two ways: servers may actively probe each other and broadcast the probing results. This approach generates O(#*servers*^{3}) total network traffic and therefore only scales to small networks. As an alternative, MEDYM can utilize state-of-the-art techniques [16][22] to approximately *estimate* server locations with much lower overhead. Note that inaccurate server location information or even inconsistent information across servers does not affect the correctness of dynamic multicast, which is guaranteed by the routing invariants. In Section 5, we present experimental results of using both probing and the available GNP estimation service [16]. More detailed simulation results of using [22] can be found in [5].

Matching Table. In a pub-sub network, servers often specialize in publishing only certain kinds of events. In MEDYM, a server maintains a matching table, with an entry (*serverID, sum_of_subscriptions*) for every other server in the system, which records the sum of subscriptions from that server that are relevant to local publication interest. To make a new subscription or to cancel a previous one (so-called *unsubscibe*), a server broadcasts a *Subscribe* or *Unsubscribe* message via dynamic multicast; servers receiving the message update their matching tables. As an optimization, servers may first broadcast *advertisements* on their publication interests, so that subscriptions are sent (via dynamic multicast) only to servers with relevant advertisements.

Scalability. We do not expect MEDYM routing tables or matching tables to introduce major storage or maintenance overhead for small or medium scale pub-sub networks. First, as each pub-sub server is expected to support a large number of end users, routing tables are expected to be much smaller and more stable than the matching tables. Second, for any pub-sub network to achieve the highly desirable *quenching* capability ([21]), i.e. to filter off events that nobody wants locally, publication servers must know the sum of all (relevant) subscriptions in the network. Servers in MEDYM and the two existing approaches discussed in Section 2 all have the quenching capability, though they differ in subscription replication formats and optimization techniques. We compare their subscription replication cost in detail in Section 5.3.

4 H-MEDYM

MEDYM requires servers to know about all other servers in the network and the sum of their subscriptions. We believe such information needs are practical for service networks with up to thousands of servers. Beyond this point, the storage and maintenance cost of the server states can become the system scalability bottleneck. Hierarchy is an effective method that makes IP routing extremely scalable. However, different from IP addresses, content-based subscriptions from servers geographically close are not necessarily similar and may not be succinctly summarized. Therefore, a similar hierarchy structure for pub-sub network can impose heavy load on servers at the upper level of the hierarchy [6][9].

Based on our experience from an earlier work [4], we propose a different hierarchical solution called for MEDYM, called *H-MEDYM* for *Hierarchical MEDYM*. An H-MEDYM network is partitioned along two dimensions: geographically, servers are clustered based on their network locations; content-wise, the event space is partitioned into non-overlapping *topics*. Each event falls into one topic, while a subscription may overlap with multiple topics (Event space partitioning will be discussed later in more detail). In each cluster, for each topic, one or more servers are designated as *matchers*, which will be responsible for matching events falling into that topic.

An example of event delivery in H-MEDYM is shown in Fig. 9. When an event is published, the publication server identifies the topic the event belongs to, and sends it the closest matcher for that topic in local cluster. At the matcher, the event is matched against subscriptions for that topic, and then dynamic-multicast to two sets of destinations: matched servers in the local cluster, and matched matchers for that topic from remote clusters. At each remote matcher, the event is matched again with subscriptions from servers in that matcher's cluster and dynamic-multicast to the matched servers.

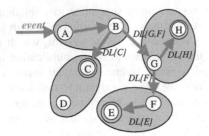

Matchers:

Cluster \ Topic	T1	T2
C1	A	B
C2	D	C
C3	H	G
C4	E	F

◎ Servers with matching subscriptions

Fig. 9. Event delivery in H-MEDYM. Server *A* publishes an event in topic *T2*. It sends the event to matcher *B*, which matches the event and dynamic-multicasts it to matched servers in the local cluster (not shown) as well as to matched matchers *C, G, F* in other clusters. The event is matched again at *C, G, F* and dynamic-multicast to the matched servers in their local clusters.

4.1 Cluster Configuration and Server States

Unlike in MEDYM, servers in H-MEDYM need to know about only a subset of other servers and subscriptions. Specifically, the first row in Table 2 describes the content of the routing and matching tables at a server that is a matcher: the routing table contains only servers in the same cluster and other matchers for the same topic; the matching table contains only subscriptions from this subset of servers that overlap with that topic (subscriptions overlapping with multiple topics can be divided into smaller subscriptions each covering one topic). A server that is not a matcher (not shown in Table 2) maintains a routing table only for servers in the same cluster, and no matching table.

Table 2. Server states at an H-MEDYM matcher for topic t in cluster c. N: #servers, C: #clusters, T: #topics.

	Routing table	Matching table
Table content	Network location of servers in c and matchers for t	Subscriptions in topic t from servers in c and matchers for t
Table size, as a fraction of global knowledge	$\sim 1/C + \max(1/T, C/N)$	$\sim \max(C/N, 1/T)$

The second row in Table 2 provides an approximate estimate of the table sizes, normalized as a fraction of global information, i.e. it shows the fraction of all servers or subscriptions in the system that a server needs to know about. The results can be intuitively explained as follows: increasing the number of topics T partitions the event space at finer level, and reduces the number of subscriptions that need to be replicated for each topic and the number of matchers for each topic. However, increasing T beyond N/C no longer reduces matching table size at an average server, as the server now has to match for more than one topic; on the other hand, it continues to increase the routing table size, as the server needs to know about more other matchers. We expect a good H-MEDYM configuration to be around $T \sim N/C \sim N^{1/2}$, in which case the matching table size is reduced by a factor of $O(N^{1/2})$ compared to that in MEDYM. (We do not focus on routing tables, as they are usually much smaller and more stable than matching tables, as mentioned in Section 3.2). Such reduction can be quite substantial in a large-scale network. In Section 5.2, we present simulation results of H-MEDYM server states under various configurations.

4.2 Scalability Analysis

Compared to MEDYM, H-MEDYM improves scalability in several aspects. First, it reduces server states as described above. Second, event delivery is divided into two steps: dynamic multicast within each server cluster, and among matchers for the same topic. As each step involves only a small subset of servers, messages carry shorter destination lists. Third, events are no longer matched at publication servers. Separation of publication and matching responsibility allows for more flexible load management, as replication of subscriptions and the workload of event matching can now be allocated based on server capabilities rather than determined by the publication interests of their nearby end users.

On the other hand, H-MEDYM introduces new overheads. An event is now matched twice, at local and remote matchers, before reaching a destination server. The event may also traverse matchers that are not be interested in it. The quenching capability is moved from publication server to the first matcher the event is sent to. Finally, managing server clusters and content space partitions introduces additional cost.

Overall, H-MEDYM trades off efficiency in event delivery for lower server states overhead, and is applicable to very large pub-sub networks where such overhead is the scalability bottleneck. We will evaluate these tradeoffs quantitatively in Section 5.

4.3 Other Issues

Several orthogonal design and algorithmic issues need to be addressed in building an H-MEDYM system. This paper does not make new contributions in these areas. Instead, we explore the possibility of applying existing technologies, and expect these issues to be fertile ground for further optimization and evaluation in the future.

Event Space Partitioning. In H-MEDYM, it is desirable that event space be partitioned into topics with balanced load, and with few subscriptions overlapping with more than one topic. The partition should also be easy to maintain and adaptive to data changes. Many pub-sub applications have inherent concepts of topics, such as news categories, stock industries or geographic area partitions, which are natural candidates for the partitioning in H-MEDYM. In [4] we propose to partition the space into continuous zones, possibly using multi-dimensional partitioning techniques [12][17][24]. Event clustering in Channelization is also an alternative, although the process can be relatively complex and results sensitive to data distribution. Note that unlike Channelization, H-MEDYM matches each event accurately with user subscriptions, and delivers events only to matched servers or matchers. A bad event space partition is likely to affect the load distribution and server states reduction in H-MEDYM, but will not lead to high extraneous event traffic.

Matcher Selection. When assigning H-MEDYM servers as matchers for topics, subscription replication and the workload of event matching should be allocated consistently with server capabilities. Load distribution is a well-studied problem in parallel and distributed computing [10], and even in pub-sub itself [24]. In H-MEDYM, locality is another key issue: it is desirable that servers match for events that are of local publication or subscription interests, so as to reduce the probability of sending events to matchers who are not interested in them. How to best assign matchers given these potentially conflicting goals is an interesting area for future work.

5 Evaluation

We evaluate our work and compare with existing solutions through qualitative analysis, quantitative simulations and real-world experiments.

5.1 Simulation Methodology

We developed a message-level, event-driven pub-sub network simulator. The IP topology is generated using the GT-ITM transit-stub model [3] with 2500 routers and 8938 links in total. 1000 pub-sub servers are randomly attached to the routers. Each event message has a payload of 200 bytes and a TCP/IP header of 44 bytes. MEDYM/H-MEDYM destination lists have server IDs of 2 bytes each. For simplicity and without loss of generality, we use integers as event and subscription values and perform only equality matching. The results presented are independent of data types or matching algorithms used.

We compare five architectural approaches: MEDYM and H-MEDYM with the SPMST routing algorithm; two versions of CBF: CBF_MST as in [6], where a single CBF tree is built as the minimum spanning tree across all servers, and CBF_SPT as in [7], where CBF trees are shortest path trees rooted at publication servers; Channelization approach as in [18], using Forgy K-Means algorithm to cluster events into 50 channels, as this algorithm was found to produce the best partition results in the paper.

A major challenge in evaluation of pub-sub systems has been the lack of representative application data. In the absence of this, we attempt to gain a comprehensive understanding of the performance of different systems under various distinguishing scenarios. We define a key parameter, *matching ratio*, as the fraction of servers with matching subscriptions for an event, or equivalently, the fraction of events that a server's subscriptions match. We examine scenarios with widely varying matching ratios and our results can be interpreted in several ways: first, low matching ratios imply highly selective subscriptions and high matching ratios represent popular events. We are interested to see how systems perform for these different scenarios. Second, for a given matching ratio, we can understand performance results not only in "absolute" terms, e.g. resource usage numbers, but also in "relative" terms, i.e. how far is the performance from the optimal case. For example, with 10% matching ratio, a server that receives 20% of all published events can be seen as carrying 100% traffic overhead. Third, a pub-sub network may scale along three dimensions: number of servers, number of total user subscriptions, and volume of event publications. As we focus on evaluation of per event delivery, we do not consider the third factor in this paper. Table 3 shows three scaling scenarios as combinations of the first two dimensions. Users can infer system scalability in these three scenarios from results with different matching ratios. Finally, we have experimented with different event and subscription data distributions, such as uniform, Zipf, exponential and normal distributions. We found that only Channelization is sensitive to data distribution; its clustering is more effective when both event and subscription distributions are highly skewed and have the same peaks. Even so, in all realistic settings, the relative positions of different approaches are the same under all distributions. Due to space limitations, we present results only with uniformly randomly generated event and subscription values, as this provides the most basic and clear understanding of system's performance. Results for many other distributions can in fact be computed as the weighted-sums of the results with different matching ratios.

Table 3. Pub-sub network scaling scenarios

Scenario	Total subscriptions	Number of servers	Matching ratio
A	↑	–	↑
B	↑	↑	–
C	–	↑	↓

5.2 H-MEDYM Configuration

We first look at the configuration of H-MEDYM networks. We use the Hierarchical Agglomerate Clustering (HAC) algorithm [14] to cluster servers based on their network locations, and partition the event space into continuous ranges with equal lengths. Fig. 10 shows the average size of routing tables and matching tables at H-MEDYM servers, normalized as a percentage of global information (see Table 2). The results validate our quantitative analysis in Section 4.1. Partitioning in both dimensions is necessary to reduce server state in H-MEDYM: when there is only 1 topic or 1 server per cluster (i.e. 1000 clusters), servers maintain 100% of global information. Increasing the number of topics is effective in reducing server states only when there are more servers in each cluster than the number of topics. In subsequent simulations, we use the configuration in Fig. 10 that is closest to our choice of $T \sim N/C \sim N^{1/2}$ in Section 4.1: 20 topics and 50 clusters. In this case, on average, each server knows about 10% of other servers, and 5% of total subscriptions.

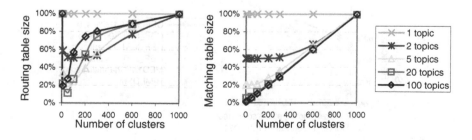

Fig. 10. H-MEDYM server states under different configurations

5.3 Subscription Replication

Subscription replication is a major source of storage and maintenance cost in pub-sub networks. This cost differs across systems in three ways:

First, the number of remote subscriptions a server needs to replicate depends on its matching responsibility. In MEDYM and Channelization, servers only match for locally published events, and therefore only need to replicate subscriptions that are relevant to their publication interests. In H-MEDYM, a server replicates subscriptions that fall into the topics it matches for, and the replication is independent of its own publication interest. In CBF, a server needs to replicate all subscriptions for which it appears on the CBF tree path between the subscriber and any possibly matching publisher. The number of such subscriptions is dependent on other servers' publication and subscription interests, not just its own.

Second, replicated subscriptions can be *aggregated* ([23][26]) to achieve more efficient storage and update. In MEDYM and H-MEDYM matching tables, only subscriptions from the same server can be aggregated. In CBF forwarding tables, subscriptions from all servers in the same direction in the CBF tree can be aggregated, since the server needs only determine in which directions to forward an event. In Channelization, all subscriptions in the network can be aggregated, as the publication server only needs to know whether an event matches any subscription in the system, for the purpose of quenching. Therefore, Channelization offers greater opportunity for optimization by aggregation than CBF, which in turn offers greater opportunity than MEDYM and H-MEDYM.

Subscription aggregation is a difficult problem whose solution and effectiveness heavily depends on pub-sub data type and distribution. It can also make canceling subscriptions difficult, as mentioned in [7]. Therefore, in Fig. 11, we look at subscription replication assuming no aggregation. In the figure, the x-axis shows an average server's publication interest, measured as a percentage of the entire event space; the y-axis shows the number of subscriptions replicated on an average server, measured as a percentage of all subscriptions in the system. For the CBF approach, we show two curves that represent different subscription selectivity: an average server subscribes to events falling into 1% or 100% of the event space. For example, if each

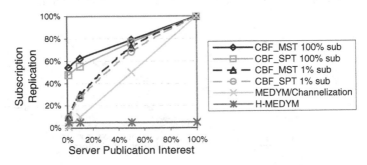

Fig. 11. Subscription replication, without aggregation

server publishes 1% of events and subscribes to (not necessarily the same) 1% of events, an average server needs to replicate 8% of total subscriptions. This figure can be combined with the effectiveness of a particular subscription aggregation scenario to estimate the subscription replication storage cost in a system.

In the face of network changes, subscription replication in CBF is likely to be more expensive to maintain than in other systems, as discussed in Section 2.1.

Overall, we expect H-MEDYM to be an effective way to reduce subscription replication, while a quantitative comparison between the other approaches is likely to be dependent on application properties.

5.4 Server Processing Load

For generality and comparability, we measure the processing load at a server by the number of events the server receives. Note that to route each event, the content-based forwarding process in CBF is likely to be more computationally expensive than the address-based routing in Channelization and MEDYM/H-MEDYM, though the concrete results depend on the data type, subscription size, and matching algorithms used. Fig. 12 plots the number of events a server receives, as a percentage of all events published in the system, under varying matching ratios. Channelization servers receive the most events, showing the ineffectiveness of clustering in filtering out extraneous event traffic. When matching ratio is higher than 15%, almost every Channelization server joins all the multicast groups and receives all the events. CBF servers receive much fewer events, due to its accurate per-step filtering. MEDYM servers receive the fewest possible events, i.e. only the events that they subscribe to. H-MEDYM introduces a small overhead over MEDYM, as events can be sent to irrelevant matchers. The difference between the approaches is most apparent when matching ratio is low. For example, a server that subscribes to only 1% events receives 1% events in MEDYM, 2% in H-MEDYM, 8% in CBF_MST, 9% in CBF_SPT, and 29% in Channelization. For very high matching ratios, all approaches converge to broadcast.

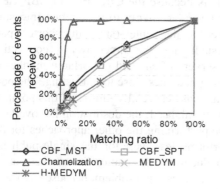

Fig. 12. Average server processing load

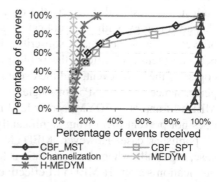

Fig. 13. Cumulative distribution of server processing load, with 10% matching ratio

Next, we look at the distribution of processing load across pub-sub servers. Fig. 13 shows the percentage of servers that receive no more than a given number of events,when each server matches 10% of total events. We see that all MEDYM servers receive 10% events each, while most Channelization servers receive more than 90% of total events. CBF server load is in between, but is highly imbalanced: about 40% of servers receive only 10% events each, while 20% servers in CBF_MST and 10% in CBF_SPT receive more than 80% events each. As expected in Section 2.1, these heavily loaded servers are located at the center of the network, and route for many irrelevant servers. The imbalance problem is more serious in CBF_MST than in CBF_SPT, because CBF_SPT has multiple CBF trees and higher routing diversity.

5.5 Server Bandwidth Consumption

Server bandwidth is a very precious resource in service networks. Fig. 14 shows the average bandwidth a server consumes in the process of delivering one event. Different from Fig. 12, MEDYM servers only achieve *close to* minimum bandwidth consumption; the difference between its curve and the optimal line shows its destination list overhead. While the overhead is small for low matching ratios, for high large matching ratios (above 90%) it makes MEDYM server bandwidth surpass that of CBF and Channelization by a small amount. H-MEDYM server bandwidth consumption is higher than MEDYM when matching ratio is low, due to events traversing irrelevant matchers, but it is lower than MEDYM when matching ratio is high, due to its shorter destination lists.

Unlike the average case, the maximum server bandwidth consumption can be sensitive to publisher distribution. In Fig. 15 and Fig. 16, we study two extreme scenarios: the *all-publisher* scenario, in which every server publishes the same number of events, and the *single-publisher* scenario, in which only one server publishes all the events. In both cases, the maximum bandwidth consumption in both CBF approaches is much higher than the average consumption, again showing the load imbalance across servers. Different form the processing load case, CBF_SPT has more serious bandwidth imbalance than CBF_MST. This is because the CBF trees in CBF_SPT, built as shortest-path trees on the overlay layer, are likely to degenerate into star-shaped topology with the publication servers at the center (since the shortest path between a publisher and a subscriber is usually just the direct overlay connection between them). Therefore, the publication servers often send out a large number of copies of the same event, and the event routing becomes close to unicasting. The poor performance of CBF_SPT for single-publisher case especially illustrates this point. In MEDYM and H-MEDYM, server load is well balanced; the destination list overhead does not prevent them from significantly outperforming the other approaches for the all-publisher case. However, MEDYM performs less well for the single-publisher case, especially when matching ratio is high, due to the destination list overhead at the publication server. H-MEDYM effectively alleviates this problem, because even with a single publication server, the destination lists are first generated at different matchers. Interested readers can refer to [5] for a dynamic multicast routing algorithm we developed to balance MEDYM server bandwidth.

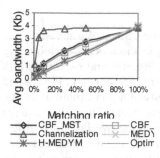

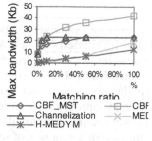

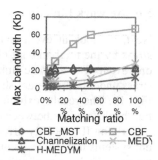

Fig. 14. Average server band-width consumption

Fig. 15. Maximum server bandwidth consumption in all-publisher case

Fig. 16. Maximum server bandwidth consumption in single-publisher case

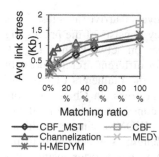

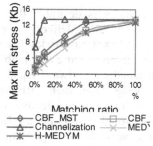

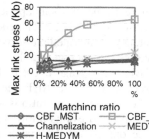

Fig. 17. Average link stress

Fig. 18. Maximum link stress in all-publisher case

Fig. 19. Maximum link stress in single-publisher case

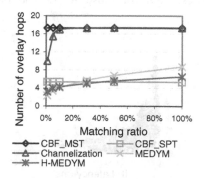

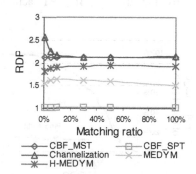

Fig. 20. Average event path length in simulation

Fig. 21. Relative Delay Penalty (RDP) of event paths in simulation

5.6 Network Link Stress

Next, we look at event traffic load on underlying network links. We measure *link stress* by the total amount of data transferred over a link in the process of delivering one event. The average link stress results are shown in Fig. 17, and maximum link stress under both all-publisher and single-publisher scenarios are shown in Fig. 18 and Fig. 19. The results exhibit similar trends as server bandwidth consumption results, but the differences between different approaches are of less extent. This is because the underlying IP topology offers lower routing diversity than at the overlay layer: different systems may route events through different sets of servers, but the messages often traverse similar sets of underlying network links, especially when there are only a few long-distance links across IP domains. We expect that in larger IP networks the difference between the approaches would be more significant, and the results would be more favorable to MEDYM and H-MEDYM.

5.7 Event Delivery Latency

In real-time pub-sub applications, it is desirable that events arrive at subscribers within short latency. The end-to-end event delivery latency consists of the processing latency at intermediate servers and the transmission latency on network links. Fig. 20 shows the average number of servers in an event path in different architectures. In CBF, the average event path lengths are always equal to the diameters of the CBF tree(s), with CBF_SPT trees being flatter than CBF_MST trees. In Channelization, when the matching ratio is low, clustering is effective in constructing small multicast groups, and events are routed through fewer servers. In MEDYM, since a multicast tree only spans the matched servers, the average path length is about equal to the logarithm of the number of matched servers. H-MEDYM has shorter event paths thanMEDYM, because of the two-level event routing hierarchy. Fig. 21 presents the average Relative Delay Penalty (RDP) of event paths. RDP is defined as the ratio of the sum of network latency of event routing in the pub-sub network over the latency of IP routing between the publication server and the destination server. With shortest path routing trees, CBF_SPT achieves lowest RDP of close to 1. The other

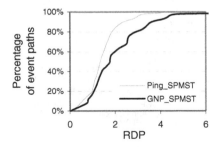

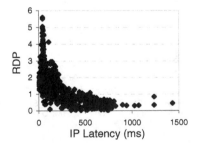

Fig. 22. Cumulative Distribution of RDP in MEDYM deployment

Fig. 23. RDP vs. IP latency using GNP in MEDYM deployment

approaches all route events along minimum spanning trees or its approximations. RDP in MEDYM and H-MEDYM is lower than in CBF and Channelization, due to the smaller trees MEDYM and H-MEDYM build. H-MEDYM has higher RDP than MEDYM because events are "detoured" to matchers first. Fig. 20 and Fig. 21 can be used, together with the event processing latency at intermediate servers and the IP latency between publication and destination servers, to estimate the end-to-end delivery for events with certain matching ratios.

5.8 MEDYM Implementation Results

We deployed a prototype of MEDYM on PlanetLab test bed [15]. MEDYM servers are run on 86 PlanetLab sites, 68 in the United States and 18 abroad. Experimental results for server processing load and bandwidth consumption confirm our simulation results above, and are not presented here due to space limitations. To understand event delivery performance in real networks, we focus on network latency results.

In the experiments, we measure server locations in two ways: first, each server randomly pings another server in every 10 seconds, and broadcasts the pinging results every 10 minutes; as an alternative, we used the GNP [16] service to estimate server locations: each MEDYM server pings one of the 8 GNP servers every minute. Based on the pinging results, it computes an 8 dimensional virtual coordinate, and broadcasts its coordinates once every 8 minutes. Distance matrices are then computed locally using the servers' coordinates. Fig. 22 presents the RDP (as defined in Section 5.7) for the event paths. It shows that the routing latency using pair-wise pinging is consistent with our expectation and the overhead of using GNP is quite acceptable. We observe that the inaccuracy of GNP estimation happens most when servers that are geographically close and derive similar coordinates in GNP in fact have high IP latencies between them, possibly due to congestions or configurations. This can also be seen from Fig. 23, which shows that event paths with high RDP typically have low IP latencies. Overall, Fig. 22 and Fig. 23 confirm our expectation that MEDYM constructs high-quality event routing paths, and network location estimation as by GNP is a promising scalable solution.

6 Conclusions and Future Work

We have presented the design and evaluation of MEDYM, a new architecture for content-based pub-sub service networks, and H-MEDYM, an approach to extend the architecture to a hierarchical structure for greater scale. While these architectures each have their challenges and limitations, we believe that they achieve some important advantages over existing approaches in performance, flexibility and manageability that are highly desirable for many pub-sub applications.

A key goal of our research has been to gain a comprehensive understanding of the characteristics of different content-based pub-sub network designs for different application circumstances. Our evaluation in this paper leads us to the following conclusions.

CBF is an elegant design that achieves accurate event delivery; however, its in-network event processing can be computationally intensive, and the server states that are tightly associated with network topology can be expensive to maintain in a dynamically changing network environment. Therefore, we expect CBF to be suitable for stable pub-sub networks with abundant computational resource. Channelization incurs low computation and subscription replication overhead, but its routing quality heavily depends on pub-sub data distribution and can be very poor when the distributions do not offer very promising clustering opportunity. It is mostly suitable for applications whose user interests can be approximated by a small number of groups with high accuracy.

MEDYM achieves low and well-balanced routing load on servers and network links by sending events only to interested servers via customized routes; its major overhead comes from the servers' global knowledge of location and sum-of-subscription information of all other servers, and the destination lists in its messages. It is well-suited for pub-sub networks with up to a few thousand servers; beyond this point, H-MEDYM is likely to be more suitable: it effectively reduces both the number of servers and the amount of subscription information each server needs to know about, and the destination list overhead. Its overheads are its complexity and the routing constraints it imposes on event delivery paths. MEDYM and H-MEDYM appear to perform well across a range of circumstances; compared to CBF and Channelization, they are most advantageous when user subscriptions are highly selective and diversified. We observe that this is exactly the scenario in which intelligence and efficiency of a pub-sub service is most needed, and therefore their properties would be highly desirable for many applications.

To better understand the characteristics of realistic pub-sub workloads and their implications for architectural tradeoffs, in addition to extrapolating and inferring characteristics from existing information access systems, we plan to deploy a public pub-sub service on PlanetLab [15] and collect real workloads to drive further research. We also plan to investigate several open questions raised in this paper, such as dynamic multicast route caching, event space partitioning and matching distribution in H-MEDYM.

References

1. M. K. Aguilera, R. E. Strom, D. C. Sturman, M.Astley, and T. D. Chandra, "Matching events in a content-based subscription system," In *Proc. of ACM PODC*, 1999.
2. R. Boivie et al., "Explicit Multicast (Xcast) Basic Specification", Internet draft, *draft-ooms-xcast-basic-spec-03.txt*.
3. K. Calvert, E. Zegura, and S. Bhattacharjee. "How to Model an Internet-work". In *Proc. of IEEE INFOCOM*, 1996.
4. F. Cao, J. P. Singh, "Efficient event routing in content-based publish-subscribe service network". In *Proc. of IEEE INFOCOM* 2004.
5. F. Cao, J. P. Singh, "Towards scalable publish-subscribe service networks". *Technical Report, Princeton University*, 2005.
6. A. Carzaniga, D. Rosenblum, and A. Wolf, "Design and evaluation of a wide-area event notification service," In *Proc. of ACM TOCS*. 2001.
7. A. Carzaniga, A.L. Wolf, "A routing scheme for content-based networking". In *Proc. of IEEE INFOCOM 2003*.
8. A. Carzaniga, A.L. Wolf, "Forwarding in a Content-Based Network". In *Proc. of ACM SIGCOMM 2003*.
9. G. Cugola, E. Di Nitto, A. Fuggetta, "The JEDI Event-based Infrastructure and its Application to the Development of the OPSS WFMS", in *IEEE Transc. on Soft. Eng.*, 2001.

10. D. Culler, J. P. Singh, "Parallel Computer Architecture: A Hardware-Software Approach", *Morgan Kaufmann*, 1998
11. Z. Ge, M. Adler, J. Kurose, D. Towsley and Steve Zabele, "Channelization problem in large scale data dissemination," In ICNP, 2001.
12. A. Guttman. "R-Trees: A Dynamic Index Structure for Spatial Searching". In *Proc. of SIGMOD Conference* 1984
13. C. P. Hall, A. Carzaniga, J. Rose and A. L. Wolf , "A content-based networking protocol for sensor networks". Tech. Report CU-CS-979-04, University of Colorado, 2004.
14. A.K. Jain, M. N. Murty, and P.J. Flynn, "Data clustering: a review." In *Proc. of ACM Computing Surveys* 31, 3 (1999), 264—323.
15. PlanetLab Testbed: http://planet-lab.org
16. T. S. E. Ng and H. Zhang. "Predicting Internet Network Distance with Coordinates-Based Approaches." In *Proc. of IEEE INFOCOM* 2002.
17. S. Ratnasamy, P. Francis, et al. "A Scalable Content-Addressable Network", In *Proc. of ACM SIGCOMM*, 2001
18. A. Riabov, Z. Liu, J. Wolf, P. Yu and L. Zhang, "Clustering Algorithms for content-based publication-subscription systems," In *Proc. of ICDCS* 2002.
19. Riabov, Z. Liu, J. Wolf, P. Yu and L. Zhang, "New Algorithms for content-based publication-subscription systems", In *Proc. of ICDCS* 2003.
20. J. Saltzer, D. Reed, and D. Clark. "End-to-end arguments in system design". In *ACM Trans. Computer System,* 2(4), pp. 277--88, 1984.
21. B. Segall, D. Arnold. "Elvin has left the building: A publish/subscribe notification service with quenching". In *Proc. of AUUG97*, Brisbane, 1997.
22. L. Tang, M. Crovella. "Virtual Landmark for the Internet", In *Proc. of ACM SIGCOMM Internet Measurement Conference*, 2003
23. P. Triantafillou, A. Economides. "Subscription summarization: A new paradigm for efficient publish/subscribe systems". In *Proc. of ICDCS* 2004.
24. Y. Wang, L. Qiu, et. al. "Subscription Partitioning and Routing in Content-based Publish/Subscribe Networks." In *Proc. of Intl. Symp. on Dist. Comp.* (DISC), 2002.
25. T. Wong, R. Katz, and S. McCanne. "An evaluation of preference clustering in large scale multicast applications," In *Proc. of IEEE INFOCOM* 2000.
26. Y. Zhao, D. Sturman and S. Bhola, "Subscription propagation in highly-available publish/subscribe middleware". In *Proc. ACM/IFIP/USENIX Middleware Conference*, 2004.

Generic Middleware Substrate Through Modelware*

Charles Zhang, Dapeng Gao, and Hans-Arno Jacobsen

University of Toronto
{czhang, gilbert, jacobsen}@eecg.toronto.edu

Abstract. Conventional middleware architectures suffer from insufficient module-level reusability and the ability to adapt in face of functionality evolution and diversification. To overcome these deficiencies, we propose the Modelware methodology adopting the Model Driven Architecture (MDA) approach and aspect oriented programming (AOP). We advocate the use of models and views to separate intrinsic functionalities of middleware from extrinsic ones. This separation effectively lowers the concern density per component and fosters the coherence and the reuse of the components of middleware architectures. Comparing to the conventionally designed version, Modelware improves the standard benchmark performance by as much as 40% through architectural optimizations. Our evaluation also shows that Modelware considerably reduces coding efforts in supporting the funcitonal evolution of middleware and dramatically different application domains.

1 Introduction

The construction of system software such as middleware is complex. A contributing factor to this complexity, as we have observed first hand, is that the code-level design reusability in conventional middleware architectures is incapable of adequately dealing with "change" in two dimensions: *time* (functional evolution) and *space* (functional diversification).

The reusability in conventionally developed software components is insufficient due to the lack of explicit means to effectively distinguish *intrinsic* and *extrinsic* architectural elements. Borrowing terms from subject-oriented programming [10], we use the term "intrinsic" to characterize middleware architectural elements that are essential, invariant, and repeatedly used despite the variations of the application domains. These "common abstractions" are typically pattern-based designs, such as proxy, forwarder-receiver [7], and acceptor [16]. Contrarily, we use the term "extrinsic" to denote elements that are vulnerable to refinements or can become optional when the application domains change. A simple example of an "extrinsic" property is "thread-level concurrency," including patterns such as leader/follower [16], which can become redundant when threading policies are controlled by user applications or if the underlying platform, such as

---

* This research was supported by an IBM CAS Fellowship and an NSERC grant.

G. Alonso (Ed.): Middleware 2005, LNCS 3790, pp. 314–333, 2005.

```
JacORB:
  private final static void _write4int
     (final byte[] buf, final int _pos, final int value) {
       buf[_pos]   = (byte)((value >> 24) & 0xFF);
       buf[_pos+1] = (byte)((value >> 16) & 0xFF);
       buf[_pos+2] = (byte)((value >>  8) & 0xFF);
       buf[_pos+3] = (byte) (value        & 0xFF);
  }
Sun CORBA:
  private final void writeBigEndianLong(int x) {
       bbwi.buf[bbwi.index++] = (byte)((x >>> 24) & 0xFF);
       bbwi.buf[bbwi.index++] = (byte)((x >>> 16) & 0xFF);
       bbwi.buf[bbwi.index++] = (byte)((x >>>  8) & 0xFF);
       bbwi.buf[bbwi.index++] = (byte)(x & 0xFF);
  }
ORBacus:
  public void write_long( int value) {
       buf_.data_.[buf_.pos_++] = (byte) (value >>> 24);
       buf_.data_.[buf_.pos_++] = (byte) (value >>> 16);
       buf_.data_.[buf_.pos_++] = (byte) (value >>>  8);
       buf_.data_.[buf_.pos_++] = (byte) value;
  }
```

Fig. 1. Data marshaling of type **long** in A:JacORB, B:Sun ORB, and C:ORBacus

Java Card[1], does not support threads at all. As we have reported in our previous work [24], "intrinsic" and "extrinsic" properties interact non-modularly in conventional middleware architectures. Consequently, middleware architects are faced with immense architectural complexities because the concern density per-module is high. The code-level reusability of the "common abstractions"is also drastically reduced because the generality of intrinsic components is restricted by the "extrinsic" properties in face of domain variations.

Conventional middleware architectures also lack effective means to reuse "extrinsic" properties, especially ones that are crosscutting [13] in nature, i.e., not localized within modular boundaries. We illustrate this problem through the example of *data marshalling*: a major CORBA feature converting the "typed" application data to an array of bytes. We study three popular implementations of CORBA, namely ORBacus [2], a commercial ORB, JacORB [3], an open source ORB, and Sun's ORB, shipped with every Java2.0 SDK. Figure 1 lists the implementations of the marshalling of the data type **long**. These three independent implementations are nearly identical in terms of structure and algorithm. Two design concepts are reused by all of the implementers: the *"buffer"*, holding a byte array representing the raw data, and the *"shifting and masking"* algorithm for decomposing four bytes of a **long** value into four byte values. The desired approach is to package this marshalling functionality for type **long**, along with the about 20 other data types in CORBA, as part of a marshalling library, so that it becomes a reusable development artifact. Conventional architectures have fallen short of doing so because they are incapable of componentizing and reusing crosscutting concerns as analyzed in our previous work [25]. Our investigation

---

[1] Java Card. http://java.sun.com/products/javacard/index.jsp
[2] ORBacus. http://www.iona.com/orbacus
[3] JacORB. http://www.jacorb.org

has revealed similar problems with many other major CORBA functionalities. Being able to componentize and to reuse these functionalities tremendously facilitates the construction of middleware systems.

To tackle the afore-mentioned problems, we propose a new architectural paradigm, Modelware, which embodies the "multi-viewpoints" [14] approach. We capture "intrinsic properties", or common abstractions, in a *base view* consisting of a set of coherent components free of crosscutting concerns. We use *role-based aspect views* and aspect libraries to capture "extrinsic properties", i.e., domain variations. we adopt the Model Driven Architecture (MDA) [4] in both types of views as the vehicle for the mapping abstractions to implementations. Concrete middleware instances can be produced by the *realization* process: selecting implementations for abstractions in both kinds of views, and the *projection* process: creating ontological relationships between elements in both aspect views and the base view.

In describing our experience of the Modelware paradigm, we make the following contributions in this paper:

1. We present Modelware, a model-driven approach, to separate middleware architectural concerns into multiple "viewpoints": an "intrinsic view" implementing common middleware functionalities through simple and coherent modules, and "aspect views" providing abstractions for crosscutting concerns.
2. We present the implementation details of the views in Modelware. More specifically, we describe the "realization" process for both the base view and aspect views and the "projection" process for integrating aspect view onto the base view.
3. We present a thorough evaluation of the Modelware paradigm to illustrate both the performance benefit and the high-level code reuse in supporting functional variations in both space and time.

The rest of the paper is organized as follows: we first introduce generic models including both the intrinsic models and aspect models of Modelware in Section 3; we then describe in Section 4 how transformations can be used to concretize generic models and to integrate aspect models to support flexible compositions of middleware functionalities; evaluations of Modelware are presented in Section 5.

2   Background and Related Work

Background and related work can be classified into two categories: aspect-oriented programming approaches and model-driven approaches. We will present these categories in turn and discuss similarities and difference to our approach.

Aspect-oriented Programming. *Aspects* modularize crosscutting concerns, coding concerns that are not localized, hence, not modularized. Aspect-oriented programming (AOP) allows the developer to cleanly encapsulated crosscutting

---

[4] MDA. http://www.omg.org/mda

concerns in separate modules [13]. Aspect-oriented languages, such as AspectJ[5], defines a set of new language constructs to support two kinds of crosscutting: *dynamic crosscutting* and *static crosscutting*. Dynamic crosscutting is defined by means of *join points* that denote well-defined points in the execution of a program. A *pointcut* refers to a collection of join points and parameters associated with these join points. A method-like construct, referred to as an *advice*, is used to define aspect code executed *before*, *after* or *in place* of a join point. Static crosscutting affects the static structure of a program, such as classes, interfaces, and the type hierarchy. *Inter-type declarations* are used to *introduce* new fields and methods into classes or interfaces. The *declare parents* construct is used to modify the existing type hierarchy. An aspect module includes pointcuts, the associated advices, inter-type declarations, and declare parents constructs.

In the context of middleware, we refer to *aspect-oriented programming approaches* as existing software platforms that expose hooks for applications using these platforms to adapt, alter, modify, or extend the normal execution flow of a service requested. In that sense, the CORBA interceptor mechanisms, although not explicitly positioned as an aspect-oriented approach, belongs to this category. Other recent examples, explicitly positioning themselves as aspect-oriented approaches, are the JBoss AOP approach [3] and the Spring AOP approach [1]. The key difference to our work is that these approaches expose a number of hooks for enabling the use of the middleware in an aspect-oriented style. However, our main objective is to build aspect-oriented middleware through the use of aspect-oriented programming techniques, with the goal of increasing the modularity of the resulting middleware, to improve the concern separation in the middleware implementation, and to ultimately enable an automated model-driven approach.

AspectJ2EE [5] is a new aspect-oriented language, specifically targeted at the generalized implementation of J2EE application servers and applications. It is a programming language that could form the basis for an approach like ours.

Other approaches have used aspects for the development of middleware, for example, Facet [11] illustrates the use of aspects for the development of an event channel. We have shown how middleware implementations can be successfully refactored with aspects, increasing modularity and configurability [24,22]. None of these approaches investigates reusability of aspects and effects of aspects on the evolution, as is our objective with Modelware.

Some work has been done on designing reusable aspects. Clarke and Walker[4] suggest the use of compositional patterns to better decouple the implementation of crosscutting concerns from the base classes of a system. Soares *et al.* [19] show how the use of *abstract aspects* effects the re-usability of aspects refactored from a health-care management system. Both approaches are very different from the role-based approach of designing aspect-oriented libraries presented in this paper.

Model-driven Development. Generally speaking, model-driven development refers to a software development process that based on models of the software synthesized code. The Model Driven Architecture process (MDA) is one promi-

---

[5] AspectJ, http://www.eclipse.org/~aspectj

nent examples of a model-driven development approach. MDA advocates developing complex systems through multiple and hierarchical viewpoints. The "Platform Independent Viewpoint" and the associated "Platform Independent Model" does not specify the details necessary for running the system on a particular platform, which makes it suitable for abstracting the essential functionalities of a system across a number of middleware platforms. By combining the specifications of the PIM with the details of how to use a particular type of platform, a "Platform Specific Model" is established. A set of mapping rules relate a PIM to its PSM that lays out the details with respect to a given middleware platform. How mappings can be effectively realized is still in question. The approach suggested in this paper is one possible realization for automating the mapping between different views and models.

Other approaches aiming at realizing a model-driven approach are [17,2]. CoSMIC [17] defines a set of domain-specific tools for composing and deploying distributed real-time and embedded middleware-based applications. Bonnet *et al.* [2] describe a model-driven software process for the automated configuration and personalization of smart card software. Both approaches do not employ aspect-oriented techniques, which is central to our approach.

3   Generic Models in Modelware

The orthogonal natures among middleware functionalities allow Modelware to enable multiple viewpoints at the architectural level: a *base view* containing common middleware functionalities through a conventional layered hierarchy of modules, and a collection of *aspectual views*, each containing an "extrinsic" functionality. We raise the levels of abstractions in both kinds of views through models and achieve the following benefit: 1. the components of base view modules become much simpler and more coherent, thus, more tolerant to variations of application contexts; 2. leveraging traditional object-oriented design principles, both core and aspectual functionalities can be flexibly supported with different

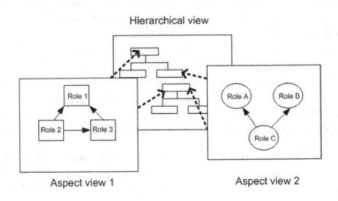

Fig. 2. Base view and aspectual views

concrete implementations; 3. the models in the base view carry many invariant properties which foster the creation of middleware-specific aspect libraries. Modelware can be thought as methodology for attacking the problem of commonality and variability [6] through the combination of conventional modules and aspects.

Before details of the models are discussed, we want to rephrase a few MDA nomenclatures in the context of Modelware. Our definition of the *Platform Independent Model* (PIM) refers to abstract concepts in both the base view and aspect views. We define the *Platform Specific Model* (PSM) as the refined models of these concepts for specific functional requirements or deployment platforms. For aspect views, in addition to PIM and PSM models, we introduce *role models* as abstractions for the behavior of aspects. As illustrated in Figure 2, each aspect view contains its own set of role models. An aspect view interacts with base view models via roles in a non-localized manner.

3.1 Invariant Concepts in Base View

It has long been recognized in literatures [7,16,21] that design patterns play essential roles in middleware architectures. In their specific problem contexts, design patterns exhibit invariance in both space and time. The Modelware base view is composed of a collection of *"invariant concepts"* including patterns as well as a number of design choices which we believe to represent common and essential functionalities of middleware.

3.1.1 Models of Invariant Concepts
The primary responsibility of the "invariant concepts" in the base view is to support the transparent interpretation and transportation of PRC operations. We enumerate a few essential elements and describe their semantics with respect to how they interpret the application requests made through RPC:

1. *Proxies (stub and skeleton)*: Stubs and skeletons are entities masking the middleware substrate as native programming facilities of the user application. Proxies see the application requests as regular method invocations.
2. *Connection facilities (acceptor and connector)*: Acceptors and connectors *"decouple the connection and initialization of peer services ... from the processing these peer services perform after they are connected and initialized"* [16]. Connection facilities see the application requests as a sequence of bytes sent to or received from network hosts.
3. *Protocols (initiator and responder)*: Protocol initiators and responders (also called forwarder-receiver [7]) leverage *connection facilities* and implement a particular sequence of message exchange between clients and servers. Protocols see the application requests as a set of generic messages subject to a specific temporal order and a specific spatial structure.
4. *Request sessions and service sessions*: A request session and a service session represents an instance of interaction among elements of *proxies* and *protocols* in the client and the server side, respectively. Sessions see application requests as instances of collaborations between *proxies* and *protocols*.

5. *Buffer:* Buffer is a commonly used data structure for encapsulating the application data. Buffer represents the application requests as a bounded array of bytes and provides interfaces to manipulate this array.
6. *Messages (outgoing and incoming):* Messages, including both outgoing and incoming messages, represent the encoding and decoding of byte-oriented data in `Buffer` with respect to type-oriented data in user applications. Messages see application requests as typed and directional data traversing the middleware stack.
7. *Servant:* Servant is the internal representation in Modelware of the hosted servers. It serves as a level of indirection between `Protocols` and `Skeletons` to facilitate management tasks. It sees application requests as invocation requests to be dispatched to the destination services.

3.1.2 Simplicity and Invariance

There are two important goals driving our design of the base view models: simplicity and invariance. In Modelware, models of these concepts are kept simple and minimal. On average, there are only around two operations associated with each entity, and most of these operations accept a single input parameter. This kind of simplicity is not arbitrary but derived from a small middleware core refactored out of its complex original version. In other words, this base view is intended to capture the smallest common denominator of middleware architectural variations. In fact, an implementation of this base view is capable of supporting CORBA-style RPC on platforms as small as Java Card, discussed in detail in Section 5.

More importantly, the base view concepts are stable designs surviving evolutions and variations in many middleware implementations. In addition to design patterns, some concepts are specified as standards, such as *request* (specified as streams in CORBA) and *servant* (specified as the object adaptor in CORBA). Others are widely adopted practices, such as *buffer* and *session*[6]. Being resilient to evolution is crucial to the base view in Modelware as it provides the foundation, i.e., architectural invariance, for establishing and integrating aspect views. As summarized by Grady Booch[7], we adhere to the *"simplicity via common abstractions and mechanisms"* principle to manage the complexity of change in middleware architectures.

3.2   Aspect views

Aspect models and views re-distribute the complexity of middleware implementation from a single flat module hierarchy to multiple separated and independent implementations of specialized middleware concerns. In Modelware, each view is oriented upon one or many *roles* specifying a specific interpretation of the Modelware base view. These interpretations are encapsulated within the aspect view in

---

[6] These design elements are present in all of the three major open source Java CORBA implementations, namely JacORB, ORBacus, and Sun ORB.

[7] Grady Booch. The Complexity of Programming Models. Keynote speech at AOSD 2005.http://www.booch.com/architecture/blog/artifacts/Complexity.ppt

the form of additional program states (*role attributes*), interactions among roles within the view (*role relationships*), and interfaces for transferring control between aspectual views and the base view (*contracts*). Each aspect view interacts with the base view through "*projection*": a process of establishing an ontological relationship by mapping aspect roles to base view entities and fulfilling the aspect contracts on them. There are two types of contracts: abstract interception points (or `pointcut` in AOP terms) and abstract operations enforced by roles. Abstract operations link the behavior of a role to an base-view entity. Abstract pointcuts define points of execution and associated computation contexts of the base view for aspect views to intervene. Each aspect view is modularized as one or many reusable aspect components.

Different from generic roles in design patterns as well as conventional aspect oriented treatments of patterns [12,9], we make heavy use of domain-specific roles that know about the base view abstractions such as *buffer* or *transport*. This dependency is necessary for making a large number of middleware functionalities reusable such as the synchronous communication model, the marshalling/unmarshalling of data types, and many others. We believe this dependency does not restrict the flexibility of the architecture for two reasons: 1. due to the strong invariance of the base view, the pointcut mapping is stable because the modular structures and the dynamic behaviours of the base view models are unlikely to change rapidly; 2. the dependency is made upon abstract models, therefore, stay unaffected by the platform specific implementations. To further illustrate aspect views, we present two concrete implementations: the thread-level concurrency library and the data type marshalling library. The projection process of aspect views is presented in Section 4.

3.2.1 Thread-Level Concurrency View

Description: Threads are common concurrency primitives popular in middleware implementations for achieving efficient request handling. From the perspective of the thread-level concurrency view (TC view for short), entities in the base view are of three kinds: non-concurrent, thread owners, and objects carrying the logic for the concurrent task. Currently, the TC view supports two well-studied middleware concurrency models, thread-per-connection and thread pool[8]. The *thread-per-connection* model detaches a new thread for a new network client. The *thread-pool* concurrency model initializes a fixed number of threads to execute tasks simultaneously. Threads in the *thread-pool* model are reused upon the completion of the task instead of being destroyed. The behaviour of threads is implemented in the library and automatically applied to the objects in the base view if these objects "*play*" the prescribed roles through specific projection transformations as illustrated in Figure 3. We discuss details of these transformations in Section 4.

---

[8] A third concurrency model, Reactive, as used in TAO [18], is also implemented as a separate view. Due to the length limit, we defer the discussion to an extended version of the paper.

Type: Domain independent. The TC view does not depend on any abstractions in the base view.

Roles and role relationships: The basic roles in the TC view are *Thread Owner* and *Thread Worker*. The *thread worker* contains the program logic to be executed concurrently, and the *thread owner* is an object in which the *thread worker* is created. Through projection, the *thread owner* role transforms the corresponding base view entities to different types of thread containers, and the *thread worker* role forces the corresponding base view object to conform to a uniform interface used by the internal threads of the library. Each role has two sub-roles to support the afore-mentioned two concurrency models.

Attributes: The common attributes of all thread owners are the base name of the thread, the thread group, and the synchronization primitive. This synchronization primitive is used if the execution thread of the owner needs to wait for the completion of the task in the thread. The *thread-per-connection* owner contains a repository of created threads. The *thread-pool* owner contains a repository of threads, a data buffer, and the size of the thread pool. No additional attributes are associated with the *thread worker* role. View-specific attributes are "mixed-in" with base view entities through AspectJ capabilities as shown in Section 4.

Role contracts: Each *thread owner* role is associated with a set of abstract operations and pointcuts. For instance, threads in the TC view are associated with states, much like Java threads. These states are often required to coordinate with the running state of the base view objects, e.g., observing the creation, the activation, or the disposal of the thread owners. The "stateTranslate" operation defined by the *thread owner* role forces base view objects which "play" this role to provide concrete mappings of base view states. Every *thread owner* is also associated with a set of abstract pointcuts, among which the most fundamental ones are to denote when threads need to be created and destroyed. In the case of the thread-pool model, an additional pointcut is used to define the point when the new data arrive, and a sleeping thread can be awoken to consume them.

3.2.2 Data Type View

Description: Data marshalling/unmarshalling is an essential middleware functionality responsible for translating typed information in the middleware user application into an ordered array of bytes. The data type view is an aggregation of a number of primitive type views, each specializing in dealing with a single middleware data type.

Type: Domain-dependent. The data type view makes use of the *Buffer* abstraction in the base view.

Roles: The data type view consists of two roles, the *marshaller* role and the *unmarshaller* role. They represent entities responsible for encoding and decoding the user application data of the middleware.

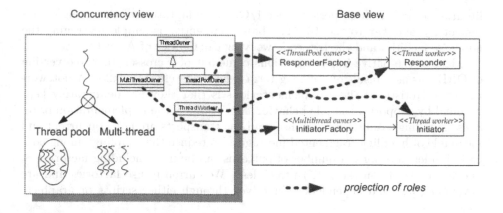

Fig. 3. Roles in concurrency view

Role relationships, attributes: No relationships are implemented between the *marshaller* role and the *unmarshaller* role as they represent two independent directions of data conversion. The data type roles do not have attributes because they are operation-oriented.

Role contracts: Both roles force the projected base view objects to implement an interface for retrieving the underlying data, i.e., a *Buffer* instance.

4   Transformation

The transformation process in Modelware consists of two independent operations: 1. *realization*, mapping base view models and aspect view models to concrete implementations; 2. *projection*, mapping aspect libraries to concrete implementations of the base view. The *realization* operation relies on an implementation library that stores *simple* and *coherent* implementation models. We discuss all the transformation within the Java language framework as it provides a mature environment for supporting both the base view and aspect views. The following sections describe the realization and the projection processes in detail.

4.1   Realization: PIM to PSM Transformations

The PIM to PSM mapping is to establish mappings between abstract model elements and their concrete implementations through either sub-typing or direct substitution. Central to this process is the Modelware implementation library which aggregates two types of reusable components: functional implementations and public application programming interfaces (APIs). The implementation of models can be native, if it is part of the implementation library, or foreign, if it already exists in third-party libraries. Proper adaptation of foreign implementations might be needed to conform to the operations of Modelware entities. For example, Modelware can leverage zero-copy buffers in the Java NIO libraries to achieve high performance I/O. The adaptation of the foreign component `ByteBuffer` to the `IBuffer` base view entity is simple leveraging the language facilities and the bytecode weaving capabilities of AspectJ.

Most of the native implementations come out of a crosscutting free version of ORBacus as a result of our long term refactoring efforts [23,25]. A noteworthy characteristic of these implementations is that they are deliberately kept minimal by supporting simple behavior. For instance, the implementation of request handling assumes no response, and the transports are non-concurrent and incapable of handling fragmented messages. To reduce the coupling among concrete implementations, a number of patterns can be used including factories [8] and inversion of control (IOC) principles[9]. We currently use factories and are developing external dependency directives through either scripts or graphical tools.

The Modelware implementation library also contains modules defining public application programming interfaces. A particular set of public APIs represents a predefined "look and feel" for accessing middleware services. For instance, there are multiple public APIs for enabling the pluggability of network transports in CORBA such as the Extensible Transport Framework (ETF), defined by the OMG, and the Open Communications Interface (OCI), defined in ORBacus[10]. Conventionally, public APIs are typically hardwired to implementations at the development time by a type hierarchy. In Modelware, the base view models serve as a level of indirection between the implementations and the public APIs, so that public APIs can be plugged in and changed at post-compilation time. As illustrated in Figure 4, by separately managing the implementation and the interface, better flexibility and reusability can be achieved by creating the appropriate "look and feel" under external transformation directives.

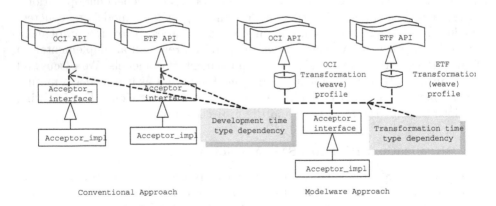

Fig. 4. Transform-time API dependency in Modelware

---

[9] Martin Fowler. Inversion of Control Containers and the Dependency Injection pattern `http://www.martinfowler.com/articles/injection.html`

[10] ORBacus   OCI   `http://www.orbacus.com/support/new_site/manual/4.2.1/users_guide/index.html`

4.2   Projection: Transformation of Aspect Views

The transformation of aspect models and views consists of both "realization" and "projection" operations. The purpose of the "realization" operation is to select concrete implementations for the aspect functionality. This is identical to the "realization" operation in the base view. The "projection" operation consists of two steps. We first determine the correspondence between entities in the base view and the roles in the aspect view. In the aspect library code, roles are represented by Java interfaces and instrumented with additional operations and states through AspectJ. Leveraging AspectJ's capability of type hierarchy modification, this mapping operation is straightforward and affects every concrete implementation of the mapped base view entity. Once the mapping is established, we need to fulfill the contracts declared by the aspect view. This is a process of locating concrete interception points and providing implementations of new operations for the base view classes, as the result of "role playing". Since contracts are composed of abstract programming elements, the enforcement can be accomplished by the AspectJ compiler.

To further illustrate the mapping process, we present a usage scenario of the concurrency aspect view. Figure 5 shows the Modelware implementation of the server-side request handling. While the focus is not the exact semantics of these statements, we want to illustrate a typical "simplistic" Modelware implementa-

```
1 public void ready() {
2     ITransport transport = acceptor_.accept();
3     IProtocolResponder responder =
4         ProtocolResponderFactory.instance().getResponder(reg_,transport);
5     responder.process();
6 }
```
A. Server Request Processing

```
public abstract aspect Threading {
A.      public abstract pointcut createThreadOnInstance();
B.      Object around(ThreadOwner owner):createThreadOnInstance()
1               &&this(owner)&&!within(Threading){
2           WorkerThread t = this.makeThread(..);
3           ThreadWorker worker = (ThreadWorker) proceed(owner);
4           t.setWorker(worker);
5           t.start();
6           return worker;
        }
```
B. Generic Threading Library

```
1 declare parents: ProtocolResponderFactory implements ThreadOwner;
2 declare parents: ProtocolResponder implements ThreadWorker;
3 public pointcut createThreadOnInstance():call(ProtocolResponder+.new(..));
4 public pointcut etherizeActiveMethodCall():call(* ProtocolResponder+.process(..))&&!(within(Threading+));
5 public void ProtocolResponder.doWork(){
6           process();
    }
```
C. Projection code

Fig. 5. Transformation of the thread-level concurrency view

tion – it is only about the operational logic of request processing. Many common concerns are absent such as iterative processing, thread safety, and concurrency. Instead of hardwiring into code as in conventional ways, we illustrate how we enable the "thread-per-connection" concurrency support with a minimal coding effort using the Modelware threading aspect library.

Figure 5(B) is a code snippet showing only the core operations of the thread library. Line A defines a contract using an `abstract pointcut` to capture the constructor invocation of the `ThreadWorker` made by the `ThreadOwner`. Lines B2-B5 create a thread before the constructor call, assign the newly constructed `ThreadWorker` to the thread, start the thread, and return the created `Thread-Worker` instance. The "thread-per-connection" concurrency model requires the base view operation (line 5 in Figure 5(A)) to execute in a separate thread. Therefore, the base-view class `ProtocolResponder` plays the `ThreadWorker` role, and the base-view class `ProtocolResponderFactory` (line 4) the `ThreadOwner` role. Figure 5(C) shows the projection code: line 1-2 modify the type hierarchy of the base view entities; line 3 fulfills the *abstract pointcut* contract by specifying the constructor call of all subtypes of `ProtocolResponder`; line 4 cancels the invocation to the to-be-made-concurrent method "`process`" in the main thread, and line 5-6 fulfills another contract by specifying the method "`process`" is to be executed concurrently. The actual functionality of our thread library[11] is more complex including thread lifecycle management, state transition support, synchronization support, and others. Our experience, also as shown in this simplified example, is that, once the roles are mapped, the code needs to be created is simple and small in size. In addition, since the projection code itself is an aspect module, many different projections can be implemented to support additional concurrency models without intrusive changes to the base view entities. In addition, in scenarios where middleware threading is not required or cannot be used, the plain implmentations can still be used.

5   Evaluation

Our assessment of Modelware examines both the performance characteristic and the programming effort for the use of Modelware models and libraries in building common middleware operations. For this purpose, we choose to support CORBA interfaces as a case study, although Modelware is not designed specifically for CORBA. For the performance evaluation, we compare the Modelware CORBA (MORB) implementation with ORBacus using Benchie [20], an open source CORBA benchmark suite. We also quantify the programming effort in three case studies: 1. creating CORBA-like middleware; 2. supporting functionality evolution of middleware in time; 3. supporting functional diversity in space, i.e., different computing platforms from Java Card, to mobile devices, and to desktop environment.

---

[11] Please visit Modelware website for details of the implementations.
`http://www.msrg.utoronto.ca/code/Modelware`

5.1   Modelware Functionalities

The key base view elements of Modelware are implemented largely by generically reusing ORBacus components such as buffer, acceptor, connector, transport, and GIOP encoding/decoding algorithms. The following properties are implemented in aspect libraries: data types such as long and char, two way communication model, thread-level concurrency, thread safety, codeset support, Java NIO support(including reactive request handling), and many others. These properties are largely orthogonal to each other and can be flexibly combined. The base view elements, without any aspect libraries, are capable of handling remote invocations with octet and integer data types. The reliability of messaging passing is guaranteed at the network level, and the receiving side processes requests passively.

5.2   Runtime Characteristics

In this set of performance evaluations, we primarily want to demonstrate the benefit of the architectural flexibility of Modelware in competing with ORBacus on the same set of benchmark measurements of Benchie. The performance delta should not be influenced much by algorithmic factors but mainly architectural ones since almost all of the critical Modelware functions, such as data marshalling/unmarhalling, GIOP protocol stack, and connection management, are just reused ORBacus implementations. The benchmark tests are performed on Pentium 4 2GHZ PC running Linux Redhat 8.0. We disable the concurrency protection of user applications for both MORB and ORBacus[12].

We present three categories of benchmark tests: a. roundtrip pings representing the minimum cost of CORBA stack traversals; b. data marshalling/-unmarshalling operations representing the performance of client-encoding and server-decoding capabilities; c. multi-server tests representing the dispatching capabilities of CORBA. We customize[13] MORB for these three categories as follows: since the concurrency support is not necessary for tests in categories a and b, "threading" and "thread-safe locks" become redundant and are configured out of the architecture. We denote this configuration as "MORB_A". We enable the "concurrency" support and disable all other features such as "interceptor" and "context" for category c Benchie tests in the "MORB_B" configuration. We have created 12 configurations of MORB for the complete tests. Due to the length limit, we present the more detailed and complete benchmarking results in an extended version of this paper. We show the results of benchmark tests for both MORB configurations and ORBacus in Figure 6. Figure 6:A shows that, for 10,000 pings, MORB shows dramatic performance improvements over ORBacus, as the shape of the histogram of "MORB_A" shifts to the left of that of ORBacus. The average invocation time for MORB is 105 microseconds, a 43% speed-up comparing to 183 microseconds found with ORBacus. We believe this is

---

[12] This is the default policy of ORBacus.

[13] A reminder that our customization only involves changing the selections of compiled classes for bytecode weaving.

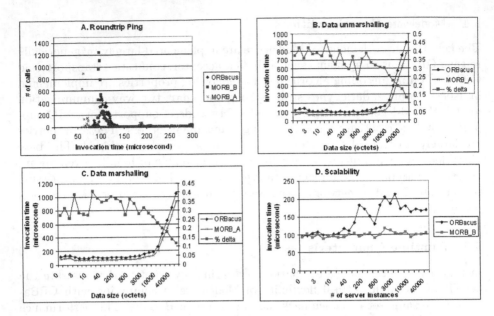

Fig. 6. Benchmark comparison of Modelware to ORBacus

primarily due to the Modelware's ability of lifting concurrency overheads since, once we enable "concurrency" and "thread-safe" features in "MORB_B", the average invocation time increases to 161 microseconds. In the marshalling and unmarshalling performance comparisons (Figure 6 B and C), the improvement decreases from 40% to 12%, as the descending differential curves on both graphs show. This confirms the fact that MORB reuses the encoding/decoding algorithms of ORBacus, and the performance difference tends to diminish, as the data exchange work dominates the request processing. Figure 6 D shows that, in the absence of facilities such as "interceptors" and "context", the dispatching can be more efficient in MORB compared to ORBacus, an architectural flexibility enabled by Modelware to optimize for performance.

5.3   Transformation for Evolution in Time: Platform Evolution

In many performance-sensitive application domains, high performance is often a mandatory requirement in addition to the location transparency. This translates to low overhead and fast response for request processing in the middleware layer. TAO [18] is a successful example of high-performance implementations exploiting techniques such as zero-copy buffer, reactive communication models, and the high speed network I/O. For a lot of conventional middleware implementations, many such techniques are not employed because of the limitations of the underlying OS and VM at the time of the design. The evolution of OSs or VMs might lift these design limitations in the infrastructure but not easily in the middleware architecture. This is because leveraging new capabilities often requires systematic, i.e., crosscutting, changes to many middleware architectural layers such as the data representation and the network communication design. The new I/O introduced in Java 1.4 platforms[14] is an example of VM evolution having profound impacts on Java-based middleware architectures. Its zero-copy buffer and asynchronous I/O primitives can be used to dramatically improve the performance of traditional stream-oriented middleware message passing. In Modelware, this improvement is captured entirely in a separate aspect library and can be transparently applied to the base view at post-compilation time.

The core entities of the `Async` aspect library consist of a reactor and four roles: `AsyncAccpetor`, `AsyncConnector`, `AsyncTransport`, and `AsyncWorker`. The primary function of the library is to disable the blocking operations in conventional Java network I/O, initialize and install "channels" onto appropriate roles, and register these roles with the `Reactor`. The `Reactor` dispatches incoming data to corresponding `AsyncWorker`s based on their registration keys. There are two different approaches of projecting this library to the base view, one being mapping these four roles to the base view model entities. The "async" functionality thus affects all concrete implementations of `Acceptor`, `Connector`, and `Transport`. However, in foreseeing future non-socket based connection management in Modelware, we chose to project onto the concrete implementations instead[15]. The library is 30KB in zipped byte-code size. The projection code only involves base view models and their implementations. Therefore, no new code is created for MORB to become reactive except the mapping of an abstract pointcut. This mapping starts the `Reactor` when MORB is initialized by standard CORBA APIs.

To quantify the performance improvement, we simulate a multi-connection scenario as follows: we host MORB on a IBM ThinkPad T41 running WindowsXP, and we start a number of clients on a Pentium 4 2G box running the Linux 2.4 kernel. The two computers are on a wireless LAN. Each client uses 300 "oneway" calls to warm up, and the time is taken for the completion of the next 300 calls. All the clients are separate processes synchronized by a semaphore to try to create as many simultaneous connections on the server side as possible. Table 1 summarizes the average time for each scenario comparing the reactive MORB with the proactive version (unit is in milliseconds). Our results confirms the findings [15] that request processing based on asynchronous I/O greatly alleviates the middleware overhead of threading when the number of simultaneous incoming connections is large (over 50 in our case). In Modelware, these two communication facilities can be inter-changed at the bytecode level.

5.4   Support Evolution in Space: Platform Diversity

Application domains of middleware systems have diverged from traditional enterprise environments to mobile and embedded devices due to the popularity of ubiquitous computing. Differences of computing environments manifest in the

---

[14] Java NIO. http://java.sun.com/j2se/1.4.2/docs/guide/nio/

[15] As we mentioned earlier, projection is done through "declare parents" statements and very easy to modify.

Table 1. Improvements of using Java New I/O in Modelware

Number of clients	10	50	100	500
Ave. Reactive	43.3	476.98	250.49	620.59
Ave. Proactive	73.1	195.02	135.53	208.67
Improvements percentage	0%	60%	46%	66%

middleware architecture as different APIs, communication styles, data types, and many others, even though the RPC semantic does not change. In conventional architectures, evolving middleware into different platforms or domains often results in non-modular modifications to the architecture so that the code reusability of common functionalities is dramatically reduced.

The focus of this experiment is to measure how well Modelware supports reusability in creating middleware platforms for three dramatically different application domains: smart cards (Java Card), mobile devices (J2ME), and traditional environments (J2SE). We measure reusability as the ratio of the code size (LOC) between reused components in the implementation library and the entire middleware implementation. We distinguish between two types of usability:

Table 2. Reusability study of Modelware in supporting different application platforms

Platform: Standard desktop platform (J2SE)
Overall reusability: 91.36% (cross-domain 16.56%, intra-domain 74.8%)   *Cross-domain reuse:* Buffer, GIOP Protocol, messages, stub, request, response, servant.   *Intra-domain reuse:* Object reference, concurrency control, transport, type support, two-way communication, protocol initiator and responder, OMG interfaces   *Newly created:*ORB interface impl, OMG interface adaptation for Modelware components
Platform: Mobile devices (J2ME)
Overall reusability: 97.5% (cross-domain 24.15%, intra-domain 73.28%)   *Cross-domain reuse:* Buffer, GIOP Protocol, messages, stub, request, response, servant.   *Intra-domain reuse:* Object reference, concurrency control, type support except float & double, two-communication, transport, protocol initiator, protocol responder, OMG interfaces   *Newly created:* J2me version of the ORB interface implementation, OMG interface adaptations as mentioned previously.
Platform: Embedded devices (Java Card)
Overall reusability: 97% (cross-domain 63.53%, intra-domain 34.27%)   *Cross-domain reuse:* Buffer, GIOP Protocol, messages, stub, request, response, servant.   *Intra-domain reuse:* Transport, protocol responder, Modelware hashtable, Modelware vector   *Newly created:* Java card ORB interface implementation

inter-domain reusability, where components are reused in all three platforms, and intra-domain reusability, where components are selected for a specific platform. We have implemented three Modelware-based CORBA implementations: the Java Card platform (872 LOC and 56.1k bytecode size), the J2ME platform (1894 LOC and 219k bytecode size for the full configuration), and MORB (3346 LOC and 283k bytecode size for the full configuration). The J2ME version is created and tested using the Nokia Series 60 emulator[16]. The Java Card version is created and tested on the Sun Java Card toolkit 2.2.1. The Java Card implementation is significantly smaller than the J2SE and J2ME versions because Java Card applications always play a passive role in the master-slave model[17]. Therefore, we only implement the request processing functionality for the Java Card instance of Modelware.

In Table 2, we report our measurements of both inter-platform and intra-platform reusability for these three implementations. For each implementation, we also list the features being reused or created. Our experimental implementations show that different flavors of ORBs can be created with a high degree of reusability. The code to be newly created to support new platforms ranges from 2% to 9% of the entire ORB code size.

6 Conclusion

We believe one of the main reasons for insufficient component reuse in system software such as middleware is the presence of crosscutting concerns. We have observed two major characteristics of this deficiency. Firstly, many middleware abstractions, such as design patterns and usage idioms, live persistently across evolution stages, but their implementations do not exist as development artifacts that can be directly reasoned and reused. Second, many designs and algorithms are repeatedly applied in conventional architectures. Unfortunately, due to their crosscutting nature, no effective ways exist in explicitly representing, evolving, and reusing them.

Our solution to overcome these difficulties is through Modelware in applying the model-driven approach to the middleware architecture itself. The foundation of our approach is to enable "multiviews" in the middleware architecture. That is, we explicitly represent the intrinsic properties or the internal logic of the middleware through platform independent models in the "base view" of the middleware architecture. The implementations of these abstract concepts, i.e., the Platform Specific Model, are stored in the implementation library. The transformation between PIM and PSM models are in form of dependency descriptions. In addition to the base view, we model and encapsulate crosscutting properties of the middleware architecture in individual aspect views. Aspect views dilute the density of the per-module design complexity by exploiting the orthogonalities among middleware design concerns. In our case studies, we are able to add new computing capabilities to Modelware through reusable aspect libraries.

---

[16] Nokia Series 60 Platform. http://forum.nokia.com

[17] Java Card: http://www.javaworld.com/javaworld/jw-03-1998/jw-03-javadev.html

We have also illustrated that supporting functional diversification in space with Modelware only requires relatively small coding efforts.

We are currently continuing in evaluating Modelware approaches in the following directions: we are working fervently in supporting the complete set of CORBA functionalities through Modelware in order to conduct a more thorough comparison; we are working on facilitating the configuration process through tool support and automated reasoning. At the same time, we are also interested in how Modelware supports other flavors of middleware systems besides those based on RPC. Modelware will be serving as an important platform for experimenting with the properties of aspect oriented middleware – our long term research focus.

References

1. Chapter 5. Spring AOP: Aspect oriented programming with spring. In *www.springframework.org*, Accessed 05/2005.
2. Stephane Bonnet and Olivier Potonnie. A model-driven approach for smart card configuration. In *GPCE*, Vancouver, October 24-28 2004.
3. Bill Burke and Adrian Brock. Aspect-oriented programming and JBoss. In *ON Java.com*, 05/28/2003.
4. Siobhn Clarke and Robert J. Walker. Composition patterns: An approach to designing reusable aspects. In *ICSE*, pages 5–14, Toronto, Canada, May 2001.
5. Tal Cohen and Joseph Gil. AspectJ2EE = AOP + J2EE. In *ECOOP*, pages 219–243, 2004.
6. James Coplien, Daniel Hoffman, and David Weiss. Commonality and variability in software engineering. *IEEE Softw.*, 15(6):37–45, 1998.
7. Frank Buschmann et al. *A System of Patterns*. John Wiley & Sons, 1997.
8. Erich Gamma, Richard Helm, Ralph Johnson, and John Vlissides. *Design Patterns*. Addison-Wesley, 1995.
9. Jan Hannemann and Gregor Kiczales. Design Pattern Implementation in Java and AspectJ. In *Proceedings of the 17th ACM SIGPLAN Conference on Object-Oriented Programming, Systems, Languages, and Applications*, pages 161–173. ACM Press, 2002.
10. William Harrison and Harold Ossher. Subject-oriented programming: a critique of pure objects. In *Proceedings of the eighth annual conference on Object-oriented programming systems, languages, and applications*, pages 411–428. ACM Press, 1993.
11. Frank Hunleth and Ron Cytron. Footprint and Feature Management using Aspect-Oriented Programming Techniques. In *Languages, Compilers, and Tools for Embedded Systems (LCTES'02)*, 2002.
12. Elizabeth A. Kendall. Role model designs and implementations with aspect-oriented programming. In *OOPSLA '99: Proceedings of the 14th ACM SIGPLAN conference on Object-oriented programming, systems, languages, and applications*, pages 353–369. ACM Press, 1999.
13. Gregor Kiczales, John Lamping, Anurag Menhdhekar, Chris Maeda, Cristina Lopes, Jean-Marc Loingtier, and John Irwin. Aspect-oriented programming. In Mehmet Akşit and Satoshi Matsuoka, editors, *Proceedings European Conference on Object-Oriented Programming*, volume 1241, pages 220–242. Springer-Verlag, Berlin, Heidelberg, and New York, 1997.

14. Bashar Nuseibeh, Jeff Kramer, and Anthony Finkelstein. A framework for expressing the relationships between multiple views in requirements specification. *IEEE Trans. Softw. Eng.*, 20(10):760–773, 1994.
15. D. C. Schmidt. ACE: An Object-Oriented Framework for Developing Distributed Applications. In *the 6th USENIX C++ Technical Conference*, Cambridge, MA, April 1994. USENIX Association.
16. Douglas Schmidt, Michael Stal, Hans Rohnert, and Frank Buschmann. *Pattern-Oriented Software Architecture Patterns for Concurrent and Networked Objects*, volume 2 of *Software Design Patterns*. John Wiley & Sons, Ltd, 1 edition, 1999.
17. Douglas C. Schmidt, Aniruddha Gokhale, Balachandran Natarajan Sandeep Neema, and et al. CoSMIC: An MDA generative tool for distributed real-time and embedded component middleware and applications. In *OOPSLA 2002 Workshop on Generative Techniques in the Context of Model Driven Architecture*, Seattle, WA, November 2002.
18. Douglas C. Schmidt, David L. Levine, and Sumedh Mungee. The design of the tao real-time object request broker. *Computer Communications*, 21(4), April 1998.
19. Sergio Soares, Eduardo Laureano, and Paulo Borba. Implementing distribution and persistence aspects with AspectJ. In *OOPSLA*, pages 174–190, 2002.
20. Petr Tuma and Adam Buble. Open CORBA Bench Marking. *SPECTS 2001*. URL: `http://nenya.ms.mff.cuni.cz/~bench`.
21. Uwe Zdun, Michael Kircher, and Markus Volter. Remoting patterns. In *IEEE Internet Computing*, number 6, pages 60–68, November/December 2004.
22. Charles Zhang, Dapeng Gao, and Hans-Arno Jacobsen. Towards Just-in-time Middleware Platforms. In *4th International Conference on Aspect Oriented Systems and Design*, Chicago, IL, March 2005.
23. Charles Zhang and Hans-Arno Jacobsen. Quantifying Aspects in Middleware Platforms. In *2nd International Conference on Aspect Oriented Systems and Design*, pages 130–139, Boston, MA, March 2003.
24. Charles Zhang and Hans-Arno Jacobsen. Refactoring Middleware with Aspects. *IEEE Transactions on Parallel and Distributed Systems*, 14(11):1058–1073, November 2003.
25. Charles Zhang and Hans-Arno Jacobsen. Resolving Feature Convolution in Middleware Systems. In *Proceedings of the 19th ACM SIGPLAN conference on Object-oriented Programming, Systems, Languages, and Applications*, September 2004.

Deep Middleware for the Divergent Grid

Paul Grace, Geoff Coulson, Gordon S. Blair, and Barry Porter

Computing Department, Lancaster University, Lancaster, UK
{gracep, geoff, gordon, porterbf}@comp.lancs.ac.uk

Abstract. Next-generation Grid applications will be highly heterogeneous in nature, will run on many types of computer and device, will operate within and across many heterogeneous network types, and must be explicitly configurable and runtime reconfigurable. We refer to this future Grid environment as the "divergent Grid". In this paper, we propose a "deep middleware" approach to meeting key requirements of the divergent Grid. Deep middleware reaches down into the network to provide highly flexible network support that underpins a rich, extensible and reconfigurable set of application-level "interaction paradigms" (such as publish-subscribe, multicast, tuple spaces etc.). In our Gridkit middleware platform, these facilities are encapsulated in two key component frameworks: the interaction framework and the overlay framework, which are the subject of this paper. The paper also evaluates the two frameworks in terms of their configurability (e.g. ability to be profiled for different device types) and reconfigurability (e.g. to self-optimise as the environment changes).

1 Introduction

As Grid computing continues to evolve, there is an accelerating trend towards diversity both in terms of application domains and, crucially, in terms of the underlying networked infrastructures in use. For example, with the emergence of the "pervasive Grid" [11], we can envisage a spectrum ranging from very large cluster computers interconnected with high-speed networks through to tiny embedded devices interconnected by often intermittent and low bandwidth wireless networks.

A more detailed analysis of heterogeneity at the infrastructure level of the Grid reveals the following:

- *At the network level*. Beginning with dedicated intra-cluster networking, the range of network types in use has grown to include: high-speed local networks; lower-speed wide-area networks; infrastructure-based wireless networks; adhoc wireless networks (themselves ranging from relatively static to highly dynamic configurations); and specialised sensor networks.
- *At the middleware level*. Beginning with basic point-to-point interactions (e.g. SOAP messaging and RPC), the range of middleware-level communications services in use is expanding to encompass a wide range of "interaction paradigms" such as: reliable and unreliable multicast; workflow; media streaming; publish-subscribe; generative communication; and peer-to-peer based resource location or file sharing.

G. Alonso (Ed.): Middleware 2005, LNCS 3790, pp. 334–353, 2005.

We characterise these trends as the *divergent Grid*. As a more concrete illustration of the divergent Grid, consider the following scenario which is currently being realised at Lancaster University [15]: *A river and estuary are instrumented with a range of sensor devices e.g. to monitor temperature, water levels, flow rates, pollution levels, coastal erosion etc. Some of these devices (e.g. fixed sensors in tidal defence walls) are networked using standard wired technologies such as Ethernet, while others employ various wireless technologies (e.g. IEEE 802.15.4 or 802.11 radios; or longwave radios for underwater use). Using this infrastructure, scientists in widely-dispersed locations selectively store sensor data for future analysis, integrate and process live sensor data on their workstations, cooperatively visualise this data in real-time (supported by a video conferencing system), and use both stored and live data to computationally steer long running environmental simulations on computational clusters.*

Note that this divergent Grid scenario clearly involves highly heterogeneous device and networking technologies, and also that it demands a wide range of interaction paradigms (e.g. ad-hoc multicast for sensor data dissemination, publish-subscribe for sensor data collection, multicast and streaming for collaboration, and secure channels for database access). Dealing with such extreme heterogeneity is a fundamental challenge for future Grid middleware, and one that is demonstrably not addressed by existing platforms (as is also argued in [7]). In this paper, we propose a platform called Gridkit that tries to address these deficiencies. Gridkit adopts and builds on our previous approach to the development of reflective middleware [4]: it utilises components, reflection and component frameworks to yield a configurable, reconfigurable and evolvable architecture.

But the most novel contribution of Gridkit is that it explores the notion of *deep middleware* in which the middleware platform reaches down into the (heterogeneous) network to provide flexible communications services with which to support a range of distributed interaction paradigms at the application level. Deep middleware can either build on support from an active or programmable network, or can leverage the notion of *overlay networks* [12]. In our previous work [9] we have explored the former; in the present work we explore an overlay-based approach which has the key advantage that it can be applied in 'black box' network environments.

In outline, Gridkit has at its heart two layered component frameworks. The higher layer is an *interaction framework* that takes plug-in interaction paradigms; the lower layer is an *overlay framework* which takes plug-in overlay implementations. See figure 1. In previous work [15], we have provided an outline of the wider Gridkit architecture which supports an API based on web-services and also in-

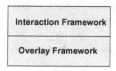

Fig. 1. The overall architecture

cludes frameworks for Grid-based resource discovery, service discovery, resource management, and security. In this paper we focus on the 'heart' of Gridkit: the above-mentioned interaction and overlay frameworks. In particular, we demonstrate how the deep middleware approach can support a rich, extensible and reconfigurable set of application-level interaction paradigms in and across a variety of network types and on a variety of devices.

The remainder of the paper is structured as follows. Sections 2 and 3 respectively discuss the interaction and overlay frameworks. Section 4 then presents a study of the configurability of the two frameworks (how they can be instantiated on different device types) and their reconfigurability. The reconfigurability study focuses especially on self-managing functionality offered by the overlay framework. Following this, we discuss related work in section 5 and present our conclusions and plans for future work in section 6.

2   The Interaction Framework

2.1   Motivation

Grid Middleware that offers only a single interaction paradigm (e.g. RPC) cannot cope with the diversity of application requirements needed by next-generation Grid applications [7]. This is illustrated clearly in the environmental informatics scenario of section 1 which, as explained, involves at least publish-subscribe, multicast-based group interaction and media streaming.

One possible solution to this problem is to *employ separate middleware implementations* for each interaction paradigm required. This solution is implicit in the piece-meal nature of current Grid middleware: e.g. SOAP for messaging, JMS for publish-subscribe, GridFTP for data streaming, and OGSA-DAI for database access. However, this ad-hoc approach has numerous problems:

- being responsible for middleware composition and integration adds considerable complexity to the load on the application developer;
- it is unlikely that all implementations of the same interaction paradigm will support the same programming model, programming language and operation syntax, which further increases the cognitive load on the developer;
- the middleware infrastructure becomes redundant and heavyweight due to potentially common functionality being duplicated across multiple implementations (e.g. network transport, resource management, and security);
- individual interaction paradigm implementations may only operate in certain environments and/or under certain network conditions (e.g. different publish subscribe implementations are typically used for infrastructure-based and for ad-hoc networks) this again leads to redundant deployment, this time of individual interaction paradigms.

2.2   Overview of the Interaction Framework

To address these problems, Gridkit's interaction framework provides a common environment for an extensible set of so-called pluggable interaction paradigms, or PIPs.

The design of the framework is guided by the following principles:

1. the selection and use of PIPs by applications should be straightforward;
2. the programming model of each PIP should be independent of how it is implemented over different (overlay) network types and conditions;
3. the configuration of PIPs, including their underlying overlay support, should be managed automatically based on an (optional) declarative specification of desired behaviour;
4. the configuration of PIPs should also be informed by the currently available network infrastructure and environmental conditions.

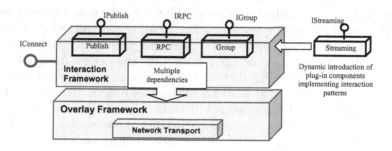

Fig. 2. The interaction framework

The overall architecture and context of the interaction framework is illustrated in figure 2. Separating the interaction framework from the overlay framework has the effect of promoting the reuse of overlays and thus conserving resources i.e. different interactions may re-use overlay configurations that are already in place (for example, a topic-based publish-subscribe PIP and a reliable multicast PIP might both share a multicast tree overlay - see section 3.2). Additionally, figure 2 shows that a *network transport framework* is plugged into the overlay network framework; this provides components (e.g. TCP, UDP etc.) that implement communications services that are used directly by overlays, and that are used directly by PIPs that do not require sophisticated overlay support (e.g. RPC).

The interaction framework does not impose any specific structure on its plugins except that it requires that each plug-in is encapsulated as a single component. However, as our OpenCOM v2 component model [8] supports composite components, this imposes no real constraint.

2.3   Interaction Framework APIs

In line with principles 1 and 2 set out above, we have made every effort to simplify the API of the interaction framework. General experience in the development of reflective middleware has taught us that highly configurable systems are often a two edged sword: configurability is certainly a good thing, but too often its benefits are outweighed by the inconvenience and complexity of having to write many lines of baroque code to achieve a desired configuration. In many cases, this complexity is so great that developers are likely to ignore the available flexibility and use only a small number of default configurations. This is especially relevant in the case of the interaction framework as (unlike the overlay framework) it is generally used directly by application developers.

Because of the variety of interaction paradigms and the need to support future extensibility, it is unrealistic to define universal, fixed, interfaces to PIPs. Instead, we adopt an approach to API provision that relies on the definition of an (extensible) set of *generic APIs*. The expectation is that each generic API will be exported by a potentially large family of underlying PIPs. In cases where a PIP requires a modification of the generic API closest to its needs, the framework recommends that interface inheritance be used wherever possible to avoid a proliferation of top-level APIs. Avoiding a proliferation of top-level APIs is crucial in giving applications some level of stability and consistency, and in enabling them to accumulate transferable knowledge. As an example, a new group communication PIP that addresses message ordering issues could not directly use a group API that is silent on message ordering. However, the PIP developer should extend this generic API rather than add an entirely new one.

In addition to providing recommendations for the structuring of PIP APIs, we have attempted to simplify the way in which applications *select and configure* PIPs. Our approach here employs a notion of so-called *binding contracts* that is in turn inspired by the idea of 'trading' in RM-ODP [23]. More specifically, PIP interfaces have attached to them sets of *name-value pairs* that embody PIP-specific information such as the name of the PIP, its purpose, constraints on its use, and the QoS it provides. Correspondingly, the receptacles (a receptacle is a 'required' interface [8]) of application components that want to use PIPs have *predicates* attached to them whose terms refer to the name-value pairs attached to potentially-matching PIP interfaces. The binding contract elements (i.e. name-value pairs and predicates) are attached to receptacles and interfaces using native facilities of our component model (i.e. the 'interface' meta-model as described in [3]).

Based on binding contracts, we provide a simple generic API to the interaction framework of the form *connect(receptacle)* to which the potential user of a PIP submits its receptacle. Given this, the interaction framework selects, instantiates, and configures a PIP instance based on the following information:

- the set of available PIPs that are currently registered with the framework;
- the predicates attached to the offered receptacle;
- the advice of a *context engine* [5] which supports additional name-value pairs, the value of which varies dynamically according to the context of the host machine (e.g. battery life, network connectivity etc.)

During the process of finding a suitable PIP, the predicate attached to the user's receptacle must evaluate to *true* when bound to the name-value pairs from both the selected PIP interface and the context engine. Section 4 has specific examples of the use of binding contracts and related machinery.

Additionally, the interaction framework (optionally) supports *dynamic monitoring* of binding contracts. Using this facility, any party to the binding contract (including the context engine) can force a re-evaluation of the contract by altering their respective 'side' of the contract. For example, the user can drive reconfiguration of a PIP (e.g. by reconfiguring its underlying overlay stack; see section 3) by altering the predicates attached to its receptacle. To detect such changes, the component model's 'interception' meta-model [3] is used to attach a 'dynamic contract evaluator' to the receptacle-interface binding. This is executed each time a call is made across the binding, and raises an exception if it finds the binding contract to be no longer valid. This exception can either be handled by the user or by the framework itself, e.g., to delete the PIP instance or to attempt to reconfigure it. As an example, the context engine might change a name-value pair to reflect the fact that a live Ethernet MAC layer no longer exists, and the framework might, on that basis, change the underlying overlay from IP-based flooding to an ad-hoc network based flooding. Again, see section 4 for examples and more detail.

3   The Overlay Framework

3.1   Background on Overlays

Overlay networks are virtual communication structures that are logically "laid over" an underlying physical network such as the Internet or a wireless ad-hoc networking environment. They are typically implemented by deploying appropriate application-level routing functionality at strategic places in the network (in principle both at the network edges and in the core). Overlays have to date mainly been motivated by two concerns: i) to alleviate the effects of slow or sporadic deployment of new services in the Internet (e.g. application-level multicast); and ii) to directly provide application-level functionality that is out-of-scope for the underlying network (e.g. large-scale peer-to-peer file sharing). Examples of overlay types are: reliable multicast overlays such as SRM; content dissemination networks; unstructured peer-to- peer overlays such as Gnutella; structured dynamic hashtable (DHT)-based peer-to-peer overlays such as Chord; resilient overlay networks (RONs); gossip overlays; and the wide variety of routing overlays used in ad-hoc or wireless sensor networks. See [15] for a survey.

3.2   Overview of the Overlay Framework

Gridkit's overlay framework supports the design, deployment and management of plug-in overlay networks. In terms of design, the framework mandates that per-host overlay plug-ins are structured in terms of three standard elements (components). These (see figure 3) are: i) a *control component* that cooperates with its peers on other hosts to build and maintain a virtual network topology, ii) a *forwarding component* that routes messages over the virtual topology, and iii) a *state component* that encapsulates key state such as nearest neighbours. This tri-partite structure provides a useful pattern for developers, promotes the

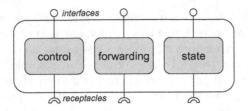

Fig. 3. Structure of an overlay plug-in

dissemination of experience and expertise in overlay development, and facilitates deployment and management. Note also in figure 3 that each of the 3 elements exposes an interface to the higher layer and a receptacle to the lower layer.

In terms of *deployment*, the overlay framework allows one to dynamically instantiate new overlays in a straightforward and lightweight manner. This is supported in a recursive fashion by using overlays to deploy overlays (PIPs are also deployed in this way). For example, a flooding-based overlay (e.g. Gnutella [14]) can be used to disseminate a message that (a filtered subset of) receiving hosts act upon by deploying a node of a new overlay of some desired type (e.g. an application-level multicast overlay). This is achieved by employing a *stack structure* for overlay implementations, and adopting an associated message handling regime that is inspired by the Ensemble communications framework [29]. In brief, the forwarding elements of overlays are organised such that when an incoming message is not recognised, it is passed up to the forwarding component of the overlay above. Given this arrangement, one can place a 'dummy' overlay at the top of the overlay stack that responds to deployment request messages. Such requests will necessarily reach the top of the stack as they will not have been recognised by any of the lower forwarding components.

Apart from its use in deployment, the general notion of stacking overlays is a powerful one, and there are numerous cases in which one overlay can usefully be employed as a substrate for another. For example, one could layer a keyword search overlay such as Gnutella over a DHT-based network such as Chord (as DHT networks do not support keyword search). Or, one could layer a content dissemination overlay such as TBCP [21] over a resilient overlay such as RON [2] to enhance dependability. All such scenarios can be achieved very easily using the overlay framework's stacking structure.

As well as stacking whole overlays, the overlay framework also supports *partial stacking* in which the control, forwarding, and state elements can be separately stacked. For example, we have designed a variant of Gnutella [17] that builds a more structured network than the completely unstructured topology constructed by standard Gnutella. This variant can be deployed simply as a <*control, state*> pair, and an existing standard Gnutella forwarding component in the layer below can be used directly. Another example of partial stacking could be the stacking of a multicast overlay over a DHT-based overlay. Here, the multicast overlay would only need to provide a forwarding component, as the control and state components of the underlying DHT overlay could be used directly.

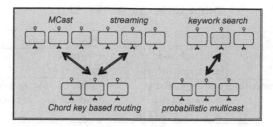

Fig. 4. Example configuration of the overlay framework

Partial stacking not only saves developer effort it also potentially conserves resources, as functionality common to a set of stacked overlays can be reused, thus saving end-system resources and potentially reducing network traffic.

Figure 4 illustrates an example configuration of the overlay framework that involves two multi-layered overlay instantiations: first, a group overlay and streaming overlay are both supported by an instance of the Chord DHT overlay; second, a keyword search overlay is supported by a probabilistic multicast overlay. This demonstrates how multiple overlay networks, both related and unrelated, can co-exist within a single middleware platform instance; and how overlays can be configured on top of other overlays to construct higher-level, more application-specific semantics.

As well as stacking, the overlay framework also promotes horizontal cooperation between different overlays. For example, as explored in section 4, a gossip-based overlay can be used to gossip about crashed nodes in a different overlay, and thus be used to provide a general failure detection service for other overlays. Similarly, an overlay that provides a dependability service for the nodes of other overlays could exploit a third overlay to search for suitable hosts on which overlay nodes could be redundantly checkpointed. As a third example, separate infrastructure-based and ad-hoc-based multicast overlays could cooperate side-by-side to underpin a publish subscribe PIP that must simultaneously operate in both network environments.

Finally, in terms of the *management* of deployed overlays, the overlay framework employs plug-in 'component configurators' [19] that builds on another of the component model's reflective meta-models - this time the 'architecture' meta-model [3]. But in addition, some management functions can be carried out by overlays themselves. Within a single overlay, it is the responsibility of the control part of the implementation to manage, maintain, and repair the overlay topology. But it is also possible to use specialised overlays to manage other overlays. Examples of this relating to failure detection and dependability have already been given above and are pursued in section 4.

3.3   Overlay Framework APIs

The general approach of interfacing users to the overlay framework is identical to that adopted by the interaction framework (see section 2.3): viz. the convention of an extensible set of generic APIs that can each support a family of related

Table 1. Generic overlay APIs

	DHT	Cast
Control	*join(networkId)* *leave(networkId)*	*join(grpId)* *leave(grpId)*
Forwarding	*put (key, data)* *remove (key)* *value = get (key)*	*multicast(msg, grpId)* *anycast(msg, grpId)*
State	*nodes = neighbours()* *addneighbour(node)*	*nodes = neighbours()* *addneighbour(node)*

underlying overlays. In addition, the framework uses the *'connect()'* API and binding contracts to select, configure and dynamically monitor overlays.

Our current set of generic APIs, which are taken almost directly from [10] except that they are factored into control, forwarding and state categories, is shown in table 1. This shows two generic APIs for DHT-based and for cast-based overlays respectively. Following Dabek et al's experience we have found that these generic APIs can be used by a large family of overlay plug-ins. For example, the generic DHT API can give access to Chord, Pastry, Tapestry etc., and the cast API can give access to multicast overlays, ad-hoc routing protocols etc. The complete set of overlays that we have implemented is listed in section 6.

Finally, note that in the case of the overlay framework, the *'connect()'* process naturally recurses to drive the instantiation of stacks of overlays: i.e., if the initial *connect()* call instantiates a new overlay plug-in, the instantiation of this might in turn drive the instantiation of another below it. And so on.

4   Case Studies of Configuration and Reconfiguration

4.1   Configuration

In this section we demonstrate the *configurability* of Gridkit on different computer and device types, showing how different PIPs can be automatically configured and underpinned with overlay configurations in a way that is appropriate to different environmental conditions. In particular, we discuss scenarios in which we configure two different types of PIP on two different types of device: a PC and a PDA. We also concretise the discussion on binding contracts in section 2.3 by giving examples of the use of binding contracts and their associated machinery.

Consider a Gridkit installation that is described by table 2. This shows the plug-ins that are currently registered with the interaction and overlay frameworks, and the context on each of the two device types we are considering. It also shows the current set of name-value pairs for the plug-ins and the per-device context. *RelMsg* means reliable messaging; *GrpMem* means group membership services; and *Net* means network type (i.e. fixed or ad-hoc).

Given this installation, consider the processing of a request on the interaction framework of the form *connect(publish-receptacle)* for an IPublish generic API

Table 2. An example Gridkit installation

Framework	Generic API	Item	Name-value pairs
Interaction	IPublish	Publish	RelMes: F
	IGroup	Group1	RelMes: F; GrpMem: T
		Group2	RelMes: F; GrpMem: F
Overlay	IGroupMessage	ALM	RelMes: F; Net: fixed
	IGroupMessage	ProbMcast	RelMes: F; Net: adhoc
	IGroupMembers	Gossip	RelMes: F; Net: fixed; Net:adhoc
Context	N/A	PC	Net: fixed
		PDA	Net: adhoc

where there is a predicate of the form *RelMes=F* attached to *publish-receptacle*. The steps involved in processing this request are as follows (please refer to figure 5):

- Step 1: the *connect(publish-receptacle)* call is issued by the application on the interaction framework as already described.
- Step 2: the interaction framework picks a PIP that exports the specified generic API, and retrieves from the context engine the set of contextual name-value pairs that are relevant to the type of this PIP - in this case it picks *Publish* and retrieves *Net: fixed* if running on a PC, or *Net: adhoc* if running on a PDA (the name-value pairs deemed relevant for a given PIP are designated by the PIP developer when the PIP is first registered with the framework).
- Step 3: a pattern-matching algorithm (similar to that used in [5]) is used to select a per-PIP 'configuration script' on the basis of the receptacle predicate and the name-value pairs from the context engine and from candidate PIPs (again, this configuration script is provided when the PIP is first registered).
- Step 4: the script instantiates the PIP and then decides on a suitable overlay type to underpin the PIP; in this case it will pick the *IGroupMessage* generic API underpinned by an Application Level Multicast (*ALM*) implementation [21] on the PC because *ALM's RelMes* and *Net* values satisfy both the publish-receptacle's predicate of *RelMes=F* and the *Net* value provided by the context engine; it will, however, be underpinned by *ProbMcast* on the PDA due to the fact that this exports *Net: adhoc* which matches the Net value exported by the context engine; the script also derives a suitable predicate for the overlay receptacle *alm-receptacle* (in this case the predicate will be *RelMes: F*), and attaches this to the *alm-receptacle*.
- Step 5: the script issues a *connect(alm-receptacle)* call on the overlay framework.

From this point on, steps 6, 7 and 8 are analogous to the steps already described above except that they are executed by the overlay framework rather than the interaction framework. The final results are shown in figure 6. Note that the *connect()* process may be carried out multiple times by the overlay framework in the case of a request that indicates a stack of overlays.

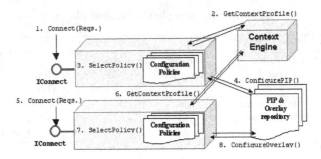

Fig. 5. Steps involved in processing a *connect()* request

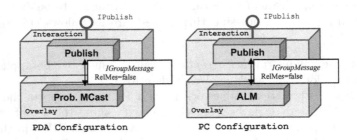

Fig. 6. Applying publish configurations on the PC and the PDA

Now consider a consider a request on the interaction framework for a Group PIP with a receptacle predicate of *RelMes=F* and *GrpMem=T*. A similar process to the above will be carried out with the *Group1* PIP being selected (because of the specification of *GrpMem=T*), and underpinned by *ALM* and *Gossip* overlays on the PC, and *ProbMcast* and *Gossip* overlays on the PDA (again due to contextual differences). The Gossip overlay is used to gossip about group membership (as required by the *GrpMem=T* predicate). The outcomes are shown in figure 7.

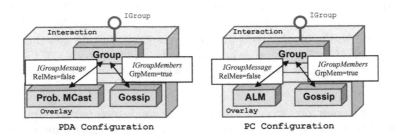

Fig. 7. Applying group configurations on the PC and PDA

Note that the above processes rely on an 'ontology' of names (*RelMes*, *Grp-Mem* etc) which are commonly understood across the two frameworks and the context engine. Although it leads to a degree of 'coupling' between the frameworks, this is a necessary evil in realising automatic configuration of PIPs/overlays. In general it is not as much of a problem as it might initially seem, as a natural convention emerges under which PIP developers build on a canonical set of names used by the lower level frameworks.

Table 3. Memory footprint sizes of the four configurations

Configuration	Static Memory Footprint (KBytes)	Configuration Time (ms)
Publish-Subscribe with ALM (PC)	171	616
Pub-Subscribe with ProbMcast (PDA)	223	3012
Group with ALM (PC)	221	591
Group with ProbMcast (PDA)	276	3776

Overhead Evaluation. For completeness we briefly present the times taken to generate the above configurations and the memory footprint incurred. These are presented in table 3. The experiments were carried out on the following platforms. The PC was a Dell Optiplex workstation with a 3.0 GHz Pentium 4 processor and 1Gbyte of RAM with a fixed network connection and running Windows XP. The PDA was a Compaq iPaq H360 2002 with a 233Mhz StrongARM processor and 32Mbytes of RAM with an ad-hoc network connection and running Windows Pocket PC. Details of the implementation environment of the frameworks are given in section 6.

4.2 Reconfiguration

We now present a case study that demonstrates one way in which *dynamic reconfiguration* of the overlay framework can benefit the overall performance of Gridkit. As previously described, it is possible to simultaneously support multiple overlays in a single overlay framework configuration. However, there is a potential source of redundancy in multi-overlay configurations in that individual overlays often provide (in their 'control' elements) their own proprietary network monitoring and repair mechanisms which may have overlapping functionality. In this case study, we investigate the potential for dynamically replacing individual overlay monitoring mechanisms with a generic mechanism that can be shared across overlays, thus reducing network messaging overhead.

We consider two overlays, each of which we have re-implemented to fit the requirements of the overlay framework: Chord [28] is a DHT-based overlay that performs key-based routing, and Scribe [6] is a tree-based overlay that performs multicast/anycast routing of messages under different 'topics' atop a keybased routing mechanism (e.g. Chord). In terms of overlay maintenance, Chord nodes continuously monitor and repair their network structure by sending control messages to their logical neighbours. Similarly, Scribe nodes periodically send 'heartbeats' to their child nodes, and receive heartbeats from their parents. A detected change in either network (due to the arrival of new nodes or node failures) triggers the execution of a proprietary repair algorithm.

The architecture of our Chord and Scribe implementations is illustrated in figure 8. It can first be seen that Scribe is stacked on top of Chord in the manner discussed in section 3.2. The figure also shows two versions of the control elements of each overlay: an *active* and a *passive* version. In each case, the active version encapsulates the overlay's proprietary monitoring and repair algorithm (as described above), whereas in the passive versions we have removed the monitoring aspect of the algorithm and left only the repair aspect. The intention is that the monitoring element, in each case, will be provided by a common monitoring service.

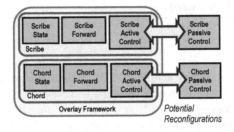

Fig. 8. Chord and Scribe overlays with alternative control elements

Our implementation of this common monitoring service (see figure 9) is based on a gossip failure detection scheme proposed by [31]. The basic operation of each gossip overlay node is to 'gossip' a given message to a specified random subset (K_{gossip}) of its neighbours. On top of this overlay, we have implemented a special-purpose *monitoring overlay*, the nodes of which periodically gossip a heartbeat counter indicating their 'alive' status to local neighbours. Each node monitors heartbeat activity, and if it hasn't received a heartbeat update from a given node in a given time period, it declares the node 'dead'.

In operation, therefore, the intention is that the monitoring and gossip overlays are used to send messages across all nodes in both the Scribe and Chord overlays about fails and joins, and this information is used to replace Scribe's and Chord's proprietary monitoring mechanisms and to drive their passive control elements.

To confirm the benefits (in terms of overall network overhead) of reconfiguring from an active to a passive control strategy, we set up an experimental configuration that involved 10 instances of the overlay framework running on 5 workstations. One of these workstations, designated as the *test host*, was set up to measure the total number of failure detection related control messages originating from that host.

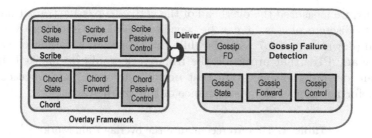

Fig. 9. Configuration of overlay framework with gossip failure detection

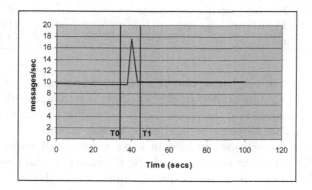

Fig. 10. Investigation of control message throughput in the overlay framework

We then configured the overlay framework to switch from an active to a passive control strategy when a threshold rate of 11 messages/sec of measured control messages was exceeded. Given this set up, we proceeded as follows (please refer to figure 10): We first instantiated a Chord overlay on all the experimental hosts; this produced a control message rate of approximately 10 messages/sec. Then, after 35 seconds (time T_0) we instantiated a two Scribe trees on top of Chord (these were configured so that the nodes on the test host acted as parent to three child nodes in one tree, and one in the other). The Scribe trees produced an additional 8 messages/sec; so at this point the combined number of control messages (18) exceeded the configured threshold (11) and forced the following reconfiguration to occur: i) the gossip and failure detection overlays were instantiated (with a heartbeat/monitoring period of 500ms and a K_{gossip} parameter of 5 neighbours); ii) each active control component was replaced by the corresponding passive version; and iii) the passive control components were connected to the failure detection component. That is, framework configuration changed, at time T_1, from the view of figure 8 to the view of figure 9. Under these conditions, the test host measured a message rate of approximately 10 messages/sec which is a significant reduction of the prior rate of 18. Note also that this rate will remain constant no matter how many overlays share the failure detection service.

Finally, we measured the overhead of the active-to-passive transition, broken down into discrete phases. It can be seen from table 4 that there was a total overhead (downtime) of 1.7 seconds while the transition is taking place; during this time any PIPs that are using the framework would be blocked. However, this is an 'out-of-band' operation that occurs only once, and once completed does not further impact the performance of the middleware.

Table 4. Time to reconfigure the overlay framework

Operation	Time(ms)
Configure Gossip Failure Detection	547
Replace 2 active control components	94
Connect FD to running overlays (Java to C++ bridge)	1141
Total Time	1782

It is important to emphasise that this failure detection approach cannot be applied under all circumstances. In particular, it is only applicable to overlays that are 'fully connected' in the sense that it is possible to reach all nodes from any given node. This property is required to be able to deploy the Gossip overlay according to the scheme outlined in section 3.2 on all nodes that require monitoring. Also, it might not necessarily be the case that the Gossip approach leads to overlays being repaired as quickly and/ or effectively as their proprietary mechanisms achieve. Nevertheless it is a clear illustrative example of the potential benefits of 'horizontally' composing overlays which is facilitated by our framework.

5   Related Work

We are not aware of any other work that is specifically addressing the provision of integrated support for pluggable overlay networks or interaction paradigms in Grid environments. However, there is a considerable amount of related work in the various sub-areas.

In terms of Grid middleware, there are platforms, notably ICENI [13], that support the notion of software components. However, these platforms, so far as we are aware, support components only at the application level: there is no infrastructure level componentisation. In terms of wider, non-Grid-specific, middleware, there are many platforms that take a component-oriented approach at the infrastructure level, and feature plug-ins to extend system functionality. Among these are DynamicTAO [19], UIC [26], ExORB [25], Arctic Beans [1] and RAPIDware [27]. However, none of these support the notion of pluggable interaction paradigms or overlay networks.

There is, of course, considerable research in the narrower field of overlay networks themselves; but this work is largely orthogonal to our focus: we are interesting in wrapping and applying overlay technologies rather than in developing new ones. In terms of generic support platforms for overlays, researchers at the University of Toronto have developed a generic platform called *iOverlays* [20] that supports the implementation of overlays. Essentially, iOverlays is a low-level software cross-connect that forwards messages according to a script that embodies the semantics of a particular overlay. It is thus orthogonal to our interests. Our work also differs in focusing more on co-existence of, and cooperation across, multiple overlay instances which is required to simultaneously support multiple PIPs in the same application. Also in the field of generic overlay support, [10] has presented APIs for common overlay services such as distributed key-based routing, distributed hashtables, distributed object lookup and multicast behaviour. Such APIs offer the potential to simplify the development of distributed systems based upon re-usable overlay services. This is a novel approach that has influenced the design of our overlay framework (see section 3.3). However, we believe that this approach does not go far enough; it concentrates on DHT-based technologies and does not generalise to the many types of overlays that are available (as discussed above). Also, it assumes static layering of overlay types in contrast to our dynamic approach. Hence, we propose a more general approach whereby overlay networks can *arbitrarily* (albeit sensibly) depend upon one another. For example, a publish-subscribe overlay can be layered atop a DHT in one configuration, or a flooding-based overlay in another (e.g. in a small scale ad hoc or wireless sensor network).

Parvalantzas et al. [24] has previously investigated middleware with extensible PIPs (then referred to as *binding types*), and this work has been an influence. However, the present research fundamentally extends this earlier work. In particular, it builds on the availability of the overlay framework to considerably extend the richness and scope of the PIPs that can be provided (e.g. into areas of resource discovery, peer-to-peer file sharing, efficient wide area publish-subscribe, wide area multicast etc). Furthermore, we now accommodate alternative, per infrastructure, PIP implementations, together with their runtime reconfiguration, and also simultaneously support multiple PIPs. We also introduce new mechanisms to support the developer in selecting, configuring and using PIPs.

Finally, there are now a number of established frameworks that support the configuration and reconfiguration of pluggable network protocols. As we have discussed previously, the design of the Gridkit framework is built upon this earlier work; message dissemination through the framework is similar to the Cactus approach [16] i.e. a message is forwarded to interested components only; and the top-level configurator is derived from the Ensemble approach [29]. Hence, with Gridkit we do not present a new approach for the development of such frameworks, rather we apply the concept of pluggable frameworks: across a diverse set of middleware services, in heterogeneous devices and environments. Hierarchical frameworks such as Ensemble [29], Horus [30], and x-kernel [18] provide pluggable stack structures into which micro-protocols implementing smaller protocol functionality are plugged. These systems generally support a single interaction type (normally group communication), and the fine-grained nature of the micro-protocol functionality makes meaningful configuration and reconfiguration of protocols a complex task. Gridkit supports both coarse and fine-grained reconfigurability, and offers declarative methods to define configurations and re-configurations. Cactus [16] is the closest framework to Gridkit in terms of its structure and dissemination of messages through the framework; however, it does not consider the potential benefits of dynamically reconfigurable interaction types nor does it examine the benefits of supporting middleware services with overlay networks. Finally, two alternative systems in this area are Appia and SAMOA. Appia [22] supports the co-ordination of multiple channels (related to a common task) operating within the protocol stack; and SAMOA[32] examines support for the concurrent execution of events across micro-protocols in the framework. Neither of these features are addressed in our current Gridkit implementation, and offer potential areas of future research.

6   Conclusions and Future Work

In this paper we have discussed two complementary component frameworks that respectively support an extensible set of interaction paradigms and an extensible set of overlay networks. The combination of the two frameworks enables a wide range of pluggable interaction paradigms to be instantiated in a wide range of network environments and to be reconfigured at runtime. The combination thus addresses both of the major requirements of the "divergent Grid" as discussed in the introduction.

To date we have implemented the two frameworks and populated them with a substantial set of plug-ins. In the interaction framework, we have implemented the publish-subscribe and group PIPs that are discussed in this paper in C++ and Java respectively. This multi-language integration is a property of the Open-COM v2 component model [8] which we use to structure all our software. We have also implemented IIOP and SOAP-based RPC PIPs (in C++) and a streaming PIP (in Java). In terms of overlay plug-ins, Chord, Scribe and Application Level Multicast (i.e. TBCP [21]) have been implemented in Java, and Gossip and ProbMcast have been implemented in C++. The two frameworks themselves, plus the context engine, are implemented in Java. Mostly, we have used the multi-language integration feature for practical reasons to more easily accommodate already-written software into the frameworks.

Although we have made considerable progress, a lot remains to be done. We have addressed dynamic deployment of both overlays and PIPs according to the approach discussed in section 3.2, and we have experimented with reconfiguration. But there is a lot more territory to explore in the area of distributed reconfiguration as discussed in section 4.2. Also, there are a lot of interesting issues in *cross-layer* distributed reconfiguration that involves intelligent cross-coordinated reconfiguration of both frameworks. For example, a publish-subscribe PIP might be adequately underpinned by a TBCP overlay while most or all of its users are situated in the fixed network; but if the situation evolves so that at some point a significant number of users are situated in ad-hoc network environments, then the optimal underpinning of the PIP needs to be reconsidered and should ideally be supported by a coordinated federation of horizontally-composed overlays.

Additional areas of challenge that we are addressing in a follow-on project are the use of Model Driven Architecture to configure our frameworks and also to provide constraint on their reconfiguration; and the use of autonomic techniques so that the frameworks can not only adapt themselves to changing environmental conditions but can also learn from prior adaptations and make better decisions on that basis.

Acknowledgements

This work is funded by the EPSRC under the Open Overlays project (grant reference GR/S68521/01). The authors would also like to acknowledge our colleagues on the project: Chris Cooper, David Duce, Musbah Sager, Wei Li, Laurent Mathy, Wei Cai and Wai-Kit Yeung.

References

1. A. Andersen, G. Blair, V. Goebel, R. Karlsen, T. Stabell-Kul, and W. Yu. Arctic Beans: Configurable and Reconfigurable Enterprise Component Architectures. *IEEE Distributed Systems Online*, 2(7), November 2001.
2. D. Andersen, H. Balakrishnan, M. Kaashoek, and R. Morris. The Case for Resilient Overlay Networks. In *Proceedings of the 8th Workshop on Hot Topics in Operating Systems*, pages 152–157, Elmau, Germany, May 2001.
3. G. Blair, G. Coulson, A. Andersen, L. Blair, M. Clarke, F. Costa, H. Duran-Limon, T. Fitzpatrick, L. Johnston, R. Moreira, N. Parlavantzas, and K. Saikoski. The design and implementation of Open ORB 2. *IEEE Distributed Systems Online*, 2(6), September 2001.
4. G. Blair, G. Coulson, and P. Grace. Research Directions in Reflective Middleware: the Lancaster Experience. In *Proceedings of the 3rd Workshop on Reflective and Adaptive Middleware (RM2004)*, pages 262–267, Toronto, Canada, October 2004.
5. L. Capra, W. Emmerich, and C. Mascolo. CARISMA: Context-Aware Reflective mIddleware System for Mobile Applications. *IEEE Transactions on Software Engineering*, 29(10):929–945, October 2003.
6. M. Castro, P. Druschel, A. Kermarrec, and A. Rowstron. SCRIBE: A large-scale and decentralized application-level multicast infrastructure. *IEEE Journal on Selected Areas in communications (JSAC)*, 20(8):1489– 1499, October 2002.
7. J. Chin and P.V. Coveney. Towards Tractable Toolkits for the Grid: a Plea for Lightweight, Usable Middleware. RealityGrid NeSC Tech Report UKeS-2004-01, February 2004.
8. G. Coulson, G. Blair, P. Grace, A. Joolia, K. Lee, and J. Ueyama. A Component Model for Building Systems Software. In *Proceedings of the IASTED Conference on Software Engineering and Applications (SEA'04)*, Cambridge, MA, USA, November 2004.
9. G. Coulson, G. Blair, D. Hutchison, A. Joolia, K. Lee, J. Ueyama, A.T. Gomes, and Y. Ye. NETKIT: A Software Component-Based Approach to Programmable Networking. *ACM SIGCOMM Computer Communications Review (CCR)*, 33(5):55–66, October 2003.

10. F. Dabek, B. Zhao, P. Druschel, J. Kubiatowicz, and I. Stoica. Towards a Common API for Structured P2P Overlays. In *Proceedings of the 2nd International Workshop on Peer-to-Peer Systems (IPTPS)*, pages 33–44, Berkeley, CA, USA, February 2003.

11. N. Davies, A. Friday, and O. Storz. Exploring the Grid's Potential for Ubiquitous Computing. *IEEE Pervasive Computing*, 3(2):74–75, April-June 2004. see also: http://ubigrid.lancs.ac.uk.

12. D. Doval and D. OMahony. Overlay Networks: A Scalable Alternative for P2P. *IEEE Internet Computing*, 7(4):79–82, July-August 2003.

13. N. Furmento, A. Mayer, S. McGough, S. Newhouse, T. Field, and J. Darlington. ICENI: Optimisation of Component Applications within a Grid Environment. *Parallel Computing*, 28(12):1753–1772, December 2002.

14. Gnutella Protocol Specification v0.6. http://rfc-gnutella.sourceforge.net.

15. P. Grace, G. Coulson, G. Blair, L. Mathy, W.K. Yeung, W. Cai, D. Duce, and C. Cooper. GRIDKIT: Pluggable Overlay Networks for Grid Computing. In *Proceedings of the International Symposium on Distributed Objects and Applications (DOA04)*, pages 1463–1481, Cyprus, October 2004.

16. M. Hiltunen and R. Schlichting. A Configurable Membership Service. *IEEE Transactions on Computers*, 47(5):573–586, 1998.

17. D. Hughes, I. Warren, and G. Coulson. AGnuS: The Altruistic Gnutella Server. In *Proceedings of the 3rd International Conference on Peer-to-Peer Computing (P2P2003)*, pages 202–203, Linkoping, Sweden, September 2003.

18. N. Hutchinson and L. Peterson. The x-kernel: An Architecture for Implementing Network Protocols. *IEEE Transactions on Software Engineering*, 17(1):64–76, January 1991.

19. F. Kon, M. Roman, P. Liu, J. Mao, T. Yamane, L. Magalhaes, and R. Campbell. Monitoring, Security, and Dynamic Configuration with the dynamicTAO Reflective ORB. In *Proceedings of the 2nd ACM/IFIP International Conference on Middleware*, pages 121–143, New York, NY, USA, April 2000.

20. B. Li, J. Guo, and M. Wang. iOverlays: A Lightweight Middleware Infrastructure for Overlay Application Implementations. In *Proceedings of the 5th ACM/IFIP/USENIX International Conference on Middleware*, pages 135–154, Toronto, Canada, November 2004.

21. L. Mathy, R. Canonico, and D. Hutchinson. An Overlay Tree Building Control Protocol. In *Proceedings of the 3rd International COST264 Workshop on Networked Group Communication*, pages 76–87, London, UK, November 2001.

22. H. Miranda and L. Rodrigues. Communication Support for Multiple QoS Requirements. In *Proceedings of the 3rd European Research Seminar on Advances in Distributed Systems (ERSADS99)*, Madeira Island, Portugal, April 1999.

23. ISO Reference Model for Open Distributed Processing. http://www.dstc.edu.au/Research/Projects/ODP/standards.html.

24. N. Parlavantzas, G. Coulson, and G. Blair. An Extensible Binding Framework for Component-Based Middleware. In *Proceedings of the 7th IEEE International Enterprise Distributed Object Computing Conference (EDOC 2003)*, pages 252–263, Brisbane, Australia, September 2003.

25. M. Roman and N. Islam. Dynamically Programmable and Reconfigurable Middleware Services. In *Proceedings of the 5th ACM/IFIP/USENIX International Conference on Middleware*, pages 372–396, Toronto, Canada, November 2004.

26. M. Roman, F. Kon, and R. Campbell. Reflective Middleware: From Your Desk to Your Hand. *IEEE Distributed Systems Online*, 2(5), August 2001.

27. S. Sadjadi, P. McKinley, and E. Kasten. Architecture and Operation of an Adaptable Communication Substrate. In *Proceedings of the 9th IEEE International Workshop on Future Trends of Distributed Computing Systems (FTDCS'03)*, pages 46–55, San Juan, Puerto Rico, May 2003.

28. I. Stoica, R. Morris, D. Karger, M. Kaashoek, and H. Balakrishnan. Chord: A Scalable Peer-to-Peer Lookup Service for Internet Applications. In *Proceedings of the ACM SIGCOMM 2001 Conference*, pages 149–160, San Diego, CA, USA, August 2001.

29. R. van Renesse, K. Birman, M. Hayden, A. Vaysburd, and D. Karr. Adaptive Systems Using Ensemble. *Software Practice and Experience*, 28(9):963–979, August 1998.

30. R. van Renesse, K. Birman, and S. Maffeis. Horus, a Flexible Group Communication System. *Communications of the ACM*, 39(4):76–83, April 1996.

31. R. van Renesse, Y. Minsky, and M. Hayden. A Gossip-Based Failure Detection Service. In *Proceedings of the 1st IFIP International Conference on Middleware*, pages 55–70, Lake District, UK, September 1998.

32. P. Wojciechowski, O. Rutti, and A. Schiper. SAMOA: A Framework for a Synchronisation-Augmented Microprotocol Approach. In *Proceedings of the 18th IEEE Parallel and Distributed Processing Symposium*, Santa Fe, New Mexico, April 2004.

Opportunistic Overlays: Efficient Content Delivery in Mobile Ad Hoc Networks

Yuan Chen and Karsten Schwan

College of Computing, Georgia Institute of Technology, Atlanta GA 30332, USA
{yuanchen, schwan}@cc.gatech.edu

Abstract. Current content-based publish/subscribe systems assume network environments with stable nodes and network topologies. For mobile environments, one resulting problem is a mismatch between static broker topologies and dynamic underlying network topologies. This mismatch will result in inefficiencies in event delivery, especially in mobile ad hoc networks where nodes frequently change their locations. This paper presents a novel middleware approach termed *opportunistic overlays*, and its dynamically reconfigurable support framework to address such inefficiencies introduced by node mobility in publish/subscribe systems. The opportunistic overlay approach dynamically adapts event dissemination structures (i.e., broker overlays) to changes in physical network topology, in nodes' physical locations, and in network node behaviors, with the goal of optimizing end-to-end delays in event delivery. Runtime adaptations include the dynamic construction of broker overlay networks and changes of mobile clients' assignments to brokers. Experimental results demonstrate that the opportunistic overlay approach is practically applicable and that the performance advantages attained from the use of opportunistic overlays can be substantial.

1 Introduction

Publish/subscribe is a widely used method for providing anonymous, inherently asynchronous group communications in distributed settings. Past work has created numerous publish/subscribe systems, in industry and in academia [1, 7] With the increased availability of powerful mobile computing devices like laptops and PDAs, and the widespread deployment and use of wireless data communications, there is a pressing need to extend such middleware to the mobile computing domain. Moreover, certain features of publish/subscribe make it well-suited to mobile environments, including asynchronous event delivery, anonymity, multipoint communication and content-based routing [8, 10] Current systems targeting Internet-based communications, however, commonly assume distributed execution environments in which clients do not move and where the network topology remains relatively stable. Stated more technically, they assume statically deployed broker networks (i.e., overlays) mapped to static network topologies. A resulting problem for mobile environments is a mismatch between static broker topologies and dynamic underlying network topologies. This mismatch will result in inefficiencies in event delivery, a simple example being a shortest

G. Alonso (Ed.): Middleware 2005, LNCS 3790, pp. 354–374, 2005.

path in the original overlay and physical network turning into an inefficient path when the same logical overlay is used with a different physical network topology. Another example is when a node's movement (either a client, or a broker or an intermediate node) affects the underlying network topology and changes the distance between a mobile client and its assigned broker, hence resulting in sub-optimized event delivery.

This paper proposes the *opportunistic overlay* approach to managing overlays for mobile nodes in mobile ad-hoc networks. The idea is to dynamically optimize content-based event delivery by adapting event dissemination structures (i.e., broker overlays) to changes in physical network topology, in nodes' physical locations, and in network node behaviors. The term 'opportunistic' denotes the fact that the solution is one in which each broker opportunistically acts to improve its relations with both other brokers and with its clients. The key points characterizing opportunistic overlays may be summarized as follows: (1) dynamically constructing broker network topologies to match the underlying physical network, (2) dynamically changing a mobile client's broker assignment based on the client's physical location and the broker's current capabilities, and (3) when broker topologies or clients' home brokers change, recalculating overlay routing paths and then using the newly computed paths.

Opportunistic overlays are implemented with the JECho Java-based publish/subscribe infrastructure [7]. A unique attribute of this implementation is that with JECho, dynamic topology adjustments can be coupled with runtime techniques for event filtering, thereby also permitting the system to match event rates and sizes to the currently available levels of bandwidth of physical communication channels.

The performance evaluations reported in this paper use actual hardware, to assess basic performance properties and penalties, and they use emulation and simulation, to assess the effects of mobility and to better understand the scalability of our approach. Results demonstrate that the performance advantages attained from the use of opportunistic overlays can be substantial. For instance, simulation results indicate that the delay of sending a message can be improved by up to 100%. In a set of emulation experiments, the opportunistic overlay approach is able to both optimize path lengths and address broker overloads. Measurements on a small testbed comprised of three laptops running the AODV protocol [11] show more than a sixfold improvements in the end-to-end delays experienced by events in the flood watch application.

The remainder of this paper is organized as follows. We present the system model, protocols, and algorithms used by opportunistic overlays in Section 2. The prototype architecture and some implementation details are discussed in Section 3. Section 4 presents evaluation results. Related work appears in Section 5, followed by conclusions and future work in Section 6.

2   The Opportunistic Overlay Approach

We first outline the system model assumed by opportunistic overlays, followed by descriptions of the adaptation protocols and algorithms underlying the approach.

2.1   System Model

Our system model adopts an overlay network approach. As illustrated in Figure 1, an event system consists of producers, consumers, and a broker network. The latter is an overlay across the physical network, composed of broker processes connected via links. Each overlay link is a network path between a broker node pair in the physical network. Each producer/consumer (mobile client) connects to one of the brokers (usually the nearest one) via one or multiple wireless links. This broker is called the client's *home broker*. A consumer also provides a content-based subscription function termed *modulator*, which operates on event contents to dynamically tailor them to the consumer's current needs. A consumer's modulator executes in an intermediate broker's address space on behalf of the consumer. The intermediate broker can be any broker(typically its home broker) on the overlay path between producers and the consumer. An event generated by a producer is first sent to the producer's home broker, then routed from the producer's home broker to the consumer's home broker, processed using the consumer's modulator, and then delivered to the consumer via some wireless network links.

An event system with four broker nodes (A, B, C and D), one producer M1, and two consumers (M2 and M3) in a wireless ad hoc network is depicted in Figure 2. Since a broker can reside on the same nodes as producers/consumers or on separate nodes, in general, a link in the broker network is a multi-hop wireless path on the underlying physical wireless network. Similarly, a producer/consumer connects to its home broker via a multi-hop wireless path.

2.2   Basic Idea

The idea behind opportunistic overlays is to continually optimize event delivery, by dynamically changing both broker networks and mobile clients' home brokers. Updates occur in response to changes in physical network topology and in nodes'

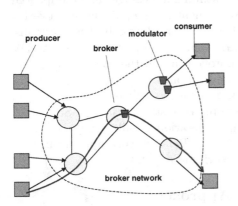

Fig. 1. System Model

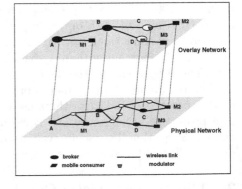

Fig. 2. A Sample Event System in Mobile Ad Hoc Networks

physical locations. Potential broker overloads are avoided by judiciously choosing clients' home brokers. The key points characterizing opportunistic overlays may be summarized as follows:

Resource awareness. An opportunistic overlay is aware of the underlying network topology used for transporting events from producers to consumers. It is also aware of the respective locations of both and of their current state (e.g., CPU Load, Memory availability).

Dynamic construction of broker overlay networks. Dynamic broker network topology construction uses a global state routing protocol [12]. Each broker maintains a local view of the broker network topology. At runtime, an opportunistic overlay dynamically monitors client location, physical network topology, and resources (e.g. latency, bandwidth, broker computation load). Periodically, each broker updates its local view of broker network topology, by changing its neighboring brokers and by propagating changes to its neighbors. Neighbor broker information is acquired by querying the network protocols' routing tables or via neighbor discovery operations [13]. When a broker receives propagated information from its neighbors, it updates its broker topology accordingly.

Dynamic change of home broker. A mobile client periodically checks the brokers in its vicinity via a 'nearest broker search'. It identifies to its home broker a found candidate broker that is closer to its current physical location. Upon receiving such a report from a client, the home broker initiates a broker selection protocol. This protocol uses an approach that combines shortest path selection with load balancing methods. Specifically, the home broker first calculates the path length from the producer to the candidate broker, and then determines whether or not to change the client's home broker based on both the network distance and the candidate broker's current capabilities. Preference is given to the closer broker unless that broker is currently overloaded.

Dynamic overlay routing. Changes in broker network topology and in mobile clients' home brokers will result in rebuilding broker-level routing tables. Opportunistic overlays use source routing for event delivery. Whenever a broker's local view of broker topology changes or whenever a client receiving events from a broker changes its home broker, new event paths are calculated using a shortest path algorithm. We next discuss some of these protocols in more detail.

2.3   Dynamic Construction of Broker Networks

Broker network topologies are kept congruent with the underlying physical network topology by periodically re-constructing global knowledge about the broker network, using a global state routing protocol [12]. Toward this end, each broker maintains its knowledge about the current broker network topology in a topology table T. Periodically, each broker receives its neighboring broker's T, updates its own T, and then propagates found topology updates to its neighbors. Each broker keeps track of the other brokers in its vicinity by querying the routing table maintained by the wireless network routing protocol used in each broker machine, or via a neighbor discovery protocol like the Expanding Ring Search described in [13].

The broker topology update protocol can be summarized as follows.

Step 1: Broker Neighbor Discovery. Each broker periodically updates its neighboring brokers using the Expanding Ring Search. If a neighbor broker moves too far away from a broker, then the original overlay link between the broker and that neighbor is removed from the broker network. If a broker moves into the vicinity of another broker, a new broker link between them is created.

Step 2: Broker Topology Propagation. Once a broker completes updating its topology table by neighbor discovery, the broker sends to its neighbors those items in its topology table that have changed since the prior propagation period. A sequence number is associated with each such update.

Step 3: Broker Topology Update. When a broker receives updated information from its neighbor, it compares the sequence number of the incoming message with its topology table's corresponding items, replaces old items with new ones, and marks the items changed if the incoming items have a higher sequence number.

Step 4: Broker Routing Table Rebuilding. A broker's topology table T changes either due to its own execution of the periodic neighbor update or due to the receipt of topology propagation from its neighbors. When such changes occur, the broker rebuilds its routing table by recalculating its shortest path to other brokers henceforth uses the new routing table for delivering events.

Figure 3 depicts an example. At the beginning, all four brokers (A, B, C and D) have the same view of the global broker network topology A—B, B—C and B—D. At some point, node 2 moves away from B and 1, and closer to C. As a result, two old wireless links 2—B and 2—1 are removed and one new wireless

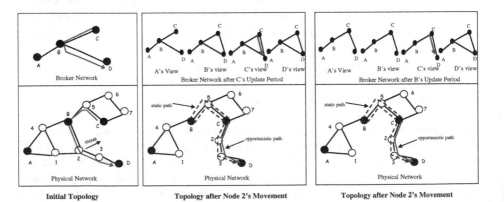

Fig. 3. An Example of Dynamic Broker Network Construction

link 2—C is created. Let's assume C is the first to start its update period. C adds D's as its new neighbor. Then C updates it topology table accordingly and propagates the change to its neighboring brokers B and D. After receiving updated information from C, each of B and D updates its topology table by adding the broker link C—D. B, C and D will rebuild their overlay routing tables based on the new broker network topology A—B, B—C, B—D and C—D. As a result of C's routing table update, opportunistic overlays deliver events from C to D using the wireless path C→2→3→D, compared with the static broker approach's C→5→B→5→C→2→3→D. Let's assume B is the next to start its update period. B removes D from its neighbor list and updates its broker topology knowledge accordingly. B then sends its changes since previous period to its neighbors A and C. Upon receiving updated information from B, both A and C update their topology knowledge by removing broker link B—D. A also adds the broker link C—D to its topology table. At this time, each of A, B and C has the latest broker topology knowledge. D's topology knowledge is outdated, and D's topology table will be updated either through C's propagation or via D's own running of the neighbor updates protocol, whichever comes first.

Our current protocol assumes reliable network communication channels. We leave it to future work to deal with issues like network partition, temporary broker disconnection, reconnection, and related reliability issues.

2.4 Dynamic Home Broker Change

End-to-end latency depends (1) on the network distance between a producer's home broker and a consumer's home broker, and also (2) on the distance between producers/consumers and their home brokers. By dynamically constructing a broker network, we aim to optimize the former. By dynamically changing home brokers, we improve the latter. Toward these ends, opportunistic overlays act as described next.

When a client subscribes to a broker network for the first time, it must connect to some home broker that receives events (via the broker network) on behalf of the client and delivers received events to the client via some wireless network link. Intuitively, we should choose the nearest broker as the client's home broker, thereby optimizing the delay between the client and its home broker. In ad-hoc mobile environments, therefore, home brokers must be chosen repeatedly, whenever nodes substantially change their locations. The procedure used by opportunistic overlays may be described as follows. Each client periodically (or in response to changes indicated by the underlying physical network protocol [14]) executes a protocol that searches for the broker nearest its current location. If the nearest broker is not its home broker, it notifies the current home broker of its discovery. Upon receiving this news from its client, the home broker selects new home broker based on average path length between producers and the client and the cpu load of candidate brokers. If the home broker must be changed, the modulator relocation protocol is performed.

An interesting aspect of our approach is overload control, which is important because end-to-end event delay from a producer to a consumer depends not only on the length of the network path, but also on event processing times at brokers. Processing times are determined by how fast modulators can be executed on home brokers which in turn depends on the home brokers' loads and capabilities. In mobile ad-hoc networks, with clients changing locations, broker loads are subject to substantial runtime variation. One reason would be the sudden arrival of large numbers of local users, exemplified by many mobile units converging at a meeting. Another reason is the use of complex modulators by 'thin' clients, such as modulators that implement the flexible data transcoding required by such clients [7]. In fact, the processing time of a modulator on moderately to highly loaded brokers can exceed network delays by an order of magnitude.

The protocol followed to change home brokers can be summarized as follows.

Step 1: Nearest Broker Search. Each client searches the broker nearest to its location, periodically, using the same algorithm in broker neighbor update as described in Section 2.3. When a client finds the nearest broker that is not its current home broker, it shares with its current home broker the newly discovered broker along with its distance to that broker.

Step 2: Home Broker Selection. A client's home broker is selected from its current home broker and the newly discovered broker based on their distances to the client and their CPU load.

Step 3: Modulator Relocation. The relocation protocol relocates a client's modulator from its current home broker (source broker) to a new broker (destination broker), asks all producers' home brokers to compute paths to the new home broker, and switches event delivery from the old to the new paths. The relocation protocol guarantees event order, prevent event duplication or event loss, and ensure consistent event state. For applications that do not need such strict semantics, lighter weight protocols are used to loosen the requirements

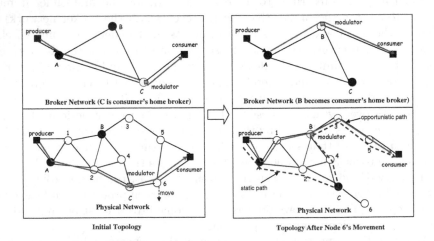

Fig. 4. An Example of Dynamic Home Broker Change

of event state consistency or modulator consistency or both. Additional detail about the relocation protocols appears in [15].

An example of dynamic home broker change is shown in Figure 4. A consumer originally receives events from broker C via the path producer→A→C→consumer corresponding to the physical network path producer→A→2→C→6→consumer. Broker C is the consumer's home broker. The consumer's modulator is also placed on C and executes there. At some point in time, with node 6 moving away from the consumer and node 5, during the consumer's nearest broker discovery period, it discovers that it is closer to B than C. When the consumer detects this, it sends a home broker change request along with B's information to C. C will choose B as the consumer's new home broker, since A→B→consumer is shorter than A→C→consumer under the new network topology. C then performs the modulator relocation protocol. After the change, the event delivery path from producer to consumer becomes producer→A→1→B→3→5→consumer. In contrast, without changing home brokers, the old overlay path producer→A→C→ consumer corresponds to the physical network path producer→ A→2→C→4→B →3→5→ consumer, which is 2 hops longer than the path used by opportunistic overlays.

3   Software Architecture and Selected Implementation Detail

3.1   Overview of JECho

Opportunistic overlays are realized with the JECho distributed event system [7]. JECho implements a publish/subscribe communication paradigm, providing services to distributed, concurrently executing components via event channels. Using JECho's *modulators*, individual event consumers can dynamically tailor event flows to their own needs, thereby adapting to runtime changes in component behaviors and needs and/or changes in platform resources. Modulators are implemented as Java objects, executed in a source's or broker's address space on behalf of clients.

3.2   Overview of Software Architecture

Opportunistic overlays are implemented as depicted in Figure 5. The architecture makes it easy to implement alternate adaptation methods, and the architecture itself is easy to reconfigure and extend.

The basic component layer provides the lower level functionalities of resource monitoring and broker information management necessary for implementing different adaptations. Event-driven adaptations are implemented by defining a set of actions to react to specific events received from basic components. By using services provided by basic components, adaptation code focuses on high level protocol only without needing to handle lower level details. The interaction between basic component layer and adaptation layer uses a set of consistent program interfaces and system events. As a result, it is easy for different brokers to define different adaptations based on their capabilities and requirements. In

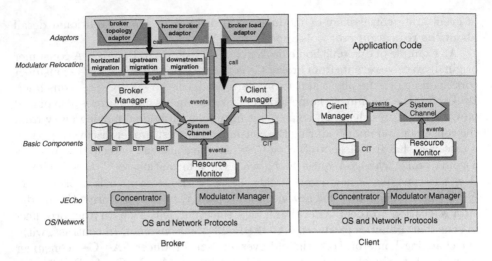

Fig. 5. Opportunistic Overlays Software Architecture

fact, the implementation of an adaptation protocol within the current system is straightforward, as exemplified by the home broker change adaptation that has less than 50 lines Java code. It is also easy to reconfigure and extend the system with new adaptations, such as those needed to handle physical network partition. For future work, we are considering adding a policy layer that permits users to define high-level policies concerning the adaptations being carried out [15].

3.3 Basic Component Layer

The basic component layer layer is composed of a resource monitor, broker manager, and client manager. Components in this layer provide the core functionality implementing the adaptation protocols described in Section 2.2. Each component in this layer defines a set of program interfaces for other components to access its services (i.e., a set of 'get' and 'set' functions). Each component notifies other components and high level protocols by sending events containing the relevant information to an internal 'system' channel. Other components receive this information by registering their interests about certain events.

Resource Monitor. The Resource Monitor collects, aggregates, processes, and delivers data about local resource availability and about its communication costs to other brokers. Local resource information includes CPU load, memory availability, and modulator execution time.

Broker Manager. The Broker Manager maintains four tables, which are the Broker Neighbor Table (BNT), the Broker Information Table (BIT), the Broker Topology Table (BTT), and the Broker Routing Table (BRT). The set of program interfaces provided by the Broker Manager to higher level protocols include functions for accessing and changing broker-related information, and operations that propagate its broker topology to neighboring brokers. The Broker Manager is also responsible for sending notifications to higher level components when it receives them.

Client Manager. The Client Manager maintains information about each client for which the broker is currently acting as home broker, including its name, IP address, physical location, as well as related path information (e.g., current routing path and communication overhead of the path). This information is stored in the Client Information Table (CIT).

3.4   Modulator Relocation Layer

Layered above the basic component layers are three modulator relocation operations: horizontal relocation, upstream relocation, and downstream relocation. Relocation operations perform the task of relocating a client's modulator from current broker to another broker, and of changing event delivery paths accordingly. Relocation operations are the basic functionality needed to support home broker changes and dynamic load balancing.

3.5   Adaptation Protocol Layer

The adaptation protocol layer implements a variety of protocols, including 'dynamic broker network construction' and 'dynamic home broker change'. Each such protocol is implemented with a Java object called an *adaptor*. An adaptor can register with the system event channel by specifying its interests in certain events delivered by the Resource Monitor, Broker Manager, and Client Manager. For the broker topology adaptor, interesting events are a time event and a broker propagation event. The interesting event for the home broker adaptor is a broker discovery message received from a client. The code in the adaptor is implemented in the event handler method "process( )", which is invoked whenever an interesting event is received. This code implements changes, such as reconfiguring the broker network, changing the home broker, or rebuilding a routing table. Using adaptors and the services provided by basic components, system developers can create potentially complex adaptation policies. Our prototype implementation has three adaptors: a broker topology construction adaptor, a home broker change adaptor and a broker load balancing adaptor. Each adaptor performs the task for which it is named.

3.6   Client Component

The final element of opportunistic overlays are client-resident components that interact with the broker overlay. These include a Resource Monitor and Client Manager.

4   Performance Evaluation

4.1   Simulation

Simulation techniques are used to evaluate the opportunistic overlay approach under various wireless network configurations. In all experiments reported in this section, the network consists of 100 mobile nodes that randomly roam in a 1000 x 1000 meter square. The random waypoint mobility model [16] is used with a pause time of 10 seconds. The radio transmission range of each node is 250 meters. Each simulation spans 600 seconds of simulated time.

Currently, our simulation study is limited to high level overlay routing, for which link layer details and physical layer characteristics are not modeled explicitly. Since aspects like control overheads or link contention are not taken into account, a high routing packet load, for instance, does not interfere as much with data transmissions as it might in reality. Also, there are no transmission errors and delays associated with overlay routing packets (i.e., broker network topology propagation and broker neighbor discovery). Future work should address these limitations by constructing a more comprehensive simulator with a MAC layer model (e.g., IEEE 802.11 MAC). The point of this section's simulation results is to compare the relative performance of the opportunistic approach to overlay routing vs. static approaches.

Performance of the Broker Network. The first set of experiments evaluate the average lengths of network paths across broker overlays with vs. without opportunistic overlay protocols. Measurements consider only brokers, not clients. 40 nodes among 100 nodes are randomly chosen as brokers. We vary the experimental configurations with different broker topology update intervals. The path length from broker B1 to broker B2 is the corresponding physical network distance of the shortest broker path between B1 and B2, which is computed based on B1's local knowledge of current broker topology. The average path length from each broker to all other brokers is computed and averaged over all brokers. In order to establish a basis for comparison, we also measure the average length of the physical network path between each pair of brokers. In addition, the overheads of broker topology update with different update intervals are evaluated.

Timeline of Path Length. Figure 6 shows how path length changes in a simulation with an update interval of 50 seconds and mobility speeds between 1

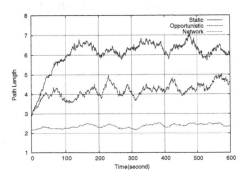
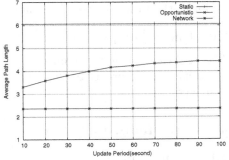
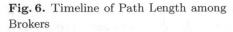

Fig. 6. Timeline of Path Length among Brokers

Fig. 7. Average Path Length among Brokers versus Update Period

m/s and 20m/s. As shown in the figure, the opportunistic approach can deliver events more efficiently than the static approach at almost all time points. At the beginning, both the static and the opportunistic approaches have similar path lengths, since the initial broker network matches physical network topology. As time passes, the path lengths of the static approach increase rapidly because the initial broker topology cannot reflect changes in physical network topology caused by node mobility. Compared with the static approach's 6.06 hops and the network's 2.36 hops, the opportunistic approach has an average path length of only 4.17 hops.

Average Path Length versus Broker Update Period. Figure 7 shows the average path length versus the update interval, the latter varying from 10 to 100 seconds. As expected, with increased update intervals, path length increases since larger update intervals imply slower reactions to changes in physical network topology. However, as shown in the figure, the change in path length is not rapid with the increase of update periods, e.g. 4.43 hops with an interval of 100 seconds versus 3.32 hops with one of 10 seconds. Even with a relatively low update period of 100 seconds, the opportunistic approach still outperforms the static approach significantly, 4.43 hops vs. 6.06 hops.

Update Overhead versus Broker Update Period. The overheads of broker network updates are shown in Figure 8. Overhead is computed as the average bandwidth requirement of each broker for propagating its broker topology knowledge to its neighbors, the argument being that network resources tend to be scarce in pervasive systems. As shown in the figure, a total of 2.4 Kbps bandwidth is used with an update period of 50 seconds. This constitutes moderate bandwidth usage in modern network infrastructures.

Performance of Event Delivery between Mobile Clients. Most relevant to our work, of course, is the end-to-end performance experienced by end users, i.e., clients. In the following experiments, we randomly choose 20 brokers, 10 event producers, and 60 event consumers from 100 mobiles nodes. In this set of

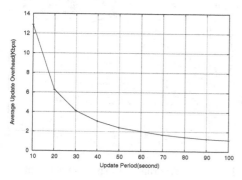

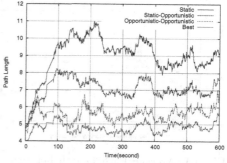

Fig. 8. Update Overhead versus Update Period

Fig. 9. Timeline of Average Path Length between Producers and Consumers

experiments, the broker network update interval is fixed at 20 seconds, and we vary mobile clients' home broker discovery periods as well as mobility speed. Four different approaches are evaluated in terms of the resulting average path lengths between each pair of producer and receiver: (1) the static approach changes neither the broker network topology nor the home broker of mobile clients; (2) the static-opportunistic approach change mobile client's home broker only; (3) the opportunistic-opportunistic changes both the broker network topology and mobile client's home broker; and (4) the best approach keeps updating the broker network whenever the physical network changes and calculates shortest broker paths based on up-to-date physical network topology data. Although the best approach is not practical, we have included it to establish a basis for comparison.

Timeline of Path Length. Figure 9 shows the performance results of a simulation with a home broker discovery period of 10 seconds. We can see that the opportunistic-opportunistic approach performs best among the three realistic approaches, shortening the delivery paths up to 5 hops compared with the static approach. Even the static-opportunistic approach can improve event delivery significantly compared with the static approach.

Average Path Length versus Nearest Broker Discovery Period. Studies assessing path lengths versus home broker discovery periods are reported in Figure 10. With increased closest broker discovery periods, path lengths increase slightly. As discussed in Section 2, the mobile client can find the nearest broker by querying its routing table or by using an expanding ring protocol. Either way, the costs are small compared with the overheads of broker update operations. More frequent closest broker discovery results in more frequent home broker changes, hence more frequent modulator relocations. Additional simulation results not reported here due to space limitations demonstrate the fact that modulator relocation costs are much smaller than the overheads of broker topology change (see [15] for more detail).

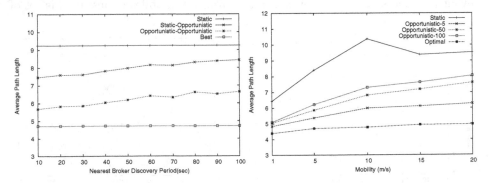

Fig. 10. Average Path Length between Producers and Consumers versus Nearest Broker Discovery Period

Fig. 11. Average Path Length between Producers and Consumers versus Mobility

Average Path Lengths versus Mobility. Average path lengths at different mobility speeds is shown in Figure 11. The figure shows that more frequent nearest broker discovery achieves shorter event delivery paths. In particular, when the nodes move at a very fast speed, increasing the discovery frequency can improve the performance significantly.

Simulation Conclusions. Multiple insights result from the simulation experiments described in this section. First, client or broker mobility in ad-hoc networked systems demand dynamic changes to the overlay networks used for event propagation. Without runtime overlay adjustments, event delivery paths and therefore, average event delays increase substantially and may not remain viable for realistic systems and applications. Interestingly, even relatively 'slow' overlay adjustments performed by the opportunistic overlay approach attain much improved results compared to static solutions (e.g., with 100 second update intervals, the opportunistic approach results in an average of 4.43 hops for packets vs. the static approach's 6.06 hops). Second, end-to-end delays in packet delivery to clients are improved further when overlay adjustments are complemented with changes in the assignment of home brokers to clients. Since it is cheaper to change home brokers than to reconfigure broker overlays, the former changes can be (and should be) more frequent than the latter. Finally, change frequencies are strongly correlated with mobility speeds.

4.2 System Emulation

In order to evaluate the effects of load balancing, we have conducted a set of experiments on an ad-hoc wireless network emulator. The mobility emulator runs on a Linux cluster of 20 nodes with MobiEmu [17] running on each node. The cluster network is a gigabit Ethernet switch. MobiEmu is a software platform for testing and analyzing ad-hoc network protocols and applications. With control software running on each node, MobiEmu mimics dynamic connectivity among nodes by dynamically installing or removing packet filters for specific MAC addresses. Since we focus on load balancing in this set of experiments, we use the 'best-case' ad-hoc routing provided by MobiEmu software. These protocols always deliver packets via shortest network paths. More detail about this system appears in [17].

The emulated mobile network consists of 20 mobile nodes, of which 5 nodes are event brokers, 5 are event producers and 15 are event consumers (5 brokers reside at event receiver nodes). In our experiments, mobile nodes move in a space of 750m x 500m and use random waypoint mobility with a pause time of 30 seconds and speeds between 1m/s and 20m/s. Due to the relatively small network size, the broker update period is set to 5 seconds and the nearest broker discovery period to 1 second. We vary the average load of the broker network and measure the maximum load during execution.

Results appear in Figure 12. As shown in the figure, when broker load is relatively light (i.e., less than 30%), there are no overloaded brokers and both approaches behave the same, where the nearest broker to a mobile client is always chosen as the client's home broker. With increased system load, without

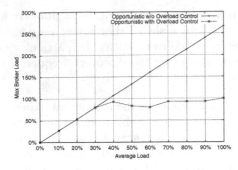 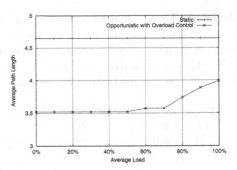

Fig. 12. Maximum Broker Load versus Average System Load

Fig. 13. Path Length versus System Load

overload control, some brokers become overloaded. The load balancing algorithm ameliorates this problem, because a client's home broker will not be moved to an overloaded node, even if that node is closer than the old one. The positive outcomes of load management reported in these measurements are moderate, of course, since in random waypoint mobility, nodes move independently. Load balancing is more important and will have more significant effects when nodes move in groups, as exemplified by conference participants moving from one presentation venue to another, for instance.

Figure 13 depicts path length versus system load. When system load is less than 70%, the opportunistic approach always chooses the nearest broker as home broker, and the delivery path can be more than 1 hop shorter than in static approach. With increased system load, load balancing selects broker with lighter loads on relatively longer paths, resulting in increased path lengths. However, the opportunistic approach continues to outperform the static approach even when system load reaches 100%.

The simple conclusion from these measurements is that realistic implementations of dynamic overlay networks for MANET should not ignore broker loads, especially when overlays perform meaningful application-level processing actions.

4.3   Testbed

The last set of experiments demonstrate the practical utility of our approach, by running a sample application on an actual wireless testbed. The testbed consists of 3 laptops A, B and C. Wireless connectivity is provided by Orinoco 802.11b cards. These cards are set to ad-hoc mode on channel 8. No WEP encryption is used. All three laptops use the UoB JAODV version 0.2, an AODV implementation in Java [11]. In order to simulate network connectivity changes, we dynamically set filters at the MAC layer. In a network consisting of 3 nodes A,B and C, there are four possible network topologies without network partitions: A-B-C, A-B-C-A , A-C-B and B-A-C.

The experiments being performed run a flood watch application on the testbed, comparing the event delivery latency of the opportunistic with the static

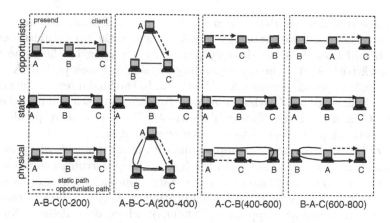

Fig. 14. Experiment Configuration

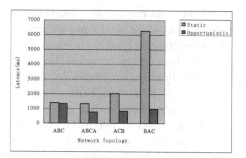

Fig. 15. Average Latency (100% data)   **Fig. 16.** Average Latency (10% data)

approach using the 4 different network topologies. The application consists of two programs and works as follows. PreSend reads precipitation data from a file and places normalized precipitation data on event channel. A client program subscribes to the channel and provides a modulator that calculates water depth from precipitation data and terrain topology data using a runoff model. The client is typically interested in flood information in some specific area, which can be defined by a two-dimensional bounding box. Flood data that is outside the bounding box will be filtered (i.e., removed) before data is sent to the channel. The output of full-size flood data is a double array of 100 x 100.

In our experiment, PreSend is running on laptop A and the client program runs on laptop C. Broker programs run on both A and B. The physical network topology changes every 200 time units. Experiment configuration is shown in Figure 14. The initial physical network topology is A-B-C. B is C's home broker. Both approaches use the same event delivery path A→B→C. After 200 time units, the network topology changes to A-B-C-A, so that the opportunistic approach chooses A as C's home broker and relocates its modulator from B to A, hence resulting the shorter delivery path A→C. During the time interval of 400 to 600, the network topology is A-C-B, where the opportunistic overlay approach still uses A→C as delivery path corresponding to the same physical network path A→C. The corresponding physical network path of A→B→C used by static approach becomes A→C→B→C. In the final interval, the network topology changes to B-A-C, where the opportunistic approach still uses the same path A→C, and the static approach's path A→B→C now corresponds to the physical network path A→B→A→C, with overlap at A.

Figure 15 shows the latency comparisons with four topologies when the client is interested in all data. As shown in the figure, the opportunistic approach can deliver data up to 6 times faster than the static approach. The static approach has its worst performance in the configuration of B-A-C (6000ms compared with to the opportunistic approach's 1000ms), where data delivery following the path A→B→A→C results not only in a longer path but also in additional network bandwidth usage at A, since at the physical layer, every event is actually delivered twice at A.

When a client is interested in only 10% of the area data, the opportunistic approach coupled with its use of modulators shows additional improvements. Results depicted in Figure 16 show that by relocating C's modulator from B to A, the opportunistic approach not only delivers data following a shorter path but also delivers less data, hence improving the application's performance significantly: the average latency is less than 200ms under all network configurations.

The key result of the testbed experiments presented here is that it is important to dynamically adjust the middleware overlays used in pervasive systems. The opportunistic overlay approach described and evaluated in our research is one method for runtime overlay management and by using it, significant performance improvements can be attained compared to non-adaptive approaches.

5   Related Work

5.1   Content-Based Event Systems

Publish/subscribe systems [1, 18, 4–7] have been investigated for many years, but most implementations have focused on systems where nodes don't move, broker networks remain fixed, and broker network topologies are defined at deployment time. As a result, their fixed event dissemination structures make them unsuitable for applications in mobile environments where physical network topology and node locations change continuously. In addition, most publish/subscribe systems perform event filtering with predicate-based subscriptions; they do not support the general event processing needed for the complex data conversions occurring in multimedia, business, or scientific applications. Opportunistic overlays are realized with the JECho pub/sub infrastructure [7]. JECho generalizes the capabilities of other event systems, by using consumer-provided functions, termed event modulators [7]. The intent is to address the severe resource limitations existing in many mobile and embedded systems, by permitting event consumers to deploy application-specific functions that manipulate event content into event sources and/or brokers, so as to precisely meet their current needs, and to avoid needless data transfers. Generic function-based subscription makes the opportunistic overlay system more feasible for developing applications in pervasive systems and mobile environments.

Previous research on event-based middleware for wireless networks has addressed applications in which mobile nodes make use of the wireless network to connect to a fixed network infrastructure [19, 20, 10, 21, 14, 10, 8, 14]. The opportunistic overlays presented in this paper differ from these systems in that they are designed for mobile ad hoc networks, support dynamic reconfiguration of event event dissemination structure and offer behaviors transparent to applications.

[22] presents an algorithm for topological reconfiguration in content-based publish/subscribe due to changes in underlying connectivity. Compared with opportunistic overlays, reconfiguration in [22] involves only link removal or insertion, and no details are given on how to apply the proposed approach to handle changes in mobile environments. In addition, the approach assumes a tree-based topology between dispatchers, which makes it hard to achieve robustness, since a single link failure partitions the tree. Another approach to dynamic broker network configuration is described in [23]. The idea is to place 'close' to each other brokers that manage similar subscriptions. This is complementary to our work, which focuses on resource awareness, where reconfiguration in the opportunistic overlays is based on nodes' physical locations and the underlying physical network topology. Similar to the approach in [22], the topology used in [23] must remain acyclic, whereas the opportunistic overlay approach supports general broker overlay topologies.

5.2   Content-Based Event Systems in Mobile Ad-Hoc Networks

Steam [24] is an event-based middleware service designed for ad-hoc wireless networks. It targets application scenarios where nodes are more likely to interact when they are in close proximity to each other. We consider more general uses of publish/subscribe in ad-hoc networks. Further, Steam uses an implicit event model without intermediate broker nodes.

[25] presents a distributed protocol to construct optimized publish/subscribe trees in ad-hoc wireless networks. The protocol builds multicast trees directly on top of lower level radio broadcast primitives. Our work relies on the underlying network infrastructure's ability to provide basic network connectivity. Another difference is that their approach assumes a relatively stable environment with occasional reconfigurations followed by periods of stability. Opportunistic overlays do not make that assumption, and they can actually handle high levels of mobility as shown by our experimental results.

[26] proposes a publish/subscribe system for MANET that integrates an extended ODMRP (On-Demand Multicast Routing Protocol [27]) with content-based subscriptions. Similar to [25], ODMRP-PUB/SUB delivers events by creating multicast groups. The difference is that ODMRP-PUB/SUB uses a mesh-based approach instead of the tree-based one used in [25]. Since a consumer's

subscription is a general function applied to events in our system, the approach of combining a multicast protocol and subscription aggregation/match is not readily applicable in our case. Further, ODMRP-PUB/SUB focuses on the routing between brokers and does not address the issue of delivery from brokers to producers/consumers. The purpose of ODMRP- PUB/SUB is to optimize network throughput, while our opportunistic method focuses on providing timely event delivery.

5.3   Overlay Multicast Protocols in Mobile Ad-Hoc Networks

AMRoute [28] and PAST-DM [13] are two ad-hoc multicast protocols that use the overlay approach. AMRoute uses a static virtual mesh and has low efficiency due to the increasing mismatch between virtual topology and physical network topology, as shown in [13]. PAST-DM addresses the efficiency problem by dynamically adapting the virtual topology to changes in the physical network. That brokers need to process events distinguishes our system from multicast systems where nodes perform data routing and participate as relays. Although opportunistic overlay approach uses a similar dynamic virtual overlay construction technique as PAST-DM [13], the dynamic routing path in opportunistic approach involves not only path changes in event routing, but also subscription code relocation, which makes the existing dynamic delivery technique in PAST-DM is not readily applicable to our system. In addition, the processing of events will consume a broker's computational resources, which implies that brokers' computational capabilities need to be taken into account.

Finally, in PAST-DM, all member nodes are considered to be equivalent peers and participate in overlay routing. In contrast, opportunistic overlays conceptually divide nodes into brokers which are organized into an overlay broker network, and clients(producers/consumers) which send/receive events via the broker network. This model is more suitable for content-based routing since overlay routing through 'thin' nodes with very limited resources will present burden on such nodes and may result in inefficiency of content delivery in mobile systems. Dynamic reconfiguration using by opportunistic overlays adapts both the overlay broker network and the connections between brokers and clients.

6   Conclusions and Future Work

This paper presents an approach to optimizing content-based event delivery in mobile ad-hoc networks. In response to changes in physical network topology and to node mobility, the opportunistic overlay approach dynamically changes broker network topology, clients' assignments to brokers, and event delivery paths, with the goal of optimizing end-to-end delays in event delivery. Opportunistic overlays are prototyped with the JECho pub/sub system [7]. Comprehensive performance evaluations are performed via simulation, emulation, and with representative applications on a physical testbed. Experimental results for mobile ad hoc networks demonstrate that the opportunistic overlay approach can significantly improve event delivery delays compared to static approaches, even with high levels of mobility. Results also show that the overheads of dynamic adaptation are moderate. Using a flood watch application and a wireless testbed, the opportunistic overlay approach is practically applicable in an actual ad hoc wireless network.

Future work should address some deficiencies of our current implementation, as well as generalize upon the basic concept of opportunistic overlays. First, our current implementation assumes a reliable network environment and therefore does not consider dynamic disconnection, reconnection, and network partition. Future work will add application-specific failure recovery to broker overlays. Second, we will extend the opportunistic approach to optimize performance metrics other than end-to-end latency, including network bandwidth and power usage. We may also explore optimizing multi-dimensional performance metrics. A final topic of interest is a performance study that uses a more comprehensive simulator with a MAC layer model (e.g., IEEE 802.11 MAC).

References

1. Strom, R., Banavar, G., et.al: Gryphon: An information flow based approach to message brokering. Technical report, IBM TJ Watson Research Center (1998)
2. Carzaniga, A., Rosenblum, D.S., Wolf, A.L.: Achieving scalability and expressiveness in an internet-scale event notification service. In: Proceedings of the Nineteenth Annual ACM Symposium on Principles of Distributed Computing(PODC 2000), Portland, Oregon (2000) 219–227
3. Cugola, G., Nitto, E.D., Fuggetta, A.: The "jedi" event-based infrastructure and its application to the development of the opss wfms. In: IEEE Transactions on Software Engineering in 2001. (2001)
4. Segall, B., Arnold, D.: Elvin has left the building: A publish/subscribe notification service with quenching. In: Proceedings of A UUG97. (1997)
5. Fiege, L., Mühl, G., Gärtner, F.C.: A modular approach to build structured event-based systems. In: Proceedings of the 2002 ACM Symposium on Applied Computing (SAC'02). (2002) 385–392
6. Eisenhauer, G., Bustamante, F.E., Schwan, K.: Event services in high performance systems. Cluster Computing 4 (2001) 243–252
7. Zhou, D., Schwan, K., Eisenhauer, G., Chen, Y.: Supporting distributed high performance application with java event channels. In: Proceedings of the 2001 International Parallel and Distributed Processing Symposium (IPDPS 2001). (2001)
8. Huang, Y., Garcia-Molina, H.: Publish/subscribe in a mobile environment. In: Proceedings of the 2nd ACM International Workshop on Data Engineering for Wireless and Mobile Access (MobiDE'01). (2001) 27–34
9. Cugola, G., Jacobsen, H.A.: Using Publish/Subscribe Middleware for Mobile Systems. ACM SIGMOBILE Mobile Computing and Communications Review 6 (2002) 25–33
10. Fiege, L., Gärtner, F.C., Kasten, O., Zeidler, A.: Supporting mobility in content-based publish/subscribe middleware. In: ACM/IFIP/USENIX International Middleware Conference (Middleware 2003). (2003) 103–122
11. : Uob-jadhoc aodv implementation, rfc 3561. http://www.aodv.org/ (2004)
12. Chen, T.W., Gerla, M.: Global state routing: A new routing scheme for ad-hoc wireless networks. In: Proceedings of IEEE ICC'98. (1998)

13. Gui, C., Mohapatra, P.: Efficient overlay multicast for mobile ad hoc networks. In: Proceedings of IEEE Wireless Communications and Networking Conference. (2003)
14. Chen, Y., Schwan, K., Zhou, D.: Opportunistic channels: Mobility-aware event delivery. In: ACM/IFIP/USENIX International Middleware Conference (Middleware 2003). (2003) 182–201
15. Chen, Y.: Opportunistic Overlays: Efficient Content Delivery in Mobile Environments. PhD thesis, Georgia Institute of Technology (2005)
16. Johnson, D.B., Maltz, D.A.: Dynamic source routing in ad hoc wireless networks. Mobile Computing **353** (1996)
17. Zhang, Y., Li, W.: An integrated environment for testing mobile ad-hoc networks. In: Proceedings of the Third ACM International Symposium on Mobile Ad Hoc Networking and Computing (MobiHoc'02). (2002)
18. Carzaniga, A., Rosenblum, D.S., Wolf, A.L.: Design and evaluation of a wide-area event notification service. ACM Transactions on Computer Systems **19** (2001) 332–383
19. Cugola, G., Nitto, E.D., Picco, G.P.: Content-based dispatching in a mobile environment. In: Proceedings of WSDAAL 2000. (2000)
20. Sutton, P., Arkins, R., Segall, B.: Supporting disconnectedness - transparent information delivery for mobile and invisible computing. In: CCGrid 2001 IEEE International Symposium on Cluster Computing and the Grid. (2001)
21. Caporuscio, M., Inverardi, P., Pelliccione, P.: Formal analysis of clients mobility in the siena publish/subscribe middleware. Technical report, Department of Computer Science, University of L'Aquila (2002)
22. Picco, G.P., Cugola, G., Murphy, A.L.: Efficient content-based event dispatching in the presence of topological reconfiguration. In: Proceedings of the 23rd International Conference on Distributed Computing Systems (ICDCS 03). (2003) 234–243
23. Virgillito, A., Beraldi, R., Baldoni, R.: On event routing in content-based publish/-subscribe through dynamic networks. In: Proceedings of the Ninth IEEE Workshop on Future Trends of Distributed Computing Systems (FTDCS 2003), IEEE (2003) 322–328
24. Meier, R., Cahill, V.: Steam: Event-based middleware for wireless ad hoc networks. In: In Proceedings of the 1st International Workshop on Distributed Event-Based Systems (DEBS'02). (2002)
25. Huang, Y., Garcia-Molina, H.: Publish/subscribe tree construction in wireless ad-hoc networks. In: Proceedings of the 4th International Conference on Mobile Data Management(MDM 2003). (2003) 122–140
26. Yoneki, E., Bacon, J.: An adaptive approach to content-based subscription in mobile ad hoc networks. In: Proceedings of The First International Workshop on Mobile Peer-to-Peer Computing (MP2P'04). (2004) 92–97
27. Lee, S.J., Su, W., Gerla, M.: On-demand multicast routing protocol in multihop wireless mobile networks. MONET **7** (2002) 441–453
28. Liu, M., Talpade, R.R., McAuley, A.: AMRoute: Adhoc Multicast Routing Protocol. Technical Report 99, The Institute for Systems Research, University of Maryland (1999)

I-RMI: Performance Isolation in Information Flow Applications

Mohamed Mansour and Karsten Schwan

College of Computing, Georgia Institute of Technology,
Atlanta, GA 30332-0280
{mansour, schwan}@cc.gatech.edu

Abstract. A problem with many distributed applications is their behavior in lieu of unpredictable variations in user request volumes or in available resources. This paper explores a performance isolation-based approach to creating robust distributed applications. For each application, the approach is to (1) understand the performance dependencies that pervade it and then (2) provide mechanisms for imposing constraints on the possible 'spread' of such dependencies through the application. Concrete results are attained for J2EE middleware, for which we identify sample performance dependencies: in the application layer during request execution and in the middleware layer during request de-fragmentation and during return parameter marshalling. *Isolation points* are the novel software abstraction used to capture performance dependencies and represent solutions for dealing with them, and they are used to create (2) I(solation)-RMI, which is a version of RMI-IIOP implemented in the WebSphere service infrastructure enhanced with isolation points. Initial results show the approach's ability to detect and filter ill-behaving messages that can cause an up to a 85% drop in performance for the Trade3 benchmark, and to eliminate up to a 56% drop in performance due to misbehaving clients.

1 Introduction

Modern middleware and programming technologies are making it ever easier to rapidly develop complex distributed applications for heterogeneous computing and communication systems. Typical software platforms are Microsoft's .NET, Sun Microsystems' Java 2 Enterprise Edition (J2EE) specification, and vendor implementations of these specifications like IBM's WebSphere, BEA's WebLogic, and open source efforts like JBoss. Businesses use these platforms to link different enterprise components across the wide spectrum of hardware and applications that are part of their daily operation. Science and engineering applications benefit from their rich functionality to capture data from remote sensors and instruments, access shared information repositories, and create remote data and collaboration services.

The software platforms identified above are mapped to hardware infrastructures in which end clients are concerned with data capture or presentation (Tier 1), supported by two server-level tiers that implement application and storage services, respectively. The J2EE architecture follows this 3-tier model by defining three container types to host each of the tiers, where containers offer sets of standard services to cover

G. Alonso (Ed.): Middleware 2005, LNCS 3790, pp. 375–389, 2005.

non-functional requirements like transactions, messaging, and security. The goal is for developers to be able to focus on business logic and processes rather than having to deal with dependencies on client or server hardware and software systems.

A barrier to creating the system-independent services envisioned by application development platforms is the level of performance robustness of the distributed applications created with them, in lieu of unpredictable variations in user behavior or in the resources available for satisfying user requests. Recognition of this fact has resulted in a multiplicity of techniques for dealing with behaviors like bursty request volumes, including dynamic load balancing and migration, server replication, and similar runtime methods [2, 6, 26]. For media-rich or data-intensive applications, bursty loads can be combated by reducing the fidelity of media content, skipping media frames, or using application-specific techniques for reducing computation and communication loads [36].

Our interest is to use application- or environment-specific techniques like those listed above to create more performance-robust distributed applications. The goal is to better *isolate* applications from each other with respect to their performance behaviors. The consequent technical contributions of this paper are the following. First, experimental evidence demonstrates the importance of performance isolation toward creating well-behaved distributed applications. Specifically, we show that the unusual behavior of even a single client can substantially diminish a data-intensive J2EE server's ability to provide suitable levels of service to its other clients. Second, we propose an approach to achieving performance isolation that (1) exposes system resource information to the middleware layer, (2) enriches the middleware layer with methods for analyzing and adapting application behavior, *isolation points* and *adaptation modules*, (3) permits the middleware layer to execute these solutions when or if necessary, the latter based on (4) user-defined SLAs (Service Level Agreements). A final contribution is the description of a general architecture for performance-isolated messaging both for J2EE applications and for the popular publish/subscribe programming model.

The concrete artifact produced by and evaluated in this research is I(solation)-RMI, a version of RMI-IIOP enhanced with functionality that enables applications to detect and react in meaningful ways to violations of performance isolation SLAs. Our initial results attained with I-RMI are encouraging. For the well-known Trade benchmark, for example, we are able to sustain high throughput in the presence of resource-intensive requests (a 85% improvement over traditional RMI-IIOP). We also report the complete elimination of side-effects (an up to 56% drop in throughput) resulting from slow clients. These results are achieved by using a sliding window algorithm at two different isolation points.

In summary, the idea of performance isolation is to understand the causes of performance dependencies in distributed applications and then provide middleware-based solutions that prevent their 'spread' through the distributed client/server system. In the remainder of this paper, the next section elaborates on the motivation behind our work as well as gives a detailed overview of I-RMI design and implementation. In Section 3 we list the software platforms and applications we experimented with. Experimental results are presented in Section 4. Conclusions and future work are given in Section 5.

2   I-RMI - Motivation, Design, and Implementation

2.1   Motivation

There is a plethora of work addressing runtime performance management in distributed server systems, ranging from system-level solutions like process/load migration or request throttling [26, 27, 32], to application-level tradeoffs in the quality of server responses produced for clients vs. server response time [10, 18], to the creation of new middleware or system abstractions that support the runtime adaptation of applications and systems in response to changes in user requirements or platform resources [7, 13, 15, 20, 24, 25].

The premise of our research is that modern distributed applications created with development platforms like those based on the J2EE standard are sufficiently complex to make it difficult, if not impossible, to design application-wide methods for optimizing their runtime behavior. Instead, we address the simpler problem of curtailing or limiting the spread of performance problems across distributed client/server subsystems. Examples of this problem occur in the enterprise system run by one of our industrial partners: (1) a backup job run by an administrator during system operation can generate a sufficient level of I/O to slow down file system operations for another subsystem running on the same machine, or (2) the logging of operational data contained in files to a backend database slows down other subsystems that use or produce this file data. One result of such slowdowns is that they cause other subsystems' request queues to build up, including those from the front ends used by clients, potentially leading to operational failures (e.g., inappropriately long response times) or revenue loss (e.g., clients going to alternate sites). The problem, of course, is that performance degradation in one part of the system (i.e., the storage subsystem) leads to performance degradation elsewhere. In other words, the system does not adequately deal with or *isolate* the *performance dependencies* inherent to this distributed application.

Our approach to limiting performance dependencies in distributed enterprise applications like those described in [5, 35] is to enhance middleware with functionality that offers improved levels of performance isolation, thereby creating a performance analogue of the firewalls used in computer security: (1) by examining middleware to identify points along the code path that are vulnerable to performance dependencies, termed *isolation points*, and (2) by re-coding these points and enhancing them with a generic and extensible API that permit developers to define runtime reactions to violations of application-specified measures of performance exhibited by applications, represented as *adaptation modules*. The outcome is the creation of performance 'firewalls' that prevent the spread of performance problems across different components of distributed applications. Our implementation approach addresses the broad class of web service-based applications, by associating instrumentation and support for performance firewalls with the RMI/IIOP implementations used in interactions between web, application, and backend servers.

2.2 Architecture and Implementation

Isolation Points
Isolation points (IP) are associated with identified performance vulnerabilities, enhancing them with a monitoring and control architecture [23] [34]. An *isolation point* uses resource monitoring to detect performance issues and reacts through its enforcement mechanism to prevent their further spread. The specific actions taken are determined by user- or developer- defined policies.

I(solation)-RMI
I(solation)-RMI (I-RMI) is a version of RMI-IIOP enhanced with several isolation points. Our current implementation uses the three isolation points listed below to cover intra- and inter- process interaction. The monitoring and adaptation methods used at these points utilize well-established techniques. The goal is to create an implementation of I-RMI suitable for the information-flow architectures prevalent in today's enterprise computing systems rather than developing new techniques. I-RMI currently defines three isolation points as shown in **Fig. 1**, an interesting aspect being that they are backed by occurrences in enterprise software observed by our industrial partners. We note here that as with related abstractions developed in earlier work [14, 20, 28], the changes made by isolation points occur at the middleware level and can be realized and carried out without requiring modifications to application code.

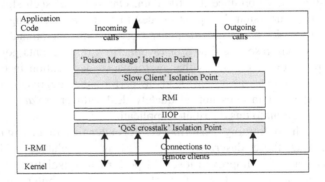

Fig. 1. Overview of I-RMI

Slow Client
The idea of isolation points applies both to client-server- and event-based distributed applications. Consider the structure of typical enterprise information systems described in [21]. Events generated at the edge of a system trigger chains of message passing and processing inside the system, where each processing step augments, personalizes, or otherwise transforms the original event. An example of such a system is deployed at one of our industrial partners, a major airline company, which feeds ticket reservation events into a revenue estimation system. Each event results in 20-30 subsequent calls to other modules inside this system. The application uses asynchronous messaging to decouple senders from receivers.

Message-based distributed applications have to be constructed and administered so that the rates of delivering messages into queues do not exceed the rates of extracting messages from queues and processing them. Jitter in rates [9] can both lead to queue buildup and put pressure on servers' available memory resources. This in turn can deteriorate server performance and its ability to meet target performance levels. A concrete set of examples studied in this paper addresses data-intensive applications, our intent being to explore the uses of J2EE infrastructures for manipulating the large data items implied by future applications in tele-medicine or -presence, remote collaboration, remote access to rich data sources [3], and data mining. For example, for the multimedia or document management applications described in Liferay Portal [1], we expect message sizes to be quite large, and any additional delays in processing queued messages by remote clients can result in substantial server-level performance degradation.

The 'slow client' isolation point added to RMI-IIOP is intended as a generic mechanism for handling the case described above. This point is inserted in the call path before call argument marshalling. The logic we inject into the path monitors queue behavior (system or application-level queues) indirectly, by monitoring the respective incoming and outgoing request rates[1]. By combining estimates of queue lengths with resource utilization on the local and remote nodes, the injected code can detect situations where a slow node is causing serious queue buildup that might lead to performance degradation on the server. A sliding window is used to measure these rates, one window per causally connected incoming and outgoing APIs, one window for local resource information, and a third window for resource information on each remote machine. The specific action taken to reduce queue buildup is decided at runtime by user-supplied logic. Possible actions include: decreasing the sizes of call parameters to reduce the processing required on the target server, rerouting the call to another host, rejecting the call and having the sender deal with this exception, etc.

Poison Messages
Our next scenario is derived from an airline enterprise information system (EIS). System administrators strive to provide consistent performance levels for the operation of their system. An occasional surge in resource usage, traced back to a particular uncommon request type, can cause other subsystems' requests to build up, including those from the front ends used by clients, ultimately threatening operational failure (e.g., inappropriately long response times) or revenue loss (e.g., clients going to alternate sites). Such uncommon request/message types are termed *Poison Messages*.

The poison message isolation point addresses this class of isolation problems. We monitor a server's steady state throughput (see **Fig. 2**) using request counting methods similar to [13]. When a sudden drop in throughput (L_1) and at the same time, a sharp increase in resource utilization is detected, we identify a potential 'poison' state. A snapshot (S_1) of every request currently executing in the J2EE is taken and stored.

---

[1] Understanding the causal relations between incoming and outgoing requests is necessary in order to translate request rates into meaningful queue behaviors. The detection of such causal relations is beyond the scope of this work. Aguilera et al [2] articulate possible ways to automatically detect such relations.

When the server later recovers and throughput rises (L_2) again, we take another snapshot (S_2) of all requests currently executing in the server. The set difference $(S_1 - S_2)$ represents a list of requests that are potential suspects. This procedure is repeated every time we encounter such abnormal behavior and eventually, the suspect list narrows down to a few request types. The specific action against the potential suspects is left to the user to define, possible actions are reject or re-route to another server.

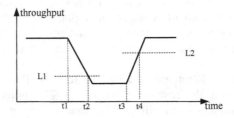

Fig. 2. Dynamically detecting poison messages at runtime

Our current implementation identifies requests only by their API names. To deal with server overload caused by changes in request parameters, the implementation has to be extended to also scan and analyze request parameters [37]. Additional detection logic is necessary if poison state is caused by a sequence of messages.

'QoS Crosstalk' due to Parallel Concurrent Streams
Tennenhouse describes `QoS crosstalk` as the effect of multiple concurrent streams on server performance [31]. We include an isolation point in I-RMI to manage and minimize such crosstalk effects. This section describes its implementation and demonstrates the potential of poor performance isolation in the presence of multiple concurrent request streams with varying request sizes. Such request streams are common in information flow applications between front-end Web/UI servers and backend business process servers.

The RMI-IIOP implementation we use dedicates a separate reader thread per client connection. When a server is subjected to invocations from multiple clients, all of the corresponding reader threads are activated, as they all receive notifications of data being available on their underlying sockets. It is up to the underlying kernel thread scheduler to decide which thread to run next. Assuming a round-robin scheduler and equal buffer sizes on all connections, it is common for streams with very small request sizes to receive better treatment compared to streams with large request sizes. Note that this analysis also applies to writer threads.

Behaviors like those explained in the previous paragraph can be unacceptable for certain application deployments or client connections. Known control methods addressing them include changing the socket buffer sizes for certain connections, altering threads priorities, or both. Setting the right buffer size for each connection requires that such a value be calculated uniformly for all connections. Toward these ends, we insert an isolation point at the IIOP reader thread level, and we re-implement parts of RMI-IIOP to use a single reader thread and non-blocking I/O. The single reader thread provides a single point of control where the 'right' buffer sizes can be calculated and applied. The resource monitor is responsible for tracking how many parallel streams are active. The enforcement logic dynamically adjusts the buffer sizes for each connection to achieve the desired relative weights. This modified implementation is backwards compatible and also scales better than the original implementation.

3 Representative Applications and Experimental Results

To demonstrate the importance of performance isolation in the J2EE environment, we select WebSphere as a representative software platform. We use the *Trade3* application [16] developed by IBM as our test bed. The Trade3 benchmark models an online stock brokerage application and is built to cover most of J2EE's programming model, including JSPs, EJBs, transactional aspects and database access. We deployed the Trade3 benchmark with the UI web component on a separate machine from the backend EJB components, WebSphere dynamic caching was not enabled in our experiments.

Experimental Setup
Experiments are run in Georgia Tech's enterprise computing laboratory, using Version 5.1 of IBM WebSphere J2EE server running on an x345 IBM server (hostname: dagobah), a dual 2.8GHz Xeon machine with 4GB memory and 1GB/s NIC, running RedHat Linux 9.0. The server runs against Version 8.1 of DB2 which runs on a separate machine with an identical configuration. Clients, secondary servers and load generators run on an IBM BladeCenter with 14 HS20 blade servers installed (hostnames awing1-awing14). Each blade has dual 2.8GHz Xeon processors with 1GB RAM and 1 Gb/s NIC card running RH Linux 9.0. We use the Tomcat 5.0.25 servlet container for hosting the front end of the Trade3 benchmark. Httperf [22] is used to generate the workload for the trade benchmark.

3.1 'Slow Client' Isolation Point

Consider the distributed application shown in Fig. 3. The external source injects events into the system, by sending messages to a primary server where they are queued for processing. A worker thread selects messages from the queue and sends them to the secondary server. The primary server also provides auxiliary services to an external client. The external event source generates a 512KB message every 10ms. A client makes repeated requests to the server; each request carries a return parameter of 1MB, the server caches the 1MB object and uses it to serve all client requests.

The average round trip time for the client is listed in Table 1. In the first case, "Unloaded", the secondary client runs with a very light load. Under these conditions, the average queue length is under 3 units, and the client average RTT is 35 ms/call. The second scenario, "Stress Load", imposes a heavy workload on the secondary server. We use the stress utility to run 8 CPU intensive threads. This results in a significant drop in the ability of the secondary server to process its requests and subsequently, creates queue buildup on the primary server. As a result of this buildup,

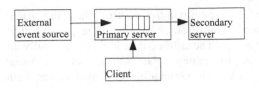

Fig. 3. Abstract view of nodes in an operational information system (OIS)

Table 1. Average round trip time for client calls

Scenario	Average RTT [from client side]
Unloaded secondary server	35 ms/call
Secondary server stress loaded	80 ms/call
Secondary server stress loaded + Primary server uses I-RMI	35 ms/call

available free memory drops on the primary server and garbage collection is triggered more often (JVM memory was set to max. to 120MB). This results in an increase in client average RTT to 80ms/call and a 56% drop in throughput. These can be attributed to increased garbage collection on the primary server (see Table 2) due to memory pressure resulting from queue buildup.

To demonstrate I-RMI effectiveness in controlling such effects, we repeat the above experiment using I-RMI on the primary server. Fig. 5 shows the rate of calls coming in and going out of the primary server. Rates are measured by dividing the number of calls that occurred during the last N seconds, where N is the width of the sliding window we use. At T=10000 the secondary server is subjected to CPU stress load, and queue buildup is evident from the difference between the rates of incoming and outgoing calls. The increased garbage collection (GC) activity (as shown in Fig. 4) leads to a drop in the server's ability to service events from the external event source. As the CPU utilization crosses a predefined threshold (1.0 in this experiment), the isolation logic decides to cancel calls outgoing to the secondary server (occurring at about T=14,000). This results in the apparent increase in the rate of outgoing calls. The application is unaware of the short circuit applied by the isolation logic, still thinking that its calls are being completed. Note that this example uses the simplistic approach of call elimination, to focus on the performance isolation properties of our approach. Realistic systems will use any number of techniques, including request rerouting, queuing for later submission, application-specific reductions in request volume [12] and others.

Table 2. Number of times primary server garbage collects per 100 client calls

Scenario	GC
Unloaded secondary server	6
Secondary server stress loaded	102

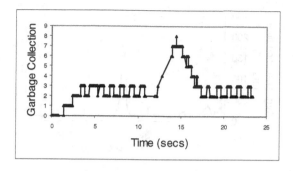

Fig. 4. Garbage collection at Primary Server

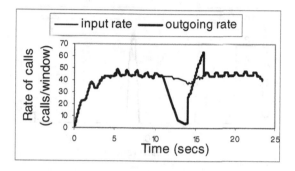

Fig. 5. Call rates measured at the primary server

3.2 'Poison Message' Isolation Point

To demonstrate the effect of a poison message, we run a steady state workload against the Trade3 benchmark. The workload generator (httperf) simulates 4 concurrent sessions with 0.1 seconds think time. The resulting server average request execution times are shown in Fig. 6, respectively (from T=0 to T=50). The small spikes at T=(3, 10, 24, ...) are due to garbage collection on the server. At T=59, we manually call a special API added to the benchmark application. This API allocates 10KB byte arrays in a tight loop for 4 seconds. The effects of this API are evident in the graphs as a sudden sharp increase in the average execution times for requests, a drop in server throughput, and a dramatic increase in garbage collection activity on the server (Fig. 7). The rising edge at T=59 triggers our detection algorithm, and it takes a snapshot of all requests currently in the server. As the poison API finishes and server load levels return to normal, the falling edge at T=63 triggers the detection algorithm and it takes another snapshot of all API currently executing on the server. The difference between these two snapshots correctly reveals the poison API in this simple example. Subsequent calls to this API are filtered by the isolation point.

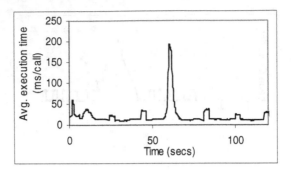

Fig. 6. Average call execution time (ms/call)

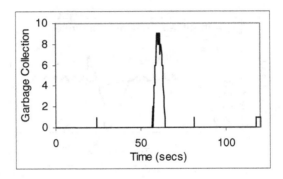

Fig. 7. Garbage collection frequency at the Primary Server

3.3 'QoS Crosstalk' Isolation Point

In this experiment, we demonstrate QoS effects in WebSphere and how I-RMI can provide some control over such behavior. All times reported here represent the time needed to read data for a request at the IIOP level. Request assembly time increases proportionally with message size in the case of one client communicating with the server. In the presence of a second client sending messages of constant 2K size, the time needed to assemble the large request message more than doubles. In Fig. 8, the lower curve shows message assembly times for a client, and the top curve shows message assembly times for the same client in the presence of a secondary request stream of size 2KB/request. This is attributed to the fact that the server processes both streams with equal priority. We ameliorate the above behavior by controlling the socket buffer size for each connection. A larger buffer enables us to read more data per system call. We note here that this approach works only if there is data available at the server socket for reading. This observation indicates the need to associate additional system-level knowledge with isolation points.

In Fig. 9, we plot assembly time against message size for a request stream running against a 2K/request secondary stream. The different lines represent different socket buffer size settings. The top curve labeled '1x' represents equal buffer sizes for both

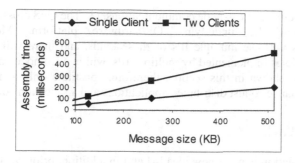

Fig. 8. Time to assemble a request for one vs. two clients

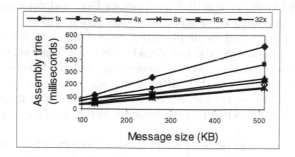

Fig. 9. Time to assemble a request at different buffer sizes

streams. For the next curve, labeled '2x', we set the socket buffer size for the main stream to be twice that of the secondary stream and so on. A larger buffer size clearly reduces the time needed to assemble a large request and therefore, reduces the effects of parallel request streams.

Our implementation replaces the one-reader-thread-per-connection IIOP model in WebSphere with a single reader thread using non-blocking socket I/O. A single reader thread constitutes a single point at which an enforcement mechanism can be realized. Its presence also removes dependencies on the underlying thread scheduler. Care is taken to prevent blocking of this single reader thread. Processing the socket data and handling it to the ORB for assembly is done in a non-blocking manner through utilization of intermediate hand-off queues. The experiments shown in Figs. 8 and 9 are based on a partial implementation, not employing a dynamic resource monitor, using pre-defined buffer sizes for each connection, and without a decoupling queue between the reader thread and the ORB.

3.4 Discussion of Experiments

Beyond the performance results attained with the isolation points used and evaluated in this section, note that they are representative of the three different kinds of isolation points needed for building performance isolation firewalls for distributed service implementations. (1) The poison message IP monitors and controls behaviors that involve the APIs exposed by the application components on a single node. (2) The slow client IP monitors cross-node communications. (3) The QoS crosstalk IP concerns interactions with the underlying OS/hardware platform. More generally, implementations will use multiple IPs of these kinds, and there will be interactions between the policies implemented by multiple IPs, within each node and across nodes. The experiments shown in this section, therefore, constitute only a first step toward creating performance-robust distributed applications and application components.

4 Related Work

Performance isolation is not a new idea [4] and in addition, prior work has developed many methods for dealing with performance problems in server applications. The latter include request deletion in web servers [27], request prioritization or frame dropping in multi-media or real-time applications [30], and the creation of system-level constructs supporting these application-level actions [25, 33]. Essentially, such methods are specific examples of the more general methods for dynamic system adaptation developed during the last decade [29, 38]. They share with adaptive techniques the use of runtime system monitoring and of dynamically reacting to certain monitoring events, but they differ in that the policy-level decisions made in response to certain events are focused on limiting performance dependencies rather than on exploiting them to optimize the behavior of the distributed system exhibiting these dependencies.

This paper advocates an isolation-based approach to performance management, but differs from prior work in that it also considers performance dependencies that exist across different layers of abstraction existing in current systems, such as dependencies across system-level communication protocols and the middleware-level messaging systems that use them. The specific results attained in this paper for Java RMI-IIOP and J2EE-level method calls are related to earlier work done by our group on the IQ-RUDP [15] data transport protocol, which coordinates middleware-level and transport-level adaptations to better meet application needs. What is new here, however, is that we consider explicit characteristics of the more complex Java middleware environments, including Java's garbage collection techniques.

Hardware, kernel, and application-level protection and isolation have been studied extensively for single Java virtual machines [8]. [17] applies the concept of a Java resource accounting interface to isolate applications inside a JVM at the granularity of isolates to J2EE platforms. In comparison, our work focuses on performance isolation at single request granularity (even within the same application), and we identify three kinds of performance dependences embedded in the middleware implementation of J2EE and WebSphere. Since detection logic is placed into middleware prior to application execution, resource reservation approaches like those described in [17] can be used as an enforcement mechanism, where thresholds are set dynamically by a resource monitor. Note that some of the scenarios present in this paper are not addressed by the isolate mechanism, such as when the vulnerability point is in the lower levels of the middleware before the message is parsed and dispatched to its target application (isolate).

Finally, we point to recent work in performance management for cluster-based web services [19]. A central router classifies and schedules incoming requests to maximize a user-defined utility function based on performance measurements collected from the cluster. While traffic classes represent high-level business value, requests in each class can still have very different operational footprints and can therefore, still experience the performance vulnerabilities presented in this work.

5 Conclusions and Future Work

This paper builds on previous work in the autonomic and adaptive system domains to address end-to-end performance issues in service-oriented software architectures. The specific issue addressed is *performance isolation*, which refers to the ability to isolate service components from each other with respect to the performance dependencies pervading distributed applications and the systems on which they run. Performance isolation is a necessary element of any solution that seeks to attain end user-desired Service Level Objectives or Agreements (SLAs), preventing the violation of SLAs through circumstances beyond the explicit control of individual services.

To attain performance isolation, our research offers novel middleware abstractions, termed *isolation points*, which both capture performance dependencies and provide functionality that deals with them. The paper first demonstrates the prevalence of performance dependencies in enterprise applications created with J2EE RMI-IIOP-based software platforms and that these dependencies can lead to the *spread* of performance problems through entire enterprise applications. For example, if a 'poison message' causes one server to slow down, this server will act as a slow client to its callers, causing their performance to degrade and propagating undesirable performance effects across the entire distributed application. Second, isolation points (IPs) are created to dynamically capture and react to performance dependencies, thereby providing middleware mechanisms for managing and preventing them. Third, a concrete product of this work is I-RMI, which is RMI-IIOP enhanced with isolation points representative of the three different types of IPs required for performance isolation in distributed enterprise applications: (1) IPs guarding service APIs, (2) IPs for inter-node interactions, and (3) IPs for interactions with underlying operating systems and hardware. I-RMI has been integrated and used with IBM's WebSphere J2EE infrastructure. When using standard J2EE benchmarks, we are able to eliminate performance degradations of up to 56% observed in traditional RMI-IIOP in one case, and up to 85% in another case.

Future work will consider solutions in which multiple IPs cooperate to address potentially complex performance dependencies, across sets of distributed services and service nodes. In addition, we will address the fact that performance dependencies and the need for performance firewalls implemented with IPs are not specific to Java. They appear both in the synchronous call-reply model of RMI and in the message-oriented asynchronous middleware of operational information systems like the one used by our industrial partners [11].

References

1. Liferay: Open source enterprise portal, 2005.
2. Aweya, J., Ouellette, M., Montuno, D.Y., et al. An adaptive load balancing scheme for web servers. *International Journal Network Management, 12* (1). 3--39.

3. Barclay, T., Slutz, D.R. and Gray, J. TerraServer: A Spatial Data Warehouse *Proceedings of the 2000 ACM SIGMOD International Conference on Management of Data*, 2000.
4. Barham, P., Dragovic, B., Fraser, K., et al. Xen and the art of virtualization *Proceedings of the 19th ACM Symposium on Operating Systems Principles (SOSP 2003)*, 2003.
5. Bernadat, P., Lambright, D. and Travostino, F. Towards a Resource-safe Java for service guarantees in uncooperative environments *IEEE Workshop on Programming Languages for Real-Time Industrial Applications*, 1998.
6. Cardellini, V., Casalicchio, E., Colajanni, M., et al. The state of the art in locally distributed Web-server systems. *ACM Computing Surveys, 34* (2). 263--311.
7. Cowan, C., Cen, S., Walpole, J., et al. Adaptive methods for distributed video presentation. *ACM Computing Surveys, 27* (4). 580--583.
8. Czajkowski, G. Application isolation in the Java Virtual Machine *Proceedings of the 15th ACM SIGPLAN conference on Object-oriented programming, systems, languages, and applications (OOPSLA '00)*, 2000.
9. Diot, C. Adaptive Applications and QoS Guaranties (Invited Paper) *Proceedings of the International Conference on Multimedia Networking (MmNet '95)*, 1995.
10. Fox, A., Gribble, S.D., Chawathe, Y., et al. Cluster-Based Scalable Network Services *Symposium on Operating Systems Principles (SOSP 97)*, 1997.
11. Gavrilovska, A., Oleson, V. and Schwan, K. Adaptable Mirroring in Cluster Servers *10th International Conference on High-Performance Distributed Computing (HPDC-10)*, 2001.
12. Gavrilovska, A., Schwan, K. and Oleson, V. A Practical Approach for 'Zero' Downtime in an Operational Information System *The 22nd International Conference on Distributed Computing Systems (ICDCS-2002)*, 2002.
13. Gheith, A. and Schwan, K. CHAOSarc: kernel support for multiweight objects, invocations, and atomicity in real-time multiprocessor applications. *ACM Transactions Computer Systems, 11* (1). 33--72.
14. Hamilton, G., Powell, M.L. and Mitchell, J.G. Subcontract: A Flexible Base for Distributed Programming *Proceedings of the Fourteenth ACM Symposium on Operating System Principles*, 1993.
15. He, Q. and Schwan, K. IQ-RUDP: Coordinating Application Adaptation with Network Transport *Proceedings of the 11 th IEEE International Symposium on High Performance Distributed Computing (HPDC'11)*, 2002.
16. IBM. WebSphere Application Server, Trade3 benchmark.
17. Jordan, M.J., Czajkowski, G., Kouklinski, K., et al. Extending a J2EE^{TM} Server with Dynamic and Flexible Resource Management *International Middleware Conference (Middleware 2004)*, 2004.
18. Krishnamurthy, B. and Wills, C.E. Improving web performance by client characterization driven server adaptation *Proceedings of the eleventh international conference on World Wide Web (WWW '02)*, 2002.
19. Levy, R.M., Nagarajarao, J., Pacifici, G., et al. Performance Management for Cluster Based Web Services *IFIP/IEEE Eighth International Symposium on Integrated Network Management (IM 2003)*, 2003.
20. Loyall, J.P., Schantz, R.E., Zinky, J.A., et al. Specifying and measuring quality of service in distributed object systems *1st International Symposium on Object-Oriented Real-Time Distributed Computing (ISORC)*, 1998.
21. Mansour, M., Wolf, M. and Schwan, K. StreamGen: A Workload Generation Tool for Distributed Information Flow Applications *Proceedings of the 2004 International Conference on Parallel Processing (ICPP'04)*, 2004.
22. Mosberger, D. and Jin, T. httperf - a tool for measuring web server performance. *SIGMETRICS Performance Evaluation Review, 26* (3). 31-37.
23. Oreizy, P., Gorlick, M., Taylor, R., et al. An Architecture-Based Approach to Self-Adaptive Software *IEEE Intelligent Systems*, 1999.

24. Plale, B. and Schwan, K. dQUOB: Managing Large Data Flows Using Dynamic Embedded Queries *Proceedings of the Ninth IEEE International Symposium on High Performance Distributed Computing (HPDC'00)*, 2000.
25. Poellabauer, C., Schwan, K., West, R., et al. Flexible User/Kernel Communication For Real-Time Applications In Elinux *Proceedings of the Workshop on Real Time Operating Systems and Applications*, 2000.
26. Powell, M.L. and Miller, B.P. Process migration in DEMOS/MP *Proceedings of the 9th ACM symposium on Operating Systems Principles (SOSP '83)*, 1983.
27. Provos, N. and Lever, C. Scalable Network I/O in Linux *Proceedings of the USENIX Technical Conference, FREENIX track*, 2000.
28. Pyarali, I., Schmidt, D.C. and Cytron, R. Techniques for enhancing real-time CORBA quality of service. *Proceedings of the IEEE, 91* (7). 1070-1085.
29. Rosu, D., Schwan, K. and Yalamanchili, S. FARA: A Framework for Adaptive Resource Allocation in Complex Real-Time Systems *he 4th IEEE Real-Time Technology and Applications Symposium (RTAS '98)*, 1998.
30. Sundaram, V., Chandra, A., Goyal, P., et al. Application performance in the QLinux multimedia operating system *Proceedings of the 8th ACM International Conference on Multimedia 2000*, 2000.
31. Tennenhouse, D.L. Layered Multiplexing Considered Harmful. Rudin, H. and Williamson, R. ed *Protocols for High-Speed Networks*, 1989.
32. Welsh, M., Culler, D. and Brewer, E. SEDA: an architecture for well-conditioned, scalable internet services *Proceedings of the eighteenth ACM symposium on Operating systems principles (SOSP '01)*, 2001.
33. West, R. and Schwan, K. Dynamic Window-Constrained Scheduling for Multimedia Applications *Proceedings of the IEEE International Conference on Multimedia Computing and Systems (ICMCS '99)*, 1999.
34. White, S.R., Hanson, J.E., Whalley, I., et al. An Architectural Approach to Autonomic Computing *1st International Conference on Autonomic Computing (ICAC 2004)*, 2004.
35. Wiseman, Y., Schwan, K. and Widener, P. Efficient End to End Data Exchange Using Configurable Compression *24th International Conference on Distributed Computing Systems (ICDCS 2004)*, 2004.
36. Wolf, M., Cai, Z., Huang, W., et al. SmartPointers: personalized scientific data portals in your hand *Proceedings of the 2002 ACM/IEEE conference on Supercomputing (Supercomputing '02)*, 2002.
37. Xie, T. and Notkin, D. Checking Inside the Black Box: Regression Testing Based on Value Spectra Differences *IEEE International Conference on Software Maintenance (ICSM 2004)*, 2004.
38. Yuan, W. and Nahrstedt, K. Process group management in cross-layer adaptation *Multimedia Computing and Networking 2004*, 2004.

Matrix: Adaptive Middleware for Distributed Multiplayer Games

Rajesh Krishna Balan[1], Maria Ebling[2], Paul Castro[2], and Archan Misra[2]

[1] Carnegie Mellon University, 5000 Forbes Avenue, Pittsburgh, PA 15213, USA
[2] IBM Research Watson, 19 Skyline Drive, Hawthorne, NY 10532, USA

Abstract. Building a distributed middleware infrastructure that provides the low latency required for massively multiplayer games while still maintaining consistency is non-trivial. Previous attempts have used static partitioning or client-based peer-to-peer techniques that do not scale well to a large number of players, perform poorly under dynamic workloads or hotspots, and impose significant programming burdens on game developers. We show that it is possible to build a scalable distributed system, called Matrix, that is easily usable by game developers. We show experimentally that Matrix provides good performance, especially when hotspots occur.

1 Introduction

Online gaming is a rapidly growing market segment estimated to reach 100 million players and a USD $5 billion market value by 2008 [9]. A popular form of multiplayer gaming is the rapidly growing [24] class of massively multiplayer online games (MMOG) such as *Everquest* [19] and *Final Fantasy XI* [20], where hundreds or even thousands of players from across the world interact in a real-time shared virtual world.

To support these virtual worlds, most MMOGs currently use a centralized server model, with players connecting to a single game server that handles the entire game world. However, each server can handle at most 30,000 clients [7] whereas games like Final Fantasy XI claim to have at least one million registered players [21]. To handle more players, some MMOGs [7] use multiple servers that are statically assigned different parts of the game world even though this approach is known to be unresponsive to unexpected workload variations or dynamic localized hotspots in the game.

To overcome this limitation, static partitioning schemes either significantly overprovision the number of servers used for the game and/or impose artificial limits on the number of players that can be in any part of the map. Unfortunately, overprovisioning incurs extra costs and artificial limits may detract from the gaming experience. It would be better instead, to use a distributed system that can handle arbitrary game loads by dynamically and automatically adjusting the number of servers used by the game in a scalable and efficient manner. This system could either be used on its own or in combination with static partitioning schemes (as a mechanism to handle unexpected load changes).

Building this dynamic distributed system for MMOGs, however, is a non-trivial problem. To preserve the interactive feel of a MMOG, the client response latency must be low [3]. But, maintaining complete consistency between distributed nodes requires

G. Alonso (Ed.): Middleware 2005, LNCS 3790, pp. 390–400, 2005.

increasingly larger amounts of time as the amount of traffic and number of nodes in the system increases (due to increased player activity). However, a lack of consistency could lead to an unsatisfactory experience for the game player. The challenge lies in satisfying these conflicting latency and consistency goals, especially for a system with a large number of nodes and a high volume (O(Gbps)) of network traffic.

The key insight that allows us to overcome this problem is the observation that MMOGs are an example of a *nearly decomposable system* [18]. Such a system is one in which the number of interactions among subsystems, in some geometric space, is of a lower order of magnitude than the number of interactions within an individual subsystem. For MMOGs, this behaviour typically manifests itself through a "radius" or "zone of visibility" associated with each game player. It is usually sufficient to update players with only those events that occur in their zone of visibility. For example, if a tank is destroyed in a battlefield game, it is enough to only send this information to other tanks that can see the victim, rather than to all the tanks in the game.

Using this insight, we built a scalable low-latency distributed middleware infrastructure, called *Matrix*, that provides pockets of locally-consistent state. This weaker form of consistency allows Matrix to provide low latency responses, while still giving adequate consistency to game clients even when the number of nodes in the system increases. Matrix also provides low latency mechanisms to handle infrequent global interactions. Another key Matrix design goal was ease of use. We achieved this by providing a clean and clear layering that hides the consistency maintainence details within an easy-to-use API (not shown due to space constraints). This API allows Matrix to be used with only minimal changes to existing MMOGs. The layering also allows Matrix to support the distributed operation of various MMOGs without actually needing to understand the game logic. Finally, unlike static partitioning techniques, Matrix can dynamically add and remove servers as necessary to handle transient hot-spots and dynamic loads caused by players joining and leaving the game.

We validated both Matrix's system-level performance as well as its effectiveness at satisfying real game players. In particular, we show that Matrix's overhead is reasonable and also that it outperforms a statically partitioned system when unexpected load patterns occur. Due to space constraints, we present a summary of these results.

In Section 2, we describe Matrix's design criteria while Section 3 presents the design and implementation of Matrix. Section 4 presents a summary of the evaluation while Section 5 presents related work.

2   Matrix Design Criteria

In this section, we describe the two key design criteria (and their corresponding implications) used to build the Matrix middleware. In particular, Matrix was specifically designed to allow MMOG game developers to focus mainly on their game's core logic and delegate the task of scalably distributing their games to Matrix.

2.1   Attractive and Easy for Game Developers

The first key criteria was to make Matrix attractive for game developers to use. Most game companies usually focus on core game-specific technologies, such as 3D graphics modeling, and typically have very little in-house distributed systems expertise. Hence, being able to leverage a distributed game middleware that scales and maintains adequate consistency as the user population grows would be of great benefit for them. To appeal to developers, Matrix has the following characteristics:

No Change in Security Model: A primary concern for online game developers is cheating and denial-of-service (DoS) attacks. In particular, they are quite resistant to any middleware that will lower their ability to tackle these issues. This concern naturally eliminates the use of peer-to-peer mechanisms, which fundamentally change the client-server interaction and security model. Matrix thus uses the same game developer preferred client-server architecture, as shown in Section 3, allowing the developer to reuse existing anti-cheating and anti-DoS mechanisms.

Separation of Concerns: To make developing distributed games easier, Matrix provides a clean "separation of concerns" programming model where Matrix would handle the distributed computing aspects of a game such as consistency, scalability, resource provisioning and fault-tolerance, leaving the MMOG developer to focus on the core game logic.

Support Multiple Gaming Platforms: Game developers frequently develop games for multiple gaming platforms; having to write new Matrix routines for each platform would hinder adoption. Our APIs do not require any new Matrix-specific routines for a new platform.

Simplicity: Building and debugging a large distributed system is a tricky endeavour. As such, Matrix intentionally uses the simplest possible algorithms and APIs. The simple algorithms allow Matrix to be easier to debug and maintain, and the API allows existing games to be quickly and easily modified for use with Matrix.

2.2 Supports Game Requirements

The second key criteria was that Matrix must support the performance requirements of massively multiplayer games. In particular Matrix must provide:

Low Response Latency: Response latency, the time between a game client's action and the observed reaction in the game world, is a crucial factor influencing a player's overall gaming experience. Matrix ensures that this latency is as low as possible by not unnecessarily buffering packets and by using an $O(1)$ route lookup mechanism to determine where to send packets (explained further in Section 3.2).

Localized Consistency: It is vital that Matrix ensure that the MMOG players are consistent with nearby objects, thus allowing these players to correctly interact with these objects. Because MMOGs are nearly decomposable, it is unnecessary to provide global consistency. Matrix thus provides fast, yet effective, localized consistency mechanisms (explained further in Section 3.1).

Automatically Handle Load Spikes: Load spikes are caused when a large number of players simultaneously decide to visit the same location in an MMOG. It is important that Matrix is automatically able to handle these load spikes without a significant increase in latency. It would also be useful, to conserve resources, if Matrix is able to dynamically change its server usage based on the current game load. We describe how we achieve this in Section 3.2.

3 Matrix Design and Implementation

In this section, we describe Matrix's design and implementation, focusing primarily on the overall architecture and major technology components.

3.1 Providing Localized Consistency

To build an easy to use localized consistency mechanism, we observed that all games have some notion of geometric space that allows distances between game objects to be computed using a game-specific distance metric. If Matrix was aware of an individual game's *spatial coordinates* and its *radius of visibility* (the range over which local consistency is typically required), it could confine the propagation of any game state update to an easily computable region, without having to maintain game-specific relationship trees or other data structures. Matrix uses this insight to require game developers to merely forward all game packets, appropriately tagged with the spatial coordinates (in the game world) of the packet's origin and destination, to the local Matrix server. Matrix uses these spatial tags, together with the game's radius of visibility, to route these packets to the other game servers that manage objects within this radius of visibility (and thus need to maintain consistency).

Matrix assigns unique portions of the MMOG's spatial map to different servers. Each server is only responsible for clients located within its assigned partition. Formally, Matrix partitions the overall space Z of an MMOG into N non-overlapping partitions, $\{P_1, P_2, \ldots, P_N\}$, and assigns each partition P_i to a distinct server S_i. To handle load spikes, the number of servers N, and the specific partition managed by any server S_i can change dynamically.

Because games have a non-zero radius of visibility, changes in the MMOG state at any point, σ_i, handled by server S_i, that is within the radius of visibility of a client located on server S_j, must be consistently applied at both servers S_i and S_j. In general,

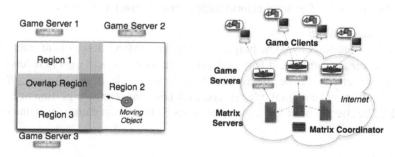

(a) Overlap Region between 3 Matrix Servers   (b) Matrix Architecture

Fig. 1. Matrix Components

given a spatial partition and a radius of visibility R, every point σ in Z has a set of servers associated with it, called the *consistency set* of σ or $C(\sigma)$. This set contains all the servers whose partitions overlap the circle (or sphere) of radius R centered at σ and therefore need to be aware of any update or activity in σ. If $d(x,y)$ represents the distance-metric between points x and y,

$$C(\sigma \in P_i) = \{S_j | j \neq i \ \wedge \ \exists \sigma' \in P_j \ s.t. \ d(\sigma,\sigma') \leq R\} \tag{1}$$

From Equation 1, we observe that if R is infinite, *all* updates must be globally propagated, making localized consistency impossible. However, if R is small compared to the size of partition P_i, most of the interior points of P_i will have empty consistency sets. Only the relatively small number of periphery points, whose $C(\sigma) \neq \emptyset$ (i.e, whose radius of visibility extends into adjoining partitions) will require consistency to be maintained between servers. Games usually have limited player visibility radii and Matrix efficiently utilize this sparseness by forming groups, called "overlap regions", of all points that have identical non-empty consistency sets (shown in Figure 1a).

Intuitively, an overlap region denotes a portion of the map, such that an update at any point in that overlap region requires all the servers in that overlap region to be informed of the update. Overlap regions allow Matrix servers to quickly determine the consistency set for any game packet they receive by merely doing a table lookup (of the set of overlap regions).

Matrix assumes that most players in a game have the same radius of visibility. The Matrix API does allow game servers to specify different visibility radii for exceptions, and internally creates distinct sets of overlap regions, each for a different R. We decided to use overlap regions instead of other geometric data structures, like spanners [4], to determine the consistency set of any object because overlap regions do not require costly (in terms of latency) hop-by-hop lookups and they work well even when the map space changes dynamically (which happens during splits and reclamations).

3.2 Matrix Architecture

Figure 1b shows the Matrix architecture, that satisfies the design criteria in Section 2. A MMOG is deployed using Matrix with the MMOG developers providing game clients and game servers and the Matrix infrastructure providing Matrix servers and a Matrix coordinator (MC). The architectural components interact as follows:

3.2.1 Game Clients
The clients are used by game players to play the MMOG. Each client interacts with a game server and provides it with updates on the player's activity and receives updates on nearby activity. Game clients must be able to switch servers *dynamically* because the MMOG may be on multiple servers, each handling a unique portion of the MMOG world. The client is informed of these switches by its current game server and is unaware of Matrix.

3.2.2 Game Servers
The game server is the software that stores the state of the game world and coordinates the activity of the players in the game. In most commercial games, they are also the only point of contact between game clients and the game world to protect against cheating

and unauthorized collusion; problems that are particularly acute in multiplayer games. The game server must be designed for use in a multiserver environment. In particular, it must identify players using globally unique IDs (such as callsigns) instead of locally generated IDs. Game servers are usually located on the same physical machine as a Matrix server (to minimize the network latency). In our current implementation, the Matrix server is a separate process from the game server. In the future, we may compile the Matrix server into the game server (as a separate library) to improve performance.

When a game server starts, it sends Matrix the visibility radius of clients in the game (to allow overlap regions to be correctly computed). The game server then forwards all client packets (after spatially tagging them) to its Matrix server for further processing. The game server also periodically reports its current load to Matrix. If the server is overloaded, Matrix will split the game world between the overloaded server and a newly created game server and inform both the new and overloaded game servers of their new map ranges. The overloaded game server will then forward all game specific state (e.g., map objects such as trees, buildings, etc.) to the new game server via Matrix. Finally, the overloaded game server will redirect any clients (and their corresponding state) that are not in its new map range to the appropriate game server (Matrix provides the identity of the appropriate game server). Moving these clients to other game servers will decrease the load on the overloaded game server. However, if it is still overloaded, Matrix will split the still overloaded game server again until it has shed enough load.

3.2.3 Matrix Servers

Matrix servers, the heart of our distributed middleware, provide the necessary consistency, reliability and latency semantics for MMOGs. Each Matrix server is aware of the map range currently managed by the game server connected to it. On receiving spatially tagged game packets from its game server, the Matrix server checks its overlap tables, provided by the MC, to see if any peer Matrix servers are within that packet's consistency set. If so, the packet is forwarded to these peer servers which then forward the packet, after verifying the packet's range, to their own game servers for processing. Because Matrix handles packet routing, individual game servers do not need to know about other game servers serving the MMOG.

Matrix splits map partitions using purely local decisions to improve scalability and minimize latency. On detecting that its game server is overloaded (through explicit load messages from the game server or via system performance measurements), a Matrix server will first check, using some non-Matrix external entity, for an available Matrix server. If a server is available, it will split its current map, keeping control of a sub-portion of the map, while transferring responsibility for the remaining portion to a new Matrix server. Currently, Matrix uses a simple "split-to-left" splitting technique where each map is split into two equal pieces with the left piece handed off to the new server. Though simple, this algorithm still provides good performance as shown in Section 4.

The new Matrix server will then create a new game server and orchestrate the transfer of the global state, from the original (overloaded) game server to this newly-created game server. The overloaded game server will then switch game clients to this new server to ease its load. The amount of state associated with switching game clients is minimal (based on experience with the games used to test Matrix) and Matrix has efficient mechanisms (not described due to space constraints) to transfer this state. Newly started game servers also need to obtain the static state of the game, like the map textures, that can be hundreds of megabytes in size. However, because this state is static, it can be pre-cached on all new servers, requiring only pointers to the cached state to be sent.

The Matrix server that performed the split will be the parent of the newly created Matrix server. When a Matrix server detects that its game server is underutilized (again, through explicit load notifications or via system performance measurements), it first checks if it has any children. If it does and if their load levels are low enough, the parent Matrix server will reclaim the partition and game state held by the child. All the game clients on the child's game server will be transfered to the parent's game server, after which the child Matrix server and game server will be removed from the game and returned to the resource pool. Matrix uses simple heuristics (not described) to prevent oscillations and ensure stability in the splitting / reclamation process.

3.2.4   Matrix Coordinator (MC)

The MC creates the overlap tables used by Matrix servers to route spatially tagged packets. When a new Matrix server is used for the game, it informs the MC of the current map range and radius of visibility. The MC then computes the overlap regions for all the Matrix servers in the game using geometric algorithms to calculate bounding boxes between spatial regions; a particularly easy computation, using well known axis-aligned bounding box computation algorithms, if the map partitions are rectangular in shape. The MC will then inform each Matrix server of their overlap regions along with the set, $C(\sigma)$, of Matrix servers that should be informed about an event in that region. The MC recomputes and redistributes overlap regions every time a new Matrix server is used or whenever an existing Matrix server is reclaimed (the MC is informed of the new map ranges whenever reclamations occur).

We used a central MC to minimize the latency of the packet forwarding process. In the common case where players are only interacting with nearby objects, each Matrix server can do an instant $O(1)$ lookup to determine the consistency set for any game packet using the overlap regions provided by the MC. Even in uncommon cases involving non-proximal interactions, the Matrix server can consult the MC to determine the consistency set for that particular interaction. Matrix could use alternate lookup methods (such as DHTs [22]), but that would result in increased latency (e.g., DHT schemes usually need $O(log(N))$ lookups for N Matrix servers). Although a centralized approach can lead to performance bottlenecks, the MC is only used when the MMOG world partitioning changes due to splits or reclamations (which should occur infrequently for a stable game). This centralized approach can scale to large server populations as the MC is not used in the latency-critical packet forwarding process (except for the rare non-proximal interactions). The MC can also be made reliable using well understood replication techniques.

4   Evaluation Highlights

Due to space constraints, we present just one detailed result showing that Matrix can handle dense hotspots automatically. The detailed evaluation results will appear in a longer version of this paper.

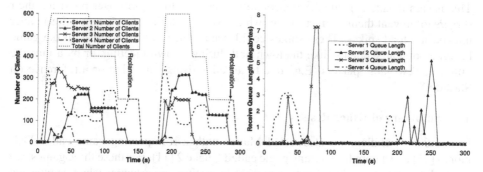

This Figure shows Matrix responding to a 600 client hotspot. The left graph shows how the total number of clients were shared among the various servers. Note that a server is overloaded when it has 300+ clients. The right graph shows the receive queue length of the various servers. Matrix used up to four server to handle the load caused by the hotspots. However, Matrix reclaimed those extra servers as shown by the reclamation points on the left graph when the load eased. The second reclamation took longer as the child server took longer to become underloaded (< 150 clients).

Fig. 2. Hotspot caused by 600 clients

4.1 Behaviour Under Load and Hotspots

Matrix was designed to gracefully react to unexpected heavy loads and dense hotspots. We tested this by subjecting Matrix to loads far higher than what a static partitioning scheme could handle.

Figure 2 shows an experiment in which a hotspot of 600 clients (for a real shooting game called Bzflag [16]), far higher than a static partitioning could handle (results not shown), was introduced at around the 10 second mark for about 75 seconds, after which the entire hotspot gradually disappeared (indicated by 200 clients disappearing at fixed intervals). The hotspot was reintroduced at a different position in the world at 170 seconds, for about 50 seconds, and then gradually removed. Matrix relieved the initial spike in the receive queue caused by 600 clients joining (shown at time=10 in Figure 2) by spawning server 2 (at time=10) and giving it half the map. However, this did not ease the load as the hotspot was on the map portion retained by server 1. Hence, server 1 spawned another server, server 3, (at time=10) and split its current map with it (servers 1 and 3 have 1/4 of the map each with server 2 having the rest). Server 3's map range contained the hotspot and a large number of clients were switched to it easing server 1's load. However, server 3 now experienced a load spike (at time=60). This process continues recursively until the load on all the servers is acceptable. As clients leave the game, servers become underloaded and Matrix reacts by consolidating the load onto a smaller number of servers. For example, after 200 clients left the game (at time=75), server 3 became underloaded and reclaimed its "child" server (server 4). Matrix was similarly able to handle the subsequent appearance and disappearance of another hotspot (introduced at t=170) located at a different part of the map.

This result clearly demonstrates that Matrix, unlike static partitioning schemes, is able to deploy additional servers to react quickly and effectively to sudden load changes.

This is significant, as game developers no longer have to a-priori over-provision their servers to prevent them from crashing (which would mar the game's reputation) under unexpected load spikes. These spikes could occur when particular areas in the game become popular suddenly, like the town hall during a town meeting, or by a massive influx of new game players (E.g., due to an advertising campaign or a reference on Slashdot).

4.2 Summary of Other Results

In addition to Bzflag, we also tested Matrix with a role playing game called Daimonin [23] and a popular shooting game called Quake 2 [11]. For these three games, we showed that Matrix is able to outperform static partitioning schemes when unexpected loads or hotspots occur. In particular, Matrix is able to automatically use extra servers to handle the load while the static partitioning schemes just fail.

We also conducted microbenchmarks that showed that Matrix's overheads, in terms of switching latency and bandwidth usage, were acceptable. In particular, the overhead of using a central coordinator was negligible and the amount of traffic sent between Matrix servers corresponded directly to the size of the overlap regions.

We then conducted a simple user study, using Bzflag, that showed that Matrix is completely transparent to real game players. Even under heavy load, requiring Matrix to add servers, game players did not perceive any significant Matrix-induced performance degradation.

Finally, we performed a simplistic asymptotic analysis of Matrix. This analysis reaffirmed the microbenchmarks and suggested that a) Matrix can scale to a large player population ($> 1,000,000$ players and $10,000$ servers) only if the number of players in the overlap regions is small relative to the total number of game players, and b) that Matrix scalability is ultimately limited by the maximum I/O capacity of individual servers.

5 Related Work

There have been previous attempts at using scalable "grids" of servers to build a distributed architectures for MMOGs [5,17]. However, these solutions are still mostly in a formative stage. Peer-to-peer (p2p) architectures have also been proposed as a solution for MMOGs [12]. In these systems, players form localized groups and exchange messages directly with other players in the group, thereby allowing the system to scale. However, these mechanisms are unable to effectively handle hotspots and they do not clearly separate the game from the infrastructure, requiring each game to be intimately designed with the p2p network in mind. They also allow players to directly exchange game messages with one another, compounding the problems associated with collusion and cheating.

Commercial MMOG systems, such as Everquest [19] and Final Fantasy XI [20], carefully partition the game world between different servers to reduce the communication overhead between servers. To handle hotspots, they allocate multiple tightly-coupled (completely consistent) servers to handle the same partition, an approach that is neither efficient nor very scalable. Instead, Matrix techniques can be used by these systems, together with careful static partitioning, to efficiently and effectively handle hotspots and load fluctuations.

The notion of radius of visibility has been used extensively in the field of computer graphics where only objects in the immediate field of view are rendered. However, we are applying this technique to the domain of multiplayer games. The use of localized consistency has also been used in previous systems to achieve lower latency updates at the expense of complete correctness. These include distributed shared memory systems [2,13], databases [1,6], and network protocols [10]. However, unlike these previous systems, multiplayer games are nearly decomposable. This allows Matrix to use localized consistency to reduce latency without sacrificing any correctness.

Finally, there have been a number of algorithms to split virtual worlds among different servers. These include algorithms optimized for reducing inter-server communications [14,15] and for preserving locality [8]. Our work complements these solutions and Matrix can use these algorithms to perform more optimal splits.

6   Conclusion

In this paper, we have shown that it is possible to build, using localized consistency and on-demand mechanisms, an easy to use distributed middleware architecture that is able to satisfy the latency and scalability requirements of MMOGs. We have implemented Matrix and used its simple API to allow three games (BzFlag, Quake2 and Daimonin) to use Matrix. The Matrix design is specially attractive because of its layered approach; by completely shielding the game from the actual mechanisms used to implement consistency, reliability and map partitioning, Matrix allows a game developer to use it with almost no modifications to the game client, and relatively simple modifications to the server code.

References

1. Adya, A. and Liskov, B. Lazy consistency using loosely synchronized clocks. *Proceedings of the 16th Annual ACM Symposium on Principles of Distributed Computing (PODC '97)*, Santa Barbara, CA, Aug. 1997.
2. Agarwal, A., Chaiken, D., Johnson, K., Kranz, D., Kubiatowicz, J., Kurihara, K., Lim, B.-H., Maa, G., and Nussbaum, D. The MIT alewife machine : A large-scale distributed-memory multiprocessor. *Proceedings of Workshop on Scalable Shared Memory Multiprocessors*. Kluwer Academic, 1991.
3. Armitage, G. Lag over 150 milliseconds is unacceptable. http://gja.space4me.com/things/quake3-latency-051701.html, May 2001.
4. Basch, J., Guibas, L. J., and Hershberger, J. Data structures for mobile data. *Proceedings of the eighth annual ACM-SIAM symposium on Discrete algorithms*, pages 747–756, 1997.
5. Bauer, D., Rooney, S., and Scotton, P. Network infrastructure for massively distributed games. *Proceedings of the 1st workshop on Network and System Support for Games (Netgames)*, pages 36–43, Bruanschweig, Germany, May 2002.
6. Breitbart, Y., Komondoor, R., Rastogi, R., Seshadri, S., and Silberschatz, A. Update propagation protocols for replicated databases. *SIGMOD Record (ACM Special Interest Group on Management of Data)*, 28(2):97–108, 1999.

7. Butterfly.net. *The Butterfly Grid.* http://www.butterfly.net/, Sept. 2000.
8. Chen, J., Wu, B., Delap, M., Knutsson, B., Lu, H., and Amza, C. Locality aware dynamic load management for massively multiplayer games. *Proceedings of the tenth ACM SIGPLAN symposium on Principles and practice of parallel programming (PPoP)*, Chicago, IL, June 2005.
9. DFC Intelligence. *Challenges and Opportunities in the Online Game Market - Executive Summary.* http://www.dfcint.com/game_article/june03article.htm, June 2003.
10. Golding, R. A. A weak-consistency architecture for distributed information services. *Computing Systems*, 5(4):379–405, Fall 1992.
11. Id Software. *Quake 2 Source Code.* http://www.idsoftware.com/business/techdownloads/, Apr. 2002.
12. Knutsson, B., Lu, H., Xu, W., and Hopkins, B. Peer-to-peer support for massively multiplayer games. *Proceedings of the 23rd Conference of the IEEE Communications Society (Infocomm)*, Hong Kong, China, Mar. 2004.
13. Lenoski, D., Laudon, J., Joe, T., Nakahira, D., Stevens, L., Gupta, A., and Hennessy, J. The DASH prototype: Implementation and performance. *Proceedings of the 19th Annual International Symposium on Computer Architecture (ISCA)*, pages 92–103, Gold Coast, Australia, May 1992.
14. Lui, J. C. S. and Chan, M. F. An efficient partitioning algorithm for distributed virtual environment systems. *IEEE Transactions on Parallel and Distributed Systems*, 13(3):193–211, 2002.
15. O'Connell, K., Dinneen, T., Collins, S., Tangney, B., Harris, N., and Cahill, V. Techniques for handling scale and distribution in virtual worlds. *Proceedings of the 7th ACM SIGOPS European Workshop*, Connemara, Ireland, Sept. 1996.
16. Riker, T. Bzflag source code and online documentation. http://www.bzflag.org/, June 2003.
17. Shaikh, A., Sahu, S., Rosu, M., Shea, M., and Saha, D. Implementation of a service platform for online games. *Proceedings of the 3rd workshop on Network and System Support for Games (Netgames)*, Portland, Oregon, Sep 2004.
18. Simon, H. A. The architecture of complexity. *Proceedings of the American Philosophical Society*, 106:467–482, 1962.
19. Sony Entertainment. *Everquest Live.* http://eqlive.station.sony.com/, Mar. 1999.
20. Square Enix. *Final Fantasy XI Online.* http://www.playonline.com/ff11us/index.shtml, Oct. 2003.
21. Square Enix. *Final Fantasy XI Online Press Release.* http://www.playonline.com/ff11us/polnews/news1430.shtml, Jan. 2004.
22. Stoica, I., Morris, R., Karger, D., Kaashoek, M. F., and Balakrishnan, H. Chord: A scalable peer-to-peer lookup service for internet applications. *Proceedings of the 2001 ACM SIGCOMM Conference*, pages 149–160. ACM Press, 2001.
23. Toennies, M. Daimonin source code. http://daimonin.sourceforge.net/, Sept. 2003. (Version 0.96alpha1).
24. Woodcock, B. S. Graphing the growth of mmogs. http://pw1.netcom.com/~sirbruce/Subscriptions.html, Mar. 2004.

Overlay Networks – Implementation by Specification

Stefan Behnel and Alejandro Buchmann

Databases and Distributed Systems Group,
Darmstadt University of Technology (TUD), Germany
{behnel, buchmann}@dvs1.informatik.tu-darmstadt.de

Abstract. Implementing overlay software is non-trivial. Current projects build overlays or intermediate frameworks on top of low-level networking abstractions. This leaves implementing the topologies, their maintenance and optimisation strategies, and the routing to the developer.

We take a novel approach to overlay implementation by modelling topologies as a distributed database. This approach, named "Node Views", abstracts from low-level issues like I/O and message handling. Instead, it moves *ranking nodes* and *selecting neighbours* into the heart of the overlay software development process. It decouples maintenance components in overlay software and allows implementing them in a generic, configurable way for pluggable integration in frameworks.

1 Introduction

Recent years have seen a large body of research in decentralised, self-maintaining overlay networks like P-Grid [1], Chord [2], ODRI [3] or Gia [4]. They are commonly regarded as building blocks for Internet-scale distributed applications.

Contrary to this expectation, current overlay implementations are built with incompatible, language specific frameworks on top of low level networking abstractions. This complicates their design and hinders the comparison and integration of different topologies. Apart from a recently proposed API for the specific case of structured overlay networks [5], there is little standardisation effort in the rest of the overlay area. And a common API does by no means simplify the design of the overlay implementation itself.

Currently, programmers who want to use overlays for their applications must decide in advance, at a very early design phase, which of the distinct overlay implementations they want to use and must invest time to understand its specific usage. This effectively prohibits testing the final product with different topologies or delivering versions with specialised overlays. Therefore, the actual usefulness of overlays for application design is currently very limited.

This paper explores the design space of overlay design frameworks and the abstractions they provide. It proposes an integrative high-level approach at a data management level rather than the networking and messaging level. Similar to the way standard DBMS's have decoupled and modularised today's server applications, the presented approach allows for a separation of concerns in overlay software and for pluggable, decoupled components in overlay design frameworks.

G. Alonso (Ed.): Middleware 2005, LNCS 3790, pp. 401–410, 2005.

Section 2 investigates the major functionality blocks of overlay software and matches them with the current framework support. Section 3 then presents the Node Views abstraction that facilitates a higher level design of overlay topologies and decoupled components. The SQL-like language that we designed for topology implementation is outlined in section 4. We describe the status of our implementation in section 5.

2   Functionality of Overlay Software

Overlay networks form a layer for organisation and communication in distributed applications. This section describes their different levels of functionality as illustrated in figure 1.While the development process of overlay software deals with all of them, only few level are well supported by design aids and frameworks.

The lowest two levels comprise the general operating system support for Internet-level **network I/O** and edge-level **message passing**. These levels are not specific to overlays and are usually hidden by higher layers.

A number of overlays, such as Bamboo [6], are implemented on top of generic event-driven state machines like SEDA [7] that model **message processing** in Internet servers. While EDSMs were not designed for overlay development, they still provide a good abstraction level for scalable event processing (see 2.2).

Overlay routing protocols then deal with local routing decisions for scalable end-to-end message forwarding. They are distributed algorithms, executed at each member node, with the purpose of forwarding messages at the overlay level from senders to receivers. Routing is left out of figure 1 for clarity reasons. While situated at the message processing layer, it actually uses the topology rules as explained in the next section.

2.1   Overlay Software from the Topology Perspective

Where current frameworks focus on message forwarding and the protocol design part of overlay software, we propose raising the abstraction level to topology design. This is motivated by four more functional levels in overlay software.

Local topology rules play a major role in overlay software which makes them a very interesting abstraction level. The global topology of an overlay is established by a distributed algorithm that each member node executes. The topology rules on each node implement this algorithm by accepting neighbour candidates or objecting to them. Overlays traditionally implement these rules

Functionality	Support in current frameworks	
Topology Selection	**Node views**	
Topology Adaptation		
Topology Maintenance		(Macedon)
Topology Rules		
Message Processing	iOverlay, Macedon	Flow-Graphs, EDSMs, ...
Message Passing		Serialisation, RPC, CORBA, ...
Network I/O		Sockets, TCP/UDP, ...

Fig. 1. Framework Support for Overlay Software

implicitly as part of their routing and maintenance algorithms, which is why frameworks currently ignore this level.

There are two sides to topology rules. *Node selection* allows an application to show interest in certain nodes and ignore others based on their status, attributes and capabilities. Generally, applications are only interested in nodes that they know (or assume) to be alive, usually based on the information when the last message from them arrived. But not even all locally known live nodes are interesting to the application that can select nodes for communication based on quality-of-service requirements. Furthermore, if a heterogeneous application uses multiple overlays, its participants do not necessarily support all running protocols. Each node must see the others only in overlays that they support.

Node categorisation is the second part. Where node selection is the black-and-white decision of seeing a node or not, categorisation determines *how* nodes are seen. Nearly all overlay networks know different kinds of neighbours: close and far ones, fast and slow ones, parents and children, super-nodes and peers, or nodes that store data of type A, B or C. Node categorisation lets a node sort other nodes into different buckets to distinguish them. Overlay routing and other overlay tasks are then implemented on top of the node categorisation.

In current structured overlay networks [1,2,3,6], topology rules are stated apart from the implementation as a local invariant whose global properties are either proven by hand or found in experiments. It is a hard problem but also an interesting question to what extent the process of building routing protocols from local rules and inferring the guarantees they provide can be automated.

Topology maintenance is the perpetual process of repairing the topology whenever it breaks the rules. Above all, this means integrating new nodes (i.e. selecting and categorising them) and replacing failed ones. Support for this functionality is very limited among the current frameworks, despite its obvious importance for self-maintaining overlays.

Topology adaptation is the ability of a given overlay topology to adapt to specific requirements. As opposed to the error correction of topology maintenance, adaptation handles the freedom of choice allowed by the topology rules. The rules therefore draw the line between maintenance and adaptation. An example is Pastry where evaluations have shown [8] that redundant entries in the routing table can be exploited for adaptation to achieve better resilience and lower latency. Topology adaptation usually defines some kind of metric for choosing new edges out of a valid set of candidates. Building the "right" sub-groups of nodes in hierarchical topologies also fits into this scheme.

Current overlays are designed with some kind of adaptation in mind, whereas the available frameworks do not provide support for its implementation. What is needed here is a ranking mechanism for connection candidates. Overlays usually aim to provide an "efficient" topology. The term efficiency, however, is always based on a specific choice of relevant metrics, such as end-to-end hop-count or edge latency, but possibly also the node degree or the expected quality of query results. The respective metric determines the node ranking which in turn parametrises the global properties of the topology.

Topology selection is the choice of different topologies that an overlay application can build on. Supporting multiple topologies obviously makes sense for debugging and testing at design-time. However, it is just as useful at run-time if an application has to adapt to diverse quality-of-service requirements, such as different preferences regarding reliability, throughput and latency. A given topology may excel in one or the other and this specialisation allows it to provide high performance while keeping a simple design. Topology selection allows an application to provide optimised solutions for different cases.

Topology adaptation and selection play the most important role for QoS support in overlays. However, selection obviously relies on the integration of different overlay implementations to make their topologies available to a single application. This is especially necessary to avoid duplication in effort when maintaining multiple topologies and switching between them. It is not efficient, for example, to have an application maintain several overlays if each of them independently sends pings to determine the availability of nodes. Integrative approaches like Node Views (as presented in section 3) become crucial here.

2.2   Frameworks and Middleware for Overlay Implementation

There have been a number of recent proposals for overlay frameworks and middleware. Macedon [9] and iOverlay [10] are under development and evaluation in the corresponding projects. Other frameworks, like SEDA [7] or JXTA (http://www.jxta.org), have also been used for overlay implementations, although they do not provide any higher-level support for topologies and other overlay specific tasks.

iOverlay essentially provides a message switch abstraction for the design of the local routing algorithm. The neighbours of a node are instantiated as local I/O queues between which the user provided implementation switches messages. This generally simplifies the design of overlay algorithms by hiding the lower networking levels. However, there is no further support for topology rules, maintenance or adaptation.

Macedon is a state machine compiler for overlay protocol design and forms the most interesting approach so far. Event-driven state machines (EDSMs) have been used over decades for protocol design and specification. Macedon extends this approach to an overlay specific, C++ based language from which it generates source code for overlay maintenance and routing. In a number of different proof-of-concept overlay implementations, this was shown to be very useful for implementing and testing algorithms for routing and maintenance.

Overlays must operate autonomously. This means that they must configure themselves and automatically adapt to a changing environment. However, this is not only a matter of designing a routing protocol. Each node in an overlay needs to take local decisions. The sum of these local decisions is the distributed algorithm that maintains the overlay. What are these local decisions based on?

iOverlay bases them on the currently available connections. It does not provide means for selecting the "right" connections or categorising them, neither does it support ranking connection candidates for adaptation and fall-back mechanisms. Similarly, Macedon does not support candidate nodes or adaptability of topologies. Modelling adaptivity in state machines is even likely to be rather complex and can lead to state explosion. Consequently, in all of these incompatible and language dependent frameworks, the designer is forced to model local decisions in framework specific source code.

2.3   Local Decisions and Data About Nodes

The local decisions, that each participant in a distributed algorithm takes, rely on the local view of that node. The local view is a node's combined knowledge about the other nodes in the system, above all its neighbours in the topology.

To establish a local view, each node has to keep data about other nodes. Examples are addresses and identifiers, measured or estimated latencies and references to data stored on these nodes. Furthermore, it is generally of interest when a node was last contacted (time-stamps or history) to determine if it is alive.

Data about remote nodes is gathered from diverse sources. Some data can be determined locally (IP address, ping latency, ...), while other information is received in dedicated messages - either directly from the node it describes or indirectly via hearsay of intermediate nodes. There is often more than one way of finding equivalent data. Latencies, for example, can be measured (ping) or estimated [11,12]. A node A knows that a node B is alive if A received a ping response or other message from B, if it heard about it from other nodes (gossip), etc. Different quality-of-service levels in an overlay application can trade load against certainty by selecting different sources.

Topology rules, maintenance, adaptation and selection mainly deal with managing data about nodes. The topology rules put constraints on the data about possible neighbour nodes. Maintenance needs to keep data about fall-back candidates that may currently not be neighbours. It also deals with gathering data about nodes that joined or finding conflicts between local and remote views. Adaptation does a ranking between candidate nodes before it decides about the instantiation as neighbours or fall-backs. Topology selection then switches between different views, i.e. ranking metrics and sets of neighbours.

A data abstraction is obviously a good way of dealing with this diversity of sources, data characteristics and data management tasks. It allows an overlay to lift dependencies on specific algorithms and to take advantage of the different characteristics of different implementations as the need arises.

3   Node Views, the System Model

We propose to design overlay frameworks as data management systems using the well-known Model-View-Controller pattern [13]. The *model* is an active local database on each node, a central storage place for all data that a node knows about remote nodes. Once the data is stored in a single place, software components no longer have to care about any data management themselves. They benefit from a locally consistent data store and from notifications about changes.

The major characteristics of the overlay topology are then defined in *views* of the database. They represent sets of nodes that are of interest to the local node (such as its neighbours). Different views provide different ways of selecting and categorising nodes, and different ways of adapting topologies. Topology selection is then mainly a matter of selecting the right set of views.

As the views form the most important overlay specific part of the implementation, they are also the most crucial part for an abstract and framework-independent specification. Their definition is the main goal of the SLOSL language that is briefly presented in the next section.

The *controllers* are tiny EDSM states that operate on the views. They are triggered by events like incoming or leaving messages, timers or changes in the views and update the database according to the view definitions. They are the actual maintenance components that perform simple tasks like updating single attributes of nodes when new data becomes available or sending out messages to search new nodes that match the current view definitions. Note that the controllers do not aim to provide a global view for the model. They continuously update and repair the restricted and possibly globally inconsistent local view. The node database decouples them from other parts of the overlay software and the node views provide them with simplified, decoupled layers and a common interface to make them generic, reusable components in frameworks.

Another very important part of the architecture is an expressive *event system* for view events and messages. A notification about changes in views is fired whenever nodes enter or leave a view, or when visible node attributes change. Views filter notifications and software components only react to events from the views that they are subscribed to.

Components like message handlers or routers are still part of the overlay specific implementation, but they can now respond to specific events and use node views for their decisions. Defining messages as hierarchical structures allows components to subscribe to data fields instead of monolithic messages. This further helps in writing generic components. Database and views decouple them from the maintenance components and simplify their design considerably. Even more so, as this architecture can provide powerful operations like topology selection and

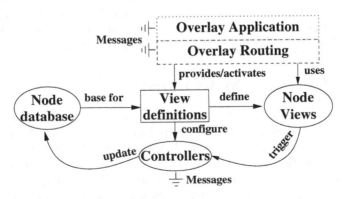

Fig. 2. Components of the System Model

adaptation with a single view selection command. The abstract view definition becomes the central point of control for the characteristics of the overlay.

4   SLOSL, the View Specification Language

For the view definitions that implement topology rules and adaptation, we developed SLOSL, the SQL-Like Overlay Specification Language [14]. We present it here using a simple example, an implementation of the Chord graph [2].

```
1  CREATE VIEW chord_fingertable
2  AS SELECT node.id, node.ring_dist, bdist=node.ring_dist−2^i
3  RANKED lowest(backups+i, node.msec_latency / node.ring_dist)
4  FROM node_db
5  WITH log_k = log(|𝒦|), backups = 1
6  WHERE node.supports_chord = true AND node.alive = true
7  HAVING node.ring_dist in (2^i : 2^{i+1})
8  FOREACH i IN (0:log_k)
```

The statements CREATE VIEW, SELECT, FROM and WHERE behave as in SQL. The WHERE clause specifically implements **node selection** based on node attributes. Note that SLOSL is not concerned with the source of the information that node attributes contain. It only constrains and categorises the presentation of locally available data. The remaining clauses do the following:

WITH. This clause defines variables or options of this view that can be set at instantiation time and changed at run-time. Here, log_k will likely keep its default value, while $backups$ allows adding redundancy at runtime.

HAVING–FOREACH. This pair of clauses aggregates the selected nodes into buckets to implement **node categorisation**. In the example, the (constant) node attribute $ring\_dist$ refers to the logical distance between the local node and the remote node. The HAVING expression states that it must lie within the given half-open interval (excluding the highest value) that depends on the bucket variable i.

The FOREACH part defines the available node buckets by declaring this bucket variable over a range (or a list, database table, . . .) of values. It defines either a single bucket of nodes, or a list, matrix, cube, etc. of buckets. The structure is imposed by the occurrence of zero or more FOREACH clauses, where each clause adds a dimension. Nodes are selected into these buckets by the optional HAVING expression.

The example shows a case where the SELECT clause gives nodes a new attribute **bdist** representing their position inside the bucket. Calculating attribute values is particularly useful for HAVING expressions that allow a node to appear in multiple buckets of the same view.

RANKED. To support **topology adaptation**, the nodes in the chord_fingertable view are chosen by the ranking function $lowest$ as the $backups + i$ top node(s) of each bucket that provide the lowest value for the given expression. Rankings are often based on the network latency, but any arithmetic expression based on node attributes can be used. The expression in the example implements a simple tradeoff between the network latency and the distance travelled in the ID space. Other overlays may require more complex expressions or user defined functions in the ranking expression.

5   Implementation, Current and Future Work

We are developing two different proof-of-concept implementations of this architecture as overlay execution environments. A first, light-weight prototype was written in Python, while our current work builds on the PostgreSQL database. It is targeted as a reference system rather than a high performance one. Once the APIs have become stable enough, we can let the architecture benefit from standard approaches used in Internet servers and application server designs.

As a major step towards simplified, abstract overlay development, we have designed a graphical editor (fig. 3) based on our system model. It allows the framework independent specification of overlay systems and outputs abstract overlay specifications in OverML [14], a new XML specification language for node attributes, SLOSL statements, messages and EDSM flow descriptions.

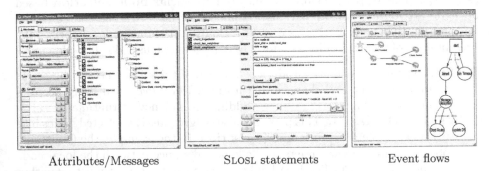

| Attributes/Messages | SLOSL statements | Event flows |

Fig. 3. The SLOSL Overlay Workbench

For the future, we hope for diverse implementations of OverML compatible frameworks as well as mappings to existing frameworks. The high abstraction level easily allows specialised environments for simulation and analysis, testing and debugging, and different deployment scenarios – without changes to the overlay specification. Deployment environments can use a rather lightweight or custom database. An interesting topic to investigate here is (partial) source code generation from SLOSL statements. This should allow customised overlay implementations for very efficient deployment.

Simulators and debuggers may prefer a single global database to enable tracing, verifying and visualising the system state. Recent proposals for scalable simulation environments [15] already take a layered approach. Simulations are carried out at a higher abstraction level and are then mapped to the network link level. We propose the database layer as a comfortable abstraction level.

Future work will also include better mechanisms for view and query optimisation. Our current PostgreSQL implementation maps SLOSL statements to rather complex, generic SQL queries. Building on the large body of literature on query modification and optimisation, we can imagine a number of ways to investigate for pre-optimising these statements. This is most interesting for views of views and for merging view definitions when sending them over the wire (like in gossip overlays [16] or hierarchical environments [17]).

6   Conclusion

This paper presented *Node Views*, a novel approach to overlay design frameworks that enables support for topology rules, maintenance, adaptation and selection at a very high level. Based on an active database, it allows for a separation of topology implementation, maintenance and message handling. This facilitates the development of generic components which enables pluggable development and integration of overlay systems.

The SLOSL language lifts the abstraction level for overlay design from messaging and routing protocols to the topology level. Its short, SQL-like statements meet the requirements for design-time specification, topology implementation and run-time adaptation of highly configurable overlay systems.

The current state of our implementation does not allow a performance comparison between the available hand-optimised overlay implementations and SLOSL based ones. In any case, the high abstraction level of Node Views will likely lead to slower systems in direct comparisons - but in a couple of hours implementation time compared to weeks for writing a traditional overlay from scratch.

Even compared to the days it takes to understand and start using one of the available overlay systems, SLOSL wins by being much easier to read and allowing overlays to gain orders of magnitude in configurability, adaptability and integration. The SLOSL Overlay Workbench makes overlay software easy and fast to write and shifts more of the development time towards testing and optimising the topology itself and choosing the right maintenance strategies. As with any other high-level language, long-term optimisations of OverML compatible platforms will improve the performance of overlays using them.

The Node Views approach encourages completely new ways of designing and testing overlays. Modifying compact SLOSL statements allows the designer to easily test and compare the impact of different selection and ranking functions on an application. Switching between different views and controllers, at design-time or run-time, enables overlay applications to adapt to the broad range from static to dynamic environments and to diverse quality-of-service requirements.

References

1. Aberer, K.: P-Grid: A Self-Organizing access structure for P2P information systems. In: Proc. of the Sixth Int. Conference on Cooperative Information Systems (CoopIS 2001), Trento, Italy. (2001)

2. Stoica, I., Morris, R., Karger, D., Kaashoek, F., Balakrishnan, H.: Chord: A scalable peer-to-peer lookup service for internet applications. In: Proc. of the 2001 ACM SIGCOMM Conference, San Diego, California, USA (2001)
3. Loguinov, D., Kumar, A., Rai, V., Ganesh, S.: Graph-theoretic analysis of structured peer-to-peer systems: Routing distances and fault resilience. [19]
4. Chawathe, Y., Ratnasamy, S., Breslau, L., Lanham, N., Shenker, S.: Making gnutella-like p2p systems scalable. [19]
5. Dabek, F., Zhao, B., Druschel, P., Stoica, I.: Towards a common API for structured peer-to-peer overlays. [18]
6. Rhea, S., Geels, D., Roscoe, T., Kubiatowicz, J.: Handling churn in a DHT. In: Proc. of the USENIX Annual Technical Conference, Boston, MA, USA (2004)
7. Welsh, M., Culler, D., Brewer, E.: SEDA: An architecture for well-conditioned, scalable internet services. In: Proc. of the 18th ACM symposium on operating systems principles, Banff, Alberta, Canada (2001)
8. Zhang, R., Hu, Y.C., Druschel, P.: Optimizing routing in structured peer-to-peer overlay networks using routing table redundancy. In: Proc. of the 9th Int. Workshop on Future Trends of Distributed Computing Systems (FTDCS'03), San Juan, Puerto Rico (2003)
9. Rodriguez, A., Killian, C., Bhat, S., Kostić, D., Vahdat, A.: MACEDON: Methodology for automatically creating, evaluating, and designing overlay networks. In: Proc. of the USENIX/ACM Symposium on Networked Systems Design and Implementation (NSDI2004), San Francisco, CA, USA (2004)
10. Li, B., Guo, J., Wan, M.: iOverlay: A lightweight middleware infrastructure for overlay application implementations. In: Proc. of the Int. Middleware Conference (Middleware2004), Toronto, Canada (2004)
11. Dabek, F., Cox, R., Kaashoek, F., Morris, R.: Vivaldi: A decentralized network coordinate system. In: Proc. of the 2004 ACM SIGCOMM Conference, Portland, Oregon, USA (2004)
12. Eugene Ng, T.S., Zhang, H.: Predicting internet network distance with coordinates-based approaches. In: INFOCOM 2002, New York, USA (2002)
13. Buschmann, F., Meunier, R., Rohnert, H., Sommerlad, P., Stal, M.: Pattern-Oriented Software Architecture: A System of Patterns. John Wiley & Sons (1996)
14. Behnel, S., Buchmann, A.: Models and languages for overlay networks. In: Proc. of the 3rd Int. VLDB Workshop on Databases, Information Systems and Peer-to-Peer Computing (DBISP2P 2005), Trondheim, Norway (2005)
15. Birck, H., Heckmann, O., Mauthe, A., Steinmetz, R.: The two-step overlay network simulation approach. In: Proc. of SoftCOM, Split, Croatia. (2004)
16. Gupta, I., Birman, K., Linga, P., Demers, A., van Renesse, R.: Kelips: Building an efficient and stable P2P DHT through increased memory and background overhead. [18]
17. Darlagiannis, V., Mauthe, A., Steinmetz, R.: Overlay design mechanisms for heterogeneous, large scale, dynamic P2P systems. Journal of Network and Systems Management, Special Issue on Distributed Management 12 (2004)
18. The 2nd International Workshop on Peer-to-Peer Systems (IPTPS03), Berkeley, CA, USA (2003)
19. The 2003 Conference on Applications, Technologies, Architectures, and Protocols for Computer Communications (SIGCOMM), Karlsruhe, Germany (2003)

Adaptive Load Diffusion for Stream Joins

Xiaohui Gu and Philip S. Yu

IBM T. J. Watson Research Center,
Hawthorne, NY 10532
{xiaohui, psyu}@ us.ibm.com

Abstract. Data stream processing has become increasingly important
as many emerging applications call for sophisticated realtime processing over data streams, such as stock trading surveillance, network traffic monitoring, and sensor data analysis. Stream joins are among the
most important stream processing operations, which can be used to detect linkages and correlations between different data streams. One major
challenge in processing stream joins is to handle continuous, high-volume,
and time-varying data streams under resource constraints. In this paper,
we present a novel load diffusion system to enable scalable execution of
resource-intensive stream joins using an ensemble of server hosts. The
load diffusion is achieved by a simple correlation-aware stream partition
algorithm. Different from previous work, the load diffusion system can
(1) achieve *fine-grained* load sharing in the distributed stream processing
system; and (2) produce *exact* query answers without missing any join
results or generate duplicate join results. Our experimental results show
that the load diffusion scheme can greatly improve the system throughput and achieve more balanced load distribution.

1   Introduction

Many emerging applications call for sophisticated realtime processing over data
streams, such as stock trading surveillance, network traffic monitoring, and sensor data analysis. In these applications, data streams from external sources
flow into a stream processing system (e.g., [5,11,12]) where they are processed
by different continuous query processing elements called operators. One of the
most important continuous query operators is sliding-window join between two
streams S_1 and S_2, called *stream join*. The output of the stream join contains
every pair of tuples (i.e., data records) $(s_1, s_2), s_1 \in S_1, s_2 \in S_2$ that satisfy a join
predicate. To handle infinite streams, each stream is associated with a sliding
window to limit the scope of stream joins. Indeed, for many applications, we only
need to correlate each newly arrived tuple with recently arrived tuples on the
other stream. The stream join can be used to detect linkages and correlations
between different data streams, which has many interesting applications. For
example, let us consider two data streams consisting of phone call records and
stock trading records, respectively. A sliding-window join between the suspicious
phone calls and anomalous trade records over the common attribute "trade identifier" can be used to generate insider trading alerts. Other application examples

G. Alonso (Ed.): Middleware 2005, LNCS 3790, pp. 411–420, 2005.

of stream joins include (1) correlate similar images between two news video for hot topic detection; and (2) associate measurements (e.g., temperature, chemical concentration) from different sensors for environment monitoring and problem diagnosis.

In many cases, stream applications require immediate on-line results, which implies that query processing should use in-memory processing as much as possible. However, given high stream rates and large window sizes, even a single sliding-window join operator can have large memory requirement [7]. Moreover, some query processing such as video analysis can also be CPU-intensive. Thus, a single server may not have enough resources to produce accurate join results while keeping up with high input rates. There are two basic solutions to address the challenge: shedding some workload by providing approximate query results [8,7], or offloading part of workload to other servers. Our research studies the latter approach, focusing on providing load diffusion scheme to efficiently execute stream joins using a cluster of servers connected by high-speed networks.

Distributed stream processing has recently received much research attention. In [10], Shah et al. studied intra-operator load distribution for processing a single windowed aggregation operator on multiple servers. However, their solution was not based on the sliding-window stream join model. In [9], Xing et al. proposed a dynamic load distribution framework that can provide coarse-grained load balancing at inter-operator level. However, the inter-operator load distribution alone is not sufficient since it does not allow a single operator to collectively use resources on multiple servers. In [4], we propose an optimal component composition scheme for distributed stream processing systems that can achieve both QoS support and load balancing. In [2], Balazinska et al. proposed a contract-based load management framework that can migrate workload among different stream processing sites based on pre-defined contracts. Different from the above work, this work focuses on supporting fine-grained load distribution, called *load diffusion* for sliding-window stream joins. For producing exact join results, the load diffusion system preserves a *correlation constraint* that correlated tuples must be sent to the same server.

In this paper, we present a novel load diffusion middleware system to dynamically distribute stream join workload among a cluster of servers. Our principle goal is to provide scalable stream joins by efficiently utilizing all available resources in the server cluster. To achieve the goal, we propose a simple correlation-aware stream partition algorithm called single stream partition (SSP). The SSP algorithm dynamically spreads the tuples of one stream called the master stream among all hosts for load diffusion, and replicates the other stream called the slave stream for preserving the correlation constraint. To adapt to dynamic stream environments, the SSP algorithm can adaptively switch the master stream and the slave stream according to the stream rate changes. We formally prove the correctness of the SSP algorithm and analyze its properties. The adaptation strategy is then derived based on the formal analysis.

We implement the load diffusion scheme as a middleware proxy service. The load diffusion proxy virtualizes a cluster of stream processing servers into a unified stream processing service. Analogous to previous middleware systems (e.g., [1]), the load diffusion middleware aims at providing a managed and transparent stream processing service, which hides complicated system management details from upper-level application developers. The major operation performed by the load diffusion proxy is to route tuples to proper servers according to the load diffusion algorithm and the load conditions of different servers. We have implemented the proposed load diffusion algorithms and conduct extensive experiments on a distributed stream processing simulation testbed. The experimental results show that the load diffusion scheme can greatly improve the system throughput and achieve more balanced load distribution compared to previous approaches.

The rest of the paper is organized as follows. Section 2 introduces the system model. Section 3 presents the correlation-aware stream partition algorithms. Section 4 presents an experimental evaluation. Finally, the paper concludes in Section 5.

2   System Model

2.1   Stream Processing Model

We now briefly describe the basic model of sliding-window stream joins illustrated by Figure 1 (a). A data stream, denoted by S_i, consists of a sequence of tuples denoted by $s_i \in S_i$. In a stream S_i, a variable number of tuples arrive in each time unit. We use r_i to denote the average arrival rate of the stream S_i. In a dynamic stream environment, the stream rate r_i can change over time. We assume that each tuple $s_i \in S_i$ carries a time-stamp $s_i.t$ to denote the time when the tuple arrives on the stream S_i. We use $S_i[W_i]$ to denote a sliding window on the stream S_i, where W_i denotes the length of the window in time units. At time t, we say s_i belongs to $S_i[W_i]$ if s_i arrives on S_i in the time interval $[t - W_i, t]$. The basic stream join operator considered in this paper is sliding-window symmetric join between two streams S_1 and S_2 over a common attribute A, denoted by $J_i = S_1[W_1] \bowtie_A S_2[W_2]$. The output of the join consists of all

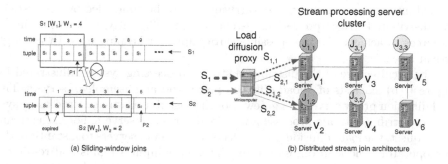

Fig. 1. The load diffusion system model

pairs of tuples (s_1, s_2) such that $s_1.A = s_2.A$ and $s_2 \in S_2[W_2]$ at time $s_1.t$ (i.e., $s_2.t \in [s_1.t - W_2, s_1.t]$) or $s_1 \in S_1[W_1]$ at time $s_2.t$ (i.e., $s_1.t \in [s_2.t - W_1, s_2.t]$). Each processing between the two tuples s_1 and s_2 is called one join operation. Each join operator maintains two queues Q_1 and Q_2 for buffering incoming tuples from the streams S_1 and S_2, respectively. When a new tuple $s_i \in S_i, 1 \le i \le 2$ arrives, it is inserted into the corresponding queue Q_i if Q_i is not full. Otherwise, the system either drops the newly arrived tuple or replace an old tuple in the buffer with the newly arrived tuple. The tuples in both queues Q_1 and Q_2 are processed according to the temporal order, i.e., if $s_1.t \in Q_1 < s_2.t \in Q_2$, s_1 is processed first. Each queue $Q_i, i = 1, 2$ maintains a pointer p_i to refer to the tuple currently processed by the join operator.

The sliding-window join algorithm processes a tuple $s_1 \in Q_1$ with the following steps: (1) update Q_2 by removing expired tuples. A tuple s_2 is expired if (a) it arrives earlier than $s_1.t - W_2$ and (b) it has been processed by the join operator (i.e., p_2 points to a tuple arrived later than s_2); (2) produce join results between s_1 and $S_2[W_2]$, denoted by $s_1 \bowtie_A S_2[W_2]$ by comparing $s_1.A$ and $s_2.A$, $\forall s_2 \in S_2[W_2]$; (3) update the pointer p_1 to refer to the next tuple in Q_1; (4) decide which tuple to process next by comparing $s_1.t$ and $s_2.t$, where s_1 and s_2 are the tuples pointed by p_1 and p_2, respectively. A symmetric procedure is followed for processing a tuple s_2 in the queue Q_2 of the stream S_2.

2.2   System Architecture

The distributed stream processing system consists of a cluster of servers connected by high-speed networks. Each server node, denoted by v_i, has a limited memory capacity M_i for buffering tuples, and a certain CPU processing speed that can process on average N_i join operations per time unit. Data streams are pushed into the distributed stream processing system from various external sources such as temperature sensors, stock tickers, and video cameras. The distributed stream processing system appears to a client as a unified stream processing service to serve a large number of continuous query processing over high volume data streams. The push-based stream environment has two unique features: (1) the tuples of a single stream can arrive in a bursty fashion (i.e., a large number of tuples can arrive in a short period of time); and (2) tuples are pushed into the system where data arrivals cannot be controlled by the system. The distributed stream processing system needs to efficiently utilize all available resources to achieve the best possible throughput for keeping up with the high arrival rates.

The architecture of the distributed stream processing system, illustrated by Figure 1 (b), consists of a load diffusion proxy and an ensemble of servers. The load diffusion proxy serves as a gateway of the distributed stream processing system to distribute stream processing workload across all servers. For each stream join request, the load diffusion proxy selects a number of servers to instantiate the join operator. The load diffusion proxy intercepts input streams and re-directs them to proper servers responsible for handling the stream joins. Due to the memory and CPU speed limits, a single server can only accommodate a certain data arrival rate in order to keep the unprocessed data in the memory. When tuples arrive too fast, the server has to drop tuples using some load shedding technique (e.g., [8]). However, dropping data can affect the accuracy of stream join results. Thus, the goal of our load diffusion scheme is to avoid dropping data as much as possible by spreading stream join workload across multiple servers.

The load diffusion proxy realizes fine-grained and balanced workload distribution using stream partitions. The stream partition algorithm can continuously split a high-volume stream into multiple substreams, each of which are sent to different servers for concurrent processing. Conceptually, the load diffusion proxy decomposes a resource-intensive join operator into multiple sub-operators executed on different servers. Each sub-operator only processes a subset of tuples on the original input streams. For example, in Figure 1 (b), the load diffusion proxy splits the stream S_1 into two substreams $S_{1,1}$ and $S_{1,2}$ that are sent to the server v_1, and v_2, respectively. Each substream has lower stream rate than the original stream. Different from load distribution for traditional distributed computing environments, our load diffusion scheme needs to send correlated data to the same server, which is called the correlation constraint. By observing the correlation constraint, the load diffusion proxy can maintain the full accuracy of stream joins. For example, let us consider a windowed stream join $S_1[W_1] \bowtie_A S_2[W_2]$. If the load diffusion proxy sends a tuple s_1 to a server node v_i, the correlated data include those tuples $s_2 \in S_2$ such that $s_2 \in S_2[s_1.t - W_2, t]$.

3   Replication-Assisted Single Stream Partition

The basic idea of the single stream partition (SSP) algorithm is to split one stream for load distribution and replicate the other stream for preserving the correlation constraint, which is illustrated by Figure 2. The partitioned stream is called the *master stream* and the replicated stream is called the *slave stream*. Each tuple of the slave stream is replicated on all the server hosts that are allocated to the join operator. Thus, we can freely partition the master stream since all the correlated tuples required by the partitioned stream are on the replicated stream, which have replicas on all server hosts. Figure 3 shows the pseudo-code of the SSP algorithm, which is described using an example as follows. Let us consider a join operator $J_i = S_1[W_1] \bowtie_A S_2[W_2]$ between the two streams S_1 and S_2 whose average arrival rates are r_1 and r_2, respectively. Suppose the sys-

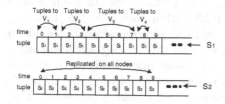

Fig. 2. The SSP example

Procedure $SSP(S_1, S_2, \{v_1, ..., v_k\})$
1. receive tuples for S_1 and S_2
3. $\forall s_1 \in S_1$, S_1: master stream
4.   send s_1 to the least-loaded host v_b
5. $\forall s_2 \in S_2$, S_2: slave stream
6.   send s_2 to all server hosts

Fig. 3. The SSP algorithm

tem allocates the host set $\{v_1, ..., v_k\}$ for executing the join operator J_i. Let us assume that S_1 is the master stream and S_2 is the slave stream. For each tuple s_1 arriving at the stream S_1, the SSP algorithm sends s_1 to one of the server hosts based on a certain selection policy (e.g., round-robin or least-loaded-first). For each tuple s_2 arrived at the stream S_2, the SSP algorithm replicates s_2 into k copies, each of which is sent to the k servers, respectively. By spreading the tuples of stream S_1 among all k servers, the workload of the join operator $J_i = S_1[W_1] \bowtie_A S_2[W_2]$ is diffused among all k servers since each server only processes a subset of all required join operations.

We now formally prove the correctness of the SSP algorithm. We define that a stream partition algorithm is correct if it executes the same set of join operations as the original join operator. We use $C(J_i)$ and $C'(J_i)$ to denote the sets of join operations performed by the original join operator and the join operations performed by the diffused join operator, respectively. We prove the correctness of the SSP algorithm by showing that $C(J_i) = C'(J_i)$.

Theorem 1. *Let $C(J_i)$ and $C'(J_i)$ denote the sets of join operations performed by the original join operator and the new join operator diffused by the SSP algorithm, respectively. We have $C(J_i) = C'(J_i)$.*

Proof. We first prove (1) $C(J_i) \subseteq C'(J_i)$ by showing that $\forall s_1$, if $s_1 \bowtie_A S_2[W_2] \in C(J_i)$, then $s_1 \bowtie_A S_2[W_2] \in C'(J_i)$, and $\forall s_2$, if $s_2 \bowtie_A S_1[W_1] \in C(J_i)$, then $s_2 \bowtie_A S_1[W_1] \in C'(J_i)$. Suppose the SSP algorithm sends s_1 to the server v_i. Because SSP replicates the stream S_2 on all servers, $S_2[W_2]$ must be present on the server v_i, too. Thus, $s_1 \bowtie_A S_2[W_2] \in C'(J_i)$. We now prove $\forall s_2$, if $s_2 \bowtie_A S_1[W_1] \in C(J_i)$, then $s_2 \bowtie_A S_1[W_1] \in C'(J_i)$. For any $s_2 \in S_2$, s_2 needs to join every tuple in $S_1[W_1]$. Suppose SSP sends $s_1 \in S_1[W_1]$ to the server v_i. Because s_2 is also present at v_i, we have $s_2 \bowtie_A s_1 \in C'(J_i)$. By aggregating all the results of $s_2 \bowtie_A s_1, \forall s_1 \in S_1[W_1]$, we have $s_2 \bowtie_A S_1[W_1] \in C'(J_i)$. Thus, we have $C(J_i) \subseteq C'(J_i)$. We then prove (2) $C'(J_i) \subseteq C(J_i)$ by showing that $\forall s_1$, if $s_1 \bowtie_A S_2[W_2] \in C'(J_i)$, then $s_1 \bowtie_A S_2[W_2] \in C(J_i)$, and $\forall s_2$, if $s_2 \bowtie_A S_1[W_1] \in C'(J_i)$, then $s_2 \bowtie_A S_1[W_1] \in C(J_i)$. The proof is straightforward since any join operation in $C'(J_i)$ follows the windowed join definition, which thus should appear in $C(J_i)$, too. Because $\forall s_1 \in S_1$, s_1 is only sent to one server, two different servers do not perform duplicated join operations. Thus, we have $C'(J_i) \subseteq C(J_i)$. Combining (1) and (2), we have $C(J_i) = C'(J_i)$. $\square$

We now analyze the properties of the SSP algorithm. Since the number of total join operations is not changed by the SSP algorithm, each server in $\{v_1, ..., v_k\}$ only processes on average one $k'th$ of the original join operations. One advantage of the SSP algorithm is that it can achieve the finest-grained spreading for the master stream at a per-tuple basis. By splitting the master stream S_1 into k substreams, the SSP algorithm can reduce the resource requirements for individual servers. Let r_1 denote the arrival rate of the master stream S_1. Each sub-stream of S_1 has an average arrival rate of r_1/k. Thus, in addition to reduce the processing workload, the SSP algorithm can reduce (1) memory requirement for buffering tuples in the sliding windows and (2) bandwidth requirement for receiving tuples.

Theorem 2. *Let r_1 and r_2 denote the rates of the two joined streams S_1 and S_2. Let W_1 and W_2 denote the sliding-window sizes of S_1 and S_2. Let m denote the average tuple size. Let k denote the server number. Let ΔM and ΔB denote the average memory reduction, average bandwidth reduction, and average processing load reduction at each server node compared to the original join operator. We have*

$$\Delta M = \frac{k-1}{k} \cdot m \cdot r_1 \cdot W_1 \tag{1}$$

$$\Delta B = \frac{k-1}{k} \cdot m \cdot r_1 \tag{2}$$

Proof. Without load diffusion, the original join operator is executed on a single server v_i. The server needs a memory space for buffering the tuples in the two sliding windows $S_1[W_1]$ and $S_2[W_2]$, which can be calculated as $m \cdot (r_1 \cdot W_1 + r_2 \cdot W_2)$. The server needs $m \cdot (r_1 + r_2)$ bandwidth for receiving the tuples. With load diffusion, the tuple arrival rate of the stream S_1 at each server is reduced to $\frac{r_1}{k}$. The memory space for buffering the tuples in the sliding windows at a single server is reduced to $m \cdot (\frac{r_1}{k} \cdot W_1 + r_2 \cdot W_2)$. The bandwidth requirement at each server is reduced to $m \cdot (\frac{r_1}{k} + r_2)$. Thus, the average memory reduction at each server is $\Delta M = m \cdot (r_1 \cdot W_1 + r_2 \cdot W_2) - m \cdot (\frac{r_1}{k} \cdot W_1 + r_2 \cdot W_2) = \frac{k-1}{k} \cdot m \cdot r_1 \cdot W_1$. The average bandwidth reduction at each server is $\Delta B = \frac{k-1}{k} \cdot m \cdot r_1$. □

We now analyze the overhead of the SSP algorithm. Since the SSP algorithm replicates the tuples of the slave stream S_2 on all allocated servers, the load diffusion proxy pushes more tuples into the server cluster than the original input streams. The system needs to spend part of CPU cycles on processing these extra tuples such as receiving the tuple from the network, extracting the time stamp and sequence number, dropping the tuple if not needed, inserting the tuple into the queue if it is useful and memory is not full, and replacing an old tuple if memory is full. We define the overhead of the SSP algorithm as the number of these extra tuples. We can easily derive that the overhead of the SSP algorithm is $(k-1) \cdot r_2$ since only S_2 is replicated on $(k-1)$ extra hosts. In order to minimize the algorithm overhead, the SSP algorithm adaptively selects the stream with lower rate as the master stream, and the other stream as the slave stream. The load diffusion proxy estimates the arrival rate of each stream by counting the number of arrived tuples on each stream within a sampling period. The average arrival rate of the input stream can be estimated by dividing the tuple number over the sampling period.

4   Experimental Evaluation

4.1   Experiment Setup

We have implemented the load diffusion middleware proxy that executes the proposed stream partition algorithm. We conduct experiments to evaluate the performance of the load diffusion proxy using a simulated stream processing cluster and a variety of stream join workloads. The source streams first arrive the load diffusion proxy and then directed to different server hosts for join processing. Each server executes the sliding-window join algorithm described in Section 2.1. The memory space of each server is randomly set in the range of [1000, 2000] tuples. The CPU speed of each server is distributed in the range of [1000, 5000] MIPS. Different values reflect the heterogeneity among different servers. The average CPU cost to process a join operation is set as 50 MIPS. The average CPU cost for processing each tuple upon receiving (i.e., insert the new tuple, drop the new tuple, or replace an old tuple with the new tuple) is set as 10 MIPS. The tuples on the input streams $S_i, i = 1, 2$ are generated at an average rate of r_i tuples per second. We use the same tuple arrival model as [7] where the inter-arrival time is uniformly selected at random between $1/2r_i$ and $2/r_i$ time units. Our experiments use different stream rates r_i to represent dynamic workloads. For comparison, we use the following metrics: (1) *throughput* that is defined as the number of join operations finished by all servers over a period of time, and (2) *effective CPU utilization* that is defined by the ratio between the CPU cycles spent on the join processing at a server per second over the server's CPU capacity. We use *LLF-Distribution* to denote the traditional least-loaded-first load distribution algorithm that instantiates a join operator on a single least-loaded server. In all experiments, we use $W_1 = W_2 = 10$ seconds. Each simulation run lasts 5000 seconds.

4.2   Results and Analysis

We first evaluate the scaling property of the SSP algorithm. The experiment executes 10 join operators using a 100 node heterogeneous cluster. The stream rates r_1 and r_2 of each join operator are randomly selected from the range of [5,20] tuples/second. Figure 4 shows the throughput of different algorithms as we gradually increase the number of servers allocated to each join operator. Each throughput value represents the total number of join operations performed by the system during the whole 5000-second simulation duration. The system randomly selects k servers for each join operator given the number of servers allocated to it. We observe that the SSP algorithm achieves best performance when each join operator is allocated with about 15 servers. The reason is that the overhead of the SSP algorithm increases proportionally to the number of allocated servers. In contrast, the throughput of the LLF-Distribution algorithm is unchanged during the above experiment since each join operator can only use one server. Figure 5 shows the average effective CPU utilization results as we gradually increase the number of servers allocated to each stream join. We observe that in the SSP algorithm, the average CPU utilization first increases as the algorithm spread the workload among all servers, and then decreases when more than 15 servers are used for each join operator since all servers are overwhelmed by excessive overhead tuples.

We then evaluate the load balancing property of the SSP algorithm. This experiment executes two stream join operators on a ten-node heterogeneous

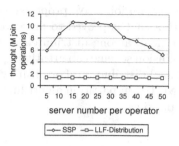

Fig. 4. Throughput results

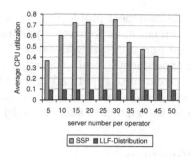

Fig. 5. CPU utilization results

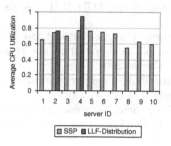

Fig. 6. Load balancing results

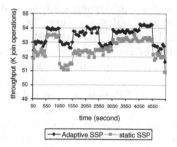

Fig. 7. Adaptation results

cluster. Figure 6 shows the average effective CPU utilization of the ten server nodes after the 5000 second simulation period. We observe that the SSP algorithm can achieve more balanced load distribution than the LLF-Distribution algorithm that can only perform load balancing at inter-operator level not at the intra-operator level. Our last experiment evaluates the adaptation strategy. The experiment runs ten stream join operators on a 100-node cluster. In the SSP algorithm, each join is allowed to use 5 servers. The initial average stream rates r_1 and r_2 are randomly selected from the range of [5,20] tuples/second. We then dynamically change the average stream rates every 500 seconds. The throughput value is sampled every 50 seconds. The throughput value at time t records the total number of join operations performed by the whole server cluster between time $[t-50, t]$. Figure 7 shows the adaptation results of the SSP algorithm that dynamically switches the master stream and the slave stream based on the rate changes. We observe that the adaptive SSP consistently achieves better performance than the static SSP algorithm that always uses the same master and slave streams.

5   Conclusion

In this paper, we presented a novel load diffusion middleware proxy to enable distributed execution of resource-intensive stream joins using a cluster of servers. To the best of our knowledge, this is the first work that studied fine-grained load management problem for sliding-window stream joins. We proposed a simple correlation-aware stream partition algorithm that is proved to preserve the stream join accuracy while spreading the workload among distributed servers. Our experimental results show that the load diffusion scheme can greatly improve the system throughput and achieve balanced load distribution. For future work, we will develop more efficient and sophisticated stream partition algorithms and extend the system to support multi-way stream joins.

References

1. C. Amza, A. Cox, W. Zwaenepoel. Consistent Replication for Scaling Back-end Databases of Dynamic Content Web Sites, Proc. of the ACM/IFIP/Usenix Middleware Conference, June, 2003.
2. M. Balazinska, H. Balakrishnan, M. Stonebraker: Contract-based Load Management in Federated Distributed Systems, Proc. of 1st Symposium on Networked Systems Design and Implementation (NSDI), March, 2004.
3. G. Cybenko: Dynamic load balancing for distributed memory multiprocessors. Journal of Parallel and Distributed Computing, 7(2):279-301, 1989.
4. X. Gu, P. S. Yu, K. Nahrstedt, Optimal Component Composition for Scalable Stream Processing, Proc. of IEEE International Conference on Distributed Computing Systems (ICDCS), June, 2005.
5. S. Krishnamurthy et al. TelegraphCQ: An Architectural Status Report. IEEE Data Engineering Bulletin, 26(1):11-18, March, 2003.
6. Arvind Krishna, Douglas C. Schmidt, and Raymond Klefstad, Enhancing Real-Time CORBA via Real-Time Java, Proceedings of the 24th IEEE International Conference on Distributed Computing Systems (ICDCS), May 23-26, 2004.
7. U. Srivastava, J. Widom: Memory Limited Execution of Windowed Stream Joins, Proc. of the 30th International Conference on Very Large Databases (VLDB), August, 2004.
8. N. Tatbul and U. etintemel and S. Zdonik and M. Cherniack and M. Stonebraker: Load Shedding in a Data Stream Manager, Proc. of the 29th International Conference on Very Large Data Bases (VLDB), September, 2003.
9. Y. Xing, S. B. Zdonik, J.-H. Hwang, Dynamic Load Distribution in the Borealis Stream Processor, Proc. of International Conference on Data Engineering (ICDE), April, 2005.
10. M. A. Shah, J. M. Hellerstein, S. Chandrasekaran, M. J. Franklin, Flux: An Adaptive Partitioning Operator for Continuous Query Systems, Proc. of the 19th International Conference on Data Engineering (ICDE), March, 2003.
11. The STREAM Group. STREAM: The Stanford Stream Data Manager. IEEE Data Engineering Bulletin, 26(1):19-26, March 2003.
12. S. Zdonik et al. The Aurora and Medusa Projects. IEEE Data Engineering Bulletin, 26(1), March 2003.

Network Processing of Documents, for Documents, by Documents

Ichiro Satoh

National Institute of Informatics,
2-1-2 Hitotsubashi, Chiyoda-ku,
Tokyo 101-8430, Japan
ichiro@nii.ac.jp

Abstract. This paper presents a content-dependent and configurable framework for the network processing of documents. Like existing compound document frameworks, it enables an enriched document to be dynamically and nestedly composed of software components corresponding to various content, e.g., text, images, and windows. It also enables each component or document to migrate over a network under its own control utilizing mobile agent technology and uses components as carriers or forwarders because it enables them to carry or transmit other components as first class objects to other locations. Since these operations are still document components, they can be dynamically deployed and customized at local or remote computers through GUI manipulations. It therefore allows an end-user to easily and rapidly configure network processing in the same way as if he/she had edited the documents.

1 Introduction

Document manipulation, such as editing, viewing, and distributing documents, is still a crucial role in modern information processing. In distributed computing systems, documents are always transmitted passively over a network by external systems, such as electronic mail systems and http servers. As a result, they cannot determine where, when, or how they should go next. However, there have been several applications whose network processing depends on the content of the documents that are transmitted over the network. For example, tasks in workflow management systems are required to be passed among multiple destinations with specified itineraries. End-users often want to define network processing for documents for them to accomplish their application-specific tasks. However, the customization and management of networking processing is too complex and difficult for end-users.

This paper addresses such a methodology and proposes a new compound document framework, called MobiDoc. Like other existing compound document frameworks, the framework enables an enriched document to be composed of visual components, e.g., text and images. It enables network protocols for documents to be implemented by a set of active documents. By using mobile agent technology, documents or components can define their own itineraries and migrate under their own control, like the programmable-packet approach in active network technology [12]. Furthermore, documents can

G. Alonso (Ed.): Middleware 2005, LNCS 3790, pp. 421–430, 2005.

transmit other documents and multimedia content as first-class objects to their destinations such as with the programmable-node approach in active network technology. The framework introduces components for network processing such as document-centric components, so that it allows an end-user to easily and rapidly configure network processing in the same way as if he/she had edited the documents.

This paper is organized as follows. We first describe the background and related work (Section 2) and then outline our compound document framework (Section 3). After this, we present component runtime systems for executing and migrating document components (Section 4) and present our component model (Section 5). We also describes its prototype implementation (Section 6) and illustrates several applications of the framework (Section 7). We conclude by providing a summary and discussing future issues (Section 8).

2   Background

Several frameworks for compound document components have been developed, such as COM/OLE [2], OpenDoc [1], and CommonPoint [6]. They enable one document to be composed of various visible parts, such as text, image, and video, created by different applications. However, existing compound documents are inherently designed as passive entities in the sense that they can be transmitted over a network by external network systems such as electronic-mail and workflow-management systems, which cannot determine where they should go next. There have been component-based technologies for distributed computing, such as Enterprise JavaBeans (EJB) [11] and Distributed COM (DCOM). However, our framework has been designed independently of these existing component frameworks, because it requires to treat each component as autonomous, mobile, and document-centric, in the sense that each component can migrate or distribute itself and other components over a network.

Several attempts have been made to support active documents, e.g., Active Mail [4] and HyperNews [5], but these haves aimed at particular application-specific documents, such as electronic mail and newspapers, so that they have not supported editing or exchanging documents with varied and complex content. The fuseONE system [13] composes GUI-based control panels for controlling appliances from active documents, i.e., GUI-based buttons and toggle switches. Like other compound document frameworks, they cannot transmit codes for viewing and editing documents. Placeless Document [3] provides a document management system for active documents. It enables a document to delegate the properties of other components like our component hierarchy, but it is not aimed at customizing the network processing of documents.

We constructed a mobile agent system, called MobileSpaces, which we discussed in a previous paper [7]. We constructed a compound document framework based on the MobileSpaces system [8,10]. Since the previous framework was inherently designed based on a mobile agent system, there were serious mismatches between mobile agent-based components and the requirements of document components. Moreover, the previous framework could not define or customize any network processing, because it was proposed only as an application of the MobileSpaces system.

3   Approach

The key idea behind the framework was to enable network protocols for documents to be implemented by a set of documents. That is, documents could define their own itineraries, like the programmable packet approach in active networks. Furthermore, documents can transmit other documents as first-class objects to their destinations such as with the programmable node approach.

3.1   Component Model

Like other existing compound-document frameworks, this framework provides document-centric components but enables them to define and manage network processing. It also introduces two notions of components. The first is the notion of a *self-contained* component, where the content of each component and its codes are inseparable even when it is migrated to another computer. Therefore, when a user receives a document, he/she can view or edit it by using its code instead of any applications deployed at its current computer. To our knowledge, no existing software component frameworks, including compound document frameworks, make the code and state of each component indivisible. The second is the notion of *hierarchical* components. Each component can be contained by at most one component and it can dynamically migrate to other components along with all its inner components. It can instruct its inner components to move to other components, marshal, and destroy them, whereas it cannot control its container component. Nevertheless, the former is still a self-contained component so that it can be removed from the latter.

3.2   Configurable Network Processing

This framework provides two approaches for enabling components to customize their own network processing. The first is to make components *mobile* in the sense that they can define their itinerary and travel among multiple computers along the itinerary by using mobile agent technology. The second enables components to define network processing for themselves. The framework also introduces a container component, called *forwarder*, that can treat its inner components as first-class objects and migrate them to other components. Components can also carry or forward other components over a network and visual components can not only contain visual components but also carrier and forwarder components. They can be customized and assembled through GUI manipulations and embedded into a document as visual components. Therefore, end-users can define and customize their application-specific network processing by combing components through GUI manipulations in the same way as if they were editing visual components in documents.

4   Design

This framework consists of two parts: runtime systems and components. It can execute components and migrate them to/from other runtime systems, even when underlying systems, i.e., operating systems and hardware, are heterogeneous, since runtime systems and components are constructed on Java language and executed on Java VM.

4.1   Component Runtime System

Each runtime system governs all the components inside it. It maintains the life-cycle state of each component, e.g., creation, execution, migration, persistence, and termination. It establishes TCP connections with other systems and exchanges control messages and components through the connection. Fig. 1 outlines the basic structure of a runtime system. When a runtime system saves or migrates a component over a network, it marshals the component, the component's inner components, and information about their containment relationships and visual layouts, called component nodes, into a bit-stream and transmits the marshaled component to its destination through an extension of the HTTP protocol. When a runtime system receives components, it unmarshals the components and information from the bit-stream later. The current implementation uses the Java object serialization package for marshaling the states of components. The package does not support the capturing of stack frames of threads. Consequently, our system cannot marshal the execution states of any thread objects. Instead, the runtime system propagates certain events to components before and after marshaling and unmarshaling them. To reduce the size of the bit-stream, the current implementation compresses the bit-stream. If inner components embedded in a component share the same codes, the runtime system can detect and remove such redundant codes from the bit-stream corresponding to the marshaled component, including its inner components.

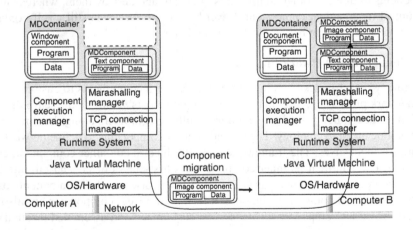

Fig. 1. Component migration between two computers

4.2   Component Hierarchy

As we can see Fig. 3, a hierarchy of components is maintained as a tree structure in which each component can contained by at most one component node. Fig. 2 shows the structure of hierarchical components. Each node is defined as a subclass of two component layout manager classes, MDContainer or MDComponent, where the first supports components, which can contain more than one component inside them and the second supports components, which cannot contain any components. The runtime

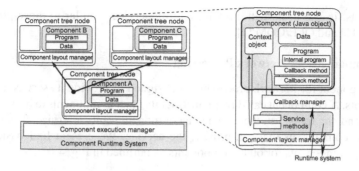

Fig. 2. Component hierarchy and structure of components

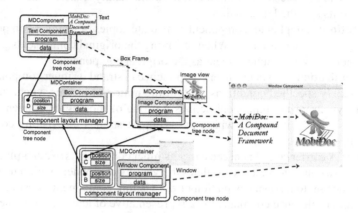

Fig. 3. Component Hierarchy

system basically provides a node derived from the `MDContainer` class for components, except for the visual components that is designed to have no inner components, e.g., text-viewer and sound-player components. For example, when a component has two other components inside it, the nodes that contains the two inner components are attached to the node that wraps the first component. Component migration in a tree is only performed as a transformation of the subtree structure of the hierarchy. When a component is moved over a network, on the other hand, the runtime system marshals the node of the component, including the nodes of its children, into a bit-stream and transmits the component and its children, and the marshaled component to the destination.

4.3 Visual Layout Management

When a component contain components inside it, its `MDContainer` object is responsible for assigning its inner components and their rectangular estates within its estate, and controlling the sizes, positions, offsets, and order of their estates. This framework provides an editing environment for manipulating the components for network processing as well as for compound documents. The environment supports GUIs for manipulating components. It also deals with in-place editing services similar to those provided by OpenDoc [1] and OLE/COM [2].

4.4 Components for Network Processing

Each component for network processing is designed to provide its service to its inner components. A component can directly instruct its inner components to move to another location, and can transform them. When a component wants a service, it migrates into one of the components that can provide the service. We present four basic network processing components for other components as outlined in Fig. 4.

- **Forwarding:** A forwarding component can redirect its inner components to other places. When it receives a component, it automatically transfers the visiting component to its specified destination.
- **Duplication:** A duplicator component can create copies of its inner components including all instance variables. When receiving the original components, the cloned components have the same content as the original components.
- **Synchronization:** A synchronizer component can strand its inner components until it can satisfy specified conditions. Within the notion of barrier synchronization, a typical synchronizer component defines a group of moving components. Until it receives all the components within the group, it strands the visiting components inside it.
- **Carrier:** A carrier component can carry its inner components to other places. When it receives a component, it encapsulates the visiting component within it and carries the component to its own destination or the visiting component's destination.
- **Linking:** A reference component is a representative of another component, which may be located at a remote computer. When it receives a component, it fetches its referring component for the visiting component.

The above components have properties that customize their processing and provide support to GUI editors.

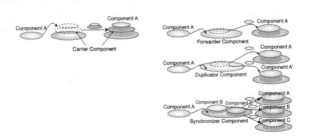

Fig. 4. Basic components for network processing

4.5 Security

Security is essential in active documents as well as mobile agents, because such documents run their own programs and access resources within the computers they visit.

The current implementation uses the standard JAR file format for passing components that can support digital signatures, allowing for authentication. It also relies on the Java security manager like existing mobile agent systems. To protect components from malicious computers, the runtime system provides an authentication mechanism for component migration borrowed from mobile agent research, so that each runtime system host can only send components to, and only receive from, trusted runtime systems.

4.6 Current Status

We implemented the framework using Java language (JDK1.4 or later version), and we developed various components for compound documents and network processing. Fig. 5 shows a screen-shot of this framework. The left window is a palette of part components and the center and right windows are compound documents contained in the components corresponding to GUI windows. When a user wants to place a component on his/her editing compound document, he/she drags the wanted component from the palette and then drops it on the estate of the document. Since the palette itself is implemented as a container component of part components, it can migrate to another computer and be saved in secondary storage. We can register new components, which may be edited or modified, in the palette through GUI-based data-transfers, e.g., drag-and-drop or copy-and-past operation.

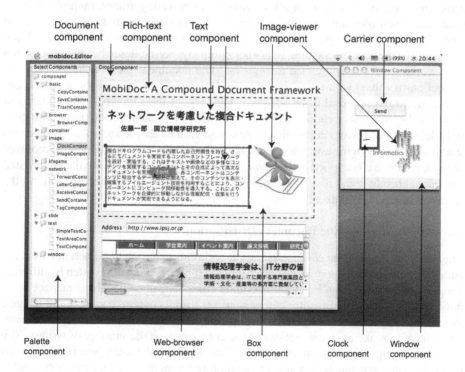

Fig. 5. Examples of compound documents

Even though our implementation was not built for performance, we conducted a basic experiment on component migration with computers (Pentium III 1.2-GHz with Windows XP and SUN JDK 1.4.2). The time for component migration measured from one container to another in the same hierarchy was 10 ms, including the cost of drawing the visible content of the moving component and checking whether the component was permitted to enter the destination component. The cost of component migration measured between two computers connected through a Fast-Ethernet was measured at 64 ms. The cost was the sum of marshaling, compression, opening a TCP connection, transmission, acknowledgment, decompression, security and consistency verification, unmarshaling, visual space layout, and drawing of content. The moving component was a simple text viewer and its size (sum of code and data) was about 9 KB (zip-compressed). The latency of component migration was reasonable for a Java-based visual environment for exchanging compound documents between computers.

5   Experiences

We developed a variety of components based on this framework. This section introduces several components and their uses.

5.1   Compound Document Letter

Most electronic mail systems disallow letters from traveling among multiple destinations along their own itinerary. We developed a legacy decision-making system, called *ringi*, for group decision-making, which has been widely used throughout Japan. When an employee proposes something to his/her company, he/she describes the proposition on a workflow document, called a *ringi-sho*. The document must be handed over to all sections involved with the proposed issue. When the managers of the sections concerned deem the proposal to be adequate, they give it their hanko, or their stamp of approval. Fig. 6 shows a ringi-sho component, which is a carrier component with multiple destinations. It has a destination table whose frames are the areas that its receivers stamp with their own hankos, where each hanko is a component and cannot be removed or modified once it is applied at the frame. The carrier can contain more than one visual component inside it and itineraries between the computers of its receivers until all the receivers stamp their hankos.

5.2   Application-Specific Document Distribution

The second example is an editing system for an in-house newsletter. Each newsletter is edited by automatically compiling one or more text parts, which are written by different people as we can see from Fig. 7. A newsletter compound document has one page component, which can contain editor components for visual content, e.g., text and images. When the newsletter is being edited, it forwards the page component to a duplicator component to make as many replicas of the component as the number of writers. The duplicator component then migrates the replicas to forwarder components so that each of the page components is forwarded to a window component on its writer's computer. When it arrives at the destination, it displays a window for its editor program on the

Ringo-sho component
Multiple destination table   Stamp (hanko) component

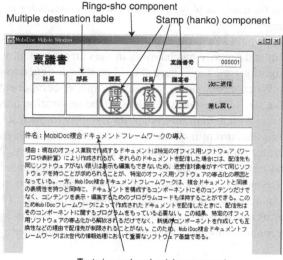

Text viewer (read-only) components

Fig. 6. Ringi-sho compound document

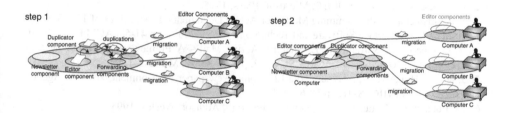

Fig. 7. Newsletter editing system

screen of the computer to assist the writer. Also, the writer can add his/her visual components to the page component. It goes back to the document after the writer finishes writing his/her text and then the document arranges the arriving components as a bound set. Since the newsletter document, duplicator, and forwarder components are still mobile, they can thus be easily deployed and coordinated according to the requirements of applications.

6   Conclusion

We presented a framework for network-enabled documents, including hypermedia. It offers five basic network processing operations for documents, i.e., forwarding, duplication, synchronization, carrying, and linking. We can achieve various types of network processing by combining these operations. Since the operations are implemented as document components, they can be dynamically deployed at remote computers. Moreover, the framework provides a GUI-based editor not only for editing documents but also for easily deploying document components for network processing at remote computers.

To conclude, we would like to point out further issues that need to be resolved. Resource management and security mechanisms in the current system were incorporated in a relatively straightforward way. These should now be designed to incorporate compound documents. When a component migrates to another component or computer, its visual resources, the size of its estate and colors, in the destination may not be the same as those in the source. Although it must adapt its visibility to the resources available in the current location, the current implementation relies on Java's layout manager. The programming interface for the current system is not yet satisfactory. We plan to design a more elegant and flexible interface for programming components. We developed an approach for the development and testing of software running on mobile computers. We are interested in applying the framework to this approach [9]. This is because the framework enables us to easily design and implement active and configurable graphical user interfaces for mobile computers as well as stationary computers.

References

1. Apple Computer Inc. OpenDoc: White Paper, Apple Computer Inc, 1994.
2. K. Brockschmidt, Inside OLE 2, Microsoft Press, 1995.
3. P. Dourish et al, A Programming Model for Active Documents, Proceedings of 13th Symposium on User Interface Software and Technology (UIST'2000), pp.41-50, ACM Press, 2000.
4. Y. Goldberg, M. Safran, and E. Shapiro, Active Mail - A Framework for Implementing Groupware, Proceedings of ACM CSCW'92, pp. 75-83, ACM Press, 1992.
5. J. Morin, HyperNews, a Hypermedia Electronic-Newspaper Environment based on Agents, Proceedings of HICSS-31, pp.58-67, 1998.
6. M. Potel and S. Cotter Inside Taligent Technology, Addison-Wesley, 1995.
7. I. Satoh, MobileSpaces: A Framework for Building Adaptive Distributed Applications Using a Hierarchical Mobile Agent System, Proceedings of International Conference on Distributed Computing Systems (ICDCS'2000), pp.161-168, IEEE Computer Society, April 2000.
8. I. Satoh, MobiDoc: A Mobile Agent-based Framework for Compound Documents, Informatica, vol.25, no.4, pp.493-500, December 2001.
9. I. Satoh, A Testing Framework for Mobile Computing Software, IEEE Transactions on Software Engineering, vol. 29, no. 12, pp.1112-1121, December 2003.
10. I. Satoh, A Compound Document Framework for Multimedia Networking, Proceedings of 1st International Conference on Distributed Frameworks for Multimedia Applications (DFMA'2005), pp.80-87, IEEE Computer Society, February 2004.
11. Sun Microsystems, Inc., Enterprise JavaBeans Technology (EJB) http://java.sun.com/products/ejb, 2002.
12. D. L. Tennenhouse et al., A Survey of Active Network Research, IEEE Communication Magazine, vol. 35, no. 1, 1997.
13. P. Werle, F. Kilander, M. Jonsson P. Lonqvist, C. G. Jansson, A Ubiquitous Service Environment with Active Documents for Teamwork Support, Proceedings of 3rd International Conference on Ubiquitous Computing (UBICOMP'2001), Lecture Notes in Computer Science, vol. 2201 pp.139-155, Springer, 2001.

Fault-Tolerant Middleware and the Magical 1%*

Tudor Dumitraş and Priya Narasimhan

Carnegie Mellon University, Pittsburgh PA 15213, USA
tdumitra@ece.cmu.edu, priya@cs.cmu.edu

Abstract. Through an extensive experimental analysis of over 900 possible configurations of a fault-tolerant middleware system, we present empirical evidence that the unpredictability inherent in such systems arises from merely 1% of the remote invocations. The occurrence of very high latencies cannot be regulated through parameters such as the number of clients, the replication style and degree or the request rates. However, by selectively filtering out a "magical 1%" of the raw observations of various metrics, we show that performance, in terms of measured end-to-end latency and throughput, can be bounded, easy to understand and control. This simple statistical technique enables us to guarantee, with some level of confidence, bounds for percentile-based quality of service (QoS) metrics, which dramatically increase our ability to tune and control a middleware system in a predictable manner.

1 Introduction

Modern computer systems are perhaps some of the most complex structures ever engineered. Together with their undisputed benefits for human society, their complexity has also introduced a few side-effects, most notably the inherent unpredictability of these systems and the increasing tuning and configuration burden that they impose on their users. The fact that large distributed systems, even under normal conditions, can exhibit unforeseen, complex behavior stresses that we are facing a veritable "vulnerability of complexity".

In this paper, we examine the unpredictability of fault-tolerant (FT) middleware. Typically used for the most critical enterprise and embedded systems to mask the effect of faults and to ensure correctness, FT middleware has higher predictability requirements than most other systems. We naturally expect that faults, which are inherently unpredictable, will have a disruptive effect on the performance of the system. In this paper, we show that *even in the fault-free case it is impossible to enforce any hard bounds on the end-to-end latency of an FT CORBA application.*

Conventional wisdom about commercial-off-the-shelf (COTS) software is that well designed and implemented ORBs behave in a sufficiently predictable manner when running on top of certain real-time operating systems. However, recent studies have independently reported that maximum end-to-end latencies of

---

* This work has been partially supported by the NSF CAREER grant CCR-0238381, the DARPA PCES contract F33615-03-C-4110, and also in part by the General Motors Collaborative Research Laboratory at Carnegie Mellon University.

G. Alonso (Ed.): Middleware 2005, LNCS 3790, pp. 431–441, 2005.

CORBA and FT-CORBA middleware can be several orders of magnitude larger than the mean values and might not follow a visible trend [1,2,3]. At [3], Thaker lists many examples of systems that produce few outliers which are several orders of magnitude larger than the average: operating systems (Linux, Solaris, TimeSys Linux), transport protocols (UDP, TCP, SCTP), group communication systems (Spread), middleware and component frameworks (TAO, CIAO, JacORB, JDK ORB, OmniORB, ORBExpressRT, Orbix, JBoss EJB, Java RMI), including our own MEAD system. Our first goal in this paper is to evaluate how much predictability we can obtain by carefully choosing a good configuration of FT middleware components (operating system, ORB, group communication package and replication mechanism) and to analyze statistically the distribution of end-to-end latencies in the resulting system.

Additionally, fault-tolerant middleware poses fundamental trade-offs between dependability, performance and resource usage. Tuning the trade-offs is a delicate and non-trivial task because in most cases, this re-calibration requires detailed knowledge of the system's implementation. We have previously advocated an approach called *versatile dependability* [4], which consists in providing high-level "knobs" to control the external properties, such as latency or availability, that are relevant to the end-users of the system. However, the unpredictability observed in COTS middleware systems poses a challenge for tuning these high-level properties, unless we can find a simple and efficient method for making deterministic guarantees based on the configuration of the system. To reliably predict the average and maximum latencies based on specific configuration parameters (*e.g.*, number of clients, request rates and sizes, replication styles and degrees), we discard the highest 1% of the measured latencies. Then, we can establish bounds on the 99th percentile of the metric monitored (*e.g.*, "the end-to-end response time will be less than 2s in 99% of the cases"). For a large class of applications, the value added by bounding the maximum latencies instead of the 99th percentile does not justify the increased efforts that are required to achieve it [5]; in this paper, our second goal is to quantify, through an extensive empirical exploration, the confidence that we can place on this kind of guarantees.

In summary, this paper makes two concrete contributions:

- We provide substantial evidence that, despite choosing a good system configuration (operating system, ORB, group communication package and replication mechanism), the remote invocation latencies of a fault-tolerant CORBA infrastructure are difficult to bound and control, regardless whether or not faults occur (Section 2);
- We show that, by filtering out 1% of the largest recorded latencies, we obtain a set of measurements with predictable properties (Section 3); we call this the "*magical 1%*" effect. This effect dramatically increases our ability to tune the system in a predictable manner by specifying QoS guarantees based on the 99th percentile of the targeted metric (*e.g.*, latency, throughput, reliability).

2   System Configuration for Achieving Predictability

In setting up the test bed for our empirical exploration, we aimed to select a configuration for our FT middleware with some of the best open source components available. We also provisioned the experimental environment to create the most favorable conditions for achieving predictable behavior.

To ensure the reproducibility of our results, we our experiments ran on the Emulab test bed [6]. We use the MEAD (Middleware for Embedded Adaptive Dependability) system [7], currently under development at Carnegie Mellon University, as our FT middleware. MEAD provides transparent, tunable fault-tolerance to distributed middleware applications. The system is based on library interposition for transparently intercepting and redirecting system calls, and features a novel architecture with components such as a tunable replicator, a decentralized resource monitor and a fault-tolerance advisor, whose task is to identify the most appropriate configurations (including the replication style and degree) for the current state of the system. MEAD implements active and passive replication based on the extended virtual synchrony model [4]. This model mandates that the same events (which can be application-generated as well as membership changes) are delivered in the same order at all the nodes of the distributed system, but without enforcing any timeliness guarantees. The extended virtual synchrony guarantees are enforced by the Spread (v. 3.17.3) group communication toolkit [8]. We have carefully tuned Spread's timeouts for our networking environment, to provide fast, reliable fault detection and steady performance. MEAD runs under the TAO real-time ORB (v. 1.4), which provide excellent average remote invocation latencies [9,3]. Our Emulab experiment uses 25 hosts connected with a 100 Mbps LAN. Each machine is a Pentium III running at 850 MHz (1697 bogomips), with 256 MB of RAM; the operating system is Linux RedHat 9.0 with the TimeSys 3.1 kernel.[1]

Since our goal is to evaluate the predictability of this system configuration (and not to assess or compare the overall performance), we believe that a micro-benchmark specifically targeting this goal is the most suited for our purpose. We have developed a micro-benchmark that measures the behavior of the system for different styles and degrees of server replication, with up to 22 connected clients. Each client sends a cycle of 10,000 requests, pausing a variable amount of time (from 0 to 32 ms) between requests. The replies from the server can also vary in size (from 16 bytes to 64 Kbytes). Each one of the physical nodes is dedicated to a single client or server. There are no additional workloads and no additional traffic imposed on the LAN to avoid interference with the experiments.

Admittedly, all these constraints imposed on the test bed make our setup somewhat unrealistic. However, our purpose was to provision the system in the best possible way for achieving predictable behavior. Since even this configuration turns out to be unpredictable (as we show in Section 2.2), it is very unlikely that a real-life industrial installation will prove to be more deterministic.

---

[1] This kernel is fully preemptible, with protection against priority inversion, $O(1)$ task scheduling complexity, and a fine timer granularity. This allows us to simulate request arrival rates with sub-millisecond precision.

Versatile Dependability. An important architectural feature of the MEAD system is the provision of tuning knobs. Adopting an approach called versatile dependability [4], MEAD defines a hierarchy of low-level and high-level knobs. Low-level knobs control the internal fault-tolerant mechanisms of the infrastructure and typically correspond to discrete (*e.g.*, the degree of replication) or even non-countable sets (*e.g.*, replication styles). In contrast, high-level knobs regulate externally-observable properties (*e.g.*, latency, availability) that are relevant to the system's users, and they should ideally have a linear transfer characteristic, with unsurprising effects. High-level knobs control the QoS goals of the system, and they are implemented based on low-level knobs; however, for defining trustworthy high-level knobs, the measured QoS values must be deterministically linked to the settings of the low-level parameters.

2.1   Experimental Methodology

In our experiments, we vary the following low-level parameters:

- *Replication style*: either active or warm passive replication;
- *Replication degree*: 1, 2 or 3 server replicas;
- *Number of clients*: 1, 4, 7, 10, 13, 16, 19 or 22 clients;
- *Request arrival rate*: the clients insert a pause of 0 ms, 0.5 ms, 2 ms, 8 ms or 32 ms. The lack of a pause (0 ms) represents bursty client activity;
- *Size of the reply messages*: 16 bytes, 256 bytes, 4 Kbytes or 64 Kbytes.

We have tested all 960 possible combinations of these parameters, collecting 9.1 Gbytes of data over a period of two weeks.[2] We statistically analyze this raw data to determine the probability distributions, the means, medians, standard deviations, the maximum and minimum values as well as the 99th percentiles, the confidence intervals and the numbers and sizes of the outliers.

2.2   Evidence of Unpredictability

Figure 1(a) shows the raw end-to-end latencies (as measured on the client side) for a configuration with an unreplicated server and 4 clients, each sending 16 byte requests at the highest possible rate (no pause between requests). A few spikes that are much larger than the average are clearly noticeable in the figure. The effect of these spikes can be further analyzed by looking at Figure 1(b), which shows the probability density function for the end-to-end latencies. The distribution has a long tail, which indicates that there are a few samples, accounting for a small percentage of the measured values, that are much larger than the rest. The distribution is skewed only to the right because latency cannot take arbitrarily low values.[3] The same information can be represented in

---

[2] The full trace is available online at www.ece.cmu.edu/~tdumitra/MEAD_trace.

[3] MEAD's latency is bounded by the round-trip time of a regular TAO invocation.

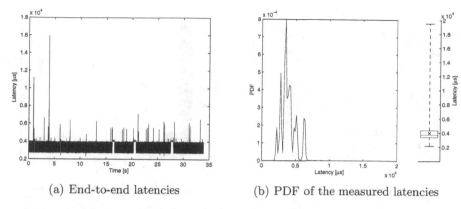

(a) End-to-end latencies   (b) PDF of the measured latencies

Fig. 1. Unpredictable behavior of end-to-end latency

a more concise way by the "box and whisker" plot on the right side of the figure.[4] From the box plot, we can tell that the distribution is skewed to the right because the median is closer to the lower end of the box and the upper whisker is much longer that the lower one. But the most striking detail is the extent to which the maximum value exceeds most of the measured samples.

Such distributions are hard to characterize with a single metric. Mean values can describe well the average expected latency, but give no indication of the jitter. Maximum values are hard to use because they are largely unpredictable. Furthermore, the spikes seem to come in bursts, which breaks the defenses of many fault-tolerant systems which assume only single or double consecutive timing faults. This difference seems to be aggravated by an increasing number of clients, but without revealing a clear trend. In Figure 2(a), we can see that the maximum values are much higher that the means and that they increase and decrease (note the exponential scale) in an uncorrelated way with respect to the number of clients. The very large latencies are seen for only a few requests.

Table 1. Impact of each parameter on the number of outliers

Replication Style		Replication Degree		# Clients	Request Rate		Request Size	
Active:	55.12%	1 replica:	28.51%	1: 9.26%	0 ms:	21.37%	16 b:	13.77%
Passive:	44.88%	2 replicas:	34.47%	4: 15.06%	0.5 ms:	20.69%	256 b:	12.10%
		3 replicas:	37.02%	7: 13.35%	2 ms:	20.50%	4 Kb:	21.14%
				10: 14.77%	8 ms:	20.16%	64 Kb:	52.99%
				13: 14.83%	32 ms:	17.28%		
				16: 12.29%				
				19: 9.24%				
				22: 9.21%				

---

[4] The box represents the size of the inter-quartile range (the difference between the 75th and 25th percentiles of the samples in the data set), while the whiskers indicate the maximum and minimum values. The mean and the median of the samples are represented by the line and the cross inside the box.

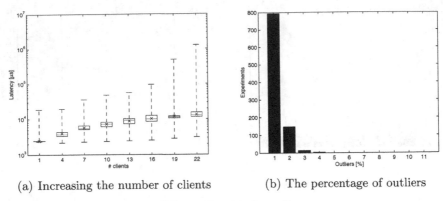

(a) Increasing the number of clients   (b) The percentage of outliers

Fig. 2. Empirical results

To determine which measurements are exceptional, we use the 3σ statistical test: any sample that deviates from the mean with more than 3σ is considered an outlier (σ is the non-biased standard deviation error). Figure 2(b) shows that, in most of our 960 experiments, the number of outliers was under 1%, with a few cases registering up to 2%, 3%, or 4%. Table 1 shows a breakdown of the numbers of outliers recorded for each value of the five parameters that we varied in our experiments. We notice that the outliers are almost uniformly distributed for all the values of these parameters (with the exception of the request size, where the 64 Kb messages produced more than half of the high latencies). This emphasizes that it is impossible to remove the outliers based on the system configuration and, knowing that outliers can be several orders of magnitude greater than the average (as shown above), we conclude that a sample of measured latencies that includes these outliers will have unpredictable maximum values.

3   The Magical 1%

Figure 2(b) shows that, in most cases, eliminating only 1% of the latencies would make all the remaining samples conform to the 3σ test. We now investigate what happens in our experiments if we remove 1% of the samples, hoping that we have isolated enough outliers to make the behavior of the system predictable. Figure 3(a) shows the high discrepancy between the means and the maximum values measured in all the experiments (in the figure, the experiments are sorted by the increasing average latencies). Note that it is hard to find a correlation between these two metrics, especially because the maximum values seem to be randomly high. If we remove the largest 1% from all these cases and we plot the data again, we get the "haircut" effect displayed in Figure 3(b): the randomness has disappeared and the 99th percentiles do not deviate significantly from the average values. Only 1% of the measured end-to-end request latencies are responsible for the unpredictable behavior; discarding this 1% when making QoS guarantees results in a far more predictable system.

3.1 Expressing the Performance QoS Goals

The magical 1% is a simple, yet powerful approach for expressing QoS goals. While providing performance guarantees based on some sort of compliance with the 3σ test is quite difficult (because the test requires all the samples), using the magical 1% approach leads to specifications of QoS objectives that guarantee that 99% of the measured samples will fall within the stipulated bounds. Such percentile-based guarantees are: (i) easy to understand and relevant to the clients, since they reflect both the average and the sub-optimal behaviors, and (ii) easy to implement by service providers because the behavior in this case is predictable, as Figure 3 suggests. Other percentiles may be used (90% and 95% are quite common in the industry [5]) if more slack is desired, but for our fault-tolerant middleware system 99% appears to work effectively.

Outlier elimination should not be haphazardly performed: *when estimating the percentile-based bounds for a certain performance metric, we must take into consideration the semantics of that metric.* Most metrics will have outliers on only one side of the distribution (leading to a skewed distribution as shown in Figure 1(b)) because there are natural bounds which prevent them from extending indefinitely in the opposite direction; however, the side where the real outliers lie depends on the specific metric. For example, end-to-end latencies cannot be arbitrarily small because they are bounded by the underlaying network delays; therefore, outliers will be on the side of high end-to-end latencies. Conversely, for throughput the outliers will be on the lower side because throughput cannot become arbitrarily high. The magical 1% should only be trimmed on the side that can become unbounded for the corresponding metric.

From low-level to high-level knobs. To implement a latency-tuning knob, we must establish the connection between the low-level parameters and the 99th percentile of the round-trip times. Our experiments reveal three trends: (i) latency increases linearly with the number of clients connected, as shown in Section 2.2; (ii) the latency decreases slightly with lower request rates; (iii) the

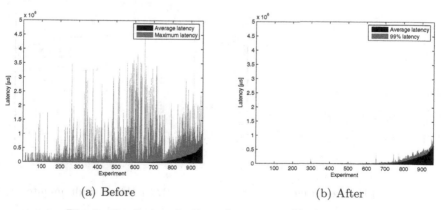

(a) Before   (b) After

Fig. 3. The "haircut" effect of removing 1% of the outliers

latency increases faster than linearly with growing reply sizes. The first and second effects occur because less clients and reduced request rates alleviate the load of the server; the severe dependence of the latency on the request size is likely the result of additional work done by the operating system and by MEAD in the fragmentation and reassembly of large messages.

3.2 Expressing the Dependability QoS Goals

Dependable systems should mask as many faults as possible without resulting in failures. The reliability of the system is the probability of correct service for a given duration of time [10]. A common metric used for representing reliability is the mean time to failure (MTTF). MEAD automatically restarts crashed replicas for improving the overall MTTF. The time between the restart and the instant when the new replica processes the first message is called the recovery time. Figure 4(a) shows the distributions of recovery times for a system with 3 replicas in the active replication style, with a request period of 2000 μs and a reply size of 4Kbytes. The recovery time depends on the number of clients connected, because the recovery algorithm must transfer the state and all the backlog of requests to the new replica. Figure 4(a) seems to indicate that recovery times are not as unpredictable as the response times, except for the case with 22 clients (compare with Figure 2(a)). This is a relatively surprising result, as the recovery process needs to perform several remote invocations to update the state of the new replica. Further investigation is needed to determine whether the "magical 1%" would be useful for making reliability guarantees.

We can convert the recovery times into mean times to failure using the formula [10]: $MTTF_{3 \text{ replicas, restart}} = \frac{2\mu^2 + 7\mu\lambda + 11\lambda^2}{6\lambda^3}$, where λ is the fault arrival rate and the recovery rate μ is the inverse of the mean recovery time. For example, at a constant rate of 1 fault per minute (which is unrealistically high), using active replication style with 3 replicas will add only 50 seconds to the $MTTF$; using the recovery strategy will raise the $MTTF$ up to 7313 hours (about 305 days). This is shown in Figure 4(b).

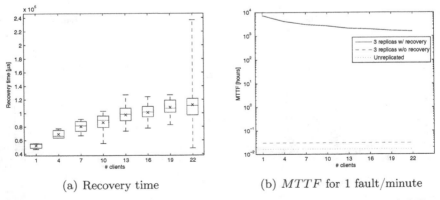

(a) Recovery time   (b) $MTTF$ for 1 fault/minute

Fig. 4. Using active replication with recovery to improve the system reliability

4   Discussion

The source of the apparently random behavior reported here cannot be easily isolated to the operating system, the network, the fault-tolerant infrastructure, the ORB, or the application. In fact, most operating systems exhibit seemingly unbounded latencies – at least for network operations, but in some cases for IPC and scheduling as well [3]. Furthermore, even systems built on top of the best designed, hard real-time operating operating systems manifest the same symptoms when combined with off-the-shelf ORBs and group communication packages. This behavior is likely the result of combining COTS components that: (i) were not built and tested jointly, and (ii) were designed to optimize for the common case among a wide variety of workloads, rather than to enforce tight bounds for the worst-case behavior.

Breaking the Magical 1%. Our empirical observations are clearly specific to the configuration under test. While the unpredictability of maximum end-to-end latencies has been reported for many different systems [3], the effectiveness of our "magical 1%" approach remains to be verified for other settings. So far, we have not tried running the application on a wide area network, using a different OS, working in a an environment with intermittent network connectivity (*e.g.*, a wireless network), simulating flash crowds, having other workloads that compete for CPU time and produce interfering traffic, or using virtual, rather than physical computing resources. Finally, certain applications (*e.g.*, embedded systems) will not be able to use percentiles; in such cases, nothing short of predictable worst-case behavior will be sufficient to ensure safety.

5   Related Work

The Fault Tolerant CORBA standard [11] specifies ten parameters that can be adjusted for achieving the required levels of performance and fault-tolerance for every application object, but it does not provide any insight on how these parameters should be set and re-tuned over the application's lifetime [12]. Even for fixed values of these parameters, the end-to-end latencies are hard to bound because they have skewed and sometimes bimodal distributions [2] (a phenomenon we have also observed). For the CORBA Component Model, it has been noted that a small number of outliers (typically less than 1%) causes maximum latencies to be much larger than the averages [1]. Thaker [3] reports that many systems produce a few numbers of outliers several orders of magnitude larger than the average: operating systems (Linux, Solaris, TimeSys Linux), transport protocols (UDP, TCP, SCTP), group communication systems (Spread), middleware and component frameworks (TAO, CIAO, JacORB, JDK ORB, OmniORB, ORBExpressRT, Orbix, JBoss EJB, Java RMI), including our own MEAD system. A percentile-based approach for specifying QoS guarantees is a common practice in the IT industry for most systems outside the real-time domain [5]. In this paper, we evaluate the virtues of such a percentile-based approach, with an emphasis on extracting tunability out of complex systems, rather than simply a risk-mitigation approach for service providers.

6   Conclusions

In this paper, we examine the predictability of a fault-tolerant, CORBA-compliant system. We try to achieve predictable behavior by selecting a good system configuration, but we show that, for almost all 960 parameter combinations tested, the measured end-to-end latencies have skewed distributions, with maximum values several orders of magnitude larger than the averages. These high latencies are due to a few (usually less than 1%) outliers which tend to come in bursts. The number of clients, the replication style and degree or the request rates neither inhibit nor augment the number of outliers. While the exact causes for this unpredictability are hard to pinpoint in every case, this seems to be a generic side-effect of complexity and of system design goals that focus on optimizing the average behavior (rather than bounding the worst case).

We also present strong empirical evidence of a "magical 1%" effect: by removing 1% of the highest measured latencies for each configuration, the remaining samples have more deterministic properties. We show that the 99th percentile follows the trend of the mean and that it can be used for making latency guarantees. The significance of this result is that it allows us to extract tunable, predictable behavior (with respect to performance and dependability) out of fairly complex, unpredictable systems. While this percentile-based guarantees are clearly inappropriate for hard real-time systems, they can be of immense benefit to enterprise service providers and customers, who want reasonable, quantifiable and monitorable assurances. Since similar behavior has been reported for many other systems, we believe that our "magical 1%" opens an interesting avenue for further research in statistical approaches for handling unpredictability.

Acknowledgments. The authors would like to thank David O'Hallaron, Asit Dan, Daniela Roşu, Jay Wylie and the anonymous reviewers for their invaluable suggestions and ideas related to this topic.

References

1. Krishna, A.S., Wang, N., Natarajan, B., Gokhale, A., Schmidt, D.C., Thaker, G.: CCMPerf: A benchmarking tool for CORBA Component Model implementations. The International Journal of Time-Critical Computing Systems **29** (2005)
2. Zhao, W., Moser, L., Melliar-Smith, P.: End-to-end latency of a fault-tolerant CORBA infrastructure. In: Object-Oriented Real-Time Distributed Computing, Washington, DC (2002) 189–198
3. http://www.atl.external.lmco.com/projects/QoS/.
4. Dumitraş, T., Srivastava, D., Narasimhan, P.: Architecting and implementing versatile dependability. In de Lemos, R. et al., ed.: Architecting Dependable Systems III. Lecture Notes in Computer Science. Springer-Verlag (2005)

5. Alistair Croll: Meaningful Service Level Agreements for Web transaction systems. LOOP: The Online Voice of the IT Community (2005)
6. White, B. et al.: An integrated experimental environment for distributed systems and networks. In: Symposium on Operating Systems Design and Implementation, Boston, MA (2002) 255–270
7. Narasimhan, P., Dumitraş, T., Paulos, A., Pertet, S., Reverte, C., Slember, J., Srivastava, D.: MEAD: Support for real-time, fault-tolerant CORBA. Concurrency and Computation: Practice and Experience **17** (2005) 1527–1545
8. Amir, Y., Danilov, C., Stanton, J.: A low latency, loss tolerant architecture and protocol for wide area group communication. In: International Conference on Dependable Systems and Networks, New York, NY (2000) 327–336
9. Schmidt, D.C., Levine, D.L., Mungee, S.: The design of the TAO real-time Object Request Broker. Computer Communications **21** (1998) 294–324
10. Siewiorek, D., Swarz, R.: Reliable Computer Systems. 2 edn. Digital Press (1992)
11. Object Management Group: Fault Tolerant CORBA. OMG Technical Committee Document formal/2001-09-29 (2001)
12. Felber, P., Narasimhan, P.: Experiences, approaches and challenges in building fault-tolerant CORBA systems. IEEE Transactions on Computers **54** (2004) 497–511

Author Index

Lecture Notes in Computer Science

For information about Vols. 1–3695

please contact your bookseller or Springer